MW01243679

The **Mission**
and **Destiny**
of **Humankind**

An Exercise in Understanding the Qur'an

Dr. Muhammad A. Hafeez

amana publications

THE MISSION AND DESTINY OF HUMANKIND
(An Exercise in Understanding the Qur'an)

First Edition
(1433 AH/2012 AC)

Amana Publications
10710 Tucker Street, Beltsville, MD 20705-2223 USA
Tel. 301.595.5777 Fax 301.595.5888
Email amana@igprinting.com
www.amana-publications.com

Reprinted
(1438 AH/2017 AC)

CreateSpace Independent Publishing Platform
North Charleston, South Carolina

Library of Congress Cataloging-in-Publication Data

Hafeez, Muhammad A.
The Mission and Destiny of Humankind : An Exercise in Understanding the
Qur'an / Muhammad A. Hafeez.
p. cm.
Includes bibliographical references.
ISBN 10: 1979588066
ISBN 13: 978-1979588065
1. Koran--Criticism, interpretation, etc. I. Title.
BP130.4.H225 2012
297.1'226--dc23
2012043654

Because of the dynamic nature of the Internet, any Web addresses or links contained
in this book may have changed since publication and may no longer be valid.

Dedicated to Humankind - God's Trustee

"We have revealed for you (O people)
A Book in which is a Message for you.
Will you not then understand?"

- The Qur'an [Surah Al-Anbiya: 10]

Acknowledgement

The importance of learning what God commands in the Qur'an is such that people should exert all their efforts to accomplish this task, and no one is exempt from this duty. Although the Messenger was *Ummi* (unlettered), God commanded him to read, "Read in the name of your Lord Who created—created man from a clot. Read, and your Lord is Most Honorable…(Qur'an 96:1-3)" Knowledge of the Arabic language is preferable in learning the Qur'an, and in the past this was the only way to learn the Qur'an, due to a limited availability of books on the Qur'an and *Ahadith* (sayings of Prophet Muhammad) in other languages. Since translations and interpretations of the Qur'an are now available in almost every widely known language, one can also learn to understand the Qur'an in a language known to the reader. It is so important to learn what God commands in the Qur'an that nothing should stand in its way; not even the lack of ability to understand Arabic. I am, therefore, highly indebted to those religious scholars, editors, translators, and commentators whose works, even in other than the Arabic language, have been instrumental in my learning process.

In understanding the Qur'an, I have benefited from Urdu and English translations and *Tafsir* (commentary) by Syed Abul Ala Maududi, as well as from English translations by 'Abdullah Yusuf Ali, Zafar Ishaq Ansari, Muhammad Marmaduke Pickthall, M. H. Shakir, and Dr. M. M. Khan and Dr. M. T. Al-Hilali. I am indebted to the scholarly writings of Dr. Malik Ghulam Murtaza, Adil Salahi, Sheikh Ali Tantavi, Sheikh 'Abdullah Bin Muhammad Al-Muhtaj, M. Al-Ghazali, and Hamza Yusuf, and I acknowledge that their contributions have greatly helped me in my pursuit of knowledge. I am grateful to Dr. Taqiuddin Ahmed, Imam/Director of the Islamic Society of Central New York, and to Mirza Iqbal Ashraf, author of 'Introduction to World Philosophies, Islamic Philosophy of War and Peace, and Rumi's Holistic Humanism, for their invaluable review and comments.

The Qur'an was revealed for the benefit of all humankind, and God thusly enjoined Adam in Paradise: "We said: 'Get you down all from here; and if, as is sure, there comes to you guidance from Me, whosoever follows My guidance, on them shall be no fear, nor shall they grieve (Qur'an 2:38)." God also promised that, "As for those who were led to the guidance, Allah increases them in their guidance and causes them to grow in their piety (Qur'an 47:17)." Every human being is divinely blessed with a capacity to comprehend God's guidance. This has indeed encouraged me and will encourage whoever wants to learn his/her obligations as God's trustee on earth. God has reminded us in Surah Al-Qamar that, "We have indeed made the Qur'an easy to understand and remember; then is there any who will receive admonition? (Qur'an 54:17)." As members of humanity, for our own good both in this life and in the hereafter, we should say, "Yes," to God's invitation to His guidance.

Dr. Muhammad A. Hafeez

Contents

Preface

Divine knowledge has been revealed to guide people through their journey towards their destiny. It tells what is expected from them, what their character should be, and how they are to behave in this world. Lack of knowledge tends to corrupt people. God tells us in Surah Al-Rum, "Nay, the unjust people follow their selfish desires without any knowledge; so who can guide them whom God lets go astray (due to their own free will)? Such shall have no helpers (Qur'an 30:29)." It was narrated by Abu Huraira: "The Messenger said, 'No child is born except on Islam - the nature in which God created humankind, and then his/her parents make him/her Jewish, Christian, or Magian.' Then he recited verse 30 of Surah Al-Rum, 'Turn your face single-mindedly to the true faith, and adhere to the nature in which God created humankind. Let there be no change in God's religion. That is the true faith, although most people do not know.' (Sahih Bukhari 6.60.298)."

The importance of knowledge and learning is very hard to overstate. Learning to manage our affairs on earth is the first obligation of humankind after being declared as God's *Khalifah* (Trustee) on earth. Besides, God has given humankind a mind with which to think. It is quite natural that He expects us to use it, particularly in the most important issue of our existence, which is the knowledge of how and by whom we were created and for what purpose. With knowledge comes understanding, then obedience. God commands in Surah Al-'Alaq, "Read in the name of your Lord Who created. He created man from a clot. Read, and your Lord is Most Honorable, Who taught (to write) with the pen. Taught man what he knew not (Qur'an 96:1-5)." From the Qur'an people learn that:

➢ God created people with a conscience and free will, and He gave guidance to them. He asked each one of us, male or female, rich or poor, to be His trustee on earth to serve Him by implementing His commands in managing our affairs and by building a just human society in the world, i.e., an Islamic welfare society that is built on hard work, truth, justice, and

xiv

charity and that is free of corruption, discrimination, exploitation, and oppression. God desires people to be His trustees on earth. It is up us to accept or reject God's offer of trusteeship.

➢ God commands people to believe in Him, His messengers, His revelations, and the ultimate accountability for their behavior and deeds. God expects them to acknowledge their mistakes, reform, do good deeds, and establish justice under all circumstances. Life in this world is a test so that people may prove who can utilize their lives to their best purpose and potential. In this regard, God has provided people with the required guidance to succeed in their assignment as His trustee on earth.

➢ One's acts and deeds make one suffer or bring happiness. God administers absolute justice. People's actions determine their presents and their futures. It is the choices one makes, not chance, that determine individual destiny—all actions, both good and bad, have appropriate consequences. Happiness in the hereafter greatly depends on the efforts of the believers to improve all aspects of life in this world. As individuals, irrespective of their situation or status in life, each one should improve his behavior and try to help others in their struggle in life.

➢ Those who wish to be God's trustees believe in and worship Him, in order to develop a relationship and trust with Him. They learn and develop to be truly human in attitude, character, and behavior. They keep on continually reforming themselves to overcome such weaknesses of character and behavior that lead people to corruption, discrimination, exploitation, and oppression. Thus, they become capable of delivering their trust and doing good deeds. Since the believers know that God is watching over them and that they will have to give an account of how they performed during their stay on earth, they take this assignment as a challenge and a trial from Him.

Believers have the desire and intention to succeed as God's trustee on earth. Since it is through knowledge and understanding that people attain closeness to God, believers strive to gain knowledge. They strive to read and understand the Qur'an and to follow His Messenger as their role model. Divine guidance equips people with the desired character and behavior of a believer, which in turn help build a just human society on earth. Our prayers and fasting remind us of our duties and teach us the self-discipline needed to guard against the temptation to sin or to do evil and spread corruption.

Believers inculcate God's love through their belief and worship. God's love motivates and helps them to overcome the weaknesses of their character and behavior. They continually improve themselves through awareness of their mistakes and repentance, for only good people can do good deeds. They do not violate God's commands, and they do good deeds. They enforce what is right and forbid what is wrong. They strive against exploitation, oppression, injustice, and corruption in society.

Believers try to be hardworking, honest, just, and charitable throughout their lives. They act with justice in their respective areas of influence with those who deal with them in all spheres and walks of life. In contrast, the unbelievers reject the responsibility of being God's trustees on earth and face the consequence of being unfaithful to their Creator. They do not believe in the accountability for their actions, and due to this they will miss out on the beautiful rewards that are promised to people in the hereafter.

Dr. Muhammad A. Hafeez,
August 7, 2011

Foreword

For Muslims the world over, the Qur'an is the word of God, revealed to Prophet Muhammad, peace be upon him, over the course of 23 years. As such, the Qur'an is not a book merely to be read on "automatic pilot" from cover to cover in one sitting. It is not a book of fiction or light reading. Rather, it is a book that deserves our sincere study far more than any college textbook that is to be mastered before some final exam in a college course. In essence, the Qur'an is the required textbook for life's final exam, the one that we shall all take on the Day of Judgment. Just as we highlight passages and take notes from a college textbook, we should approach the Qur'an with at least the same level of zeal and study. It is a book from God that demands that we honor and respect it enough to pause frequently to think about, appreciate, and contemplate what God is telling us. In doing so, we find new meaning, insight, and understanding with each successive reading of the Qur'an, and our lives are thereby spiritually enriched.

In his latest book, The Mission and Destiny of Humankind—An Exercise in Understanding the Qur'an, Dr. Muhammad Hafeez illustrates his own personal approach to the study of the Qur'an, which emphasizes the ongoing theme that we as humans have been placed on earth to be God's trustees. Individual Qur'anic passages are studied, reflected upon, organized thematically, and often even placed in outline format within the tables that frequently grace the text. This is no robotic reading of the Qur'an devoid of thought and contemplation. This is a sincere attempt by a devoted Muslim to reach a reasoned and thoughtful understanding of God's word to us.

Abu Yahya (Jerald F. Dirks), M.Div., Psy.D.
February 29, 2012

Introduction

The Qur'an is a book for the guidance of people in general and for the believers in particular. It is the textbook of Islam. For better understanding, the Qur'an should be read at least a chapter at a time, taking notes for easy reference and highlighting God's commands, the divine laws, and the laws of nature that God has put in place. People should try their best to understand and to implement God's commands individually and in their communities. Since individual abilities vary, a person should not be discouraged. God tells people, "As for those who believe and do good deeds, We do not impose on any person a duty except to the extent of its ability; they are the dwellers of the Paradise; in it they shall abide (Qur'an 7:42)."

What is the Qur'an? Hares-b-A'war reported that Ali said: "I heard the Messenger saying: 'Behold! There will soon appear calamity.' I asked, 'What will be the way of getting out of it, O Messenger of Allah?' He said: 'The book of Allah is the way, for it contains information of what has happened before you, news of what will happen after you, and a decision regarding matters that occur among you. It is clear and not a vain discourse. Whoso among oppressors abandons it, Allah shall ruin him, and whoso seeks guidance elsewhere, Allah shall misguide him. It is the firmest rope of Allah; it is the great reminder; it is the straight path. It is that by which neither the passions do go astray nor the tongues falsify, and the learned cannot grasp it completely. It does not grow old by excessive repetitions, and its wonders do not come to an end...Whoever speaks according to it, speaks the truth. Whoever acts according to it is rewarded. Whosoever pronounces judgment according to it is just, and whoever invites people to it guides to the straight path.' (Al-Tirmidhi, Al-Hadith: Vol. III, no., 29, page 675)" It was also narrated by Abu Huraira that the Messenger said: "Interpret the Qur'an, and follow its commands. Its commands are its obligatory duties and its prescribed ordinances (Baihaqi, Al-Hadith, Vol. III, no., 579w, page 685)."

Why is it important to learn what God says in the Qur'an? God has shown us in numerous ways that He loves people. That is why He commands only those things that are good for us. God says that we should serve Him and our families, neglecting neither. It is by serving God that we learn the importance of serving our families. Who are the members of our family? They are our children, relatives, neighbors, countrymen, and the people all over the world. Islam does not distinguish between living the life for this world and living the life for the hereafter. It expects its followers to live their lives following all moral and ethical principles. How we live in this world will very much determine our life in the hereafter.

People have been commanded to respect and honor God-given positions and responsibilities. It is God who created people and gave them spouses, children, parents, brothers and sisters, and all other relatives. He gave us neighbors, friends, and servants; all these belong to one's family. People are to serve God and serve their families. No one should be proud of neglecting one's duties or be boastful of one's service. God commands us in Surah Al-Nisa: "Serve Allah, and do not associate anything with Him. Be good to your parents and relatives, and to the orphans, the needy, and your neighbors, whether near or far, and also to your companions around you and to wayfarers and those whom your right hands possess. Surely, Allah does not love him who is proud, boastful (Qur'an 4:36)." This verse virtually makes the whole of humanity our family. We have to respect each one of them and fulfill our obligations towards them to the best of our ability.

There are as many ways of learning as there are human beings, and each may be adequate, depending on the emotional - intellectual makeup of an individual and the availability of opportunities. The best is an educational system where the moral values of human character and behavior are developed along with competency in professional fields. Such educational systems are not available in contemporary secular schools. Both the religious and secular aspects of human life need to be addressed in order to nurture an honest, hardworking, and competent individual. God desires that a well balanced human personality be developed for the progress of humanity. That is why He has given people an ability to endeavor in all areas of learning, "And He taught Adam the names of all things; ... (Qur'an 2:31)." Therefore, schools that only stress either religious or secular aspects of life are not helping the society. People need an integrated educational system for the development of all human faculties.

Currently, the most prevalent route to acquiring the knowledge that helps build the required human character and behavior is through self study of the Qur'an and *Ahadith*, supplemented by the writings of religious scholars. In the past Arabic was the only way to study the Qur'an, and thus many people would recite Qur'an without understanding the meanings because of non-availability or limited availability of translations of the Qur'an. Since translations and interpretations of the Qur'an are now available in almost every widely known language, one can also learn and understand the Qur'an in one's own language. However, learning and understanding the Qur'an in its original Arabic language is highly preferred. The importance of knowing what God commands us in the Qur'an is such that nothing should discourage people, not even the lack of ability to understand Arabic.

Presentations given in this book are my notes and highlights, which were prepared during my study of the Qur'an chapter by chapter. This approach is an example to be followed, especially by those who do not know Arabic and are unable to understand the Qur'an in its original Arabic text. The translation of the Qur'an by Abdullah Yusuf Ali, with minor modifications as required for clarity, has been used in this study.

In the name of Allah, the Compassionate, the Merciful

CHAPTER 1

Guidance for Those Who Desire
FROM SURAH AL-FATIHAH (01)

God created people, gave them wisdom, free will, and guidance, and appointed each one of them, male or female, rich or poor, to be His trustee on earth and to serve Him by implementing His commands in managing their affairs, in order to build a just human society in this world. The Qur'an has been revealed for the guidance of humanity. It contains the instructions, which if followed will help people to establish a prosperous and peaceful human society based on justice and mutual respect. Life in this world is a test so that people may prove who can utilize one's life to its best purpose and potential. This requires that one should know one's duties and should live accordingly to the divine laws. God has provided the required guidance for the fulfillment of one's duties as God's trustee on earth. This guidance has been given within the human gene in the form of human conscience, and it has been taught and implemented by His messengers who lived their lives as human role models. The commands given in the Qur'an encompass all moral, economic, and sociopolitical areas of human activity that are required to be implemented to develop and protect human character and society. Before implementation, one has to know what is required. This can be learned from the Qur'an.

1 EACH INDIVIDUAL IS GOD'S TRUSTEE ON EARTH

1.1 People should serve God as His Trustee on Earth
A long time ago in the past, "Behold, your Lord said to the angels: 'I will create a vicegerent on earth.' They said: 'Will You place therein one who will make mischief therein and shed blood, while we do celebrate Your praises and glorify Your holy

1

(name)?' He said: 'I know what you know not' (Qur'an 2:30)." What the angels did not know at that time was that God will provide His trustees the needed guidance to discharge their duties properly. Since God created us, He expects that we should only serve Him: "He has commanded that you worship none but Him: that is the right religion, but most men understand not (Qur'an 12:40)."

1.2 Trustees Need Guidance to perform their Duties

After the initial orientation, "He (God) taught Adam the names of all things; then He placed them before the angels and said: 'Tell me the names of these if you are right (Qur'an 2:31).'" God provided guidance to people for the fulfillment of their duties as His trustees on earth. This guidance has been provided within the human gene in the form of human conscience, and His messengers have reminded humanity of this guidance throughout history. The teaching of the Qur'an is from God, and it is the very demand of His mercy that He should provide guidance to humankind through this teaching, for it is He Who has created man as a rational and intelligent being: "(Allah) Most Gracious! It is He Who has taught the Qur'an. He has created man. He has taught him speech (and intelligence) (Qur'an 55:1-4)."

1.3 The Guidance is there only for those who Desire

God created humankind with conscience and free will. Only those people who believe in God with all of His attributes, who have respect for Him, and who are sure about the accountability for their deeds desire His guidance. Realizing this, they say, "In the name of Allah, Most Gracious, Most Merciful. Praise be to Allah, the Cherisher and Sustainer of the worlds; Most Gracious, Most Merciful; Master of the Day of Judgment (Qur'an 1:1-4)." It is not blind faith but their rational thinking and understanding that motivate such people to declare, "You do we worship, and Your aid we seek. Show us the straight way (Qur'an 1:5-6)." These people are genuine candidates for guidance. Peoples' desire for help and guidance after the realization of their relationship with their Creator has been fulfilled in the revelations of the Qur'an and in their elaboration in the *Sunnah* of the Messenger. This guidance when implemented individually and socially will lead to, "the way of those on whom You

2

(Allah) have bestowed Your grace, those whose (portion) is not wrath, and who go not astray (Qur'an 1:7)."

2 UNIVERSE HAS BEEN ESTABLISHED ON JUSTICE

2.1 People may not transgress the Balance

God has established the entire universe on justice, precisely and equitably, and the nature of this system requires that those who dwell in it should adhere to justice within the bounds of their authority and should not disturb the balance. Humankind has been warned of the dire consequences of disobeying God, and they have been made aware that the best results, both in this world and the Hereafter, come from obeying Him. God tells people in Surah Ar-Rahman: "The sun and the moon follow courses (exactly) computed, and the herbs and the trees both prostrate in adoration. And the sky has He raised high, and He has set up the balance (of justice) in order that you may not transgress the balance. So establish weight with justice, and fall not short in the balance (Qur'an 55:5-9)."

2.2 Injustice has Adverse Consequences

God expects that people should not transgress the balance; otherwise, they will have to face the consequences of injustice in this world and in the Hereafter. God warns hypocrites and unbelievers in Surah Al-Ahzab: "Truly, if the hypocrites, and those in whose hearts is a disease, and those who stir up sedition in the city desist not, We shall certainly stir you up against them. Then will they not be able to stay in it as your neighbors for any length of time. They shall have a curse on them; whenever they are found, they shall be seized and slain. (Such was) the practice (approved) by Allah among those who lived aforetime. No change will you find in the practice of Allah (Qur'an 33:60-62)."

3 THE QUR'AN IS THE GUIDANCE FOR HUMANKIND

3.1 The Divine Commandments or the Laws of Nature

The universal truths or the laws of nature given in the Qur'an encompass all moral, economic, and sociopolitical areas of human activity. These laws are required to be followed and implemented to develop and protect human character and society.

3.2 Both Believers and Unbelievers Benefit from Laws
Individuals and society benefit from Islamic laws in this world to the extent that these laws are implemented, irrespective of whether one believes in God and the Hereafter or not. However, those who believe in God and the accountability for their deeds and are motivated by their belief will be successful in the Hereafter.

3.3 Unbelievers Benefit from their Deeds in the World
Unbelievers typically do not believe in life after death. They may think that they came into existence by an evolutionary process set in place by time and the environment and that they will die and disintegrate without facing any accountability for their deeds. As such, they may not benefit in the Hereafter from their good deeds on earth. However, each person will have to account for his behavior and deeds regardless of what he believes.

4 THE TRANSGRESSION OF THE UNIVERSAL LAWS

4.1 Implementation of the Divine Laws
Islam, i.e., correct belief and behavior as taught in the Qur'an, is not just about accumulating rewards and going to Paradise in the Hereafter. Before this can happen, one has to know how to implement God's commands, and one must then try to complete one's assignment as God's trustee on earth by implementing His commands. People have to follow God's commands in managing their personal and social affairs. This will then lead to establishing a just human society and welfare community in this world.

God assures us, "…those who believe and work righteousness—no burden do We place on any soul, but that which it can bear—they will be Companions of the Garden, therein to dwell (Qur'an 7:42)." The Qur'an also states: "Allah has promised to those among you who believe and work righteous deeds that He will, of a surety, grant them in the land inheritance (of power), as He

4

granted it to those before them; that He will establish in authority their religion—the one which He has chosen for them; and that He will change (their state), after the fear in which they (lived), to one of security and peace: 'They will worship Me and associate none with Me.' If any do reject faith after this, they are rebellious and wicked (Qur'an 24:55)."

4.2 Transgressions of the Divine Laws

As God's trustee, humankind should know its duties in this world. There are consequences for one's behavior and deeds. Although the evil consequences of unbelief are there for sure in the Hereafter, there are also consequences in this world for transgressing universal laws. There can be two types of evil consequences that one may face in this world, i.e., the evil consequences of upsetting the balance of justice and of allowing corruption to flourish.

Disregarding moral, economic, and sociopolitical laws has its consequences, regardless of whether it is done by a believing or unbelieving individual and society. For example, anarchy or lack of security is directly proportional to the magnitude of injustice in society. If we desire to build a prosperous and peaceful community, we have to establish justice.

Human society should be built on hard work, truth, justice, and charity. Such a society is almost free of corruption, discrimination, exploitation, and oppression. Our actions determine our present and our future. It is the choice one makes, knowing that all actions, either good or bad, have appropriate consequences. If most people in a society are corrupt, and if no one is trying to improve, the society will eventually be destroyed from within. Since God has discontinued sending messengers, corrupt people and communities may not be completely destroyed as happened in the past. Still God commands us to guard against and, "...fear the oppression, which affects not in particular (only) those of you who do wrong: and know that Allah is strict in punishment (Qur'an 8:25)."

CHAPTER 2

Obligations of the Believers
FROM SURAH AL-BAQARAH (02)

The contract between people and God consists of three set of obligations that believers have to fulfill during their lives on earth. These obligations are about belief and worship, society and justice, and individual livelihood. The divine contract consists of people's obligations to God and their obligations to God's creation, including their fellow people. This is a single and complete whole, each part being of equal importance. To ignore any part is to reject it altogether. By virtue of being believers, we have entered into a contract with God to live our lives in this world according to the guidelines given in the Qur'an. These guidelines are summarized in Surah Al-Baqarah. Before implementing a contract, one should know the terms of the contract. Thus, the first obligation of believers is to understand what is written in the Qur'an.

All terms of the contract must be implemented. For example, in speaking about Bani Israel, God stressed that the partial implementation of the contract is not acceptable. As described in Surah Al-Baqarah, a believer's obligations can be classified into three areas. (1) There are obligations relevant to belief in God and His worship. These obligations help to develop and nurture a relationship with the Creator and reform individual character and behavior. (2) The main body of the contract is about the relationship of individuals with their fellow humankind. These sociopolitical obligations are about providing basic human needs and establishing justice and security. Most of these obligations can only be properly fulfilled by governments enforcing laws that facilitate the establishment of peace and justice. (3) Guidelines have also been provided about the types of food that should or should not be consumed and about the forbidden means of earning one's livelihood.

1 THE ESTABLISHMENT OF JUST SOCIETIES

The ultimate objective of God's reward and punishment is to save humankind from evil. Such evil is possible because of one's possession of free will. The selfish use of free will must be eliminated by education and discipline. History tells us that evil and corruption have destroyed many nations because they worshiped false idols, false standards of conduct, and false goals of desire.

1.1 Divine Guidance is to Save Humanity from Evil

A complete description of the guidelines for human conduct is given in the Qur'an. These guidelines educate us, and their implementation makes us disciplined. "This is the Book; in it is guidance sure, without doubt, to those who fear Allah...; O people! Adore your Guardian-Lord, Who created you and those who came before you that you may have the chance to learn righteousness (Qur'an 2:2, 21)." Humanity needs discipline in order to provide a better life. People who do not follow the guidelines create problems. God says, "When it is said to them: 'Make not mischief on the earth,' they say, 'Why we only want to make peace!' Of a surety, they are the ones who make mischief, but they realize (it) not (Qur'an 2:11-12)."

1.2 Knowledge Leads to Wisdom and then to Obedience

As God's trustee on earth, learning to manage our affairs is our first obligation. With knowledge comes understanding and then obedience. One must know the guidelines before one can implement them. This makes it obligatory that believers should understand what is described in the Qur'an. To achieve this purpose, we have to study, understand, and implement the Qur'an in our lives. People are told: "Those who, when they are admonished with the revelations of their Lord, droop not down at them as if they were deaf or blind (but try to understand and act upon them) (Qur'an 25:73)...We have sent it down as an Arabic Qur'an, in order that you may learn wisdom (Qur'an 12:2)...A Book where of the verses are explained in detail—a Qur'an in Arabic for people who understand (Qur'an 41:3)...Verily, We have made this (Qur'an) easy on your tongue, in order that they may give heed (and take guidance) (Qur'an 44:58)." The Qur'an

7

contains instructions, which if followed, bring blessings to people and to society. "(Here is) a Book which We have sent down unto you, full of blessings, that they may meditate on its revelations and that men of understanding may receive admonition (Qur'an 38:29)...Those who listen to the Word, and follow the best (meaning) in it: those are the ones whom Allah has guided, and those are the ones endued with understanding (Qur'an 39:18)...And follow the best of (the courses) revealed to you from your Lord, before the penalty comes on you suddenly while you perceive not (Qur'an 39:55)."

A believer, who does not know Arabic, should try to understand the message of the Qur'an by consulting its translations in a language he knows. Believers who understand Arabic should make it their duty to provide the meanings of the Qur'an to those who do not understand Arabic. Translations and commentaries can be studied and understood in one's own language. However, a believer should be able to read the Qur'an in Arabic text during the obligatory prayers. God tells the Messenger: "We have sent down unto you the message that you may explain clearly to people what is sent for them and that they may give thought (Qur'an 16:44)...You can but admonish such a one as follows the message and fears the (Lord) Most Gracious, unseen: give such a one, therefore, good tidings, of forgiveness and a reward most generous (Qur'an 36:11)." God assures people success if they act upon His commands as given in the Qur'an: "Those who recite the Book of Allah, establish regular prayer, and spend out of what We have provided for them, secretly and openly, hope for a commerce that will never fail (Qur'an 35:29)."

2 THE IMPLEMENTATION OF THE CONTRACT

2.1 O You Who Believe, Fulfill all Obligations

In Surah Al-Baqarah, God gives the example of Bani Israel, their contract with Him, and its partial fulfillment, and He tells us that the partial fulfillment of obligations is not acceptable. Partial fulfillment of a contract is breaking the contract. "Those who break Allah's covenant after it is ratified, and who sunder what Allah has ordered to be joined, and do mischief on earth—these cause loss only to themselves (Qur'an 2:27)." This contract consists of worshiping God, social obligations, and political obligations. Most of the Israelites failed in meeting their obligations, especially those concerning human rights and security. God reminds people: "And remember We took a covenant from the Children of Israel (to this effect): worship none but Allah; treat with kindness your parents and kindred, and orphans and those in need; speak fair to the people; be steadfast in prayer; and practice regular charity. Then did you turn back, except a few among you, and you backslide (even now). And remember We took your covenant (to this effect): shed no blood among you, nor turn out your own people from your homes: and this you solemnly ratified, and to this you can bear witness. After this it is you, the same people, who slay among yourselves and banish a party of you from their homes, assist (their enemies) against them in guilt and transgression, and if they come to you as captives, you ransom them, though it was not lawful for you to banish them. Then is it only a part of the Book that you believe in, and do you reject the rest? But what is the reward for those among you who behave like this but disgrace in this life? And on the Day of Judgment, they shall be consigned to the most grievous penalty. For Allah is not unmindful of what you do (Qur'an 2:83-85)." The covenant of God with Bani Israel is summarized in the table below.

Table 2.1: Terms of Contract with Bani Israel

Worship	Social Obligations	State Obligations
Worship none but God (Qur'an 2:83).	Be good to parents, relatives, orphans, and the needy. Speak kindly (Qur'an 2:83).	Shed not the blood of your people (Qur'an 2:84).
Establish Prayer (Qur'an 2:83).	And pay *Zakah* (obligatory charity) (Qur'an 2:83).	Nor turn (some of) your people out of your dwellings (Qur'an 2:84).

2.2 Partial Fulfillment of the Obligations
Partial fulfillment of the obligations is not acceptable. Partial fulfillment of the obligations or contract is like believing in only part of the Book and rejecting the rest? God reminds us that the reward for willfully performing only partial fulfillment is

9

disgrace in this life and on the Day of the Judgment. God tells people that it is not obedience to follow only what you like and to reject what you do not like or what requires some efforts for implementation!

3 THE ISLAMIC CONTRACT

3.1 The Obligations of Those Who Believe

The believers have entered into a contract with God to live their lives according to the guidelines described in the Qur'an. Implementation of all of these obligations is required, "O you who believe! Enter into Islam wholeheartedly; and follow not the footsteps of the Satan; for he is to you an avowed enemy (Qur'an 2:208)." The obligations of believers as given in Surah Al-Baqarah are summarized below in Table 3.2 and are broken down into the three types of obligations that are specified in the Qur'an.

3.2 Individual, Social and State Obligations

Like God's contract with Bani Israel, the Islamic contract consists of three types of obligations, i.e., (1) belief and worship, (2) social obligations, and (3) state obligations. This is to illustrate that unlike other religions, Islam regulates all areas of human activity. These obligations are summarized in the table below.

Table 3.2: The Islamic Contract

Belief & Worship	Social Obligations	State Obligations
1. Believe in God, the Day of Judgment, the angels, and His books and messengers (Qur'an 2:177).	1. Spend your wealth, out of love of God, on relatives and needy, and do not eat up your property wrongly (Qur'an 2:177, 188).	1. Equitable punishment is prescribed for murderers (Qur'an 2:178).
2. Establish prayer (Qur'an 2:177).	2. Pay *Zakah* (obligatory charity) (Qur'an 2:177).	2. Establish justice; do not bribe judges (Qur'an 2:188).
3. Fasting is prescribed (Qur'an 2:183).	3. Fulfill contracts (Qur'an 2:177).	3. Fight for justice and against oppression (Qur'an 2:190, 193).

10

4. Perform *Hajj* (Qur'an 2:196).	4. Be firm and patient (Qur'an 2:177).	4. Warfare is prescribed (Qur'an 2:216).
	5. Do not marry unbelieving women or men. Women have rights similar to those of men (Qur'an 2:221, 228).	5. Write down contracts with two witnesses. Witnesses should not refuse to testify or conceal evidence (Qur'an 2:282-283).
	6. Proper distribution of inheritance is prescribed (Qur'an 2:180).	

4 PEOPLE'S RELATIONSHIP WITH GOD

4.1 Belief and Worship Help to Learn Righteousness

Belief and worship are for training the believers to learn righteousness so that they may perform their duties properly. Humankind was not created to make mischief in this world. God commands people in Surah Al-Baqarah to worship Him with the objective of transforming themselves into righteous people. "O you people! Adore your Guardian-Lord, Who created you and those who came before you, that you may become righteous (Qur'an 2:21)." Belief and worship as prescribed by God create a sense of patriotism and dedication that motivate people to establish God's laws on earth.

4.2 Worship Helps to Learn Self-restrain and Courage.

Fasting during the month of *Ramadan* is made obligatory for the believers in order to teach them self-control and patience. God tells us in Surah Al-Baqarah, "Fasting is prescribed for you as it was prescribed for those before you so that you may learn self-restraint (Qur'an 2:183)." Similarly, the establishment of prayer, performing *Hajj*, and being firm and patient during suffering, adversity, and times of panic develop the desired relationship with God that gives the strength of character and courage required to say no to evil temptations and to make people honest in performing their sociopolitical obligations.

5 SOCIOPOLITICAL OBLIGATIONS

The implementation of the sociopolitical obligations of God's contract with us necessitates a system or establishment that requires the participation of all members of society. Such a system is a government formed by believers for the establishment of financial and social security, justice, equality, and civil liberties for all of its citizens. An Islamic government or the Islamic community itself is collectively responsible for the management of *Zakah*, fulfillment of contracts, security of life and property, establishment of justice, and instituting warfare when no alternative is available. These areas of responsibility, as discussed in Surah Al-Baqarah, are summarized below.

5.1 Collection and Distribution of *Zakah* and Charity
For meeting the basic necessities of the poor, disabled, and elderly, one may pay *Zakah* individually, but this will not assure that the needy population as a whole is properly served. During the early Islamic period, *Zakah* was collected and distributed by the government to provide the basic necessities for families during times of need. Several governments of non-believing states have borrowed this concept from Islam and have implemented it in their countries.

Parallel to *Zakah*, it is also obligatory for believers to "Give your wealth out of love of God to relatives, to orphans, to needy, to travelers, and to those who ask and spend it to buy the freedom for the slaves (Qur'an 2:177)." This obligation is exclusively at an individual's discretion to give to the needy out of his/her surplus wealth. Administration of the *Zakah* is the responsibility of Islamic community. This makes its proper implementation a duty of the Islamic governments. By paying *Zakah* individually, we may be meeting the requirement of the voluntary financial help only. Therefore, the government of an Islamic country that fails to provide basic necessities to its needy citizens from *Zakah* funds or the state treasury is not meeting its obligation.

5.2 Contracts between Individuals or Groups

Individuals should fulfill their part of a contract if all of the terms of the contract are clear and if both parties equally desire its implementation. In case of differences or the failure of a party, arbitration may be needed. Therefore, governments should arrange the implementation of contracts in such cases. As a safeguard against doubt, God commands in Surah Al-Baqarah: (1) "O you who believe, when you deal with each other in transactions involving future obligations then write them down ...(Qur'an 2:282);" (2) "If the party liable is mentally deficient, or weak, or unable himself to dictate, let his guardian dictate faithfully, and get two witnesses, out of your own men, and if there are not two men, then a man and two women, such as you choose, for witnesses, so that if one of them errs, the other can remind her. The witnesses should not refuse when they are called for evidence (Qur'an 2:282);" (3) "Conceal not evidence; for whoever conceals it – his heart is tainted with sin (Qur'an 2:283)."

5.3 Provision for the Security of Life and Property

The basic aim of Islam is the creation of an orderly and just society. Through divine revelations, basic standards of human conduct have been established. Compassion for the weak, fairness in commercial dealings, security of life and property, incorruptibility in administration of justice, and equal justice for all are enjoined. In this regard, Islam tries to reform society by persuasion, e.g., believing in God and doing good deeds are the central theme of the Qur'an. Punishments are only prescribed if these are needed to check heinous crimes like murder, physical injury, adultery, and theft. For example, in Surah Al-Baqarah God tells us, "O you who believe, the law of equality is prescribed for you in cases of murder: the free for the free, the slave for the slave, the woman for the woman... (Qur'an 2:178)."

5.4 The Establishment of the Security and Justice

For the establishment of justice and to safeguard against internal oppression and external aggression, believers are commanded as follows. "Fight in the cause of Allah those who fight you, but do not transgress limits...And fight them on until there is no more oppression, and there prevail justice and faith in Allah; but if they cease, let there be no hostility... (Qur'an 2:190,193)." In sanctioning war, Islam has defined its aim and purpose. These are to suppress tyranny and persecution and to guarantee freedom of belief for all. Specific situations for waging war and making peace are given in various places in the Qur'an. God tells us in Surah Al-Baqarah: "Fighting is prescribed for you, and you dislike it. But it is possible that you dislike a thing that is good for you and that you love a thing that is bad for you. But Allah knows, and you know not...And if Allah did not check one set of people by means of another, the earth would indeed be full of mischief (Qur'an 2:216,251)."

Islamic belief and worship inculcate an attitude of God-fearing or righteousness, incorporating faith and individual behavior. Individual behavior impacts the organization of a just community. This consistent and deliberate approach highlights the essential nature of the religion of Islam. It is an integral system, an indivisible whole. Its social systems, legislative codes, and religious rituals emanate from faith, and a comprehensive world order is generated. These are all held together by a common goal of submission to and veneration of God, the Creator and the Provider, Who has instituted man as His trustee and custodian in this world. This trusteeship is conditional on the worship of God alone and on receiving all systems and laws from Him only. For the smooth operation of a just community, believers are commanded, "Do not eat up your property among yourselves for vanities, nor use it as bait for the judges, with the intent that you may eat up wrongfully and knowingly a little of (other) people's property...It is prescribed, when death approaches any of you, if he leave any goods that he make a bequest to parents and next of kin, according to reasonable usage...And women shall have rights similar to the rights against them, according to what is equitable; but men have a degree (of advantage) over them (Qur'an 2:188,180,228)."

6 FOODS AND LIVELIHOOD

Guidelines have also been given in Surah Al-Baqarah about the types of foods that should and should not be consumed. Forbidden methods of earning one's livelihood have also been articulated. God commands us, "O you people, eat of what is on earth, lawful and good, and do not follow the footsteps of the Satan, for he is to you an open enemy...O you who believe, eat of good things that we have provided for you, and be grateful to Allah, if it is Him you worship (Qur'an 2:168,172)." Concerning food and earning one's livelihood, there are three options: the permissible, the illegal, and the doubtful. The believers are commanded to avoid the illegal and the doubtful. It is narrated by An-Nu'man bin Bashir that the Prophet said, "Both legal and illegal things are obvious, and in between them are (suspicious) doubtful matters. So whoever forsakes those doubtful things, lest he may commit a sin, will definitely avoid what is clearly illegal, and whoever bravely indulges in these (suspicious) doubtful things is likely to commit what is clearly illegal (Sahih Bukhari: vol.3, book 34, no. 267)."

6.1 Meats Unfit for Human Consumption
God has forbidden eating the following four types of meats in Surah Al-Baqarah (2:173) and the fifth one in Surah Al-An'am (6:121).

1. Meat of the dead animal,
2. blood,
3. the flesh of swine, and
4. that on which any name other than of Allah has been invoked.
5. Do not eat of that on which Allah's name has not been mentioned.

6.2 The Prohibition of Intoxicants and Gambling
"They ask you concerning wine and gambling. Say: 'In them is great sin and some profit for men, but the sin is greater than the profit (Qur'an 2:219)." In Surah Al-Ma'idah the use of intoxicants and gambling is also prohibited: "O you who believe! Intoxicants and gambling, (dedication of) stones, and (divination by) arrows are an abomination of Satan's handwork; eschew such (abomination) that you may prosper. Satan's plan is (but) to excite enmity and hatred between you with intoxicants and gambling, and hinder you from the remembrance of Allah, and from prayer; will you not then abstain (Qur'an 5:90-91)?"

15

6.3 Dishonest Earnings and Bribing the Judges

The food that has been earned by concealing the truth, cheating, lying, or fraud has also been forbidden for believers. "Those who conceal Allah's revelations in the Book and purchase for them a miserable profit, they swallow into themselves nothing but fire (Qur'an 2:174)." Illegal use of each other's property and bribing judges for this purpose are forbidden. God commands, "And do not eat up your property among yourselves for vanities, nor use it as bait for the judges, with the intent that you may eat up wrongfully and knowingly a little of (other) people's property (Qur'an 2:188)."

6.4 Usury, Hoarding, and the Unfair Marketing

"Those who devour usury will not stand except as stands one whom Satan by his touch has driven to madness. That is because they say: 'Trade is like usury, but Allah has permitted trade and forbidden usury'... Allah will deprive usury of all blessing, but will give increase for deeds of charity; for He loves not creatures ungrateful and wicked (Qur'an 2:275-276)." Concerning hoarding and unfair marketing, the Qur'an dictates that one must be fair to one's fellow sellers and to consumers. Hoarding of goods for higher profit by creating an artificial shortage of goods in the marketplace is forbidden in Islam. "And let not those who covetously withhold of the gifts that Allah has given them of His grace think that it is good for them. Nay, it will be the worse for them; soon shall the things that they covetously withheld be tied to their necks like a twisted collar on the Day of Judgment (Qur'an 3:180)."

CHAPTER 3

Islam, the Sociopolitical System
FROM SURAH ALI-IMRAN (03)

The believers' objective in life is the implementation of Islam. A strong moral character, honest efforts, patience, and dedication are required to overcome the difficulties that can befall one in attempting to achieve this objective. Believers are neither afraid of difficulties nor of death, as nothing happens without the will of God. Being aware of their mission of righteousness for humanity, believers hold together in unity and discipline. They keep on improving their character and behavior, enforce justice, propagate virtue, and discourage vice. Since God loves those who do good deeds, believers are rewarded in this life and bestowed with even greater reward in the next life.

1 HUMANITY HAS A MISSION IN LIFE

Humankind has been placed on earth as God's trustee to enforce and administer Divine Law. "Behold, your Lord said to the angels: 'I will create a vicegerent (trustee) on earth' (Qur'an 2:30)."

1.1 Humankind as God's Trustee on the Earth
Being God's trustee is a great responsibility. It implies duties imposed upon all people in general and on believers in particular. The main duty is to endow humankind with righteous life and for this purpose to invite all towards good, enforcing what is right and forbidding what is wrong. Moral and sociopolitical laws have been revealed to lead humanity to observe such conduct that establishes justice in this worldly life. This results in peaceful and prosperous life in this world and is rewarded by God with the best life in the next world.

1. 2 The Life and the Mission of God's Trustee
Analyzing various incidents of hardship during the early stages of establishing the Islamic state at Madinah, God tells the believers in Surah Ali-Imran: (1) the basic principles of life and

17

death, (2) the objective of a believer's life is the implementation of Islam, and (3) how the implementation of Islam can be achieved. These areas that impact the human life on earth are highlighted in the following sections.

2 BASICS OF LIFE AND DEATH

2.1 Provision for Life, Leadership, and Honor

Provision for life, honor, difficulties, and death come only from God and at ordained time. Believers, therefore, should not be concerned about these things. God tells us to affirm: "O Allah! Lord of Power (and Rule), You give power to whom You please, and You strip off power from whom You please. You endue with honor whom You please, and You abase whom You please. In Your hand is all good. Verily, You have power over all things. You cause the night to pass into the day, and You cause the day to pass into the night. You bring the living out of the dead, and You bring the dead out of the living, and You give sustenance to whom You please without measure (Qur'an 3:26-27)."

2.2 It is God Who gives Life and Death

It is weakness of faith that makes people afraid of meeting death, of doing one's duties that involve danger, of losing one's status, honor, or even livelihood. Since nothing can happen without the will of God, a believer is neither afraid of meeting death nor afraid of any danger. God tells us: "It is Allah that gives life and death (Qur'an 3:156);" and "It is only the Satan that suggests to you the fear of his votaries. Be not afraid of them, but fear Me, if you have faith (Qur'an 3:175)."

2.3 The Difficulties and the Trials in One's Life

Testing good people with difficulties and hardship and leaving evildoers enjoying their lives is a part of God's plan of giving some freedom of choice to people. Wealth, possessions, and our personal talents, knowledge, opportunities, and misfortunes are all means of the trial. We are tested in everything that happens to us and makes our personalities. God asks us: "Did you think that you would enter Heaven without Allah testing those of you who fought hard (In His cause) and remained steadfast (Qur'an

3:142)?" What should be the attitude of believers during difficult times? God tells us: "But if you persevere patiently and guard against evil, then that will be a determining factor in all affairs (Qur'an 3:186);" and "Never will I suffer to be lost the work of any of you, be he male or female (Qur'an 3:195)." The verses of Surah Ali-Imran highlighting the basics of life and death are given in the table below.

Table 2: Basics of Life and Death

No	Surah:Verses	Meanings
		Trials in Life and God's Protection
1	3:166	1. What you suffered on the day the two armies met was with the leave of Allah, in order that He might test the believers.
	3:173	2. For us, Allah is sufficient, and He is the best disposer of affairs.
	3:179	3. Allah will not leave the believers in the state in which you are now, until He separates what is evil from what is good.
		People Live and Die as God Pleases
2	3:145	4. No one can die except by Allah's leave, the term being fixed as by writing.
	3:156	5. It is Allah that gives life and death.
	3:157	6. And if you are slain or die in the way of Allah, forgiveness and mercy from Allah are far better than all they could amass.
	3:169	7. Think not of those who are slain in Allah's way as dead. Nay, they live, finding their sustenance in the presence of their Lord.
	3:185	8. Everyone shall have a taste of death.

3 ISLAM: THE SOCIOPOLITICAL SYSTEM

3.1 Objective of the Believer's Life and His Mission

God has prescribed the best moral and sociopolitical system in Islam, and the objective of the believer's life is its implementation in his own self and its establishment in society. Nothing except Islam, the establishment of justice under all circumstances, is acceptable for believers. Believers propagate virtue and discourage vice.

19

3.2 Nothing except Islam is Acceptable to God

The contemporary nations of the world seem confused and lost. Various sociopolitical systems have been tried without success, despite the fact that God tells us: "If anyone desires a religion other than Islam, never will it be accepted of him; and in the Hereafter He will be in the ranks of those who have lost. And how shall Allah guide those who reject faith after they accepted it and bore witness that the Messenger was true and that clear revelations had come unto them? But Allah guides not a people unjust (Qur'an 3:85-86)." God is warning us of a great loss if we keep on rejecting God's revelations and do not help "those who rise up from the people to establish what is right and just." The verses of Surah Ali-Imran, defining the objective of and the consequences of not implementing Islam are given in the following table.

Table 3: The Moral and Sociopolitical System of Islam

No	Surah:Verses	Meanings
		Islam Is – the Submission to God's Will
1	3:019-020	1. The religion before Allah is Islam (submission to His will)... Say: "I have submitted my whole self to Allah and so have those who follow me."
	3:102	2. O you who believe! Fear Allah as He should be feared, and die not except in the state of Islam.
		Alternate to Islam is a painful punishment
2	3:021	1. As to those who deny the revelations of Allah and in defiance of right, slay the prophets, and slay those who teach just dealing with mankind, announce to them a grievous penalty.
	3:090	2. But those who reject faith after they accepted it, and then go on adding to their defiance of faith, never will their repentance be accepted, for they are those who have (of set purpose) gone astray.
		Establishing what is right and just is Islam
3	3:104-110	1. Let there arise out of you a band of people inviting to all that is good, establishing what is right, and forbidding what is wrong...You are the best people evolved for mankind,

		enjoining what is right and forbidding what is wrong.
3:114		2. They believe in Allah and the Last Day; they enjoin what is right and forbid what is wrong, and they hasten (in emulation) in (all) good works.

4 THE IMPLEMENTATION OF ISLAM

For the implementation of any sociopolitical system, a group of dedicated people of good moral character and behavior is required. A community or a country where Muslims are in the majority is an Islamic community. If the Muslims in such a community are true believers, they will organize to be ruled by Islamic Law. It is the responsibility of the Islamic community as a whole to implement Islam individually and in society.

4.1 Islamic Brotherhood and the Community
All believers belong to the Islamic community. Referring to community affairs, God tells us: "Be not like those who are divided among themselves and fall into disputations after receiving clear signs (instructions from Allah) (Qur'an 3:105)." In the Qur'an, there are instructions for dealing among believers and with non-believers. Believers deal gently among themselves and consult each other. They forgive each other's faults and decide to go ahead with the implementation of Islam while putting their trust in God. Although the believers are encouraged to be friendly with all people, they are commanded not to ally themselves with unbelievers against each other. Likewise, they are told not to give away their secrets to others. Further, in matters of faith, the believers should not obey the unbelievers. God tells the believers: "O you who believe, if you obey the unbelievers, they will drive you back on your heels, and you will turn back (from faith) to your own loss (Qur'an 3:149)." The working guidelines of an Islamic community are given below.

21

Table 4.1: Working Guidelines of an Islamic Community

No	Surah:Verses	Meanings
		Dealings Within the Community
1	3:028	1. Let not the believers take for friends or helpers unbelievers rather than believers, except by way of precaution that you may guard yourselves from them. If any do that, in nothing will there be help from Allah.
	3:103	2. Hold fast, all together, by the rope that Allah (stretches out for you), and be not divided among yourselves; and remember with gratitude Allah's favor on you; for you were enemies and He joined your hearts in love, so that by His grace, you became brethren...
	3:159	3. It is part of the mercy of Allah that you (the Messenger or the believing leadership) deal gently with them. Were you severe or harsh-hearted, they would have broken away from you. So pass over (their faults), and ask for (Allah's) forgiveness for them, and consult them in affairs (of moment). Then when you have taken a decision, put your trust in Allah. For Allah loves those who put their trust (in Him).
		Dealing with Hostile Non-Believers
2	3:118	1. O you who believe! Take not into your intimacy those outside your ranks. They will not fail to corrupt you. They only desire your ruin.
	3:120	2. But if you are patient and do right, not the least harm will their cunning do to you...

4.2 The Islamic Leadership

Various stages of development in the life of a believer are described at different places in the Qur'an. Believing in One God and His Messenger, along with other articles of faith, admit a person into the Islamic community. Worshiping and practicing the Islamic way, learning the proper attitude in life, and developing the moral character and behavior as prescribed by God make believers the righteous people (*Muttaqeen*). The righteous people assume the leadership role, guiding other people and reforming society by establishing what is right and just. These people are the true believers (*Momineen*). Islam

22

demands continual improvement of individual character and behavior from its followers. All believers are obligated to make honest efforts to become qualified—qualified to receive God's forgiveness and His mercy in this world and in the Hereafter. The main attributes of the believers are that they: (1) admit mistakes and reform, (2) stand firmly on justice, (3) enforce justice and keep the trust, and (4) propagate virtue and discourage vice. In meeting their responsibilities, the believers make honest efforts, spend whatever is at their disposal, and always remain earnestly engaged in good works. The qualifications, responsibilities, behavior, and the efforts of the believers, as highlighted in Surah Ali-Imran are given in the table below.

Table 4.2: Leadership Traits of the Believers

No	Surah:Verses	Summery of the Meanings
1	3:016	Those who say: "Our Lord! We have indeed believed. Forgive our sins and save us from the agony of fire."
2	3:017	Those who show patience, (firmness, and self control).
3	3:017	Those who are true (in words and deeds), and obedient.
4	3:017	Those who spend (in the way of Allah and hoard not).
5	3:017	Those who pray for forgiveness in the early hours of the morning.
6	3:021	Those who rise up from among the people to enforce justice.
7	3:075	Those who if entrusted with a hoard of gold, will (readily) pay it back.
8	3:076	Those who keep their pledges and act aright.
9	3:084	Those who believe in Allah, and in what has been revealed to us and what was revealed to Abraham, Isma'il, Isaac, Jacob, and the Tribes (of Israel), and in the books given to Moses, Jesus, and the prophets from their Lord.'
10	3:092	Those who give (freely) of what they love.
11	3:102	Those who fear Allah as He should be feared and die not except in the state of Islam.
12	3:104	Those who are inviting to all that is good, enjoining what is right, and forbidding what is

		wrong.
13	3:110 3:114	Those who enjoin what is right, forbid what is wrong, and believe in Allah. Those who believe in Allah and the Last Day, enjoin what is right, and forbid what is wrong.
14	3:114	Those who strive with one another in hastening to do good deeds.
15	3:125	Those who are patient, remain firm, and act aright.
16	3:130	Those who devour not usury ... and fear Allah.
17	3:134	Those who spend whether in prosperity or in adversity.
18	3:134	Those who control anger and are forgiving.
19	3:139	Those who neither lose heart nor grieve or despair.
20	3:146	Those who never lost heart if they met with disaster in Allah's way, nor did they weaken (in will), nor give in...but are firm and steadfast.
21	3:153	Those who do not grieve for any loss or misfortune.
22	3:161	Those who do not deceive or are false to their trust.
23	3:176	Those who grieve not at the conduct of the disbelievers.
24	3:180	Those who don't think that hoarding of wealth is better for them.
25	3:200	Those who persevere in patience and constancy, vie in such perseverance, strengthen each other, and fear Allah'

CHAPTER 4

Human Rights and Obligations
FROM SURAH AN-NISA (04)

The believers spend their lives fulfilling their obligations towards God and His people. The importance of obligations towards people is stressed in Surah An-Nisa. Besides establishing prayer, fasting, and paying *Zakah* (obligatory charity), Muslims are obligated to take active part in the struggle to establish justice for all in every circumstance. Muslims are also obligated to fight in self-defense and against injustice, discrimination, and oppression. For a believer who is interested in his salvation, believing in God, praying five times a day, fasting in the month of *Ramadan*, paying *Zakah* and performing *Hajj* once in a lifetime may not be enough. He has to take part actively in the establishment of social justice, and he has to fulfill all of his moral, social, and financial obligations towards his relatives, orphans, the poor, and other people. We should always remember that God may forgive all sins that relate to our duties towards Him, but He may not forgive anything that is due to another person until that person is ready to forgive it. Hence, a balance between these two must be restored before one can truly claim to lead an Islamic life.

1 HUMAN LIFE ON EARTH IS A TRIAL

Islam tells people that they have two types of obligations. Their obligations to God and their obligations to people are of equal importance, and neither should be ignored. In numerous places in the Qur'an wherever belief and worship are mentioned to represent our obligations to God, what follows is a statement about good deeds or righteous works representing our obligations to other among ourselves. As an illustration, God tells us in Surah Al-Baqarah: "Those who believe (in the Qur'an), and those who follow the Jewish (scriptures), and the Christians and the Sabians—any who believe in Allah and the Last Day, and work righteousness (or do good deeds), shall have their reward with their Lord; on them shall be no fear, nor shall they grieve (Qur'an 2:62)." These two types of religious obligations are commonly known as *haqooq Allah* (obligations to God) and *haqooq ul abad* (obligations to people).

1.1 People's Trial by Conduct and Deeds

God has created humankind and appointed it His trustee on earth in order to test its behavior and deeds. In Islam, the importance of one's obligations towards other human beings is no less than one's obligation towards God Himself. In many sayings of the Messenger, we have been told that God may forgive peoples' shortcomings in the fulfillment of their duties towards Him, but He may not forgive our mistreatment of each other. An unjust oppressor will have to pay back the price of his misdeeds. Since duties towards other people are part of God's commands, these obligations are to both God and His creation, making them equally important.

1.2 Obligations to Humanity

It is the duty of each and every believer that they should fulfill their obligations towards their fellow humans with the utmost care. Anything short of an honest livelihood may render one's prayers, fasting, and other acts of worship invalid. In Surah Al-Hajj God tells us, "Those who believe and work righteousness, for them is forgiveness and sustenance most generous (Qur'an 22:50)." Besides belief, regular prayers, and regular charity, God has stressed the performance of good deeds at numerous places in the Qur'an. The good deeds referred to in the above verse are those actions that are taken for the care of His creation, including humankind. God does not benefit from our obedience or compliance with His rules; we do. In a sacred *Hadith* (a report as to what Prophet Muhammad said or did with regard to religion), as narrated by Abu Dharr al-Ghifari, the Messenger quotes God as saying: "My servants, it is but your deeds that I reckon up for you and then recompense you for (in this world). Therefore, let him who finds good praise Allah, and let him who finds other than that blames no one but himself (Sahih Muslim: 32.6246)." Some verses of the Qur'an stressing the importance of good behavior and deeds are given in the table below.

Table 1: Life is a Trial – by Conduct and Deeds

No	Surah:Verses	Meanings
1	06:165	It is He Who has made you (His) trustees, inheritors of the earth. He has raised you in ranks, some above others, that He may try you in the gifts He has given you. For your Lord is quick in punishment; yet, He is indeed oft-forgiving, most merciful.
2	10:013-014	Generations before you We destroyed when they did wrong. Their messengers came to them with clear signs, but they would not believe! Thus do We requite those who sin! Then We made you heirs in the land after them, to see how you would behave.
3	11:007	He it is Who created the heavens and the earth in six days—and His throne was over the waters—that He might try you, which of you is best in conduct.
4	18:007	That which is on earth we have made but as a glittering show for the earth, in order that We may test them as to which of them are best in conduct.
5	49:013	O people! We created you from a single (pair) of a male and a female and made you into nations and tribes that you may know each other (not that you may despise each other). Verily, the most honored of you in the sight of Allah is (he who is) the most righteous of you, and Allah has full knowledge and is well acquainted (with all things).

2 ISLAM IS WORSHIPING GOD AND DOING GOOD DEEDS

Humankind, being innately inclined to worship, is impelled to worship something. If people do not worship one God, their Creator and a power above them, they will worship something else, e.g., idols of their own creation, an ideology, a personality, or whatever impresses them. Worship in Islam is not a matter of flattering God to win favors from Him. When the Qur'an says that God created people so that they might worship Him, worship does not merely mean verbal veneration and begging for benefits. Rather, it means living a life according to the

27

commandments of God. Every right action is an act of worship, and what is right is the will of God. When people are true to themselves and good to their families and fellow beings, their lives are full of worship. The true implication of worship in Islam is to be good, to nurture peace and perfection of character and behavior that is free of fear, anxiety, and stress, to bow before God in prayers, and to be thankful to Him for bestowing opportunities to fulfill all the obligations of *haqooq Allah* and *haqooq ul abad.*

"O people! Adore your Guardian-Lord, Who created you and those who came before you, that you may have the chance to learn righteousness (Qur'an 2:21)." Learning righteousness is the direct outcome of worshiping God. And what is righteousness? It is the ability and capacity to do righteous deeds. Learning righteousness is initiated with our belief in and worship of our Creator, along with overcoming our physical and moral weaknesses. This will transform us into better persons of good moral character and behavior. Humanity needs a character that makes it easier for people to be fair and just in our dealings among ourselves and with other creations of God. Believers are motivated by their conscience to fight against injustice and corruption and to do righteous deeds for the benefit and welfare of all people. When living together, many individuals of good moral character and behavior do establish just and peaceful communities by encouraging each other in performing good deeds and by discouraging deeds which are harmful to the society. In other words, Islam consists of two equally important parts: (1) belief in and worship of God, and (2) doing good deeds. What people do in respecting human rights and in fulfilling their obligations to others are good deeds. The subject matter of Surah An-Nisa consists of commandments relevant to what is stressed in the Qur'an as good deeds.

2.1 Worshiping God Should Lead People to Good Deeds
People require guidance and motivation to respond to their duties regardless of their immediate benefits. This is why various types of worship are prescribed for the believers. People take time to get used to a certain duty and to be convinced of its wisdom. Taking fasting as an example, the decree of fasting starts with

the address made to the believers, which reminds them of their essential quality, that is, they believe in God. They are then told that fasting has always been a duty of the believers in all religions. Its principle aim is their education and training so that their hearts acquire a high standard of sensitivity and purity and so that the fear of God is well established in them. "O you who believe! Fasting is prescribed for you, as it was prescribed for those before you, that you may (learn) self-restraint (Qur'an 2:183)." Similarly, prayers and the payment of *Zakah* have been commanded for the believers, "Those who believe, and do deeds of righteousness, and establish regular prayers and regular charity, will have their reward with their Lord; on them shall be no fear, nor shall they grieve (Qur'an 2:277)". Likewise, God tells us, "And complete the *Hajj* or *Umra* in the service of Allah…And fear Allah, and know that Allah is strict in punishment (Qur'an 2:196)."

2.2 Good Deeds Confirm Peoples' Sincerity in Worship

To believe in God and the Last Day and to spend out of what God has given people are all good deeds. There is a reward for good deeds from God. He will give full reward to those who believe in Him and do good deeds. Those who have believed in God's revelations and have done good deeds, whether they are men or women, will be admitted to Paradise. Various verses of the Qur'an stressing the importance of good deeds are given in the table below.

Table 2.2: Importance of Good Deeds in Islam

No	Surah:Verses	Meanings
		Good Deeds are **Better than the Wealth and the Children**
1	02:148	1. Every one has a direction to which he should turn, therefore hasten to (do) good deeds; wherever you are, Allah will bring you all together; surely Allah has power over all things
	04: 085	2. Whoever recommends and helps a good cause becomes a partner therein, and whoever recommends and helps an evil cause shares in its burden. And Allah has power over all things.

29

	04:124	3.	Those who have done good deeds, be they male or female, and have faith, they will enter Heaven, and not the least injustice will be done to them.
	18:046	4.	Wealth and children are an ornament of life of the world, but the good deeds that endure are better in your Lord's sight for reward, and better in respect of hope.
		Good Deeds are **Faith, Charity, and Forgiveness**	
2	03:134	5.	Those who spend, whether in prosperity or in adversity, and those who restrain (their) anger and pardon men – for Allah loves those who do good.
	22:077-078	6.	O you who believe! Bow down, prostrate yourselves, and serve your Lord; and do good that you may succeed. Strive hard in (the way of) Allah, (such) a striving is due to Him. He has chosen you and has imposed no difficulties on you in religion; it is the faith of your father Abraham.
	103:002-003	7.	Verily, man is in loss, except those who believe, do good deeds, exhort one another to truth, and exhort one another to endurance.

2.3 Islam is Belief, Worshiping God, and Good Deeds

Along with worship, the believers participate in all activities that build a good society according to their ability. People should honestly try to do as many good deeds as possible. God tells us in Surah Al-A'raf: "But those who believe and work righteousness—no burden do We place on any soul but that which it can bear—they will be Companions of the Garden, therein to dwell (Qur'an 7:42)." In Surah An-Nisa, God gives us the details regarding both good and sinful acts and commands us: "If you (but) eschew the most heinous of the things that you are forbidden to do, We shall expel out of you all the evil in you and admit you to a gate of great honor (Qur'an 4:31)." God also promised, "…to those among you who believe and work righteous deeds that He will, of a surety, grant them in the land, inheritance (of power), as He granted it to those before them; that He will establish in authority their religion—the one that He has chosen for them; and that He will change (their state), after the fear in which they (lived), to one of security and peace (Qur'an 24:55)." Thus, as highlighted in the table below, Islam has two equally important parts: (1) belief in and worshiping God, and (2) doing good deeds.

Table 2.3: Islam is Worshiping God and Doing Good Deeds

Those who Believe in Islam They				
ESTABLISH WORSHIP				
1	2	3	4	5
Believe in Allah's Revelations. (Qur'an 2:277)	Establish *Salah* (obligatory prayers) (Qur'an 2:277)	Pay *Zakah* (obligatory charity) (Qur'an 2:277)	Fast during the month of *Ramadan* (Qur'an 2:183)	Perform *Hajj* (Qur'an 2:196)
AND DO GOOD DEEDS				
Honest Earnings: Don't eat up each other's property wrongfully, and don't use it as bribes to judges. Give up devouring usury, and do not value the hoarding of wealth. Don't conceal truth for a miserable profit. (Qur'an 2:177, 188, 275-276)				
Character and Dealings: Keep your trusts. Fulfill your pledges, and keep your oaths. (Qur'an 3:75-76; 4:58)				
Justice: Establish justice under all circumstances. Enforce what is right, and forbid what is wrong. (Qur'an 2:188; 3:21, 104, 110, 114)				
Jihad: Fight in the way of Allah for the sake of helpless men, women, and children who, being weak, have been oppressed. (Qur'an 2:190, 193)				
Social Work: Spend out of what Allah has given you. Remain earnestly engaged in good works. "You are the best people evolved for mankind, enjoining what is right, forbidding what is wrong, and believing in Allah." (Qur'an 3:17, 110)				

3 GOOD OR RIGHTEOUS DEEDS

3.1 Working Hard to Earn an Honest Living

Concerning an honest living, God commands: "O people! Eat of what is on earth, lawful and good; and do not follow the footsteps of Satan, for he is to you an avowed enemy. For he commands you what is evil and shameful and that you should say of Allah that of which you have no knowledge (Qur'an 2:168-169)." Islam encourages everyone to work hard to earn one's livelihood. It also mandates the responsibility of the government to help people find jobs or establish a business. In Islam, work is equated with worship. Anas bin Malik narrated: "We were with the Prophet (on a journey), and the only shade one could have was the shade made by one's own garment. Those who fasted did not do any work, and those who did not fast (being exempt from fasting because of the journey) served the camels, brought water to them, and treated the sick and wounded. So the Prophet said, 'Today, those who were not fasting took all the reward' (Sahih Bukhari 4.52.140)." Anas bin Malik also narrated: "The Messenger said, 'There is none amongst the Muslims who plants a tree or sows a seed and then a bird or a person or an animal eats from it, but it is regarded as a charitable gift from him' (Sahih Bukhari 3.39.513)."

God has called an honest earning a "bounty of your Lord." Ibn 'Abbas narrated: "'Ukaz, Majanna, and Dhul-Majaz were marketplaces in the pre-Islamic period of ignorance. When Islam came, Muslims felt that marketing there might be a sin. So, the divine inspiration came: 'There is no harm for you to seek the bounty of your Lord (Qur'an 2:198)' (Sahih Bukhari 2.26.822)." Striving hard to earn one's livelihood is a form of worshiping God. When one reflects that the purpose of worship is to ensure forgiveness and consequently gain salvation, and that forgiveness can be ensured through hard work, the equation of endeavor with worship becomes clear.

3.2 Inculcation of Islamic Character and Behavior
Islam requires its followers to observe a specific Islamic character and behavior. A Muslim has a unique identity that is reflected in his manners and behavior. He is always polite, kind, and steering away from what is vulgar or obscene in words or actions. A Muslim is kind to others and always prefers what is likely to cement good relations with his fellow human beings. It is his continuous duty to evaluate his dealings with others, in order to provide a good example of what Islam means in practice, by living up to requirements of his faith. A Muslim is an exponent of every virtue and refrains from everything that does not fit with the noble attribute God has bestowed on humanity. He should bring out and enhance every good aspect in

32

human life and shun every evil tendency. The Prophet said, "When you are kindly to your neighbor, you are a believer. When you wish for others what you wish for yourself, you are a Muslim (Al-Hadith, vol. I, no.153, page 252)." The Messenger linked the quality of being a person of faith to being kind to neighbors. In addition, he attached the very idea of being a Muslim to loving for others and what one wants for oneself.

When a believer works hard, lives honestly, is kind to one's neighbor, and wishes for others what he wishes for himself, then the community belonging to such people will be entirely different from all those known on the face of the earth today. There are some communities where some of these qualities may exist in varying degrees, but there is hardly any that is accomplished in all aspects. Until we have a community where all these qualities are in full blossom, we cannot say there is a truly Islamic community. When these qualities are all lacking, then the community is not Islamic, even though all the people in that community have Muslim names and claim to believe in Islam.

3.3 Establishing Justice under all Circumstances
It is mandatory in Islam that Muslims should be just in their dealings with others. They should help to establish justice under all circumstances. Neither their self-interest, the self-interest of their parents, family, or relatives, nor anything else should interfere with justice. Neither wealth nor poverty should influence any judgment. One should not plead for the dishonest or sinful person. Efforts should be made to insure that neither blame nor sin is associated with an innocent person. God commands that believers give trust into the care of those persons who are worthy of trust and that one should judge with justice among people. In Surah An-Nisa, God commands: "O you who believe, stand out firmly for justice, as witnesses to Allah, even as against yourselves, or your parents, or your kin, and whether it be (against) rich or poor: for Allah can best protect both. Follow not the lusts (of your hearts), lest you swerve, and if you distort (justice) or decline to do justice, verily Allah is well-acquainted with all that you do (Qur'an 4:135)."

The aim of divine guidance is to serve human interest and to help people build a happy life in a community characterized by justice. Justice must be achieved at all levels—within the family, the local community, the social hierarchy and the political system. God says: "My servants, I have forbidden Myself injustice and made injustice forbidden to you. Therefore, do not act unjustly to one another (Sahih Muslim: 32.6246)." Moreover, history proves that whenever people established their system on the basis of divine guidance and applied God's law, their achievements were commendable.

3.4 Striving to Eradicate Injustice and Oppression

God commanded the believers to fight in self-defense and for the defense of Human Rights. "Why should you not fight in the cause of Allah and of those who, being weak, are ill-treated (and oppressed)?—Men, women, and children whose cry is: 'Our Lord! Rescue us from this town whose people are oppressors, and raise for us from You one who will protect, and raise for us from You one who will help!' (Qur'an 4:75)." God also ordered the believers to fight with those hypocrites and disbelievers who fight with them. "If they become rebels (and make war against you), capture them or slay them (in battle) wherever you find them. Don't take friends or helpers from their ranks (Qur'an 4:89)." However, those hypocrites are excluded from the above treatment if they have joined a people with whom Muslims have a treaty or if they are averse to fighting against you or with their own people. "Therefore, if they withdraw from you but fight you not, and (instead) send you (guarantees of) peace, then Allah Has opened no way for you (to war against them) (Qur'an 4:90)." God commanded His Messenger to fight and urged Muslims to do so because, "Whoever recommends and helps a good cause becomes a partner therein, and whoever recommends and helps an evil cause shares in its burden. And Allah has power over all things (Qur'an 4:85)." Since "Wherever you are, death will find you out, even if you are in towers built up strong and high (Qur'an 4:78)," the believers should not be afraid of death in conducting just warfare.

3.5 Social Work, Enjoining Good, and Forbidding Evil

God tells the believers, "You are the best people evolved for mankind, enjoining what is right, forbidding what is wrong, and believing in Allah (Qur'an 3:110)." Believing in God is necessary in order that those who invite to all that is good, enjoin what is right, and forbid what is wrong can proceed along their appointed course and bear all its difficulties and hardships. They have to face the tyranny of evil, the pressures of worldly desires, complacency, weakness, and narrow ambitions. As they do that, they have to be equipped with faith. Their support comes from God.

A believing community has to assign some of its members to invite others to what is good, enjoin the doing of what is right, and forbid what is wrong. A true Islamic community does not come into existence unless it has this essential quality that distinguishes it from other communities. Its invitation to all that is good, its enjoining what is right and forbidding what is wrong, in addition to believing in God, gives credence to its existence as a Muslim community, without which it loses its Islamic existence.

4 HUMAN RIGHTS AND OBLIGATIONS

A Muslim must respect and honor basic human rights, and he must fulfill his obligations to others. Specific instructions to the believers in Surah An-Nisa about the rights of the other are highlighted below.

4.1 Rights of the Orphans and the Weak

Allah enjoins believers to deal justly with orphans–the children who are weak and helpless (Qur'an 4:127). He asks us to take care of the orphan's property (Qur'an 4:2). When orphans are capable, their property should be returned to them in the presence of witnesses. A rich guardian should not use an orphan's property during the orphan's upbringing, while a poor guardian can use it in a fair manner to support the orphan (Qur'an 4:6). "Those who unjustly eat up the property of orphans fill their bellies with fire, and most surely they shall be thrown into the burning fire of Hell (Qur'an 4:10)."

4.2 Women's Rights and their Obligations

God tells us in Surah An-Nisa that: (1) men (husbands) are the protectors and maintainers of women (wives) (Qur'an 4:34); (2) men own what they earn, and women own what they earn (Qur'an 4:32); (3) both women and men have a share in inheritance (Qur'an 4:7); and (4) women should be treated with respect, and men should live with them honorably (Qur'an 4:19). Additional rights of and obligations to women, as given in Surah An-Nisa, are summarized in the following table.

Table 4.2: Women's Rights and Obligations as Wives

No	Surah:Verses	Meanings
		The Marriage and Dower
1	4:004	1. Men should willingly give the dower to the women they marry. This dower is an obligation.
	4:019	2. It is neither lawful for men to inherit women by force nor lawful to treat wives harshly in order to deprive them of part of their dower. However, women guilty of adultery may be treated harshly.
		Misconduct in Marriage
2	4:015	3. If any of your women are guilty of lewdness, take the evidence of four witnesses from among you against them; and if they testify, confine them to houses until death do claim them, or Allah ordain for them some (other) way.
	4:016	4. If two among you are guilty of lewdness, punish them both (male and female). If they repent and amend, leave them alone; for Allah is oft-returning, most merciful.
		Character of Good Wives
3	4:034	5. Virtuous women are obedient and guard the rights of their husbands carefully in their absence under the care and watch of Allah.
		Compromise in Marriage
4	4:128	6. If a wife fears cruelty or desertion on her husband's part, there is no blame on them in compromising on some points in marriage.
	4:129	7. In situations where there is more than one wife, the husband should not ignore either one of them.

		Reconciliation or Divorce
5	4:035	8. For reconciliation, appoint arbiters, one from his family and the other from hers; if they wish peace, Allah will cause their reconciliation.
	4:020	9. During separation, a husband should not take back any gift that he has given her.
	4:130	10. If spouses do separate, Allah will make each one of them independent of each other by His vast powers and limitless sources.

4.3 Rights of Relatives, the Poor, and Others

In Surah An-Nisa, people are commanded to serve Allah, associate none with Him, and show kindness and affection to parents. Be kind to relatives, orphans, and the needy. Be considerate to your neighbors, your companions, wayfarers, and those who are under your protection. In our dealings with others, we should not be proud and boastful. God does not like those who are proud and boastful. We should neither hoard wealth nor encourage others to be stingy. God stresses in this Surah that people should be careful of their duty to God, under Whose name they claim their rights from one another. The specific verses of Surah An-Nisa that highlight the rights of people are summarized in the table below.

Table 4.3: Rights of Relatives, the Poor, and Others

No	Surah:Verses	Meanings
		God Commands People to Do
1	4:001	O people! Reverence your Guardian-Lord, Who created you from a single person, created of like nature his mate, and from them twain scattered countless men and women. Reverence Allah, through Whom you demand your mutual rights, and (reverence) the wombs (that bore you).
2	4:007	1. From what is left by parents and those nearest related, there is a share for men and a share for women, whether the property be small or large, a determinate share.
	4:033	2. To those, also, to whom your right hand was pledged; give their due portion.
	4:029	3. O you who believe! Eat not up your property among yourselves in vanities, but let there be

	4:032	among you traffic and trade by mutual good will.
		4. And do not covet those things in which Allah has bestowed His gifts more freely on some of you than on others. To men is allotted what they earn, and to women what they earn.
	4:036-037	5. Serve Allah, and join not any partners with Him; and do good to parents, kinsfolk, orphans, those in need, neighbors who are near, neighbors who are strangers, the companion by your side, the wayfarer (you meet), and what your right hands possess. For Allah loves not the arrogant, the vainglorious, (nor) those who are miserly or enjoin miserliness on others, or hide the bounties which Allah has bestowed on them; for We have prepared, for those who resist Faith, a punishment that steeps them in contempt.
	4:058	6. Allah does command you to render back your trusts to those to whom they are due, and when you judge between man and man that you judge with justice.
		God Commands People to Refrain From
3	4:105	1. We have sent down to you the Book in truth that you might judge between men, as guided by Allah: so be not (used) as an advocate by those who betray their trust.
	4:112	2. But if any one earns a fault or a sin and throws it on to one that is innocent, He carries (on himself) (both) a falsehood and a flagrant sin.
	4:135	3. O you who believe! Stand out firmly for justice, as witnesses to Allah, even as against yourselves, or your parents, or your kin, and whether it be (against) rich or poor: for Allah can best protect both. Follow not the lusts (of your hearts); lest you swerve, and if you distort (justice) or decline to do justice, verily Allah is well acquainted with all that you do.
	4:148	4. Allah loves not that evil should be noised abroad in public speech, except where injustice has been done.

5 THE SUCCESSFUL AND UNSUCCESSFUL PEOPLE

5.1 The Successful People

God lists a number of characteristics of those whom He judges to be successful people in Surah An-Nisa. The verses of Surah An-Nisa that highlight the character and behavior of the successful people are summarized in the table below.

Table 5.1: The Successful People

No	Surah:Verses	Summary of the Meanings
1	4:013	Those who obey (the commandments of) Allah (and do not cross the limits).
2	4:029	Those who do not devour one another's property by unlawful ways.
3	4:031	Those who abstain from those heinous sins that have been forbidden by Allah.
4	4:057	Those who believe (Allah's revelations) and do righteous deeds.
5	4:069	Those who obey Allah and His Messengers.
6	4:074-075	Those who fight in the cause of Allah and for the sake of those weak and helpless men, women, and children who have been oppressed.
7	4:114	Those who secretly exhorts to a deed of charity or justice or conciliation between men among people for seeking the good pleasure of Allah.
8	4:122	Those who believe and do good deeds.
9	4:124	Those who do good deeds, whether men or women, provided they believe, will enter Paradise.
10	4:146	Those who repent and mend their ways and dedicate their religion sincerely to Allah.
11	4:162	Those among them who are well-grounded in knowledge and who have (true) faith—they believe in what has been revealed to you and what was revealed before you: And (especially) those who establish regular prayer and practice regular charity and believe in Allah and in the Last Day:'

5.2 The Unsuccessful People

Similarly, according God's statements in Surah An-Nisa, there are specific characteristics associated with those people whom God will judge as being unsuccessful. These characteristics are summarized in the following table.

Table 5.2: The Unsuccessful People

No	Surah:Verses	Summary of the Meanings
		Belief in God, in the Day of Judgment, and in His Angels, Books, and Messengers
1	4:018	Those who persist in their evil deeds until the dying hours and who die as non-believers.
2	4:051	Those who were given a portion of the Book, believe in sorcery and evil, and say that non-believers are more rightly guided than the believers.
3	4:056	Those who reject Allah's revelations.
4	4:136	Those who disbelieve in Allah, His angels, His scriptures, His messengers, and the Last Day.
		Opposition to the Messenger and following a Non- Believer's Way
5	4:115	Those who oppose the Messenger even after guidance has been plainly conveyed to them and follow a path other than that of the believers.
6	4:119	Those who forsake Allah and take Satan for a friend.
7	4:150	Those who deny Allah and His messengers.
8	4:167	Those who reject faith and lead others away from the path of Allah.
9	4:168	Those who disbelieve and commit injustice and iniquity.
10	4:173	Those who disdain the service of Allah and take pride in it.
		Hypocrites and Believers who are not careful about their duty to God
11	4:037	Those who hoard their wealth, enjoin avarice on others, and hide that which Allah has bestowed upon them of His bounty.
12	4:093	Those who kill a believer willfully.
13	4:097	Those who do not immigrate to avoid oppression without any reason.
14	4:137	Those who vacillate between faith and unbelief and eventually go on increasing in unbelief.

CHAPTER 5

Development of
Human Character and Society

FROM SURAH AL-MA'IDAH (05),
SURAH AL-AN'AM (06), AND SURAH AL-A'RAF (07)

God inculcates people to reflect, "Do you not see that Allah has subjected to your use all things in the heavens and on earth and has made his bounties flow to you in exceeding measure, seen and unseen? Yet there are among people those who dispute about Allah, without knowledge and without guidance, and without a Book to enlighten them…It is We Who have placed you with authority on earth and provided you therein with means for the fulfillment of your life (Qur'an 31:20; 7:10)." Why has God established people with authority on earth, and why has He provided all that they needed for the fulfillment of their lives? God describes the purpose behind the creation by saying, "We appointed you as rulers in the earth after them that We might see how you behave (Qur'an 10:14)." People have the assignment of being God's trustee on earth in order to evolve a system of life according to the dictates of their Lord and not according their own selfish desires.

Therefore, the people who are God's trustees are "Those who, if We establish them in the land, establish regular prayer and give regular charity, enjoin the right and forbid wrong: (Qur'an 22:41)." This makes it obligatory on each one of us that we should keep up the prayers, pay *Zakah*, enjoin what is good, and forbid what is evil. This is the only option we have if we want to succeed in life. Otherwise, our fate may not be any different from those destroyed societies we read about in history. "And guard yourselves against a chastisement that cannot fall exclusively on those of you who are wrongdoers, and know that Allah is severe in punishment…Truly, if the hypocrites, and those in whose hearts is a disease, and those who stir up sedition in the city, desist not, We shall certainly stir you up against them. Then will they not be able to stay in it as your neighbors for any length of time. They shall have a curse on them;

whenever they are found, they shall be seized and slain. (Such was) the practice (approved) of Allah among those who lived aforetime. No change will you find in the practice of Allah (Qur'an 8:25, 33:60-62)."

1 THE MISSION AND DESTINY OF HUMANKIND

In God's creation, there are the angels who can do only what is good. An angel cannot do something evil or disobey God. On the other hand, Satan and evil temptations, either from jinn or humans, are the opposite. They can do only evil. Humans and jinn are given the power of choice, and they determine for themselves whether to follow the guidance provided by God through his messengers or to indulge in satisfying their own wanton desires. These options are made clear for people right from their early years, and the chance to rectify one's attitude and to choose what is good is offered at every juncture. In fact, whoever errs, they can correct the error at any moment, repent, and turn to God for forgiveness. If they do so, then they are forgiven. When people abandon God's guidance, their lives on earth are nothing more than eating, drinking, and self-indulgence. God says in the Qur'an: "Verily, Allah will admit those who believe and do righteous deeds to gardens beneath which rivers flow, while those who reject Allah will enjoy (this world) and eat as cattle eat, and the fire will be their abode (Qur'an 47:12)."

1.1 God appointed Humankind as His Trustee
According to the Qur'an, people are made the master of the earth. They form a species different from animals, jinn, and angels. While Satan is disobedient to God, angels serve God without any hesitation, and people can choose to do either. Hence, people are accountable for what they choose to do. They have been placed in charge of the earth and are required to build it. By building the earth, we mean building a happy human life by following God's guidance, as explained by the prophets and messengers. God tells us that this is a test so that we may prove who among us can live a life to its best purpose and potential. God states in Surah Hud, "He it is Who created the heavens and

42

the earth in six days—and His throne was over the waters—that He might try you, which of you is best in conduct. (Qur'an 11:7)." Further, in Surah Al-Mulk we are told, "Blessed is He in Whose hand is the dominion, and He is able to do all things, Who has created death and life that He may test you, which of you is best in deed (Qur'an 67:1-2)."

1.2 God Gave Humankind the Authority on Earth

God tells people in Surah Al-A'raf, "Your Lord is Allah, Who created the heavens and the earth in six days, and He is firm in power. He throws the veil of night over the day, which it pursues incessantly. He created the sun, the moon, and the stars, made subservient to His command (Qur'an 7:54)." God then reminds people, "It is We Who have placed you with authority on earth and provided you therein with means for the fulfillment of your life (Qur'an 7:10)." God has provided sufficient means for all humankind to live in prosperity in this world. We have to exploit and properly manage these natural resources for our benefit. An Islamic society that is built on hard work, truth, justice and charity and that is free of corruption, discrimination, exploitation, and oppression will certainly provide all of the proper requirements for this effort.

1.3 People are to Serve God alone as His Trustees

God tells us, "I have only created jinn and men that they may serve Me. No sustenance do I require of them, nor do I require that they should feed Me (Qur'an 51:56-57)." Throughout the Qur'an, there are numerous verses that highlight God's creation of humankind and its objective in life. In Surah Al-Baqarah, people learn about their mission, the angels' concerns, and God's reply. "Behold, the Lord said to the angels: 'I am about to place a vicegerent (trustee) on earth.' They said: 'Will You place therein one who will make mischief therein and shed blood, while we do celebrate Your praises and glorify Your holy (name)?' He said: 'I know what you know not' (Qur'an 2:30)." What the angels did not know at that time was that God would provide His trustees the needed guidance to properly discharge their duties. Initiating this process of guidance, "He taught Adam the names of all things (every branch of knowledge); then He

43

placed them before the angels, and said: 'Tell me the names of these if you are right' (Qur'an 2:31)."

In Surah Al-An'am, God states the purpose of Adam's assignment: "It is He Who has made you (His) agents, inheritors of the earth. He has raised you in ranks, some above others, that He may try you by what He has given you. For your Lord is quick in punishment; yet, He is indeed oft-forgiving, most merciful (Qur'an 6:165)." The mission and the destiny of humankind have been elaborated further in Surah Sad in an instruction to David, "We did indeed make you a vicegerent (a ruler) on earth. So judge you between men in truth (and justice): Nor follow the lusts (of your heart), for they will mislead you from the path of Allah. For those who wander astray from the path of Allah is a penalty grievous, for that they forget the Day of Account (Qur'an 38:26)."

1.4 God has been Guiding and Helping People
In Surah Bani Israel, God assures the Messenger of His help during people's struggle to accomplish their mission: "Their purpose was to scare you off the land in order to expel you, but in that case they would not have stayed (therein) after you, except for a little while. This has been Our way with the messengers We sent before you. You will not find any change in Our way (Qur'an 17:76-77)." As motivation and reassurance of His help, God asks us in Surah Al-A'raf to, "Remember how He made you (the 'Ad) inheritors after the people of Noah, and gave you a stature tall among the nations. Remember the benefits (you have received) from Allah: that so you may prosper...And remember how He made you (Thamud) inheritors after the 'Ad people and settled you in the land: you build for yourselves palaces and castles in (open) plains and carve out homes in the mountains; so remember the benefits (you have received) from Allah; do not act corruptly in the land, making mischief (Qur'an 7:69; 7:74)."

1.5 Human Mission is to Eliminate Injustice
Human struggle and patience are prerequisites to eliminating injustice from the society. When the people of Moses complained of Pharaoh's injustice, "Moses said to his people:

44

'Pray for help from Allah, and be patient: for the earth is Allah's to give as a heritage to such of His servants as He pleases, and the end is (best) for the righteous.' They said: 'We have had (nothing but) trouble, both before and after you came to us.' He said: 'It may be that your Lord will destroy your enemy and make you inheritors in the earth; that so He may try you by your deeds' (Qur'an 7:128-129)." Eventually God helped Moses' people because they struggled patiently: "We made a people, considered weak, inheritors of lands in both east and west— lands whereon We sent down Our blessings. The good promise of your Lord was fulfilled for the Children of Israel because they bore up sufferings patiently (Qur'an 7:137)."

1.6 God eliminates Unjust Communities

In Surah Hud, the sort of human behavior that brings destruction has been described: "Generations before you, We destroyed when they did wrong. Their messengers came to them with clear-signs, but they would not believe! Thus do We requite those who sin! Then We made you heirs in the land after them, to see how you would behave (Qur'an 10:13-14)!" While Noah's people were destroyed, Noah and the believers were rescued: "But they rejected him (Noah), but We delivered him and those with him in the ark, and We made them inherit (the earth), while We overwhelmed in the flood those who rejected Our Signs. See then what was the end of the (people) warned (Qur'an 10:73)." Similarly, "We delivered him (Abraham) and (his nephew) Lot (and directed them) to the land that We have blessed for the nations. And We bestowed on him Isaac and, as an additional gift, (a grandson) Jacob, and We made righteous men of every one (of them). And We made them leaders, guiding (men) by Our command, and We sent them inspiration to do good deeds, to establish regular prayers, and to practice regular charity; and they constantly served Us (and Us only) (Qur'an 21:71-73)."

2 HUMAN MISSION AS GOD'S TRUSTEE ON EARTH

2.1 Managing Life According to the Divine Laws

What sort of lives should we lead? We have a choice at every moment in our lives. Should our lives be according to the divine laws and for what benefit? Our efforts in obeying certain rules in this world do not mean that we will only be saved from suffering in the Hereafter. Who benefits here on this earth? Does the benefit of our compliance accrue to someone else or to God? God does not benefit at all by our obedience to and compliance with His rules: we do, as is mentioned in a sacred (or *Qudsi*) *Hadith* in which the Messenger quotes God as saying: "My servants, it is but your deeds that I reckon up for you and then recompense you for (in this world), so let him who finds good praise God, and let him who finds other than that blame no one but himself (Sahih Muslim: 32.6246)."

2.2 Divine Laws Help Improve the Life on Earth

God has created humanity in a certain way and has sent messengers to guidance people to lead a happy life in accordance with divine law. A messenger's role is to highlight what behavior is beneficent and that reprieves problems and misery. What the messengers have conveyed is a complete message that outlines an integrated system devised by God, the Creator of humankind, Who knows what is appropriate and suitable for implementation in human life and that will bring happiness. Thus, whoever obeys God's rules is a beneficiary. The benefit is assured, as the rules are made to spare people affliction, contradiction, and confusion.

Our prayers and fasting do not benefit God in any way. However, our prayers certainly benefit us by keeping us on our guard against temptation and falling into sin. Fasting also teaches self-discipline. In contrast, humankind suffers by not implementing God's laws. It does not harm God in any way. The choice is there: do we do what is right and enjoy its benefits in this life as well as in the Hereafter, or do we reject it and suffer the consequences of this rejection.

2.3 The Progress of Human Character and Society

Since people have free will, perfection of their character and behavior without divine guidance is not possible. What Islam teaches is an attitude that leads to continual improvements in individual character and in society. Everyone is liable to error, and everyone makes errs. However, when believers err, they seek God's forgiveness, which is forthcoming when the request is genuine. Human character is improved with every incident of acknowledgment, regret, and the effort not to repeat the mistake again. An individual may be in error throughout one's life, but whenever he realizes his mistakes and repents, seeking God's forgiveness, God forgives everyone who turns to Him in genuine repentance. The verses of Surah Al-An'am, and Surah Al-A'raf, highlighting God's forgiveness as the motivation for continual improvement are given in the table below.

Table 2
God's Forgiveness- Motivation for Continual Improvement

No	Surah:Verses	Meanings
		God Commands People to Repent and Reform
1	6:054	1. When those come to you who believe in Our revelations, say: "Peace be on you: Your Lord has inscribed for Himself (the rule of) mercy." 2. Verily, if any of you did evil in ignorance, and thereafter repented, and amended (his conduct), lo! He is oft-forgiving, most merciful.
		Moses asked for God's Forgiveness and Mercy
2	7:155	1. Moses chose seventy of his people for Our place of meeting. When they were seized with violent quaking, He prayed: "O my Lord! If it had been Your will, You could have destroyed long before both them and me. Would You destroy us for the deeds of the foolish ones among us? 2. This is no more than Your trial; by it You cause whom You will to stray, and You lead whom You will into the right path. You are our Protector: so forgive us and give us Your mercy; for You are the best of those who forgive.
		God Forgives Those who genuinely Repent
3	7:156-157	Ordain for us that which is good in this life and in the hereafter: for we have turned unto You. He said: "With My punishment I visit whom I will; but My mercy extends to all things. That (mercy) I shall ordain (especially) for: 1. Those who do right, and 2. (Those who) practice regular charity, and 3. Those who believe in Our revelations— 4. Those who follow the Messenger, the

47

	unlettered Prophet, whom they find mentioned in their own (scriptures)—in the Torah and the Gospel ... So It is those who believe in him and honor him and help him, and follow the light which has been sent down with him, these it is that are the successful.

3 GOD GAVE LIFE TO TEST HUMANKIND

The world we live in is a small corner of the universe. Our stay here is only a small fraction of the life and our efforts are a part of the test. This could be the test in poverty or affluence or a mixture of both. Belief in God and trust in Him should result in action, so that what one does in life is governed by values and standards acceptable to God. A great number of people do not get enough to eat and live in inhuman conditions. This is due to the fact that humanity is not following what God tells us to, i.e., believe and do good deeds. Life on the earth is full of problems and pleasures. As time passes and the problems begin to be solved, they appear to be much smaller than originally thought. Either the importance of these problems was exaggerated or the ability to deal with them was underestimated. Similarly, with the passage of time, moments of great pleasure appear much smaller. This is because human beings tend to think of the present, of this moment, and of now, and consider this life on earth as the only life we have.

3.1 Materialistic Culture and Human Societies
The influence of materialistic ideology has affected the way life is being perceived. In the West, material wealth is the source of all happiness. Everything is geared towards achieving the dream of getting rich. A person who gets wealth quickly, applying whatever means necessary for that end, is often considered to be an extremely successful person. The draw of easy and fast wealth is always dangled before people's eyes. Lotteries are organized by governments, bookmakers flourish in business, and pools are offered to the young and old. They all offer the same prize of that elusive million.

48

As individuals, most people in materialistic countries are good in their own way and may be following several Islamic principles. However, as a society and a government, the Western countries have spent and are still spending untold billions on arms of mass destruction, selling them to the Third World, and encouraging the Third World to make their countries experimental battle fields. This is sapping their resources and keeping them in continuous poverty. It is true that people in the developing countries should be responsible for their misdeeds. However, but Western governments selling arms for their own material gain is working contrary to the benefit of humanity.

3.2 Human Character and Human Communities

Compare this materialistic attitude to the noble character of the believer and to a society built on Islamic principles. Happiness in the life to come greatly depends on the efforts of the believers to improve life in this world. This is very important, as individuals, irrespective of our situation or status in life, we should improve our behavior and try to help others in their struggle in life. What makes us suffer forever or makes us happy depends upon our deeds. God administers absolute justice to all. Our actions determine our present and our future. It is the choice one makes, knowing that all actions, both good and bad, have appropriate consequences.

If we look at the condition of people today; a large majority do not seem to have any specific purpose in life. This is our own fault because we are neglecting to look into the main sources of faith to determine our duties and our mission in life. It is not the accumulation of wealth and material things but the possession of human values and character that makes people human.

4 THE DEVELOPMENT OF
HUMAN CHARACTER AND SOCIETY

The Islamic concept of humankind gives this noble creature a very high position, and Islam provides every facility needed for humanity to achieve its potentials. That ensures the best results of one's efforts. Indeed, it is through such the willing con-

49

tribution to the community by all individuals in a Muslim society that Islamic civilization made its mark on history and continued to lead humanity for centuries. Every time Islam was implemented, the same sort of marvelous results were achieved. This assures us that the same thing could happen today if we, the Muslims, implement our *Deen* (religion; way of life) properly.

4.1 Basic Principals of Human Behavior

Throughout the Qur'an, God has explained and motivated us with basic principles. These principles, if followed, help reform and improve our character and behavior. Some of these principles are outlined below.

1. The guidance of Allah—that is the (only) guidance (Qur'an 2:120). One shall have the reward of what one earns, and none shall be asked for what the others did (Qur'an 2:134, 141).
2. To each is a goal to which Allah turns him; then strive together (as in a race) towards all that is good (Qur'an 2:148).
3. Nor can goodness and evil be equal. Repel (evil) with what is better (Qur'an 41:34). Repel evil with that which is best (Qur'an 23:96).
4. Allah does not love mischief (Qur'an 2:205). And did not Allah check one set of people by means of another, the earth would indeed be full of mischief (Qur'an 2:251).
5. Fulfill all obligations (Qur'an 5:1); abandon all sin, open or secret (Qur'an 6:120); seek means of approach unto Allah (Qur'an 5:35); guard your own selves (Qur'an 5:105).
6. Each person earns only on its own account; no bearer of burdens shall bear the burden of another (Qur'an 6:164).
7. Help one another in righteousness and piety, but help not one another in sin and transgression (Qur'an 5:2).
8. Whoever believes in Allah and the Last Day and work righteousness—on them shall be no fear, nor shall they grieve (Qur'an 5:69).
9. Not equal are things that are bad and things that are good, even though the abundance of the bad may dazzle you (Qur'an 5:100).

10. He that does good shall have ten times as much to his credit. He that does evil shall only be recompensed according to his evil (Qur'an 6:160).
11. To those against whom war is made, permission is given (to fight) because they are wronged, and verily Allah is most powerful for their aid (Qur'an 22:39).
12. Did not Allah check one set of people by means of another, there would surely have been pulled down monasteries, churches, synagogues, and mosques in which the name of Allah is much-remembered (Qur'an 22:40).

4.2 Righteousness, the Foundation of Human Character

What is righteousness? It is correct belief accompanied by good deeds. Righteous people believe that "kind words and the covering of faults are better than charity followed by injury (Qur'an 2:263)" and that God does not impose upon any person a duty beyond the extent of one's ability, i.e., "no burden do We place on any soul, but that which it can bear (Qur'an 6:152)."

So the righteousness is belief, charity, keeping prayers, paying *Zakah*, honoring promises, and being patient during testing times. God tells us that, "It isn't righteousness to turn our faces towards the East or the West but that righteousness is:

1. Believing in Allah, the Last Day, the angels, the Book, and the messengers;
2. Spending your substance, out of love for Him, for kin, orphans, the needy, the wayfarer, those who ask, and the ransom of slaves;
3. Being steadfast in prayer, and practicing regular charity;
4. Fulfilling the contracts that you have made;
5. Being firm and patient, in pain and adversity, and throughout all periods of panic (Qur'an 2:177)."

God loves the righteous people who are humble and strive hard fearlessly. God challenge believers in Surah Al-Ma'idah, "O Believers! Whoever from among you turns back from his faith, soon will Allah bring a people whom He will love as they will love Him—humble before the believers, mighty against the unbelievers, striving hard in the way of Allah, and never afraid of the reproaches of such as find fault. That is the grace of Allah, which He will bestow on whom He pleases (Qur'an 5:54)."

4.3 The Basic Principle of Dealing with Fellow Humans
Duties towards God, i.e., *haqooq Allah*, cannot be overly emphasized, but duties towards one's fellow human beings, i.e., *haqooq ul abad*, which are equally important, are unfortunately given a low position on the list of priorities in modern Muslim communities, both at the individual and community levels. Yet, a good balance is the main characteristic of Islam and its code of living. Little importance has also been given to the high-priority objective of Islam, namely the elimination of injustice. Yet, voices that speak against injustice remain faint, particularly among Muslim scholars. On the other hand, so much has been said and written about matters that cannot be described as being of equal importance with fighting injustice to one's family, relatives, servants, employees, neighbors, or fellow human beings. We should always remember that God may forgive all our sins that relate to our duties toward Him, but He will not forgive anything that is due to a human being until that person is ready to forgive it. Hence, balance between these two, *haqooq Allah* and *haqooq ul abad*, must be restored before we can truly claim to lead an Islamic life.

4.4 Give Full Measure while Dealings with Others
God commands people to give full measure when dealing among themselves. Truth and honesty, keeping promises and honoring trusts, fulfilling contracts and establishing justice are some of the most important socioeconomic principles to assure the peace and prosperity of communities. Whoever implements these in his life benefits from them, irrespective of whether he is a believer or an unbeliever. Implementation of Islamic socioeconomic principles leads to giving full measure with justice. In Surah Al-An'am, we are commanded: "Do not approach the orphan's property, except to improve it, until he attains the age of full strength. Give measure and weight with (full) justice—no burden do We place on any person, but that which it can bear. Whenever you speak, speak justly, even if a near relative is concerned, and fulfill the covenant of Allah. Thus does He command you, that you may remember (Qur'an 6:152)."

God commands us through His messenger Shu'ayb in Surah Al-A'raf that we should, give full measure, weight fairly, and not defraud people of their things: "He (Shu'ayb) said: 'O my people! Serve Allah. You have no other Allah save Him. Lo, a clear proof has come unto you from your Lord; so give full measure and full weight and wrong not mankind in their goods, and work not confusion in the earth after the fair ordering thereof. That will be better for you, if you are believers (Qur'an 7:85)." And again in Surah Hud, we are reminded by what Shu'ayb said to his people: "He said: 'O my people! Serve Allah, you have no god other than Him, and do not give short measure and weight. Surely I see you in prosperity, and I fear for you the punishment of an all-encompassing day. O my people! Give full measure and weight with justice. Do not diminish the goods of others, and do not act corruptly in the land, making mischief. That which is left you by Allah is best for you, if you are believers' (Qur'an 11:84-86)."

4.5 Fraud, Injustice, and Corruption Destroy People

Corruption is demeaning, inhuman, and a curse for a human society; it is an embodiment of laziness and dishonesty. In Surah Al-Furqan, people are told: "He to Whom belongs the dominion of the heavens and the earth—no son has He begotten, nor has He a partner in His dominion. It is He who created all things and ordered them in due proportions (Qur'an 25:2)." People have been commanded in Surah Bani-Israel to: "Give full measure when you measure, and weigh with a balance that is straight. That is the most fitting and the most advantageous in the final determination (Qur'an 17:35)." Again, God commands people in Surah Al-Shu'ara to: "Give just measure, and cause no loss (to others by fraud). Weigh with scales true and upright. And withhold not things justly due to men, and do not act corruptly in the earth, making mischief (Qur'an 26:181-183)." In Surah Al-Qamar, God says: "Verily, all things have We created in proportion and measure (Qur'an 54:49)." Further, God reminded people in Surah Al-Rahman that: "The heaven, He raised it high, and He has set up the balance (of justice) that you may not transgress (due) balance. So establish weight with justice, and fall not short in the balance (Qur'an 55:7-9)."

4.6. Corrupt People are Not Successful, but Cursed

Doesn't it seem that God has given us conscience and guidance for the sole purpose of reforming our dealings among ourselves? Are not the law and justice a prerequisite of humanity? God says in Surah Al-Hadid, "We sent aforetime our messengers with clear signs and sent down with them the Book and the balance (of right and wrong) that men may stand forth in justice (Qur'an 57:25)." In Surah Al-Talaq, it is confirmed that our livelihood does not depend on exploitation, injustice, and corruption, but God: "…provides for him from (sources) he never could imagine. And if any one puts his trust in Allah, sufficient is (Allah) for him, for Allah will surely accomplish his purpose. Allah indeed has appointed a measure for everything (Qur'an 65:3)." For this reason, God has cursed and even destroyed unjust communities in the past. In Surah Al-Mutaffifin, God says: "Woe to those that deal in fraud—those who, when they take from others by measure, take their full share, but who when they measure out to others or weigh out for them, they are deficient. Do they think that they will not be called to account on a mighty day, a day when all humankind will stand before the Lord of the Worlds (Qur'an 83:1-6)?"

4.7 Justice, the Foundation and Structure of the Society

In a sacred *Hadith*, the Messenger quotes God the Creator as saying: "My servants, I have forbidden Myself injustice and have made it forbidden among you, so do not be unjust to one another (Sahih Muslim: 32.6246)." God reminds believers of their covenant with Him in Surah Al-Ma'idah. He says: "…remember the favor of Allah unto you and His covenant, which He ratified with you when you said: 'We hear and we obey.' And fear Allah, for Allah knows well the secrets of your hearts (Qur'an 5:7)." Immediately following this reminder, God commands believers to be just in their dealings among themselves: "O you who believe! Stand out firmly for Allah as witnesses to fair dealing, and let not the hatred of others to you make you swerve to wrong and depart from justice. Be just—that is next to piety, and fear Allah. For Allah is well-acquainted with all that you do (Qur'an 5:8)." God asks the Messenger to remind people in Surah Al-A'raf that: "My Lord has commanded justice; and that you set your whole selves (to Him) at every time and place of prayer. And call upon Him, making your devotion sincere as in His sight. As He brought you forth in the beginning, so shall you also return (Qur'an 7:29)."

Addressing Jews and Christians, God tells them in Surah Al-Ma'idah that, if they had followed the law and established justice among themselves, they would certainly have been prosperous: "If only they had stood fast by the Torah and the Gospel and all that was revealed to them from their Lord, they would have been nourished from above them and from beneath their feet (Qur'an 5:66)." This confirms that the establishment of justice through what God has revealed brings individual and collective peace and prosperity to people. That is why God has revealed several books throughout history to guide people.

5 GOD'S COVENANT – THE IMPLEMENTATION OF HIS LAW

When a person employs reason and reflection, adopts the divine faith by way of his own free choice, and tries to implement it, he certainly attains the noblest level any creature can achieve. In contrast, when he chooses the opposite, he sinks down to the level of a base creature. However, depending on one's efforts, there can be different grades in between these two extremes. There is no "divine right" that gives a person a highest and most noble status. People can only achieve this status through their efforts in implementing God's law in their individual lives and in society.

5.1 Success or Failure—the Choice is Ours

Not every human can be included among the best of God's creation. God says in Surah Al-Tin: "We have indeed created man in the best of moulds. Then do We abase him (to be) the lowest of the low, except such as believe and do righteous deeds, for they shall have a reward never to be cut off (Qur'an 95:4-6)." These verses make it clear that a person can either attain the highest level of the creation, or sink to the lowest depth. What determines one's elevation or fall is one's response to God's message and one's implementation of that message in one's life. God has bestowed intellect and wisdom upon people. He has given them freedom of choice and has sent messengers as role models to show the way for them to fulfill their individual potential to the highest level of humanity. The messengers explained divine guidance to people and provided a practical code of living that was perfected in the message of Islam. Therefore, when people implement Islam, they reach their highest level. When they abandon this guidance, they sink into the depth of ignorance in which Satan tries hard to keep them.

5.2 God's Covenant with Jews and Christians

Citing the examples of the Children of Israel and Christians, God tells about the consequences of non-implementation of the divine law. In that regard, we are told that the Jews broke the divine covenant, resulting in their being cursed by God. Christians, on the other hand, neglected a portion of the guidance given to them, resulting in God exciting enmity and hatred among them to the day of resurrection. The verses of Surah Al-Ma'idah that highlight God's covenant with the Children of Israel and Christians are given in the table below.

Table 5.2: God's Covenant with the Jews and Christians

No	Surah:Verses	Meaning
		God's Covenant with the Jews
1	5:012-013	Allah did aforetime take a covenant from the Children of Israel, and We appointed twelve captains among them. And Allah said: "I am with you: 1. If you (but) establish regular prayers, practice regular charity, believe in my messengers, honor and assist them, and loan to Allah a beautiful loan. 2. Verily I will wipe out from you your evils, and admit you to gardens with rivers flowing beneath. 3. But whoever, after this, resists faith, he has truly wandered from the right way." But because of their breach of their covenant, We cursed them and made their hearts grow hard. 1. They change the words from their (right) places

		2. And forget a good part of the message that was sent them. 3. You shall always discover treachery in them excepting a few of them; but Forgive them, and overlook (their misdeeds): for Allah loves those who are kind.
		God's Covenant with Christians
2	5:014	(Similarly), from those, too, who call themselves Christians, We did take a covenant. 1. But they forgot a good part of the message that was sent them: so 2. We estranged among them with enmity and hatred to the Day of Judgment. And soon will Allah show them what it is they have done.

5.3 Books of Law: the Torah, the Gospel, and the Qur'an

God revealed the Torah, the Gospel, and the Qur'an. These contained detailed instructions about the development of human character, behavior, and society, and they stressed the implementation of justice under all circumstances and situations.

'The Torah was the book of law for the Jews. God mentions the Torah in Surah Al-Ma'idah when He says: "It was We who revealed the Torah. Therein was guidance and light. By its standard have been judged the Jews by the prophets who bowed to Allah's will, by the rabbis and the doctors of law: for to them was entrusted the protection of Allah's book, and they were witnesses thereto. Therefore, fear not men, but fear Me, and sell not My signs for a miserable price. If any do fail to judge by what Allah has revealed, they are (no better than) unbelievers (Qur'an 5:44)." Similarly, the Gospel was the book of law for the Christians. God also talks about the Gospel in Surah Al-Ma'idah: "And in their footsteps We sent Jesus the son of Mary, confirming the Law that had come before him. We sent him the Gospel. Therein was guidance and light and confirmation of the Law that had come before him—a guidance and an admonition to those who fear Allah. Let the people of the Gospel judge by what Allah has revealed therein. If any do fail to judge by (the light of) what Allah has revealed, they are (no better than) those who rebel (Qur'an 5:46-47)."

The Qur'an is the final book of law for humanity. God also talks about the Qur'an in Surah Al-Ma'idah: "We have revealed to you the Book (the Qur'an) with the truth, verifying what is before it of the Book and a guardian over it. Therefore, judge between them by what God has revealed, and do not follow their low desires to turn away from the truth that has come to you. To each among you have we prescribed a law and an open way? If Allah had so willed, He would have made you a single people, but (His plan is) to test you in what He has given you. So strive as in a race in all virtues. The goal of you all is to Allah; it is He that will show you the truth of the matters in which you dispute (Qur'an 5:48)." Again God stresses and commands: "Judge you between them by what Allah has revealed, and follow not their vain desires, but beware of them lest they beguile you from any of that which Allah has sent down to you. And if they turn away, be assured that for some of their crime it is Allah's purpose to punish them. And truly many of the people are rebellious. Do they then seek after a judgment of (the days of) ignorance? But who, for a people whose faith is assured, can give better judgment than Allah (Qur'an 5:49-50)?"

5.4 Why Don't People Implement the Divine Law?
God says in Surah Al-Hajj, "Among people there are such as dispute about Allah without knowledge and follow every rebellious Satan…and among people there is one who disputes about Allah without knowledge, without guidance, and without a book of enlightenment, turning away haughtily that he may lead others away from the path of Allah. For him, there is disgrace in this life and on the Day of Judgment. We shall make him taste the punishment of burning (Qur'an 22:3, 8-9)." No doubt the implementation of the divine law will result in a just society that is prosperous, peaceful, and secure. Then why do people ignore it? God tells us in Surah Al-Shura, "They became divided only after knowledge reached them—through selfish envy between themselves (Qur'an 42:14)." In Surah Al-Jathiyah, God says, "We granted them clear signs in affairs (of religion). It was only after knowledge had been granted to them that they fell into schisms, through insolent envy among themselves (Qur'an 45:17)." The verses of Surah Al-Ma'idah, Surah Al-An'am, and Surah Al-A'raf that highlight the type of people who do not

follow the commandments of God are given in the table below.

Table 5.4: People Who Do Not Follow God's Commands

No	Surah:Verses	Meanings
		What their Fathers followed is enough to the Unbelievers
3	5:104	1. When it is said to them, "Come to what Allah has revealed to the Messenger," they say, "That on which we found our fathers is sufficient for us." What! Even though their fathers were void of knowledge and guidance?
	6:111	2. Even if We did send unto them angels, and the dead did speak unto them, and We gathered together all things before their very eyes, they would not believe unless it is in Allah's plan. But most of them ignore.
	6:112	3. Likewise did We make for every messenger an enemy, Satan among men and jinn, inspiring each other with flowery discourses by way of deception. If your Lord had so planned, they would not have done it.
		Those who reject the Hereafter— Vain are their Good Deeds
4	7:145-147	We ordained laws for him (Moses) in the tablets in all matters, both commanding and explaining all things, (and said): 1. "Take and hold these with firmness, and 2. "enjoin your people to take hold of what is best thereof; 3. "soon I will show you the abode of the transgressors." Those who behave arrogantly on the earth in defiance of right - them will I turn away from My signs. Even 1. if they see all the signs, they will not believe in them; and 2. if they see the way of right conduct, they will not adopt it as the way; but 3. if they see the way of error, that is the way they will adopt. This is because they rejected our revelations and failed to take warning from them. Those who reject Our signs and the meeting in the hereafter— vain are their deeds. Can they expect to be

		rewarded except as they have wrought?
		Those who missed prayers and followed after their lusts
5	19:058-059	• Those were some of the prophets on whom Allah did bestow His grace—of the posterity of Adam, and of those whom We carried (in the ark) with Noah, and of the posterity of Abraham and Israel of those whom We guided and chose. • But after them, there followed a posterity who missed prayers and followed after lusts. Soon, then, will they face destruction.

5.5 People Who Do Not Follow the Law Are Destroyed

Surah Al-Ma'idah gets its name from the food from Heaven that was sent down by God at the request of the disciples of Jesus. "Allah said: 'I will send it down unto you, but if any of you after that resists faith, I will punish him with a penalty such as I have not inflicted on any one among all the peoples' (Qur'an 5:115)." In Surah Maryam, God says that those people who neglected their prayers and pursued their lusts will face destruction: "Except those who repent and believe, and work righteousness (Qur'an 19:60)." The verses of Surah Al-Ma'idah and Surah Al-An'am that highlight the fate of people who do not follow the divine law is given in the table below.

Table 5.5: The People who do not follow the Divine Law

No	Surah:Verses	Meaning
		The People were destroyed on account of their Misdeeds
6	5:054	O you who believe! If any from among you turn back from his faith, soon Allah will bring a people whom 1. He will love as they will love Him, 2. Lowly with the believers, mighty against the rejecters, 3. Fighting in the way of Allah, and 4. Never afraid of the reproaches of such as find fault. That is the grace of Allah, which He will bestow on whom He pleases.
	6:006	• Do they not see how many a generation We

		have destroyed before them, whom 1. We had established in the earth as We have not established you, and 2. We sent the clouds pouring rain on them in abundance, and 3. We made the rivers to flow beneath them. Then We destroyed them on account of their sins and rose up after them another generation.
		For them is a partial or Complete Destruction or Civil Wars
7	6:065	Say: "He has the power to send calamities on you from above you and from beneath your feet or to cover you with confusion, making you different parties; and making some of you taste the fighting of others."

5.6 Fate of the Previous Nations that were Destroyed

God has replaced many a people who did not implement His moral and sociopolitical laws in their lives and communities. God asks people to reflect! "Say: 'Travel through the earth, and see what was the end of those who rejected the truth' (Qur'an 6:11)." God is the most just of judges. If He punishes some people in the world, it does not mean that such were the only people who deserved punishment. Allah may choose to delay the punishment of others until the Day of Judgment. No one who disobeys God's laws may escape punishment unless God chooses to forgive. Therefore, people should always be conscious of their accountability for their deeds in this life or in Hereafter. One should remember that it is God Who has set all laws of nature in motion and that people's good and evil deeds have their built-in good and bad consequences. God reminds people: (1) "Whatever good happens to you is from Allah, but whatever evil happens to you is from your own self (Qur'an 4:79);" (2) "Why were there not among the generations before you persons possessed of balanced good sense, prohibiting (people) from mischief in the earth—except a few among them whom We saved? But the wrongdoers pursued the enjoyment of the good things of life that were given them and persisted in sin (Qur'an 11:116)." The fate of previous nations that were destroyed, as described in Surah Al-A'raf, is summarized in the table below.

Table 5.6
Previous Divine Messages and the Fate of the Unbelievers

No	Messenger	Divine Message	Punishment for Rejection
1	Noah^PBUH	"We sent Noah to his people. He said: 'O my people! Worship Allah! You have no other god but Him. I fear for you the punishment of a dreadful day' (Qur'an 7:59)."	"But they rejected him, and We delivered him and those with him in the ark: But We overwhelmed in the flood those who rejected Our signs... (Qur'an 7:64)."
2	Hud^PBUH	"To the 'Ad people, (We sent) Hud, one of their (own) brethren. He said: 'O my people! Worship Allah! You have no other god but Him. Will you not fear' (Allah) (Qur'an 7:65)?"	They said: "You come to us that we may worship Allah alone and give up the cult of our fathers? Bring us what you threaten us with; if so be that you tell the truth.... We saved him and those who adhered to him by Our mercy, and We cut off the roots of those who rejected Our signs and did not believe (Qur'an 7:70, 72)."
3	Salih^PBUH	To the Thamud people "(We sent) Salih, one of their own brethren: He said: 'O my people! Worship Allah; you have no other god but Him. Now has come unto you a clear (sign) from your Lord! This she-camel of Allah is a sign unto you. So leave her to graze on Allah's earth, and let her come to no harm, or you shall be seized with a grievous punishment' (Qur'an 7:73)."	"The arrogant party said: 'For our part, we reject what you believe in.' Then they hamstrung the she-camel and insolently defied the order of their Lord, saying: 'O Salih! Bring about your threats, if you are a messenger. So the earthquake took them unawares, and they lay prostrate in their homes in the morning' (Qur'an 7:76-78)."
4	Lot^PBUH	"We also (sent) Lot; he	"But we saved him and

		said to his people: 'Do you commit lewdness such as no people in creation (ever) committed before you? For you practice your lusts on men in preference to women: you are indeed a people transgressing beyond bounds' (Qur'an 7:80-81)."	his family, except his wife; she was of those who lagged behind. And we rained down on them a shower (of brimstone). Then see what was the end of those who indulged in sin and crime (Qur'an 7:83-84)."
5	Shu'ayb^PBUH	"To the Madyan people We sent Shu'ayb, one of their own brethren. He said: 'O my people! Worship Allah; you have no other god but Him. Now has come unto you a clear (sign) from your Lord! Give just measure and weight, nor withhold from the people the things that are their due, and do no mischief on the earth after it has been set in order. That will be best for you, if you have faith. And squat not on every road, breathing threats, hindering from the path of Allah those who believe in Him, and seeking in it something crooked. But remember how you were little, and He gave you increase. And hold in your mind's eye what was the end of those who did mischief' (Qur'an 7:85-86)."	"The leaders, the arrogant party among his people, said: O Shu'ayb! We shall certainly drive you out of our city—(you) and those who believe with you, or else you (you and they) shall have to return to our ways and religion. He said: "What! Even though we do detest (them)... (Qur'an 7:88)."

"The leaders, the unbelievers among his people, said: "If you follow Shu'ayb, be sure then you are ruined." But the earthquake took them unawares, and they lay prostrate in their homes before the morning. The men who rejected Shu'ayb became as if they had never been in the homes where they had flourished. The men who rejected Shu'ayb—it was they who were ruined (Qur'an 7:90-92)." |

6	Moses[PBUH]	"Then after them We sent Moses with Our signs to Pharaoh and his chiefs… (Qur'an 7:103)."	"…but they wrongfully rejected them. So see what was the end of those who made mischief (Qur'an 7:103)."

6 ISLAM IS A RELIGION OF PEACE AND PROSPERITY

In his book Introduction to Islam, Ali Tantawi notes that Islam doesn't demand that people ignore this world, nor does it recommend that people should make mosques their living quarters. Islam also doesn't expect that people should take shelter in caves or that they should spend all of their lives in caves. However, Islam commands believers to have excellent character and a society built on the Islamic principals of piety, hard work, justice, and charity. Further, Islam commands that believers should excel all other societies in prosperity, learning, and wisdom, in order to make Muslims the richest and most learned nation. Islam also stresses that happiness in the life to come greatly depends on the efforts of the believers to improve the life in this world, for how one lives in this world will impact the quality of one's life in the Hereafter.

6.1 Islam is the Religion of All Messengers of God

Islam is a continuation of the same religion that was revealed to all the prophets, including Adam, Noah, Abraham, Moses, and Jesus. Although God commands believers to keep inviting unbelievers to Islam so that all humankind should be united in establishing a just human society, He has also made it clear that there should not be any contention between the believers and unbelievers. God says in Surah Ash-Shura: "The same religion has He established for you as that which He enjoined on Noah—that which We have sent by inspiration to you—and that which We enjoined on Abraham, Moses, and Jesus: namely, that you should remain steadfast in religion and make no divisions therein. To those who worship other things than Allah, hard is the (way) to which you call them. Allah chooses to Himself those whom He pleases and guides to Himself those who turn (to Him) (Qur'an 42:13)." Further, God asks His Messenger to declare, "I believe in the Book that Allah has sent down, and I am commanded to judge justly between you. Allah is our Lord and your Lord. We shall have our deeds, and you shall have your deeds. There is no contention between us and you. Allah will bring us together, and to Him is the return (Qur'an 42:15)."

6.2 Islam assures Provisions and Prosperity

God reminds people: "It is We Who have placed you with authority on earth and provided you therein with means for the fulfillment of your life; small are the thanks that you give (Qur'an 7:10)!" God has provided sufficient means for all humanity to live in prosperity. We have to exploit and properly manage these natural resources for our benefit. A truly Islamic society should certainly provide all of the proper requirements for this effort. Besides, if He wills, God can increase and decrease the produce. He has promised in the Qur'an that if we believe in Him and implement His law, He will increase our provisions. "If only they had stood fast by the Torah, the Gospel, and all the revelation that was sent to them from their Lord, they would have enjoyed happiness from every side. There is from among them a party on the right course, but many of them follow a course that is evil (Qur'an 5:66). If the people of the towns had but believed and feared Allah, We should indeed have opened out to them (all kinds of) blessings from Heaven and earth (Qur'an 7:96)." God also encourages believers to make efforts to acquire good things through applying lawful means and without exceeding limits: "O you who believe! Do not forbid yourself (or make unlawful) the good things that Allah has made lawful for you, but commit no excess, for Allah does not love those who exceed the limits (Qur'an 5:87)."

6.3 The Sanctity of Human Life and Property in Islam

The Messenger stated that a believer has sanctity, meaning that he must always be respected, treated well, and be immune from assault on his person, property, and integrity. He said that a believer is a brother to every other believer. One believer never treats another unjustly, nor does he let him down or try to humiliate him. It was narrated by Ibn 'Umar that at Mina, on the Day of *Nahr* (day of sacrifice), the 10th of *Dhul-Hijja*, the Prophet stood in between the *Jamrat* during his *Hajj* and said, "No doubt, Allah made your blood, your properties, and your

65

honor sacred to one another like the sanctity of this day of yours, in this month of yours, in this town of yours (Sahih Bukhari: 2.26.798)." This means that the sanctity of a believer in God's view is greater than the sanctity of everything relevant to the Ka'bah. The word sanctity in the *Hadith* implies that all rights, minor or major, that belong to an individual must always be respected.

A person who receives injustice is sure to get God's help. The Messenger said that the supplication of a person treated unjustly goes directly to God without any hindrance. It was narrated by Abu Huraira that the Prophet said: "Three supplications are answered, there being no doubt about them: that of a father, that of a traveler, and that of one who has been wronged (Abu Dawud: 8.1531). This statement should be sufficient to make anyone who exercises any degree of power be on his guard lest he should treat anyone unjustly. Besides, mutual help between members of a believing community is highly emphasized. Try to help one with something of importance, and you are certain to receive God's help in accomplishing what you need. Yahya related that Umar ibn al-Khattab said: "Do not harm the people. Fear the supplication of the wronged, for the supplication of the wronged is answered (Malik's Muwatta. 60.1.1)."

The Messenger was the best of neighbors, and he emphasized that neighbors have a claim on our kindness. He told the believers: "Gabriel continued to recommend to me about treating neighbors kindly and politely, so much so that I thought he would order me to make them as my heirs (Sahih Bukhari: 8.73.43)." This means that the status of a neighbor, irrespective of his faith, should be viewed as comparable to that of a family member. All this gives us just an idea of the sort of emphasis Islam attaches to the rights of individuals, particularly those who are vulnerable in society.

6.4 Islam is to Establish Peace and Justice in Society
God created Adam and his posterity to be His vicegerent on earth: "Behold, your Lord said to the angels: 'I will create a vicegerent on earth.' They said: 'Will You place therein one who will make mischief therein and shed blood, while we do

66

celebrate Your praises and glorify Your holy (name)?' He said: 'I know what you know not' (Qur'an 2:30)." Contrary to the concern of the angels, the aim of divine guidance is to serve human interest and to help people build a happy life in a community characterized by justice. The implementation of justice under all circumstances eliminates all disputes and creates a peaceful society. This justice must be achieved at all levels, within the family, the local community, the social hierarchy, and the political system. God commands people: "Hold to forgiveness; command what is right, but turn away from the ignorant (Qur'an 7:199)." How important it is to command and do what is right was emphasized by the Messenger. It was narrated by Abu Huraira that Messenger said, "Whoever has wronged his brother should ask for his forgiveness before his death, as in the Hereafter there will be neither a Dinar nor a Dirham. He should secure pardon in this life before some of his good deeds are taken and paid to his brother, or if he has done no good deeds, some of the bad deeds of his brother are taken to be loaded on him in the Hereafter (Sahih Bukhari: 8.76.541)."

History proves that whenever people established their system on the basis of divine guidance and applied God's law, their achievements were indeed great. Someone may argue that in certain areas of religion there may be a need for some modification in order to make it suitable in different communities. This is not required. God's law is flexible enough to suit every community at every level of civilization. Islam lays down certain principles that provide a framework within which human society can operate. Within that framework, one can choose to produce a suitable social system. This great characteristic of Islamic law enables it to be applicable to all communities. There is, however, one main requirement for Islamic law to be properly applied. Islamic law can only be properly applied in a believing community. Verses of the Qur'an highlighting the importance of implementing Islamic law are given in the table below.

Table 6: Implementation of the Islamic Law

No	Surah:Verses	Meanings
		Islam is the Religion of Success
1	5:003	1. This day have those who reject faith given up all hope of your religion. Yet, fear them not, but fear Me. This day have I perfected your religion for you, completed My favor upon you, and have chosen for you Islam as your religion.
	3:200	2. O you who believe! Persevere in patience and constancy; vie in such perseverance; strengthen each other; and fear Allah; that you may prosper.
	5:056	3. As to those who turn (for friendship) to Allah, His Messenger, and the (fellowship of) believers, it is the fellowship of Allah that must certainly triumph.
	5:090	4. O you who believe! Intoxicants and gambling, (dedication of) stones, and (divination by) arrows are an abomination of Satan's handwork. Eschew such (abomination) that you may prosper.
	5:068	5. Say: "O People of the Book! You have no ground to stand upon unless you stand fast by the Torah and the Gospel and all the revelation that has come to you from your Lord."
	5:069	6. Those who believe (in the Qur'an), those who follow the Jewish (scriptures), and the Sabians and the Christians—any who believe in Allah and the Last Day and work righteousness—on them shall be no fear, nor shall they grieve.
		Islam is the Religion of Security
2	5:067	1. And Allah will defend you from men (who mean mischief). For Allah will not guide the unbelieving people.
	6:082	2. It is those who believe and confuse not their beliefs with wrong that are (truly) in security, for they are on (right) guidance.
	7:196	3. For my Protector is Allah, Who revealed the Book (from time to time), and He will choose and befriend the righteous.
	10:103	4. In the end, We deliver Our messengers and

68

22:038		those who believe. Thus is it fitting on Our part that We should deliver those who believe. 5. Verily Allah will defend (from ill) those who believe. Verily, Allah loves not any that is a traitor to faith, or shows ingratitude.

7 THE TRUE GUIDANCE IS FROM GOD

In response to people's prayers and need for guidance, i.e., "Show us the straight way, the way of those on whom You has bestowed Your grace, not the way of those upon whom Your wrath is brought down, nor of those who go astray (Qur'an 1:6-7)," God tells people about His guidance in Surah Yunus: "O people! There has come to you a direction from your Lord and a healing for what is in your hearts—and for those who believe, a guidance and a mercy (Qur'an 10:57)." Then in Surah Al-Anbiya, God tells people that He has revealed the Qur'an only for their benefit: "We have revealed for you a book in which is a message for you. Will you not then understand (Qur'an 21:10)?"

7.1 Divine Guidance was paced to Human Maturity

Divine guidance has been provided ever since Adam was placed on earth as God's trustee. God has sent prophets and messengers to all communities. He states in the Qur'an that someone was sent to warn every community. That person must have been a prophet, a messenger, or a person endowed with the guidance provided by earlier prophets. In that regard, the Qur'an mentions the names of several prophets sent to different communities long before the appearance of Moses. These include Noah, Hud, Salih, and Idris. God says in the Qur'an that there were many other messengers about whom He has chosen not to tell us. "We did aforetime send messengers before you. Of them, there are some whose story We have related to you, and some whose story We have not related to you (Qur'an 40:78)."

God has not left people without guidance. His guidance was tailored to match the needs and maturity of the receiving communities. With time, changes crept into the divine guidance, and this corrupted guidance lost its importance and authenticity. As a result, people turned their backs on His guidance, and even the message conveyed to the people by their prophets was distorted. Basically, all prophets and messengers conveyed the same general message as Islam

7.2 Managing Human Activities without Guidance

Some people think about religions as though they were philosophical creeds put forward by philosophers and men of knowledge. You may expect a philosopher or an economist to come up with a new doctrine that takes into account the results of human experience with previous creeds and doctrines. One may say, for example, that socialism was devised in order to overcome the social disadvantages of capitalism, just as the latter was an improvement on feudalism. However, that analogy does not apply to religions revealed by God. Reflecting on God's attributes, we find among them His perfect knowledge. Therefore, it cannot be said that a later religion is an improvement on a previous one, benefiting by the human experience with the earlier religion. God does not need that experience in order to reveal a perfect religion. Indeed, Islam is a faith that remains applicable to all human generations until the Day of Judgment. Moreover, Islam, in its broadest sense, which signifies all of the divine faith, has been applicable right from the moment when Adam and Eve were created.

Discrimination, social exclusion, economic injustice, military ambitions, lack of good governance, and geopolitical rivalries play decisive roles in shattering the peace and tranquility of human societies. Even in the case of culturally and religiously rooted conflicts, violence and extremism generally stem from the exploitation of religion for political and ideological goals. Human dignity and freedom come from God. Belief in One God frees humankind from any other bondage that results in discrimination, exploitation, and corruption. On the other hand, worship of false gods, idols, and selfish desires, and any human being degrade humanity to physical, mental, and spiritual slavery.

7.3 People Need God, His Laws, and His Guidance

God commanded that we should not serve anyone but Him: "He has commanded that you worship none but Him. That is the right religion, but most men understand not (Qur'an 12:40)." However, this is not to say that God needs people to serve Him. Rather, humanity needs God's guidance. That is why God reminds us in Surah Fatir: "O people! It is you that have need of Allah, but Allah is the One free of all wants, worthy of all praise. If He so pleased, He could blot you out and bring in a new creation. And this is not hard for Allah (Qur'an 35:15-17)."

God has provided people the guidance required for the fulfillment of their duties as His trustees on earth. This guidance has been provided within the human gene in the form of human conscience. This has been explained and elaborated by His messengers through His revelations. The teaching of the Qur'an is from God, and it is His mercy that He provides guidance to humanity and has endowed humanity with reasoning abilities. This has been confirmed in Surah Al-Rahman: "(Allah) Most Gracious! It is He Who has taught the Qur'an. He has created man; He has taught him speech (and intelligence) (Qur'an 55:1- 4)."

7.4 Morality and the Sociopolitical System of Islam
In Islam, the spiritual, economic, social, and political systems are interconnected and interwoven in such a way that they cannot be isolated from each other. Throughout the Qur'an, guidelines have been provided that address various aspects of human activity. The Qur'an is the textbook of Islam. God commands: "Give this warning to those in whose (hearts) is the fear that they will be brought (to judgment) before their Lord. Except for Him, they will have no protector or intercessor... (Qur'an 6:51)." It starts with the servitude of God alone: "Say: 'I am forbidden to serve those - others than Allah - whom you call upon.' Say: 'I will not follow your vain desires. If I did, I would stray from the path and be not of the company of those who receive guidance' (Qur'an 6:56)." The verses of Surah Al-An'am that highlight that divine guidance is the true guidance are given in the table below.

Table 7: The Divine Guidance is the True Guidance

No	Surah:Verses	Meaning
		People should obey their Lord to be Truly Human
1	6:014	1. Say: 'Shall I take for my protector any other than Allah, the Maker of the heavens and the earth? And He it is that feeds but is not fed. Say: 'Nay! But I am commanded to be the first of those who bow to Allah (in Islam), and be not you of the company of those who join gods with Allah.'''
	6:015-017	2. Say: "I would, if I disobeyed my Lord, indeed have fear of the penalty of a Mighty Day. On that day, if the penalty is averted from any, it is due to Allah's mercy, and that would be (salvation), the obvious fulfillment of all desire. If Allah touches you with affliction, none can remove it but He; if He touches you with happiness, He has power over all things."
		The guidance from God is the true guidance
2	6:071	1. Say: "Shall we indeed call on others besides Allah, things that can do us neither good nor harm. And (shall we) turn on our heels after receiving guidance from Allah, like one whom the Satan has made into a fool, wandering bewildered through the earth, his friends calling, 'Come to us," (vainly) guiding him to the path."
	6:072	2. Say: "Allah's guidance is the (only) guidance, and we have been directed to submit ourselves to the Lord of the Worlds—to establish regular prayers and to fear Allah: for it is to Him that we shall be gathered together."
		To guide, God expands one's breast for Islam
3	6:125	1. Those whom Allah (in His plan) wills to guide—He opens their breast to Islam.
	6:125	2. Those whom He wills to leave straying—He makes their breast closed and constricted, as if they had to climb up to the skies. Thus does Allah (heap) the penalty on those who refuse to believe.
	6:126	3. This is the way of your Lord, leading straight. We have detailed the signs for those who receive admonition.

8 WORSHIP, PRAYER, AND PILGRIMAGE

In Surah Al-Ma'idah, several instructions concerning worship, ablution before prayer, and the performance of pilgrimage are given. God commands Muslims to refrain from violating God's monuments and letting hatred of a people lead to exceeding proper limits in conduct. We are also instructed to help one another in goodness and piety, but not in sin and aggression. With regard to ablution, we are informed that God doesn't want to cause us difficulty, but He wants to purify us so that He may complete His favor on us, so that we may be grateful. The verses of Surah Al-Ma'idah concerning ablution before prayer and the performance of pilgrimage are given in the table below.

Table 8: Fulfilling Obligations, Ablution and Pilgrimage

No	Surah:Verses	Meanings
		Fulfill Obligations and not Exceed Limits
1	5:001	1. O you who believe! Fulfill (all) obligations. Lawful unto you (for food) are all four-footed animals, with the exceptions named. But animals of the chase are forbidden while you are in the sacred precincts or in pilgrim garb: For Allah does command according to His will and plan.
	5:002	2. O you who believe! Violate not the sanctity of the symbols of Allah, nor of the sacred month, nor of the animals brought for sacrifice, nor the garlands that mark out such animals, nor the people resorting to the sacred house, seeking of the bounty and good pleasure of their Lord.
		3. But when you are clear of the sacred precincts and of pilgrim garb, you may hunt.
		4. Let not the hatred of some people in shutting you out of the Sacred Mosque lead you to transgression (and hostility on your part).
		5. Help you one another in righteousness and piety, but help you not one another in sin and aggression; fear Allah: for Allah is strict in punishment.
		Do not Hunt Animals while on Pilgrimage
2	5:094	1. O you who believe! Allah does but make a trial of you in a little matter of game well

	5:095	within reach of your hands and your lances, that He may test who fears him unseen: any who transgress thereafter, will have a grievous penalty.
		2. O you who believe! Kill not game while in the sacred precincts or in pilgrim garb. If any of you does so intentionally, the compensation is an offering, brought to the Ka'bah, of a domestic animal equivalent to the one he killed, as adjudged by two just men among you; or by way of atonement, the feeding of the indigent; or its equivalent in fasts.
	5:096	Lawful to you is the pursuit of water-game and its use for food, for the benefit of yourselves and those who travel, but forbidden is the pursuit of land-game as long as you are in the sacred precincts or in pilgrim garb.
		When you rise up to Pray, Wash Yourself
3	5:006	• O you who believe! When you prepare for prayer, wash your faces, and your hands (and arms) to the elbows; Rub your heads (with water); and (wash) your feet to the ankles. If you are in a state of ceremonial impurity, bathe your whole body. But if you are ill, or on a journey or one of you come from the call of nature, or you have been in contact with women, and you find no water, then take for yourselves clean sand or earth, and rub therewith your faces and hands. • Allah does not wish to place you in a difficulty, but to make you clean, and to complete his favor to you, that you may be grateful.

9 THE LAW AND ORDER

9.1 Punishments for Making Mischief in the Land

In Surah Al-Ma'idah, we learn: "The (selfish) soul of the other (brother, i.e., Cain) led him to the murder of his brother (Abel): he murdered him, and became (himself) one of the lost ones...On that account: We ordained for the Children of Israel that if anyone slew a person, unless it be for murder or for spreading mischief in the land, it would be as if he slew the whole people. And if any one saved a life, it would be as if he saved the life of the whole people. Then although there came to them Our messengers with clear signs, yet, even after that, many of them continued to commit excesses in the land (Qur'an 5:30, 32)." The punishments prescribed in Surah Al-Ma'idah to guard against such people are given in the table below.

Table 9.1: Punishments for Making Mischief and Steeling

No	Surah:Verses	Meaning
		Punishments for Corruption
1	5:033-034	• The punishment of those who wage war against Allah and His Messenger and strive with might and main for mischief through the land is: 1. Execution, or crucifixion, or 2. The cutting off of hands and feet from opposite sides, or 3. Exile from the land: That is their disgrace in this world, and a heavy punishment is theirs in the Hereafter—except for those who repent before they fall into your power. In that case, know that Allah is oft-forgiving, most merciful.
		Punishments for Steeling
2	5:038 5:039	• As to the thief, male or female, cut off his or her hands: a punishment by way of example, from Allah, for their crime: and Allah is exalted in power. But if the thief repents after his crime, and amends his conduct, Allah turns to him in forgiveness, for Allah is oft-forgiving, most merciful.

9.2 Self-Defense, Support from God, and the Victory

God has set in operation certain laws in this world. They take effect by His will. So when anything happens in accordance with these laws, it takes place with God's will. As such, if believers take the necessary steps to ensure their victory, God will grant them that victory by His will, in accordance with His laws. If they do not, they will fail to achieve victory, and that will be by His will and in accordance with the laws He has set in operation.

Some verses of the Qur'an concerning defense and war are given in the table below.

Table 9.2: Permission to Fight is given to the Oppressed

No	Surah:Verses	Meaning
		The Oppression is Graver than Slaughter
3	2:217	1. They ask you concerning fighting in the prohibited month. Say: "Fighting therein is a grave (offence); 2. But graver is it in the sight of Allah to prevent access to the path of Allah, to deny Him, to prevent access to the Sacred Mosque and drive out its members. 3. Tumult and oppression are worse than slaughter. Nor will they (the unbelievers) cease fighting you until they turn you back from your faith if they can.
		Surely God will Defend those who Believe
4	22:038-040	1. Verily, Allah will defend those who believe. Verily, Allah loves not any that is a traitor to faith or shows ingratitude. 2. To those against whom war is made, permission is given (to fight) because they are wronged, and verily Allah is most powerful for their aid. 3. (They are) those who have been expelled from their homes in defiance of right, (for no cause) except that they say, "Our Lord is Allah."
		God will Help those who Help His Cause
5	22:040	Had not Allah checked one set of people by means of another, there would surely have been pulled down monasteries, churches, synagogues, and mosques in which the name of Allah is much remembered? Allah will certainly aid those who aid His (cause)—for verily Allah is full of strength, exalted in might, (able to enforce His will).

9.3 Dealing with Friendly Unbelievers

Dealing with non-Muslims must always be cordial and friendly, provided they also treat believers in the same way. Good relations with non-believers are encouraged in Islam. However, people who are hostile to Islam or try to ridicule its beliefs or practices are to be treated differently. Islam does not extend kindness to them, but instructs believers to stay away from them. Believers must not start hostilities, but should not accept humiliation. God tells believers in Surah Al-Mumtahinah that, "Allah does not forbid you with regard to those who have not made war against you on account of (your) religion and have not driven you forth from your homes that you show them kindness and deal with them justly. Surely Allah loves the doers of justice. Allah only forbids you with regard to those who made war upon you on account of (your) religion and drove you forth from your homes and backed up (others) in your expulsion that you make friends with them. And whoever makes friends with them, these are the unjust (Qur'an 60:8-9)."

9.3 Treachery and Hypocrisy are Forbidden

Being friendly with the enemy, especially during hostilities, is treachery. This cannot be permitted by any community. Traitors have caused extensive damage to their communities. That is why Islam forbids its followers to be friendly with hostile unbelievers during times of war. God commands believers in Surah Al-Mumtahinah: "O you who believe! Take not My enemies and yours as friends (or protectors), offering them (your) love, even though they have rejected the truth that has come to you and have (on the contrary) driven out the Prophet and yourselves (from your homes simply) because you believe in Allah your Lord! If you have come out to strive in My way and to seek My good pleasure, (take them not as friends), holding secret converse of love (and friendship) with them: for I know full well all that you conceal and all that you reveal. And any of you that do this has strayed from the straight path. If they were to get the better of you, they would behave to you as enemies and stretch forth their hands and their tongues against you for evil, and they desire that you should reject the truth (Qur'an 60:1-2)." Verses of the Qur'an highlighting the believers' dealings with hostile unbelievers are given in the table below.

Table 9.3: Friendship with Hostile Unbelievers is Treachery

No	Surah:Verses	Meaning
		Do not side with Unbelievers during the War
6	5:051	1. O you who believe! Take not the Jews and the Christians (who are hostile) for your friends and protectors. They are but friends and protectors to each other. And he amongst you that turns to them (for friendship) is of them. Verily Allah guides not a people unjust.
	5:057	2. O you who believe! Take not for friends and protectors those who take your religion for a mockery or sport, whether among those who received the scripture before you or among those who reject faith; but fear Allah, if you have faith.
		Withdraw from those who Mock your Religion
7	6:068	3. When you see those who enter into false discourses about Our revelations, withdraw from them until they enter into some other discourse, and if the Satan causes you to forget, then do not sit after recollection with the unjust people.
	6:069	4. On their account no responsibility falls on the righteous, but (their duty) is to remind them that they may (learn to) fear Allah.
	6:070	5. Leave alone those who take their religion to be mere play and amusement and are deceived by the life of this world. But proclaim (to them) this (truth): that every soul delivers itself to ruin by its own acts.
		Do not Abuse those whom Unbelievers Worship
8	6:108	6. Revile you not those whom they call upon besides Allah, lest they out of spite revile Allah in their ignorance. Thus have We made alluring to each people its own doings? In the end will they return to their Lord, and We shall then tell them the truth of all that they did.
	6:116	7. Were you to follow most of those on earth, they would lead you away from the way of Allah. They follow nothing but conjecture; they do nothing but lie.

10 THE PROVISION AND THE COMFORTS OF LIFE

When God created people and placed them on earth, He granted them distinguished capabilities and made them the master of this planet. God has given humans certain instincts and desires. These qualities influence people, motivate them to do things in a certain fashion, and help them to set goals in life. Without these goals and motivations, human life can degenerate into something like animal life. Considering the development of human civilization, recent advancement has been so great that one cannot even imagine a society that considered itself advanced 500 years go. Because of human intelligence, we experience the progress and advancement that are so essential to human life. Otherwise, human intelligence would be of no value. It is intelligence that distinguishes humankind from other creations. It is also an essential human characteristic to seek comfort and pleasure in all spheres of life. Islam acknowledges this and does not consider it undesirable, as long as its satisfaction does not involve disobedience to God.

This means that anyone who forbids beauty, adornments, luxuries, and comforts has no justification, as long as enjoying such matters does not involve anything forbidden. When God bestows some blessings and comforts on one of His servants, He likes to see a person enjoying the blessing, and acknowledging God's grace by doing good deeds to express his gratitude to God. If a person is given plenty of money, then God likes to see him giving his family a comfortable living, including a good house and plenty of provisions, although without being wasteful and extravagant. However, God also loves to see that person giving out his *Zakah* (obligatory charity) and helping poor people and his community in other ways as well. Islam does not advocate the rejection of life's comforts. Believers may enjoy these comforts, provided that they acquire them in a legitimate way. Further, they must not seek to acquire a position of arrogance as a result of having such comforts. They should use them to show kindness to their neighbors and to the poor in the community. If they do, then these luxuries become a means of earning reward from God.

10.1 Dress Well, Eat, and Drink, but Be not Wasteful.

Islam prescribes that people dress modestly. Some people, advocating ignorance and protesting, say: "What does religion have to do with fashion, cosmetics, or how women dress?" This logic has been characteristic of ignorant people everywhere and in all generations. There can be no clearer distortion of human nature. Ignorance distorts concepts, values, and tastes, making nakedness, which is an animal quality, an indicator of progress and advancement, while propriety is considered backward and old-fashioned. Addressing people, God says in Surah Al-A'raf: "O Children of Adam! Wear your beautiful apparel at every time and place of prayer. Eat and drink, but waste not by excess, for Allah loves not the wasters." Additionally, God states: "Say: 'Who has forbidden the beautiful (things) of Allah, which He has produced for His servants, and the things, clean and pure, (which He has provided) for sustenance?' Say: 'They are in the life of this world for those who believe, (and) purely for them on the Day of Judgment' (Qur'an 7:31-32)?" The verses of Surah Al-A'raf highlighting modest dress are given in the table below.

Table 10.1: Why People Cloth Themselves

No	Surah:Verses	Meanings
		Clothing Covers, Beautifies, and Protects
1	7:026	O Children of Adam! 1. We have bestowed raiment upon you to cover your shame, 2. As well as to be an adornment to you. 3. But the raiment of righteousness, - that is the best. Such are among the signs of Allah, that they may receive admonition.
		Nakedness is either Primitive or Uncivilized
2	7:027	O Children of Adam! 1. Let not Satan seduce you, in the same manner as He got your parents out of the Garden, stripping them of their raiment to expose their shame. 2. Satan and his tribe watch you from a position where you cannot see them. We made the Satan friends (only) to those without faith.

10.2 Good things are Lawful, but Impure are Unlawful

God says in the Qur'an: "Those who follow the Messenger, the *Ummi* (Unlettered Prophet), whom they find written down with them in the Law and the Gospel, who enjoins them good and forbids them evil, and makes lawful to them the good things and makes unlawful to them impure things, and removes from them their burden and the shackles that were upon them (Qur'an 7:157)." Therefore, anything that is clearly forbidden in Islam must be harmful. Otherwise, it would not have been forbidden to us. This is a general statement that applies universally. It is sufficient to know that, for example, pork is clearly forbidden to conclude that it is harmful. It is perfectly in order for Muslims to try to determine the cause of prohibition. However, when a cause is found, it cannot be made final because the prohibition may not only be linked to this particular cause. We cannot run the risk of superimposing our conclusion on God's legislation. This is not allowed to anyone. Billions of unbelievers eat pork, and they contend that no harm is done to them. How would one justify this? They may only be considering physical harm while there could be other reasons for this prohibition that, like many other things, we do not know. God knows the best.

10.3 Types of Animal food that We are forbidden to Eat

On four separate occasions, the Qur'an mentions the type of meat that we are forbidden to eat. In all these occasions, the same prohibition is made clear. In verse 145 of Surah Al-An'am, the instruction is given in a very limiting way and is phrased to make it absolutely clear that what is forbidden is only those four types of food: (1) carrion, which denotes any animal that dies by itself, without being slaughtered for the specific purpose of eating; (2) spilled blood, which excludes the blood that is found solid in normal conditions, such as the spleen; (3) the flesh of swine, which includes everything from pigs; and lastly (4) any animal that is slaughtered with the invocation of the name of anyone other than God.

In verse 3 of Surah Al-Ma'idah, these four types of forbidden animal foods are given in greater detail. For example, under carrion we find several types of carrion specifically mentioned. Similarly, any animal that is slaughtered as an offering in honor of a human being or an idol is also forbidden. Also in verse 121 of Surah Al-An'am God commands that we not eat of that on which God's name has not been mentioned. Apart from these dietary prohibitions, there are several types of animals that are disallowed as food. The verses of Surah Al-Ma'idah and Surah Al-An'am that are specific to what God has forbidden us to eat are given in the table below.

Table 10 2: The Forbidden Animal Meat

No	Surah:Verses	Meanings
		Meat of Dead Animals, Swine, and Blood
3	5:003	Forbidden to you (for food) are: 1. Dead meat, 2. The blood, 3. The flesh of swine, and 4. That on which has been invoked the name of other than Allah; 5. That which has been killed by strangling, or by a violent blow, or by a headlong fall, or by being gored to death; 6. That which has been (partly) eaten by a wild animal, unless you are able to slaughter it (in due form); 7. That which is sacrificed on stone (altars); (forbidden) 8. Also is the division (of meat) by raffling with arrows: that is impiety. • But if any is forced by hunger, with no inclination to transgression, Allah is indeed oft-forgiving, most merciful.
	6:145	Say: "I find not in the message received by me by inspiration any (meat) forbidden to be eaten by one who wishes to eat it 1. Unless it be dead meat, 2. Or blood poured forth, 3. Or the flesh of swine, for it is an abomination, 4. Or, what is impious, (meat) on which a name has been invoked, other than Allah's. But (even so), if a person is forced by necessity, without willful disobedience, nor transgressing due limits, your Lord is oft-forgiving, most merciful."
		Meat on which God's name has not been Invoked

4	5:003, 6:145	1.	It is a transgression (to eat meat on which) other than (the name of) Allah having been invoked.
	6:121	2.	Eat not of (meats) on which Allah's name has not been pronounced. That would be impiety.

10.4 Everything that Benefits People during Life

The provision one receives during one's life is called *Rizk* in Arabic, and it is provided by God. Some scholars say *Rizk* is everything from which a person derives benefit during his life on earth. Others say it refers to all the material possessions one has. The dominant opinion is the former, since God says, "There is no moving creature on earth but its sustenance depends on Allah (Qur'an 11:6)." Provisions for people can be divided into two kinds: inner and outer. The outward provision includes such things as food, shelter, and general prosperity, while the inner provisions include human self, its health, and looks. It includes knowledge, intellect, good character and behavior, contentment, good habits, and similar qualities. Even the people in one's life, such as relatives, friends, teachers, spouse and children, etc. are considered one's provisions. Along with the provisions that God gives, He also has given means by which one must seek out one's provisions. There should be no confusion about the means of attaining wealth and the wealth itself. When one starts to believe that his or her wealth is in the hands of another person, this creates a breeding ground for moral misbehavior, such as coveting what others have, doing whatever it takes to get it, and becoming angry when one does not receive what he or she expects.

Since the provisions and life span of an individual are written down before one's birth, no one will die until one completes the provision that God has allotted to him. It was narrated by Anas bin Malik that the Prophet said: "Allah puts an angel in charge of the mother's womb...then, if Allah wishes to complete its creation, the angel asks, 'O Lord, (will it be) a male or a female...How much will his provisions be? What will his age be?' All this is written down while the creature is still in the mother's womb." (Sahih Bukhari: 8.77.594). Therefore, one must trust God and seek refuge in Him from resorting to illicit livelihood out of fear of not having enough of it. The verses of

Surah Al-Ma'idah and Surah Al-An'am highlighting what God has allowed as good provision are given in the table below.

Table 10.3: Allowed Good Provisions

No	Surah:Verses	Meanings
		Permissible Animal and Agricultural Products
	5:005	This day are (all) things good and pure made lawful unto you. The food of the People of the Book is lawful unto you, and yours is lawful unto them.
	5:004	1. Lawful unto you are (all) things good and pure: and what you have taught your trained hunting animals (to catch) in the manner directed to you by Allah. Eat what they catch for you, but pronounce the name of Allah over it: and fear Allah; for Allah is swift in taking account.
	6:141	2. It is He Who produces gardens, with trellises and without, and dates, and crops with produce of all kinds, and olives and pomegranates, similar (in kind) and different (in variety). Eat of their fruit in their season, but render the dues that are proper on the day that the harvest is gathered. But waste not by excess: for Allah loves not the wasters.
5	6:142-144	Of the cattle are some for burden and some for meat; eat what Allah has provided for you, and follow not the footsteps of Satan: for he is to you and avowed enemy. (Take) eight (head of cattle) in (four) pairs: of sheep a pair, and of goats a pair. Say, "Has He forbidden the two males, or the two females, or (the young) that the wombs of the two females enclose? Tell me with knowledge if you are truthful." Of camels a pair, and oxen a pair; Say, "Has He forbidden the two males, or the two females, or (the young) that the wombs of the two females enclose? Were you present when Allah ordered you such a thing?" • But who does more wrong than one who invents a lie against Allah, to lead astray men without knowledge? For Allah guides not people who do wrong.
		Believing Women and Women of the People of the Book

6	5:005	3. (Lawful unto you in marriage) are (not only) chaste women who are believers, but chaste women among the People of the Book, revealed before your time, - • When you give them their due dowers and desire chastity, Not lewdness or secret intrigues. If any one rejects faith, fruitless is his work, and in the Hereafter he will be in the ranks of those who have lost (all spiritual good and deeds).

10.5 Major Sins and what God Forbids Believers to Do

The authority to forbid anything belongs only to God. Only those things mentioned in the Qur'an or the *Hadith* as forbidden can be classified as such. Again what is mentioned in the *Hadith* as forbidden is only pronounced as such on divine instructions, because the *Hadith* is only the Prophet's expression of a revelation communicated to him by God.

God has forbidden the killing of children for whatever reason. "Even so, in the eyes of most of the pagans, their 'partners' made alluring the slaughter of their children, in order to lead them to their own destruction and cause confusion in their religion. If Allah had willed, they would not have done so: But leave them and their inventions alone...Lost are those who slay their children, from folly, without knowledge, and forbid food that Allah has provided for them, inventing (lies) against Allah. They have indeed gone astray and heeded no guidance (Qur'an 6:137, 140)." Various things that God forbids and that He commands believers to do are highlighted in the table below.

Table 10.4: What God Forbids and tells Believers to do?

No	Surah:Verses	Meanings
		Sin, Rebellion, and Saying Things against God
7	7:033	Say: "The things that my Lord has indeed forbidden are: 1. Shameful deeds, whether open or secret; 2. Sins and trespasses against truth or reason; 3. Assigning of partners to Allah, for which He has given no authority; and 4. Saying things about Allah of which you have no knowledge."

		What God Forbids the Believers to Do?
8	6:150-152	Nor follow you the vain desires of (the unbelievers), 1. Such as treat our signs as falsehoods, and 2. Such as believe not in the Hereafter. 3. For they hold others as equal with their Guardian-Lord. Say: "Come, I will rehearse what Allah has really) prohibited you from." 1. Join not anything as equal with Him; 2. Be good to your parents; 3. Kill not your children on a plea of want; We provide sustenance for you and for them. 4. Come not near to shameful deeds, whether open or secret; 5. Take not life, which Allah has made sacred, except by way of justice and law. Thus does He command you, that you may learn wisdom. 6. Come not near to the orphan's property, except to improve it, until he attain the age of full strength; 7. Give measure and weight with (full) justice; No burden do We place on any soul, but that which it can bear; 8. Whenever you speak, speak justly, even if a near relative is concerned; and 9. Fulfill the covenant of Allah. Thus does He command you that you may remember.
		What God Commands the Believers to Do?
9	7:199-200	1) Hold to forgiveness, 2) Command what is right, 3) But turn away from the ignorant, 4) And if a suggestion from the Satan afflicts you, seek refuge in Allah.

CHAPTER 6

Protection of Human
Character and Society
FROM SURAH AL-ANFAL (08) AND SURAH AT-TAWBAH (09)

We need only to look at history and learn about the situations that prevailed in different parts of the world to find out what the different sociopolitical systems devised by people have achieved. History tells us that every major social change that took place in the world was achieved at a very high cost in human misery and human lives. Humankind has managed very poorly without God's guidance. We continue to achieve endless misery while resisting acknowledgment of the basic truth that divine guidance is needed. No person can legitimize one's gains or achievements in the sight of God, either by arrogance, false evidence, exploitation and bribes, or puppet governments installed by rigging elections and by the manipulation of voters.

1 THE ELIMINATION OF SOCIAL INJUSTICE

Conflicts of interest cloud human wisdom when it comes to the design and implementation of a just sociopolitical system for humankind. Various attempts have been made to improve the social condition of people at different places in the past. What have these sociopolitical systems achieved to date?

1.1 Contribution of Various Sociopolitical Systems
Every country had to go through much strife before the welfare measures for its people could be introduced and implemented. These measures were the result of a very hard struggle that was fought over a long period of time. This happened when capitalism took over from feudalism and again it was the case at the time of the industrial revolution. The privileges that workers enjoy in Western countries today were not achieved through discussions between equals in meeting rooms. The same was the case when communism and socialism took over in certain countries, such as in China and the former Soviet Union. There

87

was also a great deal of trouble when the edifice of communism crumbled down in the years that followed. All these changes were episodes in people's pursuit of a just social system. This remains an elusive goal, which is always opposed by tyranny and dictatorship. This tyranny may take the form of either the power of the capital or the dictatorship of a party or individuals, regardless of their level of development in various communities or countries. There is no man-made system that has been able to eradicate social injustice. All this injustice is the result of people turning their backs on divine guidance. True justice can only be achieved through the system that God has revealed. This is because He has tailored it for the benefit of humankind, and no one knows what suits people better than God does.

1.2 The Foundation of All Human Interaction is Justice

The aim of divine guidance is to serve human interest and to help people build a happy life in a community that is characterized by justice. Justice must be achieved at all levels, within the family, the local community, the social hierarchy, and the political system. God says in a sacred *Hadith*: "My servants, I have forbidden Myself injustice and made injustice forbidden to you. Therefore, do not act unjustly to one another (Sahih Muslim: 32.6246)." Besides, history proves that whenever people established their system on the basis of true divine guidance and applied God's law, their achievements were really great.

God's law suits every community at every level of civilization. Islam lays down certain principles that provide a framework within which human society can operate. Within that framework, we can choose to produce a social system to suit us. Islamic laws are the laws of nature, and there is nothing against nature revealed by God in the Qur'an. This makes it possible to be compatible with diverse traditions and cultures throughout the world. This is a great characteristic of Islamic law that enables it to be applicable in all communities. There is, however, a main requirement for Islamic law to be properly applied. It should be applied as a complete whole covering all aspects of human life and society. In other words, Islamic law can only be properly applied in a truly Islamic community.

2 LEARNING TO MANAGE OUR AFFAIRS ON EARTH

Learning to manage our affairs on earth is the first obligation of humankind after being appointed as God's trustee on earth. With knowledge comes understanding and then obedience. God commands in Surah Al-'Alaq: "Proclaim! (Or read!) In the name of your Lord and Cherisher, Who created—created man out of a (mere) clot of congealed blood. Proclaim! And your Lord is Most Bountiful—He Who taught (the use of) the pen, taught man that which he knew not (Qur'an 96:1-5)?" Acquiring knowledge and learning are two of the most productive activities in which people can engage to elevate themselves. "Allah will exalt those of you who believe and those who are given knowledge in high degrees, and Allah is aware of what you do (Qur'an 58:11)." Anas reported that the Messenger said: "Whoso goes out in search of knowledge is in the path of Allah till he returns (Tirmidhi, Al-Hadith: vol. I, no. 38, p. 354)."

2.1 Education: Religious and Professional

Both religious and professional types of education are essential for the development of a prosperous and peaceful society that is built by the integrity and professionalism of its members. Religion makes an individual conscious of the accountability for one's action, reminds one of what is lawful and unlawful, and guards against corruption and dishonesty. A truly religious person is honest, trustworthy, and hardworking. At the same time, he is not corrupt, dishonest, and lazy. Islam opens all the horizons of knowledge and demands from its followers to excel in them, be they men or women. This, of course, includes the knowledge of the Qur'an and the *Hadith*. In our pursuit for other horizons of knowledge, we must not neglect our basic obligation to learn the Qur'an and the *Hadith*, through which we realize the need for knowledge in other fields of learning. We need experts in all disciplines, and only qualified persons should work in their respective professions. This is why God taught Adam "the names of all things (Qur'an 2:31)," i.e., gave him all types of knowledge, along with the ability to know what is good and what is bad, as well as the willpower to implement his choice.

Religious education inculcates good character and behavior, which are prerequisites to be human. This is why the first thing God did after the creation was to give Adam the knowledge of good and evil and the willpower to implement his choice. This was his orientation for his assignment as God's trustee on earth. In a similar way, each child, whether female or male, needs education to provide guidelines about what is expected of him to excel in character and education to understand the workings of the resources provided to people for their survival. This makes it mandatory that men or women should be imparted both types of education.

Non-religious or professional education is required to explore the universe for the prosperity of society and to earn an honest livelihood. The Qur'an invites people to look around them in the universe and to try to discover its secrets. How can we do this unless we acquire appropriate knowledge? Besides, God has made everything in the universe subservient to us, and He wants us to use these to build human life. This is an assignment for humankind to complete. Education in all fields of knowledge is required to complete this assignment successfully. If the community is composed of ignorant people, then they have no hope for a good future. The task of an Islamic community is to provide a model for everything good in life. This can only be achieved through excellence in all fields of knowledge. This was how the early Muslim generations understood their task. They were able, as a result, to build a civilization that was unique in the history of humankind.

2.2 The Freedom and Equality of Humankind
The main purpose behind the establishment of divine law is to liberate humankind from submission to any authority other than God. In the sight of God, all individuals are equal. God tells us: "O people! We created you from a single (pair) of a male and a female and made you into nations and tribes that you may know each other (not that you may despise each other). Verily, the most honored of you in the sight of Allah is (he who is) the most righteous of you (Qur'an 49:13)." Islam does not allow the hegemony of one philosophy or system or nation over another. It wants the system laid down by God to replace the systems

established by His creatures. Hence, it has to move forward throughout the earth in order to liberate the whole of humanity, without discriminating between those who are within the land of Islam and those outside it.

2.3 Implementation of Human Values and Rights

Human freedom lies in the recognition of the inherent dignity and the equal and inalienable rights of all members of the human family. Only on this foundation of freedom can justice and peace be achieved in the world. Disregard and contempt for human rights have resulted in barbarous acts that have outraged the conscience of humanity. The advent of a world in which people enjoy freedom of speech and belief, freedom from fear and want, and individual respect and dignity, which do not allow the hegemony of one philosophy, system, or nation over another, has been proclaimed as the highest aspiration of the people. It seems essential that human rights should be protected by the rule of law and justice in order to avoid people's rage and rebellion against tyranny and oppression. Fundamental human rights, the equality of humankind, whether male or female, and the establishment of justice between people or states are a prerequisite for the development of friendly relations among people and nations.

All this has also been reaffirmed by the people at the United Nations in their charter on fundamental human rights. It is declared in this charter that: "The General Assembly, proclaims this Universal Declaration of Human Rights as a common standard of achievement for all peoples and all nations. This requires that every individual and every organ of society, keeping this Declaration constantly in mind, shall strive by teaching and education to promote respect for these rights and freedoms and by progressive measures, national and international, to secure their universal and effective recognition and observance, both among the peoples of various countries and among the peoples of territories under their jurisdiction." History tells us that this charter has not been implemented effectively and that some nations have used it politically (not honestly) to promote their hegemony over others. The dignity and worth of the people, the rights of men and women, social progress, and better standards of life cannot be achieved by only putting these wishes in charters. People have to implement these and other universal values honestly in their respective countries and in themselves. The law of nature that God has put in place is that God will not change the social and individual condition of a people unless they change their character and behavior.

Table 2: Corrupt Societies Suffer If not Reformed

No	Surah:Verses	Meaning
		People suffer because of Corruption
1	8:025	1. And fear tumult or oppression, which affects not in particular (only) those of you who do wrong: and know that Allah is strict in punishment.
	8:038	2. Say to the unbelievers, if they desist (from unbelief), their past would be forgiven them; but if they persist, the punishment of those before them is already (a matter of warning for them).
		God does not change a people's fate Unless they change
2	8:053	1. ...Allah will never change the grace that he has bestowed on a people until they change what is in their (own) souls: and verily Allah is He Who hears and knows (all things)...
	13:011	2. Verily, never will Allah change the condition of a people until they change what is within themselves.
		The People will not find any change in the practice of God
3	17:077	1. (This was Our) way with the messengers We sent before you. You will find no change in Our ways.
	33:062	2. (Such was) the practice (approved) of Allah among those who lived aforetime. No change will you find in the practice of Allah.
	35:043	3. But no change will you find in Allah's way (of dealing); no turning off will you find in Allah's way (of dealing).
	48:023	4. (Such has been) the practice (approved) of Allah already in the past. No change will you find in the practice of Allah.
	50:029	5. The word changes not before Me, and I do not the least injustice to My servants.

		God gives Respite to People Only for a limited Period	
4	13:032	1.	Mocked were (many) messengers before you, but I granted respite to the unbelievers, and finally I punished them. Then how (terrible) was My requital!
	14:010	2.	It is He Who invites you in order that He may forgive you your sins and give you a respite for a term appointed.
	14:042	3.	Think not that Allah does not heed the deeds of those who do wrong. He but gives them respite against a day when the eyes will fixedly stare in horror.
	16:061	4.	If Allah were to punish men for their wrongdoing, He would not leave on the (earth) a single living creature. But He gives them respite for a stated term. When their term expires, they would not be able to delay (the punishment) for a single hour, just as they would not be able to anticipate it (for a single hour).
	35:045	5.	If Allah were to punish men according to what they deserve, He would not leave on the back of the (earth) a single living creature. But He gives them respite for a stated term. When their term expires, verily Allah has in His sight all His servants.
	71:004	6.	So He may forgive you your sins and give you respite for a stated term. For when the term given by Allah is accomplished, it cannot be put forward, if ye only knew.

3 THE INCULCATION OF CORE HUMAN VALUES

A review and analysis of the early history of Islam reveals how
the Messenger managed the implementation of God's commands
by developing a group of people with integrity of character who
managed to develop a just human society on earth. This is
described in Surah Al-Jumu'ah, verse 2, and in Surah Ali-Imran,
verse 110, for his efforts in Makkah and Madinah respectively.

3 1 Development of the Core Human Values

God tells us in Surah Al-Jumu'ah: "It is He Who has sent amongst the unlettered a messenger from among themselves, to rehearse to them His revelations, to sanctify them, and to instruct them in scripture and wisdom, although they had been before in manifest error (Qur'an 62:2)." In Makkah, we see the Messenger: 1) teaching verses of the Qur'an, 2) purifying the people, 3) imparting knowledge, and 4) imparting wisdom. The objectives and the results of these activities at Makkah are summarized in the table below.

Table 3.1: The Development of Core Human Values

Messenger's Duties	Objective	Impact
1. Recites to them God's revelations.	Development of faith in God and individual responsibility	Inculcation of accountability for individual actions and deeds
2. Purifies the people.	Development of character	Professional development
3. Teaches them the Book.	Provide religious guidelines	Set life's objectives
4. Teaches them the wisdom.	Religious and professional education for social and economic development	Development of religious and professional competency

3.2 The Establishment of the Best Community

The core human values that were developed among the early followers of Islam were a prerequisite for the establishment of a just community at Madinah. The end result of these efforts to adopt good human character and behavior was that God declared: "You are the best of peoples evolved for mankind, enjoining what is right, forbidding what is wrong, and believing in Allah (Qur'an 3:110)." For the protection of such a community, God commands, "Fight in the cause of Allah with those who fight you, but do not transgress limits; for Allah loves not transgressors (Qur'an 2:190)." How core human values were implemented and protected at Madinah is illustrated in the table below.

94

Table 3.2
Phase II: The Establishment of a Just Human Community

Items	Responsibilities	Guidance from the Qur'an	Areas of Human Activity
Protection of Ideology	Piety and Character	Having faith in God. Doing and enjoining others to do what is right	Religious and professional education and practice
Protection of Freedom	Individual and social responsibilities	Refraining from what is wrong	Establishing justice under all circumstances
Protection Of Society	Economical and political responsibilities	Forbidding what is wrong and eradication of inequality, oppression, discrimination, corruption, and injustice	Economic activities, trade, Zakah, charity, taxation, and social and criminal justice
Protection of Property	International relations and defense	Fight in the way of Allah with those who fight with you.	Treaties, army, for the protection of the state

3.3 Reformation of Contemporary Communities

Efforts are required both to improve the character and behavior of the people and the character and workings of the state. It is an individual's responsibility to elect honest and trustworthy people to the government who should be ready to face accountability of their behavior, whether it is by the people or by God. Muslims cannot and should not be ruled by corrupt people or corrupt governments. Based on the *Sunnah* of the Messenger, the core protection areas that are required for the continual maintenance and progress of humanity are given in the table below

Table 3.3: Core Protection Areas

No	Core Protection Areas	Required Implementation
1	Protection of Life, Liberty, and Prosperity	Equal Access to Food, Shelter, and Medical Facilities
2	Protection of Belief and Freedom of Belief	Comprehensive Religious and Professional Education for all, male and female, poor and rich
3	Equal opportunity; Freedom from Discrimination and Exploitation.	Implementation of Justice under all circumstances; Adoption of Moral and Social Values

4	Protection of Individual and State Rights	Promoting Good and Forbidding Evil
5	Protection of Society and its Institutions	Fighting against all types Aggression and Corruption

Individually and collectively, we are all obligated and responsible, in our own spheres of influence, to develop, implement, protect, and improve these core values. Our efforts should be continuous and simultaneous, in order to ensure: (1) the basic necessities required for existence, (2) education to develop personal integrity and professionalism, (3) the inculcation of moral and social values, (4) protection of individual and state rights, and (5) protection of society and its institutions at all times and under all circumstances.

CHAPTER 7

Adoption of Moral and Social Human Values

FROM VARIOUS SURAHS OF THE QUR'AN

The purpose of education is to develop personal integrity and professionalism. Both are essential in the protection of an Islamic society. After developing a relationship with God, religion builds human character, refines human behavior, and teaches how to deal with others. It is religion that, through its set of beliefs, prayer, fasting, charity, and pilgrimage, makes people conscientious about the accountability for their actions. It also develops patience, a quality of character that is very much needed during difficult situations. To such people God assures two things: (1) He is their protector in this life and in the Hereafter, and (2) they will have all that they truly need. Various verses of the Qur'an that impact and transform a beastly human individual into a real human by improving the integrity of his character and by reforming his behavior are highlighted in this chapter.

The importance of adopting good moral and social values in society can be illustrated by a tradition mentioned in Malik's Muwatta in which it is stated how stealing, fornication, shortchanging in measure and weight, injustice, and betraying pledges impact the condition of a community. It is narrated that Yahya ibn Said heard that Abdullah ibn 'Abbas said:

1. Stealing from the spoils (or public treasury) does not appear in a people but that terror is cast into their hearts.
2. Fornication does not spread in a people but that there is much death among them.
3. A people do not lessen the measure and weight but that provision is cut off from them.
4. A people do not judge without right but that blood spreads among them.
5. A people do not betray the pledge but that Allah gives their enemies power over them (Malik's Muwatta: 21.21.13.26).

Part 1: The Islamic Moral Character

Morality is not like any other means of pleasure and luxury, from which indifference may be possible. It is the most important part of human life. It is human character that determines and defines the quality of life on earth. One can even say that without good character a human is bound to fail as God's trustee on earth, resulting in long-lasting, negative consequences for himself and others around him. That is why all of the elements of good moral character should be implemented. Islam has enumerated all these virtues and principles and has encouraged its followers to make them part of their lives, one after another.

1 FAITH IN GOD AND INDIVIDUAL MORAL VALUES

It is most important to achieve harmony between faith, piety, and implementation of the divine law in practical life, on the one hand, and work productivity and the fulfillment of the human mission on earth, on the other. It is this harmony that insured the fulfillment of God's promise to people of earlier revelations, and indeed to all communities, that they will have abundance from above and from beneath and that they will be forgiven their sins and admitted into gardens of bliss in the Hereafter. Thus, they have Paradise on earth and Paradise in Heaven. We must not forget, however, that the fundamental principle and the mainstay of the whole system are faith, piety, and the implementation of the divine way of life. This implies hard work, better productivity, and moral development. Moreover, when a person maintains a constant link with God, his values and standards are enhanced, resulting in all aspects of life being more enjoyable. This is the starting point from which everything else follows.

1.1 Faith, Reliance on God, and Righteousness

People need to develop their character and behavior, along with their physical and mental maturity, to make themselves suitable as God's trustees. Complete description of the guidelines for what human conduct should be like is given in the Qur'an. These guidelines educate, and their implementation makes us disciplined. God tells us about the Qur'an in Surah Al-Baqarah: "This is the Book. In it is the guidance, without doubt, to those who fear Allah (Qur'an 2:2)." He then commands: "O people! Worship your Lord Who created you and those who came before you that you may have a chance to learn righteousness (Qur'an 2:21)." Humanity needs guidelines and discipline to provide a better life on earth to all. The people who do not follow these guidelines create problems. God tells us: "When it is said to them, "Make not mischief on the earth," they say, "Why we only want to make peace!" Surely, they are the ones who make mischief, but they realize it not (Qur'an 2:11-12)." Verses of the Qur'an stressing the importance of faith, reliance on God, and learning righteousness are given in the table below.

Table 1.1: Faith, Reliance on God, and Righteousness

No	Surah:Verses	Characteristic
		Believers Serve God alone and Do Good Deeds
1	41:037	1. Prostrate to Allah, Who created them, if it is Him you wish to serve!
	41:030	2. Believers are those who say: "Our Lord is Allah," and, further, stand straight and steadfast.
	41:033	3. "Who is better in speech than one who calls (men) to Allah, works righteousness, and says, "I am of those who bow in Islam."
	41:034	4. Believers know that Goodness and evil cannot be equal. They repel evil with what is better.
	41:035	5. No one will be granted such goodness except those who exercise patience and self-restraint.
	41:036	6. If at any time an incitement to discord is made to the believers by the Evil One, they seek refuge in Allah.
	41:031	7. The believers are told: "We (the angels) are your protectors in this life and in the Hereafter. Therein, shall you have all that your souls shall desire; therein shall you have all that you ask for."
		Believers Learn Righteousness and Practice It
2	2:177	Righteousness is: 1. to believe in Allah and the Last Day, and the angels, and the Book, and the messengers; to spend of your substance, out of love for Him, for your kin, for orphans, for the needy, for the wayfarer, for those who ask, and for the ransom of

99

	3:092	slaves; 2. to be steadfast in prayer; 3. to practice regular charity; 4. to fulfill the contracts that you have made; 5. to be firm and patient, in suffering and adversity… By no means shall you attain righteousness unless you give of that which you love.
		Believers Put their Trust in God **And Rely on Him**
3	14:011-012 65:003	1. In Allah the believers should put their trust. No reason have we why we should not put our trust in Allah. He has guided us to the ways we (follow). We shall certainly bear with patience all the hurt you may cause us. On Allah the reliant should rely. 2. And He provides for him from (sources) he never could imagine. And if anyone puts his trust in Allah, sufficient is (Allah) for him. For Allah will surely accomplish His purpose. Verily, for all things has Allah appointed a due proportion.

1.2 Truth, Promises, Trustworthiness, and Self-Respect

God created universe on the basis of love, and He commanded people to build their lives on the foundation of truth. Humanity is instructed to be true in its words and dealings. Trustworthy people are pious, truthful, keep their words, and have self-respect. Such people do not bear witness to what is false, and they try to reform themselves and to work hard to please their Creator by behaving nobly on earth. They remember what God has said to them: "Which then is best: he that lays his foundation on piety to Allah and His good pleasure, or he that lays his foundation on an undermined sand-cliff ready to crumble to pieces?…Verily the most honored of you in the sight of Allah is (he who is) the most righteous of you (Qur'an 9:109, 49:13)." Verses of the Qur'an highlighting the believer's character are given in the table below.

Table 1.2: Be Truthful, Trustworthy and Keep Promises

No	Surah:Verses	Characteristic
		Believers are Truthful and Keep their Words
4	39:033	1. He who brings the truth and he who confirms (and supports) it—such are the men who do right.
	49:015	2. The believers are only those who believe in Allah and His Messenger; then they doubt not and struggle hard with their wealth and their lives in the way of Allah. They are the truthful ones.
	2:225; 5:089	3. Allah does not call you to account for what is vain in your oaths, but He will call you to account for what your hearts have earned.
	9:119	4. O you who believe! Fear Allah, and be with those who are true (in word and deeds).
	16:091	5. Fulfill the covenant of Allah when you have entered into it, and break not your oaths after you have confirmed them. Indeed, you have made Allah your surety...
		Believers are Trustworthy and Testify the Truth
5	4:058	6. Allah commands you to make over trusts to their owners, and when you judge between people you should judge with justice.
	2:283	7. Do not conceal testimony, and whoever conceals it, his heart is surely sinful.
	23:008-011	8. Those who faithfully observe their trusts and their covenants; and who guard their prayers—these will be the heirs who will inherit Paradise.
	25:072	9. They who do not bear witness to what is false, and when they pass by what is vain, they pass by nobly.

1.3 Courage and Self-defense define Human Behavior

People who believe get their courage by their reliance on God. After describing the behavior of the hypocrites during and after the Battle of Trench, God tells the Messenger in Surah Al-Ahzab: "Say: 'Running away (from battle) will not profit you if you are running away from death or slaughter, and even if (you do escape), no more than a brief (respite) will you be allowed to enjoy!' Say: 'Who is it that can screen you from Allah if it be His wish to give you punishment or to give you mercy?' Nor will they find for themselves besides Allah any protector or helper (Qur'an 33:16-17)." The verses of the Qur'an highlighting the source of a believer's courage are given in the table below.

Table 1.3: Believers' Courage and Self-defense

No	Surah:Verses	Characteristic
		Believers' Courage Springs from their Faith
6	3:173	1. Men said to them (believers): "A great army is gathering against you, so fear them," but it (only) increased their faith. They said: "For us Allah suffices, and He is the best disposer of affairs."
	33:022	2. When the believers saw the confederate forces, they said: "This is what Allah and his Messenger had promised us, and Allah and His Messenger told us what was true," and it only added to their faith and their zeal in obedience.
		Believers are Commanded to Defend Themselves
7	22:039	3. To those against whom war is made, permission is given (to fight) because they are wronged, and verily Allah is most powerful for their aid.
	22:060	4. And if one has retaliated to no greater extent than the injury he received and is again set upon inordinately, Allah will help him, for Allah is One that blots out (sins) and forgives (again and again).
	22:040	5. Did not Allah check one set of people by means of another, there would surely have been pulled down monasteries, churches, synagogues, and mosques in which the name of Allah is commemorated in abundant measure. Allah will certainly aid those who aid his (cause).

1.4 Generosity is Kindness, Tolerance, and Forgiveness

Islam is a religion of generosity and welfare. It likes its followers to be generous and charitable. It advises believers to be kind, act righteously, help their kinsmen, and do good and virtuous deeds. "If you disclose (acts of) charity, even so it is well, but if you conceal them and make them reach those in need, that is best for you. This will do away with some of your evil deeds...Those who spend of their goods by night and by day, in secret and in public, shall have their reward with their Lord. They shall have no fear, nor shall they grieve (Qur'an 2:271, 274)."

Since people have numerous physical and emotional weaknesses, perfection of their character and behavior without divine guidance is not humanly possible. What Islam teaches is the attitude that leads to continual improvement in individual character and in society. That is why believers are commanded to forgive people if they like to be forgiven by God. They should be kind and do good to others. God tells people that there is no other reward for kindness except the kindness itself, and He asks, "Is there any reward for good other than good? (Qur'an 55:60)."

Good relations among believers and non-believers are indeed encouraged in Islam. Dealing with unbelievers must always be cordial and friendly, provided they also treat believers in the same way. Further, believers are to be tolerant of the religious beliefs of the unbeliever and are to grant the unbelievers freedom of religious choice. God tells people: "Let there be no compulsion in religion. Truth stands out clear from error. Whoever rejects evil and believes in Allah has grasped the most trustworthy hand-hold that never breaks (Qur'an 2:256)." Verses of the Qur'an highlighting the importance of generosity, kindness, tolerance, and forgiveness are given in the table below.

Table 1.4: Generosity, Kindness, Tolerance and Forgiveness

No	Surah:Verses	Characteristic
		Reward for Kindness is Kindness Itself
	10:026	1. To those who do right is a goodly (reward)— yea, more (than in measure)! No darkness or shame shall cover their faces! They are companions of the garden; they will abide therein (for ever).
8	28:077	2. But seek with the (wealth) which Allah has bestowed on you the home of the Hereafter, nor forget your portion in this world. And do good to others as Allah has been good to you, and seek not (occasions for) mischief in the land, for Allah loves not those who do mischief.
	39:010	3. Good is (the reward) for those who do good in

	39:034		this world.
		4.	They shall have all that they wish for in the presence of their Lord; such is the reward of those who do good.
			Let there be No Compulsion in Religion
9	6:107	5.	If it had been Allah's plan, they would not have taken false gods, but We made you not one to watch over their doings, nor are you set over them to dispose of their affairs.
	6:108	6.	Revile not those whom they call upon besides Allah, lest they out of spite they revile Allah in their ignorance.
			Forgiveness is Divine as Well as Human
10	24:022	7.	Do you love that Allah should forgive you? Then, let not those of you who possess grace and abundance swear against giving to the near of kin and the poor and those who have fled in Allah's way; let them forgive and overlook.
	7:199	8.	Take to forgiveness and enjoin good and turn aside from the ignorant.

1.5 Deal with Others with Justice, Kindness, and Respect

Islam expects from its followers that their hearts should be full of humanity under the wakeful guard of their conscience, thus ensuring the protection of God's, as well as people's, rights. Believers should also protect people from injustice, exploitation, and corruption. In Surah An-Nisa believers are told: "Allah does command you to render back your trusts to those to whom they are due, and when you judge between people that you judge with justice. Verily, how excellent is the teaching that He gives you (Qur'an 4:58)." As stated in Surah Al-Baqarah, testimony is also a trust; therefore, God commands people: "Conceal not evidence; for whoever conceals it, his heart is tainted with sin (Qur'an 2:283)." Believers are also commanded to be kind and to help each other in good deeds and to: "Repel evil by what is the best (Qur'an 23:96)."

People have been asked to respect and honor God-given positions and responsibilities. It is God Who created us as humankind and gave us our spouses and children, parents, brothers and sisters, and all other relatives. He gave us neighbors, friend, and servants. All these belong to one's family. We are to serve God and serve our family. One should not be so proud as to neglect one's duties or be boastful of one's service. God commands this in Surah Al-A'raf: "Serve Allah, and join not any partners with Him, and do good to parents, kinsfolk, orphans, those in need, neighbors who are near, neighbors who are strangers, the companion by your side, the wayfarer (you meet), and what your right hands possess, for Allah loves not the arrogant, the vainglorious. (Qur'an 4:36)." This verse virtually makes the whole of humanity our family. We have to respect each one of them and fulfill our obligations towards them to the best of our ability. To accomplish this, we need to deal with each other with justice and fairness; we need to treat them with kindness and affection; we need to greet them with what is better and honor them and their privacy. Verses of the Qur'an highlighting the importance of justice, mutual kindness, and individual privacy are given in the table below.

Table 1.5: Be Just, Kind, and Respectful

No	Surah:Verses	Characteristic
		Believers Deal with People with Justice
11	6:152	1. Give measure and weight with (full) justice. Whenever you speak, speak justly, even if a near relative is concerned, and fulfill the covenant of Allah.
	57:025	2. We sent aforetime our messengers with clear instructions and sent down with them the Book and the balance (of right and wrong) that men may stand forth in justice.
		Believers Deal with People with Kindness
12	3:159	3. It is part of the mercy of Allah that you do deal gently with them. Were you severe or harsh-hearted, they would have broken away from you. So pass over (their faults), and ask for (Allah's) forgiveness for them, and consult them in (mutual) affairs. Then when you have taken a decision, put your trust in Allah.
	4:085	4. Whoever recommends and helps a good cause becomes a partner therein, and whoever recommends and helps an evil cause shares in its burden.
	41:034	5. Nor can goodness and evil be equal. Repel

			(evil) with what is better.
			Believers Greet People and Respect their Privacy
13	4:086	6.	When a greeting is offered you, meet it with a greeting still more courteous or (at least) of equal courtesy.
	24:027-028	7.	Enter not houses other than your own until you have asked permission and saluted those in them; that is best for you. If you find no one in the house, enter not until permission is given to you. If you are asked to go back, go back. That makes for greater purity for yourselves, and Allah knows well all that you do.
	24:058	8.	Let those whom your right hands possess and the (children) among you who have not come of age ask your permission (before they come to your presence) on three occasions (of privacy for you).
	24:059	9.	But when the children among you come of age, let them (also) ask for permission, as do those senior to them (in age). Thus does Allah make clear His signs to you, for Allah is full of knowledge and wisdom.

1.6 Accountable People are Moderate and Humble

People are not born to be irresponsible in this world. They are accountable for their deeds, whether good or bad, and will have to face their good or bad consequences in this world and in the Hereafter. If we reflect a little, we will realize that our doubts about the Hereafter are absolutely baseless. How can our resurrection be impossible for God Who created us in the first place from an insignificant sperm drop? We are reminded in Surah Fatir: "O people! Surely, the promise of Allah is true. Therefore, let not the life of this world deceives you, and let not Satan deceive you about Allah (Qur'an 35:5)." People are responsible for what they do, and none can bear the burden of another. However, they are only responsible to the extent of their abilities, and God does not burden people beyond what He has given them.

A number of rules governing individual responsibility have been mentioned in the Qur'an. In Surah Yunus, God tells the

Messenger to inform people that each person is only responsible for what he does: "Say: My work belongs to me and yours to you! You are free from responsibility for what I do, and I for what you do (Qur'an 10:41)." Likewise, in Surah Bani Israel, God tells people: "No bearer of burdens can bear the burden of another, nor would We visit with Our wrath until We had sent a messenger (to give warning) (Qur'an 17:15)." Still further, in Surah Al-Talaq, God tells people that they are only responsible to the extent of their abilities: "Let the people with means spend according to their means, and people whose resources are restricted, let them spend according to what Allah has given them. Allah puts no burden on any person beyond what He has given him (Qur'an 65:7)." Verses of the Qur'an highlighting that accountable people are moderate and humble in their behavior are given in the table below.

Table 1.6: Accountable People are Moderate and Humble

No	Surah:Verses	Characteristic
		Be not Extravagant or Miserly but Moderate
14	17:026	1. And render to the kindred their due rights, as (also) to those in want, and to the wayfarer. But squander not (your wealth) in the manner of a spendthrift.
	17:027	2. Spendthrifts are brothers of the Satan, and the Satan is to his Lord ungrateful.
	17:029	3. Make not your hand tied (like a miser's) to your neck, nor stretch it forth to its utmost reach so that you become blameworthy and destitute.
	25:067	4. (And Allah's servants are) those who, when they spend, are not extravagant and not miserly, but hold a just (balance) between those (extremes).
		Believers Treat Other People With Respect
15	25:063	5. And the servants of (Allah) Most Gracious are those who walk on the earth in humility, and when the ignorant address them they say, "Peace!"
	31:018	6. ...swell not your cheek (for pride) at men, nor walk in insolence through the earth, for Allah loves not any arrogant boaster.
	31:019	Be moderate in your pace, and lower your voice.

1.7 Perseverance through Patience and Prayer

Patience may soon be exhausted when the period of suffering is long and strength seems to be decreasing. At such moments, individual strength needs to be renewed. Hence, prayer is needed to support patience. Prayer is a perpetual spring that renews believers' energy and gives them new strength. Believers are then able to persevere for as long as it takes to achieve their goals. Prayer also adds to their contentment, confidence, and reassurance. People are usually weak, and when a weak person faces a difficult task beyond his limited resources, faces the turmoil of evil, finds temptations too strong, finds possible solutions too difficult, and finds resistance to tyranny and corruption too demanding, he needs to have a direct link with God, the source of all power. That is why God directs the believers to be patient, to persevere, and to resort to prayers as they face difficult situations. God encourages people to come to Him and commands the believers in Surah Al-Baqarah: "O you who believe! Seek help with patient perseverance and prayer, for Allah is with those who patiently persevere (Qur'an 2:153)."

Patience and perseverance have been frequently mentioned in the Qur'an. God knows that enormous efforts are needed to ensure that proper behavior is maintained in the face of all temptations and motivations to abandon right conduct. This requires people to be on their guard and ready to give whatever sacrifice is required. For this effort, they need to be patient. They need patience to do good works, to abstain from sin, to fight those who are corrupt, to defeat their designs, and to bear with fortitude when victory seems to be delayed. They always need patience and perseverance when their objective seems to be very far away, falsehood seems to be very strong, and help seems to be not yet available. They need patience to face dishonest, cunning, and arrogant people who are persistent in their rejection of the truth. Verses of the Qur'an highlighting the importance of patience and prayer during the difficulties of life are given in the table below.

Table1.7: Perseverance through Patience and Prayer

No	Surah:Verses	Characteristic
		Bear Misfortune Patiently and with Courage
16	2:155-156	1. Be sure we shall test you with something of fear and hunger, some loss in goods or lives or the fruits (of your toil), but give glad tidings to those who patiently persevere. Who say when afflicted with calamity: "To Allah we belong, and to Him is our return."
	3:200	2. O you who believe! Persevere in patience and constancy; vie in such perseverance; strengthen each other; and fear Allah that you may prosper.
	31:017	3. Bear patiently that which befalls you; surely these acts require courage.
	42:039	4. Those who, when an oppressive wrong is inflicted on them, (are not cowed but) help and defend themselves. (Patience does not mean that a person should not defend himself. He should defend himself patiently).
		Be Patient, Show Patience, and Forgive People
17	42:040	5. If a person forgives and makes reconciliation, his reward is due from Allah: for (Allah) loves not those who do wrong.
	42:043	6. But indeed if any show patience and forgive, that would truly be an exercise of courageous will and resolution in the conduct of affairs.
	46:035	7. Therefore, patiently persevere, as did (all) messengers of inflexible purpose, and be in no haste about the unbelievers.
	73:010	8. Have patience with what they (unbelievers) say, and leave them with noble dignity.

1.8 Managing Desires with Patience and Contentment

It is natural for humankind to be honest, hardworking, and just. People resort to wrong and illegal ways in desperation. If they are patient and try their best, they will be eventually successful. So it is the determination supported by patience that helps people in managing selfish desires. In both cases of gratitude for a favorable development and perseverance in the case of misfortune, a believer is rewarded. Believers are told in Surah Al-Rad: "Those who patiently persevere, seeking the countenance of their Lord, establish regular prayers, spend out of what We have given them for their sustenance, secretly and openly, and repel evil with what is good—for such there is the final attainment of the eternal home...Peace unto you for that you persevered in patience (Qur'an 13:22, 24)!"

The Islamic way of life is based on worship that provides support during the life's journey of a believer, strengthens the spirit, and purifies the heart. If we believe in God and worship Him, then that worship makes every obligation and its benefits acceptable to our hearts. We happily appreciate the need for that obligation and its benefits. This spares us from disobeying God's commands. Worship opens up people's heart and strengthens their relation with God. God's friendship and His help make matters easy, bring light into one's world, and provide limitless strength, confidence, reassurance, and contentment. With regard to contentment, it was narrated by Abu Said Al-Khudri that Messenger said: "Allah will ask the people of Paradise, 'Are you pleased?' They will say, 'Why should we not be pleased since You have given us what You have not given to anyone of Your creation?' Allah will say, 'I will give you something better than that.' They will reply, 'O our Lord! What is better than that?' Allah will say, 'I will bestow My pleasure and contentment upon you so that I will never be angry with you after (this) forever' (Sahih Bukhari: 8.76.557)." Verses of the Qur'an highlighting the importance of patience and contentment in managing one's desires are given in the table below.

Table 1.8: Managing Desires with Patience and Contentment

No	Surah:Verses	Characteristic
		Be Patient, Pray, and ask God's Help to Succeed
18	2:250	1. Say, "Our Lord! Pour out constancy on us, and make our steps firm. Help us against those that reject faith."
	10:109	2. Follow the inspiration sent unto you, and be patient and constant.
	7:128	3. Pray for help from Allah, and (wait) in patience and constancy.
		Manage Desires with Patience and Contentment
19	13:022	4. Those who patiently persevere, seeking the countenance of their Lord, establish regular

	18:028		prayers, spend out of what We have given them for their sustenance, secretly and openly, and repel evil with what is good—for such there is the final attainment of the eternal home.
		5.	Keep yourself content with those who call on their Lord morning and evening, seeking His goodwill, and let not your eyes pass beyond them, seeking the pomp and glitter of this life. Do not obey any whose heart We have permitted to neglect the remembrance of Us, one who follows his own desires, whose case has gone beyond all bounds.
			**Patient People will be paid their Reward in Full**
20	13:024	6.	Peace unto you for that you persevered in patience!
	25:075	7.	Those are the ones who will be rewarded with the highest place in heaven because of their patient constancy. Therein shall they be met with salutations and peace.
	39:010	8.	Good is (the reward) for those who do good in this world. Spacious is Allah's earth! Those who patiently persevere will truly receive a reward without measure.

111

Part 2: Islamic Social Behavior

God says: "Why were there not among the generations before you persons possessed of balanced good sense, prohibiting (men) from mischief in the earth...Nor would your Lord be the One to destroy communities for a single wrongdoing if its members were likely to mend (Qur'an 11:116-117)." Resurrection and the Hereafter are truths that inevitably have to take place. The people of past communities who denied the accountability for their behavior and deeds and continued their sinful lives ultimately became subject to God's punishment, even in this world. People are also accountable for their social behavior. Islam demands unity, brotherhood, mutual help, and cooperation. We are commanded to respect the feelings and emotions of the others. There are a set of rules for social gatherings, social work, and mutual discourse. Most importantly, believers are commanded to make peace between quarreling parties and to wish for others what they wish for themselves.

1 UNITY, MUTUAL RESPECT, AND COOPERATION

Happiness in the life to come also depends on the efforts of the believers to improve the life in this world. What makes us suffer or makes us happy depends upon our character and our deeds. Our choices make the difference, and all actions, good and bad, have appropriate consequences. Believers are commanded to be united for the promotion of peace and community development. They should encourage people in promoting justice, general welfare, and respect for the feelings and emotions of others. They should refrain from backbiting, suspicion, and spying on others.

1.1 Believers are a Party united for Peace and Progress

A group of dedicated people of good moral character and behavior is required for the implementation of any sociopolitical system. The responsibility for the implementation of Islam is assigned to the Islamic community. All believers are united in this community. In Surah Ali-Imran, God commands the believers: "And hold fast all together by the rope that Allah (stretches out for you), and be not divided among yourselves…be not like those who are divided amongst themselves and fall into disputations after receiving clear revelations (Qur'an 3:103, 105)." Believers deal gently among themselves and consult each other during the implementation of Islam. They forgive each other's faults and decide to go ahead for the implementation of Islam while putting their trust in God.

What attitude should the believers adopt if two groups fall into mutual fighting? The answer is that one should make peace between them. This obligation is described in Surah Al-Hujurat: "If two parties among the believers fall into a quarrel, make you peace between them. But if one of them transgresses beyond bounds against the other, then fight you (all) against the one that transgresses until it complies with the command of Allah. But if it complies, then make peace between them with justice, and be fair: for Allah loves those who are fair (and just). The believers are but a single brotherhood. So make peace and reconciliation between your two (contending) brothers, and fear Allah that you may receive mercy (Qur'an 49:9-10)." The general rule to remember is: "When those come to you who believe in Our signs, say: 'Peace be on you.' Your Lord has inscribed for Himself (the rule of) mercy. Verily, if any of you did evil in ignorance and thereafter repented and amended (his conduct), lo! He is oft-forgiving, most merciful (Qur'an 6:54)." Peacemaking is of tremendous importance in an Islamic society. Even the secret councils that are forbidden under normal circumstances become legal if they are involved in making peace. "In most of their secret talks, there is no good, but if one exhorts to a deed of charity or justice or conciliation between men (secrecy is permissible). To him who does this, seeking the good pleasure of Allah, We shall soon give a reward of the highest (value) (Qur'an 4:114)."

1.2 Believers Respect People, their Feelings, and Emotions
Believers have been commanded to safeguard against the evils that spoil mutual relationships. Mocking and taunting each other, calling others by nicknames, creating suspicions, spying into other people's affairs, and backbiting are evils that are not only sins in themselves, but they also cause corruption in society. In

113

Surah Al-Hujurat, God has mentioned these evils individually and forbids them as being unlawful: "O you who believe! Let not some men among you laugh at others; it may be that the (latter) are better than the (former). Nor let some women laugh at others; it may be that the (latter) are better than the (former). Nor defame nor be sarcastic to each other, nor call each other by (offensive) nicknames. Ill-seeming is a name connoting wickedness, (to be used of one) after he has believed, and those who do not desist are (indeed) doing wrong (Qur'an 49:11)."

There are people who laugh at honest and hardworking believers. Their disgraceful, humiliating, dishonest behavior and evil deeds will meet with a most dire end in the Hereafter. God states in Surah Al-Mutaffifin: "Those in sin used to laugh at those who believed, and whenever they passed by them used to wink at each other (in mockery), and when they returned to their own people they would return jesting (Qur'an 83:29-31)." The believers, on the other hand, will feel comforted when they see their fate in the Hereafter: "So today those who believe shall laugh at the unbelievers. Seated upon their couches, they (believers) are looking around. Surely the disbelievers are paid back for what they did (Qur'an 83:34-36)."

1.3 Being Suspicious of and Spying on others is Forbidden
Since truth has lost its importance in the present world, everybody is suspicious of and spying on others. Even some governments have made it legal to spy on its citizens. In contrast, God says in the Qur'an: "O you who believe! Avoid suspicion as much (as possible), for suspicion in some cases is a sin. Spy not on each other nor speak ill of behind their backs. Would any of you like to eat the flesh of his dead brother? Nay, you would abhor it...But fear Allah: For Allah is oft-returning, most merciful (Qur'an 49:12)." This verse establishes certain rules within human society, which protect the integrity and freedom of individuals, while at the same time teaching people how to cleanse their feelings and consciences.

Islam does not stop at this point in educating people's hearts and minds. The verse also establishes a principle that applies to mutual dealings among people. It protects individual rights, so that people may not be punished or tried on the basis of suspicion. Abu Huraira reported the Messenger as saying: "Avoid suspicion, for suspicion is the gravest lie in talk, and do not be inquisitive about one another, and do not spy upon one another (Sahih Muslim: 32.6214)." This means that people remain innocent, enjoying all their rights, freedom, and status until it is evidently clear that they have committed some offense. It is not sufficient that they are suspected of having committed something in order to pursue them with the aim of establishing whether they are guilty. This verse also shows the limits to which Islam goes in protecting people's freedom, integrity, rights, and status. Islam achieves this in real life after it establishes it in people's hearts and consciences. How does this compare with what even the best democratic countries boast of in protecting human rights? I leave this to the readers to reflect and judge.

2 COMMUNITY SERVICE AND COMMUNICATION

In any good community, there are norms of mutual help and social behavior. In the Qur'an, the general attitude of the believers and the hypocrites has been described to enable every believer to discriminate between the two. The community is always bound together by adopting certain disciplinary measures that tend to increase its strength and that discourage people from creating mischief. In Surah An-Nur, God commands the believers to take permission before leaving from a community project in which they are participating: "Only those are believers, who believe in Allah and His Messenger: When they are with him on a matter requiring collective action, they do not depart until they have asked for his leave. Those who ask for your leave are those who believe in Allah and His Messenger. So when they ask for your leave for some business of theirs, give leave to those of them whom you will, and ask Allah for their forgiveness, for Allah is oft-forgiving, most merciful (Qur'an 24:62)." Islam commands its followers not to get involved in scheming for sinful plots or revolt. They should show courtesy at public meetings and social visits. In their conversations, they should be polite, truthful and withdraw from false arguments and discourse.

2.1 Participation in Secret Counsels for Sin and Revolt
Since God knows everything, the unbelievers have been warned that due to their secret whisperings and consultations, by which they conspired and intrigued against the Messenger, and because of their hidden malice and grudge in greeting him and asking, "Why does not God punish us for what we say?" they will certainly be punished in Hell. In Surah Al-Mujadilah, God says that only unbelievers hold secret counsels for sin and revolt: "Do you not see that Allah does know (all) that is in the heavens and on earth? There is not a secret consultation between three, but He makes the fourth among them—nor between five but He makes the sixth—nor between fewer no more, but He is in their midst wherever they be. In the end will He tell them the truth of their conduct on the Day of Judgment. For Allah has full knowledge of all things. Turn not your sight towards those who were forbidden secret counsels yet revert to that which they were forbidden (to do). And they hold secret counsels among themselves for iniquity and hostility and disobedience to the Messenger. And when they come to you, they salute you, not as Allah salutes you, (but in crooked ways). And they say to themselves, 'Why does not Allah punish us for our words?' Enough for them is Hell. In it will they burn, and evil is that destination (Qur'an 58:7-8)."

After reaffirming that the whisperings of the hypocrites can do no harm to the believers; the believers have been told that they should go on doing their duty with full trust in God. In contrast to the behavior of the unbelievers, the believers have further been advised that when they talk secretly they should not talk of sin, transgression, and disobedience to the Messenger, but of goodness and piety. God commands believers in Surah Al-Mujadilah: "O you who believe! When you hold secret counsel, do it not for iniquity and hostility and disobedience to the Messenger, but do it for righteousness and self-restraint; and fear Allah, to Whom you shall be brought back. Secret counsels are only (inspired) by the Satan, in order that he may cause grief to the believers, but he cannot harm them in the least, except as

Allah permits. And on Allah let the believers put their trust (Qur'an 58:9-10)."

2.2 Show of Courtesy at Public Meetings and Social Visits

The believers were given instructions to eradicate those social evils that were prevalent among the people then, just as they are today. People sitting in an assembly were not even courteous enough to squeeze in so as to make room for the latecomers. This used to be frequently experienced in the Messenger's assemblies. Therefore, the believers were told that they should not behave selfishly in their assemblies, but they should accommodate the newcomers with an open heart. "O you who believe! When you are told to make room in the assemblies, (spread out and) make room; (ample) room will Allah provide for you. And when you are told to rise up, rise up. Allah will rise up to (suitable) ranks (and degrees) those of you who believe and who have been granted knowledge (Qur'an 58:11)." Likewise, when people go to visit others, they should not prolong their visits, realizing that it may cause hardship to the people they are visiting.

Believers have been told that in general all meetings are confidential except those in which some illegal activity is taking place. It was narrated by Jabir ibn Abdullah that the Prophet said: "Meetings are confidential except three: those for the purpose of shedding blood unlawfully, or committing fornication, or acquiring property unjustly (Abu Dawud: 41.4851)." People have also been advised to avoid sitting on paths and holding meetings there. Abu Sa'id Khudri reported the Messenger as saying: "'Avoid sitting on the paths. If you have to sit there at all, then fulfill the rights of the path.' When asked, 'What are their rights?' upon this he said: 'Lowering the gaze, refraining from doing harm, exchanging of greetings, commanding of good, and forbidding from evil' (Sahih Muslim: 26.5376)."

2.3 Believers are Polite and Converse in the Best Ways

Duties toward God cannot be overly emphasized, but duties toward fellow human beings, which are equally important, are generally given a low priority in the minds of the believers, both at the individual and community levels. Yet, a good balance is the main characteristic of Islam and its code of living. Our duties and dealings include all types of people, believers and unbelievers alike. We are commanded in Surah Al-Ankabut that we should not dispute about religion with Jews and Christians. It should be discussed in a best possible way: "Do not dispute with the People of the Book, except with means better (than mere disputation), unless it be with those of them who inflict wrong (and injury): but say, 'We believe in the revelation that has come down to us and in that which came down to you; our God and your God is one, and it is to Him we bow (in Islam).' And thus (it is) that We have sent down the Book to you. So the People of the Book believe therein, as also do some of these (pagan Arabs), and none but unbelievers reject our revelations (Qur'an 29:46-47)."

Dealings with unbelievers must always be cordial and friendly, provided, they also treat believers in the same way. Good relations with non-believers are indeed encouraged in Islam. However, people who are hostile to Islam or try to ridicule its beliefs or practices are to be treated differently. Islam does not extend kindness to them, but instructs believers to stay away from them. In Surah Al-An'am, believers are advised: "When you see men engaged in vain discourse about Our revelations, turn away from them unless they turn to a different theme. If Satan ever makes you forget, then after recollection do not sit in the company of those who do wrong. On their account, no responsibility falls on the righteous, but (their duty) is to remind them that they may (learn to) fear Allah. Leave alone those who take their religion to be mere play and amusement and are deceived by the life of this world, but proclaim (to them) this (truth): that every soul delivers itself to ruin by its own acts (Qur'an 6:68-70)."

3 ENJOIN GOOD AND FORBID WHAT IS EVIL

Islam demands that believers enjoin what is good and forbid what is evil. Islam also commands the believers to wish for their brothers what they wish for themselves. Additionally, Islam commands the believers to do righteous deeds, in order to construct a truly Islamic community.

3.1 Believers Enjoin what is Good and Forbid what is Evil

At-Tirmidhi relates on the authority of Huthaifah that the Messenger said: "By Him Who holds my soul in His hand, you will enjoin the doing of what is right and forbid what is wrong, or else God will visit you with a punishment of His own. You will, then, pray to Him, and He will not answer you (Al-Hadith: vol. I. no.71, p374)." Islamic communities have to assign some of its members with the task of inviting to all that is good, enjoining the doing of what is right, and forbidding what is wrong. An Islamic community does not come into existence unless it has this essential quality by which it is distinguished from the rest of humanity. The success of an Islamic community depends on promoting good, forbidding evil, and protecting human character and society. God commands believers in Surah Ali-Imran: "Let there arise out of you a band of people inviting to all that is good, enjoining what is right, and forbidding what is wrong. They are the ones to attain felicity...They believe in Allah and the Last Day. They enjoin what is right and forbid what is wrong, and they hasten (in emulation) in good works. They are in the ranks of the righteous (Qur'an 3:104, 114)."

Without the promotion of good and the elimination of evil, an Islamic community ceases to exist. The working of an Islamic community is very well described in Surah At-Tawbah: "The believers, men and women, are protectors one of another. They enjoin what is just and forbid what is evil. They observe regular prayers, practice regular charity, and obey Allah and His Messenger (Qur'an 9:71)." Likewise, in Surah Luqman, Luqman advises his son: "O my son! Establish regular prayer, enjoin what is just, and forbid what is wrong: and bear with patient constancy whatever betide you; for this is firmness (of purpose) in (the conduct of) affairs (Qur'an 31:17)."

3.2 Believers Wish for others as they Wish for themselves

Islam condemns the national and racial distinctions that cause universal corruption in the world. Nationalism, tribalism, favoritism to one's family, pride of ancestry, looking down upon others as inferior, and pulling down others only for the sake of establishing one's own superiority have filled the world with injustices and tyranny. God in Surah Al-Hujurat refutes this evil by stating: "We created you from a single (pair) of a male and a female and made you into nations and tribes that you may know each other, (not that you may despise each other). Verily, the most honored of you in the sight of Allah is (he who is) the most righteous of you (Qur'an 49:13)."

People have been told that the real thing is not just the verbal profession of the faith. To believe in God and His Messenger truly is to obey them in one's practical life and to exert sincerely with one's self and wealth in the cause of God. True believers are only those who adopt this attitude. This is the only way to be sincere in the true profession of faith: "Only those are believers who have believed in Allah and His Messenger and have never since doubted, but have striven with their belongings and their persons in the cause of Allah. Such are the sincere ones (Qur'an 49:15)." Additionally, believers wish for others what they wish for themselves. Anas narrated that the Prophet said: "None of you will have faith till he wishes for his brother what he likes for himself (Al-Bukhari 1.12)"

As for those who merely profess Islam orally without affirmation by the heart and then adopt an attitude as if they had done someone a favor by accepting Islam, they may be counted among the Muslims in the world and may even be treated as Muslims in society, but they cannot be counted as believers in the sight of God and in the Hereafter.

3.3 Only Righteous Deeds Make a Community Islamic
God commands believers to wish for others as they wish for themselves. Such an attitude should initiate a flurry of activities that help establish all that is good, eliminating those things that are harmful to the welfare of the people. Eventually, people's belief and their cumulative righteous activities make the whole community Islamic. Previous communities suffered because they ignored the importance of enjoining the doing of what is right and forbidding what is wrong. Abu Dawud related on the authority of Ibn Massoud that the Messenger said: "When the

children of Israel began to commit sins frequently, their scholars tried to dissuade them, but they persisted. Their scholars, nevertheless, continued to attend their social gatherings, eat and drink with them. God left them (the scholars) to stray and sealed their hearts. He also cursed them in the words of David, Solomon, and Jesus, Son of Mary. The Messenger was saying this as he reclined, but at this point he sat up and said: 'By Him Who holds my soul in His hand, you must make them turn back to what is right' (Abu Dawud: 37.4322)."

When people's character and behavior keep deteriorating and when corruption is on the rise, some corrective measures need to be taken to save the community from destruction. Amirah al-Kindi narrated that the Messenger said: "When a sin is committed on earth, a person who witnesses it and denounces it is the same as one who has not seen it. But the one who has been absent and approves of it is considered like one who has taken part in it (Abu Dawud: 37.4331)." It is, therefore, a matter of utmost importance for human individuals and society that people should repent, do good deeds, and avoid what is bad. The entire Islamic code is for the benefit of the people; it either prevents harm or brings benefit.

CHAPTER 8

Striving In the Protection of Human Society

FROM SURAH AL-ANFAL (08) AND SURAH AT-TAWBAH (09)

Jihad, the struggle to protect human society, can be a simple action, such as standing firm in defense of the cause of Islam. This may require speaking out in public against ignoring Islamic principles, writing articles, or publishing books. It may also take the form of reminding people of their Islamic duties and of motivating them to conduct their lives according to Islam. It may also take the form of fighting the enemies of Islam in battle in order to foil their attempts to smother the call of Islam. Striving, making efforts, and trying to convince oneself or others about the truth of Islam are all different aspects of Jihad. It does not mean fighting only in the battlefield. But if a situation arises where the believers are attacked, then they have no choice but to defend themselves.

1 MAINTANANCE OF PEACE AND SECURITY

1.1 Jihad seeks the freedom of belief

Jihad aims to establish God's authority and to remove tyranny. It liberates humanity from submission to any authority other than that of God. Jihad does not aim to achieve the hegemony of one philosophy or system or nation over another. It wants the system laid down by God to replace the systems established by His creatures. It does not wish to establish a kingdom of anyone among people, but to establish God's own kingdom. Hence, it has to move forward throughout the earth to liberate the whole of humanity, without discrimination between those who are within the land of Islam and those outside it. The whole earth is populated by human beings that are being subjected to tyrannical authority.

1.2 Man-made Social Systems and Jihad

The systems that exist today are all man-made. None of them has any right to dominate others. The same does not apply to the divine system that sets out to overthrow all man-made systems in order to liberate all humanity from the humiliation of submission to other human beings, so that they can submit to God alone and serve Him only without any partners. Since Islam lays down a rule stating that no compulsion is admissible in matters of belief, then why does Islam move forward to fight, and why has God bought the believers' lives and property, so that they fight for God's cause, kill, and get killed? Jihad has a reason that is totally different from compelling other people to accept Islam. It is to liberate people from the tyranny of the pharaohs of the world and to establish justice in society.

1.3 Jihad for the Liberation of Humanity

Islam liberates humanity throughout the earth from submission to unjust systems. As such, Islam always confronts tyrannical forces, systems, and regimes that seek to subjugate people and dominate their lives and that deprive people of a chance to listen to the Islamic message and to adopt it if they are convinced of its truth. Further, these systems may force people, in one way or another, to turn away from the Islamic message. That is an ugly violation of freedom of belief. For these reasons, Islam moves forward, equipped with suitable power, to overthrow tyrannical systems and to destroy their forces. It leaves people entirely free to adopt the faith they like. If they wish to be Muslims, they will have all the rights and duties that apply to Muslims. On the other hand, if they wish to maintain other religions, they may do so.

2 WHO ARE GOD'S TRUSTEES ON EARTH?

One of the main objectives of Islam is to guide and help people to achieve excellent moral character and behavior, which are reflected in truthfulness, honesty, and sincerity of action, and to provide them with ideals that constantly elevate them to a higher standard of morality. To help people to achieve this high standard of nobility and perfection, God sent messengers as role models to different nations throughout the ages to preach His message and guide people to the way of life that ensures their happiness in this life and in the life to come. Some people say: "Why does God force us to be good by bribing us with Paradise and threatening us with Hell? Why can't He love us as we are?" This argument seems like a child telling his parents: "Why do I have to go to school? I am good enough! Just love me as I am." Although success or failure depends on our efforts, divine guidance motivates and helps us to excel in life—in learning, in character, and in our worth to society. God, like parents, is interested in our success, and He wants trustworthy people to be His trustees.

2.1 Those who are the Believers in the Truth

Those people who are destined to take part actively in the protection of human societies that have been established on truth need special qualifications. The Qur'an characterizes them as: "...those who when Allah is mentioned feel a tremor in their hearts, and when they hear His revelations recited find their faith strengthened and put their trust in their Lord. Who establish regular prayers and spend out of what We have given them for sustenance. Such in truth are the believers; they have grades of dignity with their Lord and forgiveness and generous sustenance (Qur'an 8:2-4)."

2.2 Those who are Guardians of Each Other

People come across difficulties and hardships during their lives on earth. In this regard, mutual help is encouraged. People who fight for what they believe in and help each other are appreciated: "Those who believed, and adopted exile, and fought for the faith with their property and their persons in the cause of Allah, as well as those who gave (them) asylum and aid—these are friends and protectors one of another. As to those who believed but came not into exile, you owe no duty of protection to them until they come into exile, but if they seek your aid in religion it is your duty to help them, except against a people with whom you have a treaty of mutual alliance (Qur'an 8:72)."

2.3 Those to Whom God is the Dearest

To whom is God the dearest? They are those who refuse to take their unbelieving fathers and brothers for guardians. God

124

commands the believers: "O you who believe! Take not for protectors your fathers and your brothers if they love infidelity above faith. If any of you do so, they do wrong. Say: 'If it be that your fathers, your sons, your brothers, your mates, or your kindred, the wealth that you have gained, the commerce in which you fear a decline, or the dwellings in which you delight are dearer to you than Allah or His Messenger or the striving in His cause, then wait until Allah brings about His decision, and Allah guides not the rebellious' (Qur'an 9:23-24)."

2.4 Those who Enjoin Good and Forbid Evil

Encouraging in good deeds and discouraging in whatever is bad, is another characteristic of the believers. God says: "The believers, men and women, are protectors one of another: they enjoin what is just and forbid what is evil: they observe regular prayers, practice regular charity, and obey Allah and His Messenger. On them will Allah pour His mercy, for Allah is exalted in power, wise…But the Messenger and those who believe with him strive and fight with their wealth and their persons. For them are good things (in this life), and it is they who will prosper (in this life and in the Hereafter) (Qur'an 9:71, 88)." This indicates that the implementation of religious principles individually and in society benefits people in both worlds. In religious terms, the quality of the believers improves with their spirituality, which is proportional to the magnitude of their *Iman* (faith) and *Taqwa* (fearing God with regard to the accountability for their behavior and deeds).

3 JUSTIFICATION FOR AND THE REWARD OF JIHAD

3.1 Jihad is to establish Truth and Justice

At the Battle of Badr, God desired to manifest the truth of His words and to cut off the root of the unbelievers. "When Allah promised you one of the two (enemy) parties, that it should be yours, you wished that the one unarmed should be yours. But Allah willed to justify the truth according to His words and to cut off the roots of the unbelievers that He might justify truth and prove falsehood false, distasteful though it be to those who are guilty (Qur'an 8:7-8)."

125

3.2 Jihad is the Surety of God's Help and Security

God reminds the believers that when they engage in defending themselves in the way of God, He will arrange for their help like He did at Badr. "Remember you implored the assistance of your Lord, and He answered you: 'I will assist you with a thousand of the angels, ranks on ranks.' Allah made it but a message of hope and an assurance to your hearts. (In any case,) there is no help except from Allah, and Allah is exalted in power, wise (Qur'an 8:9-10)." The number of angels, one thousand at Badr and three thousand and five thousand at Uhud, is probably not to be taken literally, but to express a strength matching to what was or will be required to achieve success. This is because God was a party at the time of Badr and will be with the believers in similar situations in the future.

3.3 Jihad is Struggle against Persecution

Unfortunately, the persecution of good people has not been eliminated from society. Its eradication requires continuing efforts. That is why the believers are commanded: "Say to the unbelievers if (now) they desist (from persecution of believers), their past will be forgiven them. But if they persist, the punishment of those before them is already (a matter of warning for them), and fight them on until there is no more oppression and there prevail justice and faith in Allah altogether and everywhere. But if they cease, verily Allah does see all that they do. If they refuse, be sure that Allah is your Protector, the best to protect and the best to help (Qur'an 8:38-40)." The struggle against persecution and injustice has to continue.

3.4 Jihad is either Martyrdom or Victory

Striving in the way of God means the implementation of His commands and can only result in one of two things. It is either martyrdom or victory. God states: "Say, 'Can you expect for us (any fate) other than one of two glorious things—(martyrdom or victory)? But we can expect for you either that Allah will send his punishment from Himself or by our hands. So wait; we too will wait with you' (Qur'an 9:52)." After the delivery of His message, God sends His punishment to the unbelievers either by Himself or by having the believers administer it themselves.

4 JIHAD IN WAR AND PEACE

4.1 Preparation in the Defense of Believers

God commands the believers to be prepared for war if they want to live in peace. This discourages people from attacking the believers. "Against them make ready your strength to the utmost of your power, including steeds of war, to frighten thereby the enemy of Allah and your enemies, and others besides, whom you may not know, but whom Allah does know. Whatever you shall spend in the cause of Allah shall be repaid unto you, and you shall not be treated unjustly (Qur'an 8:60)." Since war destroys much valuable infrastructure and people, any cost incurred for defense is a good investment that will be fully repaid by maintaining peace and by discouraging the enemy from attacking.

4.2 Jihad is to be ready to maintain Peace

Believers are commanded to maintain peace by not initiating aggression. If people want to live in peace, let them live in peace. "But if the enemy is inclined to peace, do you (also) incline to peace and trust in Allah, for He is One that hears and knows. Should they intend to deceive you, verily Allah is sufficient for you. He it is Who has strengthened you with His aid and with (the company of) the believers. He has put affection between their hearts. Not if you had spent all that is in the earth could you have produced that affection, but Allah has done it, for He is exalted in might, wise. O Prophet! Allah is sufficient for you and those who follow you of the believers (Qur'an 8:61-64)." God is sufficient for those who are believers. They have no justification for wars of aggression with the aim of subjugating other people and owning their wealth or natural resources.

4.3 Jihad is to Motivate the Believers to Fight

God encourages believers to defend themselves and what they believe. He commands His Messenger to motivate believers to participate in the struggle to discourage injustice and persecution in the land. "O Prophet! Rouse the believers to the fight. If there are twenty amongst you, patient and persevering, they will vanquish two hundred. If a hundred, they will vanquish a thousand of the unbelievers, for these are a people without understanding. For the present, Allah has lightened your (task), for He knows that there is a weak spot in you. But (even so), if there are a hundred of you, patient and persevering, they will vanquish two hundred, and if a thousand, they will vanquish two thousand with the leave of Allah, for Allah is with those who patiently persevere…The unbelievers are protectors of one another. Unless you do this, (protect each other), there would be oppression on earth, and great corruption (Qur'an 8:65-66, 73)."

5 SITUATIONS REQUIRING FIGHTING

Islam allows the believers to defend themselves and those who are oppressed. Believers do not force people to accept Islam. Rather, they are commanded: "Listen not to the unbelievers, but strive against them with the utmost strenuousness with (the Qur'an) (Qur'an 25:52)." It is narrated by Anas ibn Malik that the Prophet said: "Use your property, your persons, and your tongues in striving against the polytheists (Abu Dawud: 14.2498)." However, God commands in Surah Al-Baqarah: "Let there be no compulsion in religion. Truth stands out clear from error (Qur'an 2.256)." Likewise, in Surah Qaf, God says: "We know best what they say, and you are not one to compel them by force. So admonish with the Qur'an such as fear My warning (Qur'an 50:45)." Rather than forcing Islam onto others, God tells the believers to concentrate on their own improvement. "O you who believe! Take care of your own selves. If you follow (right) guidance, no harm can come to you from those who stray. The goal of you all is to Allah. It is He Who will show you the truth of all that you do (Qur'an 5:105)." In fact the believers' duty is only to establish peace and security near at home and reform themselves, their family, and their neighborhood.

5.1 Fight with those who Break their Peace Agreements
According to Islam, breaking agreements, violating oaths, and committing aggression in international affairs are punishable crimes. God commanded the Messenger: "And proclaim a grievous penalty to those who reject faith. (But the treaties are) not dissolved with those pagans with whom you have entered

into alliance and who have not subsequently failed you in anything, nor aided anyone against you. So fulfill your engagements with them to the end of their term, for Allah loves the righteous… But if they violate their oaths after their covenant and taunt you for your faith, fight with the chiefs of unfaith, for their oaths are nothing to them, that thus they may be restrained. Will you not fight people who violated their oaths, plotted to expel the Messenger, and took to aggression by being the first (to assault) you? Do you fear them? Nay, it is Allah Whom you should more justly fear, if you believe! Fight them, and Allah will punish them by your hands, cover them with shame, help you over them, heal the breasts of believers, and still the indignation of their hearts. For Allah will turn (in mercy) to whom He will, and Allah is All-Knowing, All-Wise. Or do you think that you shall be abandoned, as though Allah did not know those among you who strive with might and main and take none for friends and protectors except Allah, His Messenger, and the (community of) believers. But Allah is well acquainted with that you do (Qur'an 9:3-4; 12-16)."

5.2 Fight with only those Unbelievers who fight with you

In an Islamic state, all able-bodied believers are required to participate in the defense of the country. "Fight in the cause of Allah those who fight you, but do not transgress limits, for Allah loves not transgressors…And fight them on until there is no more tumult or oppression and there prevail justice and faith in Allah. But if they cease, let there be no hostility except to those who practice oppression (Qur'an 2:190, 193)." Believers are commanded: "Go forth, (whether equipped) lightly or heavily, and strive and struggle with your goods and your persons in the cause of Allah. That is best for you, if you (but) knew (Qur'an 9:41)." However, this requirement is not binding on unbelievers living in the community of the believers. Since unbelievers are exempted from fighting, they are required to pay a tax (*Jizya*) for their safety and protection. God commands the believers: "Fight those who believe not in Allah or the Last Day, nor hold that forbidden which has been forbidden by Allah and His Messenger, nor acknowledge the religion of truth, (even if they are) of the People of the Book, until they pay the *Jizya* with willing submission (Qur'an 9:29)."

5.3 Strive hard against Hostile Unbelievers and Hypocrites

God does not like aggressors. That is why God has commanded us to make unyielding efforts to guide the unbelievers and hypocrites about faith. In these efforts, believers have everything under their disposal. If it is needed, they are commanded to fight in the battlefield to defend themselves: "Allah has purchased of the believers their persons and their goods, for theirs (in return) is the garden (of Paradise). They fight in His cause and slay and are slain—a promise binding on Him in truth through the Law, the Gospel, and the Qur'an, and who is more faithful to His covenant than Allah? Then rejoice in the bargain that you have concluded; that is the achievement supreme. Those that turn (to Allah) in repentance, that serve Him and praise Him, that wander in devotion to the cause of Allah, that bow down and prostrate themselves in prayer, that enjoin good and forbid evil and observe the limit set by Allah—(these do rejoice). So proclaim the glad tidings to the believers (Qur'an 9:111-112)."

5.4 Weak and Sick Believers are Excused from Fighting

Fighting in the battlefield is only for those who are not sick, handicapped, or too poor to participate. "There is no blame on those who are infirm, or ill, or who find no resources to spend (on the cause). If they are sincere to Allah and His Messenger, no ground (of complaint) can there be against such as do right, and Allah is oft-forgiving, most merciful. Nor (is there blame) on those who came to you to be provided with mounts, and when you said, 'I can find no mounts for you,' they turned back, their eyes streaming with tears of grief that they had no resources wherewith to provide the expenses. The ground (of complaint) is against such as claim exemption while they are rich. They prefer to stay with (women) who remain behind. Allah has sealed their hearts, so they know not (what they miss) (Qur'an 9:91-93)."

6 THE CONDUCT OF BELIEVERS DURING WAR

Believers are advised to stand firm, remember God much, obey their leaders, and not quarrel among themselves. They are also commanded to be patient and humble in the battlefield. God commands them in Surah Al-Anfal: "O you who believe! When you meet a force, be firm, and call Allah in remembrance much, that you may prosper: Obey Allah and His Messenger, and fall into no disputes, lest you lose heart and your power depart, and be patient and persevering, for Allah is with those who patiently persevere. And be not like those who started from their homes insolently and to be seen of men and to hinder (men) from the path of Allah, for Allah compasses round about all that they do (Qur'an 8:45-47)."

6.1 Believers Make Efforts in the Defense of Life

Sometimes it is essential to fight with the wrongdoers to save lives and secure peace. God commands the believers: "O you who believe! Give your response to Allah and His Messenger when He calls you to that which will give you life, and know that Allah comes in between a man and his heart and that it is He to Whom you shall (all) be gathered (Qur'an 8:24)."

Believers can retreat but should not run away from the battlefield. "O you who believe! When you meet the unbelievers in hostile environment, never turn your backs to them. If any do turn his back to them on such a day—unless it be in a stratagem of war or to retreat to a troop (of his own)—he draws on himself the wrath of Allah, and his abode is Hell—an evil refuge (indeed)! It is not you who slew them; it was Allah. When you threw (a handful of dust), it was not your act, but Allah's, in order that He might test the believers by a gracious trial from Himself, for Allah is He Who hears and knows (all things) (Qur'an 8:15-17)."

6.2 Believers Make Efforts to Learn and Reform

As a general rule, God tells the Messenger and the believers to make efforts to reform unbelievers and hypocrites. "O Prophet! Strive hard against the unbelievers and the hypocrites, and be firm against them. Their abode is Hell, an evil refuge indeed. They (hypocrites) swear by Allah that they said nothing (evil), but indeed they uttered blasphemy, and they did it after accepting Islam; and they meditated a plot that they were unable to carry out. This revenge of theirs was (their) only return for the bounty with which Allah and His Messenger had enriched them!

131

If they repent, it will be best for them. But if they turn back (to their evil ways), Allah will punish them with a grievous penalty in this life and in the Hereafter. They shall have none on earth to protect or help them (Qur'an 9:73-74)." Believers are commanded to make efforts to improve people's understanding of religion, especially if the people are unbelievers or hypocrites, and to motivate them to improve their character and behavior. This is an important duty, and it needs determination and patience. Therefore, some among the believers should learn about religion so that they can teach others. "Nor should the believers all go forth together (to war). If a contingent from every expedition remained behind, they could devote themselves to studies in religion and admonish the people when they return to them that thus they (may learn) to guard themselves (Qur'an 9:122)." However, God commands the believers in Surah Qaf that they are not to use force to get people to accept Islam: "You are not one to compel them by force. So admonish with the Qur'an such as fear My warning (Qur'an 50:45)."

6.3 Believers are not Unfaithful to their Trusts

Nobody can be faithful to God and His Messenger if he is not performing his duties honestly or if he is being lazy and corrupt. "O you who believe! Betray not the trust of Allah and the Messenger, nor misappropriate knowingly things entrusted to you. And know that your possessions and your progeny are but a trial and that it is Allah with Whom lies your highest reward (Qur'an 8:27-28)." It is one's perception and attitude that make even difficult tasks seem easy for people who have a positive attitude and courage. God has His own ways to change people's attitudes and perception: "Remember in your dream Allah showed them to you as few. If He had shown them to you as many, you would surely have been discouraged, and you would surely have disputed in (your) decision. But Allah saved (you), for He knows well the (secrets) of hearts. And remember when you met, He showed them to you as few in your eyes, and He made you appear as contemptible in their eyes, that Allah might accomplish a matter already enacted. For to Allah do all questions go back (for decision) (Qur'an 8:43-44)."

6.4 Believers Earn God's Forgiveness and Reward

Good deeds have a good impact on the lives of people and their societies. Although the reward of good deeds in this world is very significant, the reward in the Hereafter will be much greater. "Allah turned with favor to the Prophet, the *Muhajirs* (those who emigrated from Makkah to Madinah in order to escape persecution for being Muslims), and the *Ansar* (the people in Madinah who welcomed the Muslim emigrants) who followed him in a time of distress. After that, the hearts of a part of them had nearly swerved (from duty), but He turned to them (also), for He is unto them most kind, most merciful...O you who believe! Fear Allah, and be with those who are true (in word and deed). It was not fitting for the people of Madinah and the Bedouin Arabs of the neighborhood to refuse to follow the Messenger, nor to prefer their own lives to his, because nothing could they suffer or do but was reckoned to their credit as a deed of righteousness—whether they suffered thirst, or fatigue, or hunger in the cause of Allah, or trod paths to raise the ire of the unbelievers, or received any injury whatever from an enemy, for Allah suffers not the reward to be lost of those who do good. Nor could they spend anything (for the cause), small or great, nor cut across a valley, but the deed is inscribed to their credit, that Allah may requite their deed with the best (possible reward) (Qur'an 9:117, 119-121)."

7 THE BEHAVIOR OF UNBELIEVERS AND HYPOCRITES

7.1 Behavior of the Jews, Christians, and Polytheists

Although the Jews and Christians were commanded to serve God alone, they have taken their prophets as God's associates: "The Jews call 'Uzair (Ezra) a son of Allah, and the Christians call Christ the son of Allah. That is a saying from their mouth. (In this,) they but imitate what the unbelievers of old used to say. Allah's curse be on them; how they are deluded away from the truth! They have taken as lords beside Allah their rabbis and their monks and the Messiah son of Mary; yet, they were commanded to worship but One Allah. There is no god but He.

Praise and glory to Him; (far is He) from having the partners they associate (with Him) (Qur'an 9:30-31)."

Jews, Christians, and polytheists wish that Islam should not spread: "Fain would they extinguish Allah's light with their mouths, but Allah will not allow but that His light should be perfected, even though the unbelievers may detest (it). It is He Who has sent His Messenger with guidance and the religion of truth, to proclaim it over all religion, even though the pagans may detest (it) (Qur'an 9:32-33)." Some Jews and Christians do not give charity, but they cheat people and hoard wealth: "O you who believe, there are indeed many among (Jewish) rabbis and the (Christian) monks who in falsehood devour the substance of men and hinder (them) from the way of Allah. There are those who bury gold and silver and spend it not in the way of Allah; announce unto them a most grievous penalty (Qur'an 9:34)."

7.2 The Character and Behavior of the Hypocrites

Hypocrites are reluctant to participate in the defense of their community. "Allah give you grace! Why did you grant them (leave) until those who told the truth were seen by you in a clear light, and you had known the liars? Those who believe in Allah and the Last Day ask you for no exemption from fighting with their goods and persons, and Allah knows well those who do their duty. Only those ask you for exemption who believe not in Allah and the Last Day and whose hearts are in doubt, so that they are tossed in their doubts to and fro…If there had been immediate gain (in sight) and the journey easy, they would without doubt have followed you, but the distance was long (and weighed) on them (Qur'an 9:43-45, 42)."

Further, hypocrites are reluctant to contribute in war efforts. "Say: 'Spend (for the cause) willingly or unwillingly; not from you will it be accepted, for you are indeed a people rebellious and wicked.' The only reasons why their contributions are not accepted are that they reject Allah and His Messenger, that they come to prayer without earnestness, and that they offer contributions unwillingly. So let not their wealth or their (following in) sons dazzle you. In reality, Allah's plan is to punish them with these things in this life, and that their

134

souls may perish in their (very) denial of Allah (Qur'an 9:53-55, 85)." Hypocrites enjoin evil, forbid good, and do not spend in God's way. "The hypocrites, men and women, (have an understanding) with each other. They enjoin evil, and forbid what is just, and are close with their hands. They have forgotten Allah, so He has forgotten them. Verily, the hypocrites are rebellious and perverse...It is not Allah Who wrongs them, but they wrong their own selves (Qur'an 9:67, 70)."

Finally, hypocrites break their promises and are miserly. "Amongst them are men who made a covenant with Allah that if He bestowed on them of His bounty, they would give in charity and be truly amongst those who are righteous. But when He did bestow of His bounty, they became covetous and turned back (from their covenant), averse (from its fulfillment). So He has put as a consequence hypocrisy into their hearts (to last) till the Day (of Judgment), whereon they shall meet Him. (This is) because they broke their covenant with Allah, and because they lied...Those who slander such of the believers as give themselves freely to (deeds of) charity, as well as such as can find nothing to give except the fruits of their labor, and throw ridicule on them—Allah will throw back their ridicule on them, and they shall have a grievous penalty. Whether you ask for their forgiveness or not, (their sin is unforgivable). If you ask seventy times for their forgiveness, Allah will not forgive them because they have rejected Allah and His Messenger. Allah guides not those who are perversely rebellious (Qur'an 9:75-77; 79-80)."

CHAPTER 9

Humankind, its Mission and Performance
FROM SURAH YUNUS (10) AND SURAH HUD (11)

The creation of the universe and humankind, the purpose behind the creation, and how the performance of the human actions is judged and rewarded are highlighted in Surah Yunus and Surah Hud. God states in the Qur'an: "He it is Who created the heavens and the earth in six days—and His throne was over the waters—that He might try you, which of you is best in conduct (Qur'an 11:7)." God further states: "Blessed is He in Whose hands is the dominion, and He is able to do all things, Who has created death and life that He may test you, which of you is best in deed (Qur'an 67:1-2)." Believing in God gives a correct concept of the universe, of the relationship between the Creator and His creation, of humankind, of the purpose of its existence, and of its true position in the universe. It is from these general concepts that moral values and principles are derived. The desire to earn the pleasure of God and to avoid His displeasure motivates people to work for the implementation of these principles, which are, in turn, safeguarded by fearing God and by the authority of His law.

1 THE UNIVERSE AND THE HUMAN MISSION

1.1 The Human Mission is to live on Earth as Humans
God created people with all the beastly weaknesses, but He granted them wisdom and free will, in order to enable them to overcome their weaknesses, believe in Him, and serve Him by managing their lives according to His vision and His commands. Eventually, we all will return to Him to account for our behavior and deeds. God created the universe, which will be replaced with another universe in which He will reward with justice those who believed and lived in the state of righteousness. God created the universe with truth, and His promise of resurrection and rewarding people with justice is true. The verses of Surah Yunus that highlight the creation of the universe and the human trial are given in the table below.

136

Table 1.1: Creation of the Universe and the Human Trial

No	Surah:Verses	Meanings
		God created the Universe as a Sign and that He may Try People
1	10:005	1. It is He Who made the sun to be a shining glory and the moon to be a light (of beauty), and (He) measured out stages for her that you might know the number of years and the count (of time). Allah did not create this but in truth and righteousness. (Thus) does He explain His Signs in detail, for those who understand?
	10:006	2. Verily, in the alternation of the night and the day and in all that Allah has created in the heavens and the earth are signs for those who fear Him.
	10:067	3. He it is Who has made you the night that you may rest therein and the day to make things visible (to you). Verily, in this are signs for those who listen (to His message).
		God will Reward Believers Who did Good Deeds
2	10:003	1. Verily, your Lord is Allah, Who created the heavens and the earth in six days; then He established Himself on the throne (of authority), regulating and governing all things. No intercessor (can plead with Him) except after His leave (has been obtained). This is Allah, your Lord. Him, therefore, serve you. Will you not then be of the warned?
	10:004	2. To Him will be your return—of all of you. The promise of Allah is true and sure. It is He Who begins the process of creation and repeats it that He may reward with justice those who believe and work righteousness, but those who reject Him will have draughts of boiling fluids and a penalty grievous because they did reject Him.

1.2 The Human Mission is to Behave on Earth as Humans

Surely in the variation of the night and the day and in what God has created in the heavens and the earth, there are signs for people who guard against evil. God gives life and causes death, and to Him people shall be brought back on the Day of

137

Judgment. It is not worthy of God to destroy towns tyrannically when their people are behaving properly. Communities were only destroyed due to the evil actions and corruption of their people. Verses of Surah Yunus that highlight the creation of the universe and the establishment of justice are given in the table below.

Table 1.2: The Universe and the Establishment of Justice

No	Surah:Verses	Meanings
		Unjust People have been Destroyed
3	10:013	Generations before you We destroyed when they did wrong. Their messengers came to them with clear-signs, but they would not believe! Thus do We requite those who sin.
		People should admit that It is God Who Regulates all Affairs
4	10:031	1. Say (to people, O Muhammad): • "Who is it that sustains you (in life) from the sky and from the earth? • Or who is it that has power over hearing and sight? • And who is it that brings out the living from the dead and the dead from the living? • And who is it that rules and regulates all affairs?" They will soon say, "Allah." Say, "Will you not then show piety (to Him)?" Such is Allah, your real Cherisher and Sustainer:
	10:032	2. Such is Allah, your real Cherisher and Sustainer. Apart from truth, what (remains) but error? How then are you turned away?
	10:056	3. It is He Who gives life and Who takes it, and to Him shall you all be brought back.

2 SUCCESS IS REPENTANCE AND GOOD DEEDS

The purpose of Islam is to establish a just society in which all human being are at liberty to contribute by their good deeds, which will be rewarded in this world and in the Hereafter. "But Allah does call to the home of peace. He does guide whom He pleases to a way that is straight (Qur'an 10:25)" God has provided guidance in the Qur'an for those who: "Seek the forgiveness of your Lord, and turn to Him in repentance that He may grant you enjoyment, good (and true) for a term appointed, and bestow His abounding grace on all who abound in merit (Qur'an 11:3)." God commands people to be patient: "So persevere patiently for the end is for those who are righteous...Therefore, "O my people! Ask forgiveness of your Lord, and turn to Him (in repentance). He will send you the skies pouring abundant rain and add strength to your strength, so you turn not back in sin (Qur'an 11:49, 52)." Hardworking people who are conscientious when it comes to their character and behavior are bound to make their communities strong and prosperous. Thus, the implementation of divine guidance can assure peace and prosperity of people during their life on earth.

2.1 Good Deeds Benefit People in both Worlds

People get the best reward for their good deeds in this world. Additionally, they will be getting an even greater reward in Paradise. In contrast, for people who have earned evil, the punishment of an evil is a similar evil. Evil people get punished sometimes even on earth. When their punishment is delayed for some time, they sarcastically ask, "When will this threat be implemented?" They should know: "To every people is a term appointed. When their term is reached, not an hour can they cause delay, nor (an hour) can they advance (it in anticipation) (Qur'an 7:34; 10:49)." Besides, God will gather people on the day of resurrection when every person will be accountable for what he did on earth. On that day, those who denied their meeting with God and refused to receive true guidance will be ruined. Surely, what is in the heavens and the earth belongs to God, and His promise of reward and punishment is true. The verses of Surah Yunus that highlight the reward for good and bad deeds are given in the table below.

Table 2.1: Reward for Good and Bad Deeds

No	Surah:Verses	Meanings
		For those Who do Good is the Best
1	10:026	1. To those who do right is a goodly (reward)— yea, more (than in measure)! Neither darkness nor shame shall cover their faces! They are

	10:027		companions of the garden; they will abide therein (forever).
		2.	But those who have earned evil will have a reward of like evil. Ignominy will cover their (faces). No defender will they have from (the wrath of) Allah. Their faces will be covered, as it were, with pieces from the depth of the darkness of night. They are companions of the fire; they will abide therein (forever).
		Resurrection and Judgment Day	
2	10:028	1.	One day shall We gather them all together. Then shall We say to those who joined gods (with Us): "To your place! You and those you joined as partners (with Me). We shall separate them, and their partners shall say: "It was not us that you worshiped."
	10:030	2.	There will every soul prove (the fruits of) the deeds it sent before. They will be brought back to Allah their rightful Lord, and their invented falsehoods will leave them in the lurch.
	10:045	3.	One day, He will gather them together. (It will be) as if they had tarried but an hour of a day; they will recognize each other. Assuredly those will be lost who denied the meeting with Allah and refused to receive true guidance.
	10:047	4.	To every people (was sent) a messenger. When their messenger comes (before them), the matter will be judged between them with justice, and they will not be wronged.
		The Hereafter is True, and None will Escape	
3	10:052-053	•	At length will be said to the wrongdoers: "Taste you the enduring punishment! You get but the recompense of what you earned." They seek to be informed by you, "Is that true?" Say: "Yea! By my Lord! Verily, it is true, and you cannot escape."

2.2 The Qur'an: Guidance and Mercy for the Believers

God does not do injustice to people, but people are unjust to themselves. They do injustice by not paying attention to divine guidance. "O people! There has come to you a direction from your Lord and a healing for the (diseases) in your hearts—and

for those who believe, a guidance and a mercy (Qur'an 10:57)."
Unfortunately, the unbelievers reject the divine guidance of the
Qur'an even before knowing it. People should, at least, know
what they reject! The verses of Surah Yunus that highlight that
the Qur'an is a book of revelation from God and that many
unbelievers will refuse to accept it are given in the table below.

Table 2.2: The Qur'an is the Book of Guidance and Mercy

No	Surah:Verses	Meanings
		The Qur'an is Revelation from God
4	10:001	1. These are the verses of the book of wisdom.
	10:002	2. Is it a matter of wonderment to men that We have sent Our inspiration to a man from among themselves, that he should warn mankind (of their danger) and give the good news to the believers that they have before their Lord the lofty rank of truth? (But) say the unbelievers: "This is, indeed, an evident sorcerer."
	10:037	3. This Qur'an is not such as can be produced by other than Allah. On the contrary, it is a confirmation of (revelations) that went before it and a fuller explanation of the Book from the Lord of the Worlds, wherein there is no doubt.
	10:038	4. Or do they say, "He forged it?" Say: "Bring then a chapter like unto it, and call (to your aid) anyone you can besides Allah, if it be you speak the truth."
	10:039	5. Nay, they charge with falsehood that whose knowledge they cannot compass, even before the elucidation thereof has reached them. Thus did those before them make charges of falsehood, but see what was the end of those who did wrong.
		Unbelievers refuse to Believe that the Qur'an was Revealed
5	10:041	1. If they charge you with falsehood, say: "My work to me, and yours to you! You are free from responsibility for what I do, and I for what you do.
	10:042	2. Among them are some who (pretend to) listen to you, but can you make the deaf to hear even

	10:043	though they are without understanding? 3. And among them are some who look at you, but can you guide the blind even though they will not see?
	10:044	4. Surely, Allah does not do any injustice to men, but men are unjust to themselves.

2.3 Divine Guidance helps People to Succeed in Life

Conflicts of interest clouds human wisdom and make people selfish. This makes them unsuitable when it comes to the design and implementation of a just sociopolitical system for themselves. That is why true justice can only be achieved through the implementation of what God has revealed, which He has tailored for the benefit of people. There is none other than God, the Creator, Who knows what is best for people. Peace and prosperity are the only outcome if a society is established on righteousness, balanced dealings, and true justice, as required by divine guidance. God has assured success to those who only serve Him by not violating His laws. Such people know that it is God Who provides sustenance to all of His creatures; therefore, they adopt honest ways in the pursuit of earning their living. God increases their earning capabilities if they are patient and work hard to improve themselves by repenting and reforming their character and behavior. The verses of Surah Hud, highlighting the Qur'an as the book of guidance and mercy are given in the table below.

Table 2.3: The Qur'an: The Book of Guidance and Mercy

No	Surah:Verses	Meanings
		The Qur'an: The Book of the Guidance
6	11:001	• (This is) a book with verses basic or fundamental (of established meaning), further explained in detail from One Who is wise and well-acquainted.
		Divine Guidance is God's Mercy
7	11:002 11:003-004	1. (It teaches) that you should worship none but Allah. (Say): "Verily, I am (sent) unto you from Him to warn and to bring glad tidings." 2. Seek you the forgiveness of your Lord, and turn to Him in repentance that He may grant you enjoyment, good (and true), for a term appointed, and bestow His abounding grace

		on all who abound in merit! But if you turn away, then I fear for you the penalty of a great day. To Allah is your return, and He has power over all things.
11:006	3.	There is no moving creature on earth but its sustenance depends on Allah. He knows the time and place of its definite abode and its temporary deposit.
11:049	4.	Such are some of the stories of the unseen that We have revealed unto you. Before this, neither you nor your people knew them. So persevere patiently, for the End is for those who are righteous.
11:052	5.	O my people! Ask forgiveness from your Lord, and turn to Him (in repentance). He will send you the skies pouring abundant rain and add strength to your strength. So turn you not back in sin.

2.4 Belief, Good Deeds, and Individual Salvation

Only belief in God and good deeds can assure individual salvation. God warns people that none can save even the nearest kin from His punishment. It is narrated on the authority of 'Aisha that when the verse, "and warn your nearest kinderd," (Qur'an 26:214), was revealed, the Messenger of Allah stood up on Safa' and said: O Fatimah, daughter of Muhammad, O Safiya, daughter of Abd al-Muttalib, O sons of Abd al-Muttalib, I have nothing which can avail you against (the punishment of) Allah; you may ask me what you want of my worldly belongings (Sahih Muslim: 1.401)." Even God's messenger Noah could not save his son because his son's conduct was un-righteous, and God's messenger Lot could not save his wife. The angels who were sent to destroy Lot's people told Lot to leave the city behind and not turn back, but Lot's wife failed to follow this angelic advice and paid the consequences.

The drowning of Noah's son and the destiny of Lot's wife prove that only belief in God and good deeds can assure individual salvation. God told Noah that those who did wrong would be drowned and when: "Noah called upon his Lord, and said: 'O my Lord! Surely my son is of my family! And Your promise is true, and You are the just of judges!' God replied: 'O Noah! He is not of your family, for his conduct is unrighteous. So ask not of Me that of which you have no knowledge! I give you counsel lest you act like the ignorant' (Qur'an 11:45-46)." The verses of Surah Hud that highlight that only belief and good deeds assure individual salvation are given in the table below.

Table 2.4: Only Belief and Good Deeds Assure Salvation

No	Surah:Verses		Meanings
			Refusing Guidance Destroyed Noah's People
8	11:032-033	1.	They (Noah's people) said: "O Noah! You have disputed with us, and you have prolonged the dispute with us. Now bring upon us with which you threaten us if you speak the truth." He said: "Truly, Allah will bring it on you if He wills, and then you will not be able to frustrate it."
	11:036	2.	It was revealed to Noah: "None of your people will believe except those who have believed already! So grieve no longer over their (evil) deeds.
	11:037	3.	"But construct an ark under Our eyes and Our inspiration, and address Me no (further) on behalf of those who are in sin, for they are about to be overwhelmed."
	11:040	4.	At length, behold! There came Our command, and the fountains of the earth gushed forth! We said: "Embark therein, of each kind two, male and female, and your family—except those against whom the word has already gone forth—and the believers." But only a few believed with him.
	11:044	5.	Then the word went forth: "O earth! Swallow up your water. And O sky! Withhold (your rain)!" And the water abated, and the matter was ended. The ark rested on Mount Judi. And the word went forth: "Away with those who do wrong!"
			Even God's Messengers Could not Save their Relatives
9	11:042	6.	So the ark floated with them on the waves (towering) like mountains, and Noah called out to his son, who had separated himself (from the rest): "O my son! Embark with us,

144

			and be not with the unbelievers!"
	11:043	7.	The son replied: "I will betake myself to some mountain; it will save me from the water."
	11:043	8.	Noah said: "This day nothing can save, from the command of Allah, any but those on whom He has mercy!" And the waves came between them, and the son was among those overwhelmed in the flood.
	11:081	9.	(The messengers) said: "O Lot! We are messengers from your Lord! By no means shall they reach you! Now travel with your family while yet a part of the night remains, and let not any of you look back. But your wife, to her will happen what happens to the people. Morning is their time appointed. Is not the morning around?"

3 HUMAN NATURE, THE BELIVERS, AND UNBELIEVERS

As God's trustees, people should not be rebellious and ungrateful to Him by their actions and behavior. God reminds people: "He gives you of all that you ask for. But if you count the favors of Allah, never will you be able to number them. Verily, man is given up to injustice and ingratitude (Qur'an 14:34)." However, the nature of man's humble creation and God's favors to humanity did not help some among them because of their ungratefulness. "Yet they attribute to some of His servants a share with Him (in his godhead)! Truly is man a blasphemous ingrate avowed (Qur'an 43:15)." Therefore, God declares: "Woe to man! What has made him reject Allah; from what stuff has He created him? From a sperm-drop He has created him and then molded him in due proportions (Qur'an 80:17-19)." God warned the believers: "Were you to follow the common run of those on earth, they will lead you away from the way of Allah. They follow nothing but conjecture; they do nothing but lie...Yet, no faith will the greater part of mankind have, however ardently you do desire it (Qur'an 6:116; 12:103)." Why is this so? God tells people in Surah Al-Aliq: "Nay, but man does transgress all bounds in that he looks upon himself as self-sufficient (Qur'an

145

96:6-7)." Further, in Surah Al-Adiyat, God states: "Truly man is to his Lord ungrateful, and to that (fact) he bears witness (by his deeds) (Qur'an 100:6-7)."

3.1 Humankind – They are Unjustly Rebellious

Humankind is rebellious in nature. In Surah Yunus, God tells us that people sincerely ask for His help when in difficulty but start disobeying Him as their situation improves. "He it is Who enables you to traverse through land and sea, so that you even board ships. They sail with them with a favorable wind, and they rejoice thereat. Then comes a stormy wind, and the waves come to them from all sides, and they think they are being overwhelmed. They cry unto Allah, sincerely offering (their) duty unto Him, saying, 'If you do deliver us from this, we shall truly show our gratitude' But when He delivers them, lo, they are unjustly rebellious in the earth in defiance of right. O People! Your insolence is against your own selves. (There is) an enjoyment of the life of the present; in the end to Us is your return, and We shall show you the truth of all that you did (on earth) (Qur'an 10:22-23)." Similarly, "When trouble touches a man, He cries unto Us, lying down on his side, or sitting, or standing. But when We have solved his trouble, he passes on his way as if he had never cried to Us for a trouble that touched him (Qur'an 10:12)." Human nature is, therefore, such that: "When We make mankind taste of some mercy after adversity has touched them, behold, they take to plotting against Our signs! Say: 'Swifter to plan is Allah! Verily, Our messengers (angels) record all the plots that you make' (Qur'an 10:21)."

3.2 Humankind – They are Despairing, Ungrateful

Lack of seriousness and indifference to God's commands is a common weakness of people. Maybe this is because they lack the imagination to visualize the consequences of their mistakes in this world and because they do not believe that they will have to account for their deeds in the Hereafter. God warns us in Surah Al-Anbiya: "Closer and closer to mankind comes their reckoning. Yet, they heed not, and they turn away (Qur'an 21: 1)." In Surah Bani Israel, we are reminded: "Yet, when We bestow Our favors on man, he turns away and becomes remote on his side (instead of coming to Us), and when evil seizes him he gives himself up to despair (Qur'an 17:83)." No doubt there are many people, even among the believers, who do not know why God created them, what their mission in life is, and how they should live their lives. They are ignorant of God's commands because they have never tried to understand what God has revealed in the Qur'an. Such people enjoy the good things God has created, but they fail to know even how to thank God for all these bounties.

3.3 Following the Guidance is for People's Own Good
Divine guidance is to improve the life of the people in this world. God reminds us in Surah Yunus: "O people! Now truth has reached you from your Lord! Those who receive guidance do so for the good of their own selves. Those who stray do so to their own loss, and I am not (set) over you to arrange your affairs (Qur'an 10:108)." God asks us to declare: "Say: 'O people! If you are in doubt as to my religion, (behold!) I worship not what you worship other than Allah! But I worship Allah Who will take your souls (at death). I am commanded to be (in the ranks) of the believers, (1) and further (thus): set your face towards religion with true piety, (2) and never be of the unbelievers. (3) Nor call on any other than Allah—such will neither profit you nor hurt you. If you do, behold, you shall certainly be of those who do wrong. (4) If Allah touches you with hurt, there is none can remove it but He. If He designs some benefit for you, there is none can keep back His favor' (Qur'an 10:104-107)."

While it is natural for people to differ among themselves, "Mankind was but one nation, but differed (later). Had it not been for a word, that went forth before from your Lord, their differences would have been settled between them (Qur'an 10:19)?" God further states: "If your Lord had so willed, He could have made humankind one people: but they will not cease to dispute, except those on whom your Lord has bestowed His mercy (because they believed and did good deeds), and for this did He create them. And the Word of your Lord shall be fulfilled (about those who disbelieved): 'I will fill Hell with jinns and men all together' (Qur'an 11:118-119)."

147

People's condition is such that: "If We give man a taste of mercy from Ourselves and then withdraw it from him, behold, he is in despair and (falls into) blasphemy. But if We give him a taste of (Our) favors after adversity has touched him, he is sure to say, 'All evil has departed from me.' Behold! He falls into exultation and pride (Qur'an 11:9-10)." This makes people extremely emotional. People live between the two extreme conditions of desperation and exultation and boasting. Neither of these extreme conditions is an appropriate behavior for someone who is God's trustee and who should demonstrate patience and constancy. God tells people in Surah Hud: "Those who show patience and constancy and work righteousness—for them is forgiveness (of sins) and a great reward. (Qur'an 11:11)."

3.4 For Success, Believers should follow the Guidance

It is human nature that everyone likes to succeed in this world. None seems to care about the Hereafter. This is normal since understanding the Hereafter requires sharp foresight and divine guidance. People have to understand that following God's commands does help people succeed in both this life and the Hereafter. God promises that if you reform yourselves, He will increase your prosperity. "You seek the forgiveness of your Lord and turn to Him in repentance that He may grant you enjoyment for a term appointed and bestow His abounding grace on all who abound in merit (Qur'an 11:3)." To those who believe and work righteousness God has promised that: (1) He will guide them because of their faith; (2) they shall have no fear, nor shall they grieve; (3) they shall have good news in this world's life and in the Hereafter; and (4) in the end, their Lord will deliver them and give them success. As such, the believers are advised to avoid letting an unbeliever's speech bother them and to follow what is revealed with patience. Verses of Surah Yunus confirming that believers will receive God's help are given in the table below.

Table 3.4: Believers are destined to Receive God's Help

No	Surah:Verses	Meanings
		God's Help do Deliver **His Messengers and Those who Believe**
1	10:103	1. In the end We deliver Our messengers and those who believe. Thus, it is fitting on Our part that We should deliver those who

	10:009		believe.
		2.	Those who believe and work righteousness—their Lord will guide them because of their faith; beneath them will flow rivers in gardens of bliss.
		God's Friends have Good News in this World's life and in the Hereafter	
2	10:062	1.	Behold! Verily on the friends of Allah there is no fear, nor shall they grieve.
	10:063-064	2.	Those who believe and (constantly) guard against evil—for them are glad tidings in the life of the present and in the Hereafter. No change can there be in the words of Allah. This is indeed the supreme achievement.
	10:065	3.	Let not their speech grieve you, for all power and honor belong to Allah. It is He Who hears and knows.

3.5 People's Performance Evaluation and Rewards

There are two kinds of people in the world, the people who enforce the divine law on themselves and in society and those who do not believe in the divine law. In Surah Al-Hud God says: "These two kinds (unbelievers and believers) may be compared to the blind and deaf and those who can see and hear well. Are they equal when compared? Will you not then take heed (Qur'an 11:24)?" Since none will be able to speak before God in favor of the guilty, people will be either successful or unsuccessful strictly according to their individual performance in this world. God states in the Qur'an: "The day it arrives, no soul shall speak except by His leave. Of those (gathered), some will be wretched, and some will be blessed. Those who are wretched shall be in the fire...and those who are blessed shall be in the Garden. They will dwell therein for all the time that the heavens and the earth endure, except as your Lord wills: a gift without break (Qur'an 11:105-106, 108)." Concluding this statement, God warns people: "Be not then in doubt as to what these men worship. They worship nothing but what their fathers worshiped before (them), but verily We shall pay them back (in full) their portion without (the least) abatement (Qur'an 11:109)." Additionally, God states: "But those who believe and work righteousness and

149

humble themselves before their Lord—they will be companions of the gardens, to dwell therein forever (Qur'an 11:23)."

3.6 The Believers' Mission is to establish a Just Society

Islam means peace, and it is at this goal that Islam aims. Islam achieves the ideal of peace through a continuous struggle against evil. If evil is the dominant force in the world, as compared to the good, peace cannot exist. However, Islam is not peaceful in the sense of being tolerant of evils such as injustice, discrimination, exploitation, and oppression. If there is no war against evil, evil will prevail, and Islam will cease to exist. In this fight against evil, God has provided guidance to humanity. Throughout the Qur'an, guidelines have been provided that address all aspects of human activity. It is not natural for a community to be destroyed if its people act righteously. Verses of Surah Hud highlighting that God doesn't destroy towns while their people do good are given in the table below.

Table 3.6: God Destroy not Towns if their People Do Good

No	Surah:Verses	Meanings
		Worship your Lord, and Do Good to Succeed
3	11:112	1. Therefore, stand firm (in the straight path) as you are commanded—you and those who with you turn (unto Allah), and transgress not (from the path), for He sees well all that you do.
	11:113	2. And incline not to those who do wrong, or the fire will seize you. And you have no protectors other than Allah, nor shall you be helped.
	11:114	3. And establish regular prayers at the two ends of the day and at the approaches of the night: For those things, that are good remove those that are evil. Be that the word of remembrance to those who remember (their Lord).
	11:115	4. Be steadfast in patience, for verily Allah will not make the reward of the righteous to perish.
		Forbid Mischief and Do Good Deed to Succeed
4	11:116	1. Why were there not among the generations before you persons possessed of balanced good sense, prohibiting (people) from mischief in the earth, except a few among

	11:117		them whom We saved (from harm)? But the wrongdoers pursued the enjoyment of the good things of life that were given them and persisted in sin.
		2.	Nor would your Lord be the One to destroy communities for a single wrongdoing if its members were likely to mend.

3.7 Unbelievers neither believe in God nor the Hereafter

The unbelievers do not believe in the accountability of their behavior and deeds. They desire a free hand in the world to satisfy their selfish desires. That is why those who do not hope in meeting with God are pleased with this world's life and don't want to improve it for the benefit of others. They want to have their own rules and regulations. Therefore, they want to change or reject the Qur'an. However, God asks: "Who does more wrong than such as forge a lie against Allah or deny His revelations? But never will prosper those who sin (Qur'an 10:17)." Instead of God, the unbelievers worship whatever they like, things that no power either to help or harm them: "They serve, besides Allah, things that hurt them not nor profit them, and they say: 'These are our intercessors with Allah.' Say: 'Do you indeed inform Allah of something in the heavens or on earth (that) He knows not? Glory to Him, and far is He above the partners they ascribe to Him' (Qur'an 10:18)." God asks people to reflect: "And what think those who invent lies against Allah (and) about the Day of Judgment? Verily, Allah is full of bounty to mankind, but most of them are ungrateful (Qur'an 10:60)." Verses of Surah Yunus that highlight that unbelievers are heedless of God's revelations are given in the table below.

Table 3.7: Unbelievers are Heedless of God's Revelations

No	Surah:Verses	Meanings
		Unbelievers are Content with Life As It Is
5	10:007	Those who rest not their hope on their meeting with Us, but are pleased and satisfied with the life of the present, and those who heed not Our revelations—.
		Unbelievers do not like the Rule of the Law
6	10:015	But when Our clear signs are rehearsed unto them, those who rest not their hope on their meeting with

		Us say: "Bring us a reading other than this, or change this."

3.8 Unbelievers get rewarded for their Good Deeds

God rewards good deeds whether they are from believers or unbelievers. God tells us: "Those who desire the life of the present and its glitter—to them we shall pay (the reward of) their deeds therein, without diminution (Qur'an 11:15)." Unbelievers do not believe in the Hereafter; therefore, "They are those for whom there is nothing in the Hereafter but the fire. Vain are the designs they frame therein, and of no effect are the deeds that they do (Quran 11:16)." Only the people who are unjust forge lies against God. He does not like people who (1) hinder others from the path of God, (2) desire to make life on earth miserable with corruption and mischief, and (3) do not believe in their accountability for their deeds. Such people are those: "...who have lost their own selves, and what they forged has failed them. Without a doubt, these are the very ones who will lose most in the Hereafter (Qur'an 11:21-22)." Verses highlighting the unbelievers' excuses and their eventual fate are given in the table below.

Table 3.8: Excuses of those who will not Believe

No	Surah:Verses	Meanings
		Unbelievers say that the Qur'an is forged
7	11:012	• ...they say, "Why is not a treasure sent down unto him, or why does not an angel come down with him?" But you are there only to warn! It is Allah that arranges all affairs?
	11:013	• Or they may say, "He forged it." Say, "You bring then ten forged Surahs like unto it and call (to your aid) whomever you can other than Allah if you speak the truth."
		Unbelievers only forge lies against God
8	11:018	• Who does more wrong than those who invent a lie against Allah? They will be turned back to the presence of their Lord, and the witnesses will say, "These are the ones who lied against their Lord!" Behold! The curse of Allah is on those who do wrong.
	11:019	• Those who would hinder (people) from the

		path of Allah and would seek in it something crooked—these were they who denied the Hereafter.
		The Qur'an is a guide and a mercy from God
9	11:017	• Can they be (like) those who accept a clear (sign) from their Lord and whom a witness from Himself does teach, as did the book of Moses before it—a guide and a mercy?
	11:107	• They believe therein, but those of the sects that reject it—the fire will be their promised meeting place. Be not then in doubt thereon, for it is the truth from your Lord. Yet, many among men do not believe.

3.9 Those who Rebel against God will never Believe

Those people who rebel against their Creator will never believe. This confirms God's promise about the transgressors who serve others than God—others who can neither harm nor profit them. The unbelievers say about these false deities that they are intercessors with God, an assertion that God refutes, as seen in the following table, which highlights verses that demonstrate that those who lie against God shall not be successful.

Table 3.9: Those who lie against God shall not be Successful

No	Surah:Verses	Meanings
		Unbelievers' Deities can neither Harm nor Profit them
10	10:034	1. Say: "Of your partners (that you associate with Me), can any originate creation and repeat it?" Say: "It is Allah Who originates creation and repeats it. Then how are you deluded away (from the truth)?"
	10:035	2. Say: "Of your partners, is there any that can give any guidance towards truth?" Say: "It is Allah Who gives guidance towards truth. Is He Who gives guidance to truth more worthy to be followed or he who finds no guidance unless he is guided? What then is the matter with you? How do you judge?"
	10:036	3. But most of them follow nothing but fancy. Truly, fancy can be of no avail against truth. Verily, Allah is well aware of all that they do.
	10:068	4. They say: "Allah has begotten a son!" Glory

	10:069	be to Him! He is self-sufficient! His are all things in the heavens and on earth! You have no authority for this! You say about Allah what you know not. 5. Say: "Those who forge a lie against Allah shall not be successful."
		Believers let not Unbelievers' Speech Grieve them
11	10:065 10:066	1. Let not their speech grieve You, for all power and honor belong to Allah. It is He Who hears and knows. 2. Behold! Verily to Allah belong all creatures in the heavens and on earth. What do they follow who worship as His partners other than Allah? They follow nothing but fancy, and they do nothing but lie.

4 EFFORTS AND PATIENCE SAVED THE BELIEVERS

God has replaced many a people who did not accept His guidance. God tells people to reflect! "Say: 'Travel through the earth, and see what was the end of those who rejected truth' (Qur'an 6:11)." Such people did not believe, even though every sign about the truth came to them before they witnessed the painful punishment. Throughout history, none have benefited from belief after such an incident except the people of Yunus. When they believed, God removed the punishment from them, and they lived a normal life. God has given details about the fate of the people of Noah, Moses, and Jonah to illustrate the point. However, there is a common characteristic that saved the believers, and that is their untiring efforts and patience.

4.1 God's Mercy and Tireless Efforts of the Messengers
The stories of Noah, Moses, and Jonah represent the advocacy of the divine message on earth. These stories illustrate a cycle in which humanity is treated in a consistent and permanent manner and in which there is an ever-raging battle between good and evil, guidance and ignorance, and truth and falsehood. These examples also depict a humanity that is stubborn, hard, established in its ways, following the line drawn by arrogant leadership, and unwilling to consider the divine guidance that provides pointers to faith. There are pointers that are available

everywhere in the universe and within people's own selves, recorded in the open book of the universe and in one's soul. These pointers show an aspect of divine mercy, in that God sent messengers to rescue people from their stubborn rejection of guidance and their blind following of arrogant and erroneous leadership. These stories also paint a picture of the tireless efforts of God's messengers to provide ignorant humanity with guidance. These messengers and prophets showed unparalleled patience, despite all the adversity with which they had to contend. Additionally, they did not hope for any personal favor from those who attained faith as a result of their efforts.

4.2 Perpetual Efforts and Patience Leads to Succeess

The story of Noah is a description of the final outcome of the 950 years that Noah spent exerting tireless efforts in advocating the divine faith among his people. Nonetheless, Noah's people arrogantly and stubbornly continued to follow their wealthy and powerful leaders. Noah said to his people, "'O my people, if it be hard on your (mind) that I should stay (with you) and commemorate the signs of Allah—yet, I put my trust in Allah. Get you then an agreement about your plan and among your partners, so your plan be not to you dark and dubious. Then pass your sentence on me, and give me no respite. But if you turn back, (consider that) no reward have I asked of you. My reward is only due from Allah, and I have been commanded to be of those who submit to Allah's will (in Islam).' They rejected Him. So We delivered him and those with him in the ark, and We made them inherit (the earth), while We overwhelmed in the flood those who rejected Our signs. Then see what was the end of those who were warned (Qur'an 10:71-73)."

4.3 Justice Requires Continuing Struggle and Patience

Human struggle and patience are the prerequisites to eliminating injustice from society. When the people of Moses complained about Pharaoh's injustice: "Said Moses to his people: 'Pray for help from Allah, and (wait) in patience and constancy, for the earth is Allah's to give as a heritage to such of His servants as He pleases, and the end is (best) for the righteous.' They said: 'We have had (nothing but) trouble, both before and after you come to us.' He said: 'It may be that your Lord will destroy your enemy and make you inheritors in the earth; that so He may try you by your deeds' (Qur'an 7:128-129)." Eventually, God helped Moses' people because they struggled patiently: "We made a people, considered weak (and of no account), inheritors of lands in both east and west—lands whereon We sent down Our blessings. The fair promise of your Lord was fulfilled for the Children of Israel because they had patience and constancy (Qur'an 7:137)."

4.4 Jonah's Impatience saved his People from Ruin

A long struggle and patience are required by a messenger to purge an arrogant community from unbelief. How long will it be required? This is determined by God. Even a messenger does not have an input into it, and neither is a messenger at liberty to quit his assignment by his own free will. God cites the example of Jonah who became impatient with his people and tried to abandon them because of their arrogance and refusal to reform. The reason for this is cited in Surah Yunus: "If Allah were to hasten for men the ill (they have earned) as they would fain hasten on the good, then would their respite be settled at once. But We leave those who rest not their hope on their meeting with Us in their trespasses, wandering in distraction to and fro (Qur'an 10:11)." God tells people: "To every people (was sent) a messenger. When their messenger comes (on the Day of Judgment), the matter will be judged between them with justice, and they will not be wronged (Qur'an 10:47)." According to God's will: "To every people is a term appointed: when their term is reached, not an hour can they cause delay, or can they advance it (Qur'an 10:49)."

It is important that a nation should be given enough time to learn and reflect before punishment. When this time has expired then none can believe after seeing the God's punishment. Jonah's people were the only exception: "Those against whom the word of your Lord has been verified would not believe, even if every sign was brought unto them, until they see (for themselves) the penalty grievous. Why was there not a single township (among those We warned) that believed, so its faith should have profited it, except the people of Jonah? When they believed, We removed from them the penalty of ignominy in the life of the present and permitted them to enjoy (their lives) for a while (Qur'an 10:96-98)." In conclusion God tells the Messenger: "If it had been your Lord's will, they would all have believed, all who are on earth! Will you then compel mankind against their will to believe? No soul can believe, except by the will of Allah, and He will place doubt (or obscurity) on those who will not understand (Qur'an 10:99-100)."

5 FATES OF THE UNBELIEVING COMMUNITIES

5.1 God has been eliminating Unjust Communities
In Surah Hud, God tells about the human behavior that brings destruction: "God tells people: "We destroyed generations before you when they did wrong. Their messengers came to them with clear signs, but they would not believe! Thus do We requite those who sin. Then We made you heirs in the land after them, to see how you would behave (Qur'an 10:13-14)." While Noah's people were destroyed, Noah and the believers were rescued from the flood. Similarly, God delivered Abraham and Lot from their unjust communities: "But We delivered him and (his nephew) Lot (and directed them) to the land that We have blessed for the nations. We bestowed on him Isaac and, as an additional gift, (a grandson) Jacob, and We made righteous men of every one (of them). We made them leaders, guiding by Our command, and We sent them inspiration to do good deeds, to establish regular prayers, and to practice regular charity, and they constantly served Us (alone) (Qur'an 21:71-73)."

5.2 Believers do not Make Mischief in the Earth
The Qur'an commands: "(O people!) Call on your Lord with humility and in private, for Allah loves not those who trespass beyond bounds. Do no mischief on the earth after it has been set in order, but call on Him with fear and longing, for the Mercy of Allah is (always) near to those who do good (Qur'an 7:55-56)." One may ask: "What is the mischief-making that people should not do to assure their safety and success?" Citing examples from history, this has been elaborated at various places in the Qur'an. We should try our best not to follow the behavior of the people

of 'Ad, Thamud, Lot, and Aykah (or of Midian). These nations were destroyed because of their mischievous behavior.

5.2.1 Tyranny and Corruption Ruined the People of 'Ad
Their behavior could be characterized by the cruelty of its leaders, who were more interested in building monuments and fortresses for themselves than in fulfilling their duties to God and to their fellow humans. Their messenger asked, "Do you ('Ad) build a landmark on every high place to amuse yourselves? And do you get for yourselves fine buildings in the hope of living therein (forever)? And when you exert your strong hand, do you do it like men of absolute power? ...So they rejected him, and We destroyed them. Verily, in this is a sign, but most of them do not believe (Qur'an 26:128-130, 139)."

5.2.2 Arrogance and Extravagance Destroyed Thamud
Salih, the messenger of God to the Thamud, warned his people: "Fear Allah and obey me, and follow not the bidding of those who are extravagant, who make mischief in the land and mend not (their ways) (Qur'an 26:150-152)." They did not obey their messenger, and punishment ultimately overtook them.

5.2.3 Perversion and Evil Behavior Ruined Lot's People
Lot said to his people: "'I do detest your doings...What! Of all the creatures in the world, will you approach males and leave those whom Allah has created for you to be your mates? Nay, you are a people transgressing (all limits)!' They said: 'If you desist not, O Lot, you will assuredly be cast out' (Qur'an 26:168, 165-167)." Thus, the perverted people of Lot were destroyed.

5.2.4 Fraud and Corruption Ruined the People of Midian
Because of the cheating and corruption that were prevalent in their society, Shu'ayb asked his people to: "(1) Give just measure, and cause no loss to others by fraud. (2) And weigh with scales true and upright, (3) and withhold not things justly due to men, (4) nor do evil in the land, working mischief (Qur'an 26:181-183)." Instead of listening to their messenger, the unbelievers among Shu'ayb's people said: "'You are only one of those bewitched! You are no more than a mortal like us, and indeed we think you are a liar! Now cause a piece of the sky to

fall on us, if you are truthful'…But they rejected him. Then the punishment of a day of overshadowing gloom seized them, and that was the penalty of a great day (Qur'an 26:185-187, 189)."

5.2.5 Exploitation and Injustice Ruined Pharaoh's People

God destroyed Pharaoh and his people due to their discrimination and exploitation of Bani Israel. "Truly Pharaoh elated himself in the land and broke up its people into sections, depressing a small group among them. Their sons he slew, but he kept alive their females, for he was indeed a maker of mischief. We wished to be gracious to those who were being depressed in the land, to make them leaders and make them heirs (Qur'an 28:4-5)." Moses struggled for the liberation of Bani Israel from the slavery of Pharaoh and his people. God describes the fate of Pharaoh's people thusly: "Then Pharaoh pursued them with his forces, but the waters completely overwhelmed them and covered them up. Pharaoh led his people astray instead of leading them aright…And he was arrogant and insolent in the land beyond reason—he and his hosts. They thought that they would not have to return to Us! So We seized him and his hosts, and We flung them into the sea. Now behold what was the end of those who did wrong! And we made them (but) leaders inviting to the fire, and on the Day of Judgment no help shall they find. In this world, We made a curse to follow them, and on the Day of Judgment they will be among the loathed (Qur'an 20:78-79; 28:39-42)."

CHAPTER 10

God's Will, Mercy, and Forgiveness
FROM SURAH YUSUF (12)

Humankind, due to its very nature, is an embodiment of both self-interest and conscience. Generally speaking, self-interest leads to corruption, exploitation, and oppression. "Nor do I absolve my own self (of blame). The (human) soul is certainly prone to evil unless my Lord does bestow His mercy, but surely my Lord is oft-forgiving, most merciful (Qur'an 12:53)." Conscience, on the other hand, reproaches a person whenever he commits evil deeds. The very existence of a conscience bears testimony that each and every individual is born with the knowledge of what is right, what is wrong, and effects of each on human performance. Further, God has sent messengers to remind people what is evil, what is good, and the consequences of being evil or good. Nonetheless, life on earth is a perpetual struggle between good and evil.

God created humanity in a certain way and sent messengers to guide humans into leading a happy human life. A messengers' role was to highlight what behavior is beneficial and spares humanity from problems and misery. What they have conveyed is a complete message that outlines an integrated system, devised by God, the Creator of humankind, Who knows what is appropriate and suitable for implementation in human life. Thus, whoever obeys God's rules is a beneficiary, and that benefit is immediate.

Surah Yusuf elaborates on the struggle between good and evil, providing guidance to people along the way. The story characters may have different names in the past or in the present, but their behavior and outcome remain the same. One can find many similarities in the stories of Joseph and his brothers, Moses and Pharaoh, Muhammad and the Makkans, and the people and corrupt governments of the present day. From Surah Yusuf, we learn that:

1. God helps people by His Own divine ways and rewards righteous people, both in their lives on earth and in the Hereafter.

2. During hardship, one should be patient and seek God's help. God answers the prayers of His servants, and none despairs of God's help except the unbelieving people.

3. Efforts can avail nothing against God's will. Therefore, one should not use evil means to help resolve one's difficulties.

4. God's help turns one away from evil and indecency.

5. God has the knowledge of the unseen. He grants forgiveness to all those who repent sincerely and who try to reform.

6. Only wise people can learn from history and God's signs. Most people do not follow the divine guidance and even refuse to follow their conscience, due to their self-interest and corruption.

1 THE DIVINE GUIDANCE AND GOD'S WILL

1.1 The Qur'an is Guidance for the Humanity

The Qur'an is the last of the revealed books that contains a complete guide for humanity and that should be learned and acted upon by people, in order for them to achieve peace, prosperity, and success during their lives on earth. The stories given in the Qur'an contain lessons for all of us. The Qur'an is a narrative that could not have been forged, and it is a verification of previous religions. It contains universal principles that are applicable to various situations in life. It gives a distinct explanation of all things and guidance and mercy to the people who believe in it.

In Surah Yusuf, God tells people: "These are the verses of the Book that make things clear. We have sent it down as an Arabic Qur'an, in order that you may learn wisdom. We do relate unto you the most beautiful of stories, in that We reveal to you this (portion of the) Qur'an. Before this, you too were among those who knew it not…There is in its stories instructions for men endowed with understanding. It is not a tale invented, but a confirmation of what went before it—a detailed exposition of all things and a guide and a mercy to any such as believe (Qur'an 12:1-3, 111)."

1.2 Joseph's (Yusuf's) Dream and his Brother's Planning

Why did the Israelites go to Egypt? This question was asked by the Makkans from the Messenger to test the source of his knowledge. As a result, God revealed the whole story of Joseph. This put the Makkans in a very awkward position because it not only foiled their scheme but also administered a warning to them by comparing their behavior to that of Joseph's brothers, implying that they would meet with a fate similar to that of Joseph's brothers. Joseph's story starts with his dream, which indicated that he was to be exalted in ranks above his eleven brothers and his parents. Joseph's father told him not to tell this dream to his brothers because he was afraid that Joseph's brothers might devise a plan against him in jealousy. Joseph's father also told Joseph that God would choose Joseph and teach him the interpretation of sayings and events and make His favor complete on him and on the children of Jacob, as He made it complete before Joseph to Abraham and Isaac. The verses of Surah Yusuf highlighting that there are signs for people in the story of Joseph are given in the table below.

Table 1.2: There are Signs for People in the Story of Joseph

No	Surah:Verses	Meanings
		Vision of Joseph and his Father's Advice
1	12:004-007	• Behold! Joseph said to his father: "O my father! I did see eleven stars and the sun and the moon. I saw them prostrate themselves to me." • Said (the father): "My (dear) little son! Relate not your vision to your brothers, lest they concoct a plot against you, for Satan is to man an avowed enemy. Thus will your Lord choose you and teach you the interpretation of stories (and events) and perfect His favor on you and on the posterity of Jacob—even as He perfected it on your fathers, Abraham and Isaac, aforetime! For Allah is full of knowledge and wisdom." • Verily, in Joseph and his brethren are signs (or symbols) for seekers (after truth).

		Planning of his Brothers against Joseph
2	12:009-010	• They said: ..."Slay Joseph or cast him out to some (unknown) land, so that the favor of your father may be given to you alone. (There will be time enough) for you to be righteous after that." • Said one of them: "Slay not Joseph, but if you must do something, throw him down to the bottom of the well. He will be picked up by some caravan of travelers."

2 FULFILLMENT OF GOD'S WILL

The Qur'an cites Joseph's story to bring forth another truth, i.e., whatever God wills is fulfilled, and people can never defeat His plan with their counter plans, prevent God's plan from happening, or change God's plan in any way whatever. It often happens that a person adopts some measure and believes that he has done everything that will fulfill his objective, but in the end he finds that he had done something that was against his own objective. When Joseph's brothers threw him into the well, they believed that they had gotten rid of their obstacle. They had, however, expedited a plan that would eventually make Joseph the vizier of Egypt, before whom they would have to humble themselves in the future. Similarly, the wife of Aziz sent Joseph to prison to punish him for not fulfilling her desires, but, in fact, she provided him with an opportunity to become the vizier of Egypt and put herself to the shame of having to confess her own sin publicly. These are not the only examples that prove that even if the whole world is united to bring about the downfall of a person, they will not succeed if God wills to elevate the status of that person. For example, the very sure and effective measures that were adopted by the brothers to degrade Joseph were used by God for the success of Joseph and for the humiliation and disgrace of his brothers. On the other hand, if God wills the fall of someone, no measure, howsoever effective, will raise him high. To try to thwart the will of God only brings defeat and disgrace to those who try.

2.1 God helps People by His Own Divine Ways.

During difficulties, relief may not come as we would prefer it. Rather, God brings relief according to His Own wisdom. In Surah Yusuf, God said to a boy who has been thrown down in a well and then sold in slavery by his own brothers that he would someday inform his brothers about this affair of theirs. Then God established him in Egypt where he was provided with all the opportunities to learn and become a leader.

The situation must have appeared to be quite different at the time when Joseph was sold into slavery. Joseph must have been disappointed by his brothers' actions. His father Jacob was lost in the sorrow of losing his beloved son, while his brothers were happy in the success of their plan to get rid of the one they hated. The merchants who bought Joseph were excited about the profit they were to make by selling Joseph. However, the horizon of their imaginations was limited. God knew their deeds, feelings, and motives, and He was working out His Own plan. Neither the best nor the worst of us know where our destiny is leading, how evil plots will be defeated, and how success will come in marvelous ways. Verses of Surah Yusuf highlighting that God brings relief according to His wisdom are given in the table below.

Table 2.1: God Brings Relief according to His Wisdom

No	Surah:Verses	Meanings
		Joseph's Brothers put him in the well
1	12:015	• So they did take him away, and they all agreed to throw him down to the bottom of the well. And We put into his heart (this message): "Of a surety, you will (one day) tell them the truth of this their affair while they know (you) not."
		Joseph's Journey to Egypt is arranged
2	12:019-020	• Then there came a caravan of travelers. They sent their water-carrier (for water), and he let down his bucket (into the well). He said: "Ah there! Good news! Here is a (fine) young man!" So they concealed him as a treasure! But Allah knows well all that they do! They sold him for a miserable price, for a few dirhams counted out: in such low estimation

164

		did they hold him.
		An honorable abode is provided to Joseph
3	12:021-022	• The man in Egypt who bought him, said to his wife: "Make his stay (among us) honorable. Maybe he will bring us much good, or we shall adopt him as a son." Thus did We establish Joseph in the land that We might teach him the interpretation of stories (and events). Allah has full power and control over His affairs, but most among mankind know it not. When Joseph attained His full manhood, We gave him power and knowledge: thus do We reward those who do right

2.2 In Any difficulty, be Patient and Seek God's Help

A messenger of God had lost one of his sons due to the jealousy of his other sons. "Then they came to their father in the early part of the night, weeping. They said: "O our father! We went racing with one another, and left Joseph with our things, and the wolf devoured him. But you will never believe us, even though we tell the truth (Qur'an 12:16-17)." Jacob was sure his sons' mischief regarding Joseph. So what should he have done? He didn't throw his children out, and he resigned himself completely to the will of God and sought His help. He said to his children: "Nay, but your minds have made up a tale (that may pass) with you, (for me) patience is most fitting against that which you assert. It is Allah (alone) Whose help can be sought (Qur'an 12:18)." Verily, there is guidance for contemporary parents in this story.

2.3 God Saves His Servants from Evil and Indecency

In Surah Yusuf, there is another incident in which no one can be rescued without God's help. In contemporary terms, a person is being asked to do something illegal by his manager or employer. He should refuse, and that is what Joseph did. Under any circumstances, this is not easy. So how should one do this? One should follow Joseph's approach. He reflected on the good things God had already provided him, which was a nice place to live. So he was thankful to God by not getting involved in something forbidden. Otherwise, he would have been unjust, and surely the unjust do not prosper. Besides, the credit for our being saved from sin is due, not to our weak nature, but to God. We can only try like Joseph to be true and sincere; it is only God Who purifies and saves us from all that is wrong. Verses of Surah Yusuf that command people to seek God's refuge are given below.

Table 2.3: Seek God's Refuge; the Unjust do not Prosper

No	Surah:Verses	Meanings
		Aziz's wife invites Joseph to her love
4	12:023 12:024	• But she in whose house he was, sought to seduce him from his self. She fastened the doors and said: "Now come, you (dear one)!" He said: "Allah forbid! Truly, (your husband) is my lord! He made my sojourn agreeable! Truly, to no good come those who do wrong." • And (with passion) did she desire him, and he would have desired her, but that he saw the evidence of his Lord. Thus, (We ordered) that We might turn away from him (all) evil and shameful deeds, for he was one of Our servants, sincere and purified.
		Her husband comes to know of her Story
5	12:025 12:026-029	• So they both raced each other to the door, and she tore his shirt from the back. They both found her lord near the door. She said: "What is the (fitting) punishment for one who formed an evil design against your wife, but prison or a grievous chastisement?" • He (Joseph) said: "It was she that sought to seduce me from my (true) self." And one of her household saw (this) and bore witness, (thus): "If it be that his shirt is rent from the front, then is her tale true, and he is a liar. But if it be that his shirt is torn from the back, then she is the liar, and he is telling the truth!" So when he saw his shirt, that it was torn at the back, (her husband) said: "Behold! It is a snare of you women! Truly, mighty is your snare. O Joseph, pass this over! (O wife), ask forgiveness for your sin, for truly you have been at fault."

2.4 Surely God Answers the Prayers of His servants

Joseph was threatened with imprisonment if he refused to do what was sinful or illegal. Similarly, an employee can be fired from his job for not meeting the expectations (legal as well as illegal) of his employer, something that is quite common today in secular societies. Sometimes, innocent people get fired to save others from their corruption and become the escape goats of modern society. What should a person do under such a situation? He should follow the example set by Joseph, who was willing to go to prison rather than succumb to temptation. Joseph reflected on the possibility and said: "O my Lord! The prison is more to my liking than that to which they invite me (Qur'an 12:33)." This prayer was accepted by his Lord, and Joseph happily went to prison. This is indeed very difficult to do, but believers should try their best and expect God's help. Surely, God's help is forthcoming.

This incident also teaches people that one should remain within the limits set by the divine law in one's aims, objectives, and measures, for success and failure are entirely in God's hands. If one has honest objectives and lawful measures but fails, at least one will escape ignominy and disgrace. In contrast, if one has selfish objectives and uses unlawful measures to accomplish them, he will not only meet with ignominy and disgrace in the Hereafter, but he also runs the risk of ignominy and disgrace in this world. The verses of Surah Yusuf that highlight Joseph's desire that prison was dearer to him than the evil to which he was invited are given in the table below.

Table 2.4: Prison is dearer than the Evil to which they Invite

No	Surah:Verses	Meanings
		Aziz's wife threatens Joseph with imprisonment
6	12:030-032	1. Ladies said in the city: "The wife of the (great) 'Aziz is seeking to seduce her slave from his (true) self. Truly has he inspired her with violent love; we see she is evidently going astray. 2. When she heard of their malicious talk, she sent for them and prepared a banquet for them. She gave each of them a knife and she said (to Joseph), "Come out before them."

		3. When they saw him, they did extol him and (in their amazement) cut their hands. They said: "Allah preserves us! No mortal is this! This is none other than a noble angel." 4. She said: "There before you is the man about whom you did blame me! I did seek to seduce him from his (true) self, but he did firmly save himself guiltless! And now, if he does not my bidding, he shall certainly be cast into prison and be of the company of the vilest.
		Joseph prayed for Imprisonment rather than committing Sin
7	12:033-035	• He said: "O my Lord! The prison is more to my liking than that to which they invite me. Unless You turn away their snare from me, I should (in my youthful folly) feel inclined towards them and join the ranks of the ignorant." • So his Lord hearkened to him (in his prayer) and turned away from him their snare: Verily, He hears and knows (all things). Then it occurred to the men, after they had seen the signs, (that it was best) to imprison him for a time.

3 JOSEPH MOVES FROM PRISON TO POWER

The greatest lesson this story teaches people is that if the believer possesses true Islamic character and is endowed with wisdom, he can conquer a whole country with the strength of his character alone. We learn from the story of Joseph that a person of good moral character comes out successful even under the most adverse circumstances. When Joseph went to Egypt, he was only seventeen years old. He was a foreigner in Egypt, all alone without any provisions, and was sold there as a slave. The horrible conditions of slaves during that period in history are very well known. Then he was charged with a heinous moral crime and sent to prison for an indefinite term. Yet, throughout this period of affliction, he displayed the highest moral qualities, and these raised him to the highest rank in the country.

3.1 In Prison, Joseph Practiced What He Preached

Two prison inmates asked Joseph the interpretation of their dreams. "He (Joseph) said: 'Before any food comes (in due course) to feed either of you, I will surely reveal to you the truth and meaning of this ere it befall you. That is part of the (duty) that my Lord has taught me. I have abandoned the ways of a people that believe not in Allah and that (even) deny the Hereafter. And I follow the ways of my fathers, Abraham, Isaac, and Jacob. And never could we attribute any partners whatever to Allah; that (comes) of the grace of Allah to us and to mankind; yet, most men are not grateful. O my two companions of the prison, are many lords differing among themselves better or the One Allah, Supreme and Irresistible? If not Him, you worship nothing but names that you have named—you and your fathers—for which Allah has sent down no authority. The command is for none but Allah; He has commanded that you worship none but Him; that is the right religion, but most men understand not' (Qur'an 12:37-40)." After telling the prisoners about his religion, Joseph told them what their dreams said about their future, "O my two companions of the prison! As to one of you, he will pour out the wine for his lord to drink. As for the other, he will hang from the cross, and the birds will eat from off his head. (So) has been decreed that matter whereof you two do enquire (Qur'an 12:41)."

3.2 The King's Dream Helped Joseph to gain Power

Dreams have played an important role in God's communication with those people with whom He wishes to communicate. The commencement of divine inspiration to the Messenger was also in the form of a good dream in his sleep. Further, the Messenger never had a dream but that it came true like bright day light. Abu Sa'id Al-Khudri narrated that the Messenger said: "If anyone of you sees a dream that he likes, then it is from Allah, and he should thank Allah for it and narrate it to others. But if he sees a dream that he dislikes, then it is from Satan, and he should seek refuge with Allah from its evil, and he should not mention it to anybody, for it will not harm him (Sahih Bukhari: 9.87.114)."

Four dreams are mentioned in Surah Yusuf. In the beginning, it was Joseph's own dream. The second and third were the dreams of his prison mates, and the fourth was the dream of the king. Joseph was given the knowledge to interpret these dreams. After explaining the meaning of the prisoners' dreams, Joseph said to the prisoner who would be saved: "'Mention me to your lord.' However, Satan made him forget to mention him to his lord, and (Joseph) lingered in prison a few (more) years (Qur'an 12:42)." Thus, through a dream to the king, God initiated the process by which Joseph was released from prison and made an official in the king's court. The verses of Surah Yusuf in which Joseph advises the king to conserve food for the future are given in the table below.

Table 3.2: Joseph Advises the King to Conserve Food

No	Surah:Verses	Meanings
		The King's dream reminds the prisoner of Joseph
1	12:043-045	1. The king (of Egypt) said: "I do see (in a vision) seven fat kine, whom seven lean ones devour, and seven green ears of corn, and seven (others) withered. O you chiefs! Expound to me my vision if it be that you can interpret visions." 2. They said: "A confused medley of dreams, and we are not skilled in the interpretation of dreams." But the man who had been released, one of the two (who had been in prison) and who now bethought him after (so long) a space of time, said: "I will tell you the truth of its interpretation; send me (therefore)."
		Divine Instructed Planning for Egypt's Future
2	12:046-049	1. (The former prisoner said to Joseph): "O Joseph!" O man of truth! Expound to us (the dream) of seven fat kine whom seven lean ones devour, and of seven green ears of corn and (seven) others withered, that I may return to the people and that they may understand." 2. (Joseph) said: "For seven years shall you diligently sow as is your wont, and the harvests that you reap, you shall leave them in the ear, except a little of which you shall eat. Then will come after that (period) seven dreadful (years), which will devour what you

		shall have laid by in advance for them, except a little that you shall have (specially) guarded. Then will come after that (period) a year in which the people will have abundant water and in which they will press (wine and oil)."

3.3 The Righteousness is rewarded in Both Worlds

After the innocence of Joseph was established, "…the king said: 'Bring him unto me; I will take him specially to serve about my own person.' Therefore, when he had spoken to him, he said: 'Be assured this day you are before our own presence with rank firmly established and fidelity fully proved!' (Joseph) said: 'Set me over the storehouses of the land. I will indeed guard them as one that knows (their importance)' (Qur'an 12:54-55)." This confirms that those who exert themselves for the cause of truth and righteousness, put their trust in God, and entrust all their affairs to Him get consolation and comfort from Him. This knowledge of God's help allows people to face their opponents with confidence and courage, and they do not lose heart when they encounter the apparently terrifying measures of their enemies. They will persevere in their task without fear and leave the results to God. The verses of Surah Yusuf highlighting the establishment of Joseph's innocence are given in the table below.

Table 3.3: The Establishment of Joseph's Innocence

No	Surah:Verses	Meanings
		Joseph asked about his Innocence Before Leaving the Prison
3	12:050-052	• So the king said: "Bring you him unto me. But when the messenger came to him, (Joseph) said: "Go you back to your lord, and ask him, 'What is the state of mind of the ladies who cut their hands?' For my Lord is certainly well aware of their snare." • (The king) said (to the ladies): "What was your affair when you did seek to seduce Joseph from his (true) self?" • The ladies said: "Allah preserves us! No evil know we against him!" Said the 'Aziz's wife: "Now is the truth manifest (to all). It was I who sought to seduce him from his (true) self. He is indeed of those who are (ever) true (and

		virtuous).”
		• "This (says Joseph), in order that He may know that I have never been false to him in his absence and that Allah will never guide the snare of the false ones.”
		Good Deeds will be Rewarded Both in this World and the Hereafter
4	12:056-057	1. Thus did We give established power to Joseph in the land, to take possession therein as, when, or where he pleased. We bestow of Our mercy on whom We please, and We suffer not to be lost the reward of those who do good. 2. But verily the reward of the Hereafter is the best for those who believe and are constant in righteousness.

4 HUMAN CONSCIENCE AND THE DIVINE GUIDANCE

4.1 Humankind with Self-Interest Alone

Self-interest, along with a secular life style, takes away all human values from humanity. God tells us in the Qur'an: "We have indeed created man in the best of moulds. Then do We abase him (to be) the lowest of the low (Qur'an 95:4-5)." In Surah Al-Furqan, God asks: "Do you see such one as takes for his god his own passion (or impulse)? Could you be a disposer of affairs for him, or you think that most of them listen or understand? They are only like cattle; nay, they are worse astray in path (Qur'an 25:43-44)." Humankind is born with the self-interest of self-preservation, but has also been given a conscience. So whoever is successful in regulating his self-preservation activities with a conscience elevates himself to the higher position of God's trustee (*Khalifa*).

Human self-interest bothered the angels at the time of Adam's creation: "When your Lord said to the angels: 'I will create a vicegerent on earth,' they said: 'Will You place therein one who will make mischief therein and shed blood, while we do celebrate Your praises and glorify Your holy (name)?' He said: 'I know what you know not' (Qur'an 2:30)." This indicates that the angels were concerned about the failure of humankind in

172

their assignment of being God's trustee on earth. This is why people have to listen to their conscience and follow divine guidance to succeed. God's advice to Adam before he left Paradise was: "We said: 'Get you down all from here, and if, as is sure, there comes to you guidance from Me, whosoever follows My guidance, on them shall be no fear, nor shall they grieve' (Qur'an 2:38)."

Joseph confirmed that one's self is inclined to evil. Generally speaking, it is self-interest that leads people to corruption, exploitation, and oppression. Joseph, after all of the difficulties and turmoil in his life and when he was finally declared innocent, admitted: "I do not absolve my own self (of blame). The (human) soul is certainly prone to evil, unless my Lord does bestow His mercy. But surely my Lord is oft-forgiving, most merciful (Qur'an 12:53)." It is God's mercy that motivates people to listen to their conscience and follow divine guidance. God has also promised: "But to those who receive guidance, He increases the (light of) guidance and bestows on them their piety and restraint (from evil) (Qur'an 47:17)." It is piety that makes people truly human.

4.2 Humanity with Conscience and Guidance

People should seriously take accountability for their behavior and deeds in this life and should not exploit and oppress fellow human beings. God tells us in Surah Al-Qiyamah: "I do call to witness the Resurrection Day; and I do call to witness the self-reproaching spirit: (eschew evil). Does man think that We cannot assemble his bones? Nay, We are able to put together in perfect order the very tips of his fingers (Qur'an 75:1-4)." Self-interest regulated by human conscience and divine guidance improves the character and behavior of humankind.

Listening to one's conscience makes people righteous and God-conscious. The self-reproaching part of an individual is his conscience, for conscience reproaches a person whenever he commits evil deeds. The very existence of a conscience bears testimony that each and every individual is born with the capability to know what is good, what is bad, and the effects of each on human performance. God tells people in the Qur'an: "By

173

the soul and the proportion and order given to it, and its enlightenment as to its wrong and its right—truly, he succeeds that purifies it, and he fails that corrupts it (Qur'an 91:7-10)." One could say that God presented Adam to the angels after giving Adam his conscience and all types of knowledge. "He taught Adam the names of all things; then He placed them before the angels ... (Qur'an 2:31)."

Righteousness also makes people contented. A contented self is an individual who has not committed evil to satisfy his own self-interests or a person who has repented and reformed from his prior evil ways. It is a person who has used honest ways to satisfy his physical needs. On the Day of Judgment, it will be said to the individuals with a good conscience: "O you in (complete) rest and satisfaction! You come back to your Lord, well pleased (yourself), and well pleasing unto Him! Enter you then among My devotees! Yea, enter you My Heaven (Qur'an 89:27-30)."

4.3. Learning and Following the Divine Guidance
People are commanded to learn and implement the divine guidance in their lives and in their communities. God commands in Surah Al-Alaq: "Proclaim! (Or read!) In the name of your Lord and Cherisher, Who created—created man out of a (mere) clot of congealed blood. Proclaim! And your Lord is Most Bountiful, He Who taught (the use of) the pen, taught man that which he knew not (Qur'an 96:1-5)." After Adam and Eve committed their first mistake, they were regretful. God taught them how to ask for forgiveness: "Then learnt Adam from his Lord words of inspiration, and his Lord turned towards him, for He is oft-returning, most merciful (Qur'an 2:37)." Afterwards, God commanded Adam and Eve to: "Get down you all from here, and if, as is sure, there comes to you guidance from me, whosoever follows My guidance, on them shall be no fear, nor shall they grieve (Qur'an 2:38)." God sent His messengers as role models to explain and show what is evil, what is good, and the consequences of being good or evil.

5 GOD'S WILL AND HIS OWN DIVINE WAYS

5.1 Efforts can avail nothing against God's Will

At the start of Joseph's brothers' second journey, perhaps due to fear that if his sons entered Egypt all together during a period of famine, they might be mistaken for a group of mischief makers, their father advised them: "Further he said: 'O my sons! Enter not all by one gate; enter you by different gates. Not that I can profit you aught against Allah (with my advice). None can command except Allah. On Him do I put my trust, and let all that trust put their trust on Him.' And when they entered in the manner their father had enjoined, it did not profit them in the least against (the plan of) Allah. It was but a necessity of Jacob's soul, which he discharged. For he was, by our instruction, full of knowledge (and experience), but most men know not (Qur'an 12:67-68)." The verses of Surah Yusuf in which Joseph motivates his brothers to bring his younger brother are given in the table below.

Table 5.1: Joseph Desired to Meet His Younger Brother

No	Surah:Verses	Meanings
		Joseph told his Brothers to bring their Younger Brother Next Time
1	12:058-059	• Then came Joseph's brethren. They entered his presence, and he knew them, but they knew him not. • And when he had furnished them forth with provisions (suitable) for them, he said: "Bring unto me a brother you have of the same father as yourselves (but a different mother). Don't you see that I pay out full measure and that I do provide the best hospitality?"
		Joseph's Father could not Trust his Sons; Instead, he Trusted God
2	12:063-065	1. Now when they returned to their father, they said: "O our father! No more measure of grain shall we get (unless we take our brother). So send our brother with us that we may get our measure, and we will indeed take every care of him." 2. He (their father) said: "Shall I trust you with him with any result other than when I trusted

		you with his brother aforetime? But Allah is the best to take care (of him), and He is the most merciful of those who show mercy."
	3.	Then when they opened their baggage, they found their stock-in-trade had been returned to them. They said: "O our father! What (more) can we desire? Our stock-in-trade has been returned to us, so we shall get (more) food for our family. We shall take care of our brother and add (at the same time) a full camel's load (of grain to our provisions).

5.2 God's Plan to Retain Joseph's Brother

After meeting with his younger brother, Joseph planned a scheme to retain his brother with him. He arranged to hide his golden bowl in his brother's bag. When the bowl was discovered later from the bag of his younger brother, Joseph was able to retain his younger brother because he was accused of theft. Although the planning was done by Joseph, it would not have succeeded if it was not according to God's will. That is why God says in Surah Yusuf: "Thus did We plan for Joseph. He could not take his brother by the law of the king except that Allah willed it. We raise to degrees whom We please, but over all endued with knowledge is One All-Knowing (Qur'an 12:76)." The verses of Surah Yusuf that highlight how God planned for Joseph are given in the table below.

Table 5.2: Thus, God did Plan for Joseph

No	Surah:Verses	Meanings
		Joseph meets his Brother and Consoles him
3	12:069	• Now when they came into Joseph's presence, he received his (full) brother to stay with him. He said (to him): "Behold! I am your brother, so grieve not at their doings."
		God's Will is Essential for Successful Planning
4	12:070-075	1. At length when he had furnished them forth with provisions (suitable) for them, he put the drinking cup into his brother's saddlebag. Then shouted out a crier: "O you (in) the caravan! Behold! You are thieves, without doubt."
		2. They (Joseph's brothers) asked turning

		towards them: "What is it that you miss?"
	3.	They said: "We miss the great beaker of the king. For him who produces it, is (the reward of) a camel load; I will be bound by it."
	4.	They (Joseph's brothers) said: "By Allah! Well you know that we came not to make mischief in the land, and we are no thieves."
	5.	(The Egyptians) said: "What then shall be the penalty of this if you are (proved) to have lied?"
	6.	They said: "The penalty should be that he in whose saddlebag it is found should be held (as bondman) to atone for the (crime). Thus it is we punish the wrongdoers."

5.3 None Despairs Except the Unbelieving People.

When Jacob was told about what happened to his youngest son in Egypt, he displayed all of the qualities of a true believer. He was patient, hopeful, and believed in the help and mercy of God. He said that at this stage only patience and trust in God were his refuge. He advised his sons to go back and search for Joseph and his brother and not to despair of God's mercy. The verses of Surah Yusuf highlighting the believer's attitude when in difficulty are given in the table below.

Table 5.3: Make Effort and Despair not of God's Mercy

No	Surah:Verses	Meanings
		Believers Address their Grief and Sorrow Only to God
5	12:083-086	1. He (Jacob) said: "Nay, but you have yourselves contrived a story (good enough) for you. So patience is most fitting (for me). Maybe Allah will bring them (back) all to me (in the end), for He is indeed full of knowledge and wisdom."
		2. And he turned away from them, and said: "How great is my grief for Joseph!" And his eyes became white with sorrow, and he fell into silent melancholy.
		3. They said: "By Allah! (Never) will you cease to remember Joseph until you reach the last extremity of illness, or until you die."
		4. He said: "I only complain of my distraction

		and anguish to Allah, and I know from Allah that which you know not."
		Make Efforts! **None Despair Except the Unbelievers**
6	12:087	(Jacob said): "O my sons! Go and enquire about Joseph and his brother, and never give up hope of Allah's soothing mercy. Truly, no one despairs of Allah's soothing mercy except those who have no faith."

5.4 God Rewards the Righteous and the Patient

After their father told his sons to go and inquire about Joseph and his brother and not to despair of God's mercy, the brothers of Joseph traveled to Egypt for the third time. This time they were so distressed that they begged Joseph: "So pay us full measure, and treat it as charity to us: for Allah rewards the charitable (Qur'an 12:88)."

Since it was the right time for Joseph to disclose his identity, he asked them: "'You know how you dealt with Joseph and his brother, not knowing (what you were doing)?' They said: 'Are you indeed Joseph?' He said, 'I am Joseph, and this is my brother. Allah has indeed been gracious to us (all). Behold, he that is righteous and patient—never will Allah suffer the reward to be lost of those who do right' (Qur'an 12:89-90)." Now the brothers of Joseph were mature enough to admit their guilt. "They said: 'By Allah! Indeed has Allah preferred you above us, and we certainly have been guilty of sin' (Qur'an 12:91)." Joseph, being a true believer, forgave them and said: "This day let no reproach be (cast) on you. Allah will forgive you, and He is the most merciful of those who show mercy (Qur'an 12:92)."

6 GOD IS THE FORGIVING, THE MERCIFUL

6.1 God Makes the unknown Known as He Wishes

When Joseph's brothers left from Egypt with the shirt of Joseph, God made its smell reach Joseph's father by His Own ways. "When the caravan left (Egypt), their father said: 'I do indeed scent the presence of Joseph; nay, think me not a dotard.' They said: 'By Allah! Truly you are in your old wandering mind.' Then when the bearer of the good news came, he cast (the shirt) over his face, and he forthwith regained clear sight. He said: 'Did I not say to you, 'I know from Allah that which you know not?' (Qur'an 12:94-96)."

Joseph's father did not know what happened to Joseph in the well and during his time in slavery. This was because God choose not to tell him for His Own reasons. At that time, Joseph's father said: "Nay, but your minds have made up a tale (that may pass) with you; (for me) patience is most fitting. Against that which you assert, it is Allah Whose help can be sought' (Qur'an 12:18)." Messengers only know what God tells them. For example, God asks the Messenger in Surah Al-An'am: "Say: 'I tell you not that with me are the treasures of Allah, nor do I know what is hidden, nor do I tell you I am an angel. I but follow what is revealed to me.' Say: 'Can the blind be held equal to the seeing? Will you then consider not?' (Qur'an 6:50)."

6.2 God Always Accepts Repentance and Forgives
Perfection of individual character is not humanly possible. What God desires from us is admission of guilt; when we are guilty we should repent and reform. Joseph's brothers did this and said: "'O our father! Ask for us forgiveness for our sins, for we were truly at fault. He said: 'Soon will I ask my Lord for forgiveness for you, for he is indeed oft-forgiving, most merciful'. Then when they entered the presence of Joseph, he provided a home for his parents with himself and said: 'Enter Egypt you (all) in safety if it pleases Allah.' And he raised his parents high on the throne (of dignity), and they fell down in prostration, (all) before him. He said: 'O my father! This is the fulfillment of my vision of old! Allah has made it come true! He was indeed good to me when He took me out of prison and brought you (all here) out of the desert, (even) after Satan had sown enmity between me and my brothers. Verily, my Lord understands best the mysteries of all that He planned to do, for verily He is full of knowledge and wisdom' (Qur'an 12:97-100)." Joseph thanked God for making his dream come true and prayed, "O my Lord! You have indeed bestowed on me some power and taught me something of the interpretation of dreams and events. O You, Creator of the

179

heavens and the earth! You are my protector in this world and in the Hereafter. You take my soul (at death) as one submitting to your will and unite me with the righteous' (Qur'an 12:101)."

6.3 Only Wise People can learn from History

God has sent numerous messengers to guide humankind, and He has narrated their stories of struggle and success in life. God's help is always there for those who rely on God. However, sometimes God's help was delayed: "(Respite will be granted) until, when the messengers give up hope (for their people) and (come to) think that they were treated as liars, there reaches them Our help, and those whom We will are delivered into safety. But never will be warded off our punishment from those who are in sin (Qur'an 12:110)." Therefore, one should not despair, but one should remain earnestly engaged in good work. God commands the Messenger to say: "This is my way. I do invite unto Allah— on evidence clear as the seeing with one's eyes—I and whoever follows me. Glory to Allah! And never will I join gods with Allah! Nor did We send before you (as messengers) any but men whom we did inspire—(men) living in human habitations. Do they not travel through the earth and see what was the end of those before them? But the home of the Hereafter is best for those who do right. Will you not then understand (Qur'an 12:108-109)?"

6.4 People will not Believe unless they so Desire

Only wise people with understanding can learn from history. "There is in their stories instruction for men endued with understanding. It is not a tale invented, but a confirmation of what went before it—a detailed exposition of all things, and a guide and a mercy to any such as believe (Qur'an 12:111)." God says in the Qur'an: "Yet, no faith will the greater part of mankind have, however ardently you (Muhammad) do desire it (Qur'an 12:103)." Although this verse addresses the Messenger, it could be addressing any person who has the welfare of human individuals and society at heart. Then why do people not believe? It may be due to the fact that they do not reflect and try to understand. "And how many signs in the heavens and the earth do they pass by? Yet, they turn (their faces) away from them (Qur'an 12:105)." Such people fail because of too much involvement in their selfish desires and because: "And most of them believe not in Allah without associating (others as partners) with Him (Qur'an 12:106)." God says about the unbelievers: "Do they then feel secure from the coming against them of the covering veil of the wrath of Allah, or from the sudden coming against them of the (final) Hour while they perceive not (Qur'an 12:107)?" Normally, none can feel secure from the punishment of God, and the coming of the Hour is true! "Except such as believe and do righteous deeds, for they shall have a reward unfailing. Then what can, after this, contradict you, as to the judgment (to come)? Is not Allah the wisest of judges? (Qur'an 95:6-8)."

CHAPTER 11

God's Will, His Mercy, and the Hereafter
FROM SURAH AL-KAHF (18)

Belief in One God and in the Hereafter is based on what is absolutely true and real. People should accept this reality for their own good, improve their behavior in accordance with the divine guidance, and live in this world with the conviction that everyone is accountable to God. Otherwise, one's life will be ruined and one's efforts wasted. Surah Al-Kahf was revealed to answer three questions that the unbelievers of Makkah, in consultation with the People of the Book, had put before the Messenger in order to test him. These were: (1) who were the People of the Cave, (2) what is the story of Khidr, and (3) what do you know about Zul-Qarnain. In addition to learning the historical facts about these incidents and people, the believers were also told: (1) how previous believers faced the persecution of the unbelievers in the story of the People of the Cave, (2) God has His Own divine ways to accomplish His will in the story of Khidr, and (3) the real source behind all good deeds is God Himself in the story of Zul- Qarnain.

1 DIVINE GUIDANCE IS FOR A BETTER DESTINY

1.1 The Qur'an is to Improve Human Moral Character
The Qur'an is a book revealed by God that contains clear instructions, so that His Messenger might give warning of severe punishment from God to the unbelievers and good news to the believers who do good deeds that they shall have a good reward for their deeds (Qur'an 18:1-2). God asks His Messenger to warn those who say that God has taken a son that they speak nothing but a lie (Qur'an 18:4-5). God also tells people that whatever is on earth is nothing but a glittering show so that God may test humankind as to which of us is best in conduct (Qur'an 18:7). Eventually, the earth will turn into a bare ground without vegetation before the Day of Judgment (Qur'an 18:8). At that time, each one of us will have to be accountable for our behavior and deeds during our lives on earth.

182

1.2 Guidance is for the Benefit of Humankind

Each individual has to evaluate his own situation and his strengths and weaknesses with a critical eye. He must try to improve his situation according to his ability and available resources. Divine guidance is available to each one of us, and human intellect demands that we should be conscious of it because nothing prevents people from believing when there is guidance. We should use the divine guidance to evaluate our character and behavior and to try to improve ourselves by asking God's forgiveness. We should also be conscious about the consequences of evil behavior and should know that what happened to previous communities could also happen to us. God has given us freedom of choice, and everyone is free to believe or refuse to believe. In other words, people have a choice to reform and enjoy the benefits of good behavior or to ignore divine guidance, follow wild desires, and suffer the consequences. Since people have limited freedom of action and their existence is uncertain, God commands us that:

1. We should never commit to do anything by tomorrow without saying, "God willing."
2. We should read and try to understand what is written in the Qur'an. It is the word of God, and there is no refuge except in Him.
3. We should associate with those people who serve Him and desire His goodwill.
4. We should not associate with those who do not remember God but follow their low desires.

God reassures those who follow His commands and do good deeds that their efforts will not be wasted. They will be rewarded according to their efforts. Since God is forgiving and merciful, He does not immediately punish people following their mistakes, but He gives them respite for some time, in order that they may repent and reform. People will not find any refuge except in Him, and He has only destroyed those towns whose inhabitants were unjust and whose time limit for repentance and reform had expired. The verses of Surah Al-Kahf, which highlight the 'Qur'an, the true Guidance which none can Alter', are given in the table below.

Table 1.2: The Qur'an - the Guidance that None Can Alter

No	Surah:Verses	Meanings
		Always Remember God, and Seek His Refuge
3	18:023-024	1. Do not say of anything, "I shall be sure to do so and so tomorrow," without adding, "Unless Allah pleases." And remember your Lord when you forget this, and say, "I hope that my Lord will guide me ever closer (even) than this to the right road."
	18:027	2. Recite what has been revealed to you of the Book of your Lord. None can change His words, and none will you find as a refuge other than Him.
	18:028	3. Keep yourself content with those who call on their Lord, morning and evening, seeking His face; and let not your eyes pass beyond them, seeking the pomp and glitter of this life.
	18:028	4. Do not obey any whose heart We have permitted to neglect the remembrance of Us— one who follows his own desires, whose case has gone beyond all bounds.
	18:029	5. Say, "The truth is from your Lord. Let him who will believe, and let him who will disbelieve..."
		Be not Like those Who reject Divine Guidance
4	18:054-057	We have explained in detail in this Qur'an, for the benefit of mankind, every kind of similitude, but man is, in most things, contentious. 1. Nothing prevents men from believing when the guidance comes to them, and from praying for forgiveness from their Lord, except that which happened to the ancients should overtake them, or the wrath be brought to them face to face. 2. We only send the messengers to give good news and to give warnings. But the unbelievers dispute with vain argument, in order therewith to weaken the truth, and they treat My revelations as a jest, as also the fact that they are warned. Who does more wrong than one who is reminded of the signs of his Lord, but turns away from them, forgetting the (deeds) that his hands have sent forth?

2 THE PEOPLE OF THE CAVE

The incident in which the Companions of the Cave preferred to leave the unbelievers of their time and to take refuge in a cave, in order to save the purity of their belief and to avoid persecution, indicates that believers should migrate from their homes, if needed, to save their religion. The fact that the Companions of the Cave slept in the cave for hundreds of years before waking up demonstrates that God can certainly arrange the resurrection of people after death.

2.1 Migration is encouraged to Safeguard Religion

The story of the Companions of the Cave was related in the Qur'an to comfort and encourage the persecuted believers of the present and the future, and it shows us how some righteous people were trying to safeguard their faith in the past. In Surah Al-Kahf, we are told that the religion of the Companions of the Cave was the same religion that was being revealed in the Qur'an and that their condition was similar to the condition of the persecuted believers of Makkah. The behavior of unbelievers at the time of the Companions of the Cave and the behavior of the unbelievers of Makkah were similar with regards to how they were treating the believers. If an individual is persecuted by a cruel society for one's religion, he should not bow down before falsehood. Rather, he should emigrate from he is, if need be, with trust in God. Neither compulsion nor compromise is permissible in religion. The Messenger was instructed neither to make a compromise with his persecutors nor to consider them more important than his poor followers. The leaders of the unbelievers were also reminded that they should not be misled by the transitory pleasures of life but that they should seek after those excellences of character and behavior that make them human and that are permanent and eternal.

2.2 God is All-Powerful and can Resurrect Humankind

There is clear proof of the Hereafter in the story of the Companions of the Cave. This incident confirms that God has the power to resurrect anyone He wills, as He did in case of the Companions of the Cave, who woke up after sleeping for over three hundred years. Verses of Surah Al-Kahf confirming that resurrection and the Day of Judgment are true are given in the table below.

Table 2: Resurrection and the Day of Judgment are true

No	Surah:Verses	Meanings
		The Companions of the Cave Asked for God's Mercy
1	18:009-012	1. Do you think that the Companions of the Cave and of the inscription were wonders among our signs? 2. Behold, the youths betook themselves to the cave. They said, "Our Lord! Bestow on us mercy from Yourself, and dispose of our affair for us in the right way." 3. Then We drew (a veil) over their ears, for a number of years, in the cave, (so that they heard not). Then We roused them, in order to test which of the two parties was best at calculating the term of years for which they remained.
		The Believers took Refuge in a Cave to avoid Persecution
2	18:013-016	1. We relate to you their story with the truth. They were youths who believed in their Lord, and We advanced them in guidance. 2. We gave strength to their hearts. Behold, they stood up and said: "Our Lord is the Lord of the heavens and of the earth. Never shall we call upon any god other than Him. If we did, we should indeed have uttered an enormity. 3. "These our people have taken for worship gods other than Him. Why do they not bring forward an authority clear (and convincing proof) for what they do? Who does more wrong than such as invent a falsehood against Allah? 4. "When you turn away from them and the things they worship other than Allah, betake yourselves to the cave. Your Lord will shower His mercies on you and dispose of your affair towards comfort and ease."
		God let their Secret out to Prove the Hereafter
3	18:019-021	1. Such (being their state), We raised them up (from sleep) that they might question each

		other. Said one of them: "How long have you stayed (here)?" They said: "We have stayed perhaps a day or part of a day." (At length) they (all) said: "Allah (alone) knows best how long you have stayed here. Now send then one of you with this money of yours to the town. Let him find out which is the best food and bring some to you that (you may) satisfy your hunger therewith, and let him behave with care and courtesy, and let him not inform any one about you. For if they should come upon you, they would stone you or force you to return to their cult, and in that case you would never attain prosperity."
		2. Thus did We make their case known to the people that they might know that the promise of Allah is true and that there can be no doubt about the Hour of Judgment. Behold, they dispute among themselves as to their affair. (Some) said: "Construct a building over them." Their Lord knows best about them. Those who prevailed over their affair said: "Let us surely build a place of worship over them."
		The Companions of Cave were Resurrected after over 300 years
4	18:025-026	They remained in their cave three hundred years and some add another nine. • Say: "Allah knows best how long they stayed. With Him is (the knowledge of) the secrets of the heavens and the earth. How clearly He sees; how finely He hears (everything)! • They have no protector other than Him, nor does He share His command with any (person) whatsoever."

3 THE BEHAVIOR OF UNBELIEVERS AND BELIEVERS

The behavior of both the believers and unbelievers is elaborated in the story of the two men who are described in Surah Al-Kahf. In this story, the unbeliever who is ungrateful and arrogant is punished by God for his attitude by the destruction his wealth, all the while being reminded of Allah's blessings on him by his believing companion, thereby conforming: "…protection comes (only) from Allah, the True One. He is the best to reward, and the best to give success (Qur'an 18:44)."

3.1 Ingratitude to God results in Punishment

"(Abundant) was the produce this man had. He said to his companion, in the course of a mutual argument: 'More wealth have I than you, and more honor and power in (my following of) men.' He went into his garden in a state (of mind) unjust to himself. He said, 'I deem not that this will ever perish, nor do I deem that the Hour (of Judgment) will (ever) come. Even if I am brought back to my Lord, I shall surely find (there) something better in exchange.'" So his fruits (and enjoyment) were encompassed (with ruin), and he remained twisting and turning his hands over what he had spent on his property, which had tumbled to pieces to its very foundations, and he could only say, 'Woe is me! Would I had never ascribed partners to my Lord and Cherisher.' Nor had he numbers to help him against Allah, nor was he able to deliver himself (Qur'an 18:34-36, 42-43)."

3.2 A Believer's Reliance on God results in Success

A believer who relied on God's mercy asked to his companion, "while disputing with him: 'Do you disbelieve in Him Who created you out of dust, then out of a sperm-drop, then fashioned you into a man? But for my part that He is Allah, My Lord, and none shall I associate with my Lord. When you entered your garden, why didn't you say: 'Allah's will (be done)? There is no power but with Allah!' If you see me less than you in wealth and sons, it may be that my Lord will give me something better than your garden and that He will send on your garden thunderbolts from heaven, making it slippery sand! Or the water of the garden will run off underground so that you will never be able to find it' (Qur'an 18:37-41)."

4 THE JOURNEY OF MOSES WITH KHIDR

It was narrated by Ibn 'Abbas that Ubai bin Ka'b told him he heard the Messenger saying, "While Moses was sitting in the company of some Israelites, a man came and asked him, 'Do you know anyone who is more learned than you?' Moses replied:

'No.' So Allah inspired Moses: 'Yes, Our slave Khidr (is more learned than you).' Moses asked (Allah) how to meet him (Khidr). So Allah made the fish as a sign for him, and he was told that when the fish was lost, he should return (to the place where he had lost it) and there he would meet him (Sahih Bukhari: 4.55.612)."

4.1 Moses Journeys to Meet Khidr

So Moses went on looking for the sign of the fish in the sea: "Behold! Moses said to his servant: 'I will not cease until I reach the junction of the two seas or I will go on for years.' But when they reached the junction of the two seas, they forgot (about) their fish, which took its way through the sea, (straight) as in a tunnel. When they had gone farther, he said to his servant: 'Bring us our early meal. Truly, we have suffered much fatigue at this (stage of) our journey.' He said: 'Did you see (what happened) when we took refuge on the rock? It was then I forgot (about) the fish, and nothing made me forget to speak of it but Satan. It took its course through the sea in a marvelous way.' Moses said: 'That was what we were seeking after.' So they went back on their footsteps, following (the path they had come). So they found one of Our servants on whom We had bestowed mercy from Us and whom We had taught knowledge from Ourselves (Qur'an 18:60-65)."

4.2 God's Will and His Own Divine Ways

The story of Khidr and Moses gives comfort to the believers by indicating that one should have full faith in the wisdom of what is happening in the universe. People have limited knowledge about God's will and His ways. Reality being hidden, one cannot understand the wisdom of why something is happening the way it is happening. Sometimes it appears that things are not going the right way. When the curtain of the unseen is removed, one knows that what is happening is for the best. Even if sometimes it appears that something is going against us, in the end it will undoubtedly produce good results. This was explained by three incidents in which Khidr did as God commanded; yet, Moses questioned Khidr's actions. The verses of Surah Al-Kahf highlighting God's wisdom and His ways to accomplish His will are given in the table below.

189

Table 4: God's Will, His Own Divine Ways, and His Wisdom

No	Surah:Verses	Meanings
		Moses tries to Learn from Khidr
1	18:066-070	1. Moses said to him (Khidr): "May I follow you on condition that you teach me something of truth which you have been taught?" 2. He (Khidr) said: "Verily, you will not be able to have patience with me! And how can you have patience with things about which your understanding is not complete?" 3. He (Moses) said: "You will find me, if Allah so wills, patient: nor shall I disobey you in any matter." 4. He (Khidr) said: "If then you would follow me, ask me no questions about anything until I myself speak to you concerning it."
		Actions of Khidr during the Journey
2	18:071-077	1. So they both proceeded until when they were in the boat he scuttled it. Moses said: "Have you scuttled it in order to drown those in it? Truly, a strange thing you have done." 2. So he (Khidr) answered: "Did I not tell you that you can have no patience with me?" 3. Moses said: "Rebuke me not for forgetting, nor grieve me by raising difficulties in my case." 4. Then they proceeded until when they met a young man, he slew him. Moses said: "Have you not slain an innocent person who had slain none? Truly, you have done a foul thing." 5. He (Khidr) said: "Did I not tell you that you can have no patience with me?" 6. (Moses) said: "If ever I ask you about anything after this, keep me not in your company. Then would you have received (full) excuse from my side." 7. Then they proceeded until when they came to the inhabitants of a town, they asked them for food, but they refused them hospitality. They found there a wall on the point of falling down, but he (Khidr) set it up straight. Moses said: "If you had wished, surely you could have expected some recompense for it."

		Justification for Khidr's Actions
3	18:078-082	1. He (Khidr) said: "This is the parting between me and you. Now will I tell you the interpretation of (those things) over which you were unable to hold patience. 2. "As for the boat, it belonged to certain men in dire want. They plied on the water. I but wished to damage it, for there was after them a certain king who seized on every boat by force. 3. "As for the youth, his parents were people of faith, and we feared that he would grieve them by obstinate rebellion and ingratitude. So we desired that their Lord would give them in exchange (a son) better in purity (of conduct) and closer in affection. 4. "As for the wall, it belonged to two youths, orphans in the town. There was beneath it a buried treasure to which they were entitled. Their father had been a righteous man, so your Lord desired that they should attain their age of full strength and get out their treasure—a mercy (and favor) from your Lord. I did it not of my own accord. This is the significance of that with which you could not have patience."

5 ZUL-QARNAIN AND HIS EXPEDITIONS

5.1 The Role Model of a Righteous Ruler

Zul-Qarnain was a most powerful king, but it was God, Who in His universal plan, gave him power and provided him with the resources required for his great work. His rule extended over East and West and over people of diverse cultures. He was just and righteous, not selfish or aggressive. He protected the weak and punished the unlawful and rebellious. Three of his expeditions are described in this Surah, each embodying a great ethical principle governing the working of his kingship and power. He was a great ruler and a great conqueror, having access to enormous resources; yet, he was always grateful to his Creator. In contrast, the unbelievers of Makkah continued to rebel against God even though they were insignificant chieftains. Nonetheless, they did ask the Messenger concerning Zul-

191

Qarnain. God informed the Messenger: "Say, 'I will recite to you something of his story. Verily, We established his power on earth, and We gave him the ways and the means to all ends' (Qur'an 18:83-84)."

5.2 Trust in God, not in Material Resources

During one of his expeditions, Zul-Qarnain helped to build a wall to block the illegal activities of Gog and Magog who were making mischief in the land. Though He built one of the strongest walls for protection, his real trust was in God and not in the wall he built. He believed that the wall would protect people against their enemies as long as it was the will of God, that cracks and holes would eventually appear in it, and that it would no longer offer any protection. "He said: 'This is a mercy from my Lord, but when the promise of my Lord comes to pass, He will make it into dust, and the promise of my Lord is true' (Qur'an 18:98)." The verses of Surah Al-Kahf highlighting Zul-Qarnain and his expeditions are given in the table below.

Table 5: Zul-Qarnain and His Expeditions

No	Surah:Verses	Meanings
		Punishment for the Unjust and Reward for the Righteous
1	18:085-088	1. One (such) way he followed until, when he reached the setting of the sun, he found it set in a spring of murky water: Near it he found a People. • We said: "O Zul-Qarnain! (You have authority) either to punish them or to treat them with kindness." • He said: "Whoever does wrong, him shall we punish. Then shall he be sent back to his Lord, and He will punish him with a punishment unheard of. "But whoever believes and works righteousness— he shall have a goodly reward, and easy will be his task as we order it by our command."
		Even a Great King has his Limitations To Reform Everyone
2	18:089-091	2. Then he followed (another) way until, when he came to the rising of the sun, he found it rising on a people for whom We had provided

		no covering protection against the sun. (He left them) as they were. We completely understood what was before him.
		Being Feasible, a Wall was Built To Stop the Mischief Makers
3	18:092-097	3. Then he followed (another) way until, when he reached (a tract) between two mountains, he found beneath them a people who scarcely understood a word. • They said: "O Zul-Qarnain! The Gog and Magog (people) do great mischief on earth. Shall we then render you tribute in order that you might erect a barrier between us and them?" • He said: "(The power) in which my Lord has established me is better (than tribute). Help me, therefore, with strength (and labor). I will erect a strong barrier between you and them. Bring me blocks of iron." At length, when he had filled up the space between the two steep mountainsides, he said, "Blow (with your bellows)." Then, when he had made it (red) as fire, he said: "Bring me that I may pour over it, molten lead." Thus were they (Gog and Magog) made powerless to scale it or to dig through it.

6 WEALTH, CHILDREN, AND GOOD DEEDS

6.1 Importance of Good Deeds in the World

In talking about the life of this world, God says: "It is like the rain that we send down from the skies. The earth's vegetation absorbs it, but soon it becomes dry stubble that the winds do scatter. It is (only) Allah Who prevails over all things. Wealth and children are allurements of the life of this world, but the things that endure, good deeds, are best in the sight of your Lord, as rewards, and best as (the foundation for) hopes (in the Hereafter) (Qur'an 18:45-46)." On the Day of Judgment, none will be dealt with injustice, and the guilty will find no place other than the fire. The verses of Surah Al-Kahf highlighting that God will deal with us with justice are given in the table below.

Table 6.1: Your Lord will Deal with Justice

No	Surah:Verses	Meanings
		Your Lord is Unjust to None among People
1	18:047-049	1. One day, We shall remove the mountains, and you will see the earth as a level plain, and We shall gather them all together, nor shall We leave out anyone of them. 2. And they will be brought before your Lord in ranks (with the announcement): "Now have you come to Us (bare) as We created you first, but you thought We shall not fulfill the appointment made to you to meet (Us)!" 3. And the book (of your deeds) will be placed (before you), and you will see the sinful in great terror because of what is (recorded) therein. 4. They will say: "Ah! Woe to us! What a book is this! It leaves out nothing small or great, but takes account thereof!" They will find all that they did, placed before them, and not one will your Lord treat with injustice.
		Satan and his Offspring are Your Enemies
2	18:050-053	1. Behold! We said to the angels, "Bow down to Adam." They bowed down except *Iblis*. He was one of the jinns, and he broke the command of his Lord. 2. Will you then take him and his progeny as protectors rather than Me? And they are enemies to you! Evil would be the exchange for the wrongdoers. 3. I called them not to witness the creation of the heavens and the earth, nor (even) their own creation. Nor is it for Me to take as helpers such as lead (men) astray. 4. One day, He will say: "Call on those whom you thought to be My partners." And they will call on them, but they will not listen to them, and We shall make for them a place of common perdition. 5. And the sinful shall see the fire and apprehend that they have to fall therein. No means will they find to turn away there from.

6.2 The Importance of Good Deeds in the Hereafter

God reminds people that on the Day of Judgment the reward will be according to the deeds each individual has done in this world. The greatest losers in their deeds will be those who disbelieved in the commands of their Lord and disbelieved in the Hereafter. Although they think that they are doing good deeds, their efforts in this life will bring them no reward in the Hereafter. On the other hand, those who believed and did good deeds, they will be rewarded in this world and will get a greater reward of Paradise in the Hereafter. God commands the Messenger: "Say: 'I am but a man like yourselves, (but) the inspiration has come to me that your Allah is one Allah. Whoever expects to meet his Lord, let him work righteousness and, in the worship of his Lord, admit no one as partner' (Qur'an 18:110)." The verses of Surah Al-Kahf that highlight God's judgment and rewards are given in the table below.

Table 6.2: God's Judgment and Rewards

No	Surah:Verses	Meanings
		What will happen on the Day of Judgment
3	18:099-100	• On that Day, 1. We shall leave them (Gog and Magog) to surge like waves on one another. 2. The trumpet will be blown, and We shall collect them all together. 3. And We shall present Hell that day for unbelievers to see, all spread out.
		The Unbelievers on the Day of Judgment
4	18:101-106	• (Unbelievers) whose eyes had been under a veil from remembrance of Me, and who had been unable even to hear. 1. Do the Unbelievers think that they can take My servants as protectors besides Me? 2. Verily, We have prepared Hell for the Unbelievers for (their) entertainment. • Say: "Shall we tell you of those who lose most in respect of their deeds? 1. "Those whose efforts have been wasted in this life, while they thought that they were acquiring good by their works." 2. They are those who deny the Signs of

		their Lord and the fact of their having to meet Him (in the Hereafter). Vain will be their works, nor shall We, on the Day of Judgment, give them any weight. 3. That is their reward, Hell, because they rejected faith, and took My signs and My messengers by way of jest.
		The Believers Who also did Good Deeds
5	18:107-108	• (As for) those who believe and do good deeds, their place of entertainment shall be the gardens of Paradise. Abiding therein, they shall not desire to be removed from there.

CHAPTER 12

With Islam, Humanity Comes of Age
FROM SURAH AR-RAD (13), SURAH IBRAHIM (14)
AND SURAH AL-HIJR (15)

History confirms that generally the rulers or the so-called leaders corrupted the previous religions to further their personal political agendas. Today, contemporary politicians are still using religion to further their corrupt political objectives. Even the so-called secular governments use religion to facilitate the completion of their projects of selfish national interest. In most of the struggles for independence during the twentieth century, corrupt leaders mobilized their people by using religion, or corrupt leaders took over the countries after independence by manipulating the public afterwards. Working for the completion of the projects of self- or national interest without following the divine guidance, results in corruption, oppression, and exploitation. Conscience and the ability to reason have been given by God to humanity. Thus, using conscience and reasoning for the understanding of physical, moral, and sociopolitical laws of nature, in the light of divine guidance, and living by these laws is Islam.

1 THE CONFLICT BETWEEN
RELIGION AND SCIENCE ENDS

1.1 Corruption of Religion and its Conflict with Science
In his book entitled History of the Conflict between Religion and Science, Dr. J. W. Draper, describing the religious condition of the Romans, says that the Roman adoption of Christianity led to the spread of monotheism and Christianity throughout the Roman Empire. However, the circumstances under which the Roman Empire attained imperial power made the union of Christianity with paganism a political necessity. The debasing effect of the policy of Constantine on Christianity, Christianity's alliance with the civil power, and its incompatibility with science all led to "The Scriptures being made the standard of science (Chapter II)."

Dr. Draper continues: "The Egyptians insisted on the introduction of the worship of the Virgin Mary. They were resisted by Nestor, the Patriarch of Constantinople, but eventually, through their influence with the emperor, caused Nestor's exile and the dispersion of his followers." He further says: "Mohammed is brought in contact with the Nestorians who adopts and extends their principles, rejecting the worship of the Virgin, the doctrine of the Trinity, and everything in opposition to the unity of God. He extinguishes idolatry in Arabia, by force, and prepares to make war on the Roman Empire. His successors conquer Syria, Egypt, Asia Minor, North Africa, Spain, and invade France. As the result of this conflict, the doctrine of the unity of God was established in the greater part of the Roman Empire. The cultivation of science was restored, and Christendom lost many of her most illustrious capitals, as Alexandria, Carthage, and, above all, Jerusalem (Chapter III)."

1.2 Islam Initiated an Era of Reasoning and Science
Although a number of statements given by Dr. Draper are historically incorrect, he does establish that Christianity was corrupted by Roman politicians. The Christian scriptures are not science books and should not have been made into the standard of science. It appears that the Roman politicians corrupted Christianity and initiated a conflict between religion and science, which suffocated freedom of reasoning. As confirmed by Islam, religion and the science are complementary and not in the conflict.

Dr. Draper continues on, saying: "By the influence of the Nestorians and Jews, the Arabians are turned to the cultivation of Science. They modify their views as to the destiny of man, and obtain true conceptions respecting the structure of the world. They ascertain the size of the earth, and determine its shape. Their *Khalifahs* (rulers) collect great libraries, patronize every department of science and literature, and establish astronomical observatories. They develop the mathematical sciences, invent algebra, and improve geometry and trigonometry. They collect and translate the old Greek mathematical and astronomical works, and adopt the inductive method of Aristotle. They establish many colleges, and, with the aid of the Nestorians, organize a public-school system. They introduce the Arabic numerals and arithmetic, and catalogue and give names to the stars. They lay the foundation of modern astronomy, chemistry, and physics, and introduce great improvements in agriculture and manufactures."

2 WITH ISLAM - HUMANITY COMES OF AGE

2.1 Supernatural Miracles or the Miracle of Reasoning

People in ancient times generally did not use reasoning, but looked for miracles. "Say those without knowledge: 'Why speaks not Allah unto us, or why comes not unto us a sign?' Even thus said those before them, the like of what they say. Their hearts are alike. We have indeed made clear the signs unto any people who hold firmly to faith (Qur'an 2:118)." Here God tells us that only the people who lack knowledge and reason will ask for miracles. God is All-Powerful to cause miracles. If this is not true, then what is the universe? "Verily, when He intends a thing, His command is, 'Be,' and it is (Qur'an 36:82)." In Islam anything against truth and reason is forbidden, "Say: the things that my Lord has indeed forbidden are: Shameful deeds, whether open or secret; sins and trespasses against truth or reason; assigning of partners to Allah, for which He has given no authority; and saying things about Allah of which you have no knowledge (Qur'an 7:33)." The verses of Surah Ar-Rad, Surah Ibrahim, and Surah Al-Hijr that highlight what the unbelievers ask, i.e., "Why doesn't God speak to us or a sign comes to us?," are given in the table below.

Table 2.1: Why God Speaks not to Us or Sends a Sign?

No	Surah:Verses	Meanings
		God's Reply to the Unbelievers' Demand
1	13:007	1. And the unbelievers say: "Why is not a sign sent down to him from his Lord?" But you are truly a warner and to every people a guide.
	13:027	2. The unbelievers say: "Why is not a sign sent down to him from his Lord?" Say: "Truly Allah leaves to stray, whom He will; but He guides to Himself those who turn to Him in penitence."

		The Unbelievers' Reply to their Messengers
2	14:010-011	1. Their messengers said: "Is there a doubt about Allah, the Creator of the heavens and the earth? It is He Who invites you, in order that He may forgive you your sins and give you respite for a term appointed!" They said: "Ah! You are no more than human, like ourselves! You wish to turn us away from the (gods) our fathers used to worship. Then bring us some clear authority. Their messengers said to them: "True, we are human like yourselves, but Allah does grant His grace to such of his servants as He pleases. It is not for us to bring you an authority except as Allah permits. And on Allah let all men of faith put their trust."
	15:006-007	2. They say: "O you to whom the message is being revealed! Truly you are mad (or possessed)! Why bring you not angels to us if it be that you have the truth?"

2.2 People who lack Reasoning mock their Messengers

In response to the people who lacked reasoning, God says, "Even if We opened out to them a gate from Heaven, and they were to continue (all day) ascending therein, they would only say: 'Our eyes have been intoxicated. Nay, we have been bewitched by sorcery'… Has not the story reached you, (O people!), of those who (went) before you—of the people of Noah and 'Ad and Thamud—and of those who (came) after them? None knows them but Allah. To them came messengers with clear (signs), but they put their hands up to their mouths and said: 'We do deny (the mission) on which you have been sent, and we are really in suspicious (disquieting) doubt as to that to which you invite us' (Qur'an 15:14-15; 14:9)." People who lacked reasoning existed among all communities, and their attitude against their messengers was similar: "We did send messengers before you among the religious sects of old, but never came a messenger to them but they mocked him (Qur'an 15:10-11)." Since similar behavior yields a similar response, God tells us that all such people were eventually destroyed due to their behavior: "Mocked were (many) messengers before you, but I granted respite to the unbelievers, and finally I punished them. Then how (terrible) was my requital (Qur'an 13:32)!" The verses of Surah

200

Ar-Rad, Surah Ibrahim, and Surah Al-Hijr in which people are told that history provides many signs for people to reflect are given in the table below.

Table 2.2: History is full of Signs for the People to Reflect

No	Surah:Verses	Meanings
		Only People Who Understand Take Advice
3	14:052	Here (the Qur'an) is a message for mankind. Let them take warning there from, and let them know that He is (no other than) One Allah. Let men of understanding take advice.
		The Signs of Lot's People, Companions of the Wood, and of the Rocky Tract
4	15:072-081	1. Verily, by your life (O Prophet), in their wild intoxication, they (Lot's people) wander in distraction to and fro. But the (mighty) Blast overtook them before morning. And We turned (the cities) upside down and rained down on them brimstones hard as baked clay. Behold! In this are signs for those who by tokens do understand. And the cities were right on the high road. Behold! In this is a sign for those who believed. 2. And the Companions of the Wood were also wrongdoers. So We exacted retribution from them. They were both on an open highway plain to see. 3. The Companions of the Rocky Tract also rejected the messengers. We sent them Our signs, but they persisted in turning away from them.

1.3 People with Sight, who Reflect and Understand

In the creation of the heavens and the earth and in the past histories of people, there are signs for those who can see, reflect, and understand. "Allah is He Who raised the heavens without any pillars that you can see. Then He established Himself on the throne (of authority). He has subjected the sun and the moon (to his law)! Each one runs (its course) for a term appointed. He regulates all affairs, explaining the signs in detail that you may believe with certainty in the meeting with your Lord. And it is He who spread out the earth and set thereon mountains standing firm and (flowing) rivers and fruit of every kind He made in pairs, two and two. He draws the night as a veil over the day. Behold! Verily, in these things, there are signs for those who consider! And in the earth are tracts (diverse though) neighboring and gardens of vines and fields sown with corn, and palm trees—growing out of single roots or otherwise, water with the same water. Yet, some of them We make more excellent than others to eat. Behold! Verily, in these things, there are signs for those who understand...Is then one who knows that which has been revealed unto you from your Lord is the truth like one who is blind? It is those who are endued with understanding that receive admonition (Qur'an 13:2-4, 19)."

CHAPTER 13

God, His Message, and the Messenger
FROM SURAH AR-RAD (13), SURAH IBRAHIM (14)
AND SURAH AL-HIJR (15)

God is the One Who has created the universe. He knows everything open or concealed. He has made laws that govern the universe. He watches every person as to what he earns. There is all that is good for them who respond to their Lord. The Qur'an, the Book revealed from your Lord, is the truth. God sent the Messenger so that he might recite to the people what God had revealed to him. People should not think that God is heedless of what the unjust people do. History confirms what God says to them: "You were clearly shown how We dealt with them, and We have made (them) examples for you (Qur'an 14:45)."

1 GOD AND HIS ATTRIBUTES

Who is God? In Surah Al-Ikhlas, God Himself told people: "He is Allah, the One and Only; Allah, the Eternal, Absolute. He begets not, nor is He begotten, and there is none like unto Him (Qur'an 112:1-4)." He knows all about the seen and the unseen. There is a measure (physical, moral, and sociopolitical laws) with Him for everything. True prayer is due only to Him, and those to whom some people pray besides God give them no answer. Everything in the heavens and in the earth belongs to God. He watches each and every person as to what they earn, and for those who respond to their Lord there is a good reward.

The association of others with God in His divinity by unbelievers is actually disputing about God's divinity. The celestial bodies, angels, spirits, or saints that are said to be God's associates in His attributes, powers, and rights have never made any such claims. They do not ask unbelievers to worship or bow down before them. It is merely a contrivance by some corrupt people who, in order to establish their own control over ordinary people and to cheat them out of their earnings, have invented false gods and have misled people under the claim that they were the authorized representatives of those so-called gods. In the past, some of religious leaders have used religion for the fulfillment of their selfish desires; that is why priesthood doesn't exist in Islam. Any Muslim is qualified to lead the prayers or any other religious function as desired by the community. The verses of Surah Ar-Rad and Surah Ibrahim that highlight some of the attributes of God are given in the table below.

Table 1: God is the One, the Great, and the Most High

No	Surah:Verses	Meanings
1	13:008	1. Allah knows what every female (womb) does bear, by how much the wombs fall short (of their time or number) or do exceed. Every single thing is before His sight, in (due) proportion.
	13:009-010	2. He knows the unseen and that which is open. He is the Great, the Most High. It is the same (to Him) whether any of you conceal his speech or declare it openly, whether he lie hid by night or walk forth freely by day.
	13:012-013	3. It is He Who shows you the lightning by way both of fear and of hope. It is He Who raises up the clouds heavy with rain! Nay, thunder repeats His praises, and so do the angels with awe. He flings the loud-voiced thunderbolts, and therewith He strikes whomsoever He wills. Yet, these (are the men) who (dare to) dispute about Allah, with the strength of His power (supreme).
	13:014-015	4. For Him (alone) is prayer in truth. Any others that they call upon besides Him hear them no more than if they were to stretch forth their hands for water to reach their mouths, but it reaches them not, for the prayer of those without faith is nothing but (futile) wandering (in the mind). Whatever beings there are in the heavens and the earth prostrate themselves to Allah (acknowledging subjection)—with good will or in spite of themselves. So do their shadows in the morning and evenings.
	13:018	5. For those who respond to their Lord, are (all) good things. But those who respond not to Him, even if they had all that is in the heavens

	13:033	and on earth and as much more, (in vain) would they offer it for ransom. For them will the reckoning be terrible. Their abode will be Hell—what a bed of misery. 6. Is then He who stands over every soul (and knows) all that it does (like any others)? And yet they ascribe partners to Allah. Say: "But name them! Is it that you will inform Him of something He knows not on earth, or is it (just) a show of words?" Nay! To those who believe not, their pretence seems pleasing, but they are kept back from the path. And those whom Allah leaves to stray, no one can guide.
	14:002	Of Allah, to Whom do belong all things in the heavens and on earth! But alas for the unbelievers for a terrible penalty (their unfaith will bring them).

2 THE QUR'AN, THE MESSAGE FROM GOD

God revealed the Qur'an to the Messenger so that he may bring forth people, by God's permission from darkness into light. It is a message for people so that they may be warned thereby, that they may know that He is One God, and that those who possess understanding may take advice. God revealed the Qur'an, and most surely He is its guardian and protector. The verses of Surah Ar-Rad, Surah Ibrahim, and Surah Al-Hijr that highlight some of the attributes of the Qur'an are given in the table below.

Table 2: The Qur'an; the Divine Guidance

No	Surah:Verses	Meanings
		People Familiar with Divine Guidance Welcome the Qur'an
1	13:036	Those to whom We have given the Book rejoice at what has been revealed unto you, but there are among the clans those who reject a part thereof. Say: "I am commanded to worship Allah and not to join partners with Him. Unto Him do I call, and unto Him is my return."
		For Guidance and Protection, Learn and Follow the Qur'an
2	13:001	1. These are the verses of the Book, and that

	13:019		which is revealed to you from your Lord is the truth, but most people do not believe.
		2.	Is then one who knows that, which has been revealed unto you from your Lord, is the truth like one who is blind? It is those who are endued with understanding that receive admonition.
	13:037	3.	Thus have We revealed it to be a judgment of authority in Arabic. Were you to follow their (vain) desires after the knowledge which has reached you, then would you find neither protector nor defender against Allah.
			**The Qur'an was Revealed to Bring People out of Ignorance**
3	14:001	1.	A Book that We have revealed unto you, in order that you might lead mankind out of the depths of darkness into light, by the leave of their Lord, to the way of (Him), the Powerful, the Praiseworthy.
	14:005	2.	We sent Moses with Our signs (and the command): "Bring out your people from the depths of darkness into light, and teach them to remember the days of Allah." Verily, in this there are signs for such as are firmly patient and constant—grateful and appreciative.
	14:052	3.	Here is a message (the Qur'an) for mankind. Let them take warning there from, and let them know that He is (no other than) One Allah. Let men of understanding take heed.
	15:001-002	4.	These are the verses of revelation—of a Qur'an that makes things clear. Again and again will those who disbelieve wish that they had bowed (to Allah's will) in Islam.
	15:009	5.	We have without doubt sent down the message, and We will assuredly guard it (from corruption).
	15:087	6.	We have bestowed upon you the seven oft-repeated (verses) and the grand Qur'an.

3 THE MESSENGER AND HIS MISSION

God sent the Messenger so that he might recite to the people what He had revealed to him without any of the supernatural signs for which the unbelievers had asked. The true reason for not showing miraculous signs was not that God had no power to do so. It was because God did not want to force some people into affirming the prophethood of some prophet, but to help them attain true guidance. Such a purpose can only be achieved by reforming people's attitudes and reorienting their thinking process. Had the purpose merely been that people should believe without understanding and without being rationally convinced, then perhaps God would have shown miraculous signs. However, this purpose could also have been easily achieved by simply creating all humankind as born believers without free will, like He created the angels!

God told the Messenger to declare that: (1) God is the Lord; (2) there is no god but He; (3) on God, one should rely; (4) to Him is everyone's return; (4) God is the Creator of all things; and (5) He is the One, the Supreme. God also informed the Messenger that previous prophets and messengers had wives and children, spoke the language of the people with which they lived, and were often mocked by their people, whom God gave respite before destroying them. God commanded the Messenger not to strain his eyes after what He had given to certain groups of people to enjoy, nor to grieve for them, to be gentle with the believers, and to tell them that he is a plain warner. The verses of Surah Ar-Rad and Surah Al-Hijr highlighting the Messenger and his mission are given in the table below.

Table 3: The Messenger and his Mission

No	Surah:Verses	Meanings
		The Messenger, the Role Model for his People
1	13:030	• We have sent you (O Muhammad) among a people, before whom other peoples have passed away, that you might recite to them what We have revealed to you. Yet, they deny the Most Gracious. Say: "He is my Lord! There is no god but He! On Him is my trust, and to Him do I turn!"

207

		Previous Messengers were also Role Models
2	13:038	1. We sent messengers before you and appointed for them wives and children. And it was never the part of a messenger to bring a sign except as Allah permitted (or commanded). For each period is a book (revealed).
	14:004	2. We sent not a messenger except (to teach) in the language of his (own) people, in order to make (things) clear to them. Now Allah leaves straying those whom He pleases and guides whom He pleases, and He is the Powerful, the Wise.
		People who Refuse to Reform Deserve Punishment
3	13:032	3. Mocked were (many) messengers before you, but I granted respite to the unbelievers, and finally I punished them. Then how (terrible) was my requital?
	13:040	4. Whether We shall show you (within your lifetime) part of what we promised them or take to ourselves your soul (before it is all accomplished), your duty is to make (the message) reach them; it is our part to call them to account.
	14:044	5. So warn mankind of the Day when the wrath will reach them. Then will the wrongdoers say: "Our Lord! Respite us (if only) for a short term. We will answer Your call and follow the messengers!" What! Were you not wont to swear aforetime that you should suffer no decline?
		The Unbelievers' Rejection and the Messenger's Attitude
4	13:043	6. The Unbelievers say: "You are no messenger." Say: "Enough for a witness between me and you is Allah and such as have knowledge of the Book."
	15:003	7. Leave them alone (O Muhammad) to enjoy (the good things of this life) and to please themselves. Let (false) hope amuse them. Soon will knowledge (undeceive them).
	15:088-089	8. Strain not your eyes (wistfully) at what We have bestowed on certain classes of them, nor grieve over them, but lower your wing (in

		gentleness) to the believers. And say: "I am indeed he that warns openly and without ambiguity."
		The Messengers' Duty is to Convey the Message
5	15:085-086	9. We created not the heavens, the earth, and all between them but for just ends. And the Hour is surely coming. So overlook their faults with gracious forgiveness. Verily, it is your Lord who is the Master-Creator, knowing all things.
	15:094-099	10. Therefore expound openly what you are commanded, and turn away from those who join false gods with Allah. For sufficient are We unto you against those who scoff—those who adopt, with Allah, another god. But soon will they come to know. We do indeed know how your heart is distressed at what they say. • But celebrate the praises of your Lord, • And be of those who prostrate themselves in adoration, and • And serve your Lord until there comes unto you the Hour that is certain.

4 DESTINIES OF THE UNJUST COMMUNITIES

People are told that God is the Creator of all things and is the One, the Supreme. He creates and destroys what He pleases. He knows what every person earns, and the unbelievers shall come to know who is successful at the end. Do not think God is heedless of what the unjust do. He only respites them: "If Allah were to punish men for their wrongdoing, He would not leave on the (earth) a single living creature, but He gives them respite for a stated term. When their term expires, they will not be able to delay (the punishment) for a single hour, just as they will not be able to anticipate it (for a single hour) (Qur'an 16:61)." God tells the Messenger in Surah Al-An'am: "Mocked were messengers before you; but their scoffers were hemmed in by the thing that they mocked. Say: 'Travel through the earth, and see what the end of those was who rejected the truth' (Qur'an 6:10-11)." Verses from Surah Ar-Rad and Surah Ibrahim highlighting accountability and God's judgment are given in the table below.

Table 4: The Accountability and God's Judgment

No	Surah:Verses	Meanings
		God the Creator—He is One, the Supreme
1	13:016	1. Say: "Who is the Lord and Sustainer of the heavens and the earth?" Say:" (It is) Allah." 2. Say: "Do you then take (for worship) protectors other than Him, such as have no power either for good or for harm to themselves?" 3. Say: "Are the blind equal with those who see, or the depths of darkness equal with light? Or do they assign to Allah partners who have created (anything) as He has created, so that the creation seemed to them similar?" 4. Say: "Allah is the Creator of all things; He is the One, the Supreme and Irresistible."
		God Creates and Destroys what He pleases
2	13:039 / 13:041-042	1. Allah does blot out or confirm what He pleases. With Him is the Mother of the Book. 2. Don't they see that We gradually reduce the land (in their control) from its outlying borders? (Where) Allah commands, there is none to put back His command, and He is swift in calling to account. Those before them did (also) devise plots, but in all things the master planning is Allah's. He knows the doings of every soul, and soon will the unbelievers know who gets home in the end.
		God is not Heedless of What Unbelievers Do
3	14:042-043	• Think not that Allah does not heed the deeds of those who do wrong. He but gives them respite against a Day when the eyes will fixedly stare in horror—they are running forward with necks outstretched, their heads uplifted, their gaze returning not towards them, and their hearts a (gaping) void.
		Destiny of the Unjust after the Decreed Term
4	15:004-005 / 14:045	1. Never did We destroy a population that had not a term decreed and assigned beforehand. Neither can a people anticipate its term nor delay it. 2. And you dwelt in the dwellings of men who wronged their own souls. You were clearly shown how We dealt with them, and We have

			made (them) examples to you!
14:046		3.	Mighty indeed were the plots which they made, but their plots were (well) within the sight of Allah, even though they were such as to shake the hills!
14:047		4.	Never think that Allah would fail His messengers in His promise, for Allah is Powerful, the Lord of retribution.
15:002		5.	Again and again will those who disbelieve wish that they had bowed in Islam?
15:003		6.	Leave them alone to enjoy (the good things of this life) and to please themselves. Let (false) hope amuse them. Soon will knowledge (undeceive them).

CHAPTER 14

God's Protection and His Blessings

FROM SURAH AR-RAD (13), SURAH IBRAHIM (14)
AND SURAH AL-HIJR (15)

God provides protection and prosperity to those who follow His guidance. God tells us: "To all are degrees (or ranks) according to their deeds, for your Lord is not unmindful of anything that they do (Qur'an 6:132)." For each person, there are angels who guard him by God's command. God also does not change the good condition of a people as long as they remain good by not committing sins etc. "But when Allah wills a people's punishment, there can be no turning it back, nor will they find, besides Him, any to protect (Qur'an 13:11)." People should remember that their Lord proclaimed: "If you are grateful, I will add more (favors) unto you, but if you show ingratitude, truly My punishment is terrible indeed (Qur'an 14:7)."

This increase that comes as the result of being thankful to God includes not only rank, power, wealth, and other things associated with this world's life, but it also includes ranks of nearness to God, which are the ultimate goal and sincere desire of those whose hearts are fixed upon their Lord. This can very well be illustrated by the life histories of David and Solomon who, despite the greatness of their ranks, achievements, and all the special favors bestowed upon each one of them, remained deeply humble servants to their Lord. The Qur'an teaches us how we should thank God and how we can avoid being ungrateful to Him. We should not be friendly with Satan. God tells us that he is our enemy who can misguide the unbelievers.

1 THE CREATION OF THE UNIVERSE

1.1 Creation of the Universe and the Resurrection

Before the creation of humankind, God created the earth and sky and caused to grow on earth every suitable thing required for the existence of humanity. Although God has the power to flood the earth with these things, he provides them in a known measure.

God gives life, causes death, and will gather us all after death on the Day of Judgment for the accountability for our behavior and deeds. The verses of Surah Ibrahim and Surah Al-Hijr highlighting the creation of the universe and resurrection are given in the table below.

Table 1.1: Creation of the Universe and Resurrection

No	Surah:Verses	Meanings
		God Made the Universe Subservient to People
1	14:032-034	• It is Allah Who has created the heavens and the earth and sends down rain from the skies, and with it brings out fruits wherewith to feed you. It is He Who has made the ships subject to you, that they may sail through the sea by His command; and the rivers (also) has He made subject to you. And He has made subject to you the sun and the moon, both diligently pursuing their courses; and the night and the day has he made subject to you. 1. And He gives you of all that you ask for. 2. But if you count the favors of Allah, never will you be able to number them. 3. Verily, man is given up to injustice and ingratitude.
		God Created People and all its Subsistence
2	15:016	1. It is We Who have set out the zodiacal signs in the heavens and made them fair-seeming to (all) beholders.
	15:019	2. And the earth We have spread out (like a carpet), set thereon mountains firm and immovable, and produced therein all kinds of things in due balance.
	15:020	3. We have provided therein means of subsistence for you and for those for whose sustenance you are not responsible.
	15:021	4. There is not a thing but its (sources and) treasures (inexhaustible) are with Us, but We only send down thereof in due and ascertainable measures.
	15:022	5. We send the fecundating winds, then cause the rain to descend from the sky, therewith providing you with water, though you are not the guardians of its stores.

		God gives Life and Death and He will Resurrect
3	15:023-025	• Verily, it is We Who give life and Who give death. It is We Who remain inheritors (after all else passes away). To Us are known those of you who hasten forward and those who lag behind. Assuredly, it is your Lord Who will gather them together, for He is perfect in Wisdom and Knowledge.

1.2 *Iblis* (Satan) can Misguide the Unbelievers Only

Both Satan and his allies are too weak to be feared by any believer who relies on his Lord and His support. The only power to be feared is the One, Who can truly cause harm and benefit. That is God's power, feared by those who believe in Him. By fearing Him alone, they are the most powerful among people. All individual strength comes from God. No other force can stand up to it. "Allah (addressing Satan) said: 'Go your way. If any of them follow you, verily Hell will be the recompense of you—an ample recompense. Lead to destruction those whom you can among them with your voice; make assaults on them with your cavalry and your infantry; mutually share with them wealth and children; and make promises to them. But Satan promises them nothing but deceit. As for My servants, no authority shall you have over them.' Enough is your Lord for a Disposer of affairs (Qur'an 17:63-65)." God also said: "No authority has he (Satan) over those who believe and put their trust in their Lord. His authority is over those only who take him as patron and who join partners with Allah (Qur'an 16:99-100)." The verses of Surah Al-Hijr describing the humankind and the arrogance of *Iblis* are given in the table below.

Table 1.2: Humankind and the Arrogance of *Iblis*

No	Surah:Verses	Meanings
		God created the Jinn before Humankind
4	15:026-027	We created man from sounding clay, from mud molded into shape. And the jinn race, We had created before, from the fire of a scorching wind.
		The Angels prostrated to Humankind
5	15:028-033	1. Behold! Your Lord said to the angels: "I am about to create man, from sounding clay from mud molded into shape. When I have

		fashioned him (in due proportion) and breathed into him of My spirit, fall you down in prostration unto him."
		2. So the angels prostrated themselves, all of them together. Not so *Iblis*; he refused to be among those who prostrated themselves.
		3. He (Allah) said: "O *Iblis*! What is your reason for not being among those who prostrated themselves?"
		4. He (*Iblis*) said: "I am not one to prostrate myself to man, whom You did create from sounding clay, from mud molded into shape."
		God banishes Satan from Paradise
6	15:034-038	1. (Allah) said: "Then get you out from here, for you are rejected, accursed. And the curse shall be on you till the Day of Judgment."
		2. (*Iblis*) said: "O my Lord! Give me then respite till the Day the (dead) are raised."
		3. (Allah) said: "Respite is granted to you till the Day of the time appointed."
		Satan can only Misguide the Unbelievers
7	15:039-042	1. (*Iblis*) said: "O my Lord! Because You have put me in the wrong, I will make (wrong) fair seeming to them on the earth, and I will put them all in the wrong, except Your servants among them, sincere and purified (by Your grace)."
		2. (Allah) said: "This (way of My sincere servants) is indeed a way that leads straight to Me. For over My servants no authority shall you have, except such as put themselves in the wrong and follow you."

1.3 God's Protection, His Blessings, and His Laws

It does not make any difference whether anyone conceals one's thoughts or declares them openly. Whether one is hidden in the dark or walks openly in the day, all are under God's watch and protection. His grace encompasses everyone, and it protects again and again if people will only take His protection from harm and evil. It is not possible to take some pleasure or profit in secret from God. Angels guard each person by God's command and record all of peoples' thoughts and deeds.

God's intention is not to punish people but to facilitate their existence on earth. He created people virtuous and pure. He gave them intelligence and knowledge. He provided them with His grace and mercy. In spite of all this, if humankind goes against his own nature and God's will, God's forgiveness is available, and it is there for the asking. If in ignorance people act against their nature, away from the beautiful mold in which God has formed them, they are bound to face misfortune of their own making. This will change the favorable position in which God has placed them. In such a case, when punishment comes, it cannot be stopped. None of the things one may rely on other than God can provide protection. The governing divine principle is that if people give thanks by their behavior and deeds, God will certainly give them more, and if they are ungrateful to His favors, His punishment is truly severe. He gives people all that they ask from Him if they deserve it. God's grace comes in the form of higher status and additional responsibilities. The verses of Surah Ibrahim and Surah Al-Hijr describing God's protection, His blessings, and His laws governing humankind are given in the table below.

Table 1.3: God's Protection, His Blessings and His Laws

No	Surah:Verses	Meanings
		Law of Protection and Prosperity
8	13:011	1. For each (person) there are (angels) in succession, before and behind him. They guard him by command of Allah. 2. Allah does not change a people's lot unless they change what is in their hearts. But when Allah wills a people's punishment, there can be no turning it back, nor will they find, besides Him, any to protect.
		Belief and Good Deeds help People Prosper
9	14:006-008	Moses said to his people: "Remember the favor of Allah to you when He delivered you from the people of Pharaoh. They set you hard tasks and punishments, slaughtered your sons, and let your women-folk live. Therein was a tremendous trial from your Lord." • And remember! your Lord caused to be declared (publicly): 1. "If you are grateful, I will add more

216

		(favors) unto you, 2. "But if you show ingratitude, truly My punishment is terrible indeed." And Moses said: "If you show ingratitude, you and all on earth together—yet Allah is free of all wants, worthy of all praise."
		Disbelief and Corruption Destroy People
10	14:028-029	1. Have you not turned your vision to those who have changed the favor of Allah into blasphemy and caused their people to descend to the House of Perdition—Hell—which they will endure—an evil abode in which to stay.
	14:030	2. They set up equals with Allah that they may lead people astray from His path. Say: "Enjoy (your brief power), but verily you are making straightway for Hell!"
	14:034	And He gives you of all that you ask for. But if you count the favors of Allah, never will you be able to number them. Verily, man is given up to injustice and ingratitude.

1.4 The Believers, their Duties and Rewards

God tells people that if they perform their duties well, He will reward them both in this world and in the Hereafter. He asks us: "Is then one who does know that that which has been revealed unto you from your Lord is the truth like one who is blind? It is those who are endued with understanding that receive admonition (Qur'an 13:19)." To the believers He promises that: (1) those who believe and do good deeds are destined for happiness and a blissful life, (2) relaxed hearts and reassurance by remembering God and His commands during all daily activities, and (3) there is no reason why they should not rely on Him? The verses highlighting the duties of humankind and their rewards, as mentioned in Surah Ar-Rad and Surah Ibrahim, are given in the table below.

Table 1.4: Duties of Humankind and their Rewards

No	Surah:Verses	Meanings
		Character and Behavior of the Believers
11	13:020-024	1. Those who fulfill the covenant of Allah and fail not in their plighted word.

217

		2. Those who join together those things which Allah has commanded to be joined. 3. (Those who) hold their Lord in awe, and fear the terrible reckoning. 4. Those who patiently persevere, seeking the countenance of their Lord. 5. (Those who) establish regular prayers; 6. (Those who) spend, out of (the gifts) We have bestowed for their sustenance, secretly and openly; and 7. (Those who) repel evil with good. For such, there is the final attainment of the (eternal) home. Gardens of perpetual bliss—they shall enter there, as well as the righteous among their fathers, their spouses, and their offspring, and angels shall enter unto them from every gate (with the salutation): "Peace unto you for that you persevered in patience! Now how excellent is the final home."
		Remember God, and Follow His Commands
12	13:028-029	8. Those who believe, and whose hearts find satisfaction in the remembrance of Allah: for without doubt in the remembrance of Allah do hearts find satisfaction. 9. For those who believe and work righteousness is (every) blessedness and a beautiful place of (final) return.
		Rely on God, His Guidance, and His Mercy
13	14:012 14:014	10. No reason have we why we should not put our trust in Allah. Indeed, He has guided us to the ways we (follow). We shall certainly bear with patience all the hurt you may cause us. For those who put their trust should put their trust on Allah. 11. Verily, We shall cause you to abide in the land, and succeed them. This for such as fear the time when they shall stand before My tribunal—such as fear the punishment denounced.
		Keep Up the Prayers, and Help Each other
14	14:031	Speak to my servants who have believed, that they may establish regular prayers, and spend (in charity) out of the sustenance we have given them, secretly and openly, Before the coming of a Day in

		which there will be neither mutual bargaining nor befriending.

1.5 Guidance, Prosperity, Protection, and Peace

People need guidance, prosperity, protection, peace, and love. God tells us in the Qur'an that all these will be ours if we improve our behavior through the guidance provided in the Qur'an and *Sunnah* (traditions of the Prophet). Serve only God, be grateful to Him, and ask for His help. How should one ask for God's help? We are taught this in the form of Abraham's prayer, who said: "O my Lord! Make me one who establishes regular prayer, and also (raise such) among my offspring. O our Lord! Accept my prayer. O our Lord! Cover (us) with Your forgiveness—me, my parents, and (all) believers on the day that the reckoning will be established (Qur'an 14:40-41)!" The verses of Surah Ibrahim that contain the rest of Abraham's prayer are given in the table below.

Table 1.5: Serve God, Be Grateful to Him and Pray

No	Surah:Verses	Meanings
15	4:035-039	1. O my Lord! Make this city one of peace and security, and preserve me and my sons from worshiping idols. 2. O my Lord! They have indeed led astray many among mankind. He then who follows my (ways) is of me, but he that disobeys me—You are indeed oft-forgiving, most merciful. 3. O our Lord! I have made some of my offspring to dwell in a valley without cultivation, by Your Sacred House, in order, O our Lord, that they may establish regular prayer. So fill the hearts of some among men with love towards them, and feed them with fruits, so that they may give thanks. 4. O our Lord! Truly You know what we conceal and what we reveal, for nothing whatever is hidden from Allah, whether on earth or in heaven. Praise be to Allah, Who has granted unto me in old age Isma'il and Isaac, for truly my Lord is He, the Hearer of Prayer.

1.6 Only Unbelievers Despair of God's Mercy

The Qur'an informs us that God is always merciful. Therefore, we should not despair of God's mercy under any circumstances. Abu Huraira narrated that the Messenger said: "When Allah decreed the creation, He pledged Himself by writing in His book that is laid down with Him: 'My mercy prevails over my anger' (Sahih Muslim: 37.6628)." In Surah Yusuf, Yusuf's father said to his sons: "O my sons! Go and enquire about Joseph and his brother, and never give up hope of Allah's soothing mercy. Truly, no one despairs of Allah's soothing mercy except those who have no faith (Qur'an 12:87)."

Abraham was given the good news of a son when he was very old. Noticing Abraham's surprise at the news: "They (the angels) said: 'We give you glad tidings in truth; be not then in despair!' He said: 'Who despairs of the mercy of his Lord, but such as go astray' (Qur'an 15:55-56)." To encourage people to achieve excellence and to reform, God commanded the Messenger to tell them: "Say: 'O my servants who have transgressed against their souls! Despair not of the mercy of Allah, for Allah forgives all sins, for He is oft-forgiving, most merciful' (Qur'an 39:53)." God commands the Messenger: "Tell My servants that I am indeed the oft-forgiving, most merciful (Qur'an 15:49). Likewise, God says: "When those come to you who believe in Our revelations, say: 'Peace be on you. Your Lord has inscribed for Himself (the rule of) mercy. Verily, if any of you did evil in ignorance and thereafter repented and amended (his conduct), lo, He is oft-forgiving, most merciful' (Qur'an 6:54)."

2 GOD'S JUDGEMENT AND THE REWARD

2.1 Judgment Criteria: Good and the Evil

God informs humankind that He will keep the believers firm in this world's life and will reward them in the Hereafter, indicating that the believers who do good deeds will be successful in this life as well as in the Hereafter. God tells us in Surah Ibrahim: "But those who believe and work righteousness will be admitted to gardens beneath which rivers flow—to dwell therein forever with the leave of their Lord. Their greeting therein will be: 'Peace'…Allah will establish in strength those who believe, with the word that stands firm, in this world and in the Hereafter, but Allah will leave to stray those who do wrong. Allah does what He wills (Qur'an 14:23, 27)."

Continuing on in the same passage, good deeds are described as being similar to a good tree that is strong and fruitful: "See you not how Allah sets forth a parable? A goodly word like a goodly tree whose root is firmly fixed and its branches (reach) to the heavens—it brings forth its fruit at all times, by the leave of its Lord. So Allah sets forth parables for men, in order that they may receive admonition. And the parable of an evil word is that of an evil tree. It is torn up by the root from the surface of the earth; it has no stability (Qur'an 14:24-26)."

2.2 Behavior that is not appreciated by God

The worst type of people on earth are those who (1) love this world's life more than the Hereafter, (2) turn away from divine guidance, and (3) desire to modify the Qur'an to suit their selfish desires. We are told that they will be punished in this world's life and in the Hereafter. God will not protect such people.

People who force others to agree with them are most surely unjust people, and unjust people eventually get destroyed. Every obstinate, arrogant dictator will be disappointed with God's judgment. This has already happened in the past to many tyrants, and you will not find a change in God's ways in the future. The end of all pharaohs is failure. Verses of Surahs Ar-Rad and Ibrahim highlighting the fate of unjust people are given in the table below.

Table 2.2: Fate of all Pharaohs is Failure in both Worlds

No	Surah:Verses	Meanings
		Unsuccessful People Who are in Great Error
1	13:034	1. For them is a penalty in the life of this world, but harder, truly, is the penalty of the Hereafter: and defender has they none against Allah.
	14:003	2. Those who love this world's life more than the Hereafter and those who hinder (men) from the path of Allah and seek therein something crooked—they are astray by a long distance.
	14:013	3. And the unbelievers said to their messengers:

		"Be sure we shall drive you out of our land, or you shall return to our religion." But their Lord inspired (this message) to them: "Verily, We shall cause the wrongdoers to perish!
		Dictators who oppose Truth are Disappointed
2	14:015-017	They (the messengers) sought victory and decision (there and then), and frustration was the lot of every powerful, obstinate transgressor. In front of such a one is Hell, and he is given for drink boiling, fetid water. In gulps will he sip it, but never will he be near swallowing it down his throat. Death will come to him from every quarter; yet, will he not die, and in front of him will be a chastisement unrelenting.
		The Fate of all Pharaohs of the Past and Present is Alike
3	14:018-020	The parable of those who reject their Lord is that their works are as ashes, on which the wind blows furiously on a tempestuous day. They have no power over anything that they have earned: that is the straying far, far (from the goal). Do you not see that Allah created the heavens and the earth in truth? If He so wills, He can replace you with a new creation. This is not difficult for Allah.

2.3 Consequence of Corruption is Destruction

The communities that did not implement the divine commands in their individual and social lives were previously destroyed, and this could very well happen in the future. God tells us: "Never did We destroy a population that had not a term decreed and assigned beforehand. A people can neither anticipate its term nor delay it (Qur'an 15:4-5)." God reminds us that what people earn by unethical behavior does not benefit them. Verses of Surah Al-Hijr describing the consequences of not implementing God's moral and sociopolitical laws are given in the table below.

Table 2.3: Misbehavior Destroyed their Communities

No	Surah:Verses	Meanings
		Unnatural Behavior Destroyed Lot's People
4	15:058-077	They (angels) said: "We have been sent to a people (deep) in sin, excepting the adherents of Lot. Them we are certainly (charged) to save (from harm), all except his wife who, We have ascertained, will be

222

		among those who will lag behind."
		1. At length when the messengers arrived among the adherents of Lot, he said: "You appear to be uncommon folk." They said: "Yea, we have come to you to accomplish that of which they doubt. We have brought to you that which is inevitably due, and assuredly we tell the truth. Then travel by night with your household, when a portion of the night (yet remains), and do you bring up the rear. Let no one among you look back, but pass on whither you are ordered."
		2. We made known this decree to him that the last remnants of those (sinners) should be cut off by the morning.
		3. The inhabitants of the city came in (mad) joy (at news of the young men). Lot said: "These are my guests; disgrace me not, but fear Allah, and shame me not." They said: "Did we not forbid you (to speak) for all and sundry?" He said: "There are my daughters (to marry), if you must act." Verily, by your life (O Prophet), in their wild intoxication, they wander in distraction, to and fro.
		But the (mighty) blast overtook them before morning, and We turned (the cities) upside down and rained down on them brimstones hard as baked clay. Behold! In this are signs for those who by tokens do understand. And the (cities were) right on the high road. Behold! In this is a sign for those who believed.
		Injustice Destroyed the Dwellers of the Thicket
5	15:078-079	And the Companions of the Wood were also wrongdoers. So We exacted retribution from them. They were both on an open highway, plain to see.
		Unbelief Destroyed the Dwellers of the Rock
6	15:080-084	The Companions of the Rocky Tract also rejected the messengers. We sent them Our signs, but they persisted in turning away from them. Out of the mountains did they hew (their) edifices, (feeling themselves) secure, but the (mighty) blast seized them of a morning, and of no avail to them was all that they did (with such art and care).

2.4 God will Reward People According to their Deeds

God loves people and sent them to earth as His trustee to live there as humankind, following His commands. God will reward people according to what they did in their lives on earth, and He has set aside a Day of Judgment for this purpose. We are told in Surah Ibrahim: "One day the earth will be changed to a different earth, and so will be the heavens. And (men) will be marshaled forth before Allah, the One, the Irresistible, and you will see the sinners that day bound together in fetters—their garments of liquid pitch, and their faces covered with fire—that Allah may requite each soul according to its deserts, and verily Allah is swift in calling to account (Qur'an 14:48-51)." The verses of Surah Ar-Rad and Surah Al-Hijr that describe the righteous and the guilty on the Day of Judgment are given in the table below.

Table 2.4 : Righteous and the Guilty on the Day of Judgment

No	Surah:Verses	Meanings
		Paradise is for the Righteous
7	13:035 15:045-048	1. The parable of the garden which the righteous are promised—beneath it flow rivers. Perpetual is the enjoyment thereof and the shade therein. Such is the end of the righteous. 2. The righteous (will be) amid gardens and fountains. (Their greeting will be): "Enter here in peace and security." And We shall remove from their hearts any lurking sense of injury. (They will be) brothers, (joyfully) facing each other on thrones (of dignity). There no sense of fatigue shall touch them, nor shall they (ever) be asked to leave.
		And Hell is for the Corrupt
8	13:035, 15:043-044	• The final destination of the unbelievers is the fire...And verily, Hell is the promised abode for them all! To it are seven gates; for each of those gates is a (special) class (of sinners) assigned.
		God is Forgiving, the Merciful
9	15:049-050	• Tell My servants that I am indeed the oft-forgiving, most merciful, and that My penalty will be indeed the most grievous penalty.

CHAPTER 15

The Religion of Reason and Truth
FROM SURAH AN-NAHL (16)

Physical laws govern everything in the universe. Similarly, there are moral and socioeconomic laws that if respected by people should result in better life for all, thereby resulting in a prosperous and peaceful society. God tells in Surah Ar-Rahman: "He has set up the balance (of justice), in order that you may not transgress (due) balance. So establish weight with justice, and fall not short in the balance (Qur'an 55:7-9)." In the Qur'an, God directs humanity to look to its knowledge and reason to discover convincing proofs that are based on various signs in the universe and in man's own self. Having thus reasoned, belief in a single God emerges and leads us to equality and freedom for humanity and to a single set of moral and socioeconomic laws based on justice, equality, and human effort.

1 THE WAY AND THE LAW FOR HUMANITY

Like physical laws that govern everything in nature, there are moral and sociopolitical laws that, if implemented, should result in better life for people, thereby resulting in a prosperous and peaceful society. The sun and the moon follow exactly computed courses. Similarly, vegetation and trees follow God's will and submit to His laws in their existence, and the sky exists according to His physical laws. In the same way, He has made moral and sociopolitical laws for humankind based on equity and justice. It seems irrational that, on one hand, we acknowledge the existence of physical laws for the material world and natural laws for the animal and plant worlds, but we too often refuse to acknowledge the moral and sociopolitical laws for the world of humankind.

1.1 Physical, Moral, and Sociopolitical Laws
Moral values, sociopolitical laws, and fundamental human and state rights, along with guidelines for international affairs, have been described at various places in the Qur'an. In Islam, the

225

fundamental vehicle of economic activity is individual hard work and not capital. This stresses the development of individual capabilities and not the hoarding of capital, which is being used to exploit workers in the capitalist societies of the world. God tells us that He created us with the ability to communicate and reason, indicating the importance of the development of individual capabilities through education and merit. He has set certain laws in motion to keep the universe in proper working order. He tells us that everything is following His laws as He has intended, and He commands that we should do the same. God tells people in Surah Ar-Rahman: "(Allah) Most Gracious! It is He Who has taught the Qur'an. He has created man; He has taught him speech (and intelligence) (Qur'an 55:1-4)."

God created the universe based on certain rules and principles. These laws keep the whole universe operating perfectly: "The sun and the moon follow courses (exactly) computed, and the herbs and the trees both prostrate in adoration. And the firmament has He raised high, and He has set up the balance (of justice) (Qur'an 55:5-7)." That is why He commands people: "In order that you may not transgress (due) balance, so establish weight with justice, and fall not short in the balance (Qur'an 55:8-9)." Of course God has given people a choice; if they like they can go against these rules at an expense. Since every action has its appropriate reaction, people have to consider if they can afford the eventual consequence of their good or bad behavior, actions or deeds.

1.2 Religion Based on Reason and Truth
The Makkans challenged the Prophet over and over again to bring on that scourge about which he was warning them, noting that they not only rejected his message, but openly opposed it. Such a challenge became a by-word with them, which they frequently repeated as clear proof that Muhammad was not a true Prophet. They were asking for some miracle as a proof of the truth of his message. God has indeed forbidden, "Shameful deeds, whether open or secret and trespasses against truth and reason; … (Qur'an 7:33)." Therefore, instead of providing miracles, God says that people should use their wisdom and

reason. He shows us in the universe and in one's own self convincing proofs of a single God and refutations of other gods.

In Surah An-Nahl, the objections of the unbelievers have been answered, their arguments refuted, their doubts removed, and their false pretexts exposed. Warnings have also been given about the outcome of persisting in false ways and opposing the divine message. Using examples from His creation, God leads people to His signs and then asks to reflect, reason, ponder, listen, and then believe. This is illustrated in the table below.

Table 1.2 a: Look, Reflect, Ponder and then Believe

No	Surah:Verses	Meanings
1	16:011	Verily, in this is a sign for those who give thought.
2	16:012	Verily, in this are signs for men who are wise.
3	16:013	Verily, in this is a sign for men who celebrate the praises of Allah.
4	16:065	Verily, in this is a sign for those who listen.
5	16:067	Behold, in this is a sign for those who are wise.
6	16:069	Verily, in this is a sign for those who give thought.
7	16:079	Verily, in this are signs for those who believe.

God reminds people that, if they count His favors, they will not be able to number them. He then asks: "Is then He Who creates like one that creates not? Will you not receive admonition? If you would count up the favors of Allah, never would you be able to number them, for Allah is oft-forgiving, most merciful (Qur'an 16:17-18)." God then tells the Messenger that his duty is only to deliver the message; he cannot force people to believe. Belief must come from their own conviction. This is because: "Unto Allah leads straight the way, but there are ways that turn aside. If Allah had willed, He could have guided all of you (Qur'an 16:9)." The verses of Surah An-Nahl illustrating the signs for people in God's creation are given in the table below.

Table 1.2 b: Eighteen Signs from God's Creation

No	Surah:Verses	Meanings
		1. Creation of the Universe; 2. Humankind
1	16:003-004	1. He has created the heavens and the earth for just ends. Far is He above having the partners they ascribe to Him.

		2. He has created man from a sperm-drop, and behold this same (man) becomes an open disputer.
		3. Cattle, Horses, and Mules; **4. Things yet Unknown**
2	16:005-008	And cattle He has created for you. From them you derive warmth and numerous benefits, and of their (meat) you eat. And you have a sense of pride and beauty in them as you drive them home in the evening and as you lead them forth to pasture in the morning. And they carry your heavy loads to lands that you could not (otherwise) reach, except with souls distressed, for your Lord is indeed most kind, most merciful. 3. And (He has created) horses, mules, and donkeys for you to ride and use for show, and 4. He has created (other) things of which you have no knowledge.
		5. Rain and Water
3	16:010-011	5. It is He who sends down rain from the sky. From it you drink, and out of it (grows) the vegetation on which you feed your cattle. With it, He produces for you corn, olives, date palms, grapes, and every kind of fruit. • Verily, in this is a sign for those give thought.
		6. Night and Day; 7. Sun, Moon, and Stars
4	16:012	6. He has made subject to you the night and the day; 7. the sun and the moon and the stars are in subjection by His command. • Verily, in this are signs for men who are wise.
		8. Things in Various Colors
5	16:013	8. And the things on this earth that He has multiplied in varying colors (and qualities)— • Verily, in this is a sign for men who celebrate the praises of Allah (in gratitude).
		9. Sea: Its food, Pearls, and Ships
6	16:014	9. It is He Who has made the sea subject, that you may eat thereof flesh that is fresh and tender, and that you may extract there from ornaments to wear; and you see the ships therein that plough the waves that you may seek (thus) of the bounty of Allah and that you may be grateful.

		10. Hills, Streams, and Landmarks
7	16:015-016	10. He has set up on the Earth Mountains standing firm, lest it should shake with you, and rivers and roads that you may guide yourselves, and marks and sign-posts and by the stars (men) guide themselves.
		11. Rain that gives life to the earth
8	16:065	11. Allah sends down rain from the skies and gives therewith life to the earth after its death. • Verily, in this is a sign for those who listen.
		12. Milk; 13. Fruits from Trees
9	16:066-067	Verily, in cattle will you find an instructive sign. 12. From what is within their bodies between excretions and blood, We produce milk, pure and agreeable to those who drink it. 13. And from the fruit of the date palm and the vine, you get out wholesome drink and food. • Behold, in this also is a sign for those who are wise.
		14. Bees are Inspired to make Honey
10	16:068-069	14. Your Lord taught the bee to build its cells in hills, on trees, and in habitations; then to eat of all the produce and find with skill the spacious paths of its Lord. There issues from within their bodies a drink of varying colors, wherein is healing for men. • Verily, in this is a Sign for those who give thought.
		15. Hearing, Sight, and Hearts
11	16:078	15. It is He Who brought you forth from the wombs of your mothers when you knew nothing, and He gave you hearing and sight and intelligence and affections that you may give thanks.
		16. Birds, Constrained in the Air
12	16:079	16. Do they not look at the birds, held poised in the midst of (the air and) the sky? Nothing holds them up but (the power of) Allah. • Verily, in this are signs for those who believe.
		17. Shelter; 18. Clothing
13	16:080	17. It is Allah Who made your habitations homes of rest and quiet for you; and made for you, out of the skins of animals, (tents for)

	16:081	dwellings, which you find so light (and handy) when you travel and when you stop (in your travels), and out of their wool, and their soft fibers (between wool and hair), and their hair, rich stuff and articles of convenience (to serve you) for a time. 18. It is Allah Who made out of the things He created some things to give you shade. Of the hills He made some for your shelter. He made you garments to protect you from heat and coats of mail to protect you from your (mutual) violence. Thus does He complete His favors on you that you may bow to His will (in Islam).

1.3 Justice-Based Socioeconomic and Political Laws

Injustice, discrimination, exploitation, and oppression lead to illegal economic activities, thereby, result in abundance for the corrupt members of society and in hunger for the rest. This situation has been described in the Qur'an in a parable: "(Consider) a city enjoying security and quiet, abundantly supplied with sustenance from every place. Yet was it ungrateful for the favors of Allah, so Allah made it taste of hunger and terror (in extremes), (closing in on it) like a garment (from every side), because of the (evil) that (its people) wrought (Qur'an 16:112)." In contrast: "But verily your Lord—to those who leave their homes after trials and persecutions and who thereafter strive and fight for the faith and patiently persevere—Your Lord, after all this, is oft-forgiving, most merciful. One day every soul will come up struggling for itself, and every soul will be recompensed (fully) for all its actions, and none will be unjustly dealt with (Qur'an 16:110-111)."

Lawful economic activities and provisions lead to overall prosperity for people in a peaceful environment. "So eat of the sustenance that Allah has provided for you, lawful and good, and be grateful for the favors of Allah, if it is He Whom you serve (Qur'an 16:114)." People should be careful about what is lawful and unlawful in their dealings, and they should be truthful: "But say not, for any false thing that your tongues may put forth, 'This is lawful, and this is forbidden,' so as to ascribe false things to

Allah. Those who ascribe false things to Allah will never prosper (Qur'an 16:116)."

1.4 Implementation of Divine Law Results in Success

Belief in God should not be confined merely to lip service. Divine commands should regulate the morality and practical life of people. God tells us: "To those who do good, there is good in this world, and the home of the Hereafter is even better, and excellent indeed is the home of the righteous…They will have therein all that they wish. Thus does Allah reward the righteous (Qur'an 16:30-31)." It is absolutely easy for God to accomplish anything. He created the universe and made it subservient to various physical laws. He created animals and plants that follow set paths in their existence. He created people and made their actions result in reactions that can either be good or bad according to His moral and sociopolitical laws. God says: "To those who leave their homes in the cause of Allah, after suffering oppression, We will assuredly give a goodly home in this world, but truly the reward of the Hereafter will be greater. If they only realized! (They are) those who persevere in patience and put their trust on their Lord (Qur'an 16:41-42)."

1.5 Consequence of not following the Law is Failure

The rule of law is a universal principal, and its disregard results in punishment as ordained by God, and such punishment will happen at the appropriate time. God asks: "Do then those who devise evil (plots) feel secure that Allah will not cause the earth to swallow them up, or that the wrath will not seize them from directions they little perceive, or that He may not call them to account in the midst of their goings to and fro, without a chance of their frustrating Him, or that He may not call them to account by a process of slow wastage? (Qur'an 16:45-47)." Additional verses of Surah An-Nahl that tell of God's command coming to pass are given in the table below.

Table 1.5: God's Command will come to Pass

No	Surah:Verses	Meanings
		Surely the Corrupt will be Punished
14	16:001	(Inevitably) comes (to pass) the command of Allah (regarding those who reject His guidance). Seek you not then to hasten it. Glory to Him, and far is

		He above having the partners they ascribe unto Him.
		Why God's Punishment is Delayed?
15	16:061	• If Allah were to punish men for their wrongdoing, He would not leave on the (earth), a single living creature. But He gives them respite for a stated term. When their term expires, they would not be able to delay (the punishment) for a single hour, just as they would not be able to anticipate it.
	16:063	• By Allah, We (also) sent (Our messengers) to peoples before you, but Satan made, (to the wicked), their own acts seem alluring. He is also their patron today, but they shall have a most grievous penalty.
	16:064	We sent down the Book to you for the express purpose that 1. You should make clear to them those things in which they differ, and that 2. It should be a guide and a mercy to those who believe
		Unbelievers Knowingly Deny the Truth
16	16:083	They recognize the favors of Allah; then they deny them; and most of them are creatures ungrateful.
	16:085	• When the wrongdoers (actually) see the penalty, then It will neither be mitigated, Nor will they then receive respite.
	16:088	• Those who reject Allah and hinder (men) from the Path of Allah—for them will We add penalty to penalty; for that they used to spread mischief.

2 DO NOT SERVE *TAGHUT* AND SATAN

In economic activities, easy money drives the hard money out. Easy money is earned through illegal activities, while hard money requires honest effort and hard work. It is very important for honest and hardworking people that they should not serve *Taghut* (false deities) and Satan, as they represent only the evil ways. People may fall into this trap because of the misuse of the free will granted to them by God. Other creatures that do not have free will only serve God (by following divine laws): "And to Allah does prostrate all that is in the heavens and on earth, whether moving (living) creatures or the angels: for none are arrogant (Qur'an 16:49)."

2.1 Do Not Serve *Taghut* (False Deities)

The false deities worshiped by some people other than God may include Satan, devils, idols, stones, the sun, stars, angels, or even some human beings. Likewise, these may include saints, graves, rulers, and leaders that are falsely worshiped and wrongly followed. *Taghut*, Satan, and individual self-interest hinder efforts for the overall development and progress of humanity, which is required to elevate it above the animals. To accomplish this, God commands us to serve Him alone by following His laws: "Allah has said: 'Take not (for worship) two gods, for He is just One Allah. Then fear Me (and Me alone)' (Qur'an 16:51)." All creatures in the heavens and earth prostrate to God (follow divine laws). Those *Taghut* whom unbelievers call on besides God are things that are dead and lifeless: "Those whom they invoke besides Allah create nothing and are themselves created. (They are things) dead, lifeless: nor do they know when they will be raised up (Qur'an 16:20-21)." The verses of Surah An-Nahl that highlight the fact that those who do not follow divine laws are arrogant are given in the table below.

Table 2.1: Only arrogant people do not follow Divine Law

No	Surah:Verses	Meanings
		Behavior of those who serve False Deities
1	16:022	1. Your Allah is one Allah: as to those who believe not in the Hereafter, their hearts refuse to know, and they are arrogant.
	16:060	2. To those who believe not in the Hereafter applies the similitude of evil.
	16:024	3. When it is said to them, "What is it that your Lord has revealed?" they say, "Tales of the ancients."
	16:035	4. The worshipers of false gods say: "If Allah had so willed, we should not have worshiped anything but Him—neither we nor our fathers, nor should we have prescribed prohibitions other than His." So did those who went before them. But what is the mission of messengers but to preach the clear message?

	16:038-039	5.	They swear their strongest oaths by Allah that Allah will not raise up those who die. Nay, but it is a promise (binding) on Him in truth, but most among mankind realize it not. (They must be raised up) in order that He may manifest to them the truth of that wherein they differ and that the rejecters of truth may realize that they had indeed (surrendered to) falsehood.
	16:055-056	6.	(As if) to show their ingratitude for the favors we have bestowed on them! Then enjoy (your brief day), but soon will you know (your folly). They (even) assign to things they do not know a portion out of that which We have bestowed for their sustenance! By Allah, you shall certainly be called to account for your false inventions.
	16:072	7.	(Knowing all this), will they then believe in vain things, and be ungrateful for Allah's favors?
	16:073	8.	And worship others than Allah—such as have no power of providing them, for sustenance, with anything in the heavens or earth, and cannot possibly have such power.
		Whatever is in the Universe belongs to God	
2	16:049	1.	And to Allah does obeisance all that is in the heavens and on earth, whether moving (living) creatures or the angels, for none are arrogant (before their Lord).
	16:050	2.	They all revere their Lord, high above them, and they do all that they are commanded.
	16:053-054	3.	And you have no good thing but (that) is from Allah: and moreover, when you are touched by distress, unto Him you cry with groans. Yet, when He removes the distress from you, behold, some of you turn to other gods to join with their Lord.

2.2 Do Not Serve Any Type of Satan

Satan is the unbeliever among the jinn and humanity who became enemy of the believers due to jealousy and arrogance. Satan has power that enables him to try to seduce people away from the path of God. With his cunning, he makes use of all sorts of attractions and temptations to lure people by holding before them the prospect of immediate enjoyment and pleasure, with total disregard to what God has forbidden and what He has made lawful. As the creation of humankind and assigning to him the task of developing the earth was the occasion on which Satan committed his grave sin by disobeying God, Satan has sworn to do his utmost to seduce people into committing sins and disobeying God, so that they will share in his suffering on the Day of Judgment. To achieve this, Satan tries all methods and imposes his arguments on people to drag them to what incurs God's displeasure.

It is true that Satan has some power, but what is also true is that humanity can have far greater power. This can be acquired through faith. A person with firm belief in God and in the Hereafter is always able to defeat Satan and triumph over Satan's cunning if what God commands is uppermost in his mind. He will fare even better if he fortifies his faith with a good and continuous study of the faith. Ibn 'Abbas reported that the Messenger said: "A single religious scholar is much harder for Satan to defeat than a thousand worshipers (Al-Hadith: vol.1, no.36, p. 353)." Moreover, the Prophet taught us a method by which we can chase Satan away from our lives. That method is voluntary fasting. When we fast, we are always conscious that our abstention from eating and drinking is made for God's sake. At that time, we cannot forget God. If we remember that we can obey Satan only when we forget God, then we can appreciate why fasting is of great value to us in our battle with Satan. Fasting helps us remain conscious of God and our consciousness drives Satan away. Both Satan and his allies are too weak to be feared by any believer who relies on his Lord and has His support. The only power to be feared is the One, Who can truly cause harm and benefit. That is God's power, feared by those who believe in God. By fearing Him alone, they are the most powerful of all people. No other force can stand up to them.

With regard to the animosity of Satan, God tells people in Surah Bani Israel: "Behold! We said to the angels: 'Bow down unto Adam.' They bowed down, except *Iblis* (a jinn, who was among them). He said: 'Shall I bow down to one whom You did create from clay?' He said: 'See You? This is the one whom You have honored above me! If You will but respite me to the Day of Judgment, I will surely bring his descendants under my sway—all but a few!' (Allah) said: 'Go your way; if any of them follow you, verily Hell will be the recompense of you (all)—an ample recompense. Lead to destruction those whom you can among them, with your (seductive) voice; make assaults on them with your cavalry and your infantry; mutually share with them wealth and children; and make promises to them. But Satan promises them nothing but deceit. As for My servants, no authority shall you have over them'… (Qur'an 17:61-65)."

Table 2.2: Seek God's Refuge from accursed Satan

No	Surah:Verses	Meanings
		Guidance, mercy, and good news for those who submit
3	16:063	• By Allah, We (also) sent (Our messengers) to peoples before you, but Satan made (to the wicked) their own acts seem alluring. He is also their patron today, but they shall have a most grievous penalty.
	16:064	We sent down the Book to you for the express purpose that you should make clear to them those things in which they differ and that it should be a guide and a mercy to those who believe.
	16:089	• One day, We shall raise from all peoples a witness against them from among themselves, and We shall bring you as a witness against these (your people). And We have sent down to you the Book explaining all things, a guide, a mercy, and glad tidings to Muslims.
	16:098	When you read the Qur'an, seek Allah's protection from Satan the rejected one.
	16:099-100	• No authority has he (Satan) over those who believe and put their trust in their Lord. His authority is over those only, who take him as patron and who join partners with Allah.
		They lie who do not believe in God's Commands
4	16:101	They say, "You are a forger," but most of them understand not.
	16:102	• Say, "The Holy Spirit has brought the revelation from your Lord in truth, in order to strengthen those who believe, and as a guide

	16:103	and glad tidings to Muslims. • We know indeed that they say, "It is a man that teaches him." The tongue of him they wickedly point to is notably foreign, while this is Arabic, pure and clear.
	16:105	It is those who believe not in the signs of Allah that forge falsehood. It is they who lie.
		The wrath of God is on those Who disbelieve after having Believed.
5	16:106-109	Anyone who, after accepting faith in Allah, utters unbelief—except under compulsion, his heart remaining firm in faith—but such as open their breast to unbelief, on them is wrath from Allah, and theirs will be a dreadful penalty. This (is) because they love the life of this world better than the Hereafter, and Allah will not guide those who reject faith. 1. Those are they whose hearts, ears, and eyes Allah has sealed up, and 2. They take no heed. Without doubt, in the Hereafter they will perish.

3 PEACE AND PROSPERITY THROUGH ISLAM

By motivating people with rewards in this life and in the Hereafter, God guides people to set up a prosperous and peaceful society that is established on justice and equality and that is free of corruption, discrimination, and oppression. In such a society, everyone follows Islamic moral and social values and refrains from violating the fundamental rights of others. This is a dynamic community, continually being improved through self-evaluation, education, hard work, and good deeds, in an environment that always encourages all that is beneficial to the people and always discourages all that is harmful to society.

3.1 Establishing Justice and doing Good Deeds

"Allah commands justice, the doing of good, and liberality to kith and kin, and He forbids all shameful deeds and injustice and rebellion. He instructs you that you may receive admonition (Qur'an 16:90)." God promises a happier life to the righteous: "Whoever works righteousness, man or woman, and has faith, verily, to him will We give a new life, a life that is good and pure, and We will bestow on such their reward according to the best of their actions (in the Hereafter) (Qur'an 16:97)." As can be seen, Islam aims at empowering all people proportionate to their efforts.

Table 3.1: Oaths, Contracts, Treaties and Good Deeds

No	Surah:Verses	Meanings
		Commanded is to Honor Covenants and Oaths
1	16:091	1. Fulfill the covenant of Allah when you have entered into it, and break not your oaths after you have confirmed them. Indeed, you have made Allah your surety; for Allah knows all that you do.
	16:094	2. And take not your oaths to practice deception between yourselves, with the result that someone's foot may slip after it was firmly planted, and you may have to taste the evil (consequences) of having hindered (people) from the path of Allah, and a mighty wrath descend on you.
	16:095	3. Nor sell the covenant of Allah for a miserable price: for with Allah is (a reward) far better for you, if you only knew.
		Exploitation and Corruption is Forbidden
2	16:092	Nor take your oaths to practice deception between yourselves, lest one party should be more numerous (in gains) than another: for Allah will test you by this; and on the Day of Judgment He will certainly make clear to you (the truth of) that wherein you disagree.

3.2 Establishing a Peaceful and Prosperous Society

Since the establishment of a peaceful and prosperous society requires the efforts of dedicated individuals who have to struggle continually with the evil inclinations of the humankind in a testing environment, their objective should not be worldly benefits for themselves. Although they should look forward to the eternal reward in the Hereafter, it is lawful for them to enjoy the fruits of peace, prosperity, and justice along the way. "Whoever works righteous, male or female, and has faith, verily, to him will We give a new life, a life that is good and pure, and

238

We will bestow on such their reward according to the best of their actions (Qur'an 16:97)." Other important factors that help establish a just and peaceful society are:

1. Educating and Guiding People
"Invite (all) to the way of your Lord with wisdom and beautiful preaching, and argue with them in ways that are best and most gracious, for your Lord knows best who have strayed from His path and who receive guidance (Qur'an 16:125)."

2. Just Retribution or Patience
"And if you do punish, then punish with the like of that with which you were afflicted. But if you show patience, that is indeed the best (course) for those who are patient. And be patient, for your patience is but from Allah; nor grieve over them, and distress not yourself because of their plots (Qur'an 16:126-127)."

3. Grieve Not and Do Good Deeds
Neither grieves for those who do not participate nor distress yourself at what they plan, "For Allah is with those who restrain themselves and those who do good (Qur'an 16:128)."

3.3 Emulate Abraham: A Human Role Model
God gives us the model of Abraham as an example. "Abraham was indeed a model, devoutly obedient to Allah, (and) true in faith, and he joined not gods with Allah. He showed his gratitude for the favors of Allah, Who chose him and guided him to a straight way (Qur'an 16:120-121)." God gave Abraham good life in this world, and he will be among the righteous in the next world: "We gave him good in this world, and he will be in the Hereafter in the ranks of the righteous. So We have taught you the inspired (message), follow the ways of Abraham the true in faith, and he joined not gods with Allah (Qur'an 16:122-123)." Since God never changes His ways, He will grant the believers peace and prosperity in both worlds.

CHAPTER 16

Divine Commandments
FROM SURAH BANI ISRAEL (17)

Surah Bani Israel is a wonderful combination of warning, admonition, and instruction that have been blended together in a balanced proportion. The very first verse indicates that this Surah was revealed on the occasion of *Mi`raj* (Ascension). According to the traditions and books on the life of the Prophet, this occurred one year before *Hijrah* (the Prophet's migration to Madinah). Thus, this Surah initiated a period of preparation for living in Madinah. In this Surah, unbelievers are asked to reflect on the fate of the Israelites and other communities and to reform their ways within the period of respite given by God. They should, therefore, accept the invitation that has been extended by the Messenger and the Qur'an; otherwise, they shall be destroyed and replaced by other people. Incidentally, the Israelites, with whom Islam was soon going to come into direct contact at Madinah, were also warned that they should learn a lesson from the punishments that had previously been inflicted on them. This being the last opportunity given to them, they were advised to take advantage of the message of Islam, rather than continuing to misbehave and thus meeting with a painful torment.

The fundamental principles of morality and sociopolitical laws on which human society should be established are also highlighted in Surah Bani Israel. It is stressed that individual and collective success or failure, gain or loss, depends upon the right understanding of God, the divine message, and the Day of Judgment. Accordingly, convincing arguments are given to prove that the Qur'an is from God and that its teachings are true and genuine. Believers are commanded not to tolerate a compromise in their belief, to be patient, to remember God, and to reform their character and behavior. The believers are instructed to stick firmly to their beliefs and objectives. They should never think of compromising with unbelief. The believers are commanded to face adverse circumstances with patience and fortitude and to keep full control over their feelings and passions.

240

Five daily prayers are prescribed to reform oneself and to inculcate the high qualities of character that are essential for those who struggle in the righteous way.

1 GOD, HIS WAYS, AND HIS MESSAGE

1.1 God, His Signs, and His Ways

In the Qur'an, God appeals to human knowledge and reason to look for the convincing proofs of a single Creator in His creation. The unity of God also leads to a single set of physical, moral, and sociopolitical laws that govern the universe and human activities and that help people perform their duties as God's trustees who establish a just, peaceful, and prosperous society on earth. Throughout history, God has sent messengers to remind people to listen to the call of their conscience and to discriminate between what is good and bad in the development and maintenance of human character and a humane society. Since each individual is answerable only to God, he is at liberty either to accept or reject the divine message. However, those communities in which people do not implement divine laws in their lives and in their society are ultimately destroyed by their own behavior and deeds. God reminds us that this was the divine law previously and the divine law now.

Table 1.1: God, His Signs, and His Ways

No	Surah:Verses	Meanings
		Numerous God's Signs were Shown to the Messenger during Mi`raj
1	17:001	1. Glory to (Allah) Who did take His servant for a journey by night from the Sacred Mosque (in Makkah) to Al-Aqsa Mosque (in Jerusalem), whose precincts We did bless, in order that We might show him some of Our signs: for He is the One Who hears and sees.
		Two of God's Signs are the Night and Day
2	17:012	2. We have made the night and the day as two (of Our) signs. The sign of the night We have obscured, while the sign of the day We have made to enlighten you, that you may seek bounty for your Lord, and that you may know the number and count of the years. All things

		have We explained in detail.
		God's Will and the Ways
3	17:054	(O Messenger) It is your Lord that knows you best: 1. If He pleases, He grants you mercy, or 2. If He pleases, punishment. 3. We have not sent you to be a disposer of their affairs for them.
	17:055	• It is your Lord that knows best all beings that are in the heavens and on earth. We did bestow on some prophets more than on others: and We gave to David the Psalms.
	17:076-077	Their purpose was to scare you off the land, in order to expel you; but in that case they would not have stayed (therein) after you, except for a little while. (This was Our) way with the messengers We sent before you. You will find no change in Our ways.

1.2 The Qur'an, God's Message to Humanity

The Qur'an guides the upright people and gives good news to the believers who do good. It is a healing and a mercy to the believers, and God has revealed in it truth. Humans and jinn with all their combined efforts could never produce a book like the Qur'an. God has explained things in the Qur'an in diverse ways to make people understand His message. The Qur'an was gradually revealed in parts so that it might be recited to the people slowly and with deliberation. People may believe in it or not, but those who have knowledge fall down on their faces, making prostration when it is recited to them. The verses of Surah Bani Israel highlighting that Qur'an cannot be corrupted are given in the table below.

Table 1.2: The Guidance that cannot be Corrupted

No	Surah:Verses	Meanings
		The Qur'an – Divine Guidance for the Humanity
4	17:009-010	1. Verily this Qur'an guides to that which is most right (or stable) and gives the glad tidings to the believers who work deeds of righteousness that they shall have a magnificent reward. And to those who believe not in the Hereafter, (it announces) that We

	17:082	have prepared for them a penalty grievous.
		2. We send down (stage by stage) in the Qur'an that which is a healing and a mercy to those who believe. To the unjust, it causes nothing but loss after loss.
	17:086-087	3. If it were Our will, We could take away that which We have sent you by inspiration. Then you would find none to plead your affair in that matter as against Us—except for mercy from your Lord, for His bounty is to you (indeed) great.
	17:089	4. We have explained to man in this Qur'an every kind of similitude; yet, the greater part of men refuses (to receive it) except with ingratitude.
	17:106	5. (It is) a Qur'an that We have divided (into parts from time to time), in order that you might recite it to men at intervals. We have revealed it by stages.
		The Qur'an - Recognized only by the Learned
5	17:107	Say: "Whether you believe in it or not, it is true that those who were given knowledge beforehand, when it is recited to them, fall down on their faces in humble prostration."
		The Qur'an – Truth that cannot be Corrupted
6	17:105	1. We sent down the (Qur'an) in truth, and in truth has it descended: and We sent you but to give glad tidings and to warn (sinners).
	17:088	2. Say: "If the whole of mankind and jinns were to gather together to produce the like of this Qur'an, they could not produce the like thereof, even if they backed up each other with help and support."

2 PEOPLE ARE EITHER DIGNIFIED OR CORRUPT

2.1 The Honorable and Dignified Humans

God reminds people: "We have honored the sons of Adam, provided them with transport on land and sea, given them for sustenance things good and pure, and conferred on them special favors above a great part of our creation (Qur'an 17:70)." Although God is ever merciful and there is no other protector or helper, people are ever ungrateful to God due to lack of understanding and self-interest.

Table 2.1: God has indeed honored the children of Adam

No	Surah:Verses	Meanings
		God is most Merciful and Helps People
1	17:066-067	1. Your Lord is He that makes the ship go smoothly for you through the sea, in order that you may seek of his bounty, for He is most merciful to you. 2. When distress seizes you at sea, those that you call upon besides Himself leave you in the lurch! But when He brings you back safe to land, you turn away (from Him). Most ungrateful is man.
		None can Help People against God's Will
2	17:068-069	3. Do you then feel secure that He will not cause you to be swallowed up beneath the earth when you are on land or that He will not send against you a violent tornado so that you shall find no one to carry out your affairs for you? 4. Or do you feel secure that He will not send you back a second time to sea and send against you a heavy gale to drown you because of your ingratitude, so that you find no helper therein against Us?

2.2 Satan Cannot Corrupt the Believers

Satan, after refusing to prostrate to Adam, asked God's permission to challenge Adam's descendents with corruption, exploitation, and the worship of their own selfish desires. God gave permission to Satan after telling him that he would have no authority over the believers and would not be able to misguide and corrupt them. To warn against the schemes and designs of Satan, the Messenger described Satan's efforts in many ways. One such saying is that Satan almost runs in the veins of people. This must not be taken literally. It is a physical description of a mental fact. This is to make people aware of Satan's existence and his corrupt nature so that they can fortify themselves by remembering God, seeking His refuge, and running away from disbelief and corruption in any form. The verses of Surah Bani

Israel describing Satan's arrogance, jealousy, and efforts to misguide humanity are given in the table below.

Table 2.2
Satan's Jealousy and Efforts to Misguide Humanity

No	Surah:Verses	Meanings
		Out of Jealousy Satan Refused to Bow to Adam
3	17:061-062	1. Behold! We said to the angels: "Bow down unto Adam." They bowed down except *Iblis*. He said: "Shall I bow down to one whom You did create from clay?" 2. He (*Iblis*) said: "See You? This is the one whom You have honored above me! If You will but respite me to the Day of Judgment, I will surely bring his descendants under my sway—all but a few."
		God Permitted Satan to Misguide Humanity
4	17:063-065	3. He (Allah) said: "Go your way. If any of them follow you, verily Hell will be the recompense of you (all)—an ample recompense. 4. "Lead to destruction those whom you can among them with your (seductive) voice; make assaults on them with your cavalry and your infantry; mutually share with them wealth and children, and make promises to them. But Satan promises them nothing but deceit. "As for My servants, no authority shall you have over them. Enough is your Lord for a disposer of affairs."

2.3 Accountability of People's Behavior and Deeds

Every person is responsible for his own individual actions. Whoever does good deeds it is for his own benefit and whoever does wrong it is for his own loss. One cannot bear the burden of another, nor are people punished until they receive a messenger. When God wills to destroy a town because of its bad deeds, He sends His commandment to its people, but they transgress therein. Thus, the word proves true against them. God tells humankind that whoever desires the Hereafter, strives for it as one should strive, and is a believer, their striving shall surely be accepted.

On the other hand, whoever desires only this present life, God may give him what he wants in this worldly life, but then He assigns him to Hell. When God bestows favor on them, such people turn arrogant and behave proudly, but when evil afflicts them they are despairing. If such people acquire wealth, they don't spend it, due to the fear of poverty. They worship their belongings as their deities. Their behavior and their absence of good deeds show their lack of faith. God reaffirms: "We have fastened every man's fate on his own neck. On the Day of Judgment, We shall bring out for him a scroll, which he will see spread open. (It will be said to him): 'Read your record. Sufficient is your soul this day to make out an account against yourself' (Qur'an 17:13-14)."

Table 2.3: The Consequence of Human Behavior

No	Surah:Verses	Meanings
		Your Lord Bestows His Bounties Freely on All
5	17:020-021	1. Of the bounties of your Lord, We bestow freely on all—these as well as those. The bounties of your Lord are not closed (to anyone). 2. See how We have bestowed more on some than on others, but verily the Hereafter is more in rank and gradation and more in excellence.
		Consequence of Peoples' Behavior and Deeds
6	17:022 17:015 17:016-017	1. Take not with Allah another object of worship, or you (O people) will sit in disgrace and destitution. 2. Who receives guidance, receives it for his own benefit. Who goes astray does so to his own loss. No bearer of burdens can bear the burden of another, nor would We visit with Our wrath until We had sent a messenger. 3. When We decide to destroy a population, We (first) send a definite order to those among them who are given the good things of this life and yet transgress, so that the word is proved true against them. Then We destroy them utterly. How many generations have We destroyed after Noah? And enough is your Lord to note and see the sins of His servants.

246

	17:018	4.	If any do wish for the transitory things (of this life), We readily grant them - such things as We will, to such person as We will: in the end have We provided Hell for them: they will burn therein, disgraced and rejected.
	17:019	5.	Those who do wish for the (things of) the Hereafter and strive therefore with all due striving, and have faith, they are the ones whose striving is acceptable.
		How People Act	
7	17:083	1.	When We bestow favor on man, he turns aside and behaves proudly, and when evil seizes him he gives himself up to despair.
	17:084	2.	Say: "Everyone acts according to his own disposition, but your Lord knows best who it is that is best guided on the way."
	17:100	3.	Say: "If you had control of the treasures of the mercy of my Lord, behold, you would keep them back for fear of spending them, for man is miserly."

2.4 Corruption of Human Character and Behavior

Citing the example of Bani Israel, whom God punished because of corruption after He had saved them from the cruelty of Pharaoh and had guided them through Moses and His commandments, God reminds humanity that one of His principles is that corruption begets destruction. God illustrates this in the Qur'an by noting that Bani Israel became great tyrants and caused corruption in the earth twice, each time being punished for its misdeeds.

Table 2.4: Corruption and its Consequences

No	Surah:Verses	Meanings
		People of Pharaoh refused to reform so they were destroyed
8	17:101-103	1. Verily, We gave unto Moses nine tokens, clear proofs (of Allah's sovereignty). Do but ask the Children of Israel how he came unto them. Then Pharaoh said unto him: "Lo! I deem you one bewitched, O Moses."
		2. Moses said: "You know well that these things have been sent down by none but the Lord of the heavens and the earth as eye-opening

		evidence, and I consider you indeed, O Pharaoh, to be one doomed to destruction!" 3. So he resolved to remove them (Bani-Israel) from the face of the earth, but We did drown him and all who were with him.
		God Punished Bani-Israel for their Corruption
9	17:004-008	1. We gave (clear) warning to the Children of Israel in the Book that twice they would do mischief on the earth and be elated with mighty arrogance (and twice would they be punished). 2. When the first of the warnings came to pass, We sent against you Our servants given to terrible warfare. They entered the very inmost parts of your homes, and it was a warning (completely) fulfilled. Then did We grant you the return as against them. We gave you increase in resources and sons and made you the more numerous in manpower. 3. If you did well, you did well for yourselves. If you did evil, (you did it) against yourselves. So when the second of the warnings came to pass, (We permitted your enemies) to disfigure your faces, and to enter your temple as they had entered it before, and to visit with destruction all that fell into their power. 4. It may be that your Lord may (yet) show Mercy unto you; but if you revert (to your sins), We shall revert (to Our punishments): And we have made Hell a prison for those who reject (all Faith)

3 DIVINE LAW AND NORMAL HUMAN BEHAVIOR

3.1 Normal Human Behavior and Divine Guidance

As God's trustees, people are continually being tested and evaluated during their lives on earth. Islam considers both rational and emotional aspects of human personality for development and reform. The first aspect, i.e., the rational aspect, represents a decent and pure human nature that is inclined towards righteousness, that feels happiness in doing good, and that hates wickedness and evil. It feels remorse and sorrow about those weaknesses of character that lead to mistakes and sin. It considers that the future of its existence is in truth and justice. The second aspect of human personality consists of exciting emotions and satanic inclinations that turn people away from righteousness. They present injurious human inclinations in a glamorous way, but they only represent mean and arrogant human behavior. It is known that both rational and emotional aspects are found in people and that these two aspects are in mutual, perpetual struggle to achieve the leading role in human existence. It is conscientious choice and individual free will that decides the final victor between them. In Surah Al-Shams, we are told: "By the soul, and the proportion and order given to it, and its enlightenment as to its wrong and its right—truly, he succeeds that purifies it, and he fails that corrupts it (Qur'an 91:7-10)." Fortunately for all of us, God Himself takes the responsibility for providing divine guidance to help us overcome the inhuman qualities of pride, arrogance, and greed that compel people to indulge in injustice and miserliness, both of which are discouraged in a normal human life. "And unto Allah leads straight the way, but there are ways that turn aside. If Allah had willed, He could have guided all of you (Qur'an 16:9)."

To be worthy of God's trust, humanity needs to develop its human character and behavior along with its physical development. A complete description of the guidelines for human conduct is given in the Qur'an. These guidelines educate us, and their implementation makes us disciplined. "This is the Book; in it is guidance sure, without doubt, to those who fear Allah...O you people! Adore your Guardian-Lord, who created you and those who came before you, that you may have the chance to learn righteousness (Qur'an 2:2, 21)." Humanity needs guidelines and discipline in order to provide a better life on earth for all. The people who do not follow the guidelines create problems. God tells us: "When it is said to them, 'Make not mischief on the earth,' they say, 'Why, we only want to make peace!' Of a surety, they are the ones who make mischief, but they realize (it) not (Qur'an 2:11-12)."

249

3.2 Divine Commands, the Wisdom from Your Lord

Believers do not associate any other deity with God. They speak nicely, keep up prayer, and say: "O my Lord! Let my entry be by the gate of truth and honor, and likewise my exit by the gate of truth and honor, and grant me from Your presence an authority to aid (me) (Qur'an 17:80)." Believers acknowledge that the truth has come and that falsehood has vanished (Qur'an 17:81).

The verses of Surah Bani-Israel in which God commands humankind regarding what to do or abstain from are given in the tables 3.2a and 3.2b. Implementation of these commands enables believers to fulfill their responsibilities as God's trustees on earth. God tells us: "Of all such things, the evil is hateful in the sight of your Lord. These are among the (precepts of) wisdom, which your Lord has revealed to you (Qur'an 17:38-39)."

Table 3.2 a: What Your Lord has revealed to you of Wisdom

No	Surah:Verses	Meanings
		Violations: Which are hateful to your Lord
1	17:022-038	1. Take not with Allah another object of worship, or you (O man!) will sit in disgrace and destitution. 2. Your Lord has decreed that you worship none but Him, and 3. That you be kind to parents. Whether one or both of them attain old age in your life, say not to them a word of contempt, nor repel them, but address them in terms of honor. And, out of kindness, lower to them the wing of humility, and say: "My Lord! Bestow on them Your mercy even as they cherished me in childhood." 4. Your Lord knows best what is in your hearts: If you do deeds of righteousness, verily He is Most Forgiving to those who turn to Him again and again (in true repentance). 5. Render to the kindred their due rights, as (also) to those in want, and to the wayfarer: 6. But squander not (your wealth) in the manner of a spendthrift. Verily, spendthrifts are brothers of the Satan, and the Satan is to his Lord ungrateful. And even if you have to turn away from them in pursuit of the mercy from

your Lord that you do expect, yet speak to them a word of kindness.

7. Make not your hand tied to your neck (as a miser), nor stretch it forth to its utmost reach, so that you become blameworthy and destitute. Verily, your Lord provides sustenance in abundance for whom He pleases, and He provides in a just measure, for He knows and regards all His servants.

8. Kill not your children for fear of want. We shall provide sustenance for them, as well as for you. Verily, the killing of them is a great sin.

9. Nor come near to adultery, for it is a shameful (deed) and an evil, opening the road (to other evils).

10. Nor take life, which Allah has made sacred, except for just cause. And if anyone is slain wrongfully, we have given his heir authority (to demand compensation or to forgive), but let him not exceed bounds in the matter of taking life, for he is helped (by the law).

11. Come not near to the orphan's property, except to improve it, until he attains the age of full strength, and

12. Fulfill (every) engagement, for (every) engagement will be enquired into (on the Day of Reckoning.

13. Give full measure when you measure, and weigh with a balance that is straight. That is the most fitting and the most advantageous in the final determination.

14. Pursue not that of which you have no knowledge, for every act of hearing, or of seeing or of (feeling in) the heart will be enquired into (on the Day of Reckoning).

15. Nor walk on the earth with insolence, for you cannot rend the earth asunder nor reach the mountains in height.

16. Of all such things, the evil of it is hateful in the sight of your Lord.

Table 3.2 b: What Your Lord has revealed to you of Wisdom

No	Surah:Verses	Meanings
		Attitude, Desires, and Deeds of the Believers
2	17:039	1. Take not with Allah, another object of worship, lest you should be thrown into Hell, blameworthy and rejected.
	17:053	2. Say to My servants that they should say those things that are best, for Satan does sow dissensions among them, for Satan is to man an avowed enemy.
	17:078-079	3. Establish regular prayers—at the sun's decline till the darkness of the night, and the morning prayer and reading, for the prayer and reading in the morning carry their testimony. And pray in the small watches of the morning—(it would be) an additional prayer (of spiritual profit) for you. Soon will your Lord raise you to a station of praise and glory.
	17:080	4. Say: "O my Lord! Let my entry be by the gate of truth and honor, and likewise my exit by the gate of truth and honor.
	17:080	5. "Grant me from Your presence an authority to aid (me)."
	17:081	6. Say: "Truth has arrived, and falsehood perished, for falsehood is (by its nature) bound to perish."
	17:110	7. Say: "Call upon Allah, or call upon Al-Rahman. By whatever name you call upon Him, (it is well), for to Him belong the most beautiful names.
	17:110	8. "Neither speak your prayer aloud, nor say it in a low tone, but seek a middle course between."
	17:111	9. Say: "Praise be to Allah, Who begets no son and has no partner in (His) dominion. Nor (needs) He anyone to protect Him from humiliation. Yea, magnify Him for His greatness and glory."

4 THE UNBELIEVER'S MOTIVES AND BEHAVIOR

4.1 Why Some People have Inhuman Behavior?

Prejudice, self-interest, and arrogance generally cloud the wisdom of some people. Human conscience and the intellect are to help people to manage their weaknesses and to inculcate good moral character and behavior. Unfortunately, people too often use their intellect wrongly to justify the fulfillment of their selfish desires. Such people are so selfish that they do not want to be answerable for their behavior and deeds, not even to God. Therefore, they refuse to believe in the Hereafter. Instead of listening, reasoning, reflecting, and pondering on the divine guidance and the natural laws presented to them, they resort to name-calling. These people do not worship one God but are slaves to numerous deities and even to their own selfish desires. The verses of Surah Bani Israel in which God tells about those who do not believe in the Hereafter are given in the table below.

Table 4.1: Prejudices and Self-Interest Blinds Unbelievers

No	Surah:Verses	Meanings
		Unbelievers are those who serve other than God
1	17:041-044	• We have explained (things) in various (ways) in this Qur'an, in order that they may receive admonition, but it only increases their aversion (from the truth)! Say: "If there had been (other) gods with Him, as they say, behold, they would certainly have sought out a way to the Lord of the throne." • Glory to Him! He is high above all that they say—exalted and great (beyond measure)! The seven heavens and the earth, and all beings therein, declare His glory. There is not a thing but celebrates His praise, and yet you understand not how they declare His glory! Verily He is oft-forbearing, most forgiving.
		Unbelievers do not believe in the Hereafter
2	17:045-046	When you recite the Qur'an, We put between you and those who believe not in the Hereafter, 1. A veil invisible (of prejudice and self-interest). 2. And We put coverings over their hearts (and minds) and

		3. Deafness into their ears, lest they should understand the Qur'an.
		4. When you commemorate your Lord—and Him alone—in the Qur'an, they turn on their backs, fleeing (from the truth).
		Unbelievers resort to name calling
3	17:047-048	• We know best why it is they listen, when they listen to you, and when they meet in private conference, behold, the wicked say: "You follow none other than a man bewitched." See what similes they strike for you. But they have gone astray, and never can they find a way.
		Unbelievers cannot comprehend God's Power
4	17:049-052	• They (unbelievers) say: "What! When we are reduced to bones and dust, should we really be raised up (to be) a new creation?"
		1. Say: "Be you stones or iron, or created matter which, in your minds, is hardest (to be raised up—yet, you shall be raised up)!"
		• Then will they say: "Who will cause us to return?"
		2. Say: "He who created you first!"
		• Then will they wag their heads towards you, and say: "When will that be?"
		3. Say, "Maybe it will be quite soon. It will be on a day when He will call you, and you will answer (His call) with (words of) His praise, and you will think that you tarried but a little while."

4.2 Forging or Misinterpretation of the Qur'an

How strange! Some individuals may even be tempted to invent something else in God's name, so that the unbelievers may take them as a friend. Being ignorant of the consequences of inventing something else in God's name, some people might have tried or may try in the future to misinterpret the Qur'an. God is warning such people, while telling the Messenger that if one attempts to misinterpret the Qur'an intentionally God will double his punishment both in this life and the Hereafter.

Table 4.2: Unbelievers Desire to Interpret Islam Differently

No	Surah:Verses	Meanings
		Unbelievers Desire Us to Misinterpret the Qur'an
5	17:073	1. (O Muhammad), their purpose was to tempt you away from that which We had revealed unto you, to substitute in our name something quite different. (in that case), behold, they would certainly have made you (their) friend.
		Misinterpreting the Qur'an Carries a Penalty
6	17:074-075	2. Had We not given you strength, you would nearly have inclined to them a little. 3. In that case We should have made you taste - An equal portion (of punishment) in this life, - And an equal portion in death: - And moreover, you would have found none to help you against Us.

4.3 Unbelievers' Total Lake of Reason

Belief in God marks a definite turning point in one's life, at which one is freed from servitude and submission to all types of powers, forces, and desires, and at which one submits to God alone. It is a transformation from chaos to order, from aimlessness to purpose, and from fragmentation to unity. It is a focal point around which all humankind stands equal in the eyes of God, and it gives the whole of existence direction, balance, and coherence. Since all people are equal in the eyes of God, they should be equal in the eyes of people. This eliminates all excuses for discrimination, exploitation, and oppression of some people by others. Belief in resurrection and accountability is a belief in universal and divine justice. It is a testimony to the fact that human life on earth is not without purpose, value, or order, that good works that seem to go unrewarded shall certainly be rewarded, and that bad deeds will certainly be punished. During the time of the Messenger, instead of listening to and evaluating God's message, pondering over its principles, and observing their positive impact on people's lives, the unbelievers were making unreasonable demands for miracles. In response, as directed by God, the Messenger told them that he was only human. The verses of Surah Bani Israel that highlight the divine guidance and the unbelievers' excuses are given below.

Table 4.3: Divine Guidance and the Unbelievers' Excuses

No	Surah:Verses	Meanings
		Excuses of the Unbelievers
7	17:090-096	They (unbelievers) say: "We shall not believe in you (O Messenger), 1. "Until you cause a spring to gush forth for us from the earth. 2. "Or (until) you have a garden of date trees and vines, and cause rivers to gush forth in their midst, carrying abundant water. 3. "Or you cause the sky to fall in pieces, as you say (will happen), against us. 4. "Or you bring Allah and the angels before (us) face-to-face. 5. "Or you have a house adorned with gold. 6. "Or you mount a ladder right into the skies. No, we shall not even believe in your mounting until you send down to us a book that we can read." • Say: "Glory to my Lord! Am I aught but a man, a messenger?" What kept men back from belief when guidance came to them, was nothing but this: 7. They said: "Has Allah sent a man (like us) to be (His) messenger?" • Say: "If there were settled on earth angels walking about in peace and quiet, We should certainly have sent them down from the heavens an angel for a messenger." • Say: "Enough is Allah for a witness between me and you, for He is well acquainted with His servants and He sees (all things).
		The Unbelievers' Denial of Hereafter
8	17:097-099	On the Day of Judgment We shall gather them (the unbelievers) together, prone on their faces, blind, dumb, and deaf; their abode will be Hell. Every time it shows abatement, We shall increase for them the fierceness of the fire. That is their recompense, because they rejected Our signs, and said: "When we are reduced to bones and broken dust, should we really be raised up (to be) a new Creation?" Don't they see that Allah, Who created the heavens and the earth, has power to create the like of them (anew)? Only He has decreed a term

	appointed, of which there is no doubt. But the unjust refuse (to receive it) except with ingratitude.

4.4 Human Failing and Divine Judgment

Three things that blind human intellect to reason are wealth and power, self-interest, and Satan. Wealth and power blind people through prejudice and arrogance. Self-interest blinds people through disregard of what is legal and illegal, and temptations from Satan makes what is illegal and shameful look innocent to the tempted human mind.

God has compared being blind to the status of unbelievers in both this world and the Hereafter. "One day We shall call together all human beings with their (respective) Imams. Those who are given their record in their right hand will read it (with pleasure), and they will not be dealt with unjustly in the least. But those who were blind in this world will be blind in the Hereafter and most astray from the path (Qur'an 17:71-72)."

CHAPTER 17

God's Mercy and His Signs
FROM SURAH MARYAM (19)

People are told in Surah Al-Mulk that God is: "He Who created death and life, that He may try which of you is best in deed (Qur'an 67:2)." Humans, having free will and a strong inner self, have to be tamed for the broader good. God has provided humankind with wisdom and guidance for this purpose. God tells people: "So have We made the (Qur'an) easy in your own tongue that with it you may give glad tidings to the righteous and warnings to people given to contention (Qur'an 19:97)." Surah Maryam was revealed for the guidance of the first batch of Muslim migrants from Makkah before their journey to Habash (Ethiopia) to advise them that though they were leaving their country as persecuted emigrants for a Christian country, they should not in the least hide anything from the teachings they had received. Therefore, they should plainly say to the Christians that Prophet Jesus was not the son of God. This will be applicable to all believers in a similar situation at any time in history.

1 ARE WE HONEST TRUSTEES OR SLAVES OF OUR OWN DESIRES?

Humankind is born with free will and strong physical needs have to be guided for the broader good. God has provided people the wisdom and guidance for this purpose. This has divided humanity into two distinct groups: those who guard against evil, and those who follow their selfish desires freely.

1.1 The Slaves of Our Own Selfish Desires
The influence of materialistic ideology has affected the perception of many who view material wealth as being the source of all happiness. This view is especially prevalent in the West, where it seems that everything is geared towards achieving the dream of getting rich. A person getting wealthy quickly, applying whatever means necessary, is considered to be an extremely successful person. This is the case even though, as

258

individuals, the majority of the people in capitalistic countries is good in its own way and may be following several Islamic principles. However, as a society and a government, such countries spend and are still spending untold wealth on arms of mass destruction, which they sell to other countries, encouraging them to make their countries experimental battlefields. This is sapping the other countries' resources and keeping them in continual poverty. It is true that materialistic ideology can not be blamed for all of the world's troubles, but maintaining that capitalistic governments and societies are working for the benefit of humankind is an argument that is highly doubtful.

1.2 The Believers Guard Against the Evil

In contrast, the believers, with their noble character and behavior, help build a society free of corruption, discrimination, exploitation, and oppression by way of their hard work, truth, justice, and charity. The believers' mission in life is to establish a human society in which everyone tries to guard human values and the rights of others. What makes people suffer forever or makes them happy is their balance of good and bad deeds. God has made the universe to follow absolute justice. It is the choice people make, knowing that all actions, either good or bad, have appropriate consequences, that determines their present and their future. God commands people in Surah Maryam to emulate Yahya and guard against evil: "'O Yahya! Take hold of the Book with might:' and We gave him wisdom even as a youth, and piety from Us, and purity. He was one who guarded (against evil) (Qur'an 19:12)."

2 QUALITIES THAT INCULCATE MUTUAL LOVE

2.1 God's Worship, True Promise, and Charity

God describes Isma'il in Surah Maryam by noting: "He was (1) true to what he promised, and he was a messenger (and) a prophet. He used to (2) enjoin on his people prayer and (3) charity, and he was most acceptable in the sight of his Lord (Qur'an 19:54-55)." These three qualities of believers result in mutual respect and create a state of perpetual love among the members of a society: "On those who believe and work deeds of righteousness, will (Allah) Most Gracious bestow love (Qur'an

19:96)." Prayer precludes indecency and wrongdoing. As God states in Surah Al-Ankabut, people who perform prayer are kept away from indecency and evil. God inspires the avoidance of wrongdoing by prayer: "Recite what is sent of the Book by inspiration to you, and establish regular prayer, for prayer restrains from shameful and unjust deeds; and remembrance of Allah is the greatest without doubt. And Allah knows that you do (Qur'an 29:45)."

2.2 Neglecting Prayer Inspires Evil and Wicked Deeds
On the other hand, those who do not pray are liable to follow their selfish desires: "But after them there followed a posterity who missed prayers and followed after lusts. Soon then will they face destruction (Qur'an 19:59)." One's inner self is the commanding power and knows both depravity and how to avoid it. In other words, it is the inner self that inspires evil and wicked deeds. God relates these two features of the inner self in Surah Ash-Shams: "By the soul, and the proportion and order given to it, and its enlightenment as to its wrong and its right—truly he succeeds that purifies it (Qur'an 91:7-9)."

2.3 Indecency and Wrongdoing Eventually Destroy
The inner self is the source of all the depravities and wrong acts of people. Having such a feature, the inner self is among the most avowed enemies of humanity. The inner self is arrogant and selfish; it always wants to satisfy its own desires and vanity. It cares only about its own needs and interests, and it seeks only pleasure. It resorts to every means to tempt individuals since it is not always possible to fulfill its wishes through legitimate ways. This fact has also been explained in Surah Yusuf: "Nor do I absolve my own self (of blame). The (human) self is certainly prone to evil, unless my Lord bestows His mercy, but surely my Lord is oft-forgiving, most merciful (Qur'an 12:53)" Consequently, people get destroyed due to the indecency of their character and wrongdoing. "But how many generations before them have We destroyed? Can you find a single one of them or hear a whisper of them (Qur'an 19:98)?"

2.4 Efforts are a Prerequisite for God's Help and Mercy
God tells the believers in Surah Muhammad: "O you who believe! If you will aid (the cause of) Allah, He will aid you and

260

plant your feet firmly (Qur'an 47:7)." Throughout their lives, believers make serious efforts, following Islamic values, in all their endeavors according to their ability. On the other hand, throughout history, there have always been groups of unbelievers who have been against the believers and who have tried to hinder them through force and pressure. In the Qur'an, God states that He is always with the believers to make their affairs easy. He will help and support them. Believers who put sincere effort in God's way experience this at every single instance of their lives. God brings all their affairs to a conclusion with ease, and He gives them peace and prosperity. Even in very difficult situations, He provides ease for the believers. This is highlighted very well in Surah Maryam in the case of Mary: "And the pains of childbirth drove her to the trunk of a palm tree. She cried (in her anguish): "Ah! Would that I had died before this! Would that I had been a thing forgotten and out of sight!" But (a voice) cried to her from beneath the (palm tree): "Grieve not, for your Lord has provided a rivulet beneath you, and shake towards yourself the trunk of the palm tree. It will let fall fresh ripe dates upon you' (Qur'an 19:23-25)."

2.5 Miracles Do Happen at an Appropriate Time

Believers who are certain that God helps and supports them will never give up hope and will therefore continue their efforts. They will be patient and will wait with excitement to see how God will conclude an event. A believer, who is close to God, who takes God as his friend, and who knows He supports those who believe, will see the manifestation of God's help in every instance of his life. Surely, miracles like the birth of Yahya and Jesus are signs that show how God helps believers through imperceptible ways. If believers sincerely ponder and reflect on God's creation and the verses of the Qur'an in every incident, they can see the miracle-like manifestations of God's support and help in every situation.

3 GOD ANSWERS THE PRAYERS OF HIS SERVENTS

God tells us in Surah Al-Baqarah that He is very close to everyone and that He will answer people when they pray to Him. "When My servants ask you concerning Me, I am indeed close (to them). I listen to the prayer of every suppliant when he calls on Me. Let them also, with a will, listen to My call and believe in Me that they may walk in the right way (Qur'an 2:186)." God has infinite might and knowledge. He is the possessor of everything in the entire universe. Every being, every object, from the seemingly most powerful person to the weakest and from the magnificent celestial bodies to a tiny animal dwelling on the earth, belongs to God and is under His complete will and control. A person who has faith in this truth can pray to God for anything and can hope that God will answer those prayers.

3.1 The Miraculous Birth of the Messenger Yahya
Surah Maryam describes the story of Zakariya and Yahya, in which compassion provides both the central idea and the overall atmosphere. The story begins with a scene of earnest supplication by Zakariya in total secrecy. He is alone, addressing his appeal to God, away from watching eyes and listening ears. He wants to lay his troubled heart open before his Lord and to recount his worries. He addresses God as if he were speaking to someone who is very close. Needless to say, his Lord hears and sees without the need to be addressed or called upon, but a person troubled by worries finds comfort in vocalizing his concern. Most Gracious as He is, God knows this to be part of human nature. Hence, He likes that His servants pray to Him and reveals all that worries them: "Your Lord says: 'Call on Me; I will answer your (prayer). But those who are too arrogant to serve Me will surely find themselves in Hell—in humiliation' (Qur'an 40:60)." When people pray, they find relief from their heavy burden. They are reassured because they have assigned such burdens to the One Who is most able to help people and Most Powerful. They feel that they are in contact with the Most Merciful Who will not disappoint anyone who appeals to Him and relies on Him.

One can ask God for anything permissible. God is the only ruler and owner of the entire universe, and if He wills, He grants anyone anything he desires. God's messenger Zakariya prayed for a pleasing heir, and God answered his prayer despite his old age and his wife's barrenness.

Table 3.1: God's Mercy on Zakariya

No	Surah:Verses	Meanings
		Zakariya prayed to God for a pleasing heir
1	19:002-006	(This is) a recital of the mercy of your Lord to His servant Zakariya. Behold! He cried to his Lord in secret, praying: "O my Lord! Infirm indeed are my bones, and the hair of my head does glisten with grey, but never am I unblessed, O my Lord, in my prayer to You! Now I fear (what) my relatives (and colleagues will do) after me. But my wife is barren, so give me an heir as from Yourself, (one that) will (truly) represent me and represent the posterity of Jacob; and make him, O my Lord, one with whom You are well-pleased.
		God gives Zakariya news of Yahya's Birth
2	19:007-011	• (His prayer was answered): "O Zakariya! We give you good news of a son. His name shall be Yahya. On none by that name have We conferred distinction before." • He said: "O my Lord! How shall I have a son when my wife is barren and I have grown quite decrepit from old age?" • He said: "So (it will be). Your Lord says, 'That is easy for Me. I did indeed create you before, when you have been nothing.'" • (Zakariya) said: "O my Lord! Give me a sign". "Your sign," was the answer, "Shall be that you shall speak to no man for three nights, although you are not dumb." • So Zakariya came out to his people from his chamber: He told them by signs to celebrate Allah's praises in the morning and in the evening.
		God granted Yahya Wisdom and Humility
3	19:012-015	1. We gave him wisdom even as a youth. 2. And piety (for all creatures) as from Us, and purity. 3. He was devout and kind to his parents, and he was not overbearing or rebellious. So peace on him the day he was born, the day that he dies, and the day that he will be raised up to life (again).

3.2 Miraculous Birth of the Messenger Jesus

The birth of Jesus without a father seems miraculous to people only because it is totally different from what is familiar. We must remember that what is familiar is certainly not all that is in the universe. Further, the natural laws we know are not the only laws in the universe. We must remember that God has set natural laws into operation according to His will, which is unrestricted, free, and absolute. Regarding Jesus Christ, God says: "Christ Jesus the son of Mary was (no more than) a messenger of Allah, and His word that He bestowed on Mary, and a spirit proceeding from Him (Qur'an 4:171)." He is the same as the rest of God's messengers, e.g., Noah, Abraham, Moses, Muhammad, and the other most honorable servants of God whom He selected to convey His message to mankind at various periods in history. Perhaps the best explanation of "His word that He bestowed on Mary" is that God created Jesus through a direct command, which is described in various places in the Qur'an as meaning that when God wants to create something He only says to it, "Be," and there it is. He casts this word to Mary to create Jesus without going through the normal process involving a father and a mother. God's command can create anything from nothing. No wonder that it can create Jesus by breathing of His spirit. Previously God breathed of His spirit into the clay from which Adam was made, and thus Adam became a man. God says in the Qur'an: "Behold, your Lord said to the angels: 'I am about to create man from clay. When I have fashioned him (in due proportion) and breathed into him of My spirit, fall you down in prostration unto him' (Qur'an 38:71-72)." Similarly, in the creation of Jesus and referring to the mother of Jesus, He also says: "And (remember) her who guarded her chastity. We breathed into her of Our spirit, and We made her and her son a sign for all peoples (Qur'an 21:91)."

The spirit, to which reference is made both in Adam's as well as Jesus' birth, is the same. None of the previous believers who believed in Adam's creation and that God breathed into him of His spirit claimed that Adam was a god or a part of God, as some people allege regarding Jesus. The two cases are similar; both have spirit breathed into them and both were created in similar fashion. Adam was created without a father and a mother, while

Jesus was created only through a mother. God states in Surah Ali-Imran: "The similitude of Jesus before Allah is as that of Adam. He created him from dust; then said to him, 'Be,' and he was (Qur'an 3:59)." One wonders how personal prejudices and lingering traces of polytheism have added all this complexity to the simple issue of the creation of Jesus. The Creator who gave Adam, who had no parents, a human life that is different from that of all other creatures by breathing into him of His own spirit is the One Who has given the same human life to Jesus, who had no father. The verses of Surah Maryam describing the miraculous birth of Jesus are given in the table below.

Table 3.2: Surely Jesus was not the son of God

No	Surah:Verses	Meanings
		Mary Learns the News about the Birth of Jesus
4	19:016-021	Relate in the Book (the story of) Mary when she withdrew from her family to a place in the East. She placed a screen (to screen herself) from them. Then We sent to her our angel, and he appeared before her as a man in all respects. • She said: "I seek refuge from you to (Allah) Most Gracious. (Come not near) if you do fear Allah." He said: "Nay, I am only a messenger from your Lord (to announce) to you the gift of a holy son." • She asked: "How shall I have a son, seeing that no man has touched me, and I am not unchaste?" He replied: "So (it will be). Your Lord says, 'That is easy for Me, and (We wish) to appoint him as a sign unto men and a mercy from Us.' It is a matter decreed."
		Miraculous Birth of Jesus by God's Command
5	19:022-026	So she conceived him, and she retired with him to a remote place. • And the pains of childbirth drove her to the trunk of a palm tree. She cried (in her anguish): "Ah! Would that I had died before this! Would that I had been a thing forgotten and out of sight!" • But (a voice) cried to her from beneath the (palm tree): "Grieve not! For your Lord has provided a rivulet beneath you, and shake towards yourself the trunk of the palm tree. It

		will let fall fresh ripe dates upon you. So eat and drink and cool (your) eye.
		• And if you see any man, say, 'I have vowed a fast to (Allah) Most Gracious, and this day will I enter into no talk with any human being.'"
		Jesus, a child in cradle declares Servitude to God
6	19:027-036	At length she brought the (babe) to her people, carrying him (in her arms).
		• They said: "O Mary! Truly an amazing thing have you brought! O sister of Aaron! Your father was not a man of evil, nor your mother a woman unchaste."
		But she pointed to the babe.
		• They said: "How can we talk to one who is a child in the cradle?"
		He (Jesus) said: "I am indeed a servant of Allah. He has given me revelation and made me a prophet.
		1. "And He has made me blessed wherever I be.
		2. "And has enjoined on me prayer and charity as long as I live.
		3. "(He) has made me kind to my mother and not overbearing or miserable.
		4. "So peace is on me the day I was born, the day that I die, and the day that I shall be raised up to life (again)."
		Such (was) Jesus the son of Mary. (It is) a statement of truth about which they (vainly) dispute. It is not befitting to (the majesty of) Allah that He should beget a son. Glory be to Him! When He determines a matter, He only says to it, "Be." and it is.
		Verily, Allah is my Lord and your Lord. Him therefore you serve. This is a way that is straight.
		It is not appropriate that God should take a son
7	19:088-095	• They say: "(Allah) Most Gracious has begotten a son!" Indeed you have put forth a thing most monstrous! At it the skies are ready to burst, the earth to split asunder, and the mountains to fall down in utter ruin, that they should invoke a son for (Allah) Most Gracious.
		• For it is not consonant with the majesty of

266

	(Allah) Most Gracious that He should beget a son. Not one of the beings in the heavens and the earth but must come to (Allah) Most Gracious as a servant. He does take an account of them (all) and has numbered them (all) exactly. And every one of them will come to Him singly on the Day of Judgment.

4 ALL RELIGIONS AIM TO REFORM PEOPLE

4.1 Believe, Repent, Reform, and do Good Deeds

Islam is the same way of life that had been brought by all former prophets. History tells us that in the beginning people were very conscious of their religion and followed God's commands very sincerely, but with the passage of time future generations became corrupt and adopted wrong ways. They neglected prayers and followed their sensual desires. Since human actions have their appropriate consequences, they will meet with punishment, except those who repented, believed, and did good deeds. For people to succeed, God commands them to worship Him and to be regular and patient in His worship.

Table 4.1: The Religion of all Prophets was Islam

No	Surah:Verses	Meanings
		Those on Whom God Bestowed His Favors
1	19:051-058	1. Mention in the Book (the story of) Moses, for he was specially chosen, and he was a messenger (and) a prophet. And we called him from the right side of Mount (Sinai) and made him draw near to Us for mystic (converse). And out of Our Mercy, We gave him his brother Aaron, (also) a prophet. 2. Also mention in the Book (the story of) Isma'il. He was (strictly) true to what he promised, and he was a messenger (and) a prophet. He used to enjoin on his people prayer and charity, and he was most acceptable in the sight of his Lord. 3. Also mention in the Book the case of Idris. He was a man of truth (and sincerity) (and) a prophet, and We raised him to a lofty station.

		4. Those were some of the prophets on whom Allah did bestow His grace—of the posterity of Adam, and of those whom We carried (in the ark) with Noah, and of the posterity of Abraham and Israel—of those whom We guided and chose. Whenever the revelations of (Allah) Most Gracious were recited to them, they would fall down in prostrate adoration and in tears.
		Always There Existed Two Types of People
2	19:059-060	• But after them there followed a posterity who missed prayers and followed after lusts. Soon, then, will they face destruction. Except those who repent and believe, and work righteousness: For these will enter the Garden and will not be wronged in the least.

4.2 Migration, an Option to Avoid Persecution

During the perpetual struggle between the forces of justice and corruption, there have always been situations when people who are fighting for justice have been forced to migrate to avoid oppression. Surah Maryam recounts how Abraham was forced to leave his country because of the persecution of his father, family, and countrymen. This story provided consolation for the early Muslim emigrants who were forced to follow the footsteps of Abraham and who hoped that they would attain the same good end as he did. In contrast, the unbelievers were told that when they persecuted the early Muslims they were acting like the cruel people who had persecuted their forefather Abraham. The verses of Surah Maryam, narrating the story of Abraham are given in the table below.

Table 4.2: Surely the Messenger Abraham was Truthful

No	Surah:Verses	Meanings
		Abraham Left When His Father did not Believe
4	19:041-048	Mention in the Book (the story of) Abraham. He was a man of truth, a prophet. Behold, he said to his father: 1. "O my father! Why worship that which hears not and sees not, and can profit you nothing? 2. "O my father! To me has come knowledge that has not reached you; so follow me. I will

		guide you to a way that is even and straight. 3. "O my father! Serve not Satan, for Satan is a rebel against (Allah) Most Gracious. 4. "O my father! I fear lest a penalty afflict you from (Allah) Most Gracious, so that you become to Satan a friend." (The father) replied: "Do you hate my gods, O Abraham? If you forbear not, I will indeed stone you. Now get away from me for a good long while." • Abraham said: "Peace be on you. I will pray to my Lord for your forgiveness, for He is to me Most Gracious. And I will turn away from you (all) and from those whom you invoke besides Allah. I will call on my Lord; perhaps, by my prayer to my Lord, I shall be not unblessed."
		God Rewarded Abraham for His Servitude
5	19:049-050	When he had turned away from them and from those whom they worshiped besides Allah, We bestowed on him Isaac and Jacob, and each one of them We made a prophet. We bestowed of Our mercy on them, and We granted them lofty honor on the tongue of truth.

4.3 Following Divine Guidance Leads to Success

"Man says: 'What! When I am dead, shall I then be raised up alive?' But does not man remember that We created him before out of nothing? So, by your Lord, without doubt, We shall gather them together and (also) Satan. Then shall We bring them forth on their knees round about Hell (Qur'an 19:66-68)." However, the believers have been given the good news that they will be successful in spite of the worst efforts of the enemies of the truth: "But We shall save those who guarded against evil, and We shall leave the wrongdoers therein, (humbled) to their knees (Qur'an 19:72)." Again the divine principle is that: "Allah does advance in guidance those who seek guidance, and the things that endure, good deeds, are best in the sight of your Lord, as rewards, and best in respect of (their) eventual return. ... 'Lord of the heavens and of the earth, and of all that is between them; so worship Him, and be constant and patient in His worship:' (Qur'an 19:76, 65)."

CHAPTER 18

The Conflict between
Evil and Righteousness
FROM SURAH TA-HA (20)

Influenced by the large number of Jews and Christians in neighboring communities, Arabs generally acknowledged Moses as a messenger of God. Therefore, in relating the story of Moses, God tells the people of Makkah and humankind in general that: (1) God appoints His messengers in His Own way, just as He did in the case of Moses. Therefore, one should not consider it strange if Muhammad has been suddenly appointed as a messenger and without any public proclamation. (2) The fundamental principles of Islam, i.e., *Tauheed* and the Hereafter, are just the same as were taught to Moses at the time of his appointment. Further, (3) Muhammad has been selected to deliver the divine message among the people all by himself without any material provisions, just as Moses was entrusted with the mission to go to Pharaoh and ask him to give up his attitude of rebellion. The divine principles are that guidance is only for those who desire it and that the resurrection and accountability of peoples' behavior and deeds will take place as mentioned in the Qur'an at an appropriate time.

1 GOD, HIS GUIDANCE, AND HIS JUDGMENT

1.1 Guidance is only for the God-fearing People
God tells the Messenger that the Qur'an is not being revealed to put him unnecessarily in some great affliction. It does not demand that he perform the impossible task of inculcating the hearts of the unbelievers with faith. It is merely an admonition meant to guide to the right path those who fear God and want to save themselves from His punishment. The Qur'an is the word of the Creator of the universe, and Godhead belongs to Him alone. These facts are eternal truths, whether one believes them or not.

270

The verses of Surah Ta-Ha highlighting the attributes of God and the Qur'an are given in the table below.

Table 1.1: The Qur'an: A guide on to the Right Path

No	Surah:Verses	Meanings
		The Qur'an - a revelation from God Who created the Universe
1	20:002-005	• We have not sent down the Qur'an to you to be (an occasion) for your distress, but only as an admonition to those who fear (Allah)—a revelation from Him Who created the earth and the heavens on high. (Allah) Most Gracious is firmly established on the throne (of authority).
	20:099-100	• Thus do We relate to you some stories of what happened before, for We have sent you a message from Our Own presence. If any do turn away there from, verily they will bear a burden on the Day of Judgment.
		God – there is no god but He; His are the very Best Names
2	20:006	1. To Him belongs what is in the heavens and on earth, and all between them, and all beneath the soil.
	20:007-008	2. If you pronounce the word aloud, (it is no matter), for verily He knows what is secret and what is yet more hidden. Allah! There is no god but He! To Him belong the most beautiful names.
	20:053	3. He Who has, made for you the earth like a carpet spread out, has enabled you to go about therein by roads (and channels) and has sent down water from the sky.
	20:053-054	4. With it have We produced diverse pairs of plants, each separate from the others. Eat (for yourselves), and pasture your cattle. Verily, in this are signs for men endued with understanding.

1.2 Resurrection and Accountability of Peoples' Deeds

God has provided people with the Qur'an, which contains instructions as how to guard against evil in this world. These instructions form the basis on which people will be judged about their performance and rewarded accordingly. There will be no intercession without the approval of God or contrary to the principles of Islam as given in the Qur'an. Everyone will be rewarded according to what he did, and none will be dealt unjustly.

Table 1.2: Divine Message - the Basis of Accountability

No	Surah:Verses	Meanings
		The Qur'an Guides People about how to Guard against Evil
3	20:112-113	• But he who works deeds of righteousness and has faith will have no fear of harm or of any curtailment (of what is his due). • Thus have We sent this down—an Arabic Qur'an—and explained therein in detail some of the warnings, in order that they may fear Allah or that it may cause their remembrance (of Him).
		People will be Judged According to God's Commands
4	20:100-101	If any do turn away there from, verily they will bear a burden on the Day of Judgment; they will abide in this (state), and grievous will the burden be to them on that day.
		The Resurrection, Day of Judgment, and Accountability
5	20:105-109	They ask you concerning the Mountains. Say, "My Lord will uproot them and scatter them as dust. He will leave them as plains smooth and level. Nothing crooked or curved will you see in their place. 1. On that day will they follow the caller (straight); no crookedness (can they show) him. All sounds shall humble themselves in the presence of (Allah) Most Gracious. Nothing shall you hear but the tramp of their feet (as they march). 2. On that day shall no intercession avail except for those for whom permission has been granted by (Allah) Most Gracious and whose word is acceptable to Him.

1.3 The Messengers and Virtuous Believers

God has His own mysterious ways to accomplish His will. He catches hold of a traveler from Midian on his way to Egypt and says, "Go and fight with the greatest tyrant of the time." He didn't provide him with armies and provisions for the mission. The only thing He did was to appoint the traveler's brother as his assistant at the traveler's request. Since the messengers and the believers are assigned a mission from God, it is very important that a strong bond be developed between Him Who appoints and those who are appointed. For the success of their mission, the believers should know God's attributes and regularly communicate with Him. That is why great emphasis has been placed on regular daily prayers. This creates in the messengers, as well as in the believers, the virtues of patience, forbearance, contentment, resignation to the will of God, and self-analysis, for these are greatly needed in the implementation of the divine message. God tells Moses that: (1) He has chosen Moses; therefore, Moses should listen to what is revealed to him; (2) I am God; there is no god but I; therefore, serve Me; (3) keep up prayer for My remembrance; (4) surely the hour is coming when everyone will be rewarded according to his efforts. The verses of Surah Ta-Ha that highlight the appointment of Moses as a messenger of God and the details of his mission are given in the table below.

Table 1.3: Moses, the Messenger of God, and his Mission

No	Surah:Verses	Meanings
		Moses Receives Divine Guidance
6	20:009-016	1. Has the story of Moses reached you? Behold, he saw a fire. So he said to his family, "You wait. I perceive a fire. Perhaps I can bring you some burning brand there from or find some guidance at the fire." 2. But when he came to the fire, a voice was heard: "O Moses! Verily, I am your Lord! Therefore, (in My presence) put off your shoes. You are in the sacred valley Tuwa. I have chosen you. Listen then to the inspiration (sent to you). 3. "Verily, I am Allah. There is no god but I, so serve Me (only), and establish regular prayer for celebrating My praise. Verily, the Hour is

		coming—My design is to keep it hidden—for every soul to receive its reward by the measure of its endeavor. 4. "Therefore, let not such as believe not therein, but follow their own lusts, divert you there from, lest you perish."
		Moses Receives Two of God's Signs
7	20:017-023	1. And what is that in your right hand, O Moses?" He said, "It is my rod. On it I lean; with it I beat down fodder for my flocks, and in it I find other uses." (Allah) said, "Throw it, O Moses!" He threw it, and behold it was a snake, active in motion. (Allah) said, "Seize it, and fear not. We shall return it at once to its former condition. 2. "Now draw your hand close to your side. It shall come forth white (and shining), without harm (or stain)—as another sign—in order that We may show you (two) of our greater signs."
		Moses asks for Aaron's Assistance
8	20:024-036	1. "Go you to Pharaoh, for he has indeed transgressed all bounds." 2. (Moses) said: "O my Lord! Expand me my breast. Ease my task for me, and remove the impediment from my speech, so they may understand what I say. 3. "And give me a minister from my family, Aaron, my brother. Add to my strength through him, and make him share my task that we may celebrate Your praise without stint and remember You without stint, for You are He that (ever) regards us." 4. (Allah) said: "Granted is your prayer, O Moses."
		Moses and Aaron go to Pharaoh

| 9 | 20:041-048 | 1. "I have prepared you for Myself (for service). Go, you and your brother, with My signs, and slacken not either of you in keeping Me in remembrance. Go, both of you, to Pharaoh, for he has indeed transgressed all bounds. But speak to him mildly; perchance he may take warning or fear (Allah)."

2. They (Moses and Aaron) said: "Our Lord! We fear lest he hasten with insolence against us, or lest he transgress all bounds."

3. He (Allah) said: "Fear not, for I am with you. I hear and see (everything). So go both of you to him, and say, 'Verily, we are messengers sent by your Lord. Send forth, therefore, the Children of Israel with us, and afflict them not. With a sign, indeed, have we come from your Lord! And peace to all who follow guidance. Verily, it has been revealed to us that the penalty (awaits) those who reject and turn away.'" |

2 THE STRUGGLE IN
THE IMPLEMENTATION OF DIVINE LAW

2.1 Their Attitudes Determine People's Fates

Pharaoh employed the same tactics against Moses as the unbelievers of Makkah were employing against the Messenger and the believers, i.e., frivolous objections, accusations, and cruel persecutions. History confirms that the imperialistic rulers of the past, as well as the present, have been mimicking Pharaoh very well. The verses of Surah Ta-Ha that highlight the dialogue between Moses and Pharaoh are given in the table below.

Table 2.1: Moses in the court of Pharaoh

No	Surah:Verses	Meanings
		Moses Invitation to Guidance And Pharaoh's Response
1	20:049-052	1. (When this message was delivered), (Pharaoh) said: "Who then, O Moses, is the Lord of you two?" He said: "Our Lord is He Who gave to each (created) thing its form and nature, and further gave guidance."

		2. (Pharaoh) said: "What then is the condition of previous generations?" He replied: "The knowledge of that is with my Lord, duly recorded. My Lord never errs nor forgets."
		Most surely there are Signs in God's creation for People
2	20:053-055	1. (Moses continued): "He Who has made for you the earth like a carpet spread out has enabled you to go about therein by roads (and channels) 2. "And has sent down water from the sky." 3. With it have We produced diverse pairs of plants each separate from the others. Eat (for yourselves), and pasture your cattle. Verily, in this are signs for men endued with understanding. From the (earth) did We create you, and into it shall We return you, and from it shall We bring you out once again.
		Divine Signs were shown to Pharaoh, but he rejected them
3	20:056-060	1. And We showed Pharaoh all Our Signs, but he did reject and refuse. 2. He said: "Have you come to drive us out of our land with your magic, O Moses? But we can surely produce magic to match yours! So make between us and you an appointment, which we shall not fail to keep—neither we nor you—in a place where both shall have even chances." 3. Moses said: "Your appointment is the Day of the Festival, and let the people be assembled when the sun is well up." 4. So Pharaoh withdrew. He concerted his plan and then came (back).

2.2 The Mission Supported by God Never Fails

In Surah Ta-Ha, the believers were consoled and comforted. They were told that they should not be afraid of fighting with the Quraish (unbelievers), even though the odds were fearfully against them. After all, the mission that is supported by God comes out victorious in the end. At the same time, the believers were exhorted to follow the excellent example of the magicians of Egypt, who remained steadfast in their faith, though Pharaoh threatened them with horrible vengeance.

Table 2.2: Confrontation between Moses and the Magicians

No	Surah:Verses	Meanings
		The Magicians disputed among themselves
4	20:061-065	1. Moses said to them: "Woe to you! Forge not a lie against Allah, lest He destroy you utterly by chastisement. The forger must suffer frustration!" 2. So they disputed, one with another, over their affair, but they kept their talk secret. They said: "These two are certainly (expert) magicians. Their object is to drive you out from your land with their magic and to do away with your most cherished institutions. Therefore, concert your plan, and then assemble in ranks. He wins today who gains the upper hand." 3. They said: O Moses! Either you throw first, or let us be the first to throw."
		The Magicians Believed in the Lord of Aaron and Moses.
5	20:066-070	1. He said, "Nay, throw you first!" Then behold their ropes and their rods—so it seemed to him on account of their magic—began to be in lively motion! So Moses conceived in his mind a (sort of) fear. 2. We said: "Fear not, for you have indeed the upper hand. Throw that which is in your right hand. Quickly will it swallow up that which they have faked. What they have faked is but a magician's trick, and the magician thrives not, (no matter) where he goes." 3. So the magicians were thrown down to prostration. They said: "We believe in the Lord of Aaron and Moses."
		Pharaoh's Oppression and the Magicians' Response
6	20:071-075	1. (Pharaoh) said: "You believe in Him before I give you permission? Surely this must be your leader, who has taught you magic! Be sure I will cut off your hands and feet on opposite sides, and I will have you crucified on trunks

<table>
<tr><td></td><td>

of palm trees, so you shall know for certain which of us can give the more severe and the more lasting punishment."

2. They said: "Never shall we regard you as more than the clear signs that have come to us or than Him Who created us! So decree whatever you desire to decree, for you can only decree the life of this world.

3. "For us, we have believed in our Lord. May He forgive us our faults and the magic to which you did compel us, for Allah is best and most abiding.

4. "Verily, he who comes to his Lord as a sinner (at Judgment)—for him is Hell; therein shall he neither die nor live. But such as come to Him as believers who have worked righteous deeds—for them are ranks exalted."

</td></tr>
</table>

3 HUMAN DESTINY: DESTRUCTION OR FORGIVENESS

3.1 Perpetual Conflict between Evil and Righteous

The story of Moses illustrates various aspects of the conflict between the Messenger and the Quraish at the time of the Qur'an's revelation. As such, it also represents the conflict between evil and righteousness. In conclusion, the unbelievers are briefly admonished by being told that the Qur'an has been revealed in their own language for your own good. If they listen to it and follow its commands, they will be doing so for their own good, but if they reject it, they will meet with an evil end. God says in the Qur'an that He is most forgiving to those who repent, believe, do good deeds, and then continue to follow the right direction. The verses of Surah Ta-Ha that highlight the destiny of humanity with and without divine guidance are given in the table below.

Table 3.1 Destiny of Humankind: Forgiveness or Destruction

No	Surah:Verses	Meanings
		Pharaoh misguided his people and led them astray
1	20:077-079	• We sent an inspiration to Moses: "Travel by night with My servants, and strike a dry path

278

		for them through the sea, without fear of being overtaken (by Pharaoh) and without (any other) fear."
		• Then Pharaoh pursued them with his forces, but the waters completely overwhelmed them and covered them up. Pharaoh led his people astray instead of leading them aright.
		God Forgives those **who Repent, Believe, and do Good**
2	20:080-082	O you Children of Israel! 1. We delivered you from your enemy, and 2. We made a covenant with you on the right side of Mount (Sinai), and 3. We sent down to you manna and quails. • (Saying): "Eat of the good things We have provided for your sustenance, but commit no excess therein, lest My wrath should justly descend on you. And those on whom descends My wrath do perish indeed. • "But without doubt, I am (also) He that forgives again and again, to those who repent, believe, and do right—who, in fine, are ready to receive true guidance."

3.2 Associating others with God corrupts People

An incident from the story of the Israelites has been cited to show that no matter in what ridiculous manner the idolization of false gods and goddesses starts, the messengers of God do not tolerate even the slightest form of this erroneous practice. Therefore, Islam is following the former divine messages in opposing *Shirk* (polytheism or attributing partners to God) and the idol worship of today. The verses of Surah Ta-Ha that highlight the ease with which the people of Moses were corrupted by not following divine guidance are given below.

Table 3.2: The Trial of the Israelites

No	Surah:Verses	Meanings
		They Failed in their Trial by Worshiping Idol
3	20:083-089	(When Moses was up on the mount, Allah said:) "What made you hasten in advance of your people, O Moses?" 1. He replied: "Behold, they are close on my footsteps. I hastened to you, O my Lord, to

		please you."
		2. (Allah) said: "We have tested your people in your absence; the Samiri has led them astray."
		• So Moses returned to his people in a state of indignation and sorrow. He said: "O my people! Did not your Lord make a handsome promise to you? Did then the promise seem to you long (in coming), or did you desire that wrath should descend from your Lord on you, and so you broke your promise to me?"
		• They said: "We broke not the promise to you, as far as lay in our power. But we were made to carry the weight of the ornaments of the (whole) people, and we threw them (into the fire), and that was what the Samiri suggested. Then he brought out (of the fire) before the (people) the image of a calf. It seemed to low, so they said: 'This is your god and the god of Moses, but (Moses) has forgotten.'"
		Could they not see that it could not return them a word (for answer) and that it had no power either to harm them or to do them good?
		They refused to cease but kept Idol Worshiping
4	20:090-094	1. Aaron had already before this said to them: "O my people! You are being tested in this, for verily your Lord is (Allah) Most Gracious. So follow me, and obey my command."
		2. They had said: "We will not abandon this cult, but we will devote ourselves to it until Moses returns to us."
		3. (Moses) said: "O Aaron! What kept you back, when you saw them going wrong, from following me? Did you then disobey my order?"
		4. (Aaron) replied: "O son of my mother! Seize (me) not by my beard nor by (the hair of) my head! Truly, I feared lest you should say, 'You have caused a division among the children of Israel, and you did not respect my word.'"
		Samiri explains his Reasons for making the Idol
5	20:095-097	(Moses) said: "What then is your case, O Samiri?"
		1. He replied: "I saw what they saw not. So I took a handful (of dust) from the footprint of the messenger and threw it (into the calf).

		Thus did my soul suggest to me." 2. (Moses) said: "Get you gone! But your (punishment) in this life will be that you will say, 'Touch me not,' and moreover (for a future penalty) you have a promise that will not fail. Now look at your god, of whom you have become a devoted worshiper. We will certainly (melt) it in a blazing fire and scatter it broadcast in the sea."

3.3 The Admission of Error leads to Improvement

Using the story of Adam, God tells the unbelievers that the way they are following is the way of Satan, whereas the right way for humankind is to follow their father Adam. He was misguided by Satan, but when he realized his mistake, he plainly confessed it, repented, turned back to the servitude of God, and won His favor. On the other hand, if a person follows Satan and sticks to his error in spite of admonition, he does harm to himself.

Table 3.3
Adam's Admission of Error and God's Forgiveness

No	Surah:Verses	Meanings
		Adam has been created with weaknesses
6	20:115	We had already, beforehand, taken the covenant of Adam, but he forgot. And We found on his part no firm resolve.
		Satan did not make prostration to Adam
7	20:116-119	1. When We said to the angels, "Prostrate yourselves to Adam," they prostrated themselves. But not *Iblis*; he refused. 2. Then We said: "O Adam! Verily, this is an enemy to you and your wife. So let him not get you both out of the Garden, so that you are landed in misery. There is therein (enough provision) for you neither to go hungry nor to go naked, nor to suffer from thirst, nor from the suns heat."
		Satan made an evil suggestion to Adam
8	20:120-121	1. But Satan whispered evil to him. He said, "O Adam! Shall I lead you to the Tree of Eternity and to a kingdom that never decays?" 2. In the result, they both ate of the tree, and so their nakedness appeared to them. They began

		to sew together, for their covering, leaves from the Garden. Thus did Adam disobey his Lord and allow himself to be seduced.
		God's guidance keeps People out of Misery
9	20:122-123	1. But his Lord chose him (for His grace). He turned to him and gave him guidance. 2. He said: "Get you down, both of you all together, from the Garden, with enmity one to another. But if, as is sure, there comes to you guidance from Me, whosoever follows My guidance will not lose his way nor fall into misery."
		Consequences of Unbelief and Corruption
10	20:124-127	1. (Allah continued): "But whosoever turns away from My message, verily for him is a life narrowed down, and We shall raise him up blind on the Day of Judgment." 2. He will say: "O my Lord! Why have You raised me up blind, while I had sight (before)?" 3. (Allah) will say: "Thus did you, when Our revelations came unto you, disregard them. So will you, this day, be disregarded." Thus do We recompense him who transgresses beyond bounds and believes not in the revelations of his Lord: and the Penalty of the Hereafter is far more grievous and more enduring.

3.4 Always be Patient and Thankful to Your Lord

God has His Own scheme concerning the unbelievers. Therefore, the Messenger and the believers have been advised not to be impatient concerning their punishment. God doesn't seize them at once, but He gives them sufficient respite. Hence, one should not grow impatient, but bear persecutions with fortitude and go on conveying the message. God commands the Messenger and the believers to 1). Be patient about what unbelievers' say; 2). Glorify their Lord during the night and the day; 3). Wish not for what We have given the unbelievers because what We have given you is better; and 4). Enjoin prayer on your followers and steadily adhere to it.

Table 3.4: Take Heed and Pray to your Lord

No	Surah:Verses	Meanings
		Corruption Destroys Nations after their Appointed Term is Over
11	20:128-129	• Is it not a warning to such men (to know) how many generations before them We destroyed, in whose dwellings they (now) move? Verily, in this are signs for men endued with understanding. • Had it not been for a word that went forth before from your Lord, (their punishment) must necessarily have come, but there is a term appointed (for respite).
		Be Patient, Establish Prayer and be Contented
12	20:130-132	• Therefore, be patient with what they say— 1. And celebrate the praises of your Lord before the rising of the sun and before its setting, Yea, celebrate them for part of the hours of the night, and at the sides of the day, that you may have joy. 2. Nor strain your eyes in longing for the things We have given for enjoyment to parties of them, the splendor of the life of this world, through which We test them. 3. But the provision of your Lord is better and more enduring. 4. Enjoin prayer on your people, and be constant therein. ...

CHAPTER 19

The Conflict between Truth and Falsehood
FROM SURAH AL-ANBIYA (21)

In Surah Al-Anbiya, the conflict between the Messenger and the leaders of unbelievers is discussed. The objections and doubts put forward about Messenger's divine backing and the belief in *Tauheed* and the Hereafter are answered. The leaders of the unbelievers at Makkah are also criticized for their plotting against the Messenger, and they are warned about the consequences of their wicked activities. They are admonished to give up their indifference and the heedlessness that they were showing to the message. In conclusion, the unbelievers are told that the person whom they consider to be a distress and affliction has in reality come to them as a blessing.

1 THE MESSENGERS: THEIR MISSION AND EFFORTS

1.1 All Messengers were Human
The objection of the unbelievers that a human being could not be a messenger is refuted. God tells people that He sent none other than men as His messengers to whom He sent His revelation. If someone does not already know this, this can be confirmed by the People of the Book. None of these messengers was given bodies that ate no food, nor were they exempt from death. The unbeliever's multifarious and contradictory objections against the Messenger and the Qur'an are also negated. The unbelievers thought that life was merely a sport and pastime, that it had no purpose behind or before it, and that there was no accountability for their actions. This concept of life, which was responsible for their indifference and heedless attitude towards the divine message, is proven to be wrong.

Table 1.1: Argument of Unbelievers against the Messenger

No	Surah:Verses	Meanings
		God Answers the Unbelievers' Remarks
1	21:001-009	Closer and closer to mankind comes their reckoning. Yet, they heed not, and they turn away. Never comes to them of a renewed message from their Lord, but they listen to it as in jest, their hearts toying as with trifles. The wrongdoers conceal their private counsels, (saying), "Is this (one) more than a man like yourselves? Will you go to witchcraft with your eyes open?" • Say: "My Lord knows (every) word (spoken) in the heavens and on earth. He is the One that hears and knows." "Nay," they say, "(these are) medleys of dreams! Nay, he forged it. Nay, he is (but) a poet!" → Let him then bring us a Sign like the one that were sent to (prophets) of old. 1. (As to those) before them, not one of the populations which We destroyed believed. Will these believe? 2. Before you, also, the messengers We sent were but men to whom We granted inspiration. If you realize this not, ask of those who possess the message. 3. Nor did We give them bodies that ate no food, nor were they exempt from death. → In the end, We fulfilled to them Our promise, and We saved them and those whom We pleased, but We destroyed those who transgressed beyond bounds.

1.2 All Messengers have their Struggles in Life

Important events from the life histories of the messengers were cited to show that all those sent by God were human and had human characteristics. They had no share in Godhead, and they had to implore God to fulfill each and every necessity of theirs. All messengers had to struggle for the completion of their mission, which was to follow the same principles as were being presented in Islam. They had to pass through distress and affliction, and their opponents did their worst to thwart their mission. However, in spite of it, the messengers came out successful by the extraordinary help from God. They had one and the same religion, the same as was being presented in Islam, the right way of life. All other ways, which were invented and introduced by corrupt people, were utterly wrong. Several verses of Surah Al-Anbiya, citing the example of Abraham and earlier messengers and highlighting how God helped His messengers, are given in the table below.

Table 1.2: God Helped Abraham and earlier Messengers

No	Surah:Verses	Meanings
		Abraham, his Father and his People
2	21:051-057	1. We bestowed aforetime on Abraham his rectitude of conduct, and well were We acquainted with him. Behold! He said to his father and his people, "What are these images to which you are devoted?" They said, "We found our fathers worshiping them." 2. He said, "Indeed you have been in manifest error—you and your fathers." They said, "Have you brought us the truth, or are you one of those who jest?" 3. He said, "Nay, your Lord is the Lord of the heavens and the earth, He Who created them, and I am a witness to this (truth). And by Allah, I have a plan for your idols after you go away and turn your backs."
		Abraham broke the Idols into pieces
3	21:058-065	4. So he broke them to pieces, (all) but the biggest of them, that they might turn (and address themselves) to it. They said: "Who has done this to our gods? He must indeed be some man of impiety." They said: "We heard a youth talk of them. He is called Abraham." They said: "Then bring him before the eyes of the people that they may bear witness. They said: "Are you the one that did this with our gods, O Abraham?" 5. He said: "Nay, this was done by—this is their biggest one! Ask them, if they can speak." So they turned to themselves and said, "Surely you are the ones in the wrong!" Then were they confounded with shame.

		(They said), "You know full well that these do not speak."
		God Saved Abraham from the Fire
4	21:066-070	6. (Abraham) said: "Do you then worship besides Allah things that can neither be of any good to you nor do you harm? Fie upon you and upon the things that you worship besides Allah! Have you no sense?" 7. They said, "Burn him and protect your gods, if you do (anything at all)." 8. We said: "O fire! Be cool and (a means of) safety for Abraham." Then they sought a stratagem against him, but We made them the ones that lost most.
		God made Abraham's Children Leaders
5	21:071-073	9. But We delivered him and (his nephew) Lot (and directed them) to the land that We have blessed for the nations. 10. And We bestowed on him Isaac and, as an additional gift, Jacob, and We made righteous men of every one (of them). 11. We made them leaders, guiding (people) by Our command, and • We sent them inspiration to do good deeds, • To establish regular prayers, and • To practice regular charity; • And they constantly served Us (alone).
		Other Messengers **and Notables Besides Abraham**
6	21:074-075	1. And to Lot, too, We gave judgment and knowledge, and We saved him from the town that practiced abominations. Truly, they were a people given to evil, a rebellious people. And We admitted him to Our mercy, for he was one of the righteous.
7	21:076-077	2. (Remember) Noah, when he cried (to Us) aforetime. We listened to his (prayer) and delivered him and his family from great distress. We helped him against people who rejected Our signs. Truly, they were a people given to evil. So We drowned them (in the flood) all together.
8	21:078-082	3. Remember David and Solomon when they

287

		gave judgment in the matter of the field into which the sheep of certain people had strayed by night. We did witness their judgment. To Solomon We inspired the (right) understanding of the matter. To each (of them) We gave judgment and knowledge. It was Our power that made the hills and the birds celebrate Our praises with David. It was We Who did (all these things). It was We Who taught him the making of coats of mail for your benefit, to guard you from each other's violence. Will you then be grateful? 4. (It was Our power that made) the violent (unruly) wind flow (tamely) for Solomon, to his order, to the land that We had blessed, for We do know all things. And of the evil ones were some who dived for him and did other work besides, and it was We Who guarded them.
9	21:083-084	5. (Remember) Job when He cried to his Lord, "Truly distress has seized me, but You are the most merciful of those that are merciful." So We listened to him. We removed the distress that was on him, and We restored his family to him and doubled their number—as a grace from Ourselves, and a thing for commemoration, for all who serve Us.
10	21:085-086	6. (Remember) Isma'il, 7. Idris, and 8. Zul-kifl, all (men) of constancy and patience. We admitted them to Our mercy, for they were of the righteous ones.
11	21:087-088	9. Remember Dhu al Nun (Jonah) when he departed in wrath. He imagined that We had no power over him! But he cried through the depths of darkness, "There is no god but You. Glory to you. I was indeed wrong!" So We listened to him and delivered him from distress, and thus do We deliver those who have faith.
12	21:089-090	10. (Remember) Zakariya when he cried to his Lord: "O my Lord! Leave me not without offspring, though You are the best of inheritors." So We listened to him: and We

		granted him Yahya (John the Baptist). We cured his wife's (barrenness) for him. These (three) were ever quick in emulation in good works. They used to call on Us with love and reverence and humble themselves before Us.
13	21:091	And (remember) her (Mary) who guarded her chastity. We breathed into her of Our spirit, and We made her and her son a sign for all peoples.

1.3 Divine Guidance is God's Mercy to People

People have been told that it is a great favor from God that He has sent His messengers to inform and guide them to the right way, the way that leads them to success in the life of this world and that will result in success in the Hereafter. The unbelievers of Makkah, who considered the coming of the Messenger an affliction instead of a blessing, were told that God sent the Messenger as a mercy to people. While God has made each person responsible for his own actions, He has also provided guidance through the Qur'an and the example of the Messenger.

Table 1.3: The Messenger, God's Mercy to People

No	Surah:Verses	Meanings
		When and How the Corrupt will be Punished?
14	21:107-011	• We sent you (O Messenger) not, but as a mercy for all creatures. Say: "What has come to me by inspiration is that your Allah is One Allah. Will you, therefore, bow to His will (in Islam)?" • But if they turn back, say: "I have proclaimed the message to you all alike and in truth; 1. "I know not whether that which you are promised is near or far. It is He Who knows what is open in speech and what you hide (in your hearts). 2. "I know not but that it may be a trial for you and a grant of (worldly) livelihood (to you) for a time."
		The Messenger Appeals to God for Judgment
15	21:112	Say: "O my Lord! Judge You in truth! Our Lord Most Gracious is the One Whose assistance should be sought against the blasphemies you utter."

2 THE POLYTHEISM IS CONFUSION AND CHAOS

2.1 Divine Guidance Benefits Humankind

God tells us that He has revealed the Qur'an, in which all facts and principles that are beneficial in the life of this world have been mentioned and explained. The benefits could be spiritual, economic, social and political. These benefits are interconnected and interwoven in such a way that they cannot be isolated from each other. The Qur'an contains all of the moral and sociopolitical laws needed to regulate and reform human character and behavior. It also motivates people to do good deeds and to develop welfare communities. God further stresses this by asserting that the universe has a purpose behind its creation, and that purpose is to establish the supremacy of truth, reason and justice.

Table 2.1: Battleground between the Truth and Falsehood

No	Surah:Verses	Meanings
		Guidance is to benefit People in this Life
1	21:010-011	1. We have revealed for you (O people!) a book in which is a message for you. Will you not then understand? 2. How many were the populations We utterly destroyed because of their iniquities, setting up in their places other peoples!
		Purpose behind the creation of the universe
2	21:016-020	We did not create the heavens and the earth and what is between them for sport. Had We wished to make a diversion, We would have made it from before Ourselves. By no means would We do it. • Nay! We cast the truth against the falsehood, so that it breaks its head, and lo it vanishes, and woe to you for what you describe. Whoever is in the heavens and the earth is His, and Those who are with Him are not proud to serve Him, nor do they grow weary. They glorify Him by night and day; they are never languid.

2.2 Polytheism: Worshiping Others along with God

The main cause of the conflict between the unbelievers and the Messenger was the unbelievers' insistence on associating idols *(Shirk)* along with a single Creator *(Tauheed)*. The doctrine of *Shirk* was refuted and the doctrine of *Tauheed* was reinforced in Islam with the Qur'an stating that: (1) if there had been any gods except God, there would be perpetual conflict among them; and (2) people who worship other gods besides Him have no proof of the divinity of those whom they worship. The unbelievers also said that the Beneficent God had taken to Himself a son! Such people should know that there is no god but God; therefore, people should serve Him only. The verses of Surah Al-Anbiya stating that there is no other god except the One God are given in the table below.

Table 2.2: Polytheism is nothing but Confusion and Chaos

No	Surah:Verses	Meanings
		Bring your proof if You are truthful
3	21:021-023 21:024	• Or have they taken (for worship) gods from the earth who can raise (the dead)? If there were in the heavens and the earth other gods besides Allah, there would have been confusion in both! But glory to Allah, the Lord of the Throne, (high is He) above what they attribute to Him! He cannot be questioned for His acts, but they will be questioned (for theirs). • Or have they taken for worship (other) gods besides him? Say, "Bring your convincing proof. This is the message of those with me and the message of those before me." But most of them know not the truth and so turn away.
		There is no god but God; therefore, serve Him
4	21:025-029	Not a messenger did We send before you without this inspiration sent by Us to him: that there is no god but I; therefore, worship and serve Me. • And they say: "(Allah) Most Gracious has begotten offspring." Glory to Him! They are (but) servants raised to honor.

		1. They speak not before He speaks, and they act (in all things) by His command. He knows what is before them, and what is behind them, and 2. They offer no intercession except for those who are acceptable, and they stand in awe and reverence of His (glory). 3. If any of them should say, "I am a god besides Him," such a one We should reward with Hell. Thus do We reward those who do wrong.
		God is He who has Created the Universe
5	21:030, 032	1. *Heavens and the Earth* Do not the unbelievers see that the heavens and the earth were joined together (as one unit of creation) before We clove them asunder? We made from water every living thing. Will they not then believe...And We have made the heavens as a canopy well guarded; yet do they turn away from the signs which these things (point to)!
	21:031	2. *Mountains and Valleys* We have set on the earth mountains standing firm, lest it should shake with them, and We have made therein broad highways (between mountains) for them to pass through: that they may receive guidance.
	21:033	3. *The Sun and the Moon* It is He Who created the night and the day, and the sun and the moon: all (the celestial bodies) swim along, each in its rounded course.

2.3 Unbelief has its Consequences in both Worlds

The unbelievers of Makkah presumed that the Messenger was a false prophet and that his warnings of a scourge from God were empty threats, just because no scourge was visiting them in spite of their persistent rejection of the Messenger. Since God's sign will come at its time, people should be patient. God tells people in Surah Al-Anbiya: "Man is a creature of haste. Soon (enough) will I show you My signs. Then you will not ask Me to hasten them (Qur'an 20:37)." God's punishment will come all of a sudden and will cause them to become confounded, and they will not have the power to avert it.

Table 2.3: The Consequence of Unbelief

No	Surah:Verses	Meanings
		The Consequence of Unbelief in this World
6	21:038-044	They say: "When will this promise come to pass, if you are telling the truth?" 1. If only the unbelievers knew (the time) when they will not be able to ward off the fire from their faces, nor yet from their backs, and (when) no help can reach them. 2. Nay, it may come to them all of a sudden and confound them. No power will they have then to avert it, nor will they (then) get respite. 3. Mocked were (many) messengers before you, but their scoffers were hemmed in by the thing that they mocked. Say: "Who can keep you safe by night and by day from (the wrath of Allah) Most Gracious?" 1. Yet they turn away from the mention of their Lord. 2. Or have they gods that can guard them from Us? They have no power to aid themselves, nor can they be defended from Us. 3. Nay, We gave the good things of this life to these men and their fathers until the period grew long for them. 4. Do they see not that We gradually reduce the land (in their control) from its outlying borders? Is it then they who will win?
		On Resurrection, God shall deal with Justice
7	21:047-049	• We shall set up scales of justice for the Day of Judgment, so that not a soul will be dealt with unjustly in the least, and if there be (no more than) the weight of a mustard seed, We will bring it (to account), and enough are We to take account. • In the past We granted to Moses and Aaron the criterion (for judgment), and a light and a message for those who would do right—those who fear their Lord in their most secret thoughts, and who hold the Hour (of Judgment) in awe.

2.4 Unity of Human Faith and Human Brotherhood

God's message was and ever is the same, and His messengers treated it as such. It is people of narrower views who break up the message and the brotherhood into different camps and sects. This is absolutely wrong and un-Islamic. God tells people: "Verily, this brotherhood of yours is a single brotherhood, and I am your Lord and Cherisher. Therefore, serve Me (Qur'an 21:92)" and "Whoever works any act of righteousness and has faith—his endeavor will not be rejected. We shall record it in his favor (Qur'an 21:94)." Therefore, only those who follow the right way will come out successfully in the final judgment of God, and those who discard it shall meet with the worst consequences in the Hereafter. The verses of Surah Al-Anbiya and Surah Al-Zumar highlighting God's final judgment in the Hereafter are given in the table below.

Table 2.4: Righteous People will Inherit Paradise

No	Surah:Verses	Meanings
		The Believers on the Day of Judgment
8	21:101-103	Those for whom the good (record) from Us has gone before will be removed far there from. Not the slightest sound will they hear of Hell; what their souls desired, in that will they dwell. The Great Terror will bring them no grief, but the angels will meet them (with mutual greetings): "This is your Day—(the Day) that you were promised.
		Righteous People will Inherit Paradise
9	21:104-106	The day that We roll up the heavens like a scroll rolled up for books (completed)—even as We produced the first creation, so shall We produce a new one: a promise We have undertaken. Truly shall We fulfill it. 1. Before this We wrote in the Psalms, after the message (given to Moses): "My servants, the righteous shall inherit the earth." 2. Verily, in this (Qur'an) is a message for people who would worship Allah.
	39:073-074	And those who feared their Lord will be led to the Garden in crowds: until behold, they arrive there. 1. Its gates will be opened, and its keepers will say: "Peace be upon you! Well have you

		done! Enter you here, to dwell therein." 2. They will say: "Praise be to Allah, Who has truly fulfilled His promise to us and has given us (this) land in heritage. 3. "We can dwell in the Garden as we will. How excellent a reward for those who work (righteousness)!"
		The Unbelievers on the Day of Judgment
10	21:095-100	• But there is a ban on any population that We have destroyed: that they shall not return, until the Gog and Magog (people) are let through (their barrier), and they swiftly swarm from every hill. • Then will the true promise draw near (of fulfillment). Then behold! The eyes of the unbelievers will fixedly stare in horror: "Ah! Woe to us! We were indeed heedless of this; nay, we truly did wrong." Verily you (unbelievers) and the (false) gods that you worship besides Allah are (but) fuel for Hell! To it will you (surely) come! If these had been gods, they would not have got there, but each one will abide therein. There, sobbing will be their lot, nor will they there hear (anything else).

CHAPTER 20

Fight against Oppression and Injustice
FROM SURAH AL-HAJJ (22)

Islam is all about one's behavior as an individual and as a member of the society. If an individual fulfills all his obligations, he is successful in this life and will be successful on the Day of Judgment. God tells people that their efforts, their striving or their *Jihad*, to which God and the Messenger calls them, will certainly preserve their lives and security. The believers are allowed and encouraged to fight against oppression and injustice. They are also given instructions to adopt the right and just attitude as and when they acquired power to rule in the land. "Those who, if We establish them in the land, establish regular prayer and give regular charity, enjoin the right and forbid wrong...(Qur'an 22:41)."

1 GOD, THE CREATOR—SOME OBEY; OTHERS DON'T

1.1 God's Servitude—Prerequisite to Success
The physical, moral, and sociopolitical laws of nature that God has set in operation favor no one person over another. When believers fall short of meeting any of these conditions, they have to accept the consequences. Being Muslims and believers does not mean that the laws of nature should be suspended or abrogated for their sakes. Implementation of God's law must be based in the first instance on submission to Him. Indeed, this is the very meaning of Islam. When people have shown their obedience, they may use their minds to identify, as much as possible, God's purpose behind His commandment or prohibition. Whether or not this purpose is stated in the Qur'an or understood by human intellect, it must be remembered that God, not people, is the final arbiter and judge. The verses of Surah Al-Hajj highlighting that whoever is in the heavens and the earth obeys God are given in the table below.

Table 1.1: All in the Heavens and the Earth Obeys God

No	Surah:Verses	Meanings
		All things in the Heavens and on Earth bow down to God
1	22:018	1. Don't you see that to Allah bow down in worship all things that are in the heavens and on earth—the sun, the moon, the stars, the hills, the trees, the animals, and a great number among mankind? 2. But a great number are (also) such as are fit for punishment, and such as Allah shall disgrace none can raise to honor, for Allah carries out all that He wills.
		God is He Who is Strong and Able to Carry out His Will
2	22:074-076	1. No just estimate have they made of Allah, for Allah is He Who is strong and able to carry out His will. 2. Allah chooses messengers from angels and from men, for Allah is He Who hears and sees (all things). 3. He knows what is before them and what is behind them, and to Allah go back all questions (for decision).

1.2 People Who Neither Serve Nor Obey God

People who claim that they believe, but who still fail to implement God's law in their lives, or who are not satisfied when God's law is enforced on them, do indeed make false claims. They say with their mouth, "We believe" while their hearts do not believe. Do some people not seek rulings in order to evade their religious duties, rather than to carry them out? They occasionally try to pay lip service to religion so that it may approve and endorse their selfish desires. Having received the divine revelation, they are guilty of ignoring their duties. Such people fall into (1) the Wavering Muslims, (2) the Polytheists or *Mushriks* and the Unbelievers.

The Wavering Muslims are those who had embraced Islam but are not prepared to endure any hardship in its way. They have been asked: "What is this faith of yours?" On the one hand, they are ready to believe in God and become His servants, provided they are given peace and prosperity, but on the other, if they meet with afflictions and hardships in His way, they discard their God and cease to remain His servants. One should understand that this wavering attitude cannot avert those misfortunes and losses that God has ordained for someone.

The Polytheists or *Mushriks* are those who associate others with God. They are warned: "You have persisted in your ideas of ignorance and trusted in your deities instead of God, though they possess no power at all, and you have repudiated the Messenger. Now yours will be the same fate as has been the doom of those like you before. You have only harmed yourselves by rejecting the Messenger and by persecuting the believers. False deities and selfish desires shall not be able to benefit or save you from the wrath of God."

The Unbelievers are those arrogant people who know that the faith is readily available to them, but they barter it away for disbelief. They are too weak to cause God any harm whatsoever. Error has no supporting basis, and falsehood has no strength. Its advocates cannot harm those who respond to God's call, although they may have for a short while forces with which they can inflict harm on the believers.

Table 1.2: Various Classes of Unbelievers

No	Surah:Verses	Meanings
		Wavering Muslims endure no hardship
3	22:011	• There are among men some who serve Allah, as it were, on the verge, If good befalls them, they are, therewith, well content. • But if a trial comes to them, they turn on their faces. They lose both this world and the Hereafter; that is loss for all to see.
		The *Mushriks* associate others with God
4	22:012	1. They call on such deities, besides Allah, as can neither hurt nor profit them; that is straying far indeed (from the way).
	22:013	2. (Perhaps) they call on one whose hurt is nearer than his profit. Evil, indeed, is the patron, and evil the companion.
	22:071	3. Yet they worship, besides Allah, things for

	22:073	which no authority has been sent down to them, and of which they have no knowledge. For those that do wrong there is no helper. 4. O people! Here is a parable set forth! Listen to it! Those on whom, besides Allah, you call, cannot create (even) a fly, if they all met together for the purpose! And if the fly should snatch away anything from them, they would have no power to release it from the fly. Feeble are those who petition and those whom they petition.
		God has Promised Fire to the Unbelievers
5	22:072	• When Our clear revelations are recited to them, you will notice a denial on the faces of the unbelievers! They nearly attack with violence those who recite to them Our revelations. • Say, "Shall I tell you of something (far) worse than this? It is the fire (of Hell)! Allah has promised it to the Unbelievers! And evil is that destination!"

2 PEOPLE ARE ACCOUNTABLE FOR THEIR DEEDS

2.1 Accountability of People's Behavior in this World

If people fulfill all their moral, financial, and sociopolitical obligations, they are successful in this life, and their communities will be prosperous, peaceful, and secure. They will also be successful on the Day of Judgment. God tells us: "O you who believe! Give your response to Allah and His Messenger when He calls you to that which will give you life, and know that Allah comes in between a man and his heart and that it is He to Whom you shall (all) be gathered (Qur'an 8:24)."

In contrast, if most of the people are unbelievers and follow their personal desires with a disregard for any moral and sociopolitical laws of nature, then that community is eventually bound to fail and to be destroyed. God commands: "And fear tumult or oppression, which affects not in particular (only) those of you who do wrong, and know that Allah is strict in punishment (Qur'an 8:25)." Then God goes on to say: "Generations before you We destroyed when they did wrong. Their messengers came to them with clear signs, but they would not believe! Thus do We requite those who sin! Then We made you heirs in the land after them, to see how you would behave (Qur'an 10:13-14)."

Table 2.1: Unjust Communities are eventually Destroyed

No	Surah:Verses	Meanings
		God gives Respite to the Unbelievers, then Overtakes Them
1	22:042-048	1. If they treat your (mission) as false, so did the peoples before them (with their prophets)—the people of Noah and 'Ad and Thamud, those of Abraham and Lot, and the Companions of the Madyan people, and Moses was rejected (in the same way). 2. But I granted respite to the unbelievers, and (only) after that did I punish them. But how (terrible) was my rejection (of them). 3. How many populations have We destroyed, which were given to wrongdoing? They tumbled down on their roofs. And how many wells are lying idle and neglected, and castles lofty and well built? 4. Do they not travel through the land, so that their hearts (and minds) may thus learn wisdom, and their ears may thus learn to hear? Truly, it is not their eyes that are blind, but their hearts that are in their breasts. 5. Yet, they ask you to hasten on the punishment! But Allah will not fail in His promise. Verily, a day in the sight of your Lord is like a thousand years of your reckoning. 6. And to how many populations did I give respites, which (populations) were given to wrongdoing? In the end, I punished them. To me is the destination (of all).
		God Forgives and gives Sustenance to Believers who do Good
2	22:049-051	Say: "O people! I am (sent) to you only to give a clear warning. 1. "Those who believe and work righteousness, for them is forgiveness and sustenance most generous. 2. "But those who strive against Our signs to

300

		frustrate them—they will be companions of the fire."

2.2 The Inevitability of Resurrection and Accountability

Only ignorant people dispute about God, and they do so without knowledge, guidance, or any other source of knowledge, turning away arrogantly to misguide others. If people desire to safeguard against their disgrace in this world and on the Day of Resurrection, which is inevitable if they keep on discussing God without first learning about Him, His creation, and His physical, moral, and sociopolitical laws, then they must learn from the divine guidance found in the Qur'an. One should know exactly what will be the consequences of violating God's laws. For example, discussing a book without first reading it will sound ridiculous, but one hears people discussing the Qur'an without first reading and understanding what exactly is written in it. Again, to those who are in doubt about their resurrection, God asks them to reflect on their own birth and the sterile land that stirs, swells, and brings forth every kind of beautiful vegetation after rain.

Table 2.2: Resurrection and Accountability of one's Deeds

No	Surah:Verses	Meanings
		The Resurrection and the Day of Judgment
3	22:001-002	O people! Fear your Lord! For the convulsion of the Hour (of Judgment) will be a thing terrible. The day you shall see it, 1. Every mother giving suck shall forget her suckling babe, and 2. Every pregnant female shall drop her load (unformed). 3. You shall see mankind as in a drunken riot, yet not drunk, but dreadful will be the Wrath of Allah.
		If in Doubt about the Resurrection, then Reflect on
4	22:005-007	*1. Your Own Birth and the Life* O people! If you have a doubt about the resurrection, (consider) that We created you out of dust, then out of sperm, then out of a leech-like clot, then out of a morsel of flesh, partly formed and partly unformed, in order that We may

301

		manifest (our power) to you. And We cause whom We will to rest in the wombs for an appointed term; then do We bring you out as babes, then (foster you) that you may reach your age of full strength. And some of you are called to die, and some are sent back to the feeblest old age, so that they know nothing after having known (so much).
		2. *Earth, Rain, and Vegetation*
		And you see the earth barren and lifeless, but when We pour down rain on it, it is stirred (to life); it swells, and it puts forth every kind of beautiful growth (in pairs).
		1. This is so,
		2. Because Allah is the Reality.
		3. It is He Who gives life to the dead, and
		4. It is He Who has power over all things.
		5. Verily, the Hour will come. There can be no doubt about it, or about (the fact) that
		6. Allah will raise up all who are in the graves.
		The Ignorant Dispute about God and follow Satan
5	22:003-004	• And yet among men there are such as dispute about Allah without knowledge and follow every evil one obstinate in rebellion! About the (Evil One), it is decreed that whoever turns to him for friendship, him will he lead astray, and he will guide him to the penalty of the fire.
	22:008-009	• Yet, there is among men such a one as disputes about Allah without knowledge, without guidance, and without a book of enlightenment, (disdainfully) bending his side, in order to lead (people) astray from the path of Allah. For him, there is disgrace in this life, and on the Day of Judgment We shall make him taste the penalty of burning (fire).
	22:010	• (It will be said): "This is because of the deeds that your hands sent forth, for verily Allah is not unjust to His servants.

2.3 Accountability on the Day of Resurrection

Islam considers every person to be a potential believer. Indeed, mankind is the material with which Islam deals in order to produce a real human society, one that is characterized by the fact that its members enjoin the doing of right, forbid what is wrong, and believe in the Oneness of God. Exercising their free will without compulsion, people can join this society and contribute to its growth by believing and doing good deeds. Since peoples' actions, either good or bad, have their own specific consequences, God will judge all people on the Day of Judgment. At that time, all people will be classified into two distinct groups: (1) unbelievers who will face the consequences of their unbelief and evil deeds, and (2) those who believed and did good deeds and whom God will make enter gardens beneath which rivers flow.

Table 2.3: Accountability of the Believers and Unbelievers

No	Surah:Verses	Meanings
		Believers, People of Scriptures, and Polytheists
6	22:017	1. Those who believe (in the Qur'an), 2. Those who follow the Jewish (scriptures), and the Sabians, Christians, Magians, and 3. Polytheists, Allah will judge between them on the Day of Judgment: for Allah is witness of all things.
		Unbelievers and Believers Who do Good Deeds
7	22:019-024	These two antagonists dispute with each other about their Lord. 1. But those who deny (their Lord)—for them will be cut out a garment of fire. Over their heads will be poured out boiling water. With it will be scalded what is within their bodies, as well as (their) skins. In addition, there will be maces of iron (to punish) them. Every time they wish to get away there from, from anguish, they will be forced back therein, and (it will be said), "Taste you the penalty of burning." 2. Allah will admit those who believe and work righteous deeds to gardens beneath which rivers flow. They shall be adorned therein with bracelets of gold and pearls, and their garments there will be of silk, for they have been guided (in this life) to the purest of speeches. They have been guided to the path of Him Who is worthy of praise.

3 VIRTUE HAS ALWAYS BEEN OPPOSED BY EVIL

Virtue, as preached by the messengers, is always opposed by the evil created by Satan's interference in the efforts of the messengers and the believers. God and belief in Him make it easier for a believer to avoid evil by ignoring Satan's invitations. People who have religious knowledge know the truth and are not easily fooled by satanic ideas and instigations. In contrast, those who disbelieve are easily fooled by Satan, who will persuade them to indulge in sin and to abandon the path that draws them nearer to God. This situation will continue until the Hour overtakes them and there comes on them the punishment of the Day of Judgment.

3.1 God Eradicates the Interference of Satan

God has given certain power to Satan that enables him to try to seduce people away from His path. With his cunning, Satan makes use of all sorts of attractions and temptations to lure people to disregard totally what God has forbidden and what He has made lawful by holding before them the prospect of immediate enjoyment and pleasure. As the creation of Adam and assigning him the task of the building the earth was the occasion at which Satan committed his grave sin by disobeying God, Satan has sworn to do his utmost to seduce people into committing sins and disobeying God so that they will share in his suffering on the Day of Judgment. To achieve this, Satan tries all methods and arguments to drag people to that which incurs God's displeasure.

That Satan has much power is true, but what is also true is that people can have far greater power. This they can acquire through faith. A person with firm belief in God and the Day of Judgment, and with the fear of God uppermost in his mind, is always able to defeat Satan and to triumph over Satan's cunning. He will fare even better if he fortifies his faith with a good and continuous study of the faith of Islam. The Prophet said: "A single scholar is much harder for Satan to defeat than a thousand worshipers (Al-Hadith: vol. 1, p. 353)." This *Hadith* is well to the point. A believer who knows the principles of Islam, understands its message, and believes in it can always foil the attempts of Satan

304

to seduce him. In his opposition to Satan, he is stronger than a thousand worshipers who simply offer their worship without supporting it with the knowledge that will keep them on the right track. The Qur'an cures us from doubts and gives us reassurance when we carefully contemplate the meaning of its verses and understand its message.

Table 3.1: God Removes Satan's Interference for Believers

No	Surah:Verses	Meanings
		Satan, a Trial for the Hypocrites and Unbelievers
1	22:052-053	1. Never did We send a messenger or a prophet before you, but when he framed a desire, Satan threw some (vanity) into his desire. 2. But Allah will cancel anything (vain) that Satan throws in. And Allah will confirm (and establish) His signs, for Allah is full of knowledge and wisdom— 3. That He may make the suggestions thrown in by Satan but a trial • For those in whose hearts is a disease and • Who are hardened of heart. Verily the wrongdoers are in a schism far (from the truth).
		Islamic Knowledge **Fortifies and Strengthen the Believers**
2	22:054-055	1. And that those on whom knowledge has been bestowed may learn that • The (Qur'an) is the truth from your Lord, • That they may believe therein, and • Their hearts may be made humbly (open) to it: 2. For Verily Allah is the guide of those who believe, to the straight way. 3. Those who reject faith will not cease to be in doubt concerning (revelation) Until the Hour (of Judgment) comes suddenly upon them, Or there comes to them the penalty of a day of disaster.
		Believers and Unbelievers on the Judgment Day
3	22:056-057	1. On that day, the dominion will be that of Allah. He will judge between them. So those who believe and work righteous deeds will be in gardens of delight.

		2. For those who reject faith and deny Our signs, there will be a humiliating punishment.

3.2 Each Community has a Way of Worship

Specific ways of worship were prescribed by the earlier messengers for their individual communities. Similarly, Islam has a particular way of worship for its community. No one is entitled to dispute this because this is the way that is suitable for the present age. God says in Surah Al-Kafirun: "Say: 'O you that reject faith! I worship not that which you worship, nor will you worship that which I worship. And I will not worship that which you have been wont to worship, nor will you worship that which I worship. To you be your way, and to me mine (Qur'an 109:1-6)." In Surah Al-Hajj, God tells the believers that there is a way of worship prescribed for every people: "To every people have We appointed rites and ceremonies that they follow. Let them not then dispute with you on the matter, but do you invite (them) to your Lord, for you are assuredly on the right way. If they do wrangle with you, say, 'Allah knows best what it is you are doing. Allah will judge between you on the Day of Judgment concerning the matters in which you differ' (Qur'an 22:67-69)."

3.3 Virtuous People Respect God's Signs

The believers were told that the unbelievers of Makkah had no right to prohibit them from visiting the Sacred Mosque. They had no right to prevent anyone from performing *Hajj* because the Sacred Mosque is God's sign and not their private property. This objection was not only justified, but it also acted as an effective political argument against the Quraish. It posed a question to the other tribes of Arabia, i.e., were the Quraish mere attendants of the Sacred Mosque or its owners? If the Quraish succeeded in debarring the Muslims from *Hajj* without any protest from others, they would feel encouraged in the future to debar from *Hajj* and *Umrah* the people of any other tribe who happened to have strained relations with the Quraish. Further, the history of the Sacred Mosque confirmed that it was built by Abraham by God's command and that God had invited all people to perform *Hajj* there. That is why those coming from outside the area had enjoyed equal rights by the local people from the very beginning. It was also clarified that the Sacred Mosque was not built for the

306

rituals of whatever partners they associated with God, but for the worship of the One God.

Table 3.3: Sacred Mosque was built to Worship One God

No	Surah:Verses	Meanings
		Pilgrimage should be Facilitated, not Hindered
4	22:025	As to those who have rejected (Allah) and would keep back (men) from the way of Allah and from the Sacred Mosque, which We have made (open) to (all) men, equal is the dweller there and the visitor from the country. And any whose purpose therein is profanity or wrong-doing, them will We cause to taste of a most grievous penalty.
		Pilgrimage to Makkah is to Worship One God
5	22:026-029	1. Behold! We gave the site, to Abraham, of the (Sacred) House, (saying): "Associate not anything (in worship) with Me, and sanctify My House for those who compass it round, or stand up, or bow, or prostrate themselves (therein in prayer). 2. "And proclaim the pilgrimage among men. They will come to you on foot and (mounted) on every kind of camel, lean on account of journeys through deep and distant mountain highways • "That they may witness the benefits (provided) for them and celebrate the name of Allah through the days appointed over the cattle that He has provided for them (for sacrifice). Then eat you thereof and feed the distressed ones in want. • "Then let them complete the rites prescribed for them, perform their vows, and (again) circumambulate the Ancient House."
		Respect for God's Signs indicate Piety of Hearts
6	22:030-033	1. Such (is the pilgrimage). Whoever honors the sacred rites of Allah, for him it is good in the sight of his Lord. Lawful to you (for food in pilgrimage) are cattle, except those mentioned to you (as exceptions), but shun the abomination of idols, and shun the word that is false— 2. Being true in faith to Allah and never

		assigning partners to Him. If anyone assigns partners to Allah, he is as if he had fallen from heaven and been snatched up by birds, or the wind had swooped (like a bird on its prey) and thrown him into a far-distant place. 3. Such (is his state), and whoever holds in honor the symbols of Allah, (in the sacrifice of animals), such (honor) should come truly from piety of heart. In them, you have benefits for a term appointed. In the end, their place of sacrifice is near the Ancient House.
		There is Good news for those Who do Good
7	22:034-035	1. To every people did We appoint rites (of sacrifice) that they might celebrate the name of Allah over the sustenance He gave them from animals (fit for food). • But your god is One God. Submit then your wills to Him (in Islam), and give you the good news to those who humble themselves— • To those whose hearts when Allah is mentioned are filled with fear, who show patient perseverance over their afflictions, keep up regular prayer, and spend (in charity) out of what We have bestowed upon them.
	22:037	2. It is not their meat nor their blood, that reaches Allah: it is your piety that reaches Him: He has thus made them subject to you, that you may glorify Allah for His Guidance to you and proclaim the good news to all who do right.

4 THE FIGHT AGAINST OPPRESSION AND INJUSTICE

4.1 Protection and Defense of Human Society

Believers are allowed and encouraged to fight against oppression and injustice. God expects the believers to fight against oppression and injustice. If the believers ignore this, they have to accept the consequences. The laws of nature cannot be suspended or ignored for the sake of the believers. The law that protects human society is based on the fact that if God didn't stop the corruption of some people by the actions of others, the former would certainly have destroyed cloisters, churches, synagogues, and mosques in which God's name is much remembered. Therefore, the right and just attitude of the believers is that when they are given power to rule in the land, they should keep up prayer, pay the poor-rate, enjoin good, and forbid evil. The verses of Surah Al-Hajj explaining why and how the believers should defend human society are given in the table below.

Table 4.1: People should defend Their Society

No	Surah:Verses	Meanings
		Fighting in the defense of human society
1	22:039-041	To those against whom war is made, permission is given (to fight) because they are wronged—and verily Allah is most powerful for their aid. 1. (They are) those who have been expelled from their homes in defiance of right (for no cause) except that they say, "Our Lord is Allah." • Had not Allah checked one set of people by means of another, there would surely have been pulled down monasteries, churches, synagogues, and mosques in which the name of Allah is commemorated in abundant measure. • Allah will certainly aid those who aid his (cause), for verily Allah is full of strength, exalted in might, (able to enforce His will). 2. Those who, if We establish them in the land, establish regular prayer and give regular charity, enjoin the right and forbid wrong: With Allah rests the end of (all) affairs.
		God's promise to those who die in God's way
2	22:058-059	1. Those who leave their homes in the cause of Allah and are then slain or die—on them will Allah bestow verily a goodly provision. Truly, Allah is He Who bestows the best provision. 2. Verily, He will admit them to a place with which they shall be well pleased, for Allah is All Knowing, Most Forbearing.

4.2 God Helps Those Who Fight Injustice and Oppression

One of the main features of a good, virtuous, and strong society is the high esteem given to enjoining what is right and forbidding what is wrong. Such a society is rich with people who undertake this task and with ones who are ready to listen to them. It was narrated by Anas that the Messenger said, "Help your brother, whether he is an oppressor or he is an oppressed one." People asked, "O Allah's Messenger! It is all right to help him if he is oppressed, but how should we help him if he is an oppressor?" The Prophet said, "By preventing him from oppressing others" (Sahih Bukhari: 3. 43. 624). God will certainly help those who retaliate with the like of that with which they have been afflicted and oppressed. God's help is assured because it is God's promise, and He has everything that is needed to fulfill His promise.

Table 4.2: God Helps those Who Retaliate when Oppressed

No	Surah:Verses	Meanings
		God Promises Help to the Believers
3	22:038	• Verily Allah will defend (from ill) those who believe. Verily, Allah loves not any that is a traitor to faith or shows ingratitude.
	22:060	• That (is so). And if one has retaliated to no greater extent than the injury he received, and is again set upon inordinately, Allah will help him, for Allah is One that blots out (sins) and forgives.
		God has the Ability to fulfill His Promise
4	22:061-066	1. That is because Allah merges night into day, and He merges day into night, and verily it is Allah Who hears and sees (all things).
		2. That is because Allah—He is the Reality, and those besides Him whom they invoke—they are but vain falsehood. Verily, Allah is He, Most High, Most Great.
		3. Do you not see that Allah sends down rain from the sky, and forthwith the earth becomes clothed with green? For Allah is He Who understands the finest mysteries and is well acquainted (with them).
		4. To Him belongs all that is in the heavens and on earth, for verily Allah—He is free of all

		wants, worthy of all praise.
	5.	Don't you see that Allah has made subject to you (people) all that is on the earth and the ships that sail through the sea by His command?
	6.	He withholds the sky (rain) from falling on the earth except by His leave, for Allah is most kind and most merciful.
	7.	It is He Who gave you life, will cause you to die, and will again give you life. Truly man is a most ungrateful creature!

4.3 Believers are those Who have Islamic Behavior

When it comes to the establishment of a human community and life on the basis of Islamic values, men and women have equal opportunities and similar roles and responsibilities. This is illustrated in Surah Al-Ahzab: "For Muslim men and women, for believing men and women, for devout men and women, for true men and women, for men and women who are patient and constant, for men and women who humble themselves, for men and women who give in charity, for men and women who fast (and deny themselves), for men and women who guard their chastity, and for men and women who engage much in Allah's praise—for them has Allah prepared forgiveness and great reward (Qur'an 33:35)." These qualities grouped together in this one verse work together to form an Islamic character. These are the characteristics of: self-surrender to God, faith, devotion, being true to one's word, patience in adversity, humility before God, being charitable, fasting, being mindful of one's chastity, and remembering God at all times. Each quality has its own role to play in a believer's life.

In Surah Al-Hajj, God tells the believers that they will succeed if they bow down and prostrate themselves, serve their Lord, and do good deeds. The believers are officially given the name of Muslims, and they are the real heirs of Abraham. Muslims have been chosen to witnesses the truth to humankind. So, they should establish prayer, give charity and try to become the best models of righteous living and of striving hard in the way of God.

311

Table 4.3: Serve your Lord and do Good deeds to Succeed

No	Surah:Verses	Meanings
5	22:077-078	O you who believe! 1. Bow down, prostrate yourselves, and adore your Lord, and 2. Do good (deeds) that you may prosper. 3. And strive in His cause as you ought to strive, (with sincerity and under discipline). He has chosen you and has imposed no difficulties on you in religion. It is the cult of your father Abraham. It is He Who has named you Muslims, both before and in this (revelation); that the Messenger may be a witness for you, and you be witnesses for mankind! Therefore, 1. Establish regular prayer, 2. Give regular charity, and 3. Hold fast to Allah! He is your protector—the best to protect and the best to help!

CHAPTER 21

Criteria for Self-Evaluation and Success

FROM SURAH AL-MU'MINUN (23), SURAH AN-NUR (24),
SURAH AL-AHZAB (33), SURAH AL-HUJURAT (49), SURAH
AL-FURQAN (25), AND SURAH AL-QALAM (68)

Part 1
Righteous Character and Behavior
FROM SURAH AL-MU'MINUN (23)

Humanity is the God's trustee on earth. The very nature of this assignment demands that the believers should possess the required moral character and behavior, without which it is unlikely they can succeed. The complexity of its formation and operation of the universe, including humanity, provides clear signs that confirm the existence of a Creator and His message, which is to guide humanity regarding the requirements of being a trustee. No believer can doubt that God, Who has already created the universe, has the power to resurrect people to have them account for their performance on earth.

Success and prosperity in the worldly life is not a criterion for success in the sight of God. If some people are enjoying prosperity, wealth, power, etc. in this world, it does not necessarily mean that they are favorites of God. Similarly, poverty and adversity are not a proof of God's displeasure. The important thing is not whether a person is rich or poor. It is what he does in the situation in which he finds himself. Does he make faith the factor that determines his actions, or does his fortune determine the degree of influence his faith has over his behavior? If one earns money in a lawful way, without exploiting or cheating, and if one uses it for lawful purposes, not forgetting one's religious and social obligations, then wealth is likely to increase one's reward from God. The real criterion for success is the morality of people.

313

1 ISLAM AIMS AT DEVELOPING PEOPLE

1.1 Build a Home in Paradise with Your Character

There are numerous *Ahadith* in which the Messenger stressed the importance of individual character and behavior of people. If we desire the Messenger's affection, if we like our faith to be perfect, if we want to worship God all the time, or if we want to assure our place in the heaven, then we can achieve all this by perfecting our character and behavior by following God's commands as given in the Qur'an. It was narrated by Abdullah bin Amr that the Messenger used to say: "The most beloved to me amongst you is the one who has the best character and manners (Sahih Bukhari: 5.57.104)." It was narrated by Abu Huraira that the Prophet said: "The most perfect believer with respect to faith is he who is best of them in manners (Abu Dawud: 40.4665)." A'ishah, *Ummul Mu'minin* (mother of the believers), narrated that the Messenger said: "By his good character, a believer will attain the degree of one who prays during the night and fasts during the day (Abu Dawud: 41.4780)." It was narrated by Abu Darda that the Prophet said: "There is nothing heavier put in the scale of a believer on the Day of Resurrection than good character (Abu Dawud: 41.4781)." Finally, it was narrated by Abu Umamah that the Prophet said: "I guarantee a house in the surroundings of Paradise for a man who avoids quarrelling, even if he was in the right, a house in the middle of Paradise for a man who avoids lying, even if he was joking, and a house in the upper part of Paradise for a man who made his character good (Abu Dawud: 41.4782)."

1.2 Build a Paradise on Earth with Your Morality

The ten short verses in the beginning of Surah Al-Mu'minun outline a code of morality that covers private and public situations, as well as relations with God and social dealings. Thus, humility in prayers symbolizes man's relationship with God to whom prayers are addressed, while turning away from frivolity indicates following a code of serious morality. Charity is a fulfillment of a social duty by which the rich look after the poor so that no one is left without being looked after. Maintaining virtuous standards in the fulfillment of sexual desire

314

means that sex must be confined within the bounds of marriage. No excess is permissible in Islam. This preserves a standard of purity and cleanliness in family and community relations that is bound to benefit everyone—parents and children, as well as the community as a whole. Fulfillment of trust and pledges sets relationships within society on a basis of complete honesty and sincerity. This makes for a much closer community in which every individual finds support and in which the whole community prospers. When such standards are maintained, the result is virtuous life in this world and Heaven in the Hereafter. This is a double success.

Qur'anic morality and good manners are much wider and more varied than what these ten short verses sum up. It is in this light that we should read the Prophet's own statement: "I have been sent with my message only to perfect good manners and morality (Malik, Muwatta: 47.1.8)." Thus, setting moral standards on a level of perfection is the objective of the final divine message, which remains the point of reference for all humanity at all times. When we say that the Prophet's manners were an embodiment of the Qur'anic teachings, we are confirming his perfect morality. Hence, it is not surprising that he is described in the Qur'an as having a "great moral standard (Qur'an 68:4)." That is why none can do better than to emulate the Prophet in all actions and situations.

2 SIGNS WHICH CONFIRM THE TRUTH OF ISLAM

2.1 Islamic Moral Character and Behavior

The fact that the people who accepted Islam started reforming their character confirms the truth of the message. These qualities can also be used as criteria to judge oneself or others regarding to how good a believer he/she is? The five characteristics that make believers successful are that they: (1) offer their prayers with solemnity and full submissiveness, (2) guard their chastity except before their mates or those whom their right hands possess, (3) keep aloof from what is vain, (4) are the givers of charity, and (5) keep their trusts and their promises. Such people, according to the Qur'an are the heirs and shall inherit the Paradise.

Table 2.1: Successful Indeed are the Believers

No	Surah:Verses	Meanings
		Paradise on the Earth
1	23:001-006 23:008-009	The believers must (eventually) win through. Those 1. Who humble themselves in their prayers, 2. Who avoid vain talk. 3. Who are active in deeds of charity. 4. Who abstain from sex, except with those joined to them in the marriage bond, or whom their right hands possess—for (in their case) they are free from blame... 5. Those who faithfully observe their trusts and their covenants, and 6. Who (strictly) guard their prayers.
		The Paradise in the Hereafter
2	23:010-011	These will be the heirs who will inherit Paradise; they will dwell therein (forever).

2.2 Creation of the Universe and Humankind

Divine Message, which is based on *Tauheed* and Hereafter, is only for the betterment of human life in this world. The physical, moral and sociopolitical laws of nature that God has put in place are to keep the universe and human society in proper operation. In the Hereafter, people will either be rewarded or punished, according to how they behaved on earth and what they did to prove that their behavior was really human in dealing with others.

Table 2.2: Birth and Rebirth of Humankind

No	Surah:Verses	Meanings
		Creation and the Birth of Humankind
3	23:012-014	1. Man We did create from a quintessence (of clay). 2. Then We placed him as (a drop of) sperm in a place of rest, firmly fixed. Then We made the sperm into a clot of congealed blood; then of that clot We made a (fetus) lump; then we made out of that lump bones and clothed the

			bones with flesh; then We developed out of it another creature. So blessed be Allah, the best to create.
			Death and Resurrection of Humankind
4	23:015-016	1.	After that, at length you will die.
		2.	Again, on the Day of Judgment, you will be raised up.

2.3 The Universe and its Laws Confirm Resurrection

People have been invited to observe the complexity of the formation and operation of themselves and the universe. The universality of a single set of physical, moral, and sociopolitical laws leads one to reflect that such laws could have come only from a single source, i.e., the One God. This provides a clear proof that confirms the truth of Islam. Citing the examples from the universe, an attempt has been made to convince people about the truth of resurrection. The verses of Surah Al-Mu'minun that highlight that God has enough power to resurrect people are given in the table below.

Table 2.3: God has Power to Resurrect People

No	Surah:Verses		Meanings
			God is He Who has Created the Universe
5	23:017	1.	*The Universe:* We have made above you seven tracts, and We are never unmindful of (our) creation.
	23:018	2.	*Water:* We send down water from the sky according to (due) measure, and We cause it to soak in the soil; and We certainly are able to drain it off (with ease).
	23:019-020	3.	*Vegetation:* With it We grow for you gardens of date palms and vines. In them you have abundant fruits, and of them you eat—also a tree springing out of Mount Sinai, which produces oil and relish for those who use it for food.
	23:021-022	4.	*Cattle and Milk:* In cattle (too), you have an instructive example. From within their bodies We produce (milk) for you to drink. There are in them numerous (other) benefits for you, and of their (meat) you eat, and on them, as well as on ships, you ride.
	23:078-079	5.	*Humankind:* It is He Who has created for you

	23:080	(the faculties of) hearing, sight, feeling, and understanding; little thanks it is you give! He has multiplied you through the earth, and to Him shall you be gathered back. 6. *Life and Death:* It is He Who gives life and death, and to Him (is due) the alternation of night and day. Will you not then understand?
		What Unbelievers say about Resurrection
6	23:081-083	On the contrary, they say things similar to what the ancients said. 1. They say: "What! When we die and become dust and bones, could we really be raised up again? 2. "Such things have been promised to us and to our fathers before! They are nothing but tales of the ancients!"

2.4 The Unbelievers admit that Universe belongs to God

People have been asked to look for God's supernatural signs in the universe and in themselves. If they look, they will certainly discover these clear proofs of the truth of Islam. We are told that if we ask the unbelievers, they will surely admit that the universe belongs to God alone. This provides another proof from the inner selves of the unbelievers of the existence of a single God.

Table 2.4: Exalted is God above they associate with Him

No	Surah:Verses	Meanings
7	23:084-090	1. Say: "To whom belong the earth and all beings therein? (Say) if you know." • They will say, "To Allah!" Say: "Yet will you not receive admonition?" 2. Say: "Who is the Lord of the seven heavens and the Lord of the throne (of glory) supreme? • They will say, "(They belong) to Allah." Say: "Will you not then be filled with awe? 3. Say: "Who is it in whose hands is the governance of all things? Who protects (all), but is not protected (by any)? (Say) if you know." • They will say, "(It belongs) to Allah." Say: "Then how are you deluded?" 4. We have sent them the truth, but they indeed practice falsehood.

2.5 God has taken neither a Son nor any other god

God did not have a son, nor has He any associates in His divinity. "No son did Allah beget, nor is there any god along with Him. (If there were many gods), behold, each god would have taken away what he had created, and some would have lorded it over others! Glory to Allah! (He is free) from the (sort of) things they attribute to Him! He knows what is hidden and what is open. Too high is He for the partners they attribute to Him (Qur'an 23:91-92)." In conclusion, God commands the Messenger and believers: "Say: 'O my Lord! If You will show me (in my lifetime) that which they are warned against, then O my Lord, put me not among the people who do wrong!' We are certainly able to show you (in fulfillment) that against which they are warned (Qur'an 23:93-95)."

2.6 The Consequences of Unbelief and Accountability

People's objections against and their doubts about the message of Islam are not new. These were there against the former messengers, whom the unbelievers of Makkah themselves acknowledged as messengers of God. Therefore, they should learn from their stories and judge for themselves who were proven right at the end. The stories of the past messengers and their communities have been cited as historical evidence of the truth of the divine message. The message of *Tauheed* (One God) and Hereafter (the accountability) that Islam is conveying is the same message as was revealed to the former messengers. Therefore, people should accept it. All prophets brought one and the same religion from God, and they all belonged to one and the same religious community. All other religions as they exist today were corrupted by their religious and political leaders who were motivated by their own self-interests.

People should also learn from the consequences met by those communities who rejected the message of their messengers. In all these cases, the same message was given, and the unbelievers' response and the messengers' supplication were similar. As a result, all of these communities that rejected their messenger were eventually destroyed. About Moses, we are told: "Then We sent Moses and his brother Aaron with Our signs and authority manifest to Pharaoh and his chiefs. But these behaved insolently; they were an arrogant people. They said: 'Shall we believe in two men like ourselves? And their people are subject to us!' So they accused them of falsehood, and they became of those who were destroyed (Qur'an 23:45-48)."

3 THE ABSENCE OF ACCOUNTABILITY IS NOT SUCCESS

3.1 Success is not Abundance of Wealth and Children

This clarification was needed because the people who opposed the Messenger were the chiefs of Makkah, and they and their followers were equating their own prosperity with a sign that God was well pleased with them. On the other hand, they argued that the fact that the Messenger and his followers were poor and in a state of helplessness was an indication that God was not pleased with them and that they were under the curse of their deities. Because of their hoarded wealth, even contemporary imperialistic and materialistic societies think that their behavior, no matter how corrupt, should be appreciated by others. God asks people: "Do they think that because We have granted them abundance of wealth and sons, We would hasten them on in every good? Nay, they do not understand (Qur'an 23:55-56)"

Table 3.1: What is the Real Success?

No	Surah:Verses	Meanings
		Success Is Belief and Good Deeds
1	23:057-062	1. Verily, those who live in awe for fear of their Lord, 2. Those who believe in the revelations of their Lord, 3. Those who join not partners (in worship) with their Lord, 4. And those who dispense their charity with their hearts full of fear because they will return to their Lord— 5. It is these who hasten in every good work, and these who are foremost in them. 6. On no soul do We place a burden greater than it can bear. Before Us is a record that clearly shows the truth. They will never be wronged.

320

		Success Is Not in Hoarding Material Things
2	23:063-067	1. But their hearts are in confused ignorance of this, and there are, besides that, deeds of theirs that they will (continue) to do— 2. Until, when We seize in punishment those of them who received the good things of this world, behold, they will groan in supplication! 3. (It will be said): "Groan not in supplication this day, for you shall certainly not be helped by Us." 4. My revelations used to be recited to you, but you used to turn back on your heels in arrogance, talking nonsense about the (Qur'an), like one telling fables by night.

3.2 The Success is not Freedom from Accountability

Why are the unbelievers averse to the belief that only tries to help them elevate themselves to the higher status of humankind as God's trustee? God informs us that since faith does not follow the unbelievers' low desires, it does not suit the unbelievers. "If the truth had been in accord with their desires, truly the heavens and the earth and all beings therein would have been in confusion and corruption! Nay, We have sent them their admonition, but they turn away from their admonition (Qur'an 23:71)." Since the unbelievers follow their low desires and seek their fulfillment in freedom from any guiding principles, they will not be able to face the accountability in the Hereafter. That is why the unbelievers reject faith. Two things common to all unbelievers are that: (1) the truth does not help fulfill their selfish desires, and (2) their deeds are such that they cannot face their accountability.

Table 3.2: Why Unbelievers Reject the Faith?

No	Surah:Verses	Meanings
		Truth does not fulfill unbelievers' Desires
3	23:068	1. Do they not ponder over the Word (of Allah), or has anything (new) come to them that did not come to their fathers of old?
	23:069	2. Or do they not recognize their Messenger that they deny him?
	23:070	3. Or do they say: "He is possessed?" Nay, he has brought them the truth, but most of them

	23:072	hate the truth. 4. Or is it that you ask them for some recompense? But the recompense of your Lord is best: He is the Best of those who give sustenance.
		Unbelievers' Deeds Cannot Face Accountability
4	23:074-077	1. Verily, those who believe not in the Hereafter are deviating from that way. 2. If We had mercy on them and removed the distress that is on them, they would obstinately persist in their transgression, wandering in distraction to and fro. 3. We inflicted punishment on them, but they humbled not themselves to their Lord, nor do they submissively entreat (Him)— 4. Until We open on them a gate leading to a severe punishment. Then Lo! They will be plunged in despair therein.

4 WHAT IS SUCCESS AND HOW TO ACHIEVE IT

4.1 Success is to Repel Evil with what is the Best

The Messenger and the believers were told not to adopt to retaliate in wrong ways to counteract the evil ways of their enemies and to guard against the incitement of Satan. Following these injunctions will ultimately lead to the success. "Repel evil with that which is best: We are well acquainted with the things they say. And say, "O my Lord! I seek refuge with You from the suggestions of the evil ones, and I seek refuge with You, O my Lord, lest they come near me (Qur'an 23:96-98)."

4.2 Success is to Believe and Do Righteous Deeds

The enemies of the truth are warned that they will have to render an account in the Hereafter and bear the consequences of their persecution and oppression. Therefore, they should rethink their behavior. Meanwhile, the believers are motivated to do good deeds to achieve a successful life both in this world and in the Hereafter. "Then when the trumpet is blown, there will be no more relationships between them that day, nor will one ask after another! Then those whose balance (of good deeds) is heavy, they will attain salvation (Qur'an 23:101-102)." To succeed, God

322

commands the believers: "Say: "O my Lord! Grant forgiveness and mercy, for You are the best of those who show mercy (Qur'an 23:118)."

Table 4.2: Belief and Good Deeds Make People Successful

No	Surah:Verses	Meanings
		Believers and Unbelievers on the Judgment Day
1	23:103-111	But those whose balance is light will be those who have lost their souls. In Hell will they abide. The fire will burn their faces, and they will therein grin, with their lips displaced. "Were not My revelations recited to you, and you did but treat them as falsehoods?" • They will say: "Our Lord! Our misfortune overwhelmed us, and we became a people astray! • "Our Lord! Bring us out of this. If ever we return (to evil), then shall we be wrongdoers indeed." • He will say: "Be you driven into it (with ignominy), and speak you not to Me. "A part of My servants there was who used to pray, 'Our Lord! We believe; then do You forgive us and have mercy upon us, for You are the best of those who show mercy!' • "But you (unbelievers) treated them with ridicule, so much so that (ridicule of) them made you forget My message while you were laughing at them. • I have rewarded them this day for their patience and constancy. They are indeed the ones that have achieved bliss.
		Surely the Unbelievers shall not be Successful
2	23:115-117	Did you then think that We had created you in jest, and that you would not be brought back to Us (for account)? • Therefore, exalted be Allah, the king, the reality. There is no god but He, the Lord of the throne of honor. • If anyone invokes, besides Allah, any other god, he has no authority therefore, and his reckoning will be only with his Lord! Verily, the unbelievers will fail to win through.

Part 2
Moral Values and Social Behavior
FROM SURAH AN-NUR (24)

Surah An-Nur was revealed to strengthen the moral fabric of the Islamic community at Madinah, which had been shaken by the enormity of a previous slander against the Messenger's wife. The commandments and instructions given in this Surah highlight how the Qur'an makes use of the occasion to reform the community by the adoption of certain legal, moral, and social measures. God tells us about Surah An-Nur that it is: "A Surah that We have sent down and that We have ordained—in it have We sent down clear revelations in order that you may receive admonition (Qur'an 24:1)."

1 THE PROTECTION OF FAMILY LIFE

1.1 Legislation for the Protection of Family Life
Adultery and prostitution had already been declared a social crime in Surah An-Nisa: "If any of your women are guilty of lewdness, take the evidence of four witnesses from among you against them. And if they testify, confine them to houses until death do claim them or Allah ordain for them some (other) way. If two men among you are guilty of lewdness, punish them both. If they repent and amend, leave them alone, for Allah is oft-returning, most merciful (Qur'an 4:15-16)." In Surah An-Nur, sexual promiscuity was made a criminal offense punishable with a hundred lashes. A social boycott of adulterous men and women was put in place, and the believers were forbidden to have any marital relations with them. The accuser of adultery who failed to produce four witnesses was also made punishable with eighty lashes. The Law of *Li'an* was prescribed to decide the charge of adultery against one's own wife.

Table 1.1: Legislation for the Protection of Family Life

No	Surah:Verses	Meanings
		Adultery is made a Punishable Social Crime
1	24:002-003	1. The woman and the man guilty of adultery or fornication—flog each of them with a hundred

		stripes. Let not compassion move you in their case in a matter prescribed by Allah if you believe in Allah and the Last Day. And let a party of the believers witness their punishment. 2. Let no man guilty of adultery or fornication marries any but a woman similarly guilty or an unbeliever. Nor let any but such a man or an unbeliever marries such a woman. To the believers, such a thing is forbidden.
		False Accusation is Punishable Crime and Sin
2	24:004-005	3. Those who launch a charge against chaste women and produce not four witnesses (to support their allegations), flog them with eighty stripes, and reject their evidence ever after, for such men are wicked transgressors— unless they repent thereafter and mend (their conduct), for Allah is oft-forgiving, most merciful.
		Husband Accusing Wife without Witnesses
3	24:006-009	4. For those who launch a charge against their spouses and have (in support) no evidence but their own, their solitary evidence (can be received) if they bear witness four times (with an oath) by Allah that they are solemnly telling the truth, and the fifth (oath should be) that they solemnly invoke the curse of Allah on themselves if they tell a lie. 5. But it would avert the punishment from the wife if she bears witness four times (with an oath) by Allah that (her husband) is telling a lie, and the fifth (oath) should be that she solemnly invokes the wrath of Allah on herself if (her accuser) is telling the truth.

1.2 False Accusations not be spread in Society

Muslims are commanded to learn a lesson from the incident in which the Messenger's wife was falsely accused, i.e., one should be very cautious with regard to making charges of adultery against people, and one should not spread such rumors. A general principle was enunciated that the proper spouse for a pious man is a pious woman and the proper spouse for a pious woman is a pious man.

With regard to the Messenger's wife, it was obvious that an adulterous woman could not deceive a pious man like the Messenger with her affected behavior. One also has to consider that the accuser of the Messenger's wife was a mean person, while the accused was an innocent woman. This should have convinced people that the accusation was not worth any consideration. Further, it was not even conceivable. For this reason, God commands believers in Surah Al-Hujurat: "O you who believe! If a wicked person comes to you with any news, ascertain the truth, lest you harm people unwittingly and afterwards become full of repentance for what you have done (Qur'an 49:6)." The verses of Surah An-Nur refuting the accusation against A'ishah, the Messenger's wife, are given in the table below.

Table 1.2: Slander against A'ishah, the Messenger's Wife

No	Surah:Verses	Meanings
		A Scandal that triggered Social Reform
4	24:011-017	Those who brought forward the lie are a body among yourselves. Think it not to be an evil to you. On the contrary, it is good for you. To every man among them (will come the punishment) of the sin that he earned, and to him who took on himself the lead among them will be a penalty grievous. 1. Why did not the believers, men and women, when you heard of the affair, put the best construction on it in their own minds and say, "This (charge) is an obvious lie!" 2. Why did they not bring four witnesses to prove it? When they have not brought the witnesses, such men, in the sight of Allah, (stand forth) themselves as liars. • Were it not for the grace and mercy of Allah on you, in this world and the Hereafter, a grievous penalty would have seized you in that you rushed glibly into this affair. Behold, you received it on your tongues and said out of your mouths things of which you had no knowledge, and you thought it to be a light matter, while it was most serious in the sight of Allah.

		3. And why did you not, when you heard it, say, "It is not right of us to speak of this. Glory to Allah! This is a most serious slander!" Allah does admonish you that you may never repeat such (conduct) if you are (true) believers.
		Scandalous Mentality is Discredited
5	24:019	Those who love (to see) scandal published broadcast among the believers, will have a grievous penalty in this life and in the Hereafter. Allah knows, and you know not.
	24:021	1. O you who believe! Follow not Satan's footsteps. If any will follow the footsteps of Satan, he will (but) command what is shameful and wrong.
		2. And were it not for the grace and mercy of Allah on you, not one of you would ever have been pure. But Allah does purify whom He pleases, and Allah is One Who hears and knows.
	24:023	3. Those who slander chaste women, indiscreet but believing, are cursed in this life and in the Hereafter. For them is a grievous penalty.
	24:026	4. Women impure are for men impure, and men impure for women impure and women of purity are for men of purity, and men of purity are for women of purity.
		Forgive and Forget Attitude is Commanded
6	24:022	1. Let not those among you who are endued with grace and amplitude of means resolve by oath against helping their kinsmen, those in want, and those who have left their homes in Allah's cause.
		2. Let them forgive and overlook; do you not wish that Allah should forgive you? For Allah is oft-forgiving, most merciful.

1.3 Enter Each other's Homes only if Permitted

People are forbidden to enter the houses of others without their permission. God commands the believers in Surah An-Nur: "O you who believe! Enter not houses other than your own until you have asked permission and saluted those in them. That is best for you, in order that you may heed (what is seemly). If you find no one in the house, enter not until permission is given to you. If you are asked to go back, then go back. That makes for greater purity for yourselves, and Allah knows well all that you do. It is no fault on your part to enter houses not used for living in, which serve some (other) use for you. And Allah has knowledge of what you reveal and what you conceal (Qur'an 24:27-29)."

2 PROTECTION OF MODESTY AND CHASTITY

2.1 Both Men and Women should behave Modestly
Islam encourages Muslims to adopt certain qualities and characteristics so that they are able to cope with the problems of life and conduct their social relationships in the best way. This helps to cement relationships within the Muslim community and to maintain strong ties among its members. Islam adopts a totally different attitude from that of other communities, including modern Western civilization, which consider modesty a weakness.

Islam makes modesty part of faith, a fact that is stressed in several *Ahadith*. It is narrated on the authority of Abu Huraira that the Messenger said: "*Iman* (faith) has over seventy branches, and modesty is a branch of *Iman* (Sahih Muslim: 1.55)." The Messenger also said: "Every *Deen* (religion or way of life) has an innate character. The character of Islam is modesty (Malik's Muwatta: 47.2.9)." Modesty and faith are interlinked. If either of them is lacking, the other is lacking, too. As such, good believers are, generally speaking, modest and easy to get along with. By contrast, people who lack faith often lack modesty. This is due to the fact that when faith is lacking, the life of this world becomes people's primary preoccupation. Therefore, they try to get as much as possible out of what they hold to be important. This leads them to be presumptuous, overbearing, assertive, and trampling over the rights of others. A believer who is convinced of meeting God and having to account for what he does in this life will hesitate before stressing his own importance, let alone usurping someone else's rights. In Surah Al-Nur, it is stated that both men and women have been instructed to lower their gaze and forbidden to cast glances at each other: "Say to the believing men that they should lower their gaze and guard their modesty.

328

That will make for greater purity for them, and Allah is well acquainted with all that they do (Qur'an 24:30)."

2.2 Women should dress for their Safety in Public

After an incident in which some believing women were teased by the unbelievers, God commanded the Messenger: "Tell your wives and daughters, and the believing women, that they should cast their outer garments over their persons (when in public). That is most convenient that they should be known (as such) and not molested (Qur'an 33:59)." Women are also forbidden to appear with makeup before other men, except their servants or such relatives with whom marriage is prohibited. They were enjoined not to display their makeup and even forbidden to put on jingling ornaments when they went out of their houses. "Say to the believing women that they should lower their gaze and guard their modesty, that they should not display their beauty and ornaments except what appear thereof, that they should draw their veils over their bosoms and not display their beauty except to their husbands, their fathers, their husbands' fathers, their sons, their husbands' sons, their brothers or their brothers' sons, or their sisters' sons, or their women, or the slaves whom their right hands possess, or male servants free of physical needs, or small children who have no sense of the shame of sex, and that they should not strike their feet in order to draw attention to their hidden ornaments. O believers! Turn you all together towards Allah that you may attain bliss...Such elderly women as are past the prospect of marriage—there is no blame on them if they lay aside their (outer) garments, provided they make not a wanton display of their beauty. But it is best for them to be modest, and Allah is One Who sees and knows all things (Qur'an 24:31, 60)."

3 THE PROTECTION OF DIGNITY AND CHARACTER

3.1 Eradication of Slavery and Prostitution

To protect the modesty and chastity of the people, Islam encouraged marriage as early as possible, discouraged slavery, and prohibited prostitution. Since unmarried people help spread indecency, marriage was encouraged and enjoined even for slaves. Believers were commanded in Surah An-Nur: "Marry those among you who are single, or the virtuous ones among yourselves, male or female. If they are in poverty, Allah will give them means out of His grace, for Allah encompasses all, and He knows all things. Let those who find not the wherewithal for marriage keep themselves chaste until Allah gives them means out of His grace (Qur'an 24:32-33)."

The institution of slavery was discouraged, and people were enjoined to give financial help to the slaves to earn their freedom under the Law of *Mukatabat*: "And if any of your slaves ask for a deed in writing (to enable them to earn their freedom for a certain sum), give them such a deed if you know any good in them. Yea, give them something yourselves out of the means that Allah has given to you (Qur'an 24:33)." Since prostitution in Arabia was performed only by slave girls, the following Qur'anic injunction constituted the legal prohibition of prostitution. "But force not your maids to prostitution when they desire chastity, in order that you may make a gain in the goods of this life. But if anyone compels them, yet, after such compulsion, Allah is (to them) oft-forgiving, most merciful (Qur'an 24:33)."

3.2 Sanctity of Individual Right to Privacy
Sanctity of privacy in the home was enjoined even for servants and underage children, including one's own. They were commanded not to enter the private rooms of any man or woman without permission, especially in the morning, at noon, and at night. "O you who believe! Let those whom your right hands possess and the (children) among you who have not come of age ask your permission (before they come to your presence) on three occasions: before morning prayer, the while you doff your clothes for the noonday heat, and after the late night prayer. These are your three times of undress. Outside those times, it is not wrong for you or for them to move about attending to each other. Thus does Allah make clear the signs to you, for Allah is full of knowledge and wisdom. But when the children among you come of age, let them (also) ask for permission, as do those senior to them. Thus does Allah make clear His signs to you, for Allah is full of knowledge and wisdom (Qur'an 24:58-59)."

330

3.3 The Development of Mutual Relationship

The believers were encouraged to develop mutual relationships by taking their meals together. The nearest relatives and intimate friends were allowed to take their meals in each other's house without any formal invitation. This was to inculcate mutual affection and sincere relationships between them and to counteract any future mischief. God tells people in Surah An-Nur: "It is no fault in the blind nor in one born lame, nor in one afflicted with illness, nor in yourselves, that you should eat in your own houses, or those of your fathers, or your mothers, or your brothers, or your sisters, or your father's brothers, or your father's sisters, or your mother's brothers, or your mother's sisters, or in houses of which the keys are in your possession, or in the house of a sincere friend of yours. There is no blame on you whether you eat in company or separately. But if you enter houses, salute each other—a greeting of blessing and purity as from Allah. Thus does Allah make clear the signs to you that you may understand (Qur'an 24:61)?"

Various social superstitions were also rejected. For example, blind, lame, crippled, and sick persons had been supposed to be objects of divine displeasure and, as such, not fit to be associated with people in meals at their houses. Since no one can judge the cause of people's misfortunes, one has to be kind to them. People were told that they were free and that they should regulate their lives as they wished, so long as they acted within the framework of God's laws.

3.4 Participation in the Community Development

Along with instructions about social behavior, the general attitudes of believers and hypocrites were described to enable every believer to discriminate between the two. The community was bound together by adopting certain disciplinary measures that increased its strength and discouraged people from creating mischief. Verse 62 of Surah An-Nur highlights the attitude of the believers: "Only those are believers, who believe in Allah and His Messenger. When they are with him on a matter requiring collective action, they do not depart until they have asked for his leave. Those who ask for your leave are those who believe in Allah and His Messenger. So when they ask for your leave for some business of theirs, give leave to those of them whom you will, and ask Allah for their forgiveness, for Allah is oft-forgiving, most merciful (Qur'an 24:62). At the same time, the hypocrites were told: "Deem not the summons of the Messenger among yourselves like the summons of one of you to another. Allah does know those of you who slip away under shelter of some excuse. Then let those beware who withstand the Messenger's order, lest some trial befall them or a grievous penalty be inflicted on them (Qur'an 24:63)."

3.5 The Worst Believers are the Hypocrites
The worst people in the sight of God are those who do not do what they say. This could be due to a disease in their heart or because they doubt the judgment of God and His Messenger: "Is it that there is a disease in their hearts, or do they doubt, or are they in fear, that Allah and His Messenger will deal unjustly with them? Nay, it is they themselves who do wrong (Qur'an 24:50)." To such people, God told the Messenger: "Say: 'Obey Allah, and obey the Messenger. But if you turn away, he is only responsible for the duty placed on him and you for that placed on you. If you obey him, you shall be on right guidance. The Messenger's duty is only to preach the clear message' (Qur'an 24:54)."

3.6 God's three Promises to the Believers
In Surah An-Nur, God promises three things to the believers who do what they say, i.e., their behavior reflects their belief. The believers are those Who —
1. Serve God not associating with other gods (Qur'an 24:55).
2. Keep up the Prayers (Qur'an 24:56).
3. Pay *Zakah* (Qur'an 24:56).
4. Obey the Messenger (Qur'an 24:56).
5. Don't think that unbelievers shall escape (Qur'an 24:57).

If the believers make honest efforts as individuals and as a community in the above mentioned five areas, then God has promised them that He will most certainly, "(1) Make them rulers in the land as He made rulers those before them, (2) establish for them their religion which He has chosen for them, and (3) after their fear, give them security in exchange (Qur'an 24:55),"

Part 3
The Eradication of Social Evils
FROM SURAH AL-AHZAB (33)

Initial steps to reform the society were taken as their need became manifest, secondary to the mischief of the hypocrites and unbelievers against the Messenger's wives and other believing women. These reforms started from the house of the Messenger himself, and his wives were commanded to avoid behaving and conducting themselves in the ways of the pre-Islamic Days of Ignorance, to remain in their houses with dignity, and to exercise great caution in their conversation with men. This was the beginning of the commandment of *Hijab*.

To eradicate the concepts and customs of ignorance concerning adoption, the Messenger was told: "Allah has not made for any man two hearts in his body, nor has He made your wives whom you divorce by *Zihar* your mothers, nor has He made your adopted sons your sons. Such is (only) your (manner of) speech by your mouths. But Allah tells the truth, and He shows the way. (Qur'an 33:4)." At the same time God told the believers: "There can be no difficulty to the Prophet in what Allah has indicated to him as a duty. It was the practice (approved) of Allah among those of old that have passed away, and the command of Allah is a decree determined (Qur'an 33:38)."

1 GOOD HUMAN CHARACTER AND BEHAVIOR

1.1 The Messenger's Wives as Role Models
In Surah Al-Ahzab, God told the wives of the Messenger, who were concerned about their straitened circumstances, to choose between the world and its adornments, on the one hand, or God, His Prophet, and the Hereafter, on the other hand. If they sought the former, they were told that their poverty would be lifted. However, if they sought the latter, they should cooperate with God and His Messenger and bear their burdens patiently. This choice is also specifically applicable to the wives of all those

people who are at a position of leadership in an Islamic community and to all other believing women in general.

Table 1.1: The Responsibilities of the Messenger's Wives

No	Surah:Verses	Meanings
		The Messenger's Wives were given a Choice
1	33:028-031	O Prophet! Say to your consorts: 1. "If it be that you desire the life of this world and its glitter, then come! I will provide for your enjoyment and set you free in a handsome manner." 2. But if you seek Allah and His Messenger and the home of the Hereafter, verily Allah has prepared for the doers of good among you a great reward. 3. O Consorts of the Prophet! If any of you were guilty of evident unseemly conduct, the punishment would be doubled to her, and that is easy for Allah. 4. But any of you who is devout in the service of Allah and His Messenger and works righteousness, to her shall We grant her reward twice, and We have prepared for her a generous sustenance.
		The Messenger's Wives as Role Models
2	33:032-034	O Consorts of the Prophet! You are not like any of the (other) women. If you do fear (Allah), be not too complacent of speech, lest one in whose heart is a disease should be moved with desire, but 1. You speak a speech (that is) just. 2. And stay quietly in your houses, 3. And make not a dazzling display, like that of the former Times of Ignorance, 4. And establish regular prayer, 5. And give regular charity; 6. And obey Allah and His Messenger. Allah only wishes to remove all abomination from you, O members of the family, and to make you pure and spotless. 7. And recite what is rehearsed to you in your homes of the revelations of Allah and His wisdom, for Allah understands the finest mysteries and is well acquainted (with them).

1.2 Attributes of Believing Men and Women

After the victory at Badr, the Islamic movement began to gain strength, and by the time of the Battle of the Trench, it had become so strong that the united forces of the enemy, numbering about ten thousand, failed to crush it and had to raise the siege of Madinah after one month. Consequently, the war of aggression that the unbelievers had been waging for several years had come to an end. The Messenger himself declared that after that year the Quraish would not be able to attack the Muslims and that the Muslims could now take the offensive. "It was narrated by Sulaiman bin Surd that on the day of Al-Ahzab, after the battle, the Prophet said, 'We will go to attack them, and they will not come to attack us' (Sahih Bukhari: 5.59.435)." When the unbelievers realized that they could not defeat Islam on the battlefield, they chose the moral front to carry on a conflict that is continuing even today. Under the above circumstances, the wicked designs of the unbelievers led them to start a campaign of vilification against the Messenger and the believers, in order to destroy the bulwark of morale that was helping them to defeat their enemies. The verse of Surah Al-Ahzab highlighting those attributes that reinforce the moral behavior of the believers and provide safeguards to them under all circumstances is given in the table below.

Table 1.2: Attributes of Believing Men and Believing Women

1.	For Muslim men and women,	2.	for believing men and women,
3.	for devout men and women,	4.	for true men and women,
5.	for men and women who are patient and constant,	6.	for men and women who humble themselves,
7.	for men and women who give in charity,	8.	for men and women who fast (and restrain themselves),
9.	for men and women who guard their chastity, and	10.	for men and women who engage much in Allah's praise —
For them has Allah prepared forgiveness and great reward (Qur'an 33:35)			

2 BELIEVERS TREAT EACH OTHER WITH RESPECT

2.1 False Accusation is a Moral Disease and a Sin

The Muslims were warned that they would invite the curse and scourge of God if they offended the Messenger. In fact, they were commanded to call for blessings on the Messenger: "Allah and His angels send blessings on the Prophet. O you that believe! Send you blessings on him and salute him with all respect (Qur'an 33:56)." Further, God said that it was a heinous sin to attack the honor of or slander any believing man or woman. The verses of Surah Al-Ahzab that forbid false accusations are: "Those who annoy Allah and His Messenger—Allah has cursed them in this world and in the Hereafter and has prepared for them a humiliating punishment. And those who annoy believing men and women undeservedly bear (on themselves) a calumny and a glaring sin (Qur'an 33:57-58)."

2.2 Women are Respectable Members of Society

Women are to be treated as respectable members of society and not just as sex symbols, as they generally were and are treated in many unbelieving societies. For this reason, Muslim women were enjoined to cover themselves with their sheets if and when they had to go out of their houses. God commanded the Messenger: "Tell your wives and daughters and the believing women that they should cast their outer garments over their persons (when in public). That is most convenient, that they should be known (as such) and not molested. And Allah is oft-forgiving, most merciful (Qur'an 33:59)."

3 LACK OF MORALITY CORRUPTS THE SOCIETY

3.1 Hypocrisy and Unbelief Cripples the Society

Broadly speaking, any community consists of a specific mixture of people whose individual character and behavior may be that of a believer, a hypocrite, or an unbeliever. This seems to be a dynamic system, and its very nature determines the peace and prosperity of the community. It is not humanly possible to eradicate completely behavior stemming from hypocrisy and unbelief. However, one should try to reduce the percentage of hypocrites and unbelievers in society by educating them about the benefits of hard work, honesty, justice, and charity. This can only be done by motivating people to reform themselves. Without such reform, neither prosperity in this world nor salvation in the Hereafter can be achieved. In the early Islamic community at Madinah, about one-third of its inhabitants were hypocritical. Nonetheless, the community managed to succeed.

It is extremely important that people repent and reform in order to decrease the number of people with hypocritical behavior. God commands the believers: "Be not like those who vexed and insulted Moses, but Allah cleared him of the (calumnies) they had uttered, and he was honorable in Allah's sight. O you who believe! Fear Allah, and (always) say a word directed to the right (in order) that He may make your conduct whole and sound and forgive you your sins. He that obeys Allah and His Messenger has already attained the highest achievement (Qur'an 33:69-71)."

Table 3.1: The Hypocrites, Unbelievers, and Believers

No	Surah:Verses	Meanings
		Impact of Hypocrisy and Unbelief in this Life
1	33:060-062	Truly, if the hypocrites, and those in whose hearts is a disease, and those who stir up sedition in the city, desist not, 1. We shall certainly stir you up against them. Then will they not be able to stay in it as your neighbors for any length of time. 2. They shall have a curse on them. Whenever they are found, they shall be seized and slain. (Such was) the practice (approved) by Allah among those who lived aforetime. No change will you find in the practice by Allah.
		Impact of Hypocrisy and Unbelief in Hereafter
2	33:063-068	Men ask you concerning the Hour: Say, "The knowledge thereof is with Allah (alone)." And what will make you understand? Perchance the Hour is nigh. 1. Verily Allah has cursed the unbelievers and prepared for them a blazing fire to dwell therein forever. No protector will they find, nor helper.

		2. The day that their faces will be turned upside down in the fire, they will say: "Woe to us! Would that we had obeyed Allah and obeyed the Messenger!" 3. And they would say: "Our Lord! We obeyed our chiefs and our great ones, and they misled us as to the (right) path. Our Lord! Give them double penalty and curse them with a very great curse."
		Will Hypocrites and Unbelievers be Punished?
3	33:072-073	• We did indeed offer the trust to the heavens and the earth and the mountains, but they refused to undertake it, being afraid thereof. But man undertook it; he was indeed unjust and foolish. • (With the result) that Allah has to punish the hypocrites, men and women, and the unbelievers, men and women, and Allah turns in mercy to the believers, men and women: for Allah is oft-forgiving, most merciful.

Part 4
Moral Excellence and Equality
FROM SURAH AL-HUJURAT (49)

Nationalism, tribalism, nepotism, ethnic bigotry, racism, looking down upon others as inferior to oneself, and pulling down others only for the sake of establishing one's own superiority have filled the world with injustices and tyranny. God cut at the root of this evil by stating that all men are descendants of the same original pair of humans and that division into tribes and communities was only for the sake of recognition. There is no lawful basis for one man's superiority over another except on the basis of moral excellence. The objective of Surah Al-Hujurat is to teach people the manners worthy of real humankind.

1 THE EQUALITY AMONG INDIVIDUALS

1.1 Discrimination due to Racial and National Distinctions

The racial and national distinctions that cause corruption in the world are condemned in Islam. Looking down upon others as inferior to oneself and their pulling down others only for the sake of establishing one's own superiority are important factors that have filled the world with injustice and tyranny. God tells people, "O mankind! We created you from a single (pair) of a male and a female and made you into nations and tribes that you may know each other (not that you may despise each other). Verily, the most honored of you in the sight of Allah is (he who is) the most righteous of you. And Allah has full knowledge and is well-acquainted (with all things) (Qur'an 49:13)."

1.2 Individual Conduct, not Looks makes People Human

People have been told that the real thing is not the mere verbal profession of the faith. To believe in God and His Messenger is to obey them in practical life and to exert with ones self and wealth in the cause of God. The true believers are only those who adopt this attitude. People are born with many weaknesses and have a predisposition for self-preservation. By training and education, people overcome their weaknesses and reform their character and behavior. The informed and reformed individuals in religious reference are the believers. It is their character and behavior that makes people human.

As for those who merely profess Islam orally, without affirmation in the heart, and then adopt an attitude as if they had done someone a favor by accepting Islam, they may be counted as Muslims in the world and may even be treated as Muslims in society, but they cannot be counted as believers in the sight of God and in the Hereafter. The verses of Surah Al-Hujurat that highlight that only behavior assures people's status as humankind are given in the table below.

Table 1: Only Behavior Assures People's Status in Humanity

No	Surah:Verses	Meanings
		Saying that 'We are Believers' does not make us Believers
1	49:014-015	The desert Arabs say, "We believe." Say, "You

		have no faith, but you (only) say, 'We have submitted our wills to Allah,' for not yet has faith entered your hearts. But if you obey Allah and His Messenger, He will not belittle aught of your deeds: for Allah is oft-forgiving, most merciful." Only those are believers 1. Who have believed in Allah and His Messenger, and have never since doubted, 2. But have striven with their belongings and their persons in the Cause of Allah. 3. Such are the sincere ones.
		God is not under any obligation **if we are only 'Muslims'**
2	49:016-018	• Say: "What! Will you instruct Allah about your religion? But Allah knows all that is in the heavens and on earth: He has full knowledge of all things." They impress on you as a favor that they have embraced Islam. 1. Say, "Count not your Islam as a favor upon me: Nay, Allah has conferred a favor upon you that He has guided you to the faith, if you be true and sincere. 2. "Verily, Allah knows the secrets of the heavens and the earth, and Allah sees well all that you do."

2 TRUTHFUL AND AUTHENTIC SOCIAL DISCOURSE

2.1 Social Etiquette in Meetings and Conversation

A believer should take guidance from God, His Messenger, and the Qur'an. The norms of human behavior are highlighted in the Qur'an and *Sunnah* and therefore should be learned and followed. Instructions on how to communicate with others are given in Surah Al-Hujurat: "O you who believe! Put not yourselves forward before Allah and His Messenger; but fear Allah, for Allah is He Who hears and knows all things. O you who believe! Raise not your voices above the voice of the Prophet, nor speak aloud to him in talk, as you may speak aloud to one another, lest your deeds become vain and you perceive not. Those that lower their voices in the presence of Allah's

340

Messenger—their hearts has Allah tested for piety. For them is forgiveness and a great reward. Those who shout out to you from without the inner apartments—most of them lack understanding. If only they had patience until you could come out to them, it would be best for them. But Allah is oft-forgiving, most merciful (Qur'an 49:1-5)."

2.2 Speculations and False News Reporting is Sinful

All news for circulation in the community should be authentic and true. It is not right to believe in every piece of news blindly and to act according to it without due thought. God commanded us to investigate speculations before acting on them. If information is received about a person, a group, or a community, the reliability of the news source should carefully be determined. If the source is not reliable, it should be checked to see whether the news is authentic or not before taking any action on it. "O you who believe, if a wicked person comes to you with any news, ascertain the truth, lest you harm people unwittingly and afterwards become full of repentance for what you have done. And know that among you is Allah's Messenger. Were he in many matters to follow your (wishes), you would certainly fall into misfortune. But Allah has endeared the faith to you and has made it beautiful in your hearts, and He has made hateful to you unbelief, wickedness, and rebellion—such indeed are those who walk in righteousness (Qur'an 49:6-7)."

3 SOCIAL HARMONY AND PEACE AMONG PEOPLE

3.1 Making Peace is commanded over Mutual Fighting.

What attitude should other Muslims adopt in the case of two groups of Muslims who fall into mutual fighting? God says: "If two parties among the believers fall into a quarrel, make you peace between them. But if one of them transgresses beyond bounds against the other, then fight you against the one that transgresses until it complies with the command of Allah. But if it complies, then make peace between them with justice, and be fair, for Allah loves those who are fair (and just). The believers are but a single brotherhood. So make peace and reconciliation between your two brothers, and fear Allah that you may receive mercy (Qur'an 49:9-10)." This has far-reaching consequences, i.e., we are commanded to try to make peace when people are fighting, regardless of the circumstances and the reason.

3.2 Suspicion, Backbiting, and Spying are Social Evils
Muslims are encouraged to safeguard themselves against the evil that corrupts collective life and spoils mutual relationships. Mocking and taunting each other, calling others by offensive nicknames, creating suspicions, spying into other people's affairs, and backbiting are evils and sins that corrupt society. In the Qur'an, God mentioned all these evils individually and forbade them as being unlawful. "O you who believe! Let not some men among you laugh at others. It may be that the (latter) are better than the (former). Nor let some women laugh at others. It may be that the (latter) are better than the (former). Nor defame nor be sarcastic to each other, nor call each other by (offensive) nicknames. Ill-seeming is a name connoting wickedness, (to be used of one) after he has believed. And those who do not desist are (indeed) doing wrong. O you who believe! Avoid suspicion as much (as possible), for suspicion in some cases is a sin. And spy not on each other behind their backs. Would any of you like to eat the flesh of his dead brother? Nay, you would abhor it. But fear Allah, for Allah is oft-returning, most merciful (Qur'an 49:11-12)."

Part 5
The Behavior of Real Humans
FROM SURAH AL-FURQAN (25)

Surah Al-Furqan deals with the doubts and objections that were raised by the unbelievers against the Qur'an, the Messenger, and his teachings. Appropriate answers to each objection are given, and people are warned about the consequences of rejecting faith. In conclusion, a clear picture of the moral superiority of the believers is, one that clearly distinguishes genuine humans from the counterfeit.

1 THE MESSENGERS ONLY CONVEY THE MESSAGE

Messengers are the human role models who are assigned the responsibility of guiding people according to what God commands. However, people have freedom of choice: "If any one believes in Allah, (He) guides his heart (aright), for Allah knows all things. So obey Allah, and obey His Messenger. But if you turn back, the duty of Our Messenger is but to proclaim (the message) clearly and openly (Qur'an 64:11-12)." Given that people do have free will, one is to strive against the unbelievers with the message of the Qur'an: "Had We so willed We would have raised a warner in every town. Therefore listen not to the unbelievers, but strive against them with the strenuousness with the Qur'an (Qur'an 25:51-52)."

1.1 God's Criterion for Good and Evil

God reveals the criterion for good and evil in the Qur'an: "Blessed is He who sent down the criterion to His servant that it may be an admonition to all creatures. He to whom belongs the dominion of the heavens and the earth, no son has He begotten, nor has He a partner in His dominion—it is He who created all things and ordered them in due proportions (Qur'an 25:1-2)." However, the unbelievers, who had taken others besides God as gods questioned the authenticity of the Qur'an. Appropriate answers to each and every one of the unbelievers' objections were given in this Surah, and people were warned about the consequences of rejecting faith. The verses of Surah Al-Furqan highlighting that *'Furqan* (the criterion) is the strength for the believers' hearts' are given in the table below.

Table 1.1: *Furqan* is the Strength for Believers' Heart

No	Surah:Verses	Meanings
		Unbelievers' associate gods have created nothing
1	25:003	Yet have they (the unbelievers) taken, besides Him, gods • That can create nothing but are themselves created; that have no control of hurt or good to themselves; nor can they control death nor life nor resurrection.
		Unbelievers say that the Qur'an has been forged

2	25:004-006	But the disbelievers say (about the Qur'an): 1. "Naught is this but a lie that he has forged, and others have helped him at it." In truth it is they who have put forward an iniquity and a falsehood. 2. They say: "Tales of the ancients that he has caused to be written, and they are dictated before him morning and evening." 3. Say: "The (Qur'an) was sent down by Him who knows the mystery (that is) in the heavens and the earth. Verily, He is oft-forgiving, most merciful."
	25:032-034	Those who reject faith say (about the Qur'an): "Why is not the Qur'an revealed to him all at once?" • Thus (is it revealed), that We may strengthen your heart thereby, and We have rehearsed it to you in slow, well-arranged stages, gradually. • And no question do they bring to you but We reveal to you the truth and the best explanation (thereof). • Those who will be gathered to Hell (prone) on their faces—they will be in an evil plight, and, as to path, most astray.
		Enough is your Lord to Guide and to Help
3	25:030-031	Then the Messenger will say: "O my Lord! Truly my people took this Qur'an for just foolish nonsense." 1. Thus have We made for every prophet an enemy among the sinners, 2. But enough is your Lord to guide and to help.

1.2 Authenticity of God's Messengers

Surah Al-Furqan also deals with the doubts and objections that were raised by the unbelievers of Makkah about the authenticity of the Messenger and his teachings. Appropriate answers to each and every objection were given, and the people were warned about the consequences of rejecting the truth. God tells the Messenger and believers: "The messengers whom We sent before you were all (men) who ate food and walked through the streets. We have made some of you as a trial for others. Will you have patience (Qur'an 25:20)?"

Table 1.2: Messengers Were All Human Beings

No	Surah:Verses	Meanings
		What Unbelievers say about God's Messenger
4	25:007-010	They (unbelievers) say (about the Messenger):
		1. "What sort of a messenger is this who eats food and walks through the streets?
		2. "Why has not an angel been sent down to him to give admonition with him?
		3. "Or (why) has not a treasure been bestowed on him,
		4. "Or why has he (not) a garden for enjoyment?"
		The wicked say: You follow none other than a man bewitched.
		• See what kinds of comparisons they make about you! But they have gone astray, and never a way will they be able to find! Blessed is He who, if that were His will, could give you better (things) than those—gardens beneath which rivers flow, and He could give you palaces (secure to dwell in).
	25:041-042	When they see you, they treat you not otherwise than in mockery.
		5. "Is this the one whom Allah has sent as a messenger? He would well-nigh have led us far away from our gods, had it not been that we were constant to them!"
		Soon will they know, when they see the penalty, who it is that is most misled in path.
	25:055	6. Yet do they worship, besides Allah, things that can neither profit them nor harm them, and the disbeliever is a helper (of evil) against his own Lord.
		All Messengers were sent to deliver the Message
5	25:056-059	But We only sent you to give glad tidings and admonition. Say: "No reward do I ask of you for it but this: that each one who will, may take a (straight) path to his Lord." (Therefore,)
		1. Put your trust in Him Who lives and dies not, and celebrate his praise. Enough is He to be acquainted with the faults of His servants—
		2. He Who created the heavens and the earth and all that is between in six days and is firmly

		established on the throne (of authority): Allah Most Gracious—ask you, then, about Him of any acquainted (with such things).

2 THE SELF-INTEREST OF THE UNBELIEVERS

2.1 The Indiscriminate Perusal of Happiness Destroys

Unbelievers, since they do not believe in the resurrection and personal accountability, keep on following their base personal desires and refuse to follow the divine guidance. Consequently, their selfish behavior eventually destroys their communities. The verses of Surah Al-Furqan that highlight the reasons for the destruction of unbelieving communities are given in the table below.

Table 2.1: Unbelievers were eventually Destroyed

No	Surah:Verses	Meanings
		Unbelievers do not believe in their Accountability
1	25:040	1. They (the unbelievers) must indeed have passed by the town on which was rained a shower of evil. Did they not then see it (with their own eyes)? But they fear not the resurrection.
		Unbelievers follow their Base Personal Desires
2	25:043-044	2. Have you seen such who takes for his god his own passion (or impulse or selfish desires)? Could you be a disposer of affairs for him? 3. Or you think that most of them listen or understand? They are only like cattle—nay, they are worse astray in path.
		Unbelievers Refuse to Follow What God Commands
3	25:060	4. When it is said to them, "Prostrate to (Allah) Most Gracious!" they say, "And what is (Allah) Most Gracious? Shall we prostrate to that which you command us?" And it increases their aversion (from the truth).
	25:077	5. Say (to the unbelievers): "My Lord is not uneasy because of you if you call not on Him. But you have indeed rejected (Him), and soon will come the inevitable (punishment)."

		That is Why their Communities were Destroyed
4	25:035-039	1 *Moses and Aaron* (Before this,) We sent Moses the Book and appointed his brother Aaron with him as minister. And We commanded: "Go you both to the people who have rejected our signs." And those (people) We destroyed with utter destruction. 2 *The people of Noah* When they rejected the messengers, We drowned them, and We made them as a sign for mankind. And We have prepared for wrongdoers a grievous penalty. 3 *'Ad and Thamud* 'Ad and Thamud, and the Companions of the Rass, and many a generation between them. To each one We set forth parables and examples, and each one We broke to utter annihilation (for their sins).

2.2 Unbelievers' Desires and the Day of Judgment

After explaining what the Day of Judgment will be like, God lists the reasons behind some people's disbelief. Since the unbelievers have their personal desires as their gods, it is convenient for them not to accept the accountability for their actions and bad behavior. It is clear that if a person does not believe in the Day of Judgment and the accountability for his deeds, then he definitely does not hope to meet his Lord. This attitude encourages people to fulfill their desires by any means, whether legal or illegal. Such people will never improve and as a consequence earn punishment.

Table 2.2: Unbelievers do not Hope to meet their Lord

No	Surah:Verses	Meanings
		Day of Judgment and the Unbelievers
5	25:025-029	• The day the heaven shall be rent asunder with clouds, and angels shall be sent down, descending (in ranks)—that day, the dominion as of right and truth shall be (wholly) for (Allah) Most Merciful. It will be a day of dire difficulty for the disbelievers. • The day that the wrongdoer will bite at his hands, He will say: "Oh! Would that I had taken a (straight) path with the Messenger. Ah! Woe is me! Would that I had never taken

		such a one for a friend! He did lead me astray from the message (of Allah) after it had come to me! Ah! The Satan is but a traitor to man."
		Unbelievers reject the Hour and the Fire
6	25:011-014	1. Nay, they deny the hour (of the judgment to come), but We have prepared a blazing fire for such as deny the hour. When it sees them from a place far off, they will hear its fury and it's ranging sigh. And when they are cast, bound together into a constricted place therein, they will plead for destruction there and then! "This day plead not for a single destruction: plead for destruction oft-repeated."
		Unbelievers do not hope to meet their Lord
7	25:021-023	2. Such as fear not the meeting with Us (for judgment) say: "Why are not the angels sent down to us, or (why) do we not see our Lord?" Indeed, they have an arrogant conceit of themselves, and mighty is the insolence of their impiety. 3. The day they see the angels—no joy will there be to the sinners that day. The (angels) will say: "There is a barrier forbidden (to you) altogether!" And We shall turn to whatever deeds they did (in this life), and We shall make such deeds as floating dust scattered about.
		Unbelievers and their Deities will suffer together
8	25:017-019	4. The day He will gather them together as well as those whom they worship besides Allah, He will ask: "Was it you who led these My servants astray, or did they stray from the path themselves?" They will say: "Glory to You! It was not for us that we should take for protectors others besides You, but You did bestow on them and their fathers good things until they forgot the message, for they were a people (worthless and) lost." 5. (Allah will say): "Now have they proved you liars in what you say, so you cannot avert (your penalty) nor (get) help." And whoever among you does wrong, him shall We cause to taste of a grievous penalty.

		People have to decide for themselves
9	25:015-016	6. Say: "Is that best or the eternal garden promised to the righteous? • "For them, that is a reward as well as a goal (of attainment). • "For them there will be therein all that they wish for. They will dwell (there) forever—a promise to be prayed for from your Lord."

3 THE CHARACTER AND BEHAVIOR OF BELIEVERS

3.1 Believers are of excellent Moral Character

In conclusion, the moral behavior of the believers is described as it was done in the beginning of Surah Al-Mu'minun. This description highlights the criterion for distinguishing a genuine believer from the hypocrites and unbelievers. This is the noble character of those people who have believed in and followed the teachings of the Messenger. One may compare and contrast this type of people with those unbelievers who have not accepted the message, and who are upholding ignorance and exerting their utmost to defeat the truth.

Table 3.1: Believers are the Servants of the Beneficent

No	Surah:Verses	Meanings
1	25:063-074	The servants of (Allah) Most Gracious are those 1. Who walk on the earth in humility. 2. And when the ignorant address them, they say, "Peace." 3. Those who spend the night in adoration of their Lord prostrate and standing. 4. Those who say, "Our Lord! Avert from us the wrath of Hell, for its wrath is indeed an affliction grievous. Evil indeed is it as an abode, and as a place to rest in." 5. Those who, when they spend, are not extravagant and not miserly, but hold a just (balance) between those (extremes). 6. Those who invoke not, with Allah, any other god, 7. Nor slay such life as Allah has made sacred except for just cause,

	8. Nor commit fornication. And any that does this (not only) meets punishment, (but) the penalty on the Day of Judgment will be doubled to him, and he will dwell therein in ignominy • Unless he repents, believes, and works righteous deeds, for Allah will change the evil of such persons into good. And Allah is oft-forgiving, most merciful, • And whoever repents and does good has truly turned to Allah with an (acceptable) conversion. 9. Those who witness no falsehood. 10. (Those) if they pass by futility, they pass by it with honorable (avoidance). 11. Those who, when they are admonished with the revelations of their Lord, droop not down at them as if they were deaf or blind. 12. Those who pray, "Our Lord! Grant unto us wives and offspring who will be the comfort of our eyes, and give us (the grace) to lead the righteous."

3.2 Believers are rewarded for their Patience

Believers are those who struggle patiently for the benefit of humanity. Such people are successful in this world and will achieve their salvation in the Hereafter. Verses of Surah Al-Furqan that highlight the eventual reward for the believers are, "Those are the ones who will be rewarded with the highest place in Heaven because of their patient constancy. Therein shall they be met with salutations and peace, dwelling therein—how beautiful an abode and place of rest (Qur'an 25:75-76)."

Part 6
Reformation of Human Character
FROM SURAH AL-QALAM (68)

Human character can either be like that of the believers or of the unbelievers. The believer's behavior conforms to sublime morality while unbelievers are those who swear and defame and slander others. They hinder good deeds, transgress all bounds, and are sinful. The story of the 'Owners of a Garden' was presented in Surah Al-Qalam to show the consequences of the character of those people who, after having been blessed by God, turned ungrateful to Him by not helping the poor among them. Consequently, they were deprived of God's blessing, and they realized this when all they had was destroyed by nature. This was their fate in this world. Again, those who refuse to behave as God desires due to their own freedom of choice and selfish behavior cannot expect any favors from Him on the Day of Judgment and thus will stand disgraced and condemned in both worlds. Having denied divine guidance in this world, they cannot escape divine judgment in the Hereafter.

1 THE CHARACTER OF THE LEADERS

1.1 The Excellent Moral Character of the Messenger
God tells the Messenger: "You are not, by the grace of your Lord, mad or possessed (as the unbelievers claim). Nay, verily for you is a reward unfailing. And you (stand) on an exalted standard of character. Soon will you see, and they will see, which of you is afflicted with madness. Verily, it is your Lord Who knows best which (among men) have strayed from His path, and He knows best those who receive (true) guidance. So hearken not to those who deny (the truth). Their desire is that you should compromise with them, so they too would compromise (Qur'an 68:2-9)." Muslims and their leaders should emulate the Messenger's character, and the accusations of the unbelievers should not succeed in pressuring the believers to compromise when it comes to God's directives.

1.2 Unbelieving Leaders are Exploiters, Cruel and Sinful
The character of a prominent person, whom the people of Makkah recognized very well, from among the opponents of the Messenger, was presented without naming him, in order to show what sort of character and morals were possessed by the chiefs of Makkah who were opposing the Messenger. God commands the Messenger (and the believers): "Heed not the type of despicable man—ready with oaths, a slanderer, going about with calumnies, (habitually) hindering (all) good, transgressing

beyond bounds, deep in sin, violent (and cruel)—with all that, base-born—because he possesses wealth and (numerous) sons. When to him are recited Our revelations, 'Tales of the ancients,' he cries! Soon shall We brand (the beast) on the snout (Qur'an 68:10-16)."

2 THE CONSEQUENCE OF BAD BEHAVIOR

2.1 Bad Character can ruin the People in the World

With a parable, the people of Makkah, as well as the people of all places and times, have been warned. Any person can be put to a test similar to the one to which the owners of the garden suffered. If people do not listen to divine guidance and do not reform their character and behavior, they too can be afflicted with a punishment in this world and the greater punishment of the Hereafter.

Table 2.1: Intention and Deeds Impact People's Worldly life

No	Surah:Verses	Meanings
		The Arrogant people are not willing to Help the Poor
1	68:017-027	1. Verily, We have tried them as We tried the people of the garden when they resolved to gather the fruits of the (garden) in the morning, but made no reservation (if it be Allah's will).
		2. Then there came on the (garden) a visitation from your Lord, (which swept away) all around while they were asleep. So the (garden) became, by the morning, like a dark and desolate spot, (whose fruit had been gathered).
		3. As the morning broke, they called out one to another, "Go to your tilth in the morning, if you would gather the fruits."
		4. So they departed, conversing in secret low tones, (saying)- "Let not a single indigent person break in upon you into the (garden) this day." And they went in the morning, strong in an (unjust) resolve.
		5. But when they saw the (garden), they said:

No	Surah:Verses	Meanings
		"We have surely lost our way.
		6. "Indeed, we are shut out (of the fruits of our labor)!"
		The Punishment in the Hereafter will be worse than in the World
2	68:028-033	1. Said one of them, more just (than the rest): "Did I not say to you, 'Why not glorify (Allah)?'"
		2. They said: "Glory to our Lord! Verily, we have been doing wrong."
		3. Then they turned, one against another, in reproach. They said: "Alas for us! We have indeed transgressed.
		4. "It may be that our Lord will give us in exchange a better (garden) than this, for we do turn to Him (in repentance)."
		5. Such is the punishment (in this life), but greater is the punishment in the Hereafter, if only they knew!

2.2 Bad Behavior will ruin People in the Hereafter

Wellbeing in the Hereafter inevitably belongs to those who spend their lives in the world with full consciousness of God. It is against reason that a conscientious person should meet the same fate in the Hereafter as the guilty. The unbelievers cannot expect that God will treat them as they wish. Those who refuse to behave as God desires them to behave cannot expect any favors from Him on the Day of Judgment and thus they will stand disgraced and condemned. Having denied divine guidance, the unbelievers cannot escape divine judgment.

Table 2.2: The Day of Judgment and God's Plan

No	Surah:Verses	Meanings
		Pious and the Guilty will not be Treated Alike
3	68:034-041	Verily, for the righteous are gardens of delight in the presence of their Lord. Shall We then treat the people of faith like the people of sin?
		1. What is the matter with you? How do you judge?
		2. Or have you a book through which you learn that you shall have, through it, whatever you choose?
		3. Or have you covenants with Us on oath,

		reaching to the Day of Judgment, (providing) that you shall have whatever you shall demand? Ask you of them, which of them will stand surety for that! 4. Or have they some "partners" (in Godhead)? Then let them produce their partners, if they are truthful.
		Hypocrites shall not be Able to Prostrate
4	68:042-043	• The day that the shin shall be laid bare, and they shall be summoned to prostrate in adoration, but they shall not be able—. • Their eyes will be cast down; ignominy will cover them. They used to be called to prostrate while they were healthy and good (in the life of the world, but they refused).
		God deals with Unbelievers according to His plan
5	68:044-045	• Then leave Me alone with such as reject this message. By degrees shall We punish them from directions they perceive not. A (long) respite will I grant them. Truly, powerful is My plan.

2.3 Reformation of Human Character Should Continue

Since it is in the best interest of people, both in this world and in the Hereafter, efforts to improve human character and behavior should continue irrespective of hardship and opposition by people who are corrupt and unjust. God commands: "So wait with patience for the command of your Lord, and be not like the Companion of the Fish (Jonah) when he cried out in agony. Had not grace from his Lord reached him, he would indeed have been cast off on the naked shore in disgrace. Thus did his Lord choose him and make him of the company of the righteous. And the unbelievers would almost trip you up with their eyes when they hear the message, and they say: 'Surely he is possessed!' But it is nothing less than a message to all the worlds (humankind, jinn, and all that exists) (Qur'an 68:48-52)."

CHAPTER 22

Injustice and Corruption
Destroy Communities
FROM SURAH ASH-SHU'ARA (26)

God is All Mighty, All Powerful, and All Merciful at the same
time. History contains instances of His wrath as well as of His
mercy. Therefore, it is up to people to decide whether they
would like to deserve God's mercy or His wrath. Clear directions
have been provided in the Qur'an, and acting upon these
instructions will assure God's mercy. History confirms that the
unbelievers, past and present, have been persistently refusing, on
one pretext or the other, to accept the divine message. Like past
communities, the unbelievers of Makkah had been demanding
that the Messenger should show them a sign to convince them of
his divine mission. Sometimes, they would brand him as a poet
or a sorcerer and mock his message. Sometimes they would
ridicule his mission, saying that his followers were composed
only of a few foolish youth, the poor people, and slaves. They
argued that if his mission really had some value for people, the
nobles and the elders would have accepted it first. Surah Ash-
Shu'ara was revealed under such an environment. Addressing
the unbelievers, God asked why, if they wanted to see God's
signs, they insisted on seeing only those horrible signs that
visited doomed communities of the past. Why didn't they look at
the earth, as an example, and reflect on how a variety of fine
vegetation grows from it? No doubt there was a sign in this, but
most of them couldn't comprehend.

1 HUMAN NATURE AND ITS DESTINY

1.1 Arrogance and Self-Interest Clouds Wisdom
This Surah begins with words of consolation that were
specifically applicable to the Messenger at that time and
generally applicable to believers at any time in history. In
essence, God is saying to the Messenger, "Why do you worry
about the unbelievers? If these people have not believed in

355

Islam, it is not because they have not seen any sign, it is because they are stubborn and persist in wrongdoing due to their self-interest. They lack the maturity that is required for those who will listen to reason. Such people will only bow to a sign that will humiliate them."

Table 1.1: God's Reminder and the Unbeliever's Attitude

No	Surah:Verses	Meanings
		Believers should not Grieve Over Unbelievers Attitude
1	26:003-006	It may be that you torment yourself (O Muhammad) because they believe not. • If (such) were Our will, We could send down to them from the sky a sign to which they would bend their necks in humility. But there comes not to them a newly revealed message from (Allah) Most Gracious, but they turn away there from. • They have indeed rejected (the message). So they will know soon (enough) the truth of what they mocked at.
		There are Numerous Signs in Universe for those who Look
2	26:007-009	• Do they not look at the earth—how many noble things of all kinds We have produced therein? Verily, in this is a sign, but most of them do not believe. And verily, your Lord is He, the exalted in might, most merciful.

1.2 Guidance Should Be Judged On Its Own Merit

On one hand, the Messenger was wearied by his efforts to show his people the errors of their belief and to prove the truth that there is only One Creator of the universe Who created people and endowed them with wisdom and free will. On the other hand, the unbelievers were never tired of adopting one excuse after the other. This caused great anguish and grief to the Messenger of Islam, just as had been the case with previous messengers. God asked the people to judge the guidance given in the Qur'an on its own merit. Why didn't the people realize that the Qur'an that is being presented in their own language commands the same good behavior from them that was commanded in past scriptures?

Table 1.2: The Qur'an is from the Lord of the Worlds

No	Surah:Verses	Meanings
		The Qur'an is from God brought down by the Angel to the People
3	26:192-199	1. Verily, this is a revelation from the Lord of the Worlds. 2. With it came down the spirit of faith and truth to your heart and mind that you may admonish in the plain Arabic tongue. 3. Without doubt, it is (announced) in the mystic books of former peoples. Is it not a sign to them that the learned of the Children of Israel knew it (as true)? 4. Had We revealed it to any of the non-Arabs and had he recited it to them, they would not have believed in it.
		Satan has nothing to do with the Qur'an: It is Guidance for the People
4	26:210-212	1. No Satan has brought down this (revelation). 2. It would neither suit them nor would they be able (to produce it). 3. Indeed, they have been removed far from even (a chance of) hearing it.

1.3 Behavior of the Believers and the Unbelievers

The character and behavior of the Messenger and the believers can also be the confirmation of the authenticity of the divine message. One can ask and investigate: "Does the recipient of the Qur'an appear to be a sorcerer? Are the messenger and the believers no different from a poet and his admirers? Why don't you give up disbelief and search for the judgment of your conscience with regards to what God commands? In your hearts, you yourselves believe that the revelations of the Qur'an have nothing in common with sorcery and poetry. Then, are you not cruel and unjust to yourselves, and will you not meet the punishment destined for the cruel and unjust."

Table 1.3: The Messenger, Unbelievers, Poets, and Believers

No	Surah:Verses	Meanings
		Believers Believe in God alone and Rely on Him
5	26:213-220	So call not on any other god with Allah, or you will be among those under the penalty. 1. And admonish your nearest kinsmen. 2. And lower your wing to the believers who follow you. 3. Then if they disobey you, say: "I am free (of responsibility) for what you do." Put your trust on the exalted in might, the merciful—Who sees you standing forth (in prayer), and your movements among those who prostrate themselves, for it is He Who hears and knows all things.
		Unbelievers and Poets Say what they do not Do
6	26:221-227	Shall I inform you, (O people!), on whom it is that the evil ones descend? 1. They descend on every lying, wicked person. 2. (Into whose ears) they pour hearsay vanities, and most of them are liars. 3. And the poets—it is those straying in evil who follow them. Don't you see that they wander distracted in every valley and that they say what they practice not, except those: 1. Who believe and do good 2. And engage much in the remembrance of Allah 3. And defend themselves only after they are unjustly attacked. Soon will the unjust assailants know what vicissitudes their affairs will take.

2 THE DESTINY OF UNJUST AND CORRUPT PEOPLE

There are plenty of signs in the universe for people of knowledge and wisdom. On the other hand, even supernatural signs may fail to convince unjust and the arrogant people. Such people have never believed, even after seeing signs, whether these were signs of natural phenomena or the miracles of the messengers. These people have always adhered to their arrogant behavior and corruption till the divine punishment actually overtook them. This was illustrated by the history of seven communities that persisted in unbelief, just like the unbelievers of Makkah and the unbelievers of the modern world.

2.1 Signs in Nature and the Universe

There are natural signs of God's existence that are scattered all over the universe: "Do they not look at the earth—how many noble things of all kinds We have produced therein? Verily, in this is a sign, but most of them do not believe. And verily, your Lord is He, the exalted in might, most merciful (Qur'an 26:7-9)." By reflecting on signs in nature, an intelligent person can judge for himself the truth of what the Messenger was presenting. Like physical laws, there are also moral and sociopolitical laws of nature that are fixed as to their outcome and results. These moral and sociopolitical laws are presented in the Qur'an.

2.2 Supernatural Signs of God's Wrath

Supernatural signs are like those that were seen by Pharaoh and his people, Noah's people, the 'Ad, the Thamud, the people of Lot, and the Companions of the Wood. Now, it is for the unbelievers to decide which kind of the signs they are eager to see. Perhaps the guilty cannot escape the supernatural signs of God's displeasure. The verses of Surah Ash-Shu'ara that highlight the destiny of the unbelievers are given in the table below.

Table 2: The Destiny of the Unbelievers

No	Surah:Verses	Meanings
		Can Punishment make people Believe?
1	26:200-201	Thus have We caused it to enter the hearts of the sinners. They will not believe in it until they see the grievous penalty.
		God's Punishment will appear Suddenly
2	26:202-209	1. But the (penalty) will come to them of a sudden, while they perceive it not. Then they will say: "Shall we be given a respite?" 2. Do they then ask for Our penalty to be hastened on? You see—if We do let them enjoy (this life) for a few years, yet there comes to them at length the (punishment) that

		they were promised! It will profit them not that they enjoyed (this life).
	3.	Never did We destroy a population, but had its warners by way of reminder, and We never are unjust.

3 THE CONSEQUENCE OF HUMAN BEHAVIOR

Human nature and human interest are two fundamental instincts that mould the behavior of people. Human nature is defined by the human conscience, while human interest is governed by human needs. Human behavior is also influenced by the environment and society, the latter of which is populated by good and bad people who try to motivate an individual either to listen to one's conscience and divine guidance or to run after satisfying one's selfish interests by any means, whether moral or otherwise. Good or bad human behavior results in good or bad consequences for the society

3.1 The Conscience and Divine Guidance

Human nature desires to do good deeds, and humankind is born with the knowledge of what is good and what is bad. A normal individual feels happy if he does some good, and he is troubled if he does bad. The knowledge of what is good and bad and the feeling of happiness while doing good deeds comprise the human conscience. This is the basic element of divine guidance that has been given to each individual at the time of his birth. Along with the human conscience, God has been sending His messengers (1) to remind us of what is good and what is bad and (2) to provide a living human example in the person of the messenger, in order to demonstrate how humanity should be living. The guidance that enables humankind to fulfill its needs and interests without violating its conscience is divine guidance. This is the only way that guards individual human rights and makes people human.

3.2 Human Needs and their Selfish Interests

Fulfillment of human needs is natural and commendable if it is satisfied in good conscience and without violating the rights of others. In practice, this requires honesty, patience, and hard work. Short of these, an individual may fulfill his needs by applying any means that does not violate his conscience and the divine guidance. The human mind, in various creative ways, can find arguments to satisfy, or rather to pacify, its conscience and to justify its self-interest. Presently, this is being done by rationalizing national or personal interests as a valid reason to suspend the moral and sociopolitical laws of nature that God has put in place.

3.3 Perpetual Mentality of the Unbelievers

Due to their common disregard of moral and sociopolitical laws of nature, their conscience, and the divine guidance, the mentality of the unbelievers has been the same throughout the ages. Their arguments, objections, and excuses for not believing have been similar throughout time, and ultimately the fates that they met have also been the same. Likewise, the messengers in every age presented the same teachings, their personal character and their reasoning and arguments against their opponents were the same, and they were all similarly blessed with God's mercy. Both these patterns of behavior and conduct are found in history. Humankind has to judge for themselves to choose the type of people they want to be.

4 THE GENERAL ATTITUDE OF THE UNBELIEVERS

Briefly stated, the divine message is that your Lord Who is the Almighty, the Merciful, commands that you do not oppress others, worship only the One True God, and help the oppressed. In Surah Ash-Shu'ara, narrations about various previous unbelieving communities highlight that the unbelievers ignored divine guidance, worshiped false gods, and tried to oppress and persecute the believers.

4.1 Unbelievers' Disregard for Divine Guidance

Noah's people rejected the divine message, branding the believers as the meanest among them and threatening their messenger with death. Consequently, God delivered Noah and his followers in the laden ark and drowned the rest. The verses of Surah Ash-Shu'ara that summarize the divine message, its rejection by Noah's people, and their eventual destruction are given in the table below.

Table 4.1: The Messenger of God: Noah[PBUH]

No	Surah:Verses	Meanings
		Noah's People Rejected their Messenger
1	26:105-109	The people of Noah rejected the messengers. Behold, their brother Noah said to them: "Will you not fear (Allah)? I am to you a messenger worthy of all trust. So fear Allah, and obey me. No reward do I ask of you for it. My reward is only from the Lord of the Worlds."
	26:111	1. They said: "Shall we believe in you when it is the meanest that follow you?"
	26:116	2. They said: "If you desist not, O Noah! You shall be stoned (to death)."
		Fate of Noah's People is a Sign to Reflect
2	26:117-121	1. He (Noah) said: "O my Lord! Truly my people have rejected me. You judge, then, between me and them openly and deliver me and those of the believers who are with me." 2. So We delivered him and those with him in the ark filled (with all creatures). 3. Thereafter, We drowned those who remained behind. Verily, in this is a sign, but most of them do not believe.

4.2 Unbelievers Worship False Gods of their Fathers

At the enquiry of Abraham, the unbelievers told him that they worshiped idols only because they found their fathers doing so. They didn't ask their fathers why they worshiped false deities. Were they devoid of any wisdom? The creation of the whole universe goes to God as His credit. One may ask what the false deities have created or why these idols should be worshiped. On the Day of Judgment, neither wealth nor sons nor false deities will be helpful. People's fate will only be decided by their belief and good or bad deeds. The verses of Surah Ash-Shu'ara that highlight Abraham's conversation with the unbelievers are given in the table below.

Table 4.2: The Messenger of God: Abraham[PBUH]

No	Surah:Verses	Meanings
		Abraham's Asks his Father and Unbelievers
3	26:070, 072	Behold, he said to his father and his people: "What you worship?"...He asked (again): "Do they listen to you when you call (them) or do you good or harm?"
	26:071	1. They said: "We worship idols, and we remain constantly in attendance on them..."
	26:074	2. They said: "Nay, but we found our fathers doing thus (what we do)."
		The Creator of the Universe and False deities
4	26:077-082	(Abraham said): "For they (the false deities) are enemies to me—not so the Lord and Cherisher of the Worlds 1. Who created me, and it is He Who guides me, 2. Who gives me food and drink, 3. And when I am ill, it is He Who cures me, 4. Who will cause me to die, and then to life (again), 5. And who, I hope, will forgive me my faults on the Day of Judgment."
		Believers and Unbelievers on the Judgment Day
5	26:088-093	(Abraham said:) "The day whereon neither wealth nor sons will avail, but only he (will prosper) that brings to Allah a sound heart. 1. "To the righteous, the Garden will be brought near. 2. "And to those straying in evil, the fire will be placed in full view, and it shall be said to them: 'Where are the (gods) you worshiped besides Allah? Can they help you or help themselves?'"
	26:103-104	Verily in this is a sign, but most of them do not believe. And verily your Lord is He, the exalted in might, most merciful.
		Abraham's Desires translated in his Supplication
6	26:083-087	1. (Abraham supplicated:) "O my Lord! Bestow wisdom on me, and join me with the righteous. 2. "Grant me honorable mention on the tongue of truth among the latest (generations). 3. "Make me one of the inheritors of the Garden of Bliss.

		4. "Forgive my father, for that he is among those astray.
		5. "Let me not be in disgrace on the day when (men) will be raised up."

4.3 Unbelievers Oppress and Persecute Believers

Throughout history, unbelievers have tried to humiliate their messengers and the believers. They resorted to oppression and tyranny and have persecuted the believers. Due to their unjust behavior and arrogance, they were eventually destroyed. The verses of Surah Ash-Shu'ara that highlight the destruction of Pharaoh and his people are given in the table below.

Table 4.3: The Messengers of God: Moses[PBUH] and Aaron[PBUH]

No	Surah:Verses	Meanings
		The Divine Message is—'Do not Oppress Others'
7	26:010	Behold, your Lord called Moses: "Go to the people of iniquity."
	26:022	• (Moses said to Pharaoh:) "And this is the favor with which you do reproach me—that you have enslaved the Children of Israel."
		Pharaoh tried to Humiliate the Messenger
8	26:027, 029	1. (Pharaoh) said: "Truly your messenger who has been sent to you is a veritable madman...If you do put forward any god other than me, I will certainly put you in prison."
	26:034-035	2. (Pharaoh) said to the chiefs around him: "This is indeed a sorcerer well versed. His plan is to get you out of your land by his sorcery; then what is it you counsel?"
		Magicians said: 'We Believe in One True God'
9	26:046-048	3. Then did the sorcerers fall down, prostrate in adoration, saying: "We believe in the Lord of the Worlds, the Lord of Moses and Aaron."
		Pharaoh resorts to Oppression and Tyranny
10	26:049-051	4. Said (Pharaoh): "Believe you in Him before I give you permission? Surely he is your leader who has taught you sorcery, but soon shall you know! Be sure I will cut off your hands and your feet on opposite sides, and I will cause you all to die on the cross."
		5. They said: "No matter! For us, we shall but return to our Lord! Only, our desire is that our

		Lord will forgive us our faults that we may become foremost among the believers."
		Moses was commanded to help the Oppressed
11	26:052	6. By inspiration we told Moses: "Travel by night with my servants, for surely you shall be pursued."
		Pharaoh tried to Humiliate the Believers
12	26:053-056	7. Then Pharaoh sent heralds to (all) the cities, (saying): "These (Israelites) are but a small band, and they are raging furiously against us, but we are a multitude amply forewarned.
		The Believers were Eventually Rescued
13	26:065-067	• We delivered Moses and all who were with him; But We drowned the others. Verily, in this is a sign, but most of them do not believe. And verily your Lord is He, the exalted in might, most merciful.

5 VIOLATION OF THE MORAL AND SOCIOPOLITICAL LAWS

History confirms that cruelty and extravagance destroyed 'Ad, corruption and arrogance destroyed Thamud, perversion and unnatural behavior destroyed Lot's people, and cheating and dishonesty destroyed the Companions of the Wood. Previous divine messages, the unbelievers' response, and their eventual fates as described in Surah Ash-Shu'ara are summarized below.

5.1 Tyranny and Corruption of 'Ad People

God sent messengers to guide people to overall prosperity in human life, to an optimum balance among various aspects of people's lives, and to a harmony in their communities. In contrast, 'Ad's behavior was characterized by the cruelty and extravagance of its leaders, who were more interested in building monuments and fortresses for themselves than in the welfare of their people. Their messenger told them that building monuments and strong fortresses would not enable them to live forever. Moreover, the resources wasted on these projects were compelling them to be cruel to their people. The leaders of 'Ad failed to appreciate their messenger's advice. Instead, they called him a liar and continued to be cruel and extravagant, which eventually destroyed them.

Table 5.1: The Messenger of God: Hud[PBUH]

No	Surah:Verses	Meanings
		Extravagance and Cruelty of the 'Ad Leaders
1	26:123-135	The 'Ad (people) rejected the messengers. Behold, their brother Hud said to them: "Will you not fear (Allah)? I am to you a messenger worthy of all trust. So fear Allah and obey me. No reward do I ask of you for it. My reward is only from the Lord of the Worlds. 1. "Do you build a landmark on every high place to amuse yourselves? 2. "And do you get for yourselves fine buildings in the hope of living therein (forever). 3. "And when you exert your strong hand, do you do it like men of absolute power. "Now fear Allah, and obey me. Yea, fear Him Who has bestowed on you freely all that you know. Freely has He bestowed on you cattle and sons and gardens and springs. Truly, I fear for you the penalty of a great day."
		Leaders of 'Ad Refused to Heed and Reform
2	26:136-140	1. They ('Ad's leaders) said: "It is the same to us whether you admonish us or be not among (our) admonishers. 2. "This is no other than a customary device of the ancients, 3. "And we are not the ones to receive pains and penalties." • So they rejected him, and We destroyed them. Verily in this is a sign, but most of them do not believe. And verily your Lord is He, the exalted in might, most merciful.

5.2 Arrogance and Extravagance of Thamud

Individual and collective pride, which makes a people arrogant and waste natural resources are two major human weaknesses. The most villainous people in history were filled with arrogance and false pride. About Satan, Pharaoh, the opponents of the God's messengers, and extremely wicked tyrants since then, God says: "Those who behave arrogantly on the earth in defiance of right—them will I turn away from My signs (Qur'an 7:146)." He also says: "Thus, does Allah seal up every heart of arrogant and obstinate transgressors (Qur'an 40:35)" and "Undoubtedly, Allah does know what they conceal and what they reveal. Verily, He loves not the arrogant (Qur'an 16:23)." God's messenger Salih warned his people about the consequence of arrogance. They used to carve houses out of the mountains and were very arrogant about them. Thamud disobeyed their messenger failed to reform. This resulted in a punishment which destroyed them.

Table 5.2: The Messenger of God: Salih^{PBUH}

No	Surah:Verses	Meanings
		Thamud's Arrogance and Extravagance
3	26:141-152	The Thamud (people) rejected the messengers. Behold, their brother Salih said to them: "Will you not fear (Allah)? I am to you a messenger worthy of all trust. So fear Allah, and obey me. No reward do I ask of you for it: my reward is only from the Lord of the Worlds. 1. "Will you be left secure in (the enjoyment of) all that you have here— 2. "Gardens and springs, and "Cornfields and date palms with spathes near breaking (with the weight of fruit)? 3. "And you carve houses out of (rocky) mountains with great skill. "But fear Allah and obey me, "And follow not the bidding of those who are extravagant—who make mischief in the land and mend not (their ways).
		Thamud Refused to Listen and Reform
4	26:153-159	• They said: "You are only one of those bewitched! You are no more than a mortal like us. Then bring us a sign if you tell the truth!" • He (Salih) said: "Here is a she-camel. She has a right of watering, and you have a right of watering, (severally) on a day appointed. Touch her not with harm, lest the penalty of a great day seize you." But they hamstrung her: then did they become full of regrets. But the penalty seized them. Verily, in this is a sign, but most of them do not believe. And verily your Lord is He, the exalted in might, most merciful.

5.3 Perversion and Homosexuality of Lot's People

God made human nature such that the two sexes are attracted to each other. Since life in general is based on marriage, it is natural for the opposite sexes to be attracted to each other. In the Qur'an, people are told: "Glory to Allah, Who created in pairs all things that the earth produces, as well as their own (human) kind and (other) things of which they have no knowledge (Qur'an 36:36)." Thus, all living species, plants, animals, humans, and other creatures unknown to man are created in pairs. Such duality seems fundamental in the make up of the entire universe, let alone living species. The atom itself, which until now seemed to be the basic unit of all creations, has protons and electrons, which are positive and negative charges.

By indulging unashamedly in homosexuality, Lot's people perverted human nature. This was a strange phenomenon in human history. Such perversion can occur with individuals as a result of psychological disorders or temporary circumstances. However, if such perversion is widespread, becoming a norm for a whole community despite the presence of women and marriage possibilities, it is a most peculiar distortion of nature. Instead of listening to their messenger, Lot's people threatened him with exile if he did not stop advising them to behave. The verses of Surah Ash-Shu'ara that summarize the divine Message, its rejection by Lot's people, and their eventual destruction are given in the table below.

Table 5.3: The Messenger of God: Lot[PBUH]

No	Surah:Verses	Meanings
		Perversion and Unnatural Behavior
5	26:160-166	The people of Lot rejected the messengers. Behold, their brother Lot said to them: "Will you not fear (Allah)? I am to you a messenger worthy of all trust. So fear Allah, and obey me. No reward do I ask of you for it. My reward is only from the Lord of the Worlds. • "Of all the creatures in the world, will you approach males, "And leave those whom Allah has created for you to be your mates? "Nay, you are a people transgressing (all limits)."

		Lot's People's Refused to Reform
6	26:167-175	They said: "If you desist not, O Lot! You will assuredly be cast out." He said: "I do detest your doings. O my Lord! Deliver me and my family from such things as they do." • So We delivered him and his family—all except an old woman who lingered behind. • But the rest We destroyed utterly. We rained down on them a shower (of brimstone), and evil was the shower on those who were admonished (but heeded not). Verily in this is a sign, but most of them do not believe. And verily your Lord is He, the exalted in might, most merciful.

5.4 Fraud and Corruption of the Madyan People

God tells people: "To the Madyan people, We sent Shu'ayb, one of their own brethren. He said: 'O my people! Worship Allah; you have no other god but Him. Now has come unto you a clear (revelation) from your Lord! Give just measure and weight, nor withhold from the people the things that are their due, and do no mischief on the earth after it has been set in order. That will be best for you if you have faith. And squat not on every road, breathing threats, hindering from the path of Allah those who believe in Him, and seeking in it something crooked. But remember how you were little and He gave you increase. And hold in your mind's eye what was the end of those who did mischief. And if there is a party among you that believes in the message with which I have been sent and a party that does not believe, hold yourselves in patience until Allah does decide between us, for He is the best to decide (Qur'an 7:85-87)."

Cheating was prevalent in Shu'ayb's community. This was an evil practice that spreads corruption and tyranny in society. Shu'ayb asked his people to give full measure and not diminish things while measuring, to weigh things with a right balance, and not to defraud people by reducing their goods. Shu'ayb also advised his people not to ambush people like robbers. Instead of listening to their messenger, the unbelievers among Shu'ayb's people started name-calling. They told Shu'ayb that he was bewitched, a mortal like them, and one of those who lie. They asked Shu'ayb to cause a portion of the sky to fall upon them to prove his truthfulness. In the end, their punishment came, and they were destroyed.

Table 5.4: The Messenger of God: Shu'ayb^{PBUH}

No	Surah:Verses	Meanings
		Shu'ayb's People's Corruption and Fraud
7	26:176-184	The Companions of the Wood rejected the messengers. Behold! Shu'ayb said to them: "Will you not fear (Allah)? I am to you a messenger worthy of all trust. So fear Allah, and obey me. No reward do I ask of you for it. My reward is only from the Lord of the Worlds. 1. "Give just measure, and cause no loss (to others by fraud). 2. "And weigh with scales true and upright. 3. "And withhold not things justly due to men. 4. "Nor do evil in the land, working mischief. 5. "And fear Him Who created you and (Who created) the generations before (you)."
		Shu'ayb's People Refused to Heed and Reform
8	26:185-187	• They said: "You are only one of those bewitched. "You are no more than a mortal like us, and indeed we think you are a liar. "Now cause a piece of the sky to fall on us if you are truthful."
	26:189-190	• But they rejected him. Then the punishment of the day of overshadowing gloom seized them, and that was the penalty of a great day.

CHAPTER 23

The Crisis of Leadership
FROM SURAH AL-NAML (27)

Being human, we deserve to be guided by leaders like Solomon and Sheba. Unfortunately, perhaps due to our misdeeds, we are getting leaders like Pharaoh and his chiefs. These are people who only believe in the theory of evolution, who deny that humankind was created by God, and who believe in the survival of the fittest and in the separation of church and state. God commands us: "O you who believe! Give your response to Allah and His Messenger when He calls you to that which will give you life, and know that Allah comes in between a man and his heart and that it is He to Whom you shall (all) be gathered. And fear tumult or oppression, which affects not in particular (only) those of you who do wrong, and know that Allah is strict in punishment (Qur'an 8:24-25)."

1 THE POLITICAL INSTABILITY IN THE MUSLIM WORLD

1.1 Basics of Leadership in an Islamic Community
The quality of leadership determines the health of a community. Community leaders are the guardians and are therefore responsible for the welfare of their associates. A believer has to listen to and obey the order of his ruler, whether he likes it or not, so long as his orders do not involve disobedience to God. If an act of disobedience to God is imposed, one should not listen to the ruler or obey him. Although a democratic government in a country with a Muslim majority should govern their citizens through Islamic rules of justice and equality, most of the so-called Muslim countries fail to provide justice and the rule of law. Under such circumstances, the citizens of these countries are not obligated to listen to their rulers, whether secular or religious. This has contributed to anarchy and political turmoil that can only be improved by honest governance. The *Ahadith* from Sahih Bukhari that highlight the government-citizen relationships are given in the table below.

371

Table 1.1: Government – Citizen Relationships

No	Book:Hadith	Sahih Bukhari Translated by Dr. M. Muhsin Khan
		Everyone is a Guardian and is Responsible
1	89:252	Narrated 'Abdullah bin 'Umar: God's Messenger said, "Surely! Everyone of you is a guardian and is responsible for his charges: 1. "The *Imam* (ruler) of the people is a guardian and is responsible for his subjects. 2. "A man is the guardian of his family (household) and is responsible for his subjects. 3. "A woman is the guardian of her husband's home and of his children and is responsible for them, and 4. "The slave (employee) of a man is a guardian of his master's (company's) property and is responsible for it. 5. "Surely, every one of you is a guardian and responsible for his charges."
		Limits of Citizens' Obligations in a State
2	89:258	Narrated 'Abdullah: The Messenger said, "A Muslim has to listen to and obey the order of his ruler, whether he likes it or not, as long as his orders involve not one in disobedience to Allah. But if an act of disobedience to Allah is imposed, one should not listen to it or obey it."
		Hypocrisy: Flattery of Government Officials
3	89:289	Narrated Muhammad bin Zaid bin Abdullah bin 'Umar: Some people told to Ibn 'Umar, "When we enter upon our ruler(s), we say in their praise what is contrary to what we say when we leave them." • Ibn 'Umar said, "We used to consider this as hypocrisy."
		Accountability of Government Officials
4	89:264 89:265	1. Narrated Ma'qil: I heard the Messenger saying, "Any man whom Allah has given the authority of ruling some people and he does not look after them in an honest manner, he will never feel even the smell of Paradise." 2. Narrated Ma'qil: God's Messenger said, "If any ruler having the authority to rule Muslim subjects dies while he is deceiving them, Allah will forbid Paradise for him."

1.2 Causes of Instability in the Muslim World

The reality is that it was our fate that we were born into a Muslim family. Therefore, we will prosper only if we behave like Muslims. The most important articles of Islamic belief that impact individual behavior are the belief in a single God *(Tauheed)* and belief in the accountability for one's deeds in the Hereafter. Let us challenge ourselves: what else do we worship besides God? Does our behavior really reflect that we are accountable for our injustice done to others, our unlawful earnings, and our disregard for the rule of law? What can we expect from God if our behavior is like that of unbelievers? Are we candidates for His mercy or His wrath?

Belief in *Tauheed* motivates people against self-interest and unlawful behavior. In Surah Al-Naml, attention is drawn to some of the most glaring and visible realities of the universe, and the unbelievers are asked one question again and again: "Do these realities not testify to the truth of *Tauheed* to which the Qur'an invites you?" Then, the real cause of the unbeliever's behavior is pointed out, i.e., it is their denial of the Hereafter and of the accountability for their behavior and deeds that blinds them and makes them insensitive to every glaring reality. This makes life a very non-serious business for them. The verses of Surah Al-Naml that highlight that there is no other god than God are given in the table below.

Table 1.2: Can there be another god besides one God?

No	Surah:Verses	Meanings
5	27:059-064	Praise be to Allah, and peace on his servants whom He has chosen (for his message). (Who) is better—Allah or the false gods they associate (with Him)? 1. Or, Who has created the heavens and the earth, and Who sends you down rain from the sky? Yea, with it We cause to grow well-planted orchards full of beauty and delight. It is not in your power to cause the growth of the trees in them. (Can there be another) god besides Allah? Nay, they are a people who swerve from justice. 2. Or, Who has made the earth firm to live in,

	made rivers in its midst, set thereon mountains immovable, and made a separating bar between the two bodies of flowing water? (Can there be another) god besides Allah? Nay, most of them know not. 3. Or, Who listens to the (soul) distressed when it calls on Him, and Who relieves its suffering and makes you (O people) inheritors of the earth? (Can there be another) god besides Allah? Little it is that you heed! 4. Or, Who guides you through the depths of darkness on land and sea, and Who sends the winds as heralds of glad tidings, going before His mercy? (Can there be another) god besides Allah? High is Allah above what they associate with Him! 5. Or, Who originates creation, then repeats it, and who gives you sustenance from heaven and earth? (Can there be another) god besides Allah? Say, "Bring forth your argument if you are telling the truth."

1.3 Believers Believe in Hereafter and the Accountability

The only people who can benefit from guidance as given in the Qur'an and who can become worthy of God's bounties are those who accept the physical, moral, and sociopolitical realities presented in the Qur'an as the basic laws of the universe, and who then follow up their belief with obedience and submission in their practical lives. What de-motivates people to follow this way is the denial of the Hereafter and of their accountability for their selfish behavior. This makes them irresponsible and selfish, and it compels them to commit unlawful deeds during their worldly lives. For such people, it is impossible to accept the moral restrictions put on them in fulfilling their selfish interests and desires. The verses of Surah Al-Naml that highlight the behavior of those who believe in the Hereafter are given in the table below.

Table 1.3: Behavior of Those Who Believe in the Hereafter

No	Surah:Verses	Meanings
		Those Who Believe in the Hereafter
6	27:001-003	These are verses of the Qur'an, a book that makes (things) clear, 1. A guide and glad tidings for the believers, 2. Those who establish regular prayers and give in regular charity, 3. And also have (full) assurance of the Hereafter.
		Those Who Disbelieve in the Hereafter
7	27:004-005	As to those who believe not in the Hereafter, 1. We have made their deeds pleasing in their eyes, and so they wander about in distraction. 2. They are for whom a grievous penalty is (waiting), and in the Hereafter theirs will be the greatest loss.

1.4 Behavior of Those Who Disbelieve in the Hereafter

God informs people that those who are not serious about the Hereafter do not know much about it because they are in doubt due to their flawed reasoning. They question the possibility of resurrection from the bones and dust that survive from their dead bodies. The situation of their forefathers being resurrected is even more unimaginable to them. Although they were promised resurrection, it seems to them to be nothing more than stories from the past. On the other hand, *Tauheed* and accountability are the two most fundamental principles of the divine message, and they help to transform beastly human behavior into real human behavior. The verses of Surah Al-Naml that list the importance of the Hereafter and that warn humanity of the consequences of ignoring it are given in the table below. In these verses, things are said repeatedly in order to inculcate the importance of the Hereafter in the minds of the people, to warn them of the consequences of ignoring it, and to convince them of its existence, just as an eyewitness convinces those who were not there. It is, in fact, intended to arouse humankind from their slumber and to convince them to reform their character, behavior and deeds.

Table 1.4: Unbelievers of the Hereafter and Accountability

No	Surah:Verses	Meanings
		Unbelievers, are in Doubt about Hereafter
8	27:065-066	Say: "None in the heavens or on earth except Allah knows what is hidden, nor can they perceive when they shall be raised up (for judgment). 1. "Still less can their knowledge comprehend the Hereafter. 2. "Nay, they are in doubt and uncertainty about it. 3. "Nay, they are blind thereunto."
		What Unbelievers Say about Resurrection
9	27:067-075	1. The unbelievers say: "What! When we become dust—we and our fathers—shall we really be raised (from the dead)? 2. "It is true we were promised this—we and our fathers before (us). These are nothing but tales of the ancients." Say: "Go you through the earth and see what has been the end of those guilty (of sin)." But grieve not over them, nor distress yourself because of their plots. 3. They also say: "When will this promise (come to pass)? (Say) if you are truthful." • Say: "It may be that some of the events that you wish to hasten on may be (close) in your pursuit!" But verily your Lord is full of grace to mankind. Yet, most of them are ungrateful. • Verily, your Lord knows all that their hearts do hide, as well as all that they reveal. Nor is there anything of the unseen, in heaven or earth, but is (recorded) in a clear record.
		Only Those Who have Hearing will Listen
10	2:076-081	Verily this Qur'an does explain to the Children of Israel most of the matters in which they disagree. • It certainly is a guide and a mercy to those who believe. Verily, your Lord will decide between them by His decree, and He is exalted in might, all-knowing. So put your trust in Allah, for you are on (the path of) manifest truth. 1. Truly you cannot cause the dead to listen, nor can you cause the deaf to hear the call, (especially) when they turn back in retreat.

376

		2. Nor can you be a guide to the blind (to prevent them) from straying. Only those will you get to listen who believe in Our revelations, and they will bow in Islam.
		What People shall Sow So Shall They Reap!
11	27:082-086	And when the word is fulfilled against them (the unjust), 1. We shall produce from the earth a beast to (face) them. He will speak to them, for that mankind did not believe with assurance in Our signs. 2. One day We shall gather together from every people a troop of those who reject our signs, and they shall be kept in ranks— 3. Until, when they come (before the judgment seat), (Allah) will say: "Did you reject My signs, though you comprehended them not in knowledge, or what was it you did. 4. The word will be fulfilled against them because of their wrongdoing, and they will be unable to speak (in their defense). See they not that We have made the night for them to rest in and the day to give them light? Verily, in these are signs for any people that believe!
		Only Good Deeds will earn the Best Reward
12	27:089-090	• If any do good, good will (accrue) to them there from, and they will be secure from terror that day. • And if any do evil, their faces will be thrown headlong into the fire. Do you receive a reward other than that which you have earned by your deeds?

2 VARIOUS TYPES OF LEADERSHIP

2.1 Leadership under God and His Guidance

Accepting the invitation to serve One God alone is for the benefit of people and rejecting it is to their own loss. God's servitude frees humanity from slavery to other people and to other things created by God. Only God's commands are applicable to all people, and they should be a common heritage, set of values, and a set of rules. If people keep postponing the implementation of their faith until they saw those signs of God that will force them to believe and submit, then that will be the time for judgment, and believing only at that late time will be of no avail. People are commanded to serve God alone and to act upon His divine commands. God tells the Messenger to say: "I have been commanded to serve the Lord of this city (Makkah), Him Who has sanctified it and to Whom (belong) all things. And I am commanded to be of those who bow in Islam to Allah's will and to recite the Qur'an (and live accordingly). If any accept guidance, they do it for the good of their own souls, and if any stray, say: "I am only a warner (27:91-92)."

Leadership under divine guidance was provided by Solomon, who had been blessed by God with wealth, kingdom, and grandeur undreamed of throughout history. Since he regarded himself answerable before God and had the feeling that whatever he had was only due to God's bounty, he adopted the attitude of obedience before Him without any type of vanity or dictatorship in his rule. He even listened to an ant, perhaps the most humble resident of his state, and happily addressed her concern. The verses of Surah Al-Naml that concern the behavior of a believing leader are given in the table below.

Table 2.1: Solomon, a Believing Leader and the Messenger

No	Surah:Verses	Meanings
		The Believing Leaders are always Humble
1	27:015-016	1. We gave (in the past) knowledge to David and Solomon, and they both said: "Praise be to Allah, Who has favored us above many of his servants who believe." 2. Solomon was David's heir. He said: "O you people! We have been taught the speech of birds and on us has been bestowed (a little) of all things. This is indeed grace manifest (from Allah).
		They address the Concern of all Citizens
2	27:017-019	Before Solomon were marshaled his hosts—of jinns and men and birds, and they were all kept in order and ranks. • At length, when they came to a (lowly) valley of ants, one of the ants said: "O you ants, get into your habitations, lest Solomon and his

		hosts crush you (under their feet) without knowing it. • So he (Solomon) smiled, amused at her speech, and he said: "O my Lord! So order me that I may be grateful for Your favors, which you have bestowed on me and on my parents. "And that I may work the righteousness that will please You. "Admit me, by Your Grace, to the ranks of Your righteous servants."
		A Messenger with Divine Resources
3	27:020-028	He (Solomon) took a muster of the birds, and he said: "Why is it I see not the hoopoe, or is he among the absentees? I will certainly punish him with a severe penalty or execute him unless he brings me a clear reason (for absence)." 1. But the hoopoe tarried not far. He (came up and) said: "I have compassed (territory) that you have not compassed, and I have come to you from Saba with tidings true. 2. "I found (there) a woman ruling over them and provided with every requisite, and she has a magnificent throne. I found her and her people worshiping the sun besides Allah. Satan has made their deeds seem pleasing in their eyes and has kept them away from the path, so they receive no guidance— 3. "(Kept them away from the path) that they should not worship Allah, Who brings to light what is hidden in the heavens and the earth and knows what you hide and what you reveal." 4. "Allah! There is no god but He, Lord of the throne supreme!" (Solomon) said: "Soon shall we see whether you have told the truth or lied! Go you with this letter of mine and deliver it to them. Then draw back from them, and (wait to) see what answer they return."

2.2 Divine Guidance Helps Such Leadership

The leaders that fall into this category are generally of good nature and accept the truth whenever they find it. This type of leadership is exemplified in the person of the Queen of Sheba, who ruled over a most wealthy and well-known people in the history of Arabia. She possessed all those means of life that could cause a person to become vain and conceited. She professed a religion that was not only an ancestral way of life with her but that she had to follow in order to maintain her position as ruler. Therefore, it was much more difficult for her to give up her religion and adopt the way of *Tauheed* than it would be for a common person. However, when the truth became evident to her, nothing could stop her from accepting it. Her deviation was, in fact, due to her being born and brought up in a polytheistic environment and not because of her being a slave to her lusts and desires. Her conscience was aware of the accountability before God.

Table 2.2: Sheba, a Conscientious Leader

No	Surah:Verses	Meanings
		Solomon's Letter to Sheba and her Reply
4	27:029-035	(The queen) said: "You chiefs! Here is delivered to me a letter worthy of respect. It is from Solomon and is (as follows): 'In the name of Allah, Most Gracious, Most Merciful. "'Be not arrogant against me, but come to me in submission (to the true religion).'" 1. She said: "You chiefs! Advise me in my affair. No affair have I decided except in your presence." They said: "We are endued with strength and given to vehement war, but the command is with you, so consider what you will command." 2. She said: "Kings, when they enter a country, despoil it and make the noblest of its people its meanest. Thus do they behave. But I am going to send him a present and (wait) to see with what (answer) return (my) ambassadors."
		Solomon's Response to Sheba's Messengers
5	27:036-037	Now when (the embassy) came to Solomon, he said: "Will you give me abundance in wealth? But that which Allah has given me is better than that which He has given you! Nay, it is you who rejoice in your gift. • "Go back to them, and be sure we shall come to them with such hosts as they will never be able to meet. We shall expel them from there in disgrace, and they will feel humbled."

		Solomon's Preparations to Receive Sheba
6	27:038-040	He said (to his own men): "You chiefs! Which of you can bring me her throne before they come to me in submission?" 1. Said one audacious among the jinns: "I will bring it to you before you rise from your council. Indeed, I have full strength for the purpose and may be trusted." 2. Said one who had knowledge of the Book: "I will bring it to you within the twinkling of an eye!" Then when (Solomon) saw it placed firmly before him, he said: "This is by the grace of my Lord to test me whether I am grateful or ungrateful! And if any is grateful, truly his gratitude is (a gain) for his own soul, but if any is ungrateful, truly my Lord is free of all needs, supreme in honor.
		Sheba Visits Solomon and Submits to God
7	27:041-044	He said: "Transform her throne out of all recognition by her. Let us see whether she is guided (to the truth) or is one of those who receive no guidance." 1. So when she arrived, she was asked, "Is this your throne?" She said, "It was just like this, and knowledge was bestowed on us in advance of this, and we have submitted to Allah (in Islam)." And he diverted her from the worship of others besides Allah, for she was (sprung) of a people that had no faith. 2. She was asked to enter the lofty palace, but when she saw it, she thought it was a lake of water, and she (tucked up her skirts), uncovering her legs. He (Solomon) said: "This is but a palace paved smooth with slabs of glass." She said: "O my Lord! I have indeed wronged my soul. I do (now) submit (in Islam), with Solomon, to the Lord of the Worlds.

2.3 Unbelieving Leadership is Tyrannical and Corrupt

This type of leadership is represented by Pharaoh and his chiefs, the leaders of the Thamud, and the leaders of Lot's people. They all were heedless of the accountability for their behavior in the Hereafter. Consequently, they became the slaves of national bigotry or racial self-interests. These people did not believe even after seeing numerous signs of God's power. Rather, they turned against those who invited them to goodness and piety. They persisted in their evil ways, which were held in abhorrence by every sensible person. They did not listen to the news of the divine punishment until a moment before they were overtaken by the scourge of God.

Table 2.3: Unbelieving Leaders are Unjust and Tyrants

No	Surah:Verses	Meanings
		Pharaoh and his Chiefs had enslaved Bani Israel
8	27:007-014	Behold! Moses said to his family: "I perceive a fire; soon will I bring you from there some information, or I will bring you a burning brand to light our fuel, that you may warm yourselves." But when he came to the (fire), a voice was heard: "Blessed are those in the fire and those around, and glory to Allah, the Lord of the Worlds. O Moses! Verily, I am Allah, the exalted in might, the wise. 1. "Now you do throw your rod!" But when he saw it moving (of its own accord) as if it had been a snake, he turned back in retreat and retraced not his steps. "O Moses!" (It was said), "Fear not. Truly, in My presence, those called as messengers have no fear. But if any have done wrong and have thereafter substituted good to take the place of evil, truly, I am oft-forgiving, most merciful. 2. "Now put your hand into your bosom, and it will come forth white without stain (or harm). (These are) among the nine signs (you will take) to Pharaoh and his people, for they are a people rebellious in transgression." But when Our signs came to them that should have opened their eyes, they said: "This is sorcery manifest!" And they rejected those signs in iniquity and arrogance, though their souls were convinced thereof. So see what was the end of those who acted corruptly!
		Leaders of the Thamud Planned to Kill Salih
9	27:045-053	We sent (aforetime) to the Thamud their brother Salih, saying, "Serve Allah." But behold, they

382

		became two factions quarrelling with each other.
		3. He said: "O my people! Why ask you to hasten on the evil in preference to the good? If only you ask Allah for forgiveness, you may hope to receive mercy?"
		4. They said: "Ill omen do we augur from you and those that are with you."
		5. He said: "Your ill omen is with Allah; yea, you are a people under trial."
		6. There were in the city nine men of a family who made mischief in the land and would not reform. They said: "Swear a mutual oath by Allah that we shall make a secret night attack on him and his people and that we shall then say to his heir (when he seeks vengeance): 'We were not present at the slaughter of his people, and we are positively telling the truth.'"
		They plotted and planned, but We too planned, even while they perceived it not. Then see what the end of their plot was—this, that We destroyed them and their people, all (of them). Now such were their houses in utter ruin because they practiced wrongdoing. Verily, in this is a sign for people of knowledge. And We saved those who believed and practiced righteousness.
		Lot's People and their Unnatural Behavior
10	27:054-058	(We also sent) Lot (as a messenger). Behold, He said to his people, "Do you do what is shameful though you see (its iniquity)? Would you really approach men in your lusts rather than women? Nay, you are a people (grossly) ignorant." • But his people gave no other answer but this: they said, "Drive out the followers of Lot from your city. These are indeed men who want to be clean and pure!" But We saved him and his family, except his wife. Her We destined to be of those who lagged behind. And We rained down on them a shower (of brimstone), and evil was the shower on those who were admonished (but heeded not)!

CHAPTER 24

God's Will, His Ways, and His Justice
FROM SURAH AL-QASAS (28)

Humankind, due to its very nature, is an embodiment of self-interest and conscience. Generally self-interest leads to corruption, exploitation, and oppression. "The (human) soul is certainly prone to evil, unless my Lord does bestow His mercy. But surely my Lord is oft-forgiving, most merciful (Qur'an 12:53)." Human conscience, on the other hand, reproaches a person whenever it commits evil deeds. The very existence of conscience bears testimony that each and every individual is born with the knowledge of what is good and bad. God sent his messengers to remind us of what is evil and what is good and of the consequences of being good or evil. Life on earth is a perpetual struggle between good and evil.

The messengers' role is to highlight the behavior that is beneficent and that spares problems and misery. What the messengers conveyed is a complete message that when implemented in human life brings happiness. Thus, whoever obeys God's rules is a beneficiary. This benefit is assured because the rules are made to spare people from suffering, disunity, and anarchy. In Surah Al-Qasas, the struggle between Moses and Pharaoh is elaborated, providing guidance to people along the way. The story characters may have had different names in the past than they do in the present, but their behavior and the outcome remain the same. One can find many similarities in the present word to the stories of Yusuf and his brothers, Moses and Pharaoh, and Muhammad and the Makkans.

1 GOD DESIRES TO HELP THE OPPRESSED

God helps people by His Own divine ways and rewards righteous people in both lives. God has power and ability to accomplish whatever He Wills by whatever means He chooses. Both Pharaoh and the unbelievers of Makkah used all their resources to suppress the divine message with utmost cruelty.

384

Yet, the world knows who came out victorious in the end and who was destroyed. These incidents have been preserved in history so that the unbelievers of present and future generations should reflect and take warning.

1.1 Corrupt People Discriminate and Oppress

History proves that corrupt people practice discrimination, exploitation, and oppression to achieve their selfish goals. But God desires to make the oppressed people the leaders. "Truly Pharaoh elated himself in the land and broke up its people into sections, depressing a small group among them. Their sons he slew, but he kept alive their females, for he was indeed a maker of mischief. We wished to be gracious to those who were being depressed in the land, to make them leaders and make them heirs, to establish a firm place for them in the land, and to show Pharaoh, Haman, and their hosts, at their hands, the very things against which they were taking precautions (Qur'an 28:4-6)."

Corrupt people are not helpful, and they boast about their riches acquired through corruption. Qarun was a corrupt person who was very rich. Since God does not like arrogant and boastful people, such people are eventually destroyed. Therefore, people should not be ungrateful for God's bounties. They should discriminate between who are boastful about their achievements due to corruption and who are successful due their honesty and hard work. The verses of Surah Al-Qasas that illustrate the behavior of corrupt people and God's favor to the weak are given in the table below.

Table 1: Behavior and the Fate of the Corrupt People

No	Surah:Verses	Meanings
		Corrupt People are Not Helpful, but Boastful
1	28:076-078	• Qarun was doubtless, of the people of Moses; but he acted insolently towards them. Such were the treasures We had bestowed on him that their very keys would have been a burden to a body of strong men. • Behold! His people said to him: "Exult not, for Allah loves not those who exult. But seek, with the (wealth) that Allah has bestowed on you the home of the Hereafter, nor forget your portion

		in this world. But do you good, as Allah has been good to you, and seek not mischief in the land, for Allah loves not those who do mischief." • He said: "This has been given to me because of a certain knowledge that I have." Did he not know that Allah had destroyed, before him, generations that were superior to him in strength and greater in the amount (of riches) they had collected? But the wicked are not called (immediately) to account for their sins.
		Corrupt People are Eventually Destroyed
2	28:079-081	So he went forth among his people in the (pride of his worldly) glitter. 1. Said those whose aim is the life of this world: "Oh! That we had the like of what Qarun has got! For he is truly a lord of mighty good fortune." 2. But those who had been granted knowledge said: "Alas for you! The reward of Allah (in this world and the Hereafter) is best for those who believe and work righteousness. But this none shall attain, save those who steadfastly persevere (in good)." 3. Then We caused the earth to swallow up him and his house; and he had not (the least little) party to help him against Allah, nor could he defend himself.
		Corrupt and Ungrateful People Never Succeed
3	28:082-083	• Those who had envied his position the day before began to say on the morrow: "Ah! It is indeed Allah Who enlarges the provision or restricts it to any of His servants He pleases! Had it not been that Allah was gracious to us, He could have caused the earth to swallow us up! Ah! Those who reject Allah will assuredly never prosper." • That home of the Hereafter We shall give to those who intend not high-handedness or mischief on earth, and the end is (best) for the righteous

1.2 God Helps People by His Own Divine Ways.

God desired that Moses be brought up in Pharaoh's household, and He arranged it by having Moses' mother float her infant son in a basket on the river. "So We sent this inspiration to the mother of Moses: 'Suckle (your child), but when you have fears about him, cast him into the river. But fear not nor grieve, for We shall restore him to you, and We shall make him one of Our messengers.' Then the people of Pharaoh picked him up (from the river). (It was intended) that (Moses) should be to them an adversary and a cause of sorrow, for Pharaoh and Haman and their hosts were men of sin. The wife of Pharaoh said: '(Here is) joy of the eye for me and for you; slay him not. It may be that he will be of use to us, or we may adopt him as a son.' And they perceived not (what they were doing) (Qur'an 28:7-9)."

1.3 God's Promises and Plans are Always Fulfilled

To fulfill His plans and His promise, God at first strengthened the heart of Moses' mother and then ordained that Moses would not suckle from any foster mother. In this way, God arranged the return of Moses to his mother. "But there came to be a void in the heart of the mother of Moses. She was going almost to disclose his (case) had We not strengthened her heart (with faith), so that she might remain a (firm) believer. She said to the sister of (Moses), 'Follow him,' so she (the sister) watched him in the character of a stranger. And they knew not. We ordained that he refused suck at first, until (his sister came up and) said: 'Shall I point out to you the people of a house that will nourish and bring him up for you and be sincerely attached to him?' Thus did We restore him to his mother that her eye might be comforted, that she might not grieve, and that she might know that the promise of Allah is true (Qur'an 28:10-13)."

2 MOSES: FROM A FUGITIVE TO A MESSENGER

2.1 God Plans for Moses' Training

God provides the means and motives for whatever He wills to accomplish in His Own imperceptible ways. Thus, He arranged that the child (Moses), through whom Pharaoh was to be removed from power, was raised in his own house. Next, God said about Moses: "When he reached full age and was firmly established (in life), We bestowed on him wisdom and knowledge, for thus do We reward those who do good. And he entered the city at a time when its people were not watching, and he found there two men fighting—one of his own religion and the other of his foes. Now the man of his own religion appealed to him against his foe, and Moses struck him with his fist and made an end of him. He said: 'This is a work of evil (Satan), for he is an enemy that manifestly misleads!' He prayed: 'O my Lord! I have indeed wronged my soul! Do You then forgive me!' So (Allah) forgave him, for He is the oft-forgiving, most merciful (Qur'an 28:14-16)." This was a prelude that forced Moses to leave the land of Pharaoh and peacefully attend to the learning of wisdom and knowledge in the company of one of God's messengers.

Table 2.1: God Facilitated Moses Migration

No	Surah:Verses	Meanings
		Moses Repents and Seek God's Forgiveness
1	28:017-019	• He said: "O my Lord! For that You have bestowed Your grace on me, never shall I be a help to those who sin." • So he saw the morning in the city, looking about in a state of fear, when behold, the man who had the day before sought his help called aloud for his help (again). Moses said to him: "You are truly, it is clear, a quarrelsome fellow." • Then, when he decided to lay hold of the man who was an enemy to both of them, that man said: "O Moses! Is it your intention to slay me as you slew a man yesterday? Your intention is none other than to become a powerful violent man in the land, and not to be one who sets things right."
		Moses Receives Advice to Get Away to Security
2	28:020-021	There came a man, running from the furthest end of the city. 1. He said: "O Moses! The chiefs are taking counsel together about you to slay you, so get you away, for I do give you sincere advice." 2. He therefore got away there from, looking

		about, in a state of fear.
		3. He prayed: "O my Lord! Save me from people given to wrongdoing."

2.2 God's Help is There for the Asking

During times of hardship, one should be patient and seek God's help. God answers the prayers of His servants, and none despairs of God's help except unbelieving people. Although Moses was brought up in an unbelieving environment as a member of Pharaoh's household, he believed in God. "Then, when he turned his face towards (the land of) Madyan, he said: "I do hope that my Lord will show me the smooth and straight path (Qur'an 28:22)." Believers are patient, help others, and ask for God's help. God bestowed these qualities of behavior on Moses. That is why he helped the ladies in getting water from the well for their sheep, went back to the shade, and prayed. Moses' prayer resulted in a living arrangement and an opportunity to learn from one of the most learned people of Madyan.

Table 2.2: God Facilitated Moses' Stay in Madyan

No	Surah:Verses	Meanings
		Moses arrives in Madyan and seeks God's Help
3	28:023-025	1. When he arrived at the watering (place) in Madyan, he found there a group of men watering (their flocks).
		2. Besides them he found two women who were keeping back (their flocks). He said: "What is the matter with you?" They said: "We cannot water (our flocks) until the shepherds take back (their flocks), and our father is a very old man."
		3. So he watered (their flocks) for them. Then he turned back to the shade and said: "O my Lord! Truly am I in (desperate) need of any good that You do send me."
		Afterwards one of the (damsels) came (back) to him, walking bashfully. She said: "My father invites you that he may reward you for having watered (our flocks) for us." So when he (Moses) came to him (the old Madyan man) and narrated the story, he said: "Fear not; (well) you have escaped from unjust people."

		Moses Agreed to Stay 8 or 10 Years in Madyan
4	28:026-028	1. Said one of the (damsels): "O my (dear) father! Engage him on wages. Truly, the best of men for you to employ is the (man) who is strong and trustworthy." 2. He said: "I intend to wed one of these my daughters to you on condition that you serve me for eight years, but if you complete ten years, it will be (grace) from you. But I intend not to place you under a difficulty. You will find me, indeed, if Allah wills, one of the righteous." 3. He (Moses) said: "Be that (the agreement) between me and you. Whichever of the two terms I fulfill, let there be no ill will to me. Be Allah a witness to what we say."

2.3 God Appointed Moses His Messenger

God appointed Moses to be His messenger unexpectedly, while Moses was on a journey, and nobody knew what event took place in the wilderness at the foot of Mt. Sinai. Even Moses himself did not know a moment before with what he was going to be blessed. He, in fact, had gone to bring a piece of fire, but had returned as a God's messenger. The verses of Surah Al-Qasas that highlight the appointment of Moses as God's messenger are given in the table below.

Table 2.3: Moses, the Messenger of God

No	Surah:Verses	Meanings
		Moses Returns to Egypt with his Family
5	28:029	1. Now when Moses had fulfilled the term and was travelling with his family, he perceived a fire in the direction of Mount Tur. 2. He said to his family: "Tarry you; I perceive a fire; I hope to bring you from there some information or a burning firebrand that you may warm yourselves."
		God Appointed Moses as His Messenger
6	28:030-032	1. But when he came to the (fire), a voice was heard from the right bank of the valley, from a tree in hallowed ground: 2. "O Moses! Verily I am Allah, the Lord of the Worlds. Now throw your rod!" But when he

		saw it moving (of its own accord) as if it had been a snake, he turned back in retreat and retraced not his steps.
		3. "O Moses!" (It was said), "Draw near, and fear not, for you are of those who are secure. Move your hand into your bosom, and it will come forth white without stain (or harm), and draw your hand close to your side (to guard) against fear.
		4. "Those are the two credentials from your Lord to Pharaoh and his chiefs, for truly they are a people rebellious and wicked."
		Moses is sent to Pharaoh and his Chiefs
7	28:033-035	1. He (Moses) said: "O my Lord! I have slain a man among them, and I fear lest they slay me. And my brother Aaron—he is more eloquent in speech than I. So send him with me as a helper to confirm (and strengthen) me, for I fear that they may accuse me of falsehood."
		2. He (God) said: "We will certainly strengthen your arm through your brother and invest you both with authority, so they shall not be able to touch you. With Our signs shall you triumph—you two as well as those who follow you."

2.4 One's Fate is Always Linked to one's Behavior

Both Pharaoh and the Quraish of Makkah used all their material resources to suppress the spread of Islam. Yet, the world knows who succeeded in the end and who were destroyed. This has been preserved in history so that people of present and future generations should learn that their fates are tied to their behavior and deeds. It is not possible to defeat God's will and the law of nature that God has put in place.

Table 2.4: Behavior and the Fate of Pharaoh

No	Surah:Verses	Meanings
		Behavior of Pharaoh and his People
8	28:036-039	When Moses came to them with Our clear signs, they said: "This is nothing but sorcery faked up. Never did we hear the like among our fathers of old."
		• Moses said: "My Lord knows best who it is that

9	28:040-042	comes with guidance from Him and whose end will be best in the Hereafter. Certain it is that the wrongdoers will not prosper." • Pharaoh said: "O Chiefs! No god do I know for you but myself. Therefore, 1. "O Haman! Light me a (kiln to bake bricks) out of clay, and build me a lofty palace, that I may mount up to the god of Moses. 2. "But as far as I am concerned, I think (Moses) is a liar." • And he was arrogant and insolent in the land, beyond reason—he and his hosts. They thought that they would not have to return to Us.
		The Fate of Pharaoh and his People
9	28:040-042	• So We seized him and his hosts, and We flung them into the sea. Now behold what was the end of those who did wrong. • We made them (but) leaders inviting to the fire; on the Day of Judgment no help shall they find. • In this world, We made a curse to follow them, and On the Day of Judgment they will be among the loathed.

2.5 Only Behavior Confirms what People Believe

Success or failure very much depends on one's behavior, intentions, and effort as an individual and as a member of society. If most of the individuals fulfill all their moral and sociopolitical obligations, they are successful in this life, and their community will be prosperous, peaceful, and secure. On the other hand, if most of the people follow their personal desires and disregard the moral and sociopolitical laws of nature, then that community is bound to fail and eventually to be destroyed. Believers' behavior, intentions, and effort are directed by their conscience and by divine guidance, factors that are normally ignored by the unbelievers, resulting in their undesirable fate. Individual conscience and divine guidance inculcate good intensions in people, while people's personal interests can influence people into having bad intentions. These good or bad intentions, followed by individual efforts and God's will, result in either good or bad fate for people.

God commands people: "Fear tumult or oppression, which affects not in particular (only) those of you who do wrong, and know that Allah is strict in punishment (Qur'an 8:25)." God's punishment may afflict both the bad as well as the good people. God informs people: "Generations before you We destroyed when they did wrong. Their messengers came to them with clear signs, but they would not believe! Thus do We requite those who sin! Then We made you heirs in the land after them, to see how you would behave (Qur'an 10:13-14)." To guide humanity, God kept sending messengers and books of revelation so that people might be successful, and so that they could not complain that no messenger had been sent to them and no revelation given to them.

Table 2.5: God has been Guiding People for their Success

No	Surah:Verses	Meanings
		Our Lord! **Why did You not send us a Messenger?**
10	28:043-047	1. We did reveal to Moses the Book after We had destroyed the earlier generations, (to give) insight to men, and guidance and mercy, that they might receive admonition. 2. You were not on the western side when We decreed the commission to Moses, nor were you a witness (of those events). 3. But We raised up (new) generations, and long were the ages that passed over them. 4. You were not a dweller among the people of Madyan, rehearsing Our signs to them, but it is We Who send messengers (with inspiration). 5. Nor were you at the side of (the mountain of) Tur when we called (to Moses). Yet, (you are sent) as a mercy from your Lord, to give warning to a people to whom no warner had come before you, in order that they may receive admonition. 6. If (We had) not (sent you to the Quraish)—in case a calamity should seize them for (the deeds) that their hands have sent forth, they might say: "Our Lord! Why did You not send us a messenger? We should then have

		followed Your signs and been amongst those who believe!"
		Without Guidance **People follow their Selfish Desires**
11	28:048-050	But (now), when the truth has come to them from Ourselves, 1. They say, "Why are not (signs) sent to him like those that were sent to Moses?" Do they not then reject (the signs) that were formerly sent to Moses? 2. They say: "Two kinds of sorcery, each assisting the other!" And they say: "For us, we reject all (such things)!" • Say: "Then bring you a book from Allah that is a better guide than either of them, that I may follow it! (Do), if you are truthful." • But if they hearken not to you, know that they only follow their own lusts. And who is more astray than one who follows his own lusts, devoid of guidance from Allah? For Allah guides not people given to wrongdoing.

3 GOD'S GUIDANCE AND THE JUDGMENT

False deities may help people in this world, but they will fail them in the Hereafter. False gods, whether they be our leaders, our self-interests, our egos, or arrogance, may get some unlawful benefit for us in this world, but these will not help us in the Hereafter. Unbelievers run after immediate benefits, applying unlawful means, but only those who repent, believe, and do righteous deeds are the successful in the end. God is well aware of those who respect His commands by living a life according to them and of those who are cheating and causing corruption in this world through their self-interest and arrogance.

3.1 God Guides People to Succeed in their Lives on Earth

God has been sending His messengers and books of revelation to guide people so that their earthly lives can be successful. The Qur'an was like a refresher course for the believers of previous messengers; it was easier for them to believe in Islam. Verse 28:54 specifically refers those Christians who came to Makkah and embraced Islam when they heard the Qur'an from the Messenger. Instead of learning any lesson from this, the Makkans were so upset that their leader Abu Jahl rebuked those people in public. God gave good news of reward to them for three qualities of character: steadfastness, repelling evil with good, and spending out of what God had given them. The verses of Surah Al-Qasas highlighting that it is God Who guides those whom He wills are given in the table below.

Table 3.1: God guides those whom He Wills

No	Surah:Verses	Meanings
		God has Provided the Same Guidance to All People
1	28:051-053	• Now have We caused the word to reach them themselves, in order that they may receive admonition. Those to whom We sent the Book before this—they do believe in this (revelation). • When it is recited to them, they say: "We believe therein, for it is the truth from our Lord. Indeed, we have been Muslims (bowing to Allah's will) from before this."
		The Behavior of the Believers and their Reward
2	28:054-056	Twice will they be given their reward, for 1. That they have persevered, 2. That they avert evil with good, 3. And that they spend (in charity) out of what We have given them. 4. And when they hear vain talk, they turn away there from and say: "To us our deeds and to you yours. Peace be to you; we seek not the ignorant." 5. It is true you will not be able to guide everyone, whom you love, but Allah guides those whom He will and He knows best those who receive guidance.

3.2 Social Justice (not Wealth) Leads to Prosperity

It is not material wealth but social justice that brings prosperity to people. If divine guidance is available and people refuse to live by it, then their communities get destroyed after a time. God says: "Nor was your Lord the one to destroy a population until

He had sent to its center a Messenger, reciting to them Our revelations. Nor are We going to destroy a population except when its members practice iniquity (Qur'an 28:59)." The accumulation of wealth in the hands of a few capitalists does not assure prosperity and the success of a community as a whole. God warns people: "How many populations We destroyed that exulted in their life (of ease and plenty)! Now those habitations of theirs, after them, are deserted—all but a (miserable) few! And We are their heirs (Qur'an 28:58)."

3.3 Seeking Help from False gods Brings Ruin

As noted previously, false gods include anything we worship other than God, e.g., our leaders, our self-interests, our egos, our own arrogance, and the material riches and luxuries of this world. God reminds us: "The things that you are given are but the conveniences of this life and the glitter thereof, but that which is with Allah is better and more enduring. Will you not then be wise (Qur'an 28:60)?" The verses of Surah Al-Qasas that show the helplessness of false gods are given in the table below.

Table 3.3: False gods will never be Helpful

No	Surah:Verses	Meanings
		The Unbelievers are not like the Believers
3	28:061	1. Are (these two) alike—one to whom We have made a goodly promise, and who is going to reach its (fulfillment), 2. And one to whom We have given the good things of this life, but who, On the Day of Judgment, is to be among those brought up (for punishment)?
		False Deities will not be Able to Help the Unbelievers
4	28:062-064	1. That Day (Allah) will call to them and say, "Where are my 'partners' whom you imagined (to be such)?" 2. Those against whom the charge will be proved will say: "Our Lord! These are the ones whom we led astray. We led them astray as we were astray ourselves. We free ourselves (from them) in Your presence. It was not us they worshiped." 3. It will be said (to them): "Call upon your

		'partners' (for help)." They will call upon them, but they will not listen to them, and they will see the penalty (before them). (How they will wish) if only they had been open to guidance!
		The Answer that Unbelievers gave To the Messengers
5	28:065-067	• That day (Allah) will call to them (the unbelievers) and say: "What was the answer you gave to the messengers?" Then the (whole) story that day will seem obscure to them (like light to the blind), and they will not be able (even) to question each other. • But any that (in this life) had repented, believed, and worked righteousness will have hopes to be among those who achieve salvation.
		The is no proof of their false deities
6	28:074-075	The day that He will call on them, 1. He will say: "Where are my 'partners' whom you imagined (to be such)?" And from each people shall We draw a witness, and 2. We shall say: "Produce your proof." Then shall they know that the truth is in Allah (alone), and the (lies) that they invented will leave them in the lurch.

4 GOD'S CREATION, HIS MERCY, AND HIS JUDGMENT

The unbelievers of Makkah feared that if they gave up the polytheistic creed of the Arabs and worshiped only the One God that it would put an end to their leadership in religious, political, and economic fields. They feared that this would eventually destroy their position as the most influential tribe of Arabia and that they would be left without any refuge anywhere in the land. This was the real motive of the leaders of the Quraish for their opposition to Islam. Their doubts and objections were only the excuses that they invented to deceive people. However, God commands that truth and falsehood should not be judged only from the viewpoint of one's worldly interests.

4.1 God Creates Whatever He chooses as He pleases

God tells people that: (1) He knows what their breasts conceal and what they manifest; (2) He is God, and there is no god but He; (3) all praise is due to Him in this world and in the Hereafter; (4) His is the judgment; and (5) to Him shall all return. It is God's mercy that He has made the night and the day that people may seek rest therein, seek of His bounty, and give thanks.

Table 4.1: God, the Creator is Most Merciful

No	Surah:Verses	Meanings
		Your Lord creates whatever He pleases
1	28:068-070	1. Your Lord does create and choose as He pleases. No choice have they (in the matter). Glory to Allah, and far is He above the partners they ascribe (to Him)! 2. And your Lord knows all that their hearts conceal and all that they reveal. 3. And He is Allah. There is no god but He. To Him be praise at the first and at the last, for Him is the command, and to Him shall you (all) be brought back.
		If God made the Night or Day continuous, What will you do?
2	28:071-073	• Say: "You see? If Allah were to make the night perpetual over you to the Day of Judgment, what god is there other than Allah who can give you enlightenment? Will you not then hearken?" • Say: "See you—if Allah were to make the day perpetual over you to the Day of Judgment, what god is there other than Allah who can give you a night in which you can rest? Will you not then see? • It is out of His mercy that He has made for you night and day that you may rest therein and that you may seek of His grace—and in order that you may be grateful.

4.2 Divine Guidance and the Human Performance

God is well aware of the believers who respect His commands by living a life according to His dictates. He is also well aware of the unbelievers who are cheating and causing corruption by following their selfish interests and arrogance. "Verily, He Who ordained the Qur'an for you will bring you back to the place of return. Say: "My Lord knows best who it is that brings true guidance and who is in manifest error." And you had not expected that the Book would be sent to you except as a mercy from your Lord. Therefore, lend not you support in any way to those who reject (Allah's message). And let nothing keep you back from the signs of Allah after they have been revealed to you. And invite (people) to your Lord, and be not of the company of those who join gods with Allah. And call not, besides Allah, on another god. There is no god but He. Everything (that exists) will perish except His Own face. To Him belongs the command, and to Him will you (all) be brought back (Qur'an 28:85-88)."

CHAPTER 25

Free Will and Individual Responsibility
FROM SURAH AL-ANKABUT (29)

Human free will, freedom of thought and action, and individual responsibility all go hand in hand in Islam. God commands people: "Help one another in righteousness and piety, but help not one another in sin and transgression (Qur'an 5:2)." Surah Al-Ankabut was revealed to strengthen and encourage sincere Muslims, as well as those who were showing weakness of the faith. Since, "No person earns evil but against itself, and no bearer of burden shall bear the burden of another (Qur'an 6:164)," people were advised that parents and rulers cannot force them to obey them in sin and transgression.

How should one guard against such situations? It was narrated by Abdullah bin Mas'ud that the Messenger observed: "Never a prophet had been sent before me by Allah towards his nation who had not among his people disciples and companions who followed his ways and obeyed his command. Then there came after them their successors who said whatever they did not practice, and practiced whatever they were not commanded to do. He who strove against them with his hand was a believer. He who strove against them with his tongue was a believer, and he who strove against them with his heart was a believer, and beyond that there is no faith even to the extent of a mustard seed (Sahih Muslim: 1.81)."

1 THE COMMUNITY SHOULD ORGANISE TO REFORM

1.1 The Obligations of Community Leaders
The first obligation of leaders, both religious and secular, is to organize people to eradicate corruption from society. The affluent people that enjoy wealth, servants, luxuries, comfort, and power are prone to carelessness and decadence in their lives. Thus, they tend to lead lives of corruption, transgress all limits, trample over values, desecrate sanctions, and defile other

400

people's honor. Unless they are punished for their misdeeds, they will spread corruption and indecency throughout their community. They will debase the sound values and principles that every community needs to observe for survival. As such, their corruption leads to the loss of strength, vigor, and means of survival by the whole community. It then becomes lifeless and is soon be overtaken by destruction.

What should be done to save the community from destruction? Abu Dawud and At-Tirmidhi relate on the authority of Ibn Mas'ud that: "The Messenger said: 'When the children of Israel began to commit sins frequently, their scholars tried to dissuade them, but they persisted. Their scholars, nevertheless, continued to attend their social gatherings and eat and drink with them. God left them (the scholars) to stray and sealed their hearts. He also cursed them in the words of David, Solomon, and Jesus, Son of Mary.' The Messenger was saying this as he reclined, but at this point he sat up and said: 'By Him who holds my soul in His hand, you must make them turn back to what is right' (Abu Dawud 37.4322)." Amirah al-Kindi narrated that the Messenger said: "When a sin is committed on earth, a person who witnesses it and denounces it is the same as one who has not seen it. But the one who has been absent and approves of it is considered like one who has taken part in it (Abu Dawud: 37.4331)."

1.2 People should keep away from Corruption

Corrupt communities eventually get destroyed. This law of nature, which God has set in operation, is elaborated in Surah Bani Israel: "When We decide to destroy a population, We (first) send a definite order to those among them who are given the good things of this life and yet transgress; so that the word is proved true against them: then We destroy them utterly. How many generations have We destroyed after Noah? And enough is your Lord to note and see the sins of His servants (Qur'an 17:16-17)" When God determines that a certain community is to be destroyed, this is the natural outcome of its pursuit of ways and practices that lead to destruction. The affluent become too numerous, and no one takes any action to curb their transgressions. They spread corruption, and bit-by-bit the whole community becomes corrupt. Consequently, the effects of the

401

law that God has set in operation leads such communities to destruction. Indeed, the community itself is responsible for the destruction it suffers because it did not take the necessary action to stop corruption. Had it done so, it would have spared itself destruction.

God has willed that human life should run according to set laws that never fail or change. A cause has its effect, and the effect takes place as a result of the operation of God's will in setting this law in operation. God does not approve of indecency or transgression. However, the presence of those who are exceedingly rich is indicative that the community's fabric has become loose and that it has started to decline. This seals its fate in that it has set itself open to the operation of this law when it allowed those who are excessively rich to lead their corrupt lives. What should be done to safeguard a community from the consequences of corruption? At-Tirmidhi relates that the Messenger said: "By Him Who holds my soul in His hand, you will enjoin the doing of what is right and forbid what is wrong or else God will visit you with a punishment of His own. You will then pray to Him, and He will not answer you (Al-Hadith: vol., I, no., 71, p374)."

1.3 People should know: As You Sow So Shall You Reap
This Surah was revealed during extreme persecution of the believers at Makkah. The unbelievers were opposing and fighting Islam, and the new converts were being subjected to torture and oppression. Under such conditions, sincere Muslims, as well as those who were showing weakness of faith, needed to be strengthened and encouraged. They were reminded that they would certainly benefit from their striving and hard work. This is a law of nature that God has put in operation. Further, there can be people who adopt a hypocritical way of life because they are afraid of the oppression and extreme physical torture to which they could be subjected by dictators and tyrants who only serve their false gods and self-interests. God tells the believers that they will certainly be tried to determine their sincerity in religion.

Table 1.3: Those Who Strive, They Strive for Themselves

No	Surah:Verses	Meanings
		The Believers will be Tried and Tested
1	29:002-004	Do men think that they will be left alone on saying, "We believe," and that they will not be tested? 1. We did test those before them, and Allah will certainly know those who are true from those who are false. 2. Do those who practice evil think that they will get the better of Us? Evil is their judgment!
		People make Efforts for their Own Selves
2	29:005-007	For those whose hopes are in the meeting with Allah (in the Hereafter, let them strive), for the term (appointed) by Allah is surely coming, and He hears and knows (all things). 1. And if any strive (with might and main), they do so for their own self: for Allah is free of all needs from all creation. 2. Those who believe and work righteous deeds—from them We shall expiate all evil (that may be) in them, and We shall reward them according to the best of their deeds.

1.4 No One can Force People to Transgress the Law

No one can force people to disobey God or commit evil—not even their parents: "We have enjoined on man kindness to parents, but if they (either of them) strive (to force) you to join with Me (in worship) anything of which you have no knowledge, obey them not. You have (all) to return to me, and I will tell you (the truth) of all that you did. And those who believe and work righteous deeds—them shall We admit to the company of the righteous (Qur'an 29:8-9)."

Believers are commanded to obey their rulers if such obedience does not violate any of God's commands. It was narrated by Abdullah that the Messenger said, "A Muslim has to listen to and obey (the order of his ruler), whether he likes it or not, so long as his orders don't involve one in disobedience to God. But if an act of disobedience to God is imposed, one should not listen to it or obey it (Sahih Bukhari: 9.89.258)." Further, God commands us that we should settle our disputes according to divine guidance: "O you who believe! Obey Allah, and obey the Messenger and those charged with authority among you. If you differ in anything among yourselves, refer it to Allah and His Messenger (Qur'an 4:59)."

1.5 No One is Answerable for the Misdeeds of Others

Some people of Makkah were saying to the new converts to Islam: "Leave the question of punishment in the Hereafter to us. Listen to us, and abandon your religion. If God seizes you in the Hereafter, we will come forward and say to your Lord. 'These people are innocent; we had forced them to give up their faith; therefore, seize us in their place.'" The verses of Surah Al-Ankabut that refute such an argument are given in the table below.

Table 1.5: Each will bear the Burden of One's Own Deeds

No	Surah:Verses	Meanings
		God knows the Believers and the Hypocrite
3	29:010-011	Then there are among men such as say, 1. "We believe in Allah." But when they suffer affliction in (the cause of) Allah, they treat men's oppression as if it were the wrath of Allah! And if help comes (to you) from your Lord, they are sure to say, "We have (always) been with you!" Does not Allah know best all that is in the hearts of all creation? 2. Allah most certainly knows those who believe and, as certainly, those who are hypocrites.
		No Person will bear the Burden of Another
4	29:012-013	The unbelievers say to those who believe: 1. The unbelievers say to those who believe: "Follow our path, and we will bear (the consequences) of your faults." Never in the least will they bear their faults. In fact, they are liars. 2. They will bear their own burdens, and (other) burdens along with their own, and on the Day of Judgment they will be called to account for their falsehoods.

2 GOD'S HELP WILL CERTAINLY ARRIVE

History confirms that the messengers and the believers suffered great hardships and were treated cruelly for long periods by the unjust leaders and their collaborators before they were helped and rescued by God. Therefore, the believers should take heart and struggle on patiently. Even though a period of trial and tribulation has to be undergone, God's help will certainly come. This is another law of nature which God has put in place.

2.1 The Fate of the Corrupt Communities of the Past

The unbelievers have been warned that even though they are not being immediately punished by God that doesn't mean that they will never receive punishment. The histories of the doomed nations of the past demonstrate that punishment will come. God tells people: "Each one of them We seized for his crime. Of them, against some We sent a violent tornado (with showers of stones). Some were caught by a (mighty) blast. Some We caused the earth to swallow up, and some We drowned (in the waters). It was not Allah Who injured (or oppressed) them; they injured (and oppressed) their own souls (Qur'an 29:40)."

Table 2: Divine Message and the Fate of Corrupt People

No	Messenger	Divine Message and the Punishment for Rejection
1	Noah[PBUH]	We (once) sent Noah to his people, and he tarried among them a thousand years less fifty: but the deluge overwhelmed them while they (persisted in) sin. (Qur'an 29:14) • But We saved him and the companions of the ark, and We made the (ark) a Sign for all peoples. (Qur'an 29:15)
2	Abraham[PBUH]	(We also sent) Abraham. Behold, he said to his people, "Serve Allah, and fear Him. That will be best for you—if you understand. For you do worship idols besides Allah, and you invent falsehood. The things that you worship besides Allah have no power to give you sustenance. Then seek sustenance from Allah, serve Him, and be grateful to Him. To Him will be your return." (Qur'an 29:16-17). 1. And if you reject (the message), so did

405

		generations before you: and the duty of the messenger is only to preach publicly (and clearly). (Qur'an 29:18) 2. So naught was the answer of (Abraham's) people except that they said: "Slay him or burn him." But Allah did save him from the fire. Verily, in this are signs for people who believe. (Qur'an 29:24)
3	Lot^{PBUH}	And (Remember) Lot. Behold, he said to his people: "You do commit lewdness, such as no people in creation (ever) committed before you. Do you indeed approach men, and cut off the highway, and practice wickedness (even) in your councils?" But his people gave no answer but this: they said: "Bring us the wrath of Allah if you tell the truth." (Qur'an 29:28-29) • He said: "O my Lord! Help me against people who do mischief." (Qur'an 29:30) 1. When Our messengers came to Lot, he was grieved on their account and felt himself powerless (to protect) them. But they said: "Fear not, nor grieve. We are (here) to save you and your following, except your wife. She is of those who lag behind." (Qur'an 29:33) 2. For we are going to bring down on the people of this township a punishment from heaven, because they have been wickedly rebellious. (Qur'an 29:34) We have left thereof an evident sign for any people who understand. (Qur'an 29:35)
4	Shu'ayb^{PBUH}	To the Madyan (We sent) their brother Shu'ayb. Then he said: "O my people! Serve Allah, and fear the Last Day: nor commit evil on the earth with intent to do mischief. (Qur'an 29:36) • But they rejected him. Then the mighty blast seized them, and they lay prostrate in their homes by the morning. Satan made their deeds alluring to them and kept them back from the path, though they were gifted with intelligence and skill. (Qur'an 29:37-38)
5	Moses^{PBUH}	(Remember also) Qarun, Pharaoh, and Haman. There came to them Moses with clear signs... • But they behaved with insolence on the earth;

		Yet, they could not overreach (Us). (Qur'an 29.39)

3 PEOPLE SHOULD BUILD JUST COMMUNITIES

3.1 The Communities of Unjust and Corrupt People

Dictators and collaborators, who say what they do not practice and practice what they were not commanded to do, lead to corrupt societies and failed states. God tells people in Surah Al-Ankabut that the worship of false gods and self-interest results in unjust and corrupt communities. "The parable of those who take protectors other than Allah is that of the spider, who builds a house, but truly the flimsiest of houses is the spider's house—if they but knew...And such are the parables We set forth for mankind, but only those understand them who have knowledge. Allah created the heavens and the earth in true (proportions). Verily, in that is a sign for those who believe (Qur'an 29:41, 43-44)."

3.2 God's Remembrance Inculcates a Just Behavior

Only the true and honest remembrance of God is required to establish just, prosperous, peaceful, and stable states and societies. "*Thikr*" is the Arabic word used to denote the remembrance of God, whether such remembrance is done in secret or in public, in a whisper or aloud, or in a low voice or a loud voice. A good believer is one who practices *Thikr* very frequently. Indeed, the firmer a believer is in his faith, the more he practices *Thikr*, which keeps him always mindful of his Islamic obligations. He is thus conscious of God, and consciousness of Him provides a check against deviation from Islamic teachings. Man is always liable to forget his obligations when an immediate interest or temptation offers itself. Being conscious of God is the best safeguard against succumbing to temptations and against pursuing that which is forbidden by God. Since *Thikr* helps develop and enhance such consciousness, it is part of Islamic worship. Indeed, all Islamic worship is said to fall within the overall framework of remembering God. Therefore,

- God's remembrance is to live a life according to the

guidance given in the Qur'an and explained in the
Ahadith. The Qur'an brings mercy for those who follow
its guidance.

- God's remembrance is to know God's commands,
  implement what He asks us to do in our own lives and in
  our societies, and refrain from what He prohibits in our
  own lives and in our societies.

- God's remembrance is to follow God's commands in all
  our dealings and activities and to guard against indecency
  and corruption in our social, economical, and political
  aspects of life.

Table 3.2
God's Remembrance Provides Shelter against Corruption

No	Surah:Verses	Meanings
		Prayer guards against Indecency and Corruption
1	29:045	Recite (understand and implement) what is sent of the Book by inspiration to you, and establish regular prayer, for prayer restrains from shameful and unjust deeds. • And remembrance of Allah is the greatest (thing in life) without doubt. And Allah knows the (deeds) that you do.
		Guidance is for those who are Wise and Just
2	29:048-049	You were not (able) to recite a book before this (Book came), nor are you (able) to transcribe it with your right hand. In that case, indeed, would the talkers of vanities have doubted? • Nay, here are signs self-evident in the hearts of those endowed with knowledge, and none but the unjust reject Our signs.
		The Qur'an is Mercy for its Followers
3	29:050-051	Yet, they say: "Why are not signs sent down to him from his Lord?" Say: "The signs are indeed with Allah, and I am indeed a clear warner." • And is it not enough for them that we have sent down to you the Book that is rehearsed to them? Verily, in it is mercy and a reminder to those who believe.

3.3 Strive Hard for the Implementation of Divine Law

Addressing the believers God says: "What is the matter with you that when you are asked to go forth in the cause of Allah, you cling heavily to the earth? Do you prefer the life of this world to the Hereafter...? Unless you go forth, He will punish you with a grievous penalty, and put others in your place, but Him you would not harm in the least. For Allah has power over all things. (Qur'an 9:38-39)." The verses of Surah Al-Ankabut listing some of God's laws are summarized in the table below.

Table 3.3: The Laws of Nature that God has 'put in place'

No	Surah:Verses	Meanings
		The Believers Migrate Away from Evil
1	29:056	Truly, spacious is My earth. Therefore, serve Me (and Me alone).
		None can Avoid Death and Accountability
2	29:057	Every person shall have a taste of death. In the end, to Us shall you be brought back.
		Deeds have their Respective Consequences
3	29:058-059	But those who believe and work deeds of righteousness - to them shall We give a Home in Heaven...those who persevere in patience and put their trust in their Lord and Cherisher.
		God is He Who Grants People their Sustenance
4	29:062	Allah enlarges the sustenance (which He gives) to whichever of His servants He pleases, and He grants by (strict) measure (as He pleases).
		Violate not God's Commands to Succeed
5	29:064	What is the life of this world but amusement and play? But, verily, the home in the Hereafter—that is life, indeed.
		God Guides those Who make efforts in His Way
6	29:069	Those who strive in Our (cause)—We will certainly guide them to our paths.

409

CHAPTER 26

Integrity and Justice Lead to Success
FROM SURAH AR-RUM (30)

The Messenger quotes God as saying: "My servants, I have forbidden Myself injustice and have made it forbidden among you, so do not be unjust to one another (Sahih Muslim: 32.6246)." A just society comes into existence only through the implementation of the divine laws by individuals and by society as a whole. God tells people in Surah Hud: "O my people! Give full measure and weigh fairly, and defraud not people their things, and do not act corruptly in the land, making mischief (Qur'an 11:85)." God also commands in Surah Al-Shuara: "Do not obey the bidding of the extravagant that spread corruption in the earth and reform not (Qur'an 26:151-152)."

In Surah Ar-Rum, the great turmoil that had gripped the world due the war between the two major powers of the time, i.e., the Romans and the Persians, is cited. This conflict was caused by worshiping false gods and the failure to follow God's laws. If a people's social system is based firmly on justice, as desired by God, then there is no reason for war. Therefore, it is very important that people follow the right religion. "Then set your face steadily and truly to the faith. (Establish) Allah's handiwork according to the pattern on which He has made mankind. No change (let there be) in the work (wrought) by Allah. That is the standard religion, but most among mankind understand not (Qur'an 30:30)."

Human wisdom demands that people should reflect on the universe and the signs it contains about the greatness of its Creator and that they should worship Him alone. *Shirk*, i.e., worshiping others than God alone, is opposed to the nature of the universe, as well as to the nature of man. Whenever people have adopted this deviation, chaos has resulted. With regard to the war between the Romans and the Persians cited in Surah Ar-Rum, this chaos was also the result of *Shirk*, and all the nations who were ever involved in mischief and tyranny throughout human

410

history were also the worshipers of other than God alone, i.e., they were *Mushriks.*

1 WHAT LEADS TO SUCCESS IN THE LIFE OF THIS WORLD AND IN THE HEREAFTER

1.1 God Grants Success by His Own Divine Ways

Surah Ar-Rum begins with the news that the Romans have been overcome and that people the world over are anticipating the collapse of the empire. In the face of such anticipation, the Qur'an predicts that within a few years the defeated Romans would again become victorious. God tells people: "The Roman Empire has been defeated in a land close by, but they, (even) after (this) defeat of theirs, will soon be victorious—within a few years. With Allah is the decision, in the past and in the future. On that day shall the believers rejoice—with the help of Allah. He helps whom He wills, and He is exalted in might, most merciful. (It is) the promise of Allah. Never does Allah depart from His promise, but most men understand not (Qur'an 30:2-6)." This Surah contained not only one, but two predictions. Firstly, the Romans will be victorious; secondly, the Muslims shall also win a victory at the same time. At the time of this revelation, it appeared that there wasn't even a remote chance of either prediction being fulfilled in the next few years. Yet, history confirms that both predictions were fulfilled within the stipulated period of ten years.

1.2 Implementation of Divine Laws leads to Success

This Surah highlights a great truth, which is that people are accustomed to seeing only what is apparent and superficial, which was the case with the news of the Roman's defeat. The people thought that the Roman Empire was about to collapse, but within a few years the Romans were able to defeat their opponents. At that time, people simply couldn't foresee what was to follow the Roman defeat. If this habit to see only the apparent and superficial can lead people to such misunderstandings and miscalculations about insignificant matters of life, how disastrous will be their error if they risk their life in the Hereafter only on what is visible and apparent in this

411

worldly life. Doesn't this example confirm that divine guidance is needed to succeed in life? We learn from Surah Al-Rum that evil was the end of those who did evil. This was because they rejected the revelations of God and used to mock them.

Table 1.2: Worldly Life without Divine Guidance

No	Surah:Verses	Meanings
		People tend to forget their Accountability
1	30:007-008	1. They know but the outer (things) in the life of this world, but of the end of things they are heedless. 2. Do they not reflect in their own minds? Not but for just ends and for a term appointed did Allah create the heavens and the earth, and all between them. 3. Yet are there truly many among men who deny the meeting with their Lord.
		The Evil Outcome of people's deeds Is not divine Injustice
2	30:009-010	1. Do they not travel through the earth and see what was the end of those before them? They were superior to them in strength; they tilled the soil and populated it in greater numbers than these have done. There came to them their messengers with clear (signs) (which they rejected, to their own destruction). 2. It was not Allah Who wronged them, but they wronged their own selves. In the long run, evil in the extreme will be the end of those who do evil; for that they rejected the revelations of Allah and held them up to ridicule.

1.3 Believing in the Hereafter Leads to Success

In the Hereafter, every person will be accountable for his own actions and deeds. Although one can be rewarded or punished here in this world, each and every one of us will be brought to justice in the Hereafter. Believing in the Hereafter makes people realize that it is infinitely better to pay any claim due to other people here in this life. If one has been unfair to an employee or a servant, let alone a relative, a neighbor or a friend, then one should make amends to that person before death. Otherwise, one will has to face the consequences for one's deeds on the Day of

412

Judgment. Nothing can be done to benefit oneself after one's term in this life has expired. The verses of Surah Ar-Rum that highlight the consequences of ignoring the accountability for our actions are given in the table below.

Table 1.3: On Resurrection, the Guilty will be in Despair

No	Surah:Verses	Meanings
		None will intercede on the behalf of Guilty
3	30:011-016	• It is Allah Who begins (the process of) creation; then (He) repeats it. Then shall you be brought back to Him. • On the Day that the Hour will be established, the guilty will be struck dumb with despair. No intercessor will they have among their partners, and they will (themselves) reject their partners. • On the Day that the Hour will be established, that Day shall all be sorted out. 1. Then those who have believed and worked righteous deeds shall be made happy in a mead of delight, 2. And those who have rejected faith and falsely denied our signs and the meeting of the Hereafter—such shall be brought forth to punishment.
		Excuses will not profit on the Day of Judgment
4	30:054-057	It is Allah Who created you in a state of (helpless) weakness, then gave (you) strength after weakness. Then, after strength, (He) gave (you) weakness and a hoary head. He creates as He wills, and it is He Who has all knowledge and power. 1. On the Day that the Hour (of Reckoning) will be established, the transgressors will swear that they tarried not but an hour; thus were they used to being deluded. 2. But those endued with knowledge and faith will say: "Indeed, you did tarry, within Allah's decree, to the Day of Resurrection, and this is the Day of Resurrection, but you—you were not aware. So on that Day no excuse of theirs will avail the transgressors, nor will they be invited (then) to seek grace (by repentance).

413

1.4 Reflecting on God's Creation Leads to Success

If people look around and reflect, it won't be difficult for them to realize that it can't be impossible for the Creator of the universe to resurrect people after their death. "It is He Who brings out the living from the dead and brings out the dead from the living and Who gives life to the earth after it is dead, and thus shall you be brought out (from the dead) (Qur'an 30:19). "It is He Who begins (the process of) creation, then repeats it; and for Him it is most easy. To Him belongs the loftiest similitude in the heavens and the earth, for He is exalted in might, full of wisdom (Qur'an 30:27)." "Then contemplate the memorials of Allah's mercy— how He gives life to the earth after its death. Verily, the same will give life to the men who are dead, for He has power over all things (Qur'an 30:50)." The signs of the universe that have been presented as evidence to prove the existence of the Hereafter also support the existence of only One Creator, provided people make an effort to reflect, learn, listen, and comprehend these signs.

Table 1.4: God's Creation and His Signs

No	Surah:Verses	Meanings
5	30:020-026	1. Among His signs in this, that He created you from dust, and then behold, you are men scattered (far and wide). 2. And among His signs is this, that He created for you mates from among yourselves, that you may dwell in tranquility with them, and He has put love and mercy between your (hearts). Verily, in that are signs for those who reflect. 3. And among His signs is the creation of the heavens and the earth and the variations in your languages and your colors. Verily, in that are signs for those who know. 4. And among His signs is the sleep that you take by night and by day and the quest that you (make for livelihood) out of His bounty. Verily, in that are signs for those who hearken. 5. And among His signs, He shows you the lightning, by way both of fear and of hope, and He sends down rain from the sky and with

	it gives life to the earth after it is dead. Verily, in that are signs for those who are wise.
	6. And among His signs is this, that heaven and earth stand by His command. Then when He calls you, by a single call, from the earth, behold, you (straightway) come forth. To Him belongs every being that is in the heavens and on earth. All are devoutly obedient to Him.

2 PEOPLE'S CORRUPTION AND TYRANNY

2.1 Corrupt People Follow Their Selfish Desires

There is a direct relationship between the worship of false deities and corruption in this world. In the Qur'an, oppression is often equated with the denial of God, and non-believers are often described as oppressors, wrongdoers, and corrupt. God tells people, He "forgives not associating anything with Him, but He forgives anything else to whom He pleases; to set up partners with Allah is to devise a sin most heinous indeed (Qur'an 4:48)" and "...one who joins other gods with Allah has strayed far, far away (from the right) (Qur'an 4:116)."

Satan, devils, idols, stone, the sun, stars, angels, and human beings have all been taken as false deities and worshiped. Likewise, saints, graves, rulers, and leaders have been falsely worshiped and wrongly followed. Following one's own selfish desires and rendering obedience to any authority against the order of God is also associating others with God. "They take their priests and their anchorites to be their lords in derogation of Allah, and (they take as their Lord) Christ the son of Mary. Yet, they were commanded to worship but One Allah. There is no god but He—praise and glory to Him. (Far is He) from having the partners they associate (with Him) (Qur'an 9:31)!"

Implementation of the divine laws on an individual and societal level is essential in establishing a just society. Part of the covenant with which God has bound the believers requires that they should deal with others on the basis of absolute justice. It is a justice that is based on remaining steadfast in devotion to God

415

alone. No influences are ever allowed to tilt the balance of justice, especially when believers are mindful that God watches over them and knows what is in their hearts. God tells people: "O my people! Give just measure and weight, nor withhold from the people the things that are their due. Commit not evil in the land with the intent to do mischief (Qur'an 11:85)" and "Follow not the bidding of those who are extravagant, who make mischief in the land and mend not (their ways) (Qur'an 26:151-152)." Another example of not believing in One God leading to corruption is that of Pharaoh. "Truly Pharaoh elated himself in the land and broke up its people into sections, depressing a small group among them. Their sons he slew, but he kept alive their females, for he was indeed a maker of mischief (Qur'an 28:4)."

Table 2.1: False Deities and Corruption

No	Surah:Verses	Meanings
		Unjust People follow their Low Desires
1	30:028-029	He (Allah) does propound to you a similitude from your own (experience). Do you have partners among those whom your right hands possess, to share as equals in the wealth We have bestowed on you? Do you fear them as you fear each other? Thus do we explain the signs in detail to a people that understand? Nay, the wrongdoers (merely) follow their own lusts, being devoid of knowledge. But who will guide those whom Allah leaves astray? To them there will be no helpers.
		People who are ungrateful for God's Grace
2	30:033-037	When trouble touches men, they cry to their Lord, turning back to Him in repentance: but when He gives them a taste of mercy as from Himself: 1. Behold, some of them pay part-worship to other god's besides their Lord, (as if) to show their ingratitude for the (favors) We have bestowed on them! Then enjoy (your brief day), but soon will you know (your folly). 2. Or have We sent down authority to them that points out to them the things to which they pay part-worship? 3. When We give men a taste of mercy, they exult thereat, and when some evil afflicts them because of what their (own) hands have sent

		forth, behold, they are in despair. Don't they see that Allah enlarges the provision and restricts it to whomsoever He pleases? Verily in that are signs for those who believe.
		God and False Deities
3	30:040	1. It is Allah Who has created you; 2. He has provided you sustenance; 3. then He will cause you to die; 4. And again He will give you life. Are there any of your (false) partners who can do any single one of these things? • Glory to Him! And high is He above the partners they attribute (to him).
		Why God may let People suffer from Corruption?
4	30:041-042	1. Mischief has appeared on land and sea because of what the hands of men have earned (by oppression and evil deeds), that (Allah) may give them a taste of some of their deeds, in order that they may turn back (from evil). 2. Say: "Travel through the earth and see what was the end of those before (you). Most of them worshiped others besides Allah."
		Turn to the Right Religion before the Day of Judgment!
5	30:043-045	1. But set you your face to the right religion before there comes from Allah the day that there is no chance of averting. On that day shall men be divided (into two groups). 2. Those who reject faith will suffer from that rejection, and those who work righteousness will spread their couch (of repose) for themselves, that He may reward those who believe and work righteous deeds, out of his bounty, for He loves not those who reject faith.

2.2 Faith and God-Consciousness

Faith makes people God-conscious and human. After developing people's relationship with God, religion builds human character, refines human behavior, and teaches how to deal with others. Religion's set of beliefs, prayer, fasting, charity, and pilgrimage make people conscientious regarding the accountability for their actions. Religion develops patience, a quality of character that is very much needed to succeed in life. Payer, patience, and charity are pursued during the implementation of religion and God's laws in the lives of people, in order to avoid injustice, corruption, and tyranny. God commands: "Therefore, be patient with what they say, and celebrate the praises of your Lord before the rising of the sun, and before its setting. Yea, celebrate them for part of the hours of the night and at the sides of the day that you may have happiness (Qur'an 20:130)."

Table 2.2: Prayers, Charity, and Seeking the Pleasure of God

No	Surah:Verses	Meanings
		People should be Careful of their Duties
6	30:031	1. Turn back in repentance to Him, and fear Him. 2. Establish regular prayers, and 3. Be not among those who join gods with Allah.
		Glorifying God and Establishing Prayers
7	30:017-018 11:114 17:078-079	1. So glorify Allah, when you reach eventide and when you rise in the morning—yea, to Him be praise in the heavens and on earth—and in the late afternoon and when the day begins to decline. 2. And establish regular prayers at the two ends of the day and at the approaches of the night. For those things that are good, remove those that are evil. In that is remembrance to those who remember (their Lord). 3. Establish regular prayers—at the sun's decline till the darkness of the night, and the morning prayer and reading, for the prayer and reading in the morning carry their testimony. And pray in the small watches of the morning. (It would be) an additional prayer (or spiritual profit) for you. Soon will your Lord raise you to a station of praise and glory.
		Distinguishing between Charity and Corruption
8	30:038-039	1. So give what is due to kindred, the needy, and the wayfarer. That is best for those who seek the countenance of Allah, and it is they who will prosper. 2. That which you lay out for increase through the property of (other) people will have no

418

	increase with Allah, but that which you lay out for charity, seeking the countenance of Allah, (will increase). It is those who will get a recompense multiplied.

3. ELIMINATION OF CORRUPTION AND TYRANNY

3.1 Convey the Message with full Confidence

A parable has been presented to make the people understand that just as dead earth comes to life by a shower of rain and swells with vegetation and plant life, so is the case with dead humanity. When God sends a shower of His mercy in the form of revelation and His messenger, it gives new life to humanity. At that point, the community will prosper by God's mercy, and the advantage will be theirs. But if they do not take advantage of the divine guidance, they will harm only themselves. Since God does not desire humanity to parish, He motivates the messenger and the believers to strive hard in conveying the divine message and reassures them of His help. "So patiently persevere, for verily the promise of Allah is true. Nor let those shake your firmness who have (themselves) no certainty of faith (Qur'an 30:60)."

Table 3.1: Be Patient, the Promise of God is true

No	Surah:Verses	Meanings
		The Guidance like Rain helps Humanity to Grow
1	30:048-050	• It is Allah Who sends the winds, and they raise the clouds. Then does He spread them in the sky as He wills and break them into fragments, until you see rain drops issue from the midst thereof. Then when He has made them reach such of his servants as He wills, behold, they do rejoice. • Even though, before they received (the rain) - just before this - they were dumb with despair. Then contemplate (O man!) the memorials of Allah's mercy: 1. How He gives life to the earth after its death. 2. Verily the same will give life to the men who are dead, for He has power over all things.
		No Guidance: People should think about their Loss

419

2	30:047	• We did indeed send before you messengers to their (respective) peoples, and they came to them with clear signs. Then to those who transgressed, We meted out retribution, and it was due from Us to aid those who believed.

3.2 God's is the Command Before and After

The Islamic faith is very clear and logical. While it makes clear that all power of decision rests with God, it does not exempt people from taking the measures that are normally necessary to bring about practical results. Whether these results take effect is not part of people's responsibility because the results ultimately belong to God's overall design. Thus, Islam makes true reliance on God conditional on people taking all necessary measures in any particular situation, knowing that ultimately all decisions are left to Him. Victory or success is thus the result of the power that makes it a reality and the mercy that fulfills what is in the best interests of people. In this way, victory is an aspect of mercy for both the victors and the vanquished. God tells people: "And did not Allah check one set of people by means of another, the earth would indeed be full of mischief. But Allah is full of bounty to all the worlds (Qur'an 2:251)."

That the earth should remain free of corruption is the ultimate objective that is beneficial to all, including those who are defeated. This is God's promise. Never does God fail to fulfill His promise, but most people do not know it. They only know the outer aspects of worldly life, whereas they remain unaware about the Hereafter. If victory has been promised by God, then it will certainly come in real life. What God promises is from His will and absolute wisdom. Indeed, nothing takes place in the universe except as He wills. Thus, the fulfillment of God's promise is part of the overall universal law that is subject to no exceptions.

3.3 What Reliance on God Means to a Believer

What this means in practice is that people should think and plan as they wish, but they must always remember to rely on God's help and guidance. They should realize that they only have the faculties of thinking and deliberation that God has given them.

420

This should not diminish motivation, nor should it lead them to fall victim to laziness. On the contrary, it should give people more strength, confidence, reassurance, and resolve. Should events reveal that God's will has moved in a direction different from what they planned, they should accept this with contentedness and reassurance. We submit to God's will because it is beyond our knowledge until God makes it known. This is the method Islam instills into the minds of its followers. Hence, a Muslim does not feel alone when he plans or thinks of the future. A believer does not show any conceit or arrogance when successful, nor is he overtaken by depression and despair when he fails. In all situations, he should remember God, feel stronger for relying on Him, express gratitude to Him for his success, and be resigned to whatever God's will may determine.

CHAPTER 27

People are Either Dignified or Corrupt
FROM SURAH LUQMAN (31)

Luqman was a wise person who lived in the past. Using the example of Luqman's advice to his son, the consequences of worshiping other than the real God and of forgetting the natural law of accountability are elaborated in Surah Luqman. Reflecting on some of God's creations, one is convinced that none other than God has ever created such things and that the continuation of life after death is true. Humanity achieves nothing but self-humiliation by worshiping false deities and by refusing to accept their accountability for their character, behavior, and deeds. A dignified person is a responsible person who is accountable for his actions. How could people who are not accountable for their actions and deeds be seen as dignified or responsible? People who merely follow their selfish desires are corrupt.

1 GOD, HIS CREATION AND RESURRECTION

1.1 None Has Created the Universe but God
God's powers and the wisdom behind all His flawless planning can be observed by looking at the universe and observing how wonderfully He has placed huge celestial bodies in the outer space without any visible columns (by invisible gravitational pull). Further, He has set huge mountains on earth, in spite of which it continues to rotate. He has spread various kinds of living creatures on earth, and He brings down rain from the clouds and grows all kinds of vegetation on it. This entire universe has been created by God. If the unbelievers claim someone else has similar powers, then they should show what their false deities have created.

Table 1.1: None denies God's Signs but the Ungrateful

No	Surah:Verses	Meanings
		This is God's creation – **What have those besides Him ever Created?**
1	31:010-011	1. He created the heavens without any pillars that you can see. He set on the earth mountains standing firm, lest it should shake with you, and He scattered through it beasts of all kinds. We send down rain from the sky and produce on the earth every kind of noble creature, in pairs. 2. Such is the creation of Allah: Now show Me what is there that others besides Him have created. Nay, but the transgressors are in manifest error.
		God is the Truth – **While all they associate with Him is Falsehood**
2	31:029-030	3. Do you not see that Allah merges night into day and He merges day into night, that He has subjected the sun and the moon (to His law), each running its course for a term appointed, and that Allah is well-acquainted with all that you do? 4. That is because Allah is the (only) reality, and because whatever else they invoke besides Him is falsehood, and because Allah—He is the most high, most great.
		People are Sincere before God's Help **Then Some are Ungrateful**
3	31:031-032	Do you not see that the ships sail through the ocean by the grace of Allah—that He may show you of His signs? Verily in this are signs for all who constantly persevere and give thanks. 1. When a wave covers them like the canopy (of clouds), they call to Allah, offering Him sincere devotion. 2. But when He has delivered them safely to land, there are among them those that halt between (right and wrong). But none reject Our Signs except only a perfidious ungrateful (wretch).

1.2 God, the Creator, Has the Ability to Resurrect

Even the unbelievers acknowledge the magnificent creation of God. His power and the wisdom behind all His flawless planning and creation of the universe can be cited to prove that with such power and wisdom God can also resurrect people for the accountability of their character and deeds.

Table 1.2: God Who Created the Universe can also Recreate

No	Surah:Verses	Meanings
		Unbelievers Admit that God has Created the Universe
4	31:025-026	1. If you ask them, who it is that created the heavens and the earth. They will certainly say, "Allah." 2. Say: "Praise be to Allah!" But most of them understand not. To Allah belong all things in heaven and earth. Allah is He (that is) free of all wants, worthy of all praise.
		God has Created the Universe, So why can't He Resurrect?
5	31:028	3 The creation of you all or resurrection of you all are only as (the creation and resurrection of) an individual soul, for Allah is He Who hears and sees (all things).

2 THE RIGHTEOUS AND THE CORRUPT PEOPLE

2.1 The Behavior of the Righteous People

The direction given in the Qur'an to people on how to live their lives is based on wisdom. It contains guidance to a straight path for those who are desirous of spending their lives in a balanced and dignified manner, and it presents a means for the development of real human character and abilities. People who follow such guidance establish a society based on justice wherein they worship only the One God and pay *Zakah* (obligatory charity) to those in need. The only people who can establish a justice-based system of life believe that there is life after this worldly existence where they will be rewarded or punished according to their good or bad deeds.

424

Table 2.1: Traits of the Righteous People

No	Surah:Verses	Meanings
		Righteous People, Pray, Pay *Zakah* and Believe in the Hereafter
1	31:002-005 31:008-009	These are verses of the wise book, a guide and a mercy to the doers of good. 1. Those who establish regular prayer, and give regular charity, and have (in their hearts) the assurance of the Hereafter—these are on (true) guidance from their Lord, and these are the ones who will prosper. 2. For those who believe and work righteous deeds, there will be gardens of bliss to dwell therein. The promise of Allah is true, and He is exalted in power, wise.
		Righteous People— Submit to God and do Good Deeds
2	31:022-024	1. Whoever submits his whole self to Allah, and is a doer of good, has grasped indeed the most trustworthy handhold, and with Allah rests the end and decision of (all) affairs. 2. But if any reject faith, let not his rejection grieve you. To Us is their return, and We shall tell them the truth of their deeds, for Allah knows well all that is in (men's) hearts. We grant them their pleasure for a little while; in the end shall We drive them to a chastisement unrelenting.

2.2 The Behavior of the Corrupt People

There are some people who do not have any desire to be human in life. They do not believe in any human values and consider this worldly life and its temporary comforts as an end in itself. Thus, without any knowledge or wisdom, they go astray and try to lead other people away from the right path. They ridicule all human values and any guidance that inculcates them. These are people whose fate will entail a very humiliating punishment. Whenever the divine laws are presented to them, they turn away in extreme arrogance. Their ears seem plugged, and they hear nothing. When asked to follow what God has revealed, they say that they are only following what they found their fathers doing, even though their fathers had been ignorant. Thus, they refuse to

425

reform. The verses of Surah Luqman that highlight the attitude and behavior of such arrogant and corrupt people are given in the table below.

Table 2.2: Those Who Dispute God without Knowledge

No	Surah:Verses	Meanings
		Unbelievers turn away arrogantly and try to lead people astray
3	31:006-007	1. But there are among men those who purchase idle tales without knowledge (or meaning), to mislead (men) from the path of Allah and throw ridicule (on the path). For such there will be a humiliating penalty. 2. When Our revelations are recited to such a one, he turns away in arrogance, as if he heard them not, as if there were deafness in both his ears. Announce to him a grievous penalty.
		Unbelievers dispute about Allah without knowledge and reform not
4	31:020-021	Do you not see that Allah has subjected to your (use) all things in the heavens and on earth and has made his bounties flow to you in exceeding measure, (both) seen and unseen? 1. Yet, there are among men those who dispute about Allah without knowledge and without guidance, and without a Book to enlighten them. 2. When they are told to follow the (revelation) that Allah has sent down, they say: "Nay, we shall follow the ways that we found our fathers (following)." What! Even if it is Satan beckoning them to the penalty of the (blazing) fire!

3 GOD'S NATURAL LAWS AND HIS JUDGMENT

3.1 Luqman Advised his Son to Live with Dignity

God provided Luqman with the wisdom to reflect over the universe in the light of His guidance, and thus he drew correct conclusions. This enabled him to appreciate God's bounties.

Appreciation means utilizing His bounties according to His laws. This enhances individual abilities to their full potential. A person who denies His laws suffers, but brings no harm to God. His laws do not need any outside help to produce results. His system, with its in-built forces, continues producing beneficial results that compel appreciation from people like Luqman. Addressing his son, Luqman advised him that the first and foremost principle over which the whole edifice of human thought exists is not to associate anyone with the powers and authority of God. One should obey and follow the rule of God alone. Those who associate anyone else with God are guilty of minimizing the importance of the divine law while maximizing the status of non-divine powers. This is highly unjust.

Don't degrade yourself! Whatever powers to which people give the status of god are either some natural phenomenon or other human beings. All natural phenomena have been subjugated to humankind, and all people are equal to each other. Therefore, accepting the superiority of another person or of a natural phenomenon is actually the degradation of humanity itself.

Table 3.1: Luqman Advised his Son

No	Surah:Verses	Meanings
		Be Grateful to God by Following His Commands
1	31:012	We bestowed (in the past) wisdom on Luqman: "Show (your) gratitude to Allah. Any who is grateful does so to the profit of his own soul, but if any is ungrateful, verily, Allah is free of all wants, worthy of all praise.
		Luqman Tells his Son – How to be Grateful
2	31:013-019	1. Behold, Luqman said to his son by way of instruction: "O my son! Join not in worship (others) with Allah, for false worship is indeed the highest wrongdoing." • We have enjoined on man (to be good) to his parents. In travail upon travail did his mother bear him, and in years twain was his weaning. (Hear the command): • "Show gratitude to Me and to your parents. To Me is (your final) goal. • "But if they (parents) strive to make you

427

	join in worship with Me things of which you have no knowledge, obey them not.
	• "Yet, bear them company in this life with justice (and consideration), and follow the way of those who turn to me. In the end, the return of you all is to Me, and I will tell you the truth of all that you did."
	2. "O my son!" (said Luqman). If there be (but) the weight of a mustard seed and it were (hidden) in a rock or (anywhere) in the heavens or on earth, Allah will bring it forth, for Allah understands the finest mysteries (and) is well acquainted (with them).
	3. "O my son! Establish regular prayer, enjoin what is just, and forbid what is wrong, and
	4. "Bear with patient constancy whatever betides you, for this is firmness in (the conduct of) affairs.
	5. "Swell not your cheek (for pride) at men,
	6. "Nor walk in insolence through the earth, for Allah loves not any arrogant boaster.
	7. "Be moderate in your pace, and lower your voice, for the harshest of sounds without doubt is the braying of the ass."

3.2 Divine Law of Accountability and the Hereafter

People should always remain conscious of the divine law of accountability and be aware of the day when the result of individual deeds will be revealed. On that day, neither will the father be of any help to the son, nor will the son be able to help his father. There is no exception to the law of accountability. Therefore, one should not be misled into dishonest worldly gains. There are people who will try to misguide you in various ways. Beware of their tactics, lest they become successful in turning you away from God's ways. God warns people: "O people! Do your duty to your Lord, and fear (the coming of) a day when no father can avail anything for his son, or a son avail anything for his father. Verily, the promise of Allah is true. Let not then this present life deceives you, nor let Satan deceive you about Allah (Qur'an 31:33)."

Although the process of compiling the details of individual deeds continues, it is God alone Who knows when the last hour will come. Consider the rain, for instance. Although it pours down at a particular time, the rain formation actually started quite sometime before that. Similarly, in the case of a child's birth, the birth takes place at a particular time, but the child had earlier gone through various stages in the mother's womb, and all these stages are in God's knowledge. The knowledge of these phenomena, such as rainfall or the fetus going through various stages, can be acquired. However, God knows much more that is beyond our comprehension. "Verily the knowledge of the hour is with Allah. It is He Who sends down rain, and He Who knows what is in the wombs. Neither does anyone know what it is that he will earn on the morrow, nor does any one know in what land he is to die. Verily, with Allah is full knowledge, and He is acquainted (with all things) (Qur'an 31:34)." No one knows what is in store for anyone the next day or where one will breathe one's last; whereas God knows everything.

CHAPTER 28

The Law for Peace and Prosperity
FROM SURAH AS-SAJDA (32)

The Qur'an is not the first book that has been revealed to man from God. Before this, a book was also revealed to Moses, David, and Jesus. There is also nothing strange or unheard of in the Qur'an. It contains the same guidance that had been previously revealed. Since the Qur'an was revealed from the same God Who revealed a book to Moses, be assured that similar events will happen now as happened in the time of Moses. Leadership will be bestowed only on those who accept and implement the laws of nature that God has put in place and that are given in the Qur'an. Those who reject these will be doomed to failure.

Throughout history, unbelievers have tried to humiliate the messengers and the believers. They resorted to oppression, tyranny, and persecution. Due to their unjust behavior and arrogance, the unbelievers were eventually destroyed. Like the rain that produces an abundance of all types of vegetation, implementation of the divine laws allows humans to achieve their ultimate human potential and their communities to reach new levels of peace and prosperity. God reminds people: "Don't they see that We do drive rain to parched soil and produce therewith crops, providing food for their cattle and themselves? Have they not the vision (Qur'an 32:27)?"

1 LAWS FOR HUMAN GUIDANCE AND WELFARE

1.1 God's Revelation and the Unbeliever's Doubts
The unbelievers of Makkah used to say that the Messenger was simply forging strange tales, like saying: (1) when people have become dust, they will be resurrected and will have to account for their deeds; (2) at the end of this accountability, one will either be punished in Hell or rewarded in Paradise; (3) these gods, goddesses, and saints that you worship are nonentities; (4)

430

God alone is the only deity worth worshiping; (5) the discourses that I recite are not my own but are God's word. In response, God tells people in Surah As-Sajda: "(This is) the revelation of the Book in which there is no doubt—from the Lord of the worlds. Or do they say He has forged it? Nay, it is the truth from your Lord that you may admonish a people to whom no warner has come before you, in order that they may receive guidance (Qur'an 32:2-3)."

1.2 God Regulates the Affairs of the Universe

People can reflect and judge for themselves which things presented in the Qur'an are strange and novel. Look at the creation and operation of the heavens and the earth. Consider your own creation and structure. Don't these things testify to the teaching that the Messenger is presenting to you in the Qur'an? Does the system of the universe point to One Creator or to several gods? It is God Who has created the universe and manages its operation. "It is Allah Who has created the heavens and the earth, and all between them, in six days. Then He established Himself on the throne (of authority). You have none besides Him to protect or intercede. Will you not then receive admonition? He rules (all) affairs from the heavens to the earth. In the end, (all affairs) will go up to Him on a day the space whereof will be (as) a thousand years of your reckoning. Such is He, the knower of all things, hidden and open, the exalted, the merciful—He Who has made everything that He has created most good. He began the creation of man with clay and made his progeny from a quintessence of the nature of a fluid despised. But He fashioned him in due proportion and breathed into him something of His spirit. He gave you (the faculties of) hearing and sight and feeling (and understanding). Little thanks do you give (Qur'an 32:4-9)."

2 RESURRECTION AND ACCOUNTABILITY

Considering the whole universe and one's own creation, does anyone's intellect not confirm that the One Who has given us our present existence will certainly be able to create us once again?

2.1 The Day of Judgment is to Motivate People to Reform

One can easily imagine a group of corrupt individuals after the resurrection standing before their Lord, saying to Him, "Our Lord! We have seen, and we have heard. Now then send us back (to the world). We will work righteousness, for we do indeed (now) believe (Qur'an 32:12)." However, on the Day of Judgment, the unbelievers will not get any help. They will be told: "Taste then—for you forgot the meeting of this day of yours, and We, too, will forget you—taste the penalty of eternity for your (evil) deeds (Qur'an 32:14)." It is only a mercy from God that He doesn't seize them immediately for their errors. Instead, He warns them beforehand with small troubles, hardships, calamities, losses, or strokes of misfortune so that they may wake up, take guidance, and start preparing for their ultimate accountability for their deeds.

Table 2.1: Resurrection and Accountability

No	Surah:Verses	Meanings
		Humankind will certainly be Resurrected
1	32:010-011	They say: "What! When we lie hidden and lost in the earth, shall we indeed be in a creation renewed?" Nay, they deny the meeting with their Lord. • Say: "The Angel of Death, put in charge of you, will take your souls; then shall you be brought back to your Lord.
		Punishment is to motivate people to reform

2	32:021-022	Indeed, We will make them taste of
		  1. The penalty of this (life) prior to the supreme penalty,
		  2. In order that they may (repent and) return.
		• And who does more wrong than one to whom are recited the revelations of his Lord, and who then turns away there from?
		Verily, from those who transgress, We shall exact (due) retribution.

2.2 Believers are those who Reform and Perform

Several of the believer's characteristics have been highlighted in Surah As-Sajda. The believers diligently implement divine laws in their lives and in their communities. They remember God and act according to God's commands during their daily efforts and transactions. They are not proud of their character and good deeds. They are not lazy, and they work hard. They seek God's help with fear and hope. They spend their efforts and wealth for the benefit of the people.

Table 2.2: The Behavior of the Believers

No	Surah:Verses	Meanings
3	32:015-016	Only those believe in Our revelations, 1. Who, when they are recited to them, fall down in prostration, (believe in their truth,) and celebrate the praises of their Lord (and implement His commands). 2. They are not puffed up with pride. 3. Their limbs do forsake their beds of sleep (they are not lazy). 4. They call on their Lord in fear and hope. 5. They spend (in charity) out of the sustenance that We have bestowed on them.

2.3 Believers will be Rewarded for their Good Deeds

God tells people: "Now no person knows what delights of the eye are kept hidden (in reserve) for them as a reward for their deeds. Is then the man who believes no better than the man who is rebellious and wicked? Not equal are they (Qur'an 32:17-18)." Since believers and unbelievers are not equal, they will be treated differently. "For those who believe and do righteous deeds are gardens as hospitable homes, for their (good) deeds (Qur'an 32:19)." In contrast, "As to those who are rebellious and wicked, their abode will be the fire. Every time they wish to get away there from, they will be forced there into, and it will be said to them: 'Taste the penalty of the fire, which you used to deny (Qur'an 32:20)."

3 THE IMPACT OF DIVINE GUIDANCE

3.1 Divine Laws are for Peace and Prosperity

What is failure? The unbelievers of Makkah, as well as the unbelievers of the present, have been reminded about the demise of past communities. God asked the unbelievers of Makkah if they would like to meet the same fate as that of prior unbelieving

433

communities. They were told not to be misguided by the apparent and superficial state of their worldly affairs. At that time, no one was listening to the Messenger except a few young men, including some slaves and poor people. Curses and ugly remarks from every side were being made to the Messenger. This led the unbelievers to believe wrongly that the Messenger's mission would fail. This was only a deception of their eyes. Had they not observed a land lying absolutely barren starting to swell with vegetation and plant life just by a single shower of the rain? Nobody knew that under the layers of soil there lay hidden such treasures of greenery and vegetation. Implementation of the divine laws has a similar effect in that individuals attain their ultimate human potential and their communities achieve new levels of peace and prosperity.

Table 3.1: Past Believing and Unbelieving Communities

No	Surah:Verses	Meanings
		Guided by Moses, Children of Israel flourished
1	32:023-025	We did indeed aforetime give the Book to Moses; be not then in doubt of its receiving. 1. We made it a guide to the Children of Israel. 2. We appointed, from among them, leaders, giving guidance under Our command, 3. So long as they persevered with patience and continued to have faith in Our revelations. Verily, your Lord will judge between them on the Day of Judgment, in the matters wherein they differ (among themselves).
		Like soil without rain, Unbelievers flourish not
2	32:026-027	• Does it not teach them a lesson, how many generations We destroyed before them, in whose dwellings they (now) go to and fro? Verily, in that are signs. Do they not then listen? • Don't they see that We do drive rain to parched soil (bare of herbage) and produce therewith crops, providing food for their cattle and themselves? Have they not the vision?

3.2 Believing did not help Pharaoh while Drowning

Unbelieving people used to mock the Messenger's preaching, and they tauntingly asked him when he would be victorious. "They say: "When will this decision be, if you are telling the truth (Qur'an 32:28)?" God commanded the Messenger to reply that when the time comes, believing only at that time will not profit them, just as it did not help Pharaoh at the time of his drowning. If you are to believe, then believe now. If you intend to wait till you meet your fate, as did those God destroyed, then: "...On the Day of Decision, no profit will it be to unbelievers if they (then) believe, nor will they be granted a respite. So turn away from them, and wait; they too are waiting (Qur'an 32:29-30)."

CHAPTER 29

Human Dignity and Freedom
FROM SURAH SABA (34)

Surah Saba deals with the unbelievers' objections against Islam's message of the Oneness of God, the Hereafter, and the Messenger himself. Unbelievers are warned of the evil consequences of their behavior and stubbornness. Like in the past, religion at present is being perceived by the unbelievers as a source of hostility and hatred. From Iraq to Afghanistan, from Kashmir to Sri Lanka, from Indonesia to Israel and Palestine, it often seems that religion fuels violence and raises the stakes of war. However, the fact that religion is a factor in many contemporary crises does not mean that it is the trigger that initiated them. To support the idea that religion is one of the principle sources of violence is not only unfair, it is also dangerous because it diverts our attention from the political roots of most conflicts, roots that reflect the very behavior that religion tries to eradicate.

1 DIVINE GUIDANCE IS GOD'S MERCY

1.1 Why the Hereafter? For Justice and Awards

Unbelievers often claim that the Day of Judgment will not come. God tells believers: "Say, 'Nay! But most surely, by my Lord, it will come upon you—by Him Who knows the unseen, from Whom is not hidden the least little atom in the heavens or on earth. Nor is there anything less than that, or greater, but is in the record perspicuous (Qur'an 34:3)." This is definitely going to happen, "That He may reward those who believe and work deeds of righteousness, for such is forgiveness and a sustenance most generous (Qur'an 34:4)." Certainly, "Those to whom knowledge has come see that the (revelation) sent down to you from your Lord—that is the truth, and that it guides to the path of the exalted, worthy of all praise (Qur'an 34:6)."

436

Table 1.1: Unbelievers Say: "We will not be resurrected"

No	Surah:Verses	Meanings
		Unbelievers' Objections about the Hereafter and the Messenger
1	34:005 34:007-008	But those who strive against Our revelations, to frustrate them—for such will be a penalty, a punishment most humiliating. • The unbelievers say (in ridicule): 1. "Shall we point out to you a man that will tell you, when you are all scattered to pieces in disintegration, that you shall (then be raised) in a new creation? 2. "Has he invented a falsehood against Allah, or has a spirit (seized) him?"
		Unbelievers' Deny the Accountability and Refuse to Reform
2	34:008-009	Nay, it is those who believe not in the Hereafter that are in (real) Penalty, and in farthest error. 1. Don't they see what is before them and behind them, of the sky and the earth? 2. If We wished, We could cause the earth to swallow them up, or cause a piece of the sky to fall upon them. Verily, in this is a sign for every devotee that turns to Allah (in repentance).

1.2 The Response to the Unbelievers' Comments

The unbelievers of Makkah had not received any divine message before, "We had not given them books that they could study, nor sent messengers to them before you as warners (Qur'an 34:44)." Nonetheless, they still said: "This is only a falsehood invented…This is nothing but evident magic (Qur'an 34:43)." In response, God tells the Messenger to:

1. Say: "I do admonish you on one point: that you do stand up before Allah—in pairs or singly—and reflect (within yourselves). Your companion (the Messenger) is not possessed; he is no less than a warner to you, in (the) face of a terrible penalty" (Qur'an 34:46).

437

2. Say: "No reward do I ask of you; it is (all) in your interest; my reward is only due from Allah..." (Qur'an 34:47).
3. Say: "Verily, my Lord casts the (mantle of) truth (over His servants)—He that has full knowledge of (all) that is hidden" (Qur'an 34:48).
4. Say: "The truth has arrived, and falsehood neither creates anything new nor restores anything" (Qur'an 34:49).
5. Say: "If I am astray, I only stray to the loss of my own self, but if I receive guidance, it is because of the inspiration of my Lord to me. It is He Who hears all things and is (ever) near" (Qur'an 34:50).

Concluding the discourse, God reminds the unbelievers about the fate of those who rejected the truth in the past: "And their predecessors rejected (the truth). These have not received a tenth of what We had granted to those. Yet, when they rejected My messengers, how (terrible) was My rejection (Qur'an 34:45)."

2 THE GRATEFUL AND THE UNGRATEFUL PEOPLE

The stories of the grateful people of David and Solomon and the ungrateful people of Saba highlight the benefits of being grateful to God. A review of the historical details of these two people will lead people to reflect and judge for themselves as to which mode of life is better: the one built on belief in One God, the Hereafter, and being grateful to God; or the one based on unbelief, worship of false deities and selfish desires, and denial of the Hereafter and the accountability for one's deeds.

2.1 David, Solomon, and their People were Grateful
David and Solomon and their people were blessed by God with great powers and such grandeur and glory as had never been granted to any people before them. Still, they were not proud or arrogant. They remained grateful servants of their Lord and were never rebellious.

438

Table 2.1: David and Solomon, examples of Grateful People

No	Surah:Verses	Meanings
		People thank God By doing Good to Others
1	34:010-013	We bestowed grace aforetime on David from Ourselves. 1. O you mountains! You sing back the praises of Allah with him (David), and you birds (also)! 2. We made the iron soft for him, (commanding), "Make coats of mail, balancing well the rings of chain armor, 3. "And work righteousness, for be sure I see (clearly) all that you do." And to Solomon: 1. (We made) the wind (obedient). Its early morning (stride) was a month's (journey), and its evening (stride) was a month's (journey). 2. We made a font of molten brass to flow for him. There were jinns that worked in front of him, by the leave of his Lord, and if any of them turned aside from Our command, We made him taste of the penalty of the blazing fire. 3. They worked for him as he desired, (making) arches, images, basins as large as reservoirs, and (cooking) cauldrons fixed (in places). Work you, sons of David, with thanks! But few of My servants are grateful.

2.2 Ungrateful people of Saba denied the Hereafter

When blessed by God, the people of Saba became proud and arrogant. Their actions reflected their denial of the Hereafter and their eventual accountability. Such people, having been ungrateful, were consequently so thoroughly destroyed and dispersed as to be remembered only in myths and legends. This story includes a warning to the unbelievers of Makkah and to any modern, prosperous countries that exhibit ingratitude by being unjust and tyrannical to other nations. God warns: "That was the requital We gave them because they ungratefully rejected faith, and never do We give (such) requital except to such as are ungrateful rejecters (Qur'an 34:17)." The verses of

Surah Saba, which highlight, 'God's Punishment for Unbelievers' Ingratitude', are given in the table below.

Table 2.2: The People of Saba, the Ungrateful People

No	Surah:Verses	Meanings
		God punished them with a loss of their Provisions
2	34:015-016	• There was for Saba, aforetime, a sign in their homeland—two gardens to the right and to the left. Eat of the sustenance (provided) by your Lord, and be grateful to Him—a territory fair and happy, and a Lord oft-forgiving! • But they turned away (from Allah), and We sent against them the flood (released) from the dams, and We converted their two gardens into gardens producing bitter fruit and tamarisks and some few (stunted) lote trees.
		Ungrateful People do not believe in the Hereafter
3	34:018-021	1. Between them and the cities on which We had poured our blessings, We had placed cities in prominent positions, and between them We had appointed stages of journey in due proportion: "Travel therein, secure, by night and by day." 2. But they said: "Our Lord! Place longer distances between our journey stages," but they wronged themselves (therein). At length, We made them as a tale (that is told), and We dispersed them all in scattered fragments. Verily in this are signs for every (soul that is) patiently constant and grateful. 3. And on them did Satan prove true his idea, and they followed him, all but a party that believed. But he had no authority over them, except that We might test the man who believes in the Hereafter from him who is in doubt concerning it: and your Lord does watch over all things.

3 BELIEF IN ONE GOD AND RIGHTEOUS DEEDS

Discriminations of every kind, social exclusion, economic injustice, military ambitions, lack of good governance, and geopolitical rivalries play important roles in the waging of war.

Even in the case of culturally and religiously rooted conflicts, violence and extremism generally stem from the exploitation of religion for political and ideological goals. To correct this situation in the world, God arranged to reform people with divine guidance that could not be corrupted. "We have not sent you but as a universal (Messenger) to men, giving them glad tidings, and warning them (against sin), but most men understand not (Qur'an 34:28)." While preaching divine guidance, the Messenger was instructed to declare the universal principle of individual responsibility and accountability: "You shall not be questioned as to our sins, nor shall we be questioned as to what you do (Qur'an 34:25)." Therefore, people should think seriously about the consequences of their behavior and try their best to do good deeds.

3.1 Human Dignity and Freedom Come from God

Belief in the One God frees humanity from any bondage that results in discrimination, exploitation, and corruption. In contrast, worship of false deities, idol worship, and worship of selfish desires or of any person degrades humanity to physical, mental, and spiritual slavery. Generally speaking, self-interest leads people to corruption, exploitation, and oppression. In the words of Prophet Joseph: "Nor do I absolve my own self (of blame). The (human) self is certainly prone to evil, unless my Lord does bestow His mercy (Qur'an 12:53)." Self-interest and a secular life style take away all human values from humankind. In referring to corrupt people, God says: "We have indeed created man in the best of molds; then do We abase him (to be) the lowest of the low (Qur'an 95:4-5)." Such people were described in Surah Al-Araf as being: "Those who behave arrogantly on the earth in defiance of right—them will I turn away from My signs. Even if they see all the signs, they will not believe in them. And if they see the way of right conduct, they will not adopt it as the way. But if they see the way of error, that is the way they will adopt, for they have rejected our signs and failed to take warning from them. Those who reject Our signs and the meeting in the Hereafter—vain are their deeds. Can they expect to be rewarded except as they have wrought (Qur'an 7:146-147)?"

441

Table 3.1: False Deities are helpless in both Worlds

No	Surah:Verses	Meanings
		One Day Lord will Command Truth and Justice
1	34:022	Say: "Call upon other (gods) whom you fancy besides Allah. They have no power—not the weight of an atom—in the heavens or on earth. No (sort of) share have they therein, nor is any of them a helper to Allah.
	34: 023	• "No intercession can avail in His presence, except for those for whom He has granted permission. So far (is this the case) that when terror is removed from their hearts (at the Day of Judgment, then) will they say, 'What is it that your Lord commanded?' They will say, 'That which is true and just, and He is the most high, most great.'"
	34:026	• Say: "Our Lord will gather us together and will in the end decide the matter between us (and you) in truth and justice, and He is the one to decide, the One Who knows all."
	34: 027	• Say: "Show me those whom you have joined with Him as partners. By no means (can you). Nay, He is Allah, the exalted in power, the wise."
		God (not deities) gives Sustenance
2	34:024	1. Say: "Who gives you sustenance from the heavens and the earth?" 2. Say: "It is Allah, and certain it is that either we or you are on right guidance or in manifest error."

3.2 Belief and Charity make People Peaceful and Prosperous

The positive influence of religion can be felt in a society through the pursuit of core human values and common ideals. God urges the believers to respect both fundamental human rights and the right to live in dignity. These basic tenets articulate the fundamental requirement for peaceful relations among peoples and societies. They underpin democracy and the rule of law, and they lie at the heart of key international accords and agreements. God says: "It is not your wealth nor your sons that will bring you nearer to Us in degree, but only those who believe and work righteousness. These are the ones for whom there is a multiplied

442

reward for their deeds, while secure they (reside) in the dwellings on high (Qur'an 34:37)."

Table 3.2: Children and Wealth Do Not Assure Safety

No	Surah:Verses	Meanings
		Wealth and Children make people Arrogant
3	34:034-035 34:038	1. Never did We send a warner to a population, but the wealthy ones among them said: "We believe not in the (message) with which you have been sent." 2. They said: "We have more in wealth and in sons, and we cannot be punished. Those who strive against Our revelations, to frustrate them, will be given over into punishment.
		Existance of Charity makes that Community Prosperous
4	34:039	1. Say: "Verily, my Lord enlarges and restricts the sustenance to such of his servants as He pleases. 2. "Nothing do you spend in the least (in His cause) but He replaces it, for He is the best of those who grant sustenance.

443

CHAPTER 30

Human Dignity and Self-Respect
FROM SURAH FATIR (35)

Surah Fatir was probably revealed during the middle Makkan period when the opposition of unbelievers had grown quite strong and when every sort of mischief was being adopted to frustrate the mission of Islam. This is also the case in the present period, as the unbelieving forces of the world are gathering together to frustrate efforts to bring justice and dignity back in Muslim communities after a long tragedy of colonial rule. At present, only people's own efforts and God's help can lift nations up. Begging and extravagance are nothing but God's punishment that people earn by their evil character and behavior.

Leaders of contemporary Muslim communities should not seek honor because all honor belongs to God. The only honor available to humans is in being righteous. "O people! We created you from a single (pair) of a male and a female and made you into nations and tribes that you may know each other (not that you may despise each other). Verily, the most honored of you in the sight of Allah is (he who is) the most righteous of you (Qur'an 49:13)."

1 THE SOURCE OF HUMAN DIGNITY

1.1 Honorable Humans are Trustworthy
People have not been created to be irresponsible in this world. They are accountable for their deeds, whether good or bad, and they have to face the good or bad consequences of their deeds, both in this world and the Hereafter. If we reflect a little, we realize that our doubts about the Hereafter are absolutely baseless. How can our resurrection be impossible for God Who created us from an insignificant sperm drop? God reminds us that the resurrection is His promise and that it will eventually be fulfilled. Therefore, we should live this life being conscious of our accountability for our behavior and deeds. God reassures us:

444

"O people! Certainly the promise of Allah is true. Let not then this present life deceive you, nor let Satan deceive you about Allah. Verily, Satan is an enemy to you; so treat him as an enemy. He only invites his adherents that they may become companions of the blazing fire (Qur'an 35:5-6).

Table 1.1: Only Accountability Assures Human Dignity

No	Surah:Verses	Meanings
		O people! Remember the favor of God on You
1	35:002-003	• What Allah out of his mercy does bestow on mankind, there is none can withhold. What He does withhold, there is none can grant apart from Him, and He is the exalted in power, full of wisdom. O people! Call to mind the grace of Allah unto you! Is there a creator, other than Allah, to give you sustenance from heaven or earth?
		Honor is from God and is earned through Good Deeds
2	35:008 35:010	• Is he, then, to whom the evil of his conduct is made alluring, so that he looks upon it as good, (equal to one who is rightly guided)? For Allah leaves to stray whom He wills, and guides whom He wills. So let not your self go out in (vainly) sighing after them, for Allah knows well all that they do! If any do seek for glory and power—to Allah belong all glory and power. To Him mount up (all) words of purity. It is He Who exalts each deed of righteousness. Those that lay plots of evil—for them is a penalty terrible, and the plotting of such will be void (of result).

1.2 Honorable People Cannot Worship False Gods

Worship is a show of gratitude. How can one show gratitude to those who have done nothing. God created the universe, while those deities that people associate with God have neither created anything nor control anything. If we use some common sense and reflect, we will realize that there is no being, beside God, who might possess divine attributes, powers, and authority. "If you invoke them, they will not listen to your call, and if they were to listen, they cannot answer your (prayer). On the Day of

445

Judgment they will reject your partnership, and none can tell you (the truth) like the One Who is acquainted with all things (Qur'an 35:14)."

Table 1.2: The Creator of the Universe vs. False Gods

No	Surah:Verses	Meanings
		The Creator of the Universe vs. False Gods
3	35:011-013	Allah did create you from dust, then from a sperm-drop; then He made you in pairs. <ol><li>No female conceives or lays down (her load) but with His knowledge.</li><li>Nor is a man long-lived granted length of days,</li><li>Nor is a part cut off from his life, but is in a decree (ordained).</li><li>All this is easy to Allah.</li></ol> Nor are the two bodies of flowing water alike— the one palatable, sweet, and pleasant to drink, and the other, salt and bitter. <ol><li>Yet, from each (kind of water) do you eat flesh fresh and tender,</li><li>And you extract ornaments to wear;</li><li>And you see the ships therein that plough the waves, that you may seek (thus) of the bounty of Allah that you may be grateful.</li></ol> He merges night into day, and He merges day into night, and He has subjected the sun and the moon (to his Law): each one runs its course for a term appointed. <ul><li>Such is Allah your Lord. To Him belongs all dominion, And those whom you invoke besides Him have not the least power.</li></ul>
		Unbelievers and those Who Worship God
4	35:007	For those who reject Allah is a terrible penalty, but for those who believe and work righteous deeds, is forgiveness and a magnificent reward.

2 HUMANKIND'S MISSION OF RIGHTEOUSNESS

2.1 None Can Bear the Burden of Others

Human conscience and intellect confirm that good and evil cannot be alike! People should think and judge as to what is reasonable. Should a good person and a criminal meet with the same fate and end up in the grave without resurrection and accountability, or should a good person be requited with good and an evil person with evil?

No one can bear another's burden, not even those whom people call upon besides God. If a heavily laden person should call upon another to carry his load, none of it shall be carried by the other, even if the other is near of kin. God tells us that one can guide only those who fear and worship their Lord without seeing Him and that whoever accepts guidance does so for his own good. Therefore, people should not reject truth outright without seriously learning about it because one's decision has consequences and because everybody will be held accountable.

Table 2.1: O People, Guidance is for Your Own Good.

No	Surah:Verses	Meanings
		People Need God and His Guidance
1	35:015-017	O people! It is you that have need of Allah: but Allah is the One free of all wants, worthy of all praise. If He so pleased, He could blot you out and bring in a new creation. Nor is that difficult for Allah.
		Different Attitudes have Different Results
2	35:018-022	1. Nor can a bearer of burdens bear another's burdens if one heavily laden should call another to (bear) his load. Not the least portion of it can be carried (by the other), even though he be nearly related. 2. You can but admonish such as fear their Lord unseen and establish regular prayer. Whoever purifies himself does so for the benefit of his own soul, and the destination (of all) is to Allah. 3. The blind and the seeing are not alike, nor are the depths of darkness and the light.

447

		4. Nor are the shade and the heat of the sun, nor are alike those that are living and those that are dead.
		Denial of the Truth entails Consequences
3	35:023-026	1. You are no other than a warner. Verily, We have sent you in truth as a bearer of glad tidings and as a warner: and there never was a people without a warner having lived among them (in the past). 2. And if they reject you, so did their predecessors, to whom came their messengers with clear signs, books of dark prophecies, and the book of enlightenment. In the end did I punish those who rejected faith: and how (terrible) was My rejection!

2.2 Believers and their Mission of Righteousness

The believers have been given the good news so that they may feel strengthened and encouraged and remain steadfast on the path of the truth with full faith in the promises made by God. God tells the believers that He chose them from among the people and has given them guidance. Unfortunately, some among them have wronged themselves, and some follow a medium course. However, some, by God's leave, vie with each other in acts of goodness.

Table 2.2: The Believers

No	Surah:Verses	Meanings
		Learn about your Creator to find the Truth
4	35:027-028	1. Don't you see that Allah sends down rain from the sky? With it We then bring out produce of various colors. 2. And in the mountains are tracts white and red of various shades of color, and black intense in hue. 3. And so among men and crawling creatures and cattle, are they of various colors.
		Believers Look forward to the Profitable Trade
5	35:028-030	Those truly fear Allah, among His servants, who have knowledge, for Allah is exalted in might, oft-forgiving. 1. Those who rehearse the Book of Allah,

448

		2. Establish regular prayer, and 3. Spend (in charity) out of what We have provided for them, secretly and openly, 4. Hope for a commerce that will never fail. For He will pay them their wages in full. Nay, He will give them (even) more out of His bounty, for He is oft-forgiving, most ready to appreciate (service).
		Sinners, of the Middle, and the Righteous
6	35:032	Then We have given the Book for inheritance to such of Our servants as We have chosen: But there are among them 1. Some who wrong their own souls, 2. Some who follow a middle course, and 3. Some who are, by Allah's leave, foremost in good deeds? That is the highest grace.

3 NONE CAN ALTER THE LAWS OF NATURE

Neither the Messenger nor the message will lose anything if one does not abandon one's false gods and wishes to continue living as an irresponsible person in the world. Truth will always remain the truth, and people will suffer the consequences for not accepting it. What are those consequences? In this world, they are living in conditions infested with discrimination, exploitation, and corruption. In the next world, the consequences are much more severe.

3.1 Disbelieves will bear the burden of their unbelief

Believers have the responsibility to preach Islam, to enjoin what is right, and to forbid what is wrong. In carrying out those tasks, so long as the believers exert themselves as best they can, they do not incur any responsibility for those who persist in their errors and who do not accept and follow the right way. God tells people: "Verily, Allah knows the hidden things of the heavens and the earth. Verily, He has full knowledge of all that is in (people's) hearts. He it is Who has made you inheritors in the earth. If then any do reject (Allah), their rejection (works) against themselves. Their rejection but adds to the odium for the unbelievers in the sight of their Lord. Their rejection but adds to (their own) undoing (Qur'an 35:38-39)."

3.2 The Unjust only give Promises to Deceive

God commands: "Say: 'Have you seen (these) 'partners' of yours whom you call upon besides Allah? Show me what it is they have created in the earth. Or have they a share in the heavens?' Or have We given them a book from which they (can derive) clear (evidence)? Nay, the wrongdoers promise each other nothing but delusions (Qur'an 35:40)."

Table 3: O People, Neither be Arrogant nor Plan Evil

No	Surah:Verses	Meanings
		The Outcome of Behaving Proudly and Planning Evil
1	35:042-043	1. They swore their strongest oaths by Allah that if a warner came to them, they would follow his guidance better than any of the peoples. 2. But when a warner came to them, it has only increased their flight (from righteousness) 3. On account of their arrogance in the land and their plotting of evil. But the plotting of evil will hem in only the authors thereof.
		God gives Unbelievers Enough Time to Repent and Reform
2	35:045	If Allah were to punish men according to what they deserve. 1. He would not leave on the back of the (earth) a single living creature. 2. But He gives them respite for a stated term. 3. When their Term expires, Verily, Allah has in His sight all His Servants.

CHAPTER 31

Proclamation of the Truth
FROM SURAH YA-SEEN (36)

Tauheed, the belief in One God, and the viability of and the need for the Hereafter are presented in Surah Ya-Seen. The signs from the creation, the working of the universe, and common sense testify to the existence of One God. Likewise, these same factors, plus the existence of mankind, lead one to believe in the existence of Hereafter. Life as created by God is a continuous learning and testing process, some results of which appear in this world, while the rest will be known in the Hereafter.

1 THE MESSENGER AND HIS DIFFICULTIES

1.1 Surely You Are One of the Messengers
The Messenger was enduring all kinds of hardships in selflessly preaching the message. To reinforce the Messenger's resolve, God told him: "By the Qur'an full of wisdom—you are indeed one of the messengers, on a straight way. It is a revelation sent down by the Exalted in Might, Most Merciful, so that you may admonish a people, whose fathers had received no admonition, and who therefore remain heedless (Qur'an 36:2-6)."

1.2 Arrogance and Bias Hinder Learning
Certain individual qualities are prerequisites for successful learning. Arrogance and biases hinder learning. God tells us that because of the unbelievers' arrogance: "We have put yokes round their necks right up to their chins, so that their heads are forced up (and they cannot see) (Qur'an 36:8)." Biases cause a lack of foresight and a lack of ability to perceive the truth. With regard to such people, God says: "We have put a bar in front of them and a bar behind them, and further We have covered them up, so that they cannot see (Qur'an 36:9)." In addition, God tells the Messenger: "You can but admonish such a one as follows the message and fears the (Lord) Most Gracious, unseen. Give such

451

a one, therefore, good tidings of forgiveness and a reward most generous (Qur'an 36:11)."

1.3 The Mentality and Lack of Wisdom of Unbelievers

The unbelievers' arrogance was highlighted in their answers to questions about their corruption and lack of charity. They could never comprehend that any calamity that falls on earth might be due to their own actions. "When they are told, 'Fear that which is before you and that which will be after you, in order that you may receive mercy,' (they turn back). Not a sign comes to them from among the signs of their Lord, but they turn away there from. When they are told, 'Spend of (the bounties) with which Allah has provided you,' the unbelievers say to those who believe: 'Shall we then feed those whom, if Allah had so willed, He would have fed (Himself)? You are in nothing but manifest error' (Qur'an 36:45-47)." This surely confirms that their arrogance has clouded their reasoning and wisdom.

2 BELIEVER'S PROCLAIMATION OF THE TRUTH

2.1 Believers are Commanded to Testify to the Truth

There is always a group of people in society who are convinced that Islam teaches the truth and that, just as there are physical laws that govern the universe, there are moral laws that govern the destiny of people. Unfortunately, they sometimes watch quietly and are unconcerned about the ongoing conflict between the truth and falsehood. It is a sad reflection on such people that they remain indifferent when the enemies of truth are openly plotting. Under such conditions, unless a person's conscience is totally dead, he should rise and perform his duty.

Surah Ya-Seen, verses 13-29, tells the parable of a righteous man who stood up for the truth when his people were arguing against and mocking their messengers. Although the believer lost his life in the process, it was his faith in God that helped him to side with the truth. As told in Surah Ya-Seen, his proclamation of truth earned him an immediate place in Paradise. Once installed in Paradise, he wished that his people, including those who had killed him for speaking the truth, knew why his Lord had

452

forgiven him and honored him. "It was said: 'Enter the garden.' He said: 'Ah me! Would that my people knew (what I know)—for that my Lord has granted me forgiveness and has enrolled me among those held in honor' (Qur'an 36:26-27)!"

Table 2: The Believer's Proclamation of the Truth

No	Surah:Verses	Meanings
		The Unbelievers' lame Arguments and Threats
1	36:013-019	Set forth to them, by way of a parable, the (story of) the companions of the city. 1. Behold! There came messengers to it. When We (first) sent to them two messengers, they rejected them, but We strengthened them with a third. They said, "Truly, we have been sent on a mission to you." 2. The (people) said: "You are only men like ourselves, and (Allah) Most Gracious sends no sort of revelation. You do nothing but lie." 3. They said: "Our Lord does know that we have been sent on a mission to you. Our duty is only to proclaim the clear message." 4. The (people) said: "For us, we augur an evil omen from you. If you desist not, we will certainly stone you. A grievous punishment, indeed, will be inflicted on you by us." 5. They said: "Your evil omens are with yourselves. (Deem you this an evil omen) if you are admonished? Nay, but you are a people transgressing all bounds."
		Followers of the Right Course Do not Ask for Reward
2	36:020-025	Then there came running, from the farthest part of the City, a man, saying, 1. "O my people! Obey the messengers. Obey those who ask no reward of you (for themselves), and who have themselves received guidance. 2. "It would not be reasonable for me if I did not serve Him Who created me, and to Whom you shall be brought back. 3. "Shall I take (other) gods besides Him? If (Allah) Most Gracious should intend some

453

		adversity for me, of no use whatever will be their intercession for me, nor can they deliver me. I would, indeed, if I were to do so, be in manifest error. "For me, I have faith in the Lord of you (all). Listen, then, to me."
		The People who Denied the Truth were Destroyed
3	36:028-032	1. We sent not down against his people, after him, any hosts from heaven, nor was it needful for Us so to do. 2. It was no more than a single mighty blast, and behold! They were (like ashes) quenched and silent. 3. Alas for (My) servants! There comes not a messenger to them but they mock him. Don't they see how many generations before them we destroyed? Not to them will they return, but each one of them all will be brought before Us (for judgment).

2.2 Believers should Try to Eliminate what is Evil

Without the promotion of good and the elimination of evil, an Islamic community ceases to exist. The working of an Islamic community is very well described in Surah At-Tawbah: "The believers, men and women, are protectors one of another. They enjoin what is just and forbid what is evil. They observe regular prayers, practice regular charity, and obey Allah and His Messenger. On them will Allah pour His mercy, for Allah is exalted in power, wise (Qur'an 9:71)."

It is narrated on the authority of Abdullah b. Mas'ud that the Messenger said: "Never a prophet had been sent before me by Allah towards his nation who had not among his people disciples and companions who followed his ways and obeyed his command. Then there came after them their successors who said whatever they did not practice and practiced whatever they were not commanded to do. He who strove against them with his hand was a believer. He who strove against them with his tongue was a believer, and he who strove against them with his heart was a believer, and beyond that there is no faith even to the extent of a mustard seed (Sahih Muslim: 1.81)." Abu Saeed Al-Khudri also quotes the Messenger as saying: "The best jihad in the path of Allah is to speak a word of justice to an oppressive ruler (Abu Dawud: 37.4330)." This is very important because social evils destroy a society, and the people who mock their messengers and reformers never attain peace and prosperity.

3 GOD AND HIS ABILITY TO RESURRECT

3.1 Proofs of God's Existence and the Hereafter

Tauheed, the worship of One God and the accountability of individual deeds in the Hereafter are the most important aspects of human existence in this world. In Surah Ya-Seen, God leads people to reflect on how the earth responds after the rain! It transforms itself from being baron to productive, generating all sorts of food. Did people or someone else cause it? Who created the sun or the moon? We did not create them. The signs from creation, the working of the universe, and common sense testify to the existence of a Creator. He created the rain, the vegetation, the sun and the moon, and numerous other things for people. If one reflects on the condition of the earth before and after the rain, it leads one to believe in the existence of divine guidance and the Hereafter. True humanity starts with the application of divine moral laws and the growth of human values in society. Life is a continuous human growth process, some results of which appear in this world while the rest will be known in the Hereafter.

Table 3.1: Signs from God's Creation

No	Surah:Verses	Meanings
		Let the Dead Earth before a Rain be a Sign
1	36:033-036	• A sign for them is the earth that is dead. We do give it life and produce grain there from, of which you do eat. We produce therein orchards with date palms and vines, and We cause springs to gush forth therein that they may enjoy the fruits of this (artistry). It was not their hands that made this. Will they not

		then give thanks? Glory to Allah, Who created in pairs all things that the earth produces, as well as their own (human) kind and (other) things of which they have no knowledge
		Night and Day and Sun and Moon are Signs
2	36:037-040	• And a sign for them is the night. We withdraw there from the day, and behold they are plunged in darkness. • And the sun runs his course for a period determined for him. That is the decree of (Him), the Exalted in Might, the All-Knowing. • And the moon—We have measured for her mansions (to traverse) till she returns like the old (and withered) lower part of a date stalk. It is not permitted to the sun to catch up the moon, nor can the night outstrip the day. Each (just) swims along in (its own) orbit (according to law).
		Another Sign is that God Saved People in a Boat
3	36:041-044	• And a sign for them is that We bore their race (through the flood) in the loaded ark, and We have created for them similar (vessels) on which they ride. If it were Our will, We could drown them. Then would there be no helper (to hear their cry), nor could they be delivered, except by way of Mercy from Us and by way of convenience for a time.

3.2 When God intends anything, He says to it: "Be," so it is

God, the Creator of mankind, has endowed people with numerous faculties to help them grow in this world. God reminds people: "If it had been Our will, We could surely have blotted out their eyes. Then should they have run about groping for the path, but how could they have seen? If it had been Our will, We could have transformed them (to remain) in their places. Then should they have been unable to move about, nor could they have returned (after error). If We grant long life to any, We cause him to be reversed in nature. Will they not then understand (Qur'an 36:66-68)?" God also says: "Verily, when He intends a thing, His command is, 'Be,' and it is! So glory to Him, in Whose hands is the dominion of all things, and to Him will you

456

be all brought back (Qur'an 36:82-83)." Therefore, when He intends that people should be resurrected, it will happen.

Table 3.2: The Creator of the Universe is Able to Resurrect

No	Surah:Verses	Meanings
		Creation of Cattle is for the Benefit of Humankind
4	36:071-073	Don't they see that it is We Who have created for them – • Among the things which Our hands have fashioned—cattle, which are under their dominion— • And that We have subjected them to their (use)? Of them, some do carry them and some they eat. • And they have (other) profits from them (besides), and they get (milk) to drink. Will they not then be grateful?
		Reflect on Yourself: Who brought you into existence?
5	36:077-079	Does not man see that it is We Who created him from sperm? • Yet, behold! He (stands forth) as an open adversary! He makes comparisons for Us and forgets his own (origin and) creation. • He says, "Who can give life to (dry) bones and decomposed ones?" Say, "He will give them life Who created them for the first time! For He is well-versed in every kind of creation."
		God Who Created this Universe Can create Another!
6	36:081	Is not He Who created the heavens and the earth able to create the like thereof? Yea, indeed! For He is the Creator Supreme, of skill and knowledge (infinite).

4 INDIVIDUAL ACCOUNTABILITY AND REWARD

How can we justify an afterlife? Well, where else can the injustices of this life be rectified, if not in an afterlife? What we perceive to be injustices in this worldly life would be a poor reflection upon God's attribute of fairness if these injustices were not offset by appropriate rewards and punishments in the Hereafter. Some very corrupt people enjoy the most luxurious lives in this world. Meanwhile, some of the best people suffer terribly. Since the inequities of worldly life are clear, one cannot and will not believe or trust in the mercy and justice of the Creator if He restricts only to this worldly life the rewards of piety and the punishments of transgression.

4.1 Principles of Accountability and Reward

True belief and good deeds have a reward both in this world and in the Hereafter. The same is true with regard to unbelief and evil deeds. Since unbelievers want to benefit from the injustice done to others, they refuse to believe in God's accountability and award system. Here, the unbelievers have no choice. This has been the message of all messengers of God—each and every one of them. God created this universe to be governed by certain rules and laws, whether physical, moral or sociopolitical. These laws have consequences whenever they are broken. That is why some people and communities are punished or rewarded in this world. In addition, individuals are going to be judged in the Hereafter and then punished and rewarded for the deeds they committed in this life on earth.

God commands people: "Fear tumult or oppression, which affects not in particular (only) those of you who do wrong, and know that Allah is strict in punishment (Qur'an 8:25)." At the same time, people are assured: "Allah does advance in guidance those who seek guidance, and the things that endure, good deeds, are best in the sight of your Lord as rewards and best in respect of (their) eventual returns (Qur'an 19:76)."

458

Table 4.1: Reward is Only for the Good Deeds

No	Surah:Verses	Meanings
		People shall only be rewarded according to their deeds
1	36:054 36:065	1. Then, on that day, no one will be wronged in the least, and you shall not be rewarded except according to your deeds. 2. That day shall We set a seal on their mouths. But their hands will speak to us, and their feet bear witness to all that they did.
		People shall be rewarded as described in the Qur'an
2	36:069-070	3. We have not instructed the (Prophet) in poetry, nor is it appropriate for him. This is no less than a message and a Qur'an making things clear— 4. That it may give admonition to any (who are) alive, and that the charge may be proved against those who reject.
		People shall not be helped by deities worshiped beside God
3	36:074-075	Yet they take (for worship) gods other than Allah, (hoping) that they might be helped! They have not the power to help them, but they will be brought up (before Our court) as a troop (to be condemned).

4.2 Worldly Trials are Meant to Reform People

The trials and challenges of this world are for the benefit of humankind. God tells people: "Indeed, We will make them taste of the penalty of this (life) prior to the supreme penalty (of the Hereafter), in order that they may (repent and) return (Qur'an 32:21)." Surah Al-Qalam presents a parable about the owners of a garden, who after having been blessed by God turned ungrateful to Him. They did not listen to the advice of a good person among them. Consequently, they were deprived of the blessing and realized the error of their ways when all they had lay ruined by a natural disaster. With this parable, people have been warned that we, too, could be put to a test similar to the one to which the owners of the garden were put. If we do not listen to the divine message, we could be afflicted with a punishment in this world, and the punishment of the Hereafter is far greater.

459

Table 4.2: Intentions and Deeds impact People's Worldly life

No	Surah:Verses	Meanings
		Bad Intentions Ruined the People of the Garden
4	68:017-027	Verily, We have tried them as We tried the people of the garden • When they resolved to gather the fruits of the (garden) in the morning, but made no reservation (if it be Allah's will). • Then there came on the (garden) a visitation from your Lord, (which swept away) all around, while they were asleep. So the (garden) became by the morning like a dark and desolate spot (whose fruit had been gathered). • As the morning broke, they called out, one to another, "Go to your tilth in the morning if you would gather the fruits." So they departed, conversing in secret low tones, (saying): "Let not a single indigent person break in upon you into the (garden) this day." • They started the morning, strong in an (unjust) resolve. But when they saw the (garden), they said: "We have surely lost our way. Indeed, we are shut out (of the fruits of our labor)."
		After the Loss, **They admitted their Mistake and Repented**
5	68:028-033	1. Said one of them, more just (than the rest): "Did I not say to you, 'Why not glorify (Allah)?'" They said: "Glory to our Lord! Verily, we have been doing wrong!" 2. Then they turned, one against another, in reproach. They said: "Alas for us! We have indeed transgressed! It may be that our Lord will give us in exchange a better (garden) than this, for we do turn to Him (in repentance)!" Such is the punishment (in this life), but greater is the punishment in the Hereafter, if only they knew!

4.3 Resurrection, Accountability, and Reward

Life as created by God is a continuous learning and evaluation process for people and their communities. When people learn from divine guidance and reform themselves, their communities are rewarded accordingly. Belief and good deeds help people reform and thereby establish just, prosperous, and peaceful communities. In contrast, unbelief and evil deeds tend to ruin individuals and communities after a certain fixed time. The results of human activities on earth will also be known in the Hereafter. There will be a Day of Judgment, and all of us will be there. Then it will be far too late start thinking about changing our lives for the better. The record of our deeds will have already been compiled, and there will be no going back.

Table 4.3: Resurrection: Reward or Punishment

No	Surah:Verses	Meanings
		The Resurrection and the Day of Judgment
6	36:048-053	Further, they say, "When will this promise (come to pass), if what you say is true?" 1. They will not (have to) wait for aught but a single blast. It will seize them while they are yet disputing among themselves! No (chance) will they then have, by will, to dispose (of their affairs), nor to return to their own people. 2. The trumpet shall be sounded, when behold! From the graves, they will rush forth to their Lord! They will say: "Ah! Woe unto us! Who has raised us up from our beds of repose?" (A voice will say): "This is what (Allah) Most Gracious had promised, and true was the word of the messengers." 3. It will be no more than a single blast, when lo! They will all be brought up before Us. 4. Then on that day, no one will be wronged in the least, and you shall not be rewarded except according to your deeds.
		Paradise is for Believers who do good deeds
7	36:055-058	Verily, the companions of the Garden (of Paradise) shall that day have joy in all that they do. 1. They and their associates will be in groves of shade, 2. Reclining on thrones (of dignity).

461

		3. (Every) fruit will be there for them. 4. They shall have whatever they call for. "Peace!" - A word (of salutation) from a Lord most merciful!
		Hell is for those who disbelieve and serve Satan
8	36:059-064	O you in sin! Get you apart this day! Did I not enjoin on you, O children of Adam, 1. That you should not worship Satan, for that he was to you an enemy avowed, 2. And that you should serve Me, (for that) this was the straight way. But he did lead astray a great multitude of you. Did you not then understand? This is the Hell of which you were warned! Embrace the (fire) this day, for that you (persistently) rejected (the truth).

CHAPTER 32

The Magnificent Success
FROM SURAH AS-SAFFAT (37)

In Surah As-Saffat, some of the main traits of the unbelievers of Makkah, like prejudice, arrogance, and the worship of false deities, were criticized by God for their absurdity. The unbelievers were informed about the evil consequences of their deviations, which stood in marked contrast with the splendid results obtained from faith and righteous acts. The unbelievers were also warned that the Messenger, whom they were mocking and ridiculing, would eventually be successful. God declared: "Already has Our word been passed before (this) to our servants sent (by Us), that they would certainly be assisted and that Our forces—they surely must conquer (Qur'an 37:171-173)."

1 RESURRECTION AND REWARD FOR THE RIGHTEOUS

1.1 The Creator of the Universe Can Certainly Recreate
After referring to the universe He created and guards, God tells us: "Verily, verily, your Allah is one—Lord of the heavens and of the earth and all between them, and Lord of every point at the rising of the sun (Qur'an 37:4-5)." This God, who knows how to create, can certainly resurrect humankind in the Hereafter.

Table 1.1: God, His Creation, and the Hereafter

No	Surah:Verses	Meanings
		The Universe is well Guarded by God's Laws
1	37:006-010	1. We have indeed decked the lower heaven with beauty (in) the stars, (for beauty) and for guard against all obstinate, rebellious, evil spirits. 2. (So) they should not strain their ears in the direction of the exalted assembly, but be cast away from every side. Repulsed, for they are under a perpetual penalty, except such as snatch away something by stealth,

463

		and they are pursued by a flaming fire, of piercing brightness.
		God Knows how to Create and Recreate
2	37:011-018	1. Just ask their opinion: are they the more difficult to create, or the (other) beings We have created? Them have We created out of a sticky clay! 2. Truly do you marvel while they ridicule, and when they are admonished, pay no heed, and when they see a sign, turn it to mockery and say, "This is nothing but evident sorcery. What! When we die and become dust and bones, shall we (then) be raised up (again), and also our fathers of old?" Tell them: Yes, and you shall then be humiliated (on account of your evil).

1.2 The Day of Sorting Out

On the Day of Judgment: "They (the unbelievers) will say, 'Ah! Woe to us! This is the Day of Judgment!' (A voice will say,) 'This is the Day of Sorting Out, whose truth you denied!' 'Bring you up,' it shall be said, 'the wrongdoers and their wives, and the things they worshiped' (Qur'an 37:20-22)."

Table 1.2: The Day of Sorting Out

No	Surah:Verses	Meanings
		Unbelievers converse with their False Gods
3	37:024-033	Stop them (the wrongdoers and their false gods), for they must be asked: • "What is the matter with you that you don't help each other?" Nay, but that day they shall submit (to judgment). • They will turn to one another and question one another. They (the followers) will say: "It was you who used to come to us from the right hand (of power and authority)!" • They (the leaders) will reply: "Nay, you yourselves had no faith, nor had we any authority over you. Nay, it was you who were a people in obstinate rebellion. So now has been proved true against us the word of our Lord that we shall indeed (have to) taste

		(the punishment of our sins). We led you astray, for truly we were ourselves astray." Truly, that day, they will (all) share in the penalty.
		The Consequences for Unbelief
4	37:034-039	Verily, that is how We shall deal with sinners. 1. For they, when they were told that there is no god except Allah, would puff themselves up with pride, 2. And say: "What! Shall we give up our gods for the sake of a poet possessed?" 3. Nay! He has come with the (very) truth, and he confirms (the message of) the (previous) messengers. You shall indeed taste of the grievous penalty, but it will be no more than the retribution of (the evil) that you have wrought.

2 THE AFTERLIFE: EITHER PARADISE OR HELL

2.1 The Reward for Belief and Good Deeds

The believers, the purified servants of God, have been told that they shall be rewarded. After describing the life of the believers in Paradise and illustrating it with a dialogue between the believers and the unbelievers about their lives and encounters in the previous life, God tells people that entering Paradise is the mighty achievement.

Table 2.1: Getting into Paradise is the Mighty Achievement

No	Surah:Verses	Meanings
		Paradise: Reward for Belief and Good Deeds
1	37:040-049	But the sincere (and devoted) servants of Allah— for them is a well-measured supply of fruits, and they (shall enjoy) honor and dignity in gardens of felicity, facing each other on thrones (of dignity). 1. Round will be passed to them a cup from a clear-flowing fountain, crystal-white, of a taste delicious to those who drink (thereof), free from headiness. Nor will they suffer intoxication there from. 2. Beside them will be chaste women, restraining their glances, with big eyes (of

		wonder and beauty), as if they were (delicate) eggs closely guarded.
		Dialogue between the Believers and Unbelievers

2	37:050-061	Then they (the believers) will turn to one another and question one another. One of them will start the talk and say:
		1. "I had an intimate companion (on the earth) who used to say, 'What? Are you among those who bear witness to the truth (of the message)? When we die and become dust and bones, shall we indeed receive rewards and punishments?'"
		2. (A voice) said: "Would you like to look down?" He looked down and saw him in the midst of the fire.
		    • He said: "By Allah! You were little short of bringing me to perdition! Had it not been for the grace of my Lord, I should certainly have been among those brought (there)!
		    • "Is it (the case) that we shall not die, except our first death, and that we shall not be punished?"
		Verily, this is the supreme achievement! For the like of this, let all strive who wish to strive.

2.2 The Award for Unbelief and Corruption

The unbelievers have been warned about their refusal to listen to God's messengers and their mockery and ridicule of the divine message of the Oneness of God, the Hereafter, and the accountability for one's deeds. The unbelievers have been asked: "Is that the better entertainment or the tree of Zaqqum—for We have truly made it (as) a trial for the wrongdoers, for it is a tree that springs out of the bottom of Hellfire. The shoots of its fruit stalks are like the heads of devils. Truly, they will eat thereof and fill their bellies therewith. Then on top of that, they will be given a mixture made of boiling water. Then shall their return be to the fire. Truly, they found their fathers on the wrong path, so they (too) were rushed down on their footsteps. Truly, before them, many of the ancients went astray, but We sent aforetime among them (messengers) to admonish them. Then see what was the end, of those who were admonished (but heeded not),—except the sincere servants of Allah (Qur'an 37:62-74)."

3 GOD HAS PROMISED THE BELIEVERS VICTORY IN THIS WORLD

3.1 The Angels are God's Servants Who Cannot Disobey

The Qur'an tells people about the existence of the angels. They were created before the creation of humankind, and they always obey God. They glorify Him all the time and also pray for the forgiveness of the believers. They may take a material form or even appear as humankind, as happened with the angels who appeared before Mary to give her the news of her forthcoming pregnancy and childbirth. The angels live in heaven and come down to earth when God instructs them to do so. There is no other relationship of angels and God except that they are God's creation and His servants.

Table 3.1: Angels are only a Creation of God

No	Surah:Verses	Meanings
		Unbelievers say that the Angels are Daughters of God
1	37:149-157	Now ask them their opinion. Is it that your Lord has (only) daughters and they have sons, or that We created the angels female, and they are witnesses (thereto)? 1. Is it not that they say from their own invention (that) Allah has begotten children? But they are liars! Did He (then) choose daughters rather than sons? What is the matter with you? How do you judge? Will you not then receive admonition? 2. Or have you an authority manifest? Then you bring your Book (of authority) if you be truthful.
		Assertion of God's Relationship with Angels and Jinns is Untrue
2	37:158-166	They have invented a blood relationship between Him and the jinns, but the jinns know (quite well) that they have indeed to appear (before His court)!

		Glory to Allah! (He is free) from the things they ascribe (to Him)! Not (so do) the servants of Allah, sincere and devoted. 1. For, verily, neither you nor those you worship can lead (any) into temptation concerning Allah, except such as are (themselves) going to the blazing fire. 2. (The angels say): "Not one of us but has a place appointed. We are verily ranged in ranks (for service), and we are verily those who declare (Allah's) glory."

3.2 God has promised Victory to Messengers and Believers

The unbelievers were plainly warned that the Messenger whom they were mocking and ridiculing would eventually be successful. Their power and position would not be able to stop the army of God encamping in the very courtyards of their houses. God declared in Surah As-Saffat that the Messenger and his message would be successful. This notice was given at a time when there appeared no chance of the Messenger's success. The Muslims were being severely persecuted, about 75% of their population had already left their homes, and about 40 to 50 helpless individuals were left with the Messenger in Makkah. Under such circumstances, none of the unbelievers thought that the Messenger and his handful of ill-equipped companions would ultimately achieve dominance. Instead, they thought that the new movement would end and be buried in the valleys of Makkah. However, only 15 to 16 years later, upon the conquest of Makkah, the prophecy was fulfilled. This promise of God to help His believers is as valid today as it was at the time when Surah As-Saffat was revealed.

Table 3.2: Messengers and their Comrades shall Triumph

No	Surah:Verses	Meanings
		Unbelievers Wished for and then Rejected the Guidance
3	37:167-170	• There were those who said, "If only we had had before us a message from those of old, We should certainly have been servants of Allah, sincere (and devoted)!" But (now that the Qur'an has come), they reject it.

		But soon will they know.
		Divine Promise to the Believers is Success

4	37:171-179	Already has Our Word been passed before (this) to our servants sent (by Us)
		    1. That they would certainly be assisted,
		    2. That Our forces—they surely must conquer.
		• So turn you away from them for a little while, and watch them (how they fare), and they soon shall see (how you fare).
		• Do they wish (indeed) to hurry on Our punishment? But when it descends into the open space before them, evil will be the morning for those who were warned (and heeded not).
		So turn you away from them for a little while, and watch (how they fare), and they soon shall see (how you fare).

4 EFFORTS IMPACT THE FATE OF COMMUNITIES

4.1 Abraham's Attitude and Efforts Earned God's Respect

People's individual and collective attitudes and efforts affect their fate. This has been elaborated with the life history of Abraham, who did not show any reluctance to sacrifice his only son when he received an inspiration from God to do so. There is a lesson in this incident for Muslims, as there was for the unbelieving Quraysh, who were very proud of being Abraham's descendents. This event indicates the essence and the real spirit of Islam and how a true believer should be ready to sacrifice for the pleasure and approval of God.

Table 4.1: Abraham - The Model Believer

No	Surah:Verses	Meanings
		Abraham came to his Lord with a pure Heart
1	37:083-087	Verily, among those who followed his (Noah's) way was Abraham. Behold! He approached his Lord with a sound heart. • Behold! He said to his father and to his people, "What is that which you worship? Is

469

		it a falsehood—gods other than Allah that you desire? Then what is your idea about the Lord of the worlds?"
		Unbelievers worship what they have carved

2	37:088-098	1. Then did he cast a glance at the stars, and he said: "I am indeed sick (at heart)!" So they turned away from him, and departed.
		2. Then did he turn to their gods and said, "Will you not eat (of the offerings before you)? What is the matter with you that you speak not?"
		3. Then did he turn upon them, striking (them) with the right hand. Then came (the worshipers) with hurried steps, and faced (him).
		  • He said: "You worship that which you have (yourselves) carved, but Allah has created you and your handwork."
		  • They said, "Build him a furnace, and throw him into the blazing fire."
		(This failing), they then sought a stratagem against him, but We made them the ones most humiliated.

		Abraham Submits to God's Will and Guidance
3	37:099-102	He said: "I will go to my Lord! He will surely guide me. O my Lord! Grant me a righteous (son)!" So We gave him the good news of a boy ready to suffer and forbear. 1. Then, when (the son) reached (the age of) (serious) work with him, he said: "O my son! I see in vision that I offer you in sacrifice. Now see what your view is!" 2. (The son) said: "O my father! Do as you are commanded. You will find me, if Allah so wills, one practicing patience and constancy."
		Thus God rewards Abraham and the Doers of Good!
4	37:103-111	So when they had both submitted their wills (to Allah), and he had laid him prostrate on his forehead (for sacrifice), We called out to him, "O Abraham! You have already fulfilled the vision! • Thus indeed do We reward those who do right? For this was obviously a trial.

		• We ransomed him with a momentous sacrifice, and We left (this blessing) for him among generations (to come) in later times: "Peace and salutation to Abraham!" Thus, indeed, do We reward those who do right, for he was one of our believing servants.

4.2 People's Attitudes and Efforts Determine their Destiny

History confirms that people's attitudes and efforts make them candidates for God's help, in the case of His messengers and their followers, or God's punishment, for those who reject the divine guidance. These historical incidents are not only a warning for the unbelievers, but they are also good news for the believers who were and will be passing through highly unfavorable and discouraging conditions on account of their supporting and following God's messengers. Believers are told that they should not be disheartened at the hardships and difficulties they have to encounter in their efforts, for in the end they will be successful. The unbelievers, who may appear to be dominant at any given time in history, will eventually be overwhelmed.

Table 4.2: Past Communities either Prospered or Destroyed

No	Surah:Verses	Meanings
		Noah Prayed to God to Help him and his Followers
5	37:075-082	(In the days of old), Noah cried to Us, and We are the best to hear prayer. 1. We delivered him and his people from the great calamity and made his progeny to endure (on this earth). 2. We left (this blessing) for him among generations to come in later times: "Peace and salutation to Noah among the nations." Thus, indeed, do we reward those who do right, for he was one of our believing servants. Then the rest we overwhelmed in the flood.
		God delivered Moses, Aaron and their People
6	37:114-122	1. Again (of old), We bestowed Our favor on Moses and Aaron, and We delivered them and their people from (their) great calamity; and

471

		We helped them, so they overcame (their troubles). 2. We gave them the book that helps to make things clear; and We guided them to the straight way. We left (this blessing) for them among generations (to come) in later times: "Peace and salutation to Moses and Aaron!" Thus, indeed, do We reward those who do right, for they were two of our believing servants.
		God punished Elias's People, except His devoted Servants
7	37:123-132	So also was Elias among those sent (by Us)? Behold, he said to his people, 1. "Will you not fear (Allah)? 2. "Will you call upon Baal and forsake the Best of Creators—Allah, your Lord and Cherisher and the Lord and Cherisher of your fathers of old?" 3. But they rejected him, and they will certainly be called up (for punishment), except the sincere and devoted servants of Allah (among them). 4. We left (this blessing) for him among generations (to come) in later times: "Peace and salutation to such as Elias!" Thus, indeed, do We reward those who do right, for he was one of our believing servants.
		God delivered Lot and his Adherents- then destroyed the Rest
8	37:133-138	• So also was Lot among those sent (by Us). Behold, We delivered him and his adherents, all except an old woman who was among those who lagged behind. • Then We destroyed the rest. • Verily, you pass by their (sites) by day and by night. Will you not then understand?
		Jonah Repented and Glorified God, Who Forgave Him -
9	37:139-148	So also was Jonah among those sent (by Us)? 1. When he ran away (like a slave from captivity) to the ship (fully) laden, He (agreed to) cast lots, and he was condemned. 2. Then the big fish did swallow him, and he had

| | | done acts worthy of blame. Had it not been that he (repented and) glorified Allah, He would certainly have remained inside the fish till the Day of Resurrection.
3. But We cast him forth on the naked shore in a state of sickness, and We caused to grow over him a spreading plant of the gourd kind.
We sent him (on a mission) to a hundred thousand (men) or more. They believed; so We permitted them to enjoy (their life) for a while. |

CHAPTER 33

Civilization Built on Human Dignity
FROM SURAH SAD (38)

Human dignity springs from people's freedom and from their accountability for their actions and deeds. It is not the message of Islam, but the unbeliever's own arrogance, jealousy, and fear of change, that comes in the way of their believing the truth. They want to persist in the ideas of ignorance that their ancestors followed. The concepts of the Oneness of God, the Hereafter, and the accountability for one's deeds are not only unacceptable to them, but they are something that the unbelievers ridicule and mock. However, there are severe consequences for such unbelief. According to the law of nature that God has put in place, corrupt communities that refuse to reform will eventually be destroyed.

1 THE FATE OF UNJUST AND CORRUPT SOCIETIES

1.1 The Arrogance and Stubborn Defiance of the Unbelievers
As noted above, the actual reason for the unbelievers' denial of the divine message is not due to any defect in the message of Islam. Rather, it is due to their own arrogance, jealousy, and the fear of change. The unbelievers of Makkah were not prepared to believe in the truth proclaimed by a man from their own clan. They could not accept him as a Messenger and were unwilling to follow him. They wanted to persist in the ideas of ignorance that their ancestors followed. God tells the unbelievers (of Makkah and of future generations) that a community, which follows divine laws, in which people play a dignified role in shouldering responsibility for their own deeds, and which establishes justice, will be prosperous and peaceful, as compared with communities ruled by self-interest, injustice, exploitation, and corruption. God tells people: "But the unbelievers (are steeped) in self-glory and separatism. How many generations before them did We destroy? In the end, they cried (for mercy) when there was no longer time for being saved (Qur'an 38:2-3)."

474

Table 1.1 Unbelievers reject the Messenger and the Messege

NoSurah:Verses		Meanings
		Unbelieving Leaders Arrogantly Refuse the Message
1	38:004-007	So they wonder that a warner has come to them from among themselves. 1. And the unbelievers say: "This is a sorcerer telling lies! Has he made the gods (all) into one Allah? Truly, this is a wonderful thing!" 2. The leader among them goes away (impatiently, saying), "Walk away, and remain constant to your gods, for this is truly a thing designed (against you). We never heard (the like) of this among the people of these latter days. This is nothing but a made-up tale."
		Unbelieving Leaders Jealously Reject the Messenger
2	38:008-010	(The unbelievers say): "What! Has the message been sent to him (out of all the people) among us?" • But they are in doubt concerning My (Own) message! Nay, they have not yet tasted My punishment! 1. Or have they the treasures of the mercy of your Lord, the exalted in power, the grantor of bounties without measure? 2. Or have they the dominion of the heavens and the earth and all between? If so, let them mount up with the ropes and means (to reach that end)!

1.2 Communities that Refuse to Reform Face Destruction

The people of Noah, 'Ad, Pharaoh, and the Lord of Stakes rejected the messengers. As such, their communities were based on the rejection of the laws of nature that God has put in place. The same was the case with the Thamud, the people of Lot, and the people of Aykah. Each community called their messengers liars and refused to adjust their character and behavior according to the divine guidance. This made them something other than the true humanity that God, their Creator, desired. Therefore, they were destroyed.

Table 1.2
Fates of Corrupt Communities Which Refused to Reform

No	Surah:Verses	Meanings
		God Appoints Messengers and Compensates their Work
3	38:086-088	• Say: "No reward do I ask of you for this (Qur'an), nor am I a pretender." • This is no less than a message to (all) the worlds, and you shall certainly know the truth of it (all) after a while.
		Communities that Refused to Reform were Destroyed
4	38:012-016	1. Before them (were many who) rejected messengers—the people of Noah, and 'Ad, and Pharaoh, the Lord of Stakes, and Thamud, and the people of Lot, and the Companions of the Wood—such were the confederates. 2. Not one (of them) but rejected the messengers, but My punishment came justly and inevitably (on them). These (today) only wait for a single mighty blast, which (when it comes) will brook no delay. They say: "Our Lord! Hasten to us our sentence (even) before the Day of Account."

2 BUILDING OF A PROSPEROUS AND PEACEFUL SOCIETY

In telling the story of David and Solomon, God emphasized that His law of justice is impartial and objective. Only the right attitude of people is acceptable to Him. He calls to account and punishes every wrongdoer whoever he may be, and He likes only those people who do not persist in wrongdoing, who repent immediately after they learn their mistake, and who correct their behavior. Such people live in the world knowing that they are accountable for their behavior and deeds and will be rewarded in this world and on the Day of Judgment.

2.1 Justice and the Accountability for People's Conduct

Addressing David, God commanded all people and their leaders to do justice: "O David! We did indeed make you a vicegerent on earth. So judge between men in truth (and justice), nor follow the lusts (of your heart), for they will mislead you from the path of Allah. For those who wander astray from the path of Allah is a penalty grievous, for that they forget the Day of Account (Qur'an 38:26)." People have been advised to reflect over the verses of the Qur'an and to take advice: "(Here is) a Book that We have sent down unto you, full of blessings, that they may meditate on its revelations and that men of understanding may receive admonition (Qur'an 38:29)."

Table 2.1
Even Wise People with Clear Judgment Need Guidance

No	Surah:Verses	Meanings
		David: A man of Wisdom and Clear Judgment
1	38:017-020	Have patience at what they say, and remember our servant David, the man of strength, for he ever turned (to Allah). • It was We that made the hills declare, in unison with him, Our praises at eventide and at break of day, and the birds gathered (in assemblies). All with him did turn (to Allah). • We strengthened his kingdom and gave him wisdom and sound judgment in speech and decision.
		The Litigants said: **"Decide between us with Justice"**
2	38:021-025	Has the story of the disputants reached you? Behold, they climbed over the wall of the private chamber. 1. When they entered the presence of David, and he was terrified of them, they said: "Fear not. We are two disputants, one of whom has wronged the other. Decide now between us with truth, and treat us not with injustice, but guide us to the even path. This man is my brother. He has nine and ninety ewes, and I have (but) one. Yet, he says, 'Commit her to my care,' and is (moreover) harsh to me in speech."

477

		2. (David) said: "He has undoubtedly wronged you in demanding your ewe to be added to his (flock of) ewes. Truly, many are the partners (in business) who wrong each other. Not so do those who believe and work deeds of righteousness, and how few are they! David gathered that We had tried him. He asked forgiveness of his Lord, fell down, bowing (in prostration), and turned (to Allah in repentance). So We forgave him this (lapse). He enjoyed, indeed, a near access to Us and a beautiful place of (final) return.

2. 2 God Helps Believers Build Prosperous Communities

God expects and appreciates devotion from the believers, and believers turn to Him when in trouble and seek His help. God answers the supplications of such people and makes their efforts fruitful. "And We did try Solomon. We placed on his throne a body (without life), but he did turn (to Us in true devotion). He said, 'O my Lord! Forgive me, and grant me a kingdom that suits not another after me, for You are the grantor of bounties (without measure) (Qur'an 38:34-35)." God helps those who ask for His help in His Own divine ways.

Table 2.2
God Granted Solomon the Most Prosperous Kingdom

No	Surah:Verses	Meanings
		God Rewards the Believers for their Devotion
4	38:030-033	To David We gave Solomon (for a son)—how excellent in Our service! Ever did he turn (to Us). • Behold, there were brought before him at eventide coursers of the highest breeding and swift of foot, and he said, "Truly do I love the love of good, with a view to the glory of my Lord,"—until (the sun) was hidden in the veil (of night). "Bring them back to me." Then he began to pass his hand over (their) legs and their necks.
		God helps Believers by His Own Divine Ways
5	38:036-040	• Then We subjected the wind to his power, to

	flow gently to his order, whithersoever he willed—as also the devils, (including) every kind of builder and diver, as also others bound together in fetters. Such are Our bounties. Whether you bestow them (on others) or withhold them, no account will be asked. He enjoyed, indeed, a near access to Us and a beautiful place of (final) return.

2.3 The behavior that Makes People Successful

In describing some of His messengers, God emphasizes those traits of human behavior through which one can hope to receive His mercy and help. In mentioning the story of Job, God tells people: "Truly, We found him full of patience and constancy—how excellent in Our service! Ever did he turn (to Us) (Qur'an 38:44)." The verses of Surah Sad that highlight that patience, devotion, and the remembrance of the Hereafter always earn God's mercy are given in the table below.

Table 2.3
Patient, Devoted, and Trustworthy People are Successful

No	Surah:Verses	Meanings
		God found in Job a Patient and Most Excellent Servant
6	38:041-043	Commemorate Our Servant Job. • Behold he cried to his Lord: "The Satan has afflicted me with distress and suffering!" • (The command was given): "Strike with your foot. Here is (water) wherein to wash, cool and refreshing, and (water) to drink." We gave him (back) his people and doubled their number as a grace from Ourselves and a thing for commemoration for all who have understanding.
		The Remembrance of the Hereafter Earns Wisdom and Power
7	38:045-048	Commemorate Our Servants Abraham, Isaac, and Jacob—possessors of power and vision. 1. Verily, We did choose them for a special (purpose)—proclaiming the message of the Hereafter. 2. They were, in Our sight, truly of the

		company of the elect and the good. Commemorate Isma'il, Elisha, and Zul-Kifl. Each of them was of the company of the good.

3 PEOPLE'S BEHAVIOR IMPACTS THEIR OUTCOME

3.1 Disobedient People in the Hereafter

Those people who were disobedient to God will meet in the Hereafter, and they will find that the corrupt leaders and preachers whom they blindly followed in this world have reached Hell even before their followers. In Hell, these two groups, the corrupt leaders and their followers, will be cursing each other. Further, the unbelievers will be disappointed to find Hell void of believers, the very people whom they used to regard as contemptible in this world.

Table 3.1: Cordial Friendship between God and the Believers

No	Surah:Verses	Meanings
		Paradise: An Excellent Resort for the God-fearing
1	38:049-054	This is a message (of admonition), and verily, for the righteous is a beautiful place of (final) return—gardens of eternity, whose doors will (ever) be open to them. 1. Therein will they recline (at ease). 2. Therein can they call for fruit in abundance and (delicious) drink. 3. Beside them will be chaste women restraining their glances, (companions) of equal age. Such is the promise made to you for the Day of Account. Truly, such will be Our bounty (to you); it will never fail.
		Hell: An Evil Resort for the Unbelievers
2	38:055-058	Yea, such! But - for the wrongdoers will be an evil place of (final) return. 1. Hell! They will burn therein—an evil bed (indeed, to lie on)! 2. Yea, such—then shall they taste it, a boiling fluid and a fluid dark, murky, intensely cold— And other penalties of a similar kind to match them.
		Corrupt Inmates of Hell will be Disappointed

3	38:062-064	1. And they (Inmates of Hell) will say: "What has happened to us that we see not men whom we used to number among the bad ones?" 2. Did we treat them (as such) in ridicule, or have (our) eyes failed to perceive them? Truly that is just and fitting—the mutual recriminations of the people of the fire.

3.2 Behavior and Fate of Unbelievers and Satan is the same

Citing the story of Adam and *Iblis* (Satan), God says that all unbelievers, irrespective of place or time, possess the same arrogance and vanity that prevented *Iblis* from bowing before Adam. *Iblis* was jealous of the high rank that God gave to Adam, and he became accursed when he disobeyed God's command. Likewise, the unbelievers of Makkah were jealous of the high rank that God bestowed on the Messenger. They were not prepared to obey him, whom God has appointed as His Messenger? Therefore, they were ultimately doomed to the same fate as that of Satan.

Table 3.2
Arrogance and Vanity are Common to all Corrupt People

No	Surah:Verses	Meanings
		Haughty People could Inherit Haughty Satan
4	38:071-074	• Behold, your Lord said to the angels: "I am about to create man from clay: When I have fashioned him (in due proportion) and breathed into him of My spirit, you fall down in obeisance unto him." • So the angels prostrated themselves, all of them together. Not so *Iblis* (one of the jinn). He was haughty and became one of those who reject faith.
		God Promised to fill Hell with Satan's Followers
5	38:075-085	(Allah) said: "O *Iblis*! What prevents you from prostrating yourself to one whom I have created with my hands? Are you haughty, or are you one of the high (and mighty) ones?" 1. (*Iblis*) said: "I am better than he. You created me from fire, and him you created from clay." 2. (Allah) said: "Then you get out from here,

	for you are rejected, accursed. My curse shall be on you till the Day of Judgment." 3. (*Iblis*) said: "O my Lord! Give me then respite till the day the (dead) are raised." 4. (Allah) said: "Respite then is granted you till the day of the time appointed." 5. (*Iblis*) said: "Then, by Your power, I will put them all in the wrong—except Your servants among them, sincere and purified (by Your grace)." (Allah) said: "Then it is just and fitting—and I say what is just and fitting—that I will certainly fill Hell with you and those that follow you, every one.

3.3 A Message of Extreme Importance, Full of Guidance

Commenting on the unbelievers' reasons for their denial of Islam, God says: "By the Qur'an, full of admonition, (this is the truth). But the unbelievers (are steeped) in self-glory and separatism. How many generations before them did We destroy? In the end, they cried (for Allah's mercy) when there was no longer time for being saved (Qur'an 38:1-3)." God commanded the Messenger to tell the unbelievers that Islam is a message of extreme importance and that the Qur'an, which they are rejecting, is a reminder to all people of the world. He also warned the unbelievers of Makkah that the person whom they were ridiculing would soon overpower them. God commanded the Messenger: "Say: 'Truly am I a warner. No god is there but the One Allah, supreme and irresistible, the Lord of the heavens and the earth and all between, exalted in might, able to enforce His will, forgiving again and again.' Say: 'That is a message supreme from which you do turn away' (Qur'an 38:65-68)."

CHAPTER 34

People Need Guidance to Succeed
FROM SURAH AZ-ZUMAR (39)

Surah Az-Zumar is an eloquent and effective address that was revealed some time before the emigration of early Muslims to Ethiopia to escape the tyranny and persecution at Makkah. In it, people are told that only service to God frees people from servitude to numerous false deities. False deities, including one's own selfish desires, may have some immediate benefit for some people, but they are eventually injurious to human dignity and society.

The Qur'an is a self-consistent book containing guiding principles, the implementation of which leads people to a prosperous and peaceful life in this world and to God's mercy in the Hereafter. These guiding principles are taught to the wise and knowledgeable through reason and to those whose reasoning has been clouded by various biases and arrogance through punishments (small calamities).

1 THE CREATOR OF THE UNIVERSE AND HIS GUIDANCE

1.1 *Tauheed* is to Serve God, in Sincerity and Obedience
Islam helps people recognize their real, dignified position in the universe by freeing them from servitude to idols, other human beings, various objects of the universe, and even their own individual selfish desires. People should sincerely serve God and not contaminate their servitude with the service of anything else. Whether people serve God or not, God has no need of them. Instead, they need God, whether they know it or not.

483

Table 1.1: The Creator of the Universe is your Lord

No	Surah:Verses	Meanings
		The Creator of the Universe is your Lord
1	39:005-006	• He created the heavens and the earth in true (proportions). He makes the night overlap the day and the day overlap the night. He has subjected the sun and the moon (to His law). Each one follows a course for a time appointed. Is not He the exalted in power, He Who forgives again and again? • He created you (all) from a single person— then created of like nature his mate, and He sent down for you eight head of cattle in pairs. He makes you in the wombs of your mothers in stages, one after another, in three veils of darkness. Such is Allah, your Lord and Cherisher. To Him belongs (all) dominion. There is no god but He. Then how are you turned away?
		The Qur'an is the Truth Revealed from God
2	39:001-002	• The revelation of this Book is from Allah, the exalted in power, full of wisdom. Verily, it is We Who have revealed the Book to you in truth. So serve Allah, offering Him sincere devotion.
		The Declaration of Faith from the Believers
3	39:010-014	Say: "O you my servants who believe! Fear your Lord. Good is (the reward) for those who do good in this world. Spacious is Allah's earth! Those who patiently persevere will truly receive a reward without measure." 1. Say: "Verily, I am commanded to serve Allah with sincere devotion." 2. (Say): "I am commanded to be the first of those who bow to Allah in Islam." 3. Say: "I would, if I disobeyed my Lord, indeed have fear of the penalty of a mighty day." 4. Say: "It is Allah I serve with my sincere (and exclusive) devotion."
		Believers will be at high Places in Hereafter
4	39:019-020	• Is, then, one against whom the decree of punishment is justly due (equal to one who

		eschews evil)? Would you, then, deliver one (who is) in the fire? But it is for those who fear their Lord that lofty mansions, one above another, have been built. Beneath them flow rivers (of delight). (Such is) the promise of Allah. Never does Allah fail in (His) promise.

1.2 *Tauheed* is to Refrain from Worshiping *Taghut*

Taghut covers a wide range of meanings. It means everything worshiped other than the One God, i.e., all false deities. It may be Satan, devils, idols, stones, sun and stars, angels, or people that are worshiped. Similarly, saints, graves, rulers, and leaders are falsely worshiped and wrongly followed. It could also be ideologies like capitalism and socialism, which give undue and unnatural advantages to some sections of the society.

Table 1.2: Listen to the Command and Follow the Best of it

No	Surah:Verses	Meanings
		None can Intercede for People to God
5	39:003	1. Is it not to Allah that sincere devotion is due? But those who take for protectors other than Allah (say): "We only serve them in order that they may bring us nearer to Allah." Truly, Allah will judge between them in that wherein they differ, but Allah guides not such as are false and ungrateful.
	39:004	2. Had Allah wished to take to Himself a son, He could have chosen whom He pleased out of those whom He does create. But Glory be to Him—He is Allah, the One, the Irresistible.
	39:008	3. When some trouble touches man, he cries unto his Lord, turning to Him in repentance. But when He bestows a favor upon him as from Himself, (man) does forget what he cried and prayed for before, and he does set up rivals unto Allah, thus misleading others from Allah's path. Say, "Enjoy your blasphemy for a little while. Verily, you are (one) of the companions of the fire."

485

		Turn to God; You shall have Good News
6	39:015-018	1. ...Say: "Truly, those in loss are those who lose their own souls and their people on the Day of Judgment. Ah! That is indeed the (real and) evident loss!" 2. They shall have layers of fire above them, and layers (of fire) below them. With this does Allah warn off his servants. O My servants! Then fear Me! 3. Those who eschew evil, and fall not into its worship, and turn to Allah (in repentance)—for them is good news. So announce the good news to My servants. Those who listen to the word and follow the best (meaning) in it—those are the ones whom Allah has guided, and those are the ones endued with understanding.

1.3 *Tauheed* is to know that God is Sufficient against *Taghut*
Since Surah Az-Zumar is an address given before a group of people who were being forced to leave Makkah (the emigration to Ethiopia), due to being oppressed and persecuted, it was very important to remind these believers about the extensive powers and support of God and to tell the disbelievers that no matter what they did, their persecutions and tyrannies would never deter the believers from the way of Islam. Addressing the Messenger, God command: "Say: 'O my people! Do whatever you can; I will do (my part). But soon will you know Who it is to whom comes a penalty of ignominy and on whom descends a penalty that abides (Qur'an 39:39-40)."

Table 1.3: God is Sufficient for His Servants

No	Surah:Verses	Meanings
		Fearing *Taghut* is Senseless
7	39:036-037	• Is not Allah enough for his servant? But they try to frighten you with other (gods) besides Him! For such as Allah leaves to stray, there can be no guide. Such as Allah does guide there can be none to lead astray. Is not Allah exalted in power, (able to enforce His will), Lord of retribution?
		God is sufficient for the Believers;

486

		on Him do reliant rely

8	39:038	If indeed you ask them who it is that created the heavens and the earth. They would be sure to say, "Allah."
		 • Say: "You see then? The things that you invoke besides Allah—can they,
		    1. "If Allah wills some penalty for me, remove His penalty?
		    2. "Or if He wills some grace for me, can they keep back his grace?
		 Say: "Sufficient is Allah for me! In Him trust those who put their trust.

1.4 *Tauheed* is to know that People are not in need of Them?
God tells people that false deities can't intercede with Him and that they may not even understand what a person is asking from them. Why do we need intermediaries when God is so close to us and listens to us? This gives the lie to one of the claims of polytheists, i.e., "Those who take for protectors other than Allah (say): 'We only serve them in order that they may bring us nearer to Allah' (Qur'an 39:3)."

As far as our sins are concerned, these will be changed into good deeds if we repent and do good deeds. People are told: "Unless he repents, believes, and works righteous deeds, for Allah will change the evil of such persons into good, and Allah is oft-forgiving, most merciful (Qur'an 25:70)." Again, God is He Who enlarges and straitens the provisions of whom so ever He pleases. All this is an aspect of God's grace and mercy. It is faith and good deeds and not false deities that determine what a person receives of God's grace and mercy: "Do they not know that Allah enlarges the provision or restricts it for any He pleases (Qur'an 39:52)?"

Table 1.4: False Deities Entice People into Unjust Ways

No	Surah:Verses	Meanings
		False Deities cannot Intercede with God
9	39:043-045	What! Do they take for intercessors others besides Allah? 1. Say: "Even if they have no power whatever and no intelligence?"

487

		2. Say: "To Allah belongs exclusively (the right to grant) intercession. To Him belongs the dominion of the heavens and the earth. In the end, it is to Him that you shall be brought back." When Allah, the One and Only, is mentioned, the hearts of those who believe not in the Hereafter are filled with disgust and horror, but when (gods) other than He are mentioned, behold, they are filled with joy.
		Unbelievers' Attitudes, Behavior, and Deeds
10	39:049-051	Now, when trouble touches man, he cries to Us: 1. But when We bestow a favor upon him as from Ourselves, he says, "This has been given to me because of a certain knowledge (I have)!" Nay, but this is but a trial, but most of them understand not! 2. Thus did the (generations) before them say, but all that they did was of no profit to them. Nay, the evil results of their deeds overtook them. And the wrongdoers of this (generation)—the evil results of their deeds will soon overtake them (too), and they will never be able to frustrate (Our plan).
		Evil Consequences of Unbelievers' Behavior
11	39:046-048	• Say: "O Allah! Creator of the heavens and the earth! Knower of all that is hidden and open! It is You Who will judge between Your servants in those matters about which they have differed." • Even if the wrongdoers had all that there is on earth and as much more, (in vain) would they offer it for ransom from the pain of the penalty on the Day of Judgment, but something will confront them from Allah that they could never have counted upon. For the evils of their deeds will confront them, and they will be (completely) encircled by that at which they used to mock.

2 GUIDING PRINCIPLES FOR THE COMMON GOOD

2.1 People should Learn and Follow Divine Guidance

Like physical laws, there are moral and sociopolitical laws or principles that God has put in place. These guiding principles, as described in the Qur'an, when implemented in individual lives and in society, lead people to a prosperous and peaceful life in this world and to God's mercy in the Hereafter. Each one of us is responsible for following these principles because none shall bear the burden of others.

Table 2.1: None can bear the Burden of the Others

No	Surah:Verses	Meanings
		No one shall Bear Burden of Another
1	39:007	• No bearer of burdens can bear the burden of another. In the end, to your Lord is your return, when He will tell you the truth of all that you did (in this life). For He knows well all that is in (men's) hearts.
		The Knowing is Better than Ignorance
2	39:009	• Is one who worships devoutly during the hour of the night prostrating himself or standing (in adoration)—(he) who takes heed of the Hereafter, and who places his hope in the mercy of his Lord—(like one who does not)? Say: "Are those equal, those who know and those who do not know? It is those who are endued with understanding that receive admonition."
		Can He Who is on Islam be like Who is Not?
3	39:021-022	• Don't you see that Allah sends down rain from the sky and leads it through springs in the earth? Then He causes to grow, therewith, produce of various colors. Then it withers; you will see it grow yellow. Then He makes it dry up and crumble away. Truly, in this, is a message of remembrance to men of understanding. 1. Is one whose heart Allah has opened to Islam, so that he has received enlightenment from Allah, (no better than one hard-hearted)?

		2. Woe to those whose hearts are hardened against celebrating the praises of Allah! They are manifestly wandering (in error).

2.2 Divine Guidance Benefits Humankind

The Qur'anic teachings are repeated in different ways for the benefit of people possessing various levels of intellect. "Allah has revealed the most beautiful message in the form of a Book, consistent with itself, (yet) repeating (its teaching in various aspects). The skins of those who fear their Lord tremble thereat. Then their skins and their hearts do soften to the celebration of Allah's praises. Such is the guidance of Allah. He guides therewith whom He pleases, but such as Allah leaves to stray can have none to guide (Qur'an 39:23)." People with knowledge are motivated to implement the Islamic principles in their lives through reasoning. In contrast, those whose reasoning is adversely affected by biases and arrogance may be prompted to accept divine guidance by punishments (small calamities).

Table 2.2: The Qur'an: Revealed Guidance for Humankind

No	Surah:Verses	Meanings
		A Qur'an that People may Reform
4	39:027-028	We have put forth for men, in this Qur'an every kind of parable, in order that they may receive admonition. (It is) a Qur'an in Arabic without any crookedness (therein), in order that they may guard against evil).

	39:041	• Verily, We have revealed
		   1. The Book to you (O Messenger) in truth, for (instructing) mankind.
		   2. He, then, that receives guidance benefits his own self, but
		   3. He that strays injures his own self.

		Motivation by Persuasion or by Calamities
5	39:024-026	• Is then one who has to fear the brunt of the penalty on the Day of Judgment (and receive it) on his face, (like one guarded there from)? It will be said to the wrongdoers: "Taste (the fruits of) what you earned." Those before them (also) rejected (revelation), and so

		1. *(Calamities:)* the punishment came to them from directions they did not perceive. 2. *(Destruction:)* So Allah gave them a taste of humiliation in the present life, but 3. *(Hell:)* greater is the punishment of the Hereafter, if they only knew!
		Resurrection, Accountability, and the Rewards
6	39:030-035	Truly, you will die (one day), and truly they (too) will die (one day). 1. In the end you (all) will, on the Day of Judgment, settle your disputes in the presence of your Lord. 2. Who then does more wrong than one who utters a lie concerning Allah and rejects the truth when it comes to him? Is there not in Hell an abode for blasphemers? 3. And he who brings the truth and he who confirms (and supports) it—such are the men who do right. 4. They shall have all that they wish for in the presence of their Lord. Such is the reward of those who do good. So that Allah will turn off from them (even) the worst in their deeds and give them their reward according to the best of what they have done.

3 SELF EVALUATION ASSURES THE SUCCESS

3.1 Consciousness of Accountability of one's Deeds

God tells people: "Commemorate Our servants, Abraham, Isaac, and Jacob, possessors of power and vision. Verily, We did choose them for a special (purpose)—proclaiming the message of the Hereafter. They were in Our sight truly of the company of the elect and the good (Qur'an 38:45-47)." In these verses, God informs people that his servants proclaim the message of the Hereafter and are wise enough to realize the benefits of honesty, integrity, and hard work. Such people always admit their mistakes and reform.

Table 3.1
Believe in the Hereafter and Continually Reform Yourself

No	Surah:Verses	Meanings
		Despair not of God's Mercy, just Follow His Commands
1	39:053-060	Say: "O my servants who have transgressed against their souls! 1. "Despair not of the mercy of Allah, for Allah forgives all sins, for He is oft-forgiving, most merciful. 2. "Turn to your Lord (in repentance) and bow to His (will), before the penalty comes on you. After that you shall not be helped. "And follow the best of (the courses) revealed to you from your Lord before the penalty comes on you of a sudden while you perceive not. • "Lest the soul should (then) say: 'Ah! Woe is me, in that I neglected (my duty) towards Allah and was but among those who mocked;' • "Or (lest) it should say: 'If only Allah had guided me, I should certainly have been among the righteous;' • "Or (lest) it should say when it (actually) sees the penalty: 'If only I had another chance, I should certainly be among those who do good.' • "(The reply will be:) 'Nay, but there came to you my signs, and you did reject them. You were haughty and became one of those who reject faith.'" On the Day of Judgment will you see those who told lies against Allah; their faces will be turned black. Is there not in Hell an abode for the haughty?
		Thank your Lord by Following His Commands
2	39:061-066	But Allah will deliver the righteous to their place of salvation. No evil shall touch them, nor shall they grieve. 1. Allah is the Creator of all things, and He is the guardian and disposer of all affairs. To Him belong the keys of the heavens and the earth, and those who reject the signs of

492

| | | Allah—it is they who will be in loss. |
| | 2. | Say: "Is it someone other than Allah that you order me to worship, O you ignorant ones?" But it has already been revealed to you, as it was to those before you: "If you were to join (gods with Allah), truly fruitless will be your work (in life), and you will surely be in the ranks of those who lose (all spiritual good)." Nay, but worship Allah, and be of those who give thanks. |

3.2 People will be Judged with Justice in the Hereafter

One of the human weaknesses is that people do not give honor where it is due, especially in the case of their Creator. They enjoy all of His blessings without being thankful to Him. God reminds people: "No just estimate have they made of Allah, such as is due to Him. On the Day of Judgment the whole of the earth will be but His handful, and the heavens will be rolled up in His right hand. Glory to Him! High is He above the partners they attribute to Him (Qur'an 39:67)." The resurrection and the accountability process will start when: "The trumpet will (just) be sounded, when all that are in the heavens and on earth will faint, except such as it will please Allah (to exempt). Then will a second one be sounded, when behold, they will be standing and looking on! And the earth will shine with the glory of its Lord. The record (of the deeds) will be placed (open). The prophets and the witnesses will be brought forward and a just decision pronounced between them, and they will not be wronged (Qur'an 39:68-69)."

3.3 People will be Judged on their Intentions and Deeds

In the Hereafter, people will be judged according to their actions, along with the intensions behind their deeds. People will be directed to their abodes according to their deeds: "To every person will be paid in full (the fruit) of its deeds, and (Allah) knows best all that they do. The unbelievers will be led to Hell in crowds until, when they arrive there; its gates will be opened... (To them) will be said: 'Enter the gates of Hell to dwell therein, and evil is (this) abode of the arrogant' (Qur'an 39:70-72)." In a striking contrast, the believers will be led to Paradise: "And those who feared their Lord will be led to the garden in crowds until, behold, they arrive there. Its gates will be opened, and its keepers will say: 'Peace be upon you! Well have you done! Enter here to dwell therein.' They will say: 'Praise be to Allah, Who has truly fulfilled His promise to us and has given us (this) land in heritage. We can dwell in the garden as we will—how excellent a reward for those who work (righteousness)' (Qur'an 39:73-74)." At the conclusion of the accountability process: "You will see the angels surrounding the throne on all sides, singing glory and praise to their Lord. The decision between them (at Judgment) will be in (perfect) justice, and the cry (on all sides) will be, 'Praise be to Allah, the Lord of the worlds' (Qur'an 39:75)."

CHAPTER 35

Repentance: The Prosperity and Paradise
FROM SURAH AL-GHAFIR (40)

With the institution of repentance and forgiveness, God has provided people an opportunity for the continual improvement of their character and behavior. Although it is not possible for people to be perfect in dealing with others, the effort to improve their dealings with others produces positive results in their communities. Societies built on positive moral values are surely prosperous and peaceful. Happiness in the life to come also depends on one's efforts to improve the life in this world. This is very important, as individuals, irrespective of their situation or status in life, should improve their behavior and try to help others in their struggle in life. What makes us suffer or makes us happy are our attitudes and deeds. As God administers absolute justice to all, our actions and intentions determine our present and our future. In contrast, corrupt people, who worship their own selfish desires and like to benefit from the injustice done to others, cannot form prosperous societies. Even the so-called rich countries, where most of the wealth belongs to a few individuals or corporations, cannot be really prosperous.

1 DIVINE FORGIVENESS MOVITATES CHARACTER BUILDING

1.1 God Accepts Repentance and Forgives
The opportunity for repentance after committing a sin, i.e., an action not compatible with God's commandments, even the most serious one, is there all the time. God doesn't close the door of forgiveness to anyone who turns to Him with sincerity and true repentance. Therefore, one shouldn't lose hope. God may forgive all sins, as He has promised. The only requirement for the acceptance of repentance is that it should be made seriously and sincerely, and it should be coupled with a resolve not to repeat the sin again. God describes Himself in Surah Al-Ghafir as One: "Who forgives sin, accepts repentance, is strict in punishment,

495

and has a long reach (in all things). There is no god but He; to Him is the final goal (Qur'an 40:3)."

In contrast, the unbelievers who refuse to reform and do not improve their character and behavior get destroyed: "None can dispute about the revelations of Allah but the unbelievers. Let not then their strutting about through the land deceives you! But (there were people) before them who denied—the people of Noah and the confederates (of evil) after them, and every people plotted against their prophet to seize him and disputed by means of vanities, therewith to condemn the truth. But it was I that seized them! And how (terrible) was My requital! Thus was the decree of your Lord proved true against the unbelievers that truly they are the companions of the fire (Qur'an 40:4-6)?"

1.2 Turn to God Again and Again in Repentance
There is a rule for repentance and a condition for its acceptance. Repentance begins with a genuine regret and desisting from bad deeds and is completed through doing good deeds to prove that the repentance is serious and genuine. Good deeds produce a positive effect that favorably compensates for abandoning sin. A sin is an action that, when withdrawn, leaves a vacuum that must be filled with an action in the opposite direction. Otherwise, the feeling of emptiness makes one miss one's old sinful ways. This is a remarkable feature of the divine method of cultivating goodness within the believers. It is based on profound knowledge of human nature. God is: "He it is Who shows you his signs and sends down sustenance for you from the sky, but only those receive admonition who turn (to Him). Call you then upon Allah with sincere devotion to Him, even though the unbelievers may detest it (Qur'an 40:13-14)." God motivates people to repent and do good deeds by telling them that upon their resurrection, they will be rewarded according to what they did in the world. On that day: "...every soul shall be requited for what it earned; no injustice will there be that day, for Allah is swift in taking account (Qur'an 40:17)."

1.3 The Continual Improvement of Human Character
Perfection of character and actions is not humanly possible. What Islam teaches is the attitude that leads to continual

improvements in individual character and society. Everyone is liable to make errors and mistakes, but when the believers do, they seek God's forgiveness, which is forthcoming when the request is genuine. Human character is improved with every incident of acknowledgment, regret, and effort made not to repeat the mistakes again. A person may be in error throughout his life, but whenever he realizes his mistakes and repents, God forgives whoever turns to Him in genuine repentance—even the most wicked among people.

Table 1.3: God's Mercy and Help Depend on Repentance

No	Surah:Verses	Meanings
		Can God Accept the Repentance of Hypocrites?
1	3:090	But those who reject faith after they accepted it and then go on adding to their defiance of faith—never will their repentance be accepted, for they are those who have gone astray.
		People are Commands to Repent and Reform
2	4:017	Allah accepts the repentance of those who do evil in ignorance and repent soon afterwards; to them will Allah turn in mercy, for Allah is full of knowledge and wisdom.
	6:054	• When those come to you who believe in Our revelations, say: "Peace be on you. Your Lord has inscribed for Himself (the rule of) mercy. Verily, if any of you did evil in ignorance and thereafter repented and amended (his conduct), lo! He is oft-forgiving, most merciful."
		The Believer's Supplication and God's Response
3	7:156	• (Moses prayed:) "Ordain for us good in this world's life and in the Hereafter, for we turned unto You (in repentance)." He (God) said: "With My punishment I visit whom I will, but My mercy extends to all things. That (mercy) I shall ordain for 1. "Those who do right, and 2. "(Those who) practice regular charity, and 3. "Those who believe in Our revelations."
	7:161	And remember it was said (by Allah) to them (the people of Moses): "Dwell in this town and eat therein as you wish, but say the word of humility,

		and enter the gate in a posture of humility. We shall forgive you your faults; We shall give more to those who do good deeds.
		People should know - God Accepts Repentance
4	9:104	Know they not that Allah does accept repentance from His votaries and receives their gifts of charity and that Allah is verily He, the oft-returning, most merciful?
	9:126	1. See they not that they are tried every year once or twice? Yet, they turn not in repentance, and they take no heed.
	25:071	2. Whoever repents and does good has truly turned to Allah with an (acceptable) conversion.
	30:033	3. When trouble touches men, they cry to their Lord, turning back to Him in repentance. But when He gives them a taste of mercy as from Himself, behold, some of them pay part-worship to other god's besides their Lord.
	39:017	4. Those who eschew evil, and fall not into its worship, and turn to Allah (in repentance)— for them is good news. So announce the good news to My servants.
	40:003	5. Who forgives sin, accepts repentance, is strict in punishment, and has a long reach (in all things)—there is no god but He; to Him is the final goal.
	42:025	He is the One that accepts repentance from His servants and forgives sins, and He knows all that you do.
		David, Solomon, and Job as Human Role Models
5	38:017	Have patience at what they say, and remember our servant David, the man of strength, for he ever turned (to Us in repentance).
	38:030	1. To David We gave Solomon (for a son)—how excellent in Our service! Ever did he turn (to Us in repentance).
	38:041, 044	2. Commemorate Our servant Job. Behold he cried to his Lord: "Satan has afflicted me with distress and suffering!"...Truly, We found him full of patience and constancy—how excellent in Our service! Ever did he turn (to Us in repentance).

2 THE DIVINE LAW LEADS PEOPLE TO PROSPERITY AND PARADISE

God encourages people to strive to acquire good things through lawful means, without exceeding limits. "O you who believe! Make not unlawful the good things that Allah has made lawful for you, but commit no excess, for Allah loves not those given to excess (Qur'an 5:87)." God has also provided sufficient means in the world for all people to live in prosperity. We have to exploit and properly manage these natural resources for the benefit of all humanity. God reminds people: "It is We Who have placed you with authority on earth and provided you therein with means for the fulfillment of your life. Small are the thanks that you give (Qur'an 7:10)!"

2.1 Repent and Follow God's Commands to Prosperity

Our individual and collective prosperity depends on how seriously and effectively the divine law is implemented. God tells us that if we fail to follow these laws, we should repent, correct the situation, and continue to strive to improve our character and society. This will, with God's help and His mercy, make people and their countries prosperous. God said that Noah taught: "Ask forgiveness from your Lord, for He is oft-forgiving. He will send rain to you in abundance, give you increase in wealth and sons, and bestow on you gardens, and bestow on you rivers (of flowing water) (Qur'an 71:10-12)."

Table 2.1
Repentance → God's Forgiveness and Mercy → Prosperity

No	Surah:Verses	Meanings
		Repentance → Forgiveness → Prosperity
1	11:003	Seek the forgiveness of your Lord, and turn to Him in repentance that 1. He may grant you enjoyment, good (and true), for a term appointed, and 2. Bestow His abounding grace on all who abound in merit! 3. But if you turn away, then I fear for you the penalty of a great day.
	11:050	To the 'Ad people (We sent) Hud, one of their own brethren.

499

	11:052	1. He said: "O my people! Serve Allah! You have no other god but Him. (Your other gods) you do nothing but invent." 2. (He said) "O my people! Ask forgiveness of your Lord, and turn to Him (in repentance). He will send you the skies pouring abundant rain and add strength to your strength, so you turn not back in sin."
		Repentance → Forgiveness → God's Mercy
2	27:045-046	• We sent (aforetime) to the Thamud their brother Salih, saying, "Serve Allah." But behold, they became two factions quarrelling with each other. • He said: O my people! Why you ask to hasten on the evil in preference to the good? If only you ask Allah for forgiveness, you may hope to receive mercy?"
		The Despair (lack of rain) → The Hope (Rain)
3	30:047-050	• We did indeed send before thee messengers to their (respective) peoples, and they came to them with clear signs. Then to those who transgressed, We meted out retribution, and it was due from Us to aid those who believed. • It is Allah Who sends the winds, and they raise the clouds. Then does He spread them in the sky as He wills and break them into fragments, until you see raindrops issue from the midst thereof. Then when He has made them reach such of his servants as He wills, behold, they do rejoice, even though before they received (the rain)—just before this—they were dumb with despair. Then contemplate (O people!) the memorials of Allah's mercy—how He gives life to the earth after its death. Verily, the same will give life to the men who are dead, for He has power over all things.
		After Despair, the Rain comes as God's Mercy
4	42:028 78:014-016	He is the One that sends down rain (even) 1) After (the people) 2) And scatters His have given up all hope, mercy (far and wide). • He is the protector, worthy of all praise.

500

		And do We not send down from the clouds water in abundance that We may produce therewith corn and vegetables and gardens of luxurious growth.

2.2 Repent and Follow God's Commands to Paradise

The door of repentance is always open to admit anyone whose conscience is reawakened and who desires improvement in his character and behavior. No one is ever turned away from it, no matter who he might be or what sins he might have committed. It was related by at-Tirmidhi that the Messenger said: "Allah the Almighty said: 'O son of Adam, so long as you call upon Me and ask of Me, I shall forgive you for what you have done, and I shall not mind. O son of Adam, were your sins to reach the clouds of the sky and were you then to ask forgiveness of Me, I would forgive you. O son of Adam, were you to come to Me with sins nearly as great as the earth and were you then to face Me, ascribing no partner to Me, I would bring you forgiveness nearly as great at it. (Al-Hadith: vol. 3, no. 96, page 756).'"

Table 2.2: Paradise, the Great Achievement

No	Surah:Verses	Meanings
		This World's Life, like Vegetation is Transient
5	57:020	• Know you (all) that the life of this world is but play and amusement, pomp, and mutual boasting and multiplying (in rivalry) among yourselves, riches and children. • Here is a similitude: how rain and the growth that it brings forth delight (the hearts of) the tillers. Soon it withers; you will see it grow yellow; then it becomes dry and crumbles away. But in the Hereafter is a penalty severe (for the devotees of wrong) and forgiveness from Allah and (His) good pleasure (for the devotees of Allah). And what is the life of this world but goods and chattels of deception?
		Like Land after Rain, People will be Resurrected
6	50:009-011	We send down from the sky rain charted with blessing, and We produce therewith gardens and grain for harvests and tall (and stately) palm trees

501

		with shoots of fruit stalks, piled one over another, as sustenance for (Allah's) servants. And We give (new) life therewith to land that is dead. Thus will be the resurrection.
		Repentance + Good Deeds → God's Forgiveness
7	40:007-009	Those who sustain the throne (of Allah) and those around it sing glory and praise to their Lord, believe in Him, and implore forgiveness for those who believe. 1. "Our Lord! Your reach is over all things in mercy and knowledge. Forgive then those who turn in repentance and follow Your path, and preserve them from the penalty of the blazing fire. 2. "And grant, our Lord, that they enter the gardens of eternity that You have promised to them and to the righteous among their fathers, their wives, and their posterity, for You are (He), the exalted in might, full of wisdom. 3. "And preserve them from (all) ills. And any whom You do preserve from ills that day— on them You will have bestowed mercy indeed, and that will be truly (for them) the highest achievement."
		God accepts Repentance from His servants
8	42:025-026	• He is the One that accepts repentance from His servants and forgives sins, and He knows all that you do. He listens to those who believe and do deeds of righteousness and gives them increase of His bounty, but for the unbelievers, there is a terrible penalty.

2.3 Believers Who do Good and Evildoers are not Alike

God tells people: "Assuredly the creation of the heavens and the earth is a greater (matter) than the creation of men. Yet, most men understand not. Not equal are the blind and those who (clearly) see, nor are (equal) those who believe and work deeds of righteousness and those who do evil. Little do you learn by admonition! The Hour (of Judgment) will certainly come. Therein is no doubt. Yet, most men believe not (Qur'an 40:57-59)." God has also promised His help in this world, as well as in the Hereafter, to anyone who calls upon Him: "Your Lord says: 'Call on Me. I will answer your (prayer), but those who are too arrogant to serve Me will surely find themselves in Hell—in humiliation (Qur'an 40:60)." Since God's promise is true, people should be patient and ask for His help while trying their best.

Table 2.3: Your Lord Says: "Call Me; I will Answer You"

No	Surah:Verses	Meanings
		God helps the Messengers and those who Believe
9	40:051-052	1. We will, without doubt, help our messengers and those who believe, (both) in this world's life and on the Day (of Judgment) when the witnesses will stand forth— 2. The Day when no profit will it be to wrongdoers to present their excuses, but they will (only) have the curse and the home of misery.
		Patiently persevere, for the Promise of God is true
10	40:055-056	1. Patiently then persevere, for the promise of Allah is true. And ask forgiveness for your fault, and celebrate the praises of your Lord in the evening and in the morning. 2. Those who dispute about the signs of Allah without any authority bestowed on them— there is nothing in their breasts but (the desire of) greatness, which they shall never attain. Seek refuge then in Allah. It is He Who hears and sees (all things).

3 CONSPIRACIES AGAINST ISLAM WILL NEVER SUCCEED

3.1 God's Punishment awaits the Conspirators

With regard to the conspiracies of the unbelievers during the Messenger's time to suppress the worship of the true God, the equality of all people, the rule of justice, and belief in one's accountability in the Hereafter for one's actions in this life, these conspirators were warned by the example of Pharaoh and his minions as presented in the Qur'an. Just as Pharaoh and his army were drowned, so the conspirators against the Messenger would be doomed. No matter how strong and powerful the conspirators against Islam may appear to be, true believers should seek God's refuge in response to each and every threat they receive. If people go on fearlessly performing their mission and with full trust in God, His help will ultimately come, and the pharaohs of today will be doomed just as were the pharaohs of the past.. Until then, believers must face and bear patiently every wave of persecution that is directed against them.

Table 3.1

Pharaohs of today are Doomed as were Pharaohs of the Past

No	Surah:Verses	Meanings
		God Destroyed Unbelievers for their Sins
1	40:021-022	Do they not travel through the earth and see what was the end of those before them? • They were even superior to them in strength and in the traces (they have left) in the land: 1. But Allah did call them to account for their sins, and none had they to defend them against Allah. 2. That was because there came to them their messengers with clear (signs), but they rejected them. So Allah called them to account, for He is full of strength, strict in punishment.
		The Struggle of Unbelievers always Ends in Vain
2	40:023-025	• Of old We sent Moses, with Our signs and an authority manifest to Pharaoh, Haman, and Qarun, but they called (him) a sorcerer telling lies. • Now, when he came to them in truth, from Us, they said, "Slay the sons of those who believe with him, and keep alive their females." But the plots of unbelievers (end) in nothing but errors (and delusions).
		On the Day, None will Intercede for Unbelievers
3	40:018-020	Warn them of the Day (of Judgment) that is (ever) drawing near, when the hearts will (come) right up to the throats to choke (them). 1. Neither intimate friend nor intercessor will the wrongdoers have who could be listened to. (Allah) knows of (the tricks) that deceive with the eyes and all that the hearts (of men)

		conceal.
		2. Allah will judge with (justice and) truth, but those whom (men) invoke besides Him will not (be in a position) to judge at all.
		Verily, it is Allah (alone) Who hears and sees (all things).
		Take refuge from Arrogant Unbelievers who don't believe in the Hereafter
4	40:026-027	1. Said Pharaoh: "Leave me to slay Moses, and let him call on his Lord! What I fear is lest he should change your religion, or lest he should cause mischief to appear in the land."
		2. Moses said: "I have indeed called upon my Lord and your Lord (for protection) from every arrogant one who believes not in the Day of Account."

3.2 Stand Up for Islam if you are the Believers

All believers must be willing to testify to the truth that is Islam, regardless of the hardships such a testimonial may bring. Unless a person's conscience is dead, he should rise up and perform his duty, which is exactly what a righteous man from among the courtiers of Pharaoh did at a time when Pharaoh had made up his mind to kill Moses. The circumstances that prevent people from raising their voices did not discourage this true believer. He had full faith in God and knew that Pharaoh was powerless compared to God. How exactly should one stand up for Islam? One should actively pursue what the Messenger said: "He who among you sees something abominable should modify it with the help of his hand; and if he has not strength enough to do it, then he should do it with his tongue; and if he has not strength enough to do it, even then he should (abhor it) from his heart, and that is the least of faith (Sahih Muslim: 1.79)."

Table 3.2: A believer argues for Moses' life in Pharaoh's court

No	Surah:Verses	Meanings
		Believer Defends Moses in Pharaoh's Court
5	40:028-029	A believer, a man from among the people of Pharaoh, who had concealed his faith, said: 1. "Will you slay a man because he says, 'My Lord is Allah,' when he has indeed come to you with clear (signs) from your Lord? 2. "And if he be a liar, on him is (the sin of) his lie, but if he is telling the truth, then will fall on you something of the (calamity) of which he warns you. 3. "Truly, Allah guides not one who transgresses and lies. "O my people! Yours is the dominion this day. You have the upper hand in the land, but who will help us from the punishment of Allah should it befall us?"
		Believer Argues with his People and Pharaoh
6	40:030-037	Then said the man who believed: 1. "O my people! Truly, I do fear for you something like the day (of disaster) of the confederates (in sin)—something like the fate of the people of Noah, the 'Ad, and the Thamud, and those who came after them, but Allah never wishes injustice to his servants. 2. "O my people! I fear for you a day when there will be mutual calling (and wailing)—a day when you shall turn your backs and flee. No defender shall you have from Allah. Any whom Allah leaves to stray, there is none to guide. 3. "And to you there came Joseph in times gone by with clear signs, but you ceased not to doubt of the (mission) for which he had come. 4. "At length, when he died, you said: 'No messenger will Allah send after him.' 5. "Thus does Allah leave to stray such as transgress and live in doubt—(such) as dispute about the signs of Allah without any authority that has reached them. 6. "Grievous and odious (is such conduct) in the sight of Allah and of the believers. 7. "Thus does Allah, seal up every heart - of arrogant and obstinate transgressors."

		• Pharaoh said: "O Haman! Build me a lofty palace, that I may attain the ways and means—the ways and means of (reaching) the heavens and that I may mount up to the god of Moses. But as far as I am concerned, I think (Moses) is a liar!" Thus was made alluring in Pharaoh's eyes the evil of his deeds, and he was hindered from the path, and the plot of Pharaoh led to nothing but perdition (for him).
		Believer Offered to Guide his People and Pharaoh
7	40:038-044	The man who believed said further: 1. "O my people! Follow me. I will lead you to the path of right. 2. "O my people! This life of the present is nothing but (temporary) convenience. It is the Hereafter that is the home that will last. He that works evil will not be requited but by the like thereof, and he that works a righteous deed—whether man or woman—and is a believer—such will enter the garden (of bliss). Therein will they have abundance without measure. 3. "And O my people! How (strange) it is for me to call you to salvation while you call me to the fire. 4. "You do call upon me to blaspheme against Allah and to join with Him partners of whom I have no knowledge, and I call you to the exalted in power, Who forgives again and again. 5. "Without doubt you do call me to one who is not fit to be called to, whether in this world or in the Hereafter. Our return will be to Allah, and the transgressors will be companions of the fire. "Soon will you remember what I say to you (now). My (own) affair I commit to Allah, for Allah (ever) watches over His servants."
		God Saved the Believer and Destroyed Pharaoh's People
8	40:045-046	1. Then Allah saved him from (every) ill that they plotted (against him), but the brunt of the penalty encompassed on all sides the people of Pharaoh. In front of the fire will they be brought, morning and

		evening. And (the sentence will be) on the day that judgment will be established: "Cast you the people of Pharaoh into the severest penalty."

4 GOD, HIS SIGNS, AND HIS OWN DIVINE WAYS

4.1 Submission is only to the Lord of the Universe

Confronting the unbelievers' denial of the message and their arrogance, God points to the many proofs of His existence and power.

Table 4.1: God and the Proofs of His Existence and Power

No	Surah:Verses	Meanings
		God is He Who has Created the Universe
1	40:061-064	1. It is Allah Who has made the night for you that you may rest therein and the days as that which helps (you) to see. Verily, Allah is full of grace and bounty to men. Yet, most men give no thanks. 2. Such is Allah, your Lord, the Creator of all things. There is no god but He. Then how you are deluded away from the truth? 3. Thus are deluded those who denied the revelations of Allah. 4. It is Allah Who has made for you the earth as a resting place, And the sky as a canopy, and has given you shape and made your shapes beautiful, and has provided for you sustenance of things pure and good. Such is Allah your Lord. So glory to Allah, the Lord of the worlds.
		God is He Who has Created Humankind
2	40:065 40:067-068	• He is the living (One). There is no god but He. Call upon Him, giving Him sincere devotion. Praise be to Allah, Lord of the worlds. 1. It is He Who has created you from dust, then from a sperm-drop, then from a leech-like clot. Then does He get you out (into the light) as a child, then lets you (grow and) reach your age of full strength, then lets you become old, though of you there are some who die before,

		and lets you reach a term appointed, in order that you may learn wisdom.
		2. It is He Who gives life and death, and when He decides upon an affair, He says to it, "Be," and it is.
		Believers Submit to the Lord of the Universe
3	40:066	Say: "I have been forbidden to invoke those whom you invoke besides Allah, seeing that the clear signs have come to me from my Lord. • And I have been commanded to bow (in Islam) to the Lord of the worlds.
		Unbelievers Dispute about God and His Revelations
4	40:069-076	• Don't you see those that dispute concerning the signs of Allah? How are they turned away (from reality)? • Those who reject the Book and the (revelations) with which We sent our messengers: but soon shall they know when the yokes (shall be) round their necks, and the chains. They shall be dragged along in the boiling fetid fluid. Then in the fire shall they be burned. Then shall it be said to them: "Where are the (deities) to which you gave part-worship in derogation of Allah?" • They will reply: "They have left us in the lurch. Nay, we invoked not of old anything (that had real existence)." Thus does Allah leave the unbelievers to stray? "That was because you exulted in the land unjustly, and because you behaved insolently. Enter the gates of Hell to dwell therein, and evil is abode of the arrogant."

4.2 Believing does not help After Seeing the Signs of Doom

The unbelievers were warned again and again that if they didn't stop wrangling against the revelations of God, they would be doomed like past communities. In reply, the unbelievers asked for signs of the coming doom. Responding to this, God pointed out the fate of past communities. "But when they saw Our punishment, they said: 'We believe in Allah, the One Allah, and we reject the partners we used to join with Him.' But their

509

professing the faith when they (actually) saw Our punishment was not going to profit them. (Such has been) Allah's way of dealing with His servants, and even thus did the unbelievers perish utterly (40:84-85)."

Table 4.2: Believing Will Not Benefit after Seeing the Signs

No	Surah:Verses	Meanings
		It is not for a Messenger to bring God's Signs
5	40:078	1. We did aforetime send messengers before you: of them there are some whose story We have related to you, and some whose story We have not related to you. 2. It was not (possible) for any messenger to bring a sign except by the leave of Allah. But when the command of Allah issued, the matter was decided in truth and justice, and there perished, there and then, those who stood on falsehoods.
		God shows People His Signs, but They Ignore Them
6	40:079-081	1. It is Allah Who made cattle for you that you may use some for riding and some for food, and there are (other) advantages in them for you (besides), that you may through them attain to any need in your hearts, and on them and on ships you are carried. 2. He shows you (always) His signs. Then which of the signs of Allah will you deny?
		God asks the Unbelievers to Learn from History
7	40:082-083	Have they not journeyed in the land and seen how was the end of those before them? 1. They were more numerous than these and superior in strength and in the traces (they have left) in the land. Yet, all that they accomplished was of no profit to them. 2. For when their messengers came to them with clear signs, they exulted in such knowledge as they had, and there beset them that which they used to mock.

CHAPTER 36

God Will Bring People to Justice
FROM SURAH FUSSILAT (41)

People who are aware of the underlining bases and benefits associated with the divine laws are guided by them. If people accept the truth and correct their behavior accordingly, they will do good to themselves. If they reject it, they will be preparing their own doom. "Whoever works righteousness benefits his own self; whoever works evil, it is against his own self: nor is your Lord ever unjust (in the least) to His Servants (41:46)."

The Qur'an is divine guidance. The truth given in the Qur'an can neither be altered nor corrupted. According to the Qur'an, behavior has its consequences. To those who make efforts to propagate divine guidance and to eliminate corruption, God commands them to repel evil with good, seek refuge in Him, and be patient. Although the obstacles in the way may seem to be insurmountable, the good morals and character will prevail. Whenever Satan provokes and incites to use some evil way, seek refuge in God.

1 THE QUR'AN, THE BOOK OF DIVINE GUIDANCE

1.1 Reward for Those Who Believe and Do Good Deeds
It is God's mercy that He has revealed the guidance for people. However, some unfortunate people do not find any wisdom in the truths that have been presented in the Qur'an. This is a catastrophic misfortune for those whose faculties of listening and reasoning have been tarnished by prejudice and arrogance. It was not the duty of the Messenger nor was he required to force people who did not want to hear to comprehend. He could only make those hear and understand who were inclined to listen and learn. Whether people close their eyes and ears or put coverings on their hearts, the fact remains that there is only One God, and we are His servants. People's arrogance and stubbornness cannot change this reality in any way.

Table 1.1
The Qur'an is Good News and a Warning for the People

No	Surah:Verses	Meanings
		The Qur'an is a Revelation from God
1	41:002-005	A revelation from (Allah), Most Gracious, Most Merciful—a Book of which the verses are made plain—a Qur'an in Arabic for people who understand, giving good news and warning. Yet, most of them turn away and so they hear not. • They say: "Our hearts are under veils from that to which you do invite us, and in our ears is a deafness, and between us and you is a screen. So act, we too are acting."
		The Messenger is a Mortal Like People
2	41:006-008	Say (O Messenger): "I am but a man like you. It is revealed to me by inspiration that your Allah is one Allah. So stand true to Him, and ask for His forgiveness." • And woe to those who join gods with Allah—those who practice not regular charity and who even deny the Hereafter. • For those who believe and do good deeds are a reward that will never fail.

1.2 The Qur'an can neither be Changed nor Corrupted

The unbelievers of Makkah adopted various measures to frustrate the Messenger's mission. They would suddenly make such a noise that none could hear anything. They would misconstrue the verses of the Qur'an and spread every kind of misunderstanding among the people. They would take words and sentences out of context and add their own words, in order to create new meanings to mislead people about the Qur'an and the Messenger. They would raise strange objections, e.g., arguing that there was nothing miraculous about an Arab presenting a discourse in his mother tongue of Arabic. From there they would argue that anyone can compose something in his mother tongue and claim that he had received it from God. What would be a miracle, they argued, was if a person made an eloquent speech in a foreign language that he did not know; only then could one say that the discourse was not his own composition but a revelation from God. To refute their objections, the unbelievers were told that the Qur'an is unchangeable. Its purpose and truth cannot be altered by people's wishes and falsehoods. The verses of Surah Fussilat that list the unbeliever's attacks against the Qur'an and the refutation of those attacks are given in the table below.

Table 1.2: Well Guarded Book of Right Guidance

No	Surah:Verses	Meanings
		Unbelievers will Curse their Leaders and Seek Revenge
3	41:026-029	The Unbelievers say: "Listen not to this Qur'an, but talk at random in the midst of its (reading) that you may gain the upper hand!" • But We will certainly give the unbelievers a taste of a severe penalty, and We will requite them for the worst of their deeds. • Such is the requital of the enemies of Allah—the fire. Therein will be for them the eternal home—a (fit) requital for their denying Our revelations. The unbelievers will say: "Our Lord! Show us those among jinns and men who misled us. We shall crush them beneath our feet, so that they become the vilest (before all).
		Truth that can Neither be Changed Nor Corrupted
4	41:040-043	1. Those who pervert the truth in Our signs are not hidden from Us. Which is better—he that is cast into the fire, or he that comes safely through on the Day of Judgment? Do what you will; verily, He sees (clearly) all that you do. 2. Those who reject the message when it comes to them (are not hidden from Us), and indeed it is a Book of exalted power. • No falsehood can approach it from before or behind it. It is sent down by One full of wisdom, worthy of all praise. • Nothing is said to you that was not said to the messengers before you: that your lord has at his command (all) forgiveness as well as a most grievous penalty.

		The Qur'an is a Guidence in Arabic
5	41:044	1. Had We sent this as a Qur'an (in) other than Arabic, they would have said: "Why are not its verses explained in detail? What! (A Book) not in Arabic and (a Messenger an Arab)?" 2. Say: "It is a guide and a healing to those who believe. And for those who believe not, there is deafness in their ears, and it is blindness in their (eyes). They are (as it were) being called from a place far distant."

2 THE SERVITUDE OF NONE BUT GOD ALONE

2.1 The Unbelievers' Fate is Humiliation in Both Worlds

The unbelievers have no comprehension of the Creator Whom they refuse to serve or with Whom they associate others in divinity. It is God Who has created this extensive universe, Who is the Creator of the earth and heavens, with Whose blessings they are benefiting on the earth, and with Whose provisions they are being fed and sustained. The unbelievers set up His creatures as His associates, and when they are told the truth, they turn away in arrogance. Such behavior can result in punishments similar to those that visited the peoples of the 'Ad and the Thamud. However, this will not be the final punishment for their corruption; it will be followed by the accountability for their deeds in the Hereafter.

Table 2.1: False Gods: Humiliation of People in Both Worlds

No	Surah:Verses	Meanings
		Do you indeed disbelieve in Him Who created the Universe?
1	41:009-012	Say: "Is it that you deny Him Who created the earth in two days, and do you join equals with Him? He is the Lord of (all) the worlds." 1. He set on the (earth) mountains standing firm, high above it, and bestowed blessings on the earth, and measured therein all things to give them nourishment in due proportion, in four days, in accordance with (the needs of) those

		who seek (sustenance).
		2. Moreover, He comprehended in His design the sky, and it had been (as) smoke. He said to it and to the earth: "Come you together willingly or unwillingly." They said: "We do come (together) in willing obedience." So He completed them as seven firmaments in two days, and He assigned to each heaven its duty and command. And We adorned the lower heaven with lights and (provided it) with guard. Such is the decree of (Him), the exalted in might, full of knowledge.
		The Unbelievers are warned about the Consequences of Disbelief
2	41:013-018	But if they turn away, say: "I have warned you of a stunning punishment (of thunder and lightning) like that which (overtook) the 'Ad and the Thamud." • Behold, the messengers came to them, from before them and behind them, (telling): "Serve none but Allah." • They said: "If our Lord had so pleased, He would certainly have sent down angels (to preach). Now we reject your mission (altogether)." 1. Now the 'Ad behaved arrogantly through the land, against (all) truth and reason, and said: "Who is superior to us in strength?" What! Did they not see that Allah, Who created them, was superior to them in strength? But they continued to reject Our signs! So We sent against them a furious wind through days of disaster, that We might give them a taste of a penalty of humiliation in this life. But the penalty of a Hereafter will be more humiliating still, and they will find no help. 2. As to the Thamud, We gave them guidance, but they preferred blindness (of heart) to guidance. So the stunning punishment of humiliation seized them because of what they had earned, but We delivered those who believed and practiced righteousness.

2.2 Repel Evil with Good, Seek Refuge, and Be Patient

An environment of active resistance to the truth and of societal corruption makes it difficult for believers to lead a moral and honest life. The believers and the Messenger himself were in such a situation when Surah Fussilat was revealed. For such people, at any time in history, life becomes agony. Against the enemy and its all pervading power, the believers may feel utterly helpless and powerless. However, the believers are not powerless as long as they adhere to God and His divine guidance, for God can direct His angels to support the believers, and He encourages the believers by pointing them to their eventual rewards in the Hereafter. Although obstacles may seem insurmountable, patient perseverance and good morals and character help the believers succeed.

Table 2.2: Worship God, Not those whom He has created

No	Surah:Verses	Meanings
		Angels also accompany believers in world's life
3	41:030-032	1. In the case of those who say, "Our Lord is Allah," and, further, stand straight and steadfast, the angels descend on them (from time to time). • "Fear you not!" (they suggest), "nor grieve! But receive the glad tidings of the garden, which you were promised. 2. "We are your protectors in this life and in the Hereafter. Therein shall you have all that you shall desire. Therein shall you have all that you ask for—a hospitable gift from One oft-forgiving, most merciful!
		Good and Evil are not alike. **Repel evil with what is the Best**
4	41:033-036	1. Who is better in speech than one who calls (men) to Allah, works righteousness, and says, "I am of those who bow in Islam?" 2. Nor can goodness and evil be equal. Repel (evil) with what is better; then will he between whom and you was hatred become as it were your friend and intimate. And no one will be granted such goodness except those who exercise patience and self-restraint—none but persons of the greatest

516

		good fortune. 3. And if (at any time) an incitement to discord is made to you by the Satan, seek refuge in Allah. He is the One Who hears and knows all things.
		Prostrate to God Who has Created Everything
5	41:037-038	• Among His signs are the night and the day, and the sun and the moon. Do not prostrate to the sun and the moon, but prostrate to Allah Who created them, if it is Him you wish to serve. • But if they wax proud (and persist in their attitude, it does not matter, for) the angels near-stationed to your Lord glorify Him night and day and never grow weary.

3 THE HEREAFTER AND ACCOUNTABALITY

Just like the revival of the earth after a rain will be the resurrection of the dead. God says, "Among His signs in this: you see the earth barren and desolate, but when We send down rain to it, it is stirred to life and yields increase. Truly, He Who gives life to the (dead) earth can surely give life to (men) who are dead, for He has power over all things (Qur'an 41:39)."

3.1 God Created People, and He will Bring Them to Justice

The unbelievers refuse to believe in divine guidance. They want to benefit from their injustices to other people and from their corruption. God tells them that on the Day of Judgment, they will not be able to conceal their misdeeds. Their ears, eyes, and skins will testify against them as to what they used to do. They used to conceal their misdeeds, and they never realized that their various body parts would bear witness against them. They foolishly thought that God would not know most of what they did. This attitude about their Lord will bring them to destruction, and they will be among the losers.

Table 3.1: Denial of the Divine Guidance and Evil deeds

No	Surah:Verses	Meanings
		Sinners will not be able to conceal their Misdeeds
1	41:019-022	On the day that the enemies of Allah will be gathered together to the fire, they will be marched in ranks. • At length, when they reach the (fire), their hearing, their sight, and their skins will bear witness against them as to (all) their deeds. They will say to their skins: "Why bear witness against us?" They will say: "Allah has given us speech—(He) Who gives speech to everything. He created you for the first time, and unto Him you were to return." You did not seek to hide yourselves, lest your hearing, your sight, and your skins should bear witness against you! But you thought that Allah knew not many of the things that you used to do.
		It will not be possible to Repent on Judgment Day
2	41:023-025	But this thought of yours that you did entertain concerning your Lord, has brought you to destruction, and (now) you have become of those utterly lost. 1. If, then, they have patience, the fire will be a home for them! And if they beg to be received into favor, into favor will they not (then) be received. 2. We have destined for them intimate companions (of like nature), who made alluring to them what was before them and behind them. And the sentence among the previous generations of jinns and men who have passed away is proved against them, for they are utterly lost.

3.2 Selfish Desires Drive People Away from the Truth

None knows the timing of the Hour except God Himself, and all those whom they used to associate with God will not be able to help the unbelievers. Have the unbelievers ever considered that if the Qur'an is really from God, then what fate will they have by denying it and opposing it so bitterly? Those who do not believe will soon see with their own eyes that the message of the Qur'an has spread throughout the whole world and that they have themselves been overwhelmed by it. Then they will realize that this message is the universal truth.

Table 3.2: People are Accountabile and the Qur'an is True

No	Surah:Verses	Meanings
		People are Accountable for their Deeds
3	41:049-050	Man does not weary of asking for good (things), but if ill touches him, he gives up all hope (and) is lost in despair. • When we give him a taste of some mercy from Ourselves, after some adversity has touched him, he is sure to say, "This is due to my (merit). I think not that the Hour (of Judgment) will (ever) be established. But if I am brought back to my Lord, I have (much) good (stored) in His sight!" But We will show the unbelievers the truth of all that they did, and We shall give them the taste of a severe penalty.
		The Qur'an is from God, the Almighty
4	41:052-053	1. Say: "See you if the (revelation) is (really) from Allah, and yet do you reject it? Who is more astray than one who is in a schism far (from any purpose)?" 2. Soon will We show them our signs in the (furthest) regions (of the earth) and in their own selves, until it becomes manifest to them that this is the truth. Is it not enough that your Lord does witness all things?

519

CHAPTER 37

Shirk, the Root of All Corruption

FROM SURAH ASH-SHURA (42)

Shirk is associating anything, whether dead or alive, with God in His divinity. Islam is based on the fact that the Creator of the universe is God. He is the master and real patron of people and the universe. He alone is the ruler. He alone has the right to give people faith and law, systems of belief and practice. He judges the disputes among people and tells what truth is and what falsehood is. No other being has any right whatsoever to be the lawgiver. Like natural sovereignty, lawgiving sovereignty is also vested only in God. If a person does not recognize and accept this divine rule, it is futile for him to recognize the natural sovereignty of God.

God, being the master and real patron of people and the universe, has ordained the true religion since the very beginning. The same religion has been enjoined by God for all people since the beginning of creation, and all of His messengers have been following this religion and inviting others to follow it. This religion requires that people not only believe in it, but also introduce, establish, and enforce it. Against God's divine religion, no man-made religion can prevail in God's earth.

1 EXPLOITING OTHERS IS ALIEN TO THE BELIEVERS

1.1 Divine Guidance is For the Benefit of all People

The Messenger neither knew about the Qur'an nor the true faith during the first forty years of his life. His sudden preaching about the Oneness of God and the Hereafter is clear proof of his being a Messenger from God. In presenting his teaching as a revelation from God, that does not mean that he claimed to have spoken to God, face to face. Rather, God conveyed this guidance to him, as in the case of all other messengers, in any of three ways. God speaks to His messengers either (1) through

520

revelation, (2) from behind a veil, or (3) by sending an angel with the message.

Table 1.1: The Qur'an: Guidance Revealed By God

No	Surah:Verses	Meanings
		God revealed the Qur'an as He Revealed other Divine Books
1	42:003-005	Thus does (He) send inspiration to you as (He did) to those before you—Allah, exalted in power, full of wisdom. To Him belongs all that is in the heavens and on earth, and He is most high, most great. The heavens are almost rent asunder from above them (by His glory), and the angels celebrate the praises of their Lord and pray for forgiveness for (all) beings on earth. Behold! Verily, Allah is He, the oft-forgiving, most merciful.
		God revealed the Qur'an So People may seek Guidance
2	42:007	Thus have We sent by inspiration to you an Arabic Qur'an that you may warn the Mother of Cities (Makkah) and all around her—and warn (them) of the Day of Assembly, of which there is no doubt, (when) some will be in the garden and some in the blazing fire.
		Messages are revealed by God by various Ways
3	42:051-053	It is not fitting for a man that Allah should speak to him except by inspiration, or from behind a veil, or by the sending of a messenger (angel) to reveal, with Allah's permission, what Allah wills: for He is most high, most wise. 1. Thus have We, by Our command, sent inspiration to you. 2. You knew not (before) what was revelation and what was faith, but 3. We have made the (Qur'an) a light, wherewith We guide such of Our servants as We will. 4. Verily, you do guide (men) to the straight way—the way of Allah, to Whom belongs whatever is in the heavens and whatever is on earth. Behold, all affairs tend towards Allah.

1.2: Unbelievers Wish to Commit Excesses against Eachother
After the death of their respective messengers, selfish people
have corrupted religion again and again. Because of their vested
interests, self-conceit, and vanity, they have created new creeds
and manipulated legitimate ones. With the exception of Islam,
the true religion, all the different religions and creeds found in
the world have resulted from the corruption of what had been
divine revelations. "And they became divided only after
knowledge reached them—through selfish envy as between
themselves. Had it not been for a word that went forth before
from your Lord, (tending) to a term appointed, the matter would
have been settled between them. But truly, those who have
inherited the Book after them are in suspicious (disquieting)
doubt concerning it (Qur'an 42:14)."

The Messenger of Islam was sent to present and establish the
same original religion as had previous messengers. "The same
religion has He established for you as that which He enjoined on
Noah—that which We have sent by inspiration to you—and that
which We enjoined on Abraham, Moses, and Jesus: namely, that
you should remain steadfast in religion, and make no divisions
therein. To those who worship other things than Allah, hard is
the (way) to which you call them (Qur'an 42:13)."

The Messenger was also sent to free people from superstitious
practices, artificial creeds, and man-made religions. Instead of
being grateful, the unbelievers were angry and fought him, but
that was their folly. The arrogance of the people cannot force the
messengers to abandon their missions. They have been enjoined
to adhere to their faith at all costs and to carry out the mission
with full dedication. People should not cherish any false hopes
that to please them or their chiefs, a messenger would agree to
the same whims, superstitions, and ignorance that have corrupted
God's religion before. God commands people to establish this
religion and not dispute regarding it.

2 EFFORTS IMPACT OUR GAINS
IN BOTH WORLDS

2.1 People should only Serve God

People who know the truth are conscientious regarding their accountability for their deeds. God tells them: "To any that desires the tilth of the Hereafter, We give increase in his tilth, and to any that desires the tilth of this world, We grant somewhat thereof, but he has no share or lot in the Hereafter (Qur'an 42:20)." Therefore, people should follow and invite others to the way of God as they have been commanded, and they should not indulge in illegal activities for worldly gains.

Table 2.1: Efforts Impact People's Gains in both Worlds

No	Surah:Verses	Meanings
		Follow and Invite people to the Truth
1	42:015-016	Now then, for that (reason), call (them to the faith), and stand steadfast as you are commanded, nor follow their vain desires, but say: 1. "I believe in the Book that Allah has sent down, and I am commanded to judge justly between you. 2. "Allah is our Lord and your Lord. 3. "For us (is the responsibility for) our deeds, and for you for your deeds. 4. "There is no contention between us and you. 5. "Allah will bring us together, and to Him is (our) final goal." But those who dispute concerning Allah after He has been accepted—futile is their dispute in the sight of their Lord. On them will be a penalty terrible.
		Believers are Conscientious about their Accountability
2	42:017-019	It is Allah Who has sent down the Book in truth and the balance (by which to weigh conduct). And what will make you realize that perhaps the Hour (of Judgment) is close at hand? 1. Only those wish to hasten it who believe not in it. 2. Those who believe hold it in awe and know that it is the truth.

		• Behold, verily those that dispute concerning the Hour are far astray. Gracious is Allah to His servants. He gives sustenance to whom He pleases, and He has power and can carry out His will.

2.2 Consequence of following the Corrupted Religions

One cannot even comprehend how grave it is to follow corrupted religions and laws instead of the divine religion. It is the worst kind of *Shirk* and a grave crime, the punishment for which will be the deterioration of life for all those who enforced their own religion on God's earth, as well as for those who adopted and followed a false religion. People suffer the bad consequences of following man-made creeds that promote injustice, discrimination, exploitation, and corruption. The deterioration of a society is directly proportional to the magnitude of its corruption, irrespective of whether such community is inhabited by believers or unbelievers.

Table 2.2: Rewards, Repentance, and Answered Prayers

No	Surah:Verses	Meanings
		The Rewards of the Unjust and the Just
3	42:021-023	• What! Have they partners (in godhead) who have established for them some religion without the permission of Allah? Had it not been for the decree of judgment, the matter would have been decided between them (at once). But verily the wrongdoers will have a grievous penalty. You will see the wrongdoers in fear on account of what they have earned, and (the burden of) that must fall on them. • But those who believe and work righteous deeds will be in the luxuriant meads of the gardens. They shall have, before their Lord, all that they wish for. That will indeed be the magnificent bounty (of Allah). That is (the bounty) whereof Allah gives glad tidings to His servants who believe and do righteous deeds. Say: "No reward do I ask of you for this except the love of those near of kin." And if any one

524

		earns any good, We shall give him an increase of good in respect thereof, for Allah is oft-forgiving, most ready to appreciate (service).
		God accepts Repentance and Answers the Prayers
4	42:024-026	What! Do they say: "He has forged a falsehood against Allah?" But if Allah willed, He could seal up your heart. And Allah blots out vanity and proves the truth by His words, for He knows well the secrets of all hearts. 1. He is the One that accepts repentance from His servants and forgives sins, and He knows all that you do. 2. He listens to those who believe and do deeds of righteousness and gives them increase of His bounty, but for the unbelievers there is a terrible penalty.

2.3 Implementation of Divine Laws Leads to Prosperity

Prosperity is the overall welfare of all members of a society. It cannot come through injustice, unequal treatment, and exploitation of others. There are two fundamental sources of prosperity: agriculture and human resources. Agriculture, the main source of prosperity, depends on a combination of rain and human effort. God says: "If Allah were to enlarge the provision for His servants, they would indeed transgress beyond all bounds through the earth, but He sends (it) down in due measure as He pleases, for He is with His servants well-acquainted, watchful (Qur'an 42:27)." Whatever hardship comes to people is due to their behavior and deeds: "Whatever misfortune happens to you is because of the things your hands have wrought, and for many (of them) He grants forgiveness (Qur'an 42:30)." There is no guardian and helper other than God. God challenges people: "Nor can you frustrate through the earth, nor have you besides Allah anyone to protect or to help (Qur'an 42:31)."

Table 2.3: God's Creation and Signs of His Power

No	Surah:Verses	Meanings
		God's Provisions and Signs of His Power
5	42:028	1. (*Rain:*) He is the One that sends down rain, (even) after (men) have given up all hope, and scatters His mercy (far and wide). He is the protector, worthy of all praise.
	42:029	2. (*Living Creatures:*) Among His signs is the creation of the heavens and the earth and the living creatures that He has scattered through them, and He has power to gather them together when He wills.
	42:032-033	3. (*Wind, Sea and Ships:*) Among His signs are the ships, smooth running through the ocean, (tall) as mountains. If it be His will, He can still the wind; then would they become motionless on the back of the (ocean). Verily, in this are signs for everyone who patiently perseveres and is grateful.
		God's Forgiveness or Punishment for Sins
6	42:034-035	• ...He can cause them to perish because of the (evil) that (men) have earned, but much does He forgive. • But let those know who dispute about Our signs that there is for them no way of escape.
		Children are Granted by God as He Wills
7	42:049-050	To Allah belongs the dominion of the heavens and the earth. He creates what He wills. • He bestows (children) male or female according to His will (and plan). • ...He bestows both males and females, and He leaves barren whom He wills, For He is full of knowledge and power.

3 SUCCESS IS GOOD BEHAVIOR AND GOOD DEEDS

3.1 Divine Guidance Leads to Good Behavior and Deeds

God gives people freedom of choice. He allows them to have different viewpoints and to follow their own inclinations. This makes it possible for people to obtain special mercy from God, a mercy that is not meant for other creatures. However, this special stature is only for those people who chose to take God as their patron and guardian by a conscious and intentional exercise of their free will. God supports those who adapt to His way. He guides and helps them to do well in life, and He admits them into His mercy. However, individuals who misuse their free will by taking others as their patrons and guardians are deprived of this divine mercy. Only God can be a true patron and guardian of people. False deities are neither patrons nor powerful enough to do full justice to patronage. People's success depends on choosing God as their patron. They must take God as their guide, and they must follow Him. Success does not come to those who serve false gods or by the recommendation of false deities.

Table 3.1: Paradise is for Good Behavior and Good Deeds

No	Surah:Verses	Meanings
		Belief, Reliance on God, and Good Behavior
1	42:036-038	Whatever you are given (here) is (but) a convenience of this life, but that which is with Allah is better and more lasting. (It is) for those who believe and put their trust in their Lord. 1. Those who avoid the greater crimes and shameful deeds, and 2. (Those who) when they are angry even then forgive. 3. Those who hearken to their Lord and establish regular prayer; 4. (Those) who (conduct) their affairs by mutual consultation; 5. (Those) Who spend (in charity) out of what We bestow on them for sustenance.
		Fighting Against Oppression with Patience
2	42:039-043	6. Those who, when an oppressive wrong is inflicted on them, (are not cowed, but) help and defend themselves. 7. The recompense for an injury is an injury equal thereto (in degree), but if a person forgives and makes reconciliation, his reward is due from Allah, for (Allah) loves not those who do wrong. 8. Indeed, if any do help and defend themselves after a wrong (is done) to them, against such there is no cause of blame.

		9. The blame is only against those who oppress men and wrongdoing and insolently transgress beyond bounds through the land, defying right and justice. For such there will be a penalty grievous. But indeed if any show patience and forgives, that would truly be an exercise of courageous will and resolution in the conduct of affairs.

3.2 People Should Reform for Prosperity and Paradise

If people do not accept divine guidance and do not reform accordingly, nothing else in the world can make them human. They will, therefore, remain engaged in the same evil behavior in which people have remained involved for centuries. Such people will face the fate in this world that has been destined for wrongdoers, and they will also face punishment in the Hereafter. God tells us: "For any whom Allah leaves astray, there is no protector thereafter. You will see the wrongdoers, when in sight of the penalty, say: 'Is there any way (to affect) a return?'…Accept the command of your Lord before there comes a day that there will be no putting back, because of (the ordainment of) Allah! That day there will be for you no place of refuge, nor will there be for you any room for denial (Qur'an 42:44, 47)."

Table 3.2: People should Reform before it is too late

No	Surah:Verses	Meanings
		Unbelievers and their kindred will be the True Losers
3	42:045-046	You will see them brought forward to the (penalty) in a humble frame of mind because of (their) disgrace, (and) looking with a stealthy glance. 1. The believers will say: "Those are indeed in loss, who has given to perdition their own selves and those belonging to them on the Day of Judgment. Behold! Truly, the wrongdoers are in a lasting penalty!" 2. And no protectors have they to help them, other than Allah. And for any whom Allah leaves to stray, there is no way (to the goal).

528

		Misfortune afflicts People on account of their Misdeeds
4	42:048	(O Messenger,) if they turn away from the truth, We have not sent you as a guard over them. Your duty is but to convey (the message). And truly, when We give man a taste of a mercy from Ourselves, he does exult thereat. But when some ill happens to him on account of the deeds that his hands have sent forth, truly then is man ungrateful.

CHAPTER 38

An Argument Against *Shirk*

FROM SURAH AZ-ZUKHRUF (43)

Shirk is polytheism or the worship of others along with the One God. It also implies assigning divine attributes to anyone besides God, worshiping others than God, or believing that the source of power, harm, and blessings can be from others besides God. After rejecting the unbelievers' various practices of ignorance with rational arguments, it is pointed out in Surah Az-Zukhruf that God has no offspring, that there are no additional gods, and that there are no intercessors that can protect from God's punishment of those who knowingly adopt deviations. God is far above having children. He alone is the Lord of the whole universe. Everybody else is His servant, and none is associated in His attributes and powers. Only those who are the followers of the truth can intercede with Him, and only for those who may have adopted obedience to the truth in the world.

1 THE CREATOR OF UNIVERSE AND HIS GUIDANCE

1.1 Unbelievers Agree that God Created the Universe

The unbelievers acknowledge that God is the Creator of the earth and heavens, of themselves, and also of their deities: "If you were to question them, 'Who created the heavens and the earth?' they would be sure to reply, 'they were created by (Him), the exalted in power, full of knowledge' (Qur'an 43:9)." They also admit that the blessings from which they are benefiting have been bestowed by Him. God tells people: "(Yea, the same that) has made for you the earth spread out and has made for you roads (and channels) therein, in order that you may find guidance (on the way), that sends down (from time to time) rain from the sky in due measure—and We raise to life therewith a land that is dead even so will you be raised (from the dead), that has created pairs in all things and has made for you ships and cattle on which you ride, in order that you may sit firm and square on their backs, and when so seated, you may celebrate the favor of your

530

Lord and say, 'Glory to Him Who has subjected these to our (use), for we could never have accomplished this (by ourselves), and to our Lord, surely, must we turn back.' Yet, they attribute to some of His servants a share with Him (in his godhead)! Truly is man a blasphemous ingrate avowed (Qur'an 43:10-15)."

1.2 Divine Guidance will never Cease to Exist
Neither did God withhold the appointment of His messengers nor was revelation discontinued because of the resistance of the people to learn and reform. In Surah Az-Zukhruf, swearing by the Book, God tells people: "We have made it a Qur'an in Arabic, that you may be able to understand (and learn wisdom) (Qur'an 43:3)." God then asks: "Shall We then take away the message from you and repel (you), for that you are a people transgressing beyond bounds? But how many were the prophets We sent among the peoples of old? And never came there a prophet to them but they mocked him. So We destroyed (them)—stronger in power than these—and (thus) has passed on the parable of the peoples of old (Qur'an 43:5-8)."

2 THE UNBELIEVERS' JUSTIFICATION FOR *SHIRK*

2.1 Past Practices are used to defend False Gods
Some people believed that the angels were goddesses. They carved their images as females; they adorned them with female dresses and ornaments and called them daughters of God. They worshiped them and invoked them for the fulfillment of their needs. God asked the polytheists of Makkah how it was that they knew that the angels were female. In response, the unbelievers weakly argued that if God actually disapproved of their practice, He would have stopped them from worshiping these images. However, such a weak argument can also be used to justify theft, adultery, robbery, murder, etc. Can this argument be used to justify the occurrence of every crime and evil in the world as somehow being right and proper?

When asked if they had any other proof, apart from the above argument, for their polytheism, the unbelievers replied that they were merely following the practices of their ancestors. The unbelievers wrongly thought that evidence of past practice was a strong enough evidence for a creed to be right and true. In contrast, Abraham, who was their forefather and the basis of Makkan pride and distinction, had rejected the religion of his elders. He discarded every blind imitation of his forefathers that could not be supported by rational argument.

Table 2.1
Unbelievers Argue for the Status Quo and Refuse to Reform

No	Surah:Verses	Meanings
		The Unbelievers' Justification for the Angels being Female Deities
1	43:019-021	1. And they make into females angels who themselves serve Allah. Did they witness their creation? Their evidence will be recorded, and they will be called to account. 2. ("Ah!") they say. "If it had been the will of (Allah) Most Gracious, we should not have worshiped such (deities)!" Of that they have no knowledge! They do nothing but lie! What! Have We given them a Book before this to which they are holding fast?
		The Unbelievers Say - **They follow the Way of their Forefathers**
2	43:022-025	Nay! They say: "We found our fathers following a certain religion, and we do guide ourselves by their footsteps." 1. Just in the same way, whenever We sent a warner before you to any people, the wealthy ones among them said: "We found our fathers following a certain religion, and we will certainly follow in their footsteps." 2. He (their warner) said: "What! Even if I brought you better guidance than that which you found your fathers following?" They said: "For us, we deny that you (prophets) are sent." So We exacted retribution from them; now see what was the end of those who rejected.
		But Abraham - **One of their forefathers was not an Unbeliever**
3	43:026-030	1. Behold! Abraham said to his father and his people: "I do indeed clear myself of what you

532

		worship. (I worship) only Him Who made me, and He will certainly guide me." He left it as a word to endure among those who came after him that they may turn back (to Allah).
		2. Yea, I (God) have given the good things of this life to these (men) and their fathers until the truth has come to them, and a messenger making things clear.
		But when the truth came to them, they said: "This is sorcery, and we do reject it."

2.2 'Material Position' and 'Rank' are their Deities

The unbelievers were not inclined to believe in the Messenger because, according to them, he was neither a rich man nor a person of high worldly position and rank. Therefore, in their opinion, he was not qualified to be the Messenger of God. They maintained that had God willed to appoint a prophet among them, He would have appointed one of the great men from the cities of Makkah or Taif. On that very basis, Pharaoh had also looked down upon Moses, maintaining that if God, the king of the heavens, were to send a messenger to him, the king of the earth, He would have sent that messenger with bracelets of gold and a company of angels in attendance. Pharaoh questioned the status of Moses, who had neither wealth nor authority. In Pharaoh's mind, he was superior to Moses, for the kingdom of Egypt belonged to him and the canals of the Nile were flowing under his control.

Table 2.2
Wealth and Power is very Important to the Unbelievers

No	Surah:Verses	Meanings
		Good Character and Honesty are Better than Wealth
4	43:031-035	They (the unbelievers) say: "Why is not this Qur'an sent down to some leading man in either of the two (chief) cities?" 1. Is it they who would portion out the mercy of your Lord? It is We Who portion out between them their livelihood in the life of this world, and We raise some of them above others in ranks, so that some may

		command work from others. But the mercy of your Lord is better than the (wealth) that they amass. 2. And were it not that (all) men might become of one (evil) way of life, We would provide for everyone that blasphemes against (Allah) Most Gracious silver roofs for their houses and (silver) stairways on which to go up, and (silver) doors to their houses, and thrones (of silver) on which they could recline, and also adornments of gold. But all this were nothing but conveniences of the present life. The Hereafter, in the sight of your Lord, is for the righteous.
		Pharaoh said, **"My kingdom makes me better than Moses"**
5	43:046-056	We did send Moses aforetime with Our signs, to Pharaoh and his chiefs. He said: "I am a messenger of the Lord of the worlds. • But when he came to them with Our signs, behold, they ridiculed them. We showed them sign after sign, each greater than its fellow, and We seized them with punishment, in order that they might turn (to Us). And they said, "O you sorcerer! Invoke your Lord for us according to His covenant with you; for we shall truly accept guidance." • But when We removed the penalty from them, behold, they broke their word. 1. Pharaoh proclaimed among his people, saying: "O my people! Does not the dominion of Egypt belong to me? (Witness) these streams flowing underneath my (palace). What! Don't you see then? 2. "Am I not better than this (Moses) who is a contemptible wretch and can scarcely express himself clearly? 3. "Then why are not gold bracelets bestowed on him, or (why) come (not) with him angels accompanying him in procession?" • Thus did he make fools of his people, and

		they obeyed him, truly were they a people rebellious (against Allah). When at length they provoked Us, We exacted retribution from them, and We drowned them all. And We made them (a people) of the past and an example to later ages.

2.3 Messengers never taught that God's has Partners

When the unbelievers are asked: "Has ever a messenger or a Book from God taught people that besides God there are others who are worthy of worship?" they argued that the Christians took Jesus, the son of Mary, as the son of God and worshiped him. However, the question was not whether the community of a messenger committed *Shirk* or not; the question was whether a messenger had himself taught *Shirk*. Jesus, the son of Mary, never said that he was the son of God and that people should worship him. His own teaching was the same as every other messenger, i.e., worship God alone.

Table 2.3: Jesus Never said that He was Son of God

No	Surah:Verses	Meanings
		Unbelievers Ask - "Who is better, our deities or Jesus?"
6	43:057-058	1. When (Jesus), the son of Mary, is held up as an example, behold, your people raise a clamor thereat (to ridicule). 2. They say, "Are our gods best or he?" This they set forth to you only by way of disputation. Yea, they are a contentious people
		My Lord and your Lord is God - Worship Him alone.
7	43:059-065	He (Jesus) was no more than a servant. We granted Our favor to him, and We made him an example to the Children of Israel. And if it were Our will, We could make angels from among you, succeeding each other on the earth. 1. And (Jesus) shall be a sign (for the coming of) the Hour (of Judgment). Therefore, have no doubt about the (Hour), but follow Me. This is a Straight Way. Let not Satan hinder you, for he is to you an enemy avowed. 2. When Jesus came with clear signs, he said:

535

		"Now have I come to you with wisdom and in order to make clear to you some of the (points) on which you dispute. Therefore, fear Allah and obey me. For Allah, He is my Lord and your Lord, so you worship Him. This is a straight way." But sects from among themselves fell into disagreement. Then woe to the wrongdoers from the penalty of a grievous day.

3 UNBELIEVERS' SCHEMING AND ACCOUNTABILITY

3.1 Unbelievers' Scheming for False Deities will not Succeed

When Surah Az-Zukhruf was revealed, the unbelievers of Makkah were planning to put an end to the Messenger's life. Consultations on how to eliminate him were continuing, and an attack on his life has been planned. (This is referred to in Qur'an 43:79-80.) However, these conspirators were plainly warned that if they tried to take action against the Messenger, God would take decisive action against them. The Messenger was asked to tell the unbelievers that: (1) if God had a son, which He doesn't, he (the Messenger) would be the first to worship him (Qur'an 43:81-82); (2) with God is the knowledge of the Day of Judgment, and to God they would all be sent back (Qur'an 43:84-85); and (3) the false deities that they called upon have no power of intercession with God (Qur'an 43:86).

3.2 People shall soon be Questioned about their Behavior

If the fear of God is uppermost in his mind, a person with a firm belief in God and in the Day of Judgment is always able to defeat Satan and triumph over Satan's cunning. He will fare even better if he fortifies his faith by increasing his knowledge of Islam and by remembrance of God. Since his people were plotting against his life, the Messenger was told by God: "Even if We take you away, We shall be sure to exact retribution from them, or We shall show you that (accomplished) that We have promised them, for verily We shall prevail over them (Qur'an 43:41-42)." Since one cannot "...make the deaf to hear, or give direction to the blind or to such as (wander) in manifest error (Qur'an 43:40)," God further commands the Messenger: "So

536

hold you fast to the revelation sent down to you. Verily, you are on a straight way. The (Qur'an) is indeed the message for you and for your people, and soon shall you (all) be brought to account (Qur'an 43:43-44)."

Table 3.2: Hold Fast to What God have Revealed

No	Surah:Verses	Meanings
		Remembrance of God **Shields People from Evil Associates**
1	43:036-039	If anyone withdraws himself from remembrance of (Allah) Most Gracious, We appoint for him a devil to be an intimate companion to him. Such (devils) really hinder them from the path, but they think that they are being guided aright. • At length, when (such a one) comes to Us, he says (to his evil companion): "Would that between me and you were the distance of East and West! Ah! Evil is the companion (indeed)!" • When you have done wrong, it will avail you nothing, that day that you shall be partners in punishment.
		God never appointed False Deities **to be worshiped besides Him**
2	43:045	You question our messengers whom We sent before you. Did We appoint any deities other than (Allah) Most Gracious to be worshiped?

3.3 Day of Judgment, Accountability, and Awards

The basic Islamic concepts of life, death, resurrection, accountability, and reward ensure that a believer unhesitatingly acknowledges God's authority over people's lives on earth. The reckoning, judgment, and reward or punishment and in the Hereafter are based on what people actually do in this life. People cannot be held responsible for what they do in this world unless they are given a law that explains what is lawful and what is forbidden. This makes it necessary that there is a single authority over both this life and the Hereafter.

When a law other than God's is enforced in this world, how can people be judged in the Hereafter? Is it according to the law they implemented here or according to the divine law that they did not implement? People must realize that God will hold them to account on the basis of His own law. They must be aware that if they do not conduct their lives and establish their relationships and worship according to God's law, then this will be the first thing for which they have to account. People will also be questioned as to why they have not chosen God as their Lord on earth, preferring instead to claim other deities. This they do by following God's law in matters of worship but adopting a different law in their social, political, and economic systems, as well as in their interactions, dealings, and relationships. This means that they will have to account for denying God or associating others with Him. God forgives whomever He pleases, but only for that which is short of associating partners with him.

Table 3.3: Day of Judgment: Paradise or Hell

No	Surah:Verses	Meanings
		On that Day, **Friends will Be enemies, except the God-fearing**
3	43:066-067	Do they only wait for the Hour—that it should come on them all of a sudden, while they perceive not? Friends on that day will be foes, one to another, except the righteous.
		On that Day, **Believers shall have Nothing to Fear or Regret**
4	43:068-073	My devotees! No fear shall be on you that Day, nor shall you grieve—(being) those who have believed in Our signs and bowed (their wills to Ours) in Islam. Enter you the garden, you and your wives, in (beauty and) rejoicing. 1. To them will be passed round dishes and goblets of gold. There will be all that the souls could desire, all that their eyes could delight in, and you shall abide therein. 2. Such will be the garden of which you are made heirs for your (good) deeds (in life). You shall have therein abundance of fruit, from which you shall have satisfaction.
		On that Day, **The Guilty shall abide in Hell for being Unjust**

5	43:074-077	The sinners will be in the punishment of Hell, to dwell therein (forever). The (punishment) will not be lightened for them, and in despair will they be there overwhelmed.
		1. Nowise shall We be unjust to them, but it is they who have been unjust themselves.
		2. They will cry: "O Malik (to Hell's caretaker)! Would that your Lord put an end to us!" He will say, "Nay, but you shall abide."

CHAPTER 39

Natural Disasters and Accountability
FROM SURAH AD-DUKHAN (44),
AND SURAH AL-JATHIYA (45)

When the unbelievers of Makkah became most hostile in their attitude and conduct, the Messenger prayed for a famine. He thought that when the people would be afflicted with a calamity, they would remember God, their hearts would soften, and they would accept divine guidance. God granted his prayer, and the whole land was overtaken by such a terrible famine that the people were very distressed. Finally, some of the Quraysh chiefs, among whom Abdullah bin Mas'ud has particularly mentioned the name of Abu Sufyan, came to the Messenger and requested him to pray to God to deliver his people from the calamity. On this occasion Surah Ad-Dukhan was revealed (Sahih Bukhari: 2.17.133). The unbelievers were told that due to their chronic arrogance, they would not believe after the torment was removed from them, just as Pharaoh and his people did not honor their promise to reform after their afflictions were removed from them. Further, God warned the unbelievers that a graver disaster was about to fall upon them. They needed a severe punishment; minor misfortunes would not set them right. This can also serve as a warning to the arrogant and corrupt people of today, irrespective of what they call themselves, non-Muslims as well as Muslims.

In Surah Al-Jathiya, people are told that if there were no accountability, this would make the good and the bad, the obedient and the disobedient, and the oppressor and the oppressed all the same. Such a situation would be against all reason and justice. In such a situation, neither would a good act bear a good result, nor would an evil act bear an evil result, nor would the grievances of the oppressed be redressed, nor would the oppressor be punished, but everyone would meet the same fate. Unjust and wicked people adopt this view because they lack the courage to face the evil consequences of their deeds. God's world is not a lawless territory. The universe is built on specific

540

physical, moral, and sociopolitical principles. The injustice of good and bad being equal does not exist. Lack of accountability encourages corruption, lessens motivation to reform, and is destructive to moral fiber. The belief that there is no accountability is adopted only by those who desire the freedom to serve their lusts, which results in human nature degenerating into perversion and moral sense being killed. At this stage, guidance becomes extinct for them.

1 THE SIGNS OF GOD'S EXISTENCE AND HIS GUIDANCE

Numerous signs found in the universe, from one's own body to the earth and heavens, testify to the existence of God. If someone attentively observes the variety of animals, the day and night, the rainfall and vegetation, the winds, and the creation of humankind, and if he reflects over them intelligently and without prejudice, he will find these signs sufficiently convincing that this universe is neither godless nor under the control of many gods. It has been created by One God, and He alone is its controller and ruler. However, if an individual is determined not to acknowledge this, but remains in doubts, he cannot be blessed with faith and conviction.

1.1 Read, Reflect, and Follow What Has Been Revealed

God tells people that the Qur'an is the true guidance. People should learn it and implement its commands in their individual lives and in their communities in order to achieve success in this life and the next. The entire Islamic code is for the benefit of people; it either prevents harm or brings benefit. When God addresses the believers in the Qur'an, one finds either something good that people are encouraged to do or something evil that they are required to avoid or a combination of both. Compliance with God's commands is the only way if people wish to receive His mercy and not His punishment. God's punishment is, in reality, the consequence of a person's bad deeds. That is why whoever acts righteously does so for his own good.

Table 1.1: The Qur'an: Guidance Revealed By God

No	Surah:Verses	Meanings
		There are Signs for People who use Reason

1	45:002-006	The revelation of the Book is from Allah the exalted in power, full of wisdom.
		• Verily, in the heavens and the earth are signs for those who believe.
		  1. And in the creation of yourselves
		  2. And the fact that animals are scattered (through the earth).
		• Are signs for those of assured faith.
		  1. And in the alternation of night and day,
		  2. And the fact that Allah sends down sustenance from the sky
		  3. And revives therewith the earth after its death,
		  4. And in the change of the winds,
		• (There) are signs for those that are wise. Such are the signs of Allah, which We rehearse to you in truth.
		Then in what exposition will they believe after (rejecting) Allah and His signs?

		Who Ignore the Divine Guidance will Suffer
2	45:007-011	Woe to each sinful dealer in falsehoods. 1. He hears the signs of Allah rehearsed to him; yet, (he) is obstinate and lofty, as if he had not heard them. Then announce to him a penalty grievous. 2. When he learns something of Our signs, he takes them in jest. For such, there will be a humiliating penalty. 3. In front of them is Hell, and of no profit to them is anything they may have earned nor any protectors they may have taken to themselves besides Allah. For them is a tremendous penalty This is (true) guidance, and for those who reject the signs of their Lord is a grievous penalty of abomination.
		Who acts Righteously does so for his own Good
3	45:012-015	It is Allah Who has subjected the sea to you that ships may sail through it by His command, that you may seek of his bounty, and that you may be

		grateful.
		1. He has subjected to you, as from Him, all that is in the heavens and on earth:
		2. Behold, in that are signs indeed for those who reflect.
		• Tell those who believe to forgive those who do not look forward to the days of Allah. It is for Him to recompense (for good or ill) each people according to what they have earned.
		If anyone does a righteous deed, it ensures to the benefit of his own self. If he does evil, it works against (his own soul). In the end, you will be brought back to your Lord.

1.2 Do not follow the Selfish Desires of the Ignorant

There were some people who, due to their stubbornness, arrogance, mockery and insistence on disbelief, resist the invitation of the Qur'an, even though the Qur'an brought the same guidance that was given to the Children of Israel. When the Children of Israel failed to recognize the true worth of this blessing, they corrupted their religion and lost it. The Qur'an consists of the true moral and sociopolitical code that helps people achieve their status as God's trustee, which is much higher than the status of those who live only to fulfill their selfish needs. Only people devoid of wisdom reject such guidance. In contrast, people who adopt obedience to divine guidance and lead a life of piety and righteousness become worthy of God's mercy and friendship.

Table 1.2: People's Exploitation of Religion

No	Surah:Verses	Meanings
		Children of Israel Corrupted their own religion
4	45:016-017	We did aforetime grant to the Children of Israel the book, the power of command, and prophethood.
		1. We gave them for sustenance things good and pure, and We favored them above the nations.
		2. We granted them clear signs in affairs (of religion). It was only after knowledge had been granted to them that they fell into schisms through insolent envy among themselves.

		Verily, your Lord will judge between them on the Day of Judgment as to those matters in which they set up differences.
		The Qur'an gives the True Religion
5	45:018-020	1. Then We put you on the (right) way of religion. So follow that (way), and follow not the desires of those who know not. 2. They will be of no use to you in the sight of Allah. It is only wrongdoers (that stand as) protectors one to another, but Allah is the protector of the righteous. These are clear evidences to men and a guidance and mercy to those of assured faith.

1.3 People who Worship their Own Selfish Desires

People have been endowed with intellect and conscience to enable them to distinguish between what is good and what is bad, thus avoiding the bad consequences of bad deeds. The mission of people is to develop a human civilization based on divine principles of conduct. They are also to harness natural resources for the use of all creatures that inhabit the earth. To succeed in this endeavor, people have to use their intellect, conscience, and the divine guidance. This is a test so that people may prove who among them can utilize one's life to its best purpose and potential. God states in the Qur'an: "He Who created death and life that He may try which of you is best in deed, and He is the exalted in might, oft-forgiving (Qur'an 67:2)."

The unbelievers tend to use their brains cunningly to find justifications for the fulfillment of their own selfish desires. Usually, they are whispering like Satan to other people's ears suggestions that everything is allowed in love and war and that one shouldn't have to work hard if one plays it smart. They refuse to realize that we have been created to use our wisdom to manage and control our selfish desires, not to justify them so that we lose the ability distinguish between extortion and honest living. It is inconceivable to think that God Who is the supreme justice will not be able to distinguish between the believers who do good deeds and the evildoers.

Table 1.3: God created the World to Reward People's Efforts

No	Surah:Verses	Meanings
		God Created the World to Reward Good Deeds
6	45:021-022	What! Do those who seek after evil ways think that 1. We shall hold them equal with those who believe and do righteous deeds— 2. That equal will be their life and their death? 3. Ill is the judgment that they make. Allah created the heavens and the earth for just ends, and in order that each soul may find the recompense of what it has earned, and none of them be wronged.
		And Punish those who Worship their Low Desire
7	45:023	• Then see you such a one as takes as his god his own vain desire? • Allah has, knowing (him as such), left him astray and sealed his hearing and his heart and put a cover on his sight. Who then will guide him after Allah (has withdrawn guidance)? Will you not then receive admonition?

1.4 God's Mercy or His Wrath Depends on One's Efforts

God tells people that just as they did not become alive of their own accord, so they will not die of their own accord. They will die when God sends death to them. A time is certainly coming when all people will be gathered together. If people do not believe in this, it is because of their own ignorance and arrogance. Of a surety, the Day of Judgment will come. At that time, each person's book of conduct will delineate his good and bad deeds before God's court of justice. Then, when it is too late to repent, each person will know how dearly his denial and mockery of the Hereafter has cost him.

Table 1.4: Consequences of Peoples' Behavior and Efforts

No	Surah:Verses	Meanings
		On the Day of Judgment, **All People will be called to their Books**
8	45:028-029	You will see every sect bowing the knee. Every sect will be called to its record. This day shall you be recompensed for all that you did. • This Our record speaks about you with truth, for We have caused (all) that you did to be recorded.
		People will face **the Consequences of their Behavior and Efforts**
9	45:030-035	Then, as to those who believed and did righteous deeds, their Lord will admit them to His mercy. That will be the achievement for all to see. • But as to those who rejected Allah, (to them will be said): 1. "Were not Our revelations rehearsed to you? But you were arrogant and were a people given to sin. 2. "When it was said that the promise of Allah was true and that the Hour (of Judgment)—there was no doubt about its (coming), 3. "You used to say, 'We know not what is the hour. We only think it is an idea, and we have no firm assurance.'" 4. Then will appear to them the evil (fruits) of what they did, and they will be completely encircled by that at which they used to mock. 5. It will also be said: "This day, We will forget you as you forgot the meeting of this day of yours! And your abode is the fire, and no helpers have you! This, because you used to take the signs of Allah in jest, and the life of the world deceived you." (From) that day, therefore, they shall not be taken out thence, nor shall they be received into grace.

2 NATURAL DISASTERS MAY LEAD TO IMPROVEMENT

2.1 God took on Himself to Feed and Guide Humanity

God's providence and mercy include the provisions of life, as well as His guidance. Messengers and Books were sent for the guidance of humanity. God's decisions are eternal and cannot be altered to accommodate an individual's liking. These decisions are based on His perfect knowledge and foresight and are from the ruler of the universe. Therefore, His commands should not be taken lightly. The Qur'an bears the clear testimony that it is not the composition of an individual, but of God, the Lord of the universe.

Table 2.1: God Revealed the Qur'an on a Blessed Night

No	Surah:Verses	Meanings
		The Qur'an is God's Mercy and His Guidance to the People
1	44:001-006	By the Book that makes things clear— 1. We sent it down during a blessed night, for We (ever) wish to warn (against evil). In that (night) is made distinct every affair of wisdom, by command from Our presence, 2. For We (ever) send (revelations) as a mercy from your Lord, for He hears and knows (all things).
		The Qur'an is made Easy for People to Learn and Remember
2	44:058	Verily, We have made this (Qur'an) easy in your tongue, so that they may be mindful.

2.2 Natural Disasters Tend to Lead People to Humbleness

The famine raging in Makkah at the time of this revelation has been cited as a calamity that befell the Makkans, in order to break the arrogance of the disbelievers. It looked as if this expectation was being fulfilled to some extent, for some of the most stubborn enemies of the truth, on account of the severities of the famine, had cried out that they would believe if God would avert this torment from them. However, God told the Messenger that these people would not learn any lesson from such calamities. When they turned away from the Messenger,

547

whose life, character, works, and speech clearly show that he was God's true messenger, how would a mere famine help remove their disbelief?

Table 2.2
The Day when the Sky will bring an evident Smoke

No	Surah:Verses	Meanings
		Evil Deeds are followed by their Evil Consequences
3	44:010-011	Then watch for the day that the sky will bring forth a kind of smoke (or mist) plainly visible, enveloping the people. This will be a Penalty Grievous (44.10-11).
		Evildoers Refuse to Learn from History and to Reform
4	44:012-014	(They will say:) "Our Lord! Remove the penalty from us, for we do really believe." 1. How shall the message be (effectual) for them, seeing that a Messenger explaining things clearly has (already) come to them? 2. Yet, they turn away from him and say: "Tutored (by others), a man possessed."

2.3 Severe Punishment may be required for the Arrogant

The unbelievers of Makkah were told that, due to their chronic arrogance, they would not believe after the torment was removed from them, just like Pharaoh and his people refused to believe when disasters were removed from them during the time of Moses. God warned them that He would remove the famine just to see how sincere they were in their promise. Thereafter, a graver disaster awaited them. They needed a much more severe punishment because minor misfortunes would not set them on the right course.

Table 2.3: A Graver Disaster may follow Little Disasters

No	Surah:Verses	Meanings
		Evil Behavior and Deeds eventually Destroys
5	44:015-029	• We shall indeed remove the penalty for a while, (but) truly you will revert (to your ways). One day We shall seize you with a mighty onslaught. We will, indeed, (then)

		exact retribution. We did before them try the people of Pharaoh. 1. There came to them a messenger most honorable, saying: "Restore to me the servants of Allah. I am to you a messenger worthy of all trust, and be not arrogant as against Allah, for I come to you with authority manifest. For me, I have sought safety with my Lord and your Lord against your injuring me. If you believe me not, at least keep yourselves away from me." 2. (But they were aggressive.) Then he cried to his Lord: "These are indeed a people given to sin." 3. (The reply came:) "March forth with My servants by night, for you are sure to be pursued. And leave the sea as a furrow (divided), for they are a host (destined) to be drowned." 4. How many were the gardens and springs they left behind—and fields of grain and noble buildings and wealth (and conveniences of life), wherein they had taken such delight! Thus (was their end)! We made other people inherit (those things)! Neither heaven nor earth shed a tear over them, nor were they given a respite (again).
		God delivered the Children of Israel **And chose them above all creatures**
6	44:030-033	We did deliver aforetime the Children of Israel from humiliating punishment inflicted by Pharaoh, for he was arrogant among inordinate transgressors. We chose them aforetime above the nations knowingly and granted them signs in which there was a manifest trial.

3 RESURRECTION AND ACCOUNTABILITY

3.1 The Resurrection and the Day of God's Judgment

Unbelievers do not abide by justice, and they try to benefit from the injustice done to others. Indeed, they say: "There is nothing beyond our first death, and we shall not be raised again (Qur'an

44:35)." The unbelievers of Makkah argued with the Messenger about whether there would be a resurrection, saying: "Then bring (back) our forefathers if what you say is true! (Qur'an 44:36)." About such people, God says: "What! Are they better than the people of Tubba and those who were before them? We destroyed them because they were guilty of sin (Qur'an 44:37)." Why do people need to be resurrected and their behavior and deeds judged? God says: "We created not the heavens, the earth, and all between them merely in sport. We created them not except for just ends, but most of them do not understand (Qur'an 44:38-39)." With regard to the Day of Judgment, God tells people: "Verily, the day of sorting out is the time appointed for all of them (Qur'an 44:40)." It is also said that on that day: "No protector can avail his client anything, and no help can they receive except such as receive Allah's mercy, for He is exalted in might, most merciful (Qur'an 44:41-42)."

3.2 People will be Judged according to the Divine Law

Human values as inspired by the human conscience and stressed in the divine guidance form the bases according to which people will be judged on the Day of Judgment. People will be divided into two separate categories according to their deeds in the world, and they will be rewarded accordingly: (1) those who were arrogant and corrupt, and (2) those who were the God-fearing. People are responsible for their deeds, and they will have to account for denying God or associating partners with Him.

As for the arrogant and corrupt people: "Verily the tree of Zaqqum will be the food of the sinful. Like molten brass, it will boil in their insides like the boiling of scalding water. (A voice will cry:) 'Seize him, and drag him into the midst of the blazing fire! Then pour over his head the penalty of boiling water. Taste (this)! Truly were you mighty, full of honor! Truly, this is what you used to doubt' (Qur'an 44:43-50). On the other hand, God-fearing people "(...will be) in a position of security among gardens and springs. Dressed in fine silk and in rich brocade, they will face each other. Moreover, We shall join them to fair women with beautiful, big, and lustrous eyes. There they can call for every kind of fruit in peace and security. Nor will they there taste death, except the first death, and He will preserve them from the penalty of the blazing fire as a bounty from your Lord! That will be the supreme achievement (Qur'an 44:51-57)."

3.3 Judgment, Accountability, and Rewards

People who disbelieve in the Hereafter think that this worldly life is the only life. They believe that people simply die in the course of time or just stop functioning suddenly due to age or some ailment. According to them, the body is not survived by any soul that might be seized and then breathed again into the human body some time in the future. The unbelievers of Makkah challenged the Messenger to prove there would be a resurrection by asking him to raise their ancestors back to life. They said this because they had never seen any dead person coming back to life and returning to the world. However, the lack of such experience doesn't prove that there is no resurrection. One might ask them if they really have knowledge that there is no other life after death and that souls are not seized but are annihilated?

Table 3: Resurrection and Accountability

No	Surah:Verses	Meanings
		Unbelievers think that Death will end the Life
1	45:024-025	They say: "What is there but our life in this world? We shall die and we live, and nothing but time can destroy us." But of that they have no knowledge; they merely conjecture. • When Our clear signs are rehearsed to them, their argument is nothing but this. They say, "Bring (back) our forefathers if what you say is true."
		People will be Raised for their Accountability
2	45:026-027	• Say: "It is Allah Who gives you life, then gives you death. Then He will gather you together for the Day of Judgment about which there is no doubt." But most men do not understand. To Allah belongs the dominion of the heavens and the earth and the day that the Hour of Judgment is established. That day will the dealers in falsehood perish.

551

CHAPTER 40

God Desires People to Excel in Life
FROM SURAH AL-AHQAF (46)

God criticized the misconceptions and arrogance of the unbelievers of Makkah. These corrupt leaders and their followers thought that this world was a purposeless place where they were not answerable to anyone. They were not inclined to believe that the Qur'an was the word of their Lord. They had an erroneous concept of apostleship, on the basis of which they were proposing strange criteria in judging the Messenger's claim. In their myopic view, one proof against the truth of Islam was that their elders, important chiefs of the tribes, and so-called leaders were not accepting it and that only a few young men, poor people, and slaves believed in it. They thought that the resurrection, life after death, and the rewards and punishments of the Hereafter were fabrications whose occurrence was absolutely impossible.

God tells people: "To all are (assigned) degrees according to the deeds that they (have done), and in order that (Allah) may recompense their deeds, and no injustice be done to them. And on the day that the unbelievers will be placed before the fire, (it will be said to them): 'You received your good things in the life of the world, and you took your pleasure out of them, but today shall you be recompensed with a penalty of humiliation, for that you were arrogant on earth without just cause and that you (ever) transgressed (Qur'an 46:19-20)."

1 DIVINE GUIDENCE TO FORM JUST COMMUNITIES

1.1 The Universal Law that God has put in Place
In Surah Al-Ahqaf, the unbelievers were warned that if they refuse to follow divine guidance, as given in the Qur'an and as elaborated by the Messenger, due to their prejudices and arrogance, they would only be preparing for their own doom. If most of society is corrupt and none is trying to improve, it

cannot be a society of or for humanity. Eventually, it may be destroyed from within. As such, currently corrupt communities should guard themselves against a social punishment that will engulf all their people, irrespective of the nature of their individual character and behavior.

Table 1.1: Guidance for Humankind and Jinn

No	Surah:Verses	Meanings
		God Created the Universe with Purpose and for a Limited Time
1	46:003	We created not the heavens and the earth and all between them but for just ends and for a term appointed, but those who reject faith turn away from that whereof they are warned.
		Jinns have also been Listening to and Propagating the Qur'an
2	46:029-032	Behold, We turned towards you a company of jinns (quietly) listening to the Qur'an. When they stood in the presence thereof, they said, "Listen in silence!" When the (reading) was finished, they returned to their people, to warn (them of their sins). 1. They said, "O our people! We have heard a book revealed after Moses, confirming what came before it. It guides (men) to the truth and to a straight path. 2. "O our people, hearken to the one who invites (you) to Allah, and believe in Him. He will forgive you your faults and deliver you from a penalty grievous. 3. "If any does not hearken to the one who invites (us) to Allah, he cannot frustrate (Allah's plan) on earth, and no protectors can he have besides Allah. Such men (wander) in manifest error.

1.2 What if the Universal Laws are the Truth?

The unbelievers said that the Qur'an has been forged. If that were true, then what about the history of other messengers of God and what about our conscience? Can they all have been forged? God tells us: "The same religion has He established for you as that which He enjoined on Noah, which We have sent by inspiration to you, and that which We enjoined on Abraham, Moses, and Jesus—namely, that you should remain steadfast in religion and make no divisions therein (Qur'an 42:13)." If the Qur'an is a lie, then what about the Book of Moses?

Table 1.2: Self-Interests and Arrogance cloud the Reasoning

No	Surah:Verses	Meanings
		Universal Laws are the Truths which cannot be Forged
3	46:007-008	When Our clear signs are rehearsed to them, the unbelievers say of the truth when it comes to them, "This is evident sorcery," or do they say, "He has forged it." • Say: "Had I forged it, then can you obtain no single (blessing) for me from Allah. He knows best of that whereof you talk (so glibly)! Enough is He for a witness between me and you! And He is oft-forgiving, most merciful.
		Self- Interest and Arrogance Cloud People's Ability to take Guidance
4	46:009-010	1. Say (O Messenger:) "I am no bringer of new-fangled doctrine among the messengers, nor do I know what will be done with me or with you. I follow but that which is revealed to me by inspiration. I am but a warner open and clear." 2. Say: "You see? If (this teaching) be from Allah, and you reject it, and a witness from among the Children of Israel testifies to its similarity (with earlier scripture) and has believed while you are arrogant, truly! Allah guides not a people unjust.
		History of Messengers and our Conscience testify to the Truth
5	46:011-014	1. The Unbelievers say of those who believe: "If (this message) were a good thing, (such men who we believe are lower in rank than we are) would not have gone to it first before us!" And seeing that they guide not themselves thereby, they will say, "This is an (old) falsehood." 2. Before this, was the Book of Moses as a guide and a mercy: And this Book confirms (it) in

		the Arabic tongue to admonish the unjust and as glad tidings to those who do right. Verily, those who say, "Our Lord is Allah," and remain firm (on that path)—on them shall be no fear, nor shall they grieve. Such shall be companions of the gardens, dwelling therein (forever)— a recompense for their (good) deeds.

1.3 Reasoning Leads to the One God, the Creator

God gave people reasoning and wisdom so that they should control and regulate their selfish desires with reasoning. However, some people use their intellect to justify the fulfillment of their self-interests and arrogance. In the sight of God, such people are the lowest of the low. "We have indeed created man in the best of molds; then do We abase him (to be) the lowest of the low—except such as believe and do righteous deeds, for they shall have a reward unfailing (Qur'an 95:4-6)."

Table 1.3: Unbiased Reasoning Leads to the Truth

No	Surah:Verses	Meanings
		Only God Created the Earth and Heavens
6	46:004	Say: "Do you see what it is you invoke besides Allah? Show me what it is they have created on earth, or have they a share in the heavens? Bring me a book (revealed) before this or any remnant of knowledge (you may have), if you are telling the truth."
		False Deities are not aware that People Worship Them
7	46:005-006	• And who is more astray than one who invokes, besides Allah, such as will not answer him to the Day of Judgment, and who (in fact) are unconscious of their call (to them)? • And when mankind are gathered together (at the resurrection), they will be hostile to them and reject their worship (altogether).

1.4 Universal Laws are for the Benefit of Humanity

The laws of nature that Allah has set in operation favor no one over another. When the believers fall short of meeting any of these laws, they have to suffer the consequences. The fact that they are Muslims and believers does not mean that the laws of nature are suspended or abrogated for their sake. God has made the triumph of the truth a natural law similar to that of the creation of the heavens and the earth and the succession of night and day. It may be slow in coming, but this is only due to ensuring the fulfillment of certain goals. However, the law remains in operation, and God's promise will be fulfilled. Indeed, no one's faith is complete unless one believes in its certainty. People should know that God's promise will be fulfilled at an appointed time that will neither be hastened nor delayed.

When a society is established on hard work, truth, justice, and charity, and when it is almost free of corruption, discrimination, exploitation, and oppression, then peace and prosperity follow. This can only be achieved by following the moral and sociopolitical laws as given in the Qur'an. Further, success in the life to come greatly depends on one's efforts to improve the life in this world. God administers absolute justice, and His Laws have spontaneous consequences. It is the choice we make, knowing well that all actions, both good and bad, have appropriate consequences.

Table 1.4: Violation of the Divine Laws has its Consequences

No	Surah:Verses	Meanings
		'Ad were destroyed because they rejected the Divine Laws
8	46:021-023	Mention (Hud) one of 'Ad's (own) brethren. Behold, he warned his people about the winding sand tracts, but there have been warners before him and after him. "Worship none other than Allah. Truly, I fear for you the penalty of a mighty day." 1. They said: "Have you come in order to turn us aside from our gods? Then bring upon us the (calamity) with which you do threaten us, if you are telling the truth. 2. He said: "The knowledge (of when it will come) is only with Allah. I proclaim to you the mission on which I have been sent, but I

556

		see that you are a people in ignorance."
		'Ad could not Foresee **the Arrival of their Destruction**
9	46:024-026	Then, when they saw the (penalty in the shape of) a cloud traversing the sky, coming to meet their valleys, they said: "This cloud will give us rain!" Nay, it is the (calamity) you were asking to be hastened—a wind wherein is a grievous penalty! Everything will it destroy by the command of its Lord! Then by the morning, they—nothing was to be seen but (the ruins of) their houses! Thus do We recompense those given to sin. 1. We had firmly established them in a (prosperity and) power that We have not given to you (O Quraysh), and We had endowed them with (faculties of) hearing, seeing, heart, and intellect. 2. But of no profit to them were their (faculties of) hearing, sight, and heart and intellect when they went on rejecting the signs of Allah, and they were (completely) encircled by that at which they used to mock.
		God Repeated the Guidance **So the People may Reform**
10	46:027-028	We destroyed aforetime populations round about you, and We have shown the signs in various ways that they may turn (to Us). 1. Why then was no help forthcoming to them from those whom they worshiped as gods, besides Allah, as a means of access (to Allah)? 2. Nay, they failed them, but that was their falsehood and their invention.

2 PEOPLE ARE HARDWORKING AND JUST

2.1 Corruption is Alien to Human Nature

People are rewarded according to their behavior and deeds. People are told: "To all are (assigned) degrees according to the deeds that they (have done) and in order that (Allah) may recompense their deeds, and no injustice be done to them (Qur'an 46:19)." They will also be rewarded in the Hereafter according to their behavior and deeds on earth. "On the day that the unbelievers will be placed before the fire, (it will be said to them): 'You received your good things in the life of the world, and you took your pleasure out of them, but today you shall be recompensed with a penalty of humiliation, for that you were arrogant on earth without just cause and that you transgressed (Qur'an 46:20)."

Table 2: People Benefit from Good Deeds in their Lives

No	Surah:Verses	Meanings
		God Commands **people to Be Nice and Do Good**
1	46:015-016	1. We have enjoined on man kindness to his parents. In pain did his mother bear him, and in pain did she give him birth. The carrying of the (child) to his weaning is (a period of) thirty months. At length, when he reaches the age of full strength and attains forty years, he says: 2. "O my Lord! Grant me that I may be grateful for Your favor that You has bestowed upon me, and upon both my parents, and that I may work righteousness such as You may approve, and be gracious to me in my issue. Truly have I turned to You, and truly do I bow (to You) in Islam." Such are they from whom We shall accept the best of their deeds and pass by their ill deeds. (They shall be) among the companions of the garden—a promise of truth that was made to them (in this life).
		Unbelievers deny Hereafter and Accountability
2	46:017-018	3. But (there is one) who says to his parents, "Fie on you! Do you hold out the promise to me that I shall be raised up, even though generations have passed before me (without rising)?" They two seek Allah's aid (and rebuke the son): "Woe to you! Have faith, for the promise of Allah is true." But he says: "This is nothing but tales of the ancients." Such are they against whom is proved the sentence among the previous generations of jinns

		and men that have passed away, for they will be (utterly) lost.
		God Who can Create is Capable to Resurrect
3	46:033-034	Don't they see that Allah, Who created the heavens and the earth, and never wearied with their creation, is able to give life to the dead? Yea, verily, He has power over all things. 4. On the day that the unbelievers will be placed before the fire, (they will be asked,) "Is this not the truth?" 5. They will say: "Yea, by our Lord!" (One will say:) Then taste you the penalty, for that you were wont to deny (truth).

2.2 To Convey the Truth requires Efforts and Patience

The numerous false gods and the selfish desires that people worship make it very difficult for anyone to motivate people to be just, honest, and hardworking individuals who are content and willing to give up what does not belong to them. However difficult it may be, it is absolutely essential that efforts should continue for the improvement of human character and society. The alternative would be a society full of corruption, discrimination, exploitation, and oppression. In Surah Al-Ahqaf, God commands people: "Therefore, patiently persevere, as did (all) messengers of inflexible purpose, and be in no haste about the (unbelievers). On the day that they see the (punishment) promised them, (it will be) as if they had not tarried more than an hour in a single day. (Your duty is) to proclaim the message, but shall any be destroyed except those who transgress (Qur'an 46:35)?"

CHAPTER 41

In the Defense of Truth and Justice
FROM SURAH MUHAMMAD (47)

God commands people: "Keep up the balance with justice, and do not make the measure deficient (Qur'an 55:9)." This is because injustice and corruption must bear their inevitable fruit. The wrongdoers don't suffer because God is unjust or cruel to them, nor are they made to suffer as a deterrent to others. They suffer because their own evil deeds bear their inevitable fruit.

1 EVERY DEED HAS ITS INEVITABLE CONSEQUENCE

1.1 The Doctrine of Works and their Fruits

People are commanded to be just and avoid injustice. Such people will be told on the Day of Judgment: "O My servants! No fear shall be on you that day, nor shall you grieve—(being) those who have believed in Our signs and bowed (their wills to Ours) in Islam. You enter the garden, you and your wives, in (beauty and) rejoicing. To them will be passed round dishes and goblets of gold. There will be there all that the souls could desire, all that their eyes could delight in, and you shall abide therein (forever). Such will be the garden of which you are made heirs for your deeds (in life). You shall have therein abundance of fruit from which you shall have satisfaction (Qur'an 43: 68-73)."

According to the doctrine of works and their fruits, evil deeds must bear their inevitable fruit. "Not your desires nor those of the People of the Book (can prevail). Whoever works evil will be requited accordingly. Nor will he find, besides Allah, any protector or helper. If any do deeds of righteousness—be they male or female—and have faith, they will enter Heaven, and not the least injustice will be done to them (Qur'an 4:123-124)." Since evil deeds, like good deeds, must bear their inevitable fruit, people who do wrong suffer accordingly. However, God's grace is ever ready to offer opportunities for repentance and forgiveness. Unfortunately, unbelievers reject these opportunities and are unjust to themselves.

Table 1.1: God Shall Render their Deeds Ineffective

No	Surah:Verses	Meanings
		Disbelievers people away from Belief
1	47:001	Those who reject Allah and hinder (men) from the path of Allah—their deeds will Allah render astray (from their mark).
		Not so for those who believe and do Good
2	47:002	But those who believe and work deeds of righteousness and believe in the (revelation) sent down to Muhammad—for it is the truth from their Lord—He will remove from them their ills and improve their condition.
		Why God Renders their Deeds Ineffective
3	47:003	This (is) because those who reject Allah follow vanities, while those who believe follow the truth from their Lord. Thus does Allah set forth for men their lessons by similitude.

1.2 Their Evil Deeds Destroyed People in the Past

If not checked, corruption can destroy contemporary communities, just as it did communities in the past. A community should not think that it is superior to all that went before it. We may be heirs to all the progress in history, but this is no reason for arrogance. Rather, it adds to our responsibilities. When one reflects on past civilizations, how they flourished in people and prosperity, what opportunities they were given, and how they perished when they disobeyed God's laws, one feels a sense of humility and realizes that it was rebellion and selfish behavior that brought them down. God was more than just; He was also merciful. However, they brought their own ruin by ignoring God's moral and sociopolitical laws.

Table 1.2: God was not Unjust; they themselves were Unjust

No	Surah:Verses	Meanings
		People of Moses Rebelled to Harm Themselves
4	2:057	1. We gave you the shade of clouds and sent down to you manna and quails, saying: "Eat of the good things We have provided for you," (but they rebelled). To us they did no harm, but they harmed their own selves.
		Deniers of the Truth only Wrong Themselves
5	3:116-117	2. Those who reject faith—neither their possessions nor their (numerous) progeny will avail them anything against Allah. They will be companions of the fire, dwelling therein (forever). What they spend in the life of this (material) world may be likened to a wind that brings a nipping frost. It strikes and destroys the harvest of men who have wronged their own selves. It is not Allah that has wronged them, but they wrong themselves.
		The Unjust People of Noah, 'Ad, and Thamud
6	9:070	3. Has not the story reached them of those before them—the people of Noah and 'Ad and Thamud, the people of Abraham, the men of Midian, and the cities overthrown? To them came their messengers with clear signs. It is not Allah Who wrongs them, but they wrong their own selves.
		False Deities did not Profit Them
7	11:100-101	4. These are some of the stories of communities that We relate unto you. Of them, some are standing, and some have been mown down (by the sickle of time). It was not We that wronged them; they wronged their own selves. The deities other than Allah whom they invoked profited them no whit when there issued the decree of your Lord. Nor did they add anything but perdition.
		The Evil Results of their Deeds Overtook Them
8	16:033-034	5. Do the (ungodly) wait until the angels come to them or there comes the command of your Lord (for their doom)? So did those who went before them. But Allah wronged them not. Nay, they wronged their own selves. But the

		evil results of their deeds overtook them, and that very (wrath) at which they had scoffed hemmed them in.
		Evil in the Extreme will End those who do Evil
9	30:009-010	6. Do they not travel through the earth and see what was the end of those before them? They were superior to them in strength. They tilled the soil and populated it in greater numbers than these have done. There came to them their messengers with clear (signs). It was not Allah Who wronged them, but they wronged their own souls. In the long run, evil in the extreme will be the end of those who do evil, for that they rejected the signs of Allah and held them up to ridicule.

2 FIGHTING FOR THE TRUTH IS AN OBLIGATION

2.1 Fight with Those Who Fight With You

There were only a handful of Muslims in Madinah, and they could not gather even a thousand soldiers. Yet, they were being urged to take up the sword and clash against the entire pagan forces of Arabia. In addition, the kind of the weapons needed to equip Muslim soldiers for war could hardly be afforded by the town in which hundreds of emigrants were still homeless and unsettled. People were starving at that time because they were boycotted economically by the Arabs on all sides. Such were the conditions when Surah Muhammad was revealed and the Muslims were given initial instructions for war. They were assured of God's help and guidance, were given hope for the best rewards for offering sacrifices in the cause of God, and were assured that their struggle in the cause of truth would not go to waste. They were told that they would be abundantly rewarded both in this world and in the Hereafter.

Table 2.1: Fight for Your Values and Freedom

No	Surah:Verses	Meanings
		God Guides the Believers and Improve their Condition
1	47:004-007	1. Therefore, when you meet the unbelievers (in war), smite at their necks. At length, when you have thoroughly subdued them, bind a bond firmly (on them). Thereafter (is the time for) either generosity or ransom, until the war lays down its burdens. 2. Thus (are you commanded). But if it had been Allah's will, He could certainly have exacted retribution from them (Himself), but (He lets you fight) in order to test you, some with others. But those who are slain in the way of Allah—He will never let their deeds be lost. 3. Soon will He guide them and improve their condition, and admit them to the garden that He has announced for them. O you who believe! If you will aid Allah, He will aid you, and plant your feet firmly.
		Corruption will be the Fate of those who reject Guidance
2	47:008-011	But those who reject (Allah)—for them is destruction, and (Allah) will render their deeds astray (from their mark). 1. That is because they hate the revelation of Allah. So He has made their deeds fruitless. Do they not travel through the earth and see what was the end of those before them (who did evil)? Allah brought utter destruction on them, and similar (fates await) those who reject Allah. 2. That is because Allah is the protector of those who believe, but those who reject Allah have no protector.
		Corruption destroyed in the Past and can destroy in the Future
3	47:013-014	And how many cities, with more power than your city, which has driven you out, have We destroyed (for their sins)? And there was none to aid them. • What! Is then one who is on a clear (path) from his Lord no better than one to whom the

		evil of his conduct seems pleasing, and such as follow their own lusts?
		Living under Guidance is not the Same as indulging in Selfish Desires.
4	47:012	• Verily, Allah will admit those who believe and do righteous deeds to gardens beneath which rivers flow, while those who reject Allah will enjoy (this world) and eat as cattle eat, and the fire will be their abode.
	47:015	• (Here is) a parable of the garden that the righteous are promised. In it are rivers of water incorruptible, rivers of milk of which the taste never changes, rivers of wine, a joy to those who drink, and rivers of honey pure and clear. In it there are for them all kinds of fruits and grace from their Lord. (Can those in such bliss) be compared to such as shall dwell forever in the fire and be given to drink boiling water, so that it cuts up their bowels (to pieces)?

2.2 Fight for the Knowledge and the Wisdom

Divine guidance is for the welfare of people. It encompasses rules and regulation, which if followed, result in better individual behavior and prosperous societies. Islam provides such knowledge. It is from religion and our conscience that we learn what is right and what is wrong, what is good and what is bad, and what is beneficial and what is harmful. Therefore, it is our duty to learn because, "Those who are firmly grounded in knowledge say: 'We believe in the Book; the whole of it is from our Lord,' and none will grasp the message except men of understanding (Qur'an 3:7)."

Table 2.2: Only the Ignorant follow their Low Desires

No	Surah:Verses	Meanings
		Those Blessed with knowledge and Ignorant
5	47:016-017	1. Among them are men who listen to you, but in the end, when they go out from you, they say to those who have received knowledge, "What is it he said just then?" Such are men whose hearts Allah has sealed and who follow their own lusts.

		2. But to those who receive guidance, He increases the (light of) guidance and bestows on them their piety and restraint (from evil).
		People should Know that there is no god but God
6	47:019	Know, therefore, that there is no god but Allah. Ask forgiveness for your fault and for the men and women who believe, for Allah knows how you move about and how you dwell in your homes.

2.3 Fight with Courage and don't be Miserly

The believers have been commanded to spend their resources in the defense of truth and justice. Although they may be economically weak, the problem they confront is the very survival of Islam and of Muslims. This demands that Muslims should not only risk their lives for safeguarding themselves and their faith from the dominance of disbelief and corruption, but they should also expend their economic resources as far as possible in preparation for war. Miserliness at such times would not harm God at all, but it would result in their own destruction. If people shirk sacrificing for that in which they believe, they will eventually be removed and replaced by another group of people. The descendants of a corrupt people will have to reform to improve their condition.

Table 2.3: Fight to Eliminate Corruption and Oppression

No	Surah:Verses	Meanings
		Be not Weary and Faint-hearted, Crying for Peace
7	47:035-037	• Be not weary and faint-hearted, crying for peace, when you should be uppermost, for Allah is with you and will never put you in loss for your (good) deeds. The life of this world is but play and amusement, and if you believe and guard against evil, He will grant you your recompense and will not ask you (to give up) your possessions. If He were to ask you for all of them and press you, you would covetously withhold, and He would bring out all your ill feeling.
		If you turn back, God will bring another People
8	47:038	1. Behold, you are those invited to spend (of your substance) in the way of Allah, but

566

		among you are some that are miserly.
		2. But any who are miserly are so at the expense of their own souls. But Allah is free of all wants, and it is you who are needy.
		3. If you turn back (from the path), He will substitute in your stead another people; then they would not be like you.

2.4 Fight with Courage and be not Hypocritical

The hypocrites, posing as sincere believers, conspired with the unbelievers to save themselves from the hazards of war. Such hypocrites were plainly warned that no act and deed of those who adopt hypocrisy is acceptable to God. The basic issue against which all those who profess faith are being tried is whether they are on the side of truth or falsehood? Are one's sympathies with Islam and the Muslims or with disbelief and the unbelievers? Does one keep one's own self-interests dearer or the truth that one professes to believe in and follow? One who fails in this test is not a believer. In such a case, one's prayers, fasting, and other duties as a believer deserve no reward from God.

Table 2.4: God will make null the Deeds of the Hypocrites

No	Surah:Verses	Meanings
		Attitude of the Hypocrites about Fighting
9	47:020-023	Those who believe say: "Why is not a Surah sent down (for us)?" 1. But when a Surah of basic or categorical meaning is revealed, and fighting is mentioned therein, you will see those in whose hearts is a disease looking at you with a look of one in swoon at the approach of death. 2. But more fitting for them were it to obey and say what is just, and when a matter is resolved, it were best for them if they were true to Allah. 3. Then, is it to be expected of you, if you were put in authority, that you will do mischief in the land and break your ties of kith and kin! Such are the men whom Allah has cursed, for He has made them deaf and blinded their sight.
		God has made null the deeds of the Hypocrites

567

10	47:024-029	Do they not then earnestly seek to understand the Qur'an, or are their hearts locked up by them? 1. Those who turn back as apostates after guidance was clearly shown to them—Satan has instigated them and busied them up with false hopes. 2. This, because they said to those who hate what Allah has revealed, We will obey you in part of (this) matter; but Allah knows their (inner) secrets. • But how (will it be) when the angels take their souls at death, and smite their faces and their backs. This because they followed that which called forth the wrath of Allah, and they hated Allah's good pleasure. So He made their deeds of no effect. Or do those in whose hearts is a disease think that Allah will not bring to light their entire rancor?
		God will know who exert hard and are patient
11	47:030-032	• Had We so willed, We could have shown them up to you, and you should have known them by their marks. But surely you will know them by the tone of their speech, and Allah knows all that you do. And We shall try you until We test those among you who strive their utmost and persevere in patience, and We shall try your reported (mettle). Those who reject Allah, hinder (men) from the path of Allah, and resist the Messenger after guidance has been clearly shown to them will not injure Allah in the least, but He will make their deeds of no effect.

CHAPTER 42

The Birth of an Islamic State
FROM SURAH AL-FATH (48)

Surah Al-Fath was revealed in the lunar month of Dhul-Qadah, 6 A.H., during the return journey to Madinah after concluding the truce of Hudaibiyah with the unbelievers of Makkah. The truce of Hudaibiyah has been rightly declared as "the victory" in this Surah. Because of this treaty, the existence of the Islamic state in Arabia was duly recognized for the first time. The Quraysh recognized Islam as one of the religions of Arabia by allowing pilgrimage to the Muslims. A truce between the Muslims of Madinah and the pagans of Makkah provided full peace for the Muslims. Within two years after the truce, the number of conversions to Islam far exceeded the conversions of the previous 19 years. Whereas on the occasion of the truce of Hudaibiyah the Muslim force was only 1,400 men, two years later, in response to a violation of this treaty by the Quraysh, Makkah was invaded by an army of about 10,000 Muslims. The truce of Hudaibiyah had given the Muslims their own political identity.

1 ISLAM, THE SOCIOPOLITICAL SYSTEM

1.1 A Society Built on Islamic Principles
One of the main objectives of Islam is to establish communities based on justice. In Surah Ar-Rahman, God, describing the basic principle that governs the universe, commands that people should respect this principle: "The sky, He raised it high, and He has set up the balance (of justice), in order that you may not transgress the balance. So establish weight with justice, and fall not short in the balance (Qur'an 55:7-9)." The suspension of hostilities by the Quraysh after the treaty of Hudaibiyah provided an opportunity to establish and strengthen Islamic society into a fully functioning civilization based on Islamic principles. Being assured of peace from the south, the Muslims overpowered all opponent forces in the north and in central Arabia. Just three months after the treaty, Khaiber, a major stronghold of rebellious

Jews, was conquered. Within two years of the treaty, the balance of power in Arabia shifted from the Quraysh to the Muslims.

Table 1.1: A Clear Victory, God's Forgiveness, and Help

No	Surah:Verses	Meanings
		Victory with God's Forgiveness, Help and Faith
1	48:001-004	Verily, We have granted you a manifest victory 1. That Allah may forgive you your faults of the past and those to follow, fulfill His favor to you, and guide you on the straight way— 2. That Allah may help you with powerful help. It is He Who sent down tranquility into the hearts of the believers 3. That they may add faith to their faith, For to Allah belong the forces of the heavens and the earth, and Allah is full of knowledge and wisdom.
		Victory to Reward Believing Men and Women
2	48:005-007	4. That He may admit the men and women who believe to gardens beneath which rivers flow, to dwell therein forever, and remove their ills from them. And that is, in the sight of Allah, the highest achievement (for man). 5. That He may punish the hypocrites, men and women, and the polytheists, men and women, who imagine an evil opinion of Allah. On them is a round of evil; the wrath of Allah is on them. He has cursed them and got Hell ready for them, and evil is it for a destination. For to Allah belong the forces of the heavens and the earth, and Allah is exalted in power, full of wisdom.

1.2 A Society Built on Mutual Help and Respect

Faith and mutual help go hand in hand. God tells the Messenger: "(O Messenger), We have truly sent you as a witness, as a bringer of glad tidings, and as a warner (Qur'an 48:8)." At the same time, God tells people that He has sent the Messenger: "In order that you (O people) may believe in Allah and His Messenger, that you may assist and honor Him and celebrate His praise morning and evening. Verily, those who plight their fealty to you do no less than plight their fealty to Allah; the hand of

Allah is over their hands. Therefore, anyone who violates his oath, does so to the harm of his own soul, and anyone who fulfills what he has covenanted with Allah, Allah will soon grant him a great reward (Qur'an 48:9-10)." This all comes down to: (1) respecting God by believing and serving Him as He desires; and (2) respecting the *Sunnah* of the Messenger by developing an Islamic society in which the rights of each other are respected.

2 GOD HELPS THOSE WHO FOLLOW HIS COMMANDS

2.1 Believers Get their Courage and Reward from God

Believers do good deeds, as God have commanded, and do not follow pursuits that are prohibited by Him. Dedicated to their cause, they do not worry too much about their safety. This practice gives them confidence and makes them courageous. They draw their peace and reward from God. He sends down tranquility to them and rewards them with victories. This has been illustrated by the example of those who swore allegiance to the Messenger.

Table 2.1: Those Who Swore Allegiance to the Messenger

No	Surah:Verses	Meanings
		God rewarded Believers with a speedy Victory
1	48:018-019	Allah's good pleasure was on the believers when they swore fealty to you under the tree. He knew what was in their hearts, so He sent down tranquility to them, and He rewarded them with a speedy victory. Many gains will they acquire (besides), and Allah is exalted in power, full of wisdom.
		God Promised the Believers Additional Gains
2	48:020-021	Allah has promised you many gains that you shall acquire, and He has given you these beforehand. And He has restrained the hands of men from you that it may be a sign for the believers and that He may guide you to a straight path. And other gains that are not within your power, but which Allah has compassed. Allah has power over all things.

2.2 God has His Own Divine Ways to Accomplish His Will

The believers would have certainly been successful if a battle has happened instead of the truce at Hudaibiyah. It did not occur because God desired to save those potential believers who were living among the unbelievers of Makkah. The believers in general were satisfied when they heard this divine revelation, and the advantages of this treaty began to appear over time, one after the other, until every one became fully convinced that this peace treaty was indeed a great victory:

Table 2.2: Unbelievers Cannot Expect God's Help

No	Surah:Verses	Meanings
		Those who Disbelieve will certainly be Defeated
3	48:022-023	If the unbelievers should fight you, they would certainly turn their backs. Tthen would they find neither protector nor helper. (Such has been) the practice (approved) of Allah already in the past: no change will you find in the practice of Allah.
		Divine Justification for the truce of Hudaibiyah
4	48:024-026	It is He Who has restrained their hands from you and your hands from them in the midst of Makkah. After that, He gave you the victory over them, and Allah sees well all that you do. • They are the ones who denied revelation and hindered you from the Sacred Mosque and the sacrificial animals, detained from reaching their place of sacrifice. • Had there not been believing men and believing women whom you did not know that you were trampling down, and on whose account a crime would have accrued to you without (your) knowledge, (Allah would have allowed you to force your way, but He held back your hands) that He may admit to His mercy whom He will. 1. If they had been apart, We should certainly have punished the unbelievers among them with a grievous punishment. 2. While the unbelievers got up in their hearts pride and haughtiness—the pride and haughtiness of the time of ignorance, Allah sent down His tranquility to his Messenger

		and to the believers, and made them stick close to the command of self-restraint, and well were they entitled to it and worthy of it. And Allah has full knowledge of all things.
		God has His Own Divine Ways to Accomplish His Will
5	48:027	Truly did Allah fulfill the vision for His Messenger. You shall enter the Sacred Mosque, if Allah wills, with minds secure, heads shaved, hair cut short, and without fear, For He knew what you knew not. And He granted, besides this, a speedy victory.

3 THE BELIEVERS AND THE HYPOCRITES

Although there are two broad types of people in the world, i.e., the believers and unbelievers, there is a subgroup of so-called believers, i.e., the hypocrites. This latter type surfaced during the journey to perform Umrah (the lesser pilgrimage to Makkah) in the company of the Messenger. Although invited to accompany the Messenger, some tribes failed to participate in the journey and made excuses in order to avoid the journey's inherent danger and the possibility of conflict.

3.1 The Description of the Believers

The true practitioners of all monotheistic religions, whether that religion is Islam, Judaism, or Christianity, share certain behavior traits and moral values that they find embedded in their scriptures. For Muslims, Surah Al-Fath lists specific traits and behaviors that are indicative of true believers.

Table 3.1: The Character and Deeds of the Believers

No	Surah:Verses	Meanings
		God Sent Messengers and Guidance for People
1	48:028	It is He Who has sent His Messenger with guidance and the religion of truth, to proclaim it over all religion. And enough is Allah for a witness.
		Character, and the Behavior of the Believers
2	48:029	Muhammad is the messenger of Allah, and those

| | | who are with him
1. (They) are strong against unbelievers,
2. (But) compassionate among each other.
3. You will see them bow and prostrate themselves (in prayer),
4. Seeking grace from Allah and (His) good pleasure.
5. On their faces are their marks, (being) the traces of their prostration.
• This is their similitude in the Torah, and their similitude in the gospel is like a seed that sends forth its blade, then makes it strong. It then becomes thick, and it stands on its own stem, (filling) the sowers with wonder and delight. As a result, it fills the unbelievers with rage at them.
Allah has promised those among them who believe and do righteous deeds forgiveness and a great reward. |

3.2 The Description of the Hypocrites

Perhaps nothing is more hateful to Islam and Muslims than hypocrisy. This is due to the fact that a hypocrite is not merely a habitual liar, he is a person who thinks that he can easily deceive people and get away with it. He imagines that nobody can see through him. When hypocrisy is focused on faith, with the hypocrite claiming to be a believer when he truly does not believe, then such a hypocrite imagines that he can even deceive God. Thus, he makes fun of God's knowledge and power. "Of the people, there are some who say: 'We believe in Allah and the Last Day,' but they do not (really) believe. They desire to deceive Allah and those who believe, but they only deceive themselves and realize (it) not! In their hearts is a disease, and Allah has increased their disease. Grievous is the penalty they (incur) because they are false (Qur'an 2:8-10)." In Surah Al-Fath, people are told that the hypocrites say what is not in their hearts and are still unbelievers. God tells them that they will get opportunities to demonstrate their belief. If they are truly sincere, they will earn a good reward, and if turn back as they turned back before, He will punish them with a painful punishment.

Table 3.2: Hypocrites Argue to hide what is in their Hearts

No	Surah:Verses	Meanings
		Hypocrites say what is not in their hearts.
3	48:011-012	The desert Arabs who lagged behind will say to you: "We were engaged in (looking after) our flocks and herds, and our families. Do then ask forgiveness for us." They say with their tongues what is not in their hearts. • Say: "Who then has any power at all (to intervene) on your behalf with Allah if His will is to give you some loss or to give you some profit? But Allah is well acquainted with all that you do. Nay, you thought that the Messenger and the believers would never return to their families. This seemed pleasing in your hearts, and you conceived an evil thought, for you are a people lost (in wickedness)."
		Hypocrites will be provided Opportunities.
4	48:015-016	Those who lagged behind (will say) when you (are free to) march and take booty (in war): "Permit us to follow you." They wish to change Allah's decree. • Say: "Not thus will you follow us. Allah has already declared (this) beforehand." Then they will say, "But you are jealous of us." Nay, but little do they understand. • Say to the desert Arabs who lagged behind: "You shall be summoned (to fight) against a people given to vehement war. Then shall you fight, or they shall submit. "Then if you show obedience, Allah will grant you a goodly reward, "But if you turn back as you did before, He will punish you with a grievous penalty."

CHAPTER 43

Humanity Without Justice Is Tyranny
FROM SURAH AR-RAHMAN (55)

According to traditions, Surah Ar-Rahman was revealed quite early at Makkah and even before Surah Al-Ahqaf, which was revealed after the incident of the jinns listening to the Qur'an had occurred. This incident occurred during the Prophet's return journey from Ta'if to Makkah, which happened three years before the *Hijrah*. God tells people in Surah Ar-Rahman that He has established the entire system of the universe precisely and equitably on justice. This system requires that people adhere to justice within the bounds of their authority and should not disturb the balance. Abu Dharr reported that the Messenger said that God said: "My servants, I have made oppression unlawful for Me and unlawful for you, so do not commit oppression against one another (Sahih Muslim: 32.6246)." Both humankind and jinn, who are the other creation living on the earth and endowed with freedom of will and action, have been addressed in this Surah. They are made to realize the wonders of God's power, His countless blessings, and their own helplessness and accountability before Him. They are warned about the bad consequences of disobeying Him and told about the good results that follow from obeying Him.

1 THE JINN AND THE HUMANKIND

1.1 The Jinns, another Creation with Free Will
At several places in the Qur'an, there are clear pointers to show that the jinn are a creation endowed with freedom of will and action. They are also accountable for their character and behavior. Like humankind, jinn believe or disbelieve in the messengers and Books revealed by God. In Surah Ar-Rahman, it is confirmed that the message of the Qur'an is for both humankind and jinn and that both will be judged and rewarded according to their belief and behavior.

576

Table 1.1: Like People, Jinn are endowed with Free Will

No	Surah:Verses	Meanings
		Jinn and Men were created to serve God
1	06:130	• O you assembly of jinns and men! Came there not unto you messengers from among you, setting forth unto you My signs and warning you of the meeting of this day of yours? They will say: "We bear witness against ourselves." It was the life of this world that deceived them. So against themselves will they bear witness that they rejected faith.
	51:056	I have only created jinns and men that they may serve Me.
		God created Men and Jinn from Clay and Fire
2	15:026-027	We created man from sounding clay, from mud molded into shape, and the jinn race, We had created before from the fire of a scorching wind.
		The Qur'an is to Guide both Men and Jinn
3	17:088	1. Say: "If the whole of mankind and jinns were to gather together to produce the like of this Qur'an, they could not produce the like thereof, even if they backed up each other with help and support."
	46:029	2. Behold, We turned towards you a company of jinns (quietly) listening to the Qur'an. When they stood in the presence thereof, they said, "Listen in silence!" When the (reading) was finished, they returned to their people to warn (them of their sins).
	72:001	3. Say: "It has been revealed to me that a company of jinns listened (to the Qur'an). They said, 'We have really heard a wonderful recital.'"
		Interaction between People and Unbelieving Jinn
4	18:050	Behold! We said to the angels, "Bow down to Adam." They bowed down, except *Iblis*. He was one of the jinns, and he broke the command of his Lord. Will you then take him and his progeny as protectors rather than Me? They are enemies to you! Evil would be the exchange for the wrongdoers!

1.2 God Preferred Humankind as His Trustee on Earth

Equipped with conscience, intellect, free will, and God's guidance, people have been assigned to be God's trustees on earth, serving Him, implementing His commands in managing their affairs, and building a just human society in the world. This task will eventually be evaluated and compensated for how well it was performed. God states in the Qur'an: "That which is on earth we have made but as a glittering show for the earth, in order that We may test them, as to which of them are best in conduct (Qur'an 18:7)." Although God created jinn before humankind, God preferred humankind as His trustee. Being God's trustee on earth, only humankind is addressed in the beginning of Surah Ar-Rahman. Besides, the messengers and the divine books belong to humankind. Yet, from verse 13 onward, both humans and jinns are addressed, and the same invitation is to both. Both will be resurrected and judged for their performance in their earthly lives, and both will be rewarded or punished for their conduct and deeds.

2 NONE CAN PROGRESS WITHOUT JUSTICE

2.1 Humankind with Free Will and Wisdom

The teaching of the Qur'an is from God, and it is the very demand of His mercy that He should provide guidance to humanity through this teaching, for it is He Who created people as rational and intelligent beings. In Surah Ar-Rahman, people are reminded that it is learning and reasoning that distinguish them from other creatures on earth: "(Allah) Most Gracious! It is He Who has taught the Qur'an. He has created man; he has taught him speech (and intelligence) (Qur'an 55:1-4)."

2.2 God Created the Universe on Justice

The universe is functioning under God's sovereignty, and everything in the earth and heavens is subject to His command alone. God has established the entire system of the universe precisely and equitably on justice, and the nature of this system requires that those who live in it should adhere to justice within the bounds of their authority and should not disturb the balance. "The sun and the moon follow courses (exactly) computed, and the vegetation and the trees both prostrate in adoration. The sky has He raised high, and He has set up the balance (of justice), in order that you may not transgress (due) balance. So establish weight with justice, and fall not short in the balance (Qur'an 55:5-9)."

3 JUSTICE, THE LAW OF HUMAN BEHAVIOR

3.1 Establish Justice under All Circumstances

The Messenger defines seven classes of people who will enjoy God's shelter on the Day of Judgment, when there is no shelter other than what He provides. The first of these is a just ruler. God commands the believers: "O you who believe! Stand out firmly for Allah, as witnesses to fair dealing, and let not the hatred of others to you make you swerve to wrong and depart from justice. Be just—that is next to piety, and fear Allah, for Allah is well acquainted with all that you do (Qur'an 5:8)." God has revealed several books throughout the history to guide humankind for the establishment of justice, including the Torah, the gospel given to Jesus, and the Qur'an.

"It was We who revealed the Torah (to Moses). Therein was guidance and light. By its standard have been judged the Jews, by the prophets who bowed to Allah's will, by the rabbis and the doctors of law—for to them was entrusted the protection of Allah's book, and they were witnesses thereto. Therefore, fear not men, but fear Me, and sell not My signs for a miserable price. If any do fail to judge by (the light of) what Allah has revealed, they are (no better than) unbelievers (Qur'an 5:44)."

"And in their footsteps, We sent Jesus, the son of Mary, confirming the Torah that had come before him. We sent him the gospel. Therein was guidance and light and confirmation of the Torah that had come before him—a guidance and an admonition to those who fear Allah. Let the people of the gospel judge by what Allah has revealed therein. If any do fail to judge by (the light of) what Allah has revealed, they are (no better than) those who rebel (Qur'an 5:46-47)."

"To you, We sent the scripture in truth, confirming the scripture that came before it, and guarding it in safety. So judge between them by what Allah has revealed, and follow not their vain desires, diverging from the truth that has come to you. To each among you have we prescribed a law and an open way. If Allah had so willed, He would have made you a single people, but (His plan is) to test you in what He has given you. So strive as in a race in all virtues... (Qur'an 5:48)."

Table 3.1: Justice, the Foundation of Human Society

No	Surah:Verses	Meaning
		Purpose and the Objectives of Divine Justice
1	5:049	Therefore, judge between them by what Allah has revealed, and follow not their vain desires, but beware of them lest they beguile thee from any of that (teaching) that Allah has sent down to you.
		Judge Among People by the Divine Law
2	4:105	We have sent down to you the Book in truth that you might judge between men, as guided by Allah. So be not (used) as an advocate by those who betray their trust.
	4:135	1. O you who believe! Stand out firmly for justice, as witnesses to Allah, even as against yourselves, or your parents, or your kin, and whether it be (against) rich or poor, for Allah can best protect both. Follow not the lusts (of your hearts), lest you swerve, and if you distort (justice) or decline to do justice, verily, Allah is well acquainted with all that you do.
	5:042	2. (They are fond of) listening to falsehood, of devouring anything forbidden. If they do come to you, either judge between them, or decline to interfere. If you decline, they cannot hurt you in the least. If you judge, judge in equity between them, for Allah loves those who judge in equity.
		Justice is a Prerequisite for Peace and Prosperity
3	5:066	1. If only they had stood fast by the Torah, the gospel, and all the revelation that was sent to them from their Lord, they would have enjoyed happiness from every side.
	7:029	2. Say: "My Lord has commanded justice and

		that you set your whole selves (to Him) at every time and place of prayer, and call upon Him, making your devotion sincere as in His sight. Such as He created you in the beginning, so shall you return."

3.2 Be Just When Speaking Even against Relatives

Within the context of blood relations, there lies a human weakness. People tend to think that family relations dictate mutual support in all situations. Hence, the Qur'an provides the necessary support so that a believer's conscience prompts him to say words of truth and justice, thinking only of his relationship with God. This gives him strength, which outweighs by far any support he may have from his relatives, as he places his obligation to God above his duties to his relatives. Further, God forbids people to take sides with those who are unjust and untrue.

Table 3.2: Be Just in Speach, and Plead not for the Unjust

No	Surah:Verses	Meanings
		Plead not for the Unjust and Corrupt
4	4:107-109	Contend not on behalf of such as betray their own souls, for Allah loves not one given to perfidy and crime. • They may hide (their crimes) from men, but they cannot hide (them) from Allah, seeing that He is in their midst when they plot by night, in words that He cannot approve. And Allah does compass round all that they do. • Ah! These are the sort of men on whose behalf you may contend in this world, but who will contend with Allah on their behalf on the Day of Judgment, or who will carry their affairs through?
		Whenever you speak, be True and Just
5	6:152	Whenever you speak, speak justly, even if a near relative is concerned, and fulfill the covenant of Allah. Thus does He command you that you may remember.

3.3 Do Not Defraud People, but Give Full Measure

Duties toward God cannot be over emphasized, but duties toward fellow human beings, which are equally important, are sometimes given a low position on the list of priorities in contemporary Muslim communities, both at the individual and community levels. Yet, a good balance is the main characteristic of Islam and its code of living. Likewise, little importance is sometimes given to a high-priority objective of Islam, i.e., the elimination of all injustice. Yet, voices that speak against injustice remain faint, even among Muslim scholars. On the other hand, much has been said and written about matters that cannot be described as being equally important. We should always remember that God may forgive us all sins that relate to our duties toward Him, but He will not forgive us anything that is due to a person until that person is ready to forgive it. Hence, balance between our duties to God and our duties to our fellow humans must be restored before we can truly claim to lead an Islamic life. God warns people: "Woe to the defrauders who, when they take the measure (of their dues) from people, take it fully, but when they measure out to others or weigh out for them, they are deficient. Do they think that they will not be called to account on a mighty day, a day when all humankind will stand before the Lord of the worlds (Qur'an 83:1-6)?"

Table 3.3: The Basic Principle of Dealings among People

No	Surah:Verses	Meanings
		God has appointed a Measure for Everything
6	25:002	1. He to whom belongs the dominion of the heavens and the earth—no son has He begotten, nor has He a partner in His dominion. It is He who created all things and ordered them in due proportions.
	54:049	2. Verily, all things have We created in proportion and measure.
	57:025	3. We sent aforetime our messengers with clear signs and sent down with them the Book and the balance (of right and wrong) that men may stand forth in justice.
	65:003	4. Verily, for all things has Allah appointed a due proportion.

		Security and Ownership of Personal Property
7	2:188	1. Do not eat up your property among yourselves for vanities, nor use it as bait for the judges, with intent that you may eat up wrongfully and knowingly a little of (other) people's property.
	6:152	2. Come not near to the orphan's property, except to improve it, until he attain the age of full strength. Give measure and weight with (full) justice.
		Defraud not - Give full Measure and Weight
8	7:085	1. (Shu'ayb said:) "Give just measure and weight. Nor withhold from the people the things that are their due, and do no mischief on the earth after it has been set in order. That will be best for you if you have faith."
	11:084-086	2. (Shu'ayb said:) "Give not short measure or weight. I see you in prosperity, but I fear for you the penalty of a day that will compass (you) all round. O my people! Give just measure and weight, nor withhold from the people the things that are their due. Commit not evil in the land with intent to do mischief. That which is left you by Allah is best for you if you (but) believed! But I am not set over you to keep watch."
	17:035	3. Give full measure when you measure, and weigh with a balance that is straight. That is the most fitting and the most advantageous in the final determination.
	26:181-083	4. (Shu'ayb said:) "Give just measure, and cause no loss (to others by fraud). And weigh with scales true and upright. And withhold not things justly due to men, nor do evil in the land, working mischief."

4 CONSCIENTIOUS PEOPLE ARE GRATEFUL

4.1 God Created the Earth to Flourish Life

In Surah Ar-Rahman, besides mentioning the wonders and excellences of God's might, reference is made to God's bounties, from which the jinn and humankind are deriving benefit. God repeatedly asks: "Then which of the favors of your Lord will you deny?" Of course, this makes it impossible for conscientious people to be anything but grateful to God.

Table 4.1: Creation of Life and how it is Sustained

No	Surah:Verses	Meanings
		God Created Soil and Vegetation to Sustain Life
1	55:010-018	1. It is He Who has spread out the earth for (His) creatures. Therein are fruits and date palms, producing spathes (enclosing dates)—also grain with (its) leaves and stalk for fodder, and fragrant plants. Then which of the favors of your Lord will you deny? 2. He created man from sounding clay like unto pottery, and He created Jinns from fire free of smoke. • Then which of the favors of your Lord will you deny? 3. (He is) Lord of the two Easts and Lord of the two Wests. Then which of the favors of your Lord will you deny?
		God Created Water to Sustain Life and Trade
2	55:019-025	1. He has let free the two bodies of flowing water, meeting together. Between them is a barrier that they do not transgress. Then which of the favors of your Lord will you deny? 2. Out of them come pearls and coral. Then which of the favors of your Lord will you deny? 3. His are the ships sailing smoothly through the seas, lofty as mountains. Then which of the favors of your Lord will you deny?

4.2 Life on Earth is for a Limited Time

Both humankind and jinn have been reminded that in this universe: (1) no one except God is immortal and imperishable; (2) from the lowest insects to the highest of humanity, everyone stands in need of God for their survival; and (3) from the earth to the heavens, whatever is happening is happening under God's administration and control. God tells people: "All that is on earth will perish, but the face of your Lord will abide (forever), full of majesty, bounty, and honor. Then which of the favors of your Lord will you deny? Of Him, every creature in the heavens and on earth seeks (its need). Every day in (new) splendor does He (shine)! Then which of the favors of your Lord will you deny (Qur'an 55:26-30)?"

5 ACCOUNTABILITY OF THE JUST AND CORRUPT

5.1 No Person can escape Accountability
Both humankind and jinn have been warned that the time is fast approaching when they will be called to account. They will not be able to avoid this; it is not in their power to run away from it. God challenges people and jinns in Surah Ar-Rahman: "Soon shall We settle your affairs, O both you worlds (man and jinn)...O you assembly of jinns and men! If it be you can pass beyond the zones of the heavens and the earth, pass you! Not without authority shall you be able to pass...On you will be sent (O you evil ones twain!) a flame of fire (to burn) and a smoke (to choke). No defense will you have (Qur'an 55:31, 33, 35)."

5.2 Accountability and Consequences for the Corrupt.
Accountability will be held on the Day of Judgment. This will be a day, "When the sky is rent asunder, and it becomes red like ointment (Qur'an 55:37)." On that day, all humans and jinn who have been guilty of disobeying God in this world will be punished in Hell, the same Hell that the guilty used to deny. "On that day no question will be asked of man or jinn as to his sin. Then which of the favors of your Lord will you deny? The sinners will be known by their marks, and they will be seized by their forelocks and their feet. Then which of the favors of your Lord will you deny? This is the Hell which the sinners deny. In its midst and in the midst of boiling hot water will they wander round! Then which of the favors of your Lord will you deny (Qur'an 55:39-45)."

5.3 Accountability and Reward for the Righteous

Various rewards and blessings will be granted to the righteous people and jinn who have led pious lives and lived in the world with a clear understanding that they would have to appear before their Lord and give an account of their deeds. These rewards have been most eloquently mentioned in Surah Ar-Rahman. It is a spirited address in which, after mentioning each of the wonders of God's great power and each of the blessings bestowed by Him, jinn and men are questioned again and again as to which of the favors of God they will deny."

However, it is narrated by Abu Huraira that the Messenger said: "Allah says: 'I have prepared for My righteous slaves (such excellent things) as no eye has ever seen, nor an ear has ever heard, nor a human heart can ever think of' (Sahih Bukhari: 9.93.589)." This indicates that any description about the Hereafter, Paradise, and Hell is only an attempt to describe something that is beyond the comprehension of the people. It is a challenge to human imagination and, therefore, cannot be considered complete.

Table 5.3: Paradise for Good Behavior and for Good Deeds

No	Surah:Verses	Meanings
		A Paradise for those who are Humble and Just
1	55:046-059	But for such as fear the time when they will stand before (the judgment seat of) their Lord, there will be two gardens—then which of the favors of your Lord will you deny?— 1. Containing all kinds (of trees and delights). Then which of the favors of your Lord will you deny? 2. In them will be two springs flowing (free). Then which of the favors of your Lord will you deny? 3. In them will be fruits of every kind, two and two. Then which of the favors of your Lord will you deny? ' 4. They will recline on carpets, whose inner linings will be of rich brocade. The fruit of the gardens will be near (and easy to reach). Then which of the favors of your Lord will you

		deny? 5. In them will be (companions), chaste, restraining their glances, whom no man or jinn before them has touched—then which of the favors of your Lord will you deny?— 6. Like unto rubies and coral. Then which of the favors of your Lord will you deny?
		Another Paradise - a Reward for Good Deeds
2	55:060-078	Is there any reward for good other than good? Then which of the favors of your Lord will you deny? 1. And besides these two, there are two other gardens—then which of the favors of your Lord will you deny?— 2. Dark-green in color (from plentiful watering). Then which of the favors of your Lord will you deny? 3. In them (each) will be two springs pouring forth water in continuous abundance. Then which of the favors of your Lord will you deny? 4. In them will be fruits and dates and pomegranates. Then which of the favors of your Lord will you deny? 5. In them will be fair (companions), good, beautiful—then which of the favors of your Lord will you deny?— 6. Companions restrained (as to their glances), in (goodly) pavilions—then which of the favors of your Lord will you deny?— 7. Whom no man or jinn before them has touched—then which of the favors of your Lord will you deny?— 8. Reclining on green cushions and rich carpets of beauty. Then which of the favors of your Lord will you deny? Blessed be the name of your Lord, full of majesty, bounty, and honor!

587

CHAPTER 44

Establishment of Just Communities
FROM SARAH AL-HADID (57)

Surah Al-Hadid was revealed at Madinah, between the fourth and fifth year after the *Hijrah* during the interval between the Battle of Uhud and the Truce of Hudaibiyah. People learn from this Surah that God sent His messengers with clear instructions, so people can adhere to justice. God assures the people who support His religion at the risk of their lives and wealth that the opportunity exists for people to advance and develop by being just. However, God does not stand in need of others to accomplish His will and purpose.

1 THE MISSION OF HUMANITY AS GOD'S TRUSTEE

God created humanity for a different purpose and mission than the animals. People are entrusted with the management and development of life on earth, according to the basic principles that God has put in place through His revelations and the human consciences, the latter of which is thoroughly interpreted and explained in the Qur'an. Humans are given the power of choice. People determine for themselves whether to follow the guidance provided by God through his messengers or to behave impulsively in satisfying their own selfish desires. When people abandon God's guidance, their lives on earth are nothing more than eating, drinking, and self-indulgence.

1.1 Who is God and Who Created the Universe?
To refresh people's memory and to establish the seriousness of what God commands, the attributes of God Almighty are mentioned in this Surah. In this way, people may realize just Who is addressing them.

Table 1.1: God's Attributes

No	Surah:Verses	Meanings
1	57:001-006	Whatever is in the heavens and on earth—let it declare the praises and glory of Allah, for 1. He is the exalted in might, the wise. 2. To Him belongs the dominion of the heavens and the earth. 3. It is He Who gives life and death, and He has power over all things. 4. He is the first and the last, the evident and the hidden, and 5. He has full knowledge of all things. 6. He it is Who created the heavens and the earth in six days and is, moreover, firmly established on the throne (of authority). 7. He knows what enters within the earth and what comes forth out of it, what comes down from heaven and what mounts up to it. 8. He is with you wherever you may be; Allah sees well all that you do. 9. To Him belongs the dominion of the heavens and the earth, and 10. All affairs are referred back to Allah. 11. He merges night into day, and He merges day into night, and He has full knowledge of the secrets of (all) hearts.

1.2 God's Purpose: Establishment of Just Communities

At the most critical juncture of history, when Islam was engaged in a life and death struggle with Arab unbelievers, Surah Al-Hadid was revealed to make people realize that Islam does not merely demand a verbal affirmation and some outward practices but that its essence and spirit are sincerity towards God and His purpose. The faith of those who are devoid of this spirit, and who regard their own selves and their wealth as being dearer to them than God and His purpose, is of little worth in the sight of God.

The new Islamic State at Madinah was surrounded by unbelievers, and a few poorly equipped believers were entrenched against the combined power of the whole of Arabia. As such, the nascent Islamic community not only needed the sacrifice of life from its followers, but it also needed monetary help and assistance. To arouse the believers to action, God says: "Has not the time arrived for the believers that their hearts in all humility should engage in the remembrance of Allah and of the truth that has been revealed (to them) (Qur'an 57:16)?" Although sacrificing for the sake of God's purpose is commendable in any case, the true worth of these sacrifices is determined by the nature of the occasion. The demand and the importance of such sacrifice increases when the power of unbelief is overwhelming and when there is a danger that it might completely subdue and overcome Islam.

Table 1.2: Unusual Environment Demands Unusual Efforts

No	Surah:Verses	Meanings
		What reason do people have Not to believe in God?
2	57:007-008	1. Believe in Allah and His messenger, and spend (in charity) out of the (substance) whereof He has made you heirs. For those of you who believe and spend (in charity)—for them is a great reward. 2. What cause have you why you shouldn't believe in Allah? The Messenger invites you to believe in your Lord and has indeed taken your covenant if you are men of faith.
		What reason do people have Not to spend in God's way?
3	57:010	And what cause have you why you shouldn't spend in the cause of Allah, for to Allah belongs the heritage of the heavens and the earth. • Not equal among you are those who spent (freely) and fought before the victory (with those who did so later). • Those are higher in rank than those who spent (freely) and fought afterwards. • But to all has Allah promised a goodly (reward), and Allah is well acquainted with all that you do.

590

1.3 Whatever is spent in God's Purpose is an Investment

Whatever is spent to support God's purpose is a loan to God, and God will return it, after increasing it manifold, and give from Himself the best reward for it. God says: "Who is he that will loan to Allah a beautiful loan? For (Allah) will increase it manifold to his credit, and he will have (besides) a liberal reward (Qur'an 57:11)." Such people are assured that: in this world, they will live with respect in peaceful, prosperous, and just communities; and in the Hereafter, light will be given to those believers who spent their wealth in the cause of God. As for the hypocrites who served their own self-interests in the world, weren't concerned with justice, and let corruption prevail, they will be separated from the believers in the Hereafter, will be deprived of light, and will be counted among the disbelievers.

Table 1.3: Wealth Spent on Defense is an Investment

No	Surah:Verses	Meanings
		Great Achievement for faithful Men and Women
4	57:012	1. One day shall you see the believing men and the believing women—how their light runs forward before them and by their right hands. 2. (Their greeting will be): "Good news for you this day—gardens beneath which flow rivers to dwell therein forever! This is indeed the highest achievement."
		The hypocrites and the unbelievers are Ruined
5	57:013-014	1. One day will the hypocrites, men and women, say to the believers: "Wait for us! Let us borrow (a light) from your light!" It will be said: "Turn back to your rear! Then seek a light (where you can)!" 2. So a wall will be put up betwixt them, with a gate therein. Within it will be mercy throughout, and without it, all alongside, will be (wrath and) punishment. (Those without) will call out: "Were we not with you?" (The others) will reply, "True! But you led yourselves into temptation. You looked forward (to our ruin). You doubted (Allah's promise), and (your false) desires deceived you until there issued the command of Allah. And the Satan deceived you with respect to Allah."

2 PEOPLE SHOULD ENFORCE JUSTICE

People are asked: "Do you not see that Allah has subjected to your (use) all things in the heavens and on earth and has made his bounties flow to you in exceeding measure, (both) seen and unseen? Yet, there are among men those who dispute about Allah without knowledge and without guidance and without a Book to enlighten them...It is We Who have placed you with authority on earth and provided you therein with means for the fulfillment of your life...Then We made you heirs in the land after them to see how you would behave...Therefore, "(they are) those who, if We establish them in the land, establish regular prayer and give regular charity, enjoin the right and forbid wrong (Qur'an 31:20; 7:10; 10:14; 22.41)."

2.1 Required Resources should be Spent

God sent His messengers with His guidance and law so that people could establish justice. Muslims should not behave like the followers of earlier books, whose lives were spent in worshiping the world and whose hearts became hardened. A believer's heart melts at the remembrance of God and follows the truth. Sincere upholders of truth and true witnesses of faith are only those believers who spend their wealth in God's way and only for Him. In contrast, hypocrites and unbelievers behave proudly when God favors them with His blessings, boasting about them and showing miserliness when called upon to spend in the cause of the same God Who blessed them in the first place. Further, they counsel others to be miserly.

Table 2.1: Believers are Humble and Charitable

No	Surah:Verses	Meanings
		Believers are Humbled by God's Remembrance
1	57:016	Has not the time arrived for the believers that their hearts in all humility should engage in the remembrance of Allah and of the truth that has been revealed (to them)—that they should not become like those to whom was given revelation aforetime, but long ages passed over them and their hearts grew hard? For many among them are

		rebellious transgressors.
		Charitable Men and Women will be Rewarded
2	57:018-019	1. For those who give in charity, men and women, and loan to Allah a beautiful loan, it shall be increased manifold, and they shall have (besides) a liberal reward. 2. Those who believe in Allah and His messengers—they are the sincere (lovers of truth) and the witnesses (who testify) in the eyes of their Lord. They shall have their reward and their light.

2.2 Life of the World and Life of the Hereafter

The life of this world is like a short-lived spring and a means of pride and show. Its sports and pastimes, its adornments and decorations, its pride of place, and its wealth and possessions, for which people vie with one another, are transient. It resembles the crop that flourishes and blooms, then turns pale, and finally is reduced to chaff. The everlasting life is that of the Hereafter, where the results of individual human efforts and behavior will be rewarded. Therefore, if one competes for something, one should strive for Paradise by obeying God's commands, implementing justice under all circumstances, and spending to achieve God's purpose. Whatever hardships good people face and suffer in this world are a pre-ordained test for them by God. A true believer neither loses heart in difficulty nor feels exultant in good times.

Table 2.2: Life and its Trials and Tribulations

No	Surah:Verses	Meanings
		The World's Life is Only Sport and Play
3	57:020-021	1. Know you that the life of this world is but play and amusement, pomp and mutual boasting and multiplying (in rivalry) among yourselves, riches and children. Here is a similitude: How rain and the growth that it brings forth delight the tillers. Soon it withers; you will see it grow yellow; then it becomes dry and crumbles away. 2. But in the Hereafter is a penalty severe and forgiveness from Allah and (His) good

		pleasure. And what is the life of this world but goods and chattels of deception.
		3. Be foremost (in seeking) forgiveness from your Lord, and a garden, the width whereof is as the width of Heaven and earth, prepared for those who believe in Allah and His messengers. That is the grace of Allah, which He bestows on whom He pleases, and Allah is the Lord of grace abounding.
		Trials and Difficulties of Life are Unavoidable
4	57:022-023	No misfortune can happen on earth or in your souls but is recorded in a decree before We bring it into existence—that is truly easy for Allah, in order that you may not despair over matters that pass you by, or exult over favors bestowed upon you. For Allah loves not any vainglorious boaster.

2.3 Justice should be enforced, even with Force

God sent His messengers with His guidance and law so that people can adhere to justice. Further, He created iron so that force could be used, if required, to establish truth and justice on the earth. Thus, God wants to see people will rise up to support and fight for justice, even at the risk of their lives. God appointed messengers in the past. By their preaching, some people opted to enforce justice, but most of them persisted in corruption. Then Prophet Jesus came, whose teachings brought many moral improvements, but his community invented monasticism. Finally, God sent the Messenger of Islam. Those who affirm faith in him and pass their life fearing their accountability before God will be granted by God a double share of His mercy, and He will bless them with the light by which they will see and walk along the straight path, which lies among the crooked paths that can mislead people at every step in their lives. Although the followers of earlier revelations regard themselves as the sole heirs of God's bounties, the fact remains that God Himself controls His bounties and blesses whomever He pleases.

Table 2.3: Force can be used to enforce Justice

No	Surah:Verses	Meanings
		God Gave Iron, the Book, and the Balance
5	57:025	We sent aforetime our messengers with clear signs and sent down with them the Book and the balance (of right and wrong) that men may stand forth in justice, and We sent down iron, in which is (material for) mighty war, as well as many benefits for mankind, that Allah may test who it is that will help, unseen, Him and His messengers, for Allah is full of strength, exalted in might (and able to enforce His will).
		God rewards those who Believe
6	57:026-027	We sent Noah and Abraham, and established in their line prophethood and revelation, and some of them were on right guidance, but many of them became rebellious transgressors. Then, in their wake, We followed them up with (others of) Our messengers. 1. We sent after them Jesus, the son of Mary, and bestowed on him the gospel, and We ordained in the hearts of those who followed him compassion and mercy. 2. But the monasticism that they invented for themselves We did not prescribe for them. (We commanded) only the seeking for the good pleasure of Allah, but that they did not foster as they should have done. Yet, We bestowed on those among them who believed their (due) reward, but many of them are rebellious transgressors.
		God's Mercies: the Guidance and Forgiveness
7	57:028-029	O you who believe! Fear Allah, and believe in His Messenger, He will bestow on you a double portion of His mercy. He will provide for you a light by which you shall walk (straight in your path), and He will forgive you (your past). • For Allah is oft-forgiving, most merciful, that the People of the Book may know that they have no power whatever over the grace of Allah, that (His) grace is (entirely) in His hand, to bestow it on whomsoever He wills, for Allah is the Lord of grace abounding.

CHAPTER 45

Believers have Good Social Behavior
FROM SURAH AL-MUJADILAH (58)

After asserting that God knows everything, the unbelievers are warned that, due to their secret whisperings and consultations by which they conspired and intrigued against the Messenger, and because of their hidden malice and grudge in greeting him and in asking why God doesn't punish them for what they say, they will certainly be punished in Hell. After reaffirming that the whisperings of the hypocrites can do no harm to them, the believers are assured that they should go on doing their duty with full trust in God. Believers are also commanded to council each other about goodness, make room for others in assemblies, keep up prayer, pay the obligatory charity, and obey God and His Messenger.

1 BELIEVERS ARE KNOWN BY THEIR BEHAVIOR

1.1 Divine Social Laws Should Be Implemented
The believers are reminded that it is contrary to their faith to persist in the practices of ignorance by breaking the bounds set by God. They shouldn't behave contrary to their religious belief, and they shouldn't make their own rules and regulations that are contradictory to the spirit and injunctions of Islam. Such behavior is not only disgraceful and punishable in this world, but in the Hereafter, too, there will be a strict accountability. People are reminded: "Those who resist Allah and His Messenger will be humbled to dust, as were those before them, for We have already sent down clear signs. The Unbelievers (will have) a humiliating penalty on the day that Allah will raise them all up and show them the truth of their conduct. Allah has reckoned its (value), though they may have forgotten it, for Allah is witness to all things (Qur'an 58:5-6)."

1.2 Penalty for Uttering Hateful and False Words

The practice of pre-Islamic era to divorce a wife by *Zihar* (an oath by the husband that his wife is like his mother's back, meaning she is unlawful to him) is a sin and a crime. People who utter such hateful and false words to their wives can annul it by paying a penalty for it. God tells people in Surah Al-Mujadilah: "If any men among you divorce their wives by *Zihar* (calling them mothers), they cannot be their mothers. None can be their mothers except those who gave them birth. And in fact they use words (both) iniquitous and false... (Qur'an 58:2)."

Only unbelievers cross the limits set by God. Believers should renounce this practice and pay the penalty, "But those who divorce their wives by *Zihar*, then wish to go back on the words they uttered—(it is ordained that such a one) should free a slave before they touch each other. Thus are you admonished to perform, and Allah is well acquainted with (all) that you do. And if any has not (the wherewithal), he should fast for two months consecutively before they touch each other. But if any is unable to do so, he should feed sixty indigent ones—this that you may show your faith in Allah and His Messenger. Those are limits (set by) Allah. For those who reject (Him), there is a grievous penalty (Qur'an 58:3-4)."

2 THE UNBELIEVERS' AND BELIEVERS' SOCIAL BEHAVIOR

2.1 Social Behavior of the Unbelievers

God asks the unbelievers and hypocrites: "Do you not see that Allah does know (all) that is in the heavens and on earth? There is not a secret consultation between three, but He makes the fourth among them—nor between five but He makes the sixth, nor between fewer or more, but He is in their midst wherever they be: In the end will He tell them the truth of their conduct on the Day of Judgment, for Allah has full knowledge of all things (Qur'an 58:7)." The secret consultations against the Messenger and Islam make unbelievers suitable only for God's anger. They cannot deserve His mercy, and Hell will be their abode. God says: "Turn not your sight towards those who were forbidden secret counsels yet revert to that which they were forbidden (to do). They hold secret counsels among themselves for iniquity and hostility and disobedience to the Messenger. And when they come to you, they salute you not as Allah salutes you, (but in crooked ways). They say to themselves: 'Why does not Allah punish us for our words?' (Qur'an 58:8)."

2.2 Social Behavior of the Believers

"O you who believe! When you hold secret counsel, do it not for iniquity and hostility and disobedience to the Prophet; but do it for righteousness and self-restraint, and fear Allah to Whom you shall be brought back. Secret counsels are only (inspired) by Satan, in order that he may cause grief to the believers, but he cannot harm them in the least, except as Allah permits, and on Allah let the believers put their trust (Qur'an 58:9-10)."

The believers are given instructions to eradicate certain social evils that were prevalent among the people during pre-Islamic times, just as they are still today. People sitting in an assembly often were not courteous enough to squeeze in so as to make room for latecomers. This often used to be experienced in the Messenger's assemblies. Believers should not behave selfishly in their assemblies, but they should do accommodate newcomers with an open heart. They are told: "O you who believe! When you are told to make room in the assemblies, (spread out and) make room. (Ample) room will Allah provide for you. And when you are told to rise up, rise up. Allah will raise up to (suitable) ranks (and degrees) those of you who believe and who have been granted knowledge, and Allah is well acquainted with all you do (Qur'an 58:11)." Likewise, when people go to visit someone, they should not prolong their visit, realizing that it may cause hardship to the people they are visiting.

Another issue was that some people wished to have secret counsel individually with the Messenger without any real need. To discourage this, God imposed the restriction of giving something in charity first, a restriction that was later withdrawn after people had corrected their behavior. "O you who believe! When you consult the Messenger in private, spend something in charity before your private consultation. That will be best for you and most conducive to purity. But if you find not, Allah is oft-forgiving, most merciful. Is it that you are afraid of spending sums in charity before your private consultation (with him)? If then you do not so, and Allah forgives you, then (at least) establish regular prayer, practice regular charity, and obey Allah and His Messenger. And Allah is well acquainted with all that you do (Qur'an 58:12-13)."

3 THE MEMBERS OF GOD'S AND OF SATAN'S PARTY

3.1 Believers of Satan's Party are the Lowest

The members of a believers' community, at any time or age, is a mixture of sincere people, hypocrites, and those who are wavering. Therefore, it is important that people should know the criterion of sincerity in Islam. There are Muslims who have friendships with the enemies of Islam; they do not hesitate for the sake of their interests to be treacherous to their own religion and people. They spread doubts and suspicions against the religion and prevent people from adopting it. Since they are a part of the Muslim community, their false profession of faith serves them as a cover and shield. This category of people, however hard they may try to convince others of their faith by swearing oaths, belong to Satan's party. With regard to the destiny of such people, "Those who resist Allah and His Messenger will be among those most humiliated. Allah has decreed: 'It is I and My messengers, who must prevail,' for Allah is One full of strength, able to enforce His will (Qur'an 58:20-21)."

Table 3.1 Only Hypocrites Befriend with Hostile Unbelievers

No	Surah:Verses	Meanings
		Hypocrites Swear Falsely in the World
1	58:014-017	Turn you not your attention to those who turn (in friendship) to such as have the wrath of Allah upon them. They are neither of you nor of them, and they swear to falsehood knowingly. Allah has prepared for them a severe penalty. 1. Evil indeed are their deeds. 2. They have made their oaths a screen (for their misdeeds); thus, they obstruct (men) from the

		path of Allah. Therefore, they shall have a humiliating penalty. 3. Of no profit whatever to them against Allah will be their riches nor their sons. They will be companions of the fire, to dwell therein (forever).
		Hypocrites will Swear Falsely in the Hereafter
2	58:018-019	4. One day will Allah raise them all up (for judgment). Then will they swear to Him as they swear to you, and they think that they have something (to stand upon). No, indeed! They are but liars. 5. Satan has got the better of them, so he has made them lose the remembrance of Allah. They are the party of the evil one. Truly, it is the party of the evil one that will perish.

3.2 Believers of God's Party are Successful

However, there are believers who in the matter of their religion do not care even for their father, brothers, children, and family. They do not cherish any feeling of love for those who are the enemies of God, His Messenger, and the religion. The honor of belonging to God's party is earned only by such believers. They alone are the true Muslims. They alone will attain to true success, and with them alone is God well pleased.

Table 3.2: Believers do not befriend with Hostile Unbelievers

No	Surah:Verses	Meanings
		Even if the Unbelievers are their close Relatives
3	58:022	• You will not find any people who believe in Allah and the Last Day loving those who resist Allah and His Messenger, even though they were their fathers or their sons, or their brothers, or their kindred. For such, He has written faith in their hearts and strengthened them with a spirit from Himself.
		God is pleased with Them and They with Him
4	58:022	• He will admit them to gardens beneath which rivers flow, to dwell therein (forever). Allah will be well pleased with them, and they with Him. They are the party of Allah. Truly, it is the party of Allah that will achieve felicity.

CHAPTER 46

Banishment of Arrogant People
FROM SURAH AL-HASHR (59)

People are asked to learn a lesson from the fate of befallen tribe of Bani an-Nadir. They were very well equipped militarily, and their castles were fortified, but they were defeated because they tried to fight God and His Messenger. Their defeat was not because of any power possessed by the Muslims. Those who dare to resist the power of God will always meet with a similar fate. Further, people who joined the Muslim community without the true spirit of faith were warned of the evil consequences of their attitudes and behavior.

1 THE MANAGEMENT OF
CONQUERED TERRITORIES

1.1 God has His Own Ways to Punish the Corrupt
Although the tribe of Bani an-Nadir matched the Muslims in strength, they had far more wealth and possessions than the Muslims. They were powerfully equipped militarily, and their castles were strongly fortified. However, they could not stand a siege even for a few days and expressed their readiness to accept banishment from their century's old settlement in Madinah, even though not a single man from among them was slain. This happened because the Jews tried to fight God and His Messenger and not because of the strength of the Muslim army. God tells people in Surah Al-Hashr: "It is He Who got out the unbelievers among the People of the Book from their homes at the first gathering (of the forces). Little did you think that they would get out, and they thought that their fortresses would defend them from Allah! But the (wrath of) Allah came to them from quarters from which they little expected, and (it) cast fear into their hearts, so that they destroyed their dwellings by their own hands and the hands of the believers. Take warning then, O you with eyes! Had it not been that Allah had decreed banishment for them, He would certainly have punished them in this world, and

601

in the Hereafter they shall have the punishment of the fire. That is because they resisted Allah and His Messenger, and if any one resists Allah, verily, Allah is severe in punishment (Qur'an 59:2-4)."

1.2 State Management of Conquered Territories

During a just and lawful war, the destruction caused for military purposes does not come under the title of spreading mischief in the earth. In Surah Al-Hashr, the believers are told: "Whether you cut down the tender palm trees or you left them standing on their roots, it was by leave of Allah and in order that He might cover with shame the rebellious transgresses. What Allah has bestowed on His Messenger (and taken away) from them—for this you made no expedition with either cavalry or camelry. But Allah gives power to His messengers over any He pleases, and Allah has power over all things (Qur'an 59:5-6)." The defeat of the Bani an-Nadir was the first occasion when Muslims took control of a conquered territory. Therefore, the law concerning its control and management was laid down for the guidance of Muslims.

Table 1.2: Owners of Properties; God gave to His Messenger

No	Surah:Verses	Meanings
		Conquered Properties Belong to the State for People's Welfare
1	59:007-008	1. What Allah has bestowed on His Messenger from the people of the townships belongs to Allah, to His Messenger, and to kindred and orphans, the needy and the wayfarer, in order that it may not (merely) circulate among the wealthy among you. So take what the Messenger assigns to you, and deny yourselves that which he withholds from you. Fear Allah, for Allah is strict in punishment. 2. (Some part is due) to the indigent Muhajirs (emigrants from Makkah to Madinah), those who were expelled from their homes and their property, while seeking grace from Allah and (His) good pleasure, and aiding Allah and His Messenger. Such are, indeed, the sincere ones.
		The Successful are

		Those who are Saved from Covetousness
2	59:009-010	3. But those who before them had homes (in Madinah) and had adopted the faith show their affection to such as came to them for refuge, and entertain no desire in their hearts for things given to the (latter), but give them preference over themselves, even though poverty was their (own lot). And those saved from the covetousness of their own souls— they are the ones that achieve prosperity. 4. And those who came after them say: "Our Lord! Forgive us and our brethren who came before us into the faith, and leave not in our hearts rancor (or sense of injury) against those who have believed. Our Lord! You are indeed full of kindness, most merciful.

2 THE BEHAVIOR OF THE HYPOCRITES

2.1 The Hypocrites and Satan are Alike

During the battle against the tribe of Bani an-Nadir, the hypocrites adopted an attitude that was not expected from the believers. God asks in Surah Al-Hashr: "Have you not observed the hypocrites say to their misbelieving brethren among the People of the Book 'If you are expelled, we too will go out with you, and we will never hearken to anyone in your affair. And if you are attacked, we will help you.' But Allah is witness that they are indeed liars. If they are expelled, never will they go out with them; and if they are attacked, they will never help them. If they do help them, they will turn their backs (in cowardice); so they will receive no help (Qur'an 59:11-12)."

Table 2.1: Both Hypocrites and Satan will end up in the Fire

No	Surah:Verses	Meanings
		God will put Fear in the Hearts of the Hypocrites
1	59:013	1. Of a truth you are stronger (than they) because of the terror in their hearts (sent) by Allah. This is because they are men devoid of understanding.
		Hypocrites are Disunited and lack Courage

2	59:014	2. They will not fight you (even) together, except in fortified townships or from behind walls. Strong is their fighting (spirit) among themselves. You would think they were united, but their hearts are divided. That is because they are a people devoid of wisdom.
		Hypocrites and Satan share in their Behavior
3	59:015-017	3. Like those who lately preceded them, they have tasted the evil result of their conduct, and (in the Hereafter there is) for them a grievous penalty. 4. (Their allies deceived them), like Satan, when he says to man, "Deny Allah." But when (man) denies Allah, (Satan) says, "I am free of you. I do fear Allah, the Lord of the worlds." 5. The end of both will be that they will go into the fire, dwelling therein forever. Such is the reward of the wrongdoers.

2.2 Believers and the Hypocrites are not alike

The people who joined the Muslim community without the true spirit of faith were warned of the evil consequences of their attitudes and behavior. They were told about the real demands of faith and the difference between piety and corruption. Addressing the believers, including those who were actually hypocrites, God says: "O you who believe! Fear Allah, and let every soul look to what (provision) He has sent forth for the morrow. Yea, fear Allah, for Allah is well acquainted with that you do. And be you not like those who forgot Allah, and He made them forget their own souls! Such are the rebellious transgressors! Not equal are the companions of the fire and the companions of the garden. It is the companions of the garden that will achieve felicity (Qur'an 59:18-20)."

2.3 People should take the Qur'an Seriously

After asserting His power and attributes, God tells people that being His trustee on earth is a great responsibility and that they should take it seriously. In that regard, the required duties described in the Qur'an are for the benefit of the people. With great responsibility comes a great reward, as well as punishment, depending on individual attitudes, behavior, and deeds.

Table 2.3: God Revealed the Qur'an for People to Reflect

No	Surah:Verses	Meanings
		Who is God, and What are His Attributes?
4	59:022-024	1. He is Allah, besides Whom there is no god, the knower of the unseen and the seen. 2. He is the Most Gracious, Most Merciful. 3. He is Allah, besides Whom there is no god, the Sovereign, the Holy One, the Source of Peace, the Guardian of Faith, Preserver of Safety, the Exalted in Might, the Irresistible, the Supreme. Glory to Allah! (High is He) above the partners they attribute to Him. 4. He is Allah, the Creator, the Evolver, the Fashioner. 5. To Him belong the most beautiful names. Whatever is in the heavens and on earth declares His praises and glory 6. He is the Exalted in Might, the Wise.
		God's Trusteeship is a Great Responsibility
5	59:021	• Had We sent down this Qur'an on a mountain, verily, you would have seen it humble itself and cleave asunder for fear of Allah. Such are the similitudes which We propound to men that they may reflect.

CHAPTER 47

Relationship with Hostile Unbelievers
FROM SURAH AL-MUMTAHINAH (60)

Surah Al-Mumtahinah deals with two incidents. The first relates to Hatib bin Abz Balta'a, who, a little before the conquest of Makkah, sent a secret letter to the Quraysh leaders informing them of the Messenger's intention to attack them. This was an act of treason that even today carries a severe penalty. That is why the believers are commanded in this Surah that they should refrain from everything that might be helpful to the unbelievers in a conflict between Islam and disbelief. However, one should deal kindly and justly with those unbelievers who are not engaged in hostile activities against Islam and in persecution of Muslims.

The second incident relates to Muslim women who had started emigrating from Makkah to Madinah after the truce of Hudaibiyah. Should these women be returned to Makkah according to the conditions of the truce? This was resolved based on the fact that believing women are not lawful for unbelieving men, so they should not be returned. A further question was what these women should pledge when they take an oath of allegiance before the Messenger as believers? Speculations are that this part of the Surah was also revealed some time before the conquest of Makkah. After this conquest a large number of the Quraysh women, like men, entered Islam and had to be administered an oath of allegiance. Basically the pledge was to refrain from pre-Islamic social evils.

1 FRIENDSHIP WITH THE UNBELIEVERS

1.1 Hostile Unbelievers are not Believers' Friends
Hatib bin Abi Balta'a tried to inform the enemies of a very important war secret, hoping that it would safeguard his family still in Makkah. Had it not been intercepted, it would have caused difficulties during the conquest of Makkah, and the gains

that were to accrue from peacefully conquering Makkah would have been lost. Giving a severe warning regarding this incident, God commanded that no believer should, under any circumstances and for any motive, have relations of love and friendship with unbelievers who are actively hostile to Islam. "O you who believe! Turn not (for friendship) to people on whom is the wrath of Allah. Of the Hereafter, they are already in despair, just as the unbelievers are in despair about those (buried) in graves (Qur'an 60:13)."

Table 1.1: Befriend not with God's and Your Own Enemy

No	Surah:Verses	Meanings
		Unbelievers Hostile to Islam **Cannot be your Friends**
1	60:001-003	• O you who believe! Take not my enemies and yours as friends (or protectors), offering them (your) love, even though they have rejected the truth that has come to you and have (on the contrary) driven out the Messenger and yourselves (from your homes), (simply) because you believe in Allah your Lord! If you have come out to strive in My way and to seek My good pleasure, (take them not as friends), holding secret converse of love (and friendship) with them, for I know full well all that you conceal and all that you reveal. And any of you that does this has strayed from the straight path. 1. If they were to get the better of you, they would behave to you as enemies and stretch forth their hands and their tongues against you for evil, and they desire that you should reject the truth. 2. Of no profit to you will be your relatives and your children on the Day of Judgment. He will judge between you, for Allah sees well all that you do.
		Treat Unbelievers **like Abraham and his Companions did**
2	60:004-005	There is for you an excellent example (to follow) in Abraham and those with him, when they said to their people: "We are clear of you and of whatever you worship besides Allah. We have rejected you,

607

		and there has arisen between us and you enmity and hatred forever—unless you believe in Allah and Him alone:" but not when Abraham said to his father: "I will pray for forgiveness for you, though I have no power (to get) anything on your behalf from Allah." (Abraham and his companions prayed): 1. Our Lord! In You do we trust, and to You do we turn in repentance. To You is (our) final goal. 2. Our Lord! Make us not a (test and) trial for the unbelievers, but forgive us, our Lord! For You are the exalted in might, the wise.

1.2 Be Kind and Just to Non-Hostile Unbelievers

A believer should refrain from anything that might be helpful to hostile unbelievers during any conflict between Islam and unbelief. However, there is no harm in dealing kindly and justly with those unbelievers who are not engaged in hostile activities against Islam and in the persecution of Muslims. Rather, Islam encourages the believers to be kind and just to unbelievers. It may happen that Allah may make believers and their present enemies' mutual friends.

Table 1.2: Friendship with Non-Hostile Unbelievers

No	Surah:Verses	Meanings
		God may make the Believers and their Enemies Friends
3	60:007	It may be that Allah will grant love (and friendship) between you and those whom you (now) hold as enemies, for Allah has power (over all things), and Allah is oft-forgiving, most merciful.
		Believers are always Kind and Friendly to the Unbelievers
4	60:008-009	• Allah forbids you not, with regard to those who fight you not for (your) faith nor drive you out of your homes, from dealing kindly and justly with them, for Allah loves those who are just. • Allah only forbids you with regard to those who fight you for (your) faith, and drive you

		out of your homes, and support (others) in driving you out, from turning to them (for friendship and protection). It is such as turn to them (in these circumstances) that do wrong.

2 MIGRATION OF BELIEVING WOMEN FROM MAKKAH

2.1 Pledge to refrain from Pre-Islamic Social Evils

The Messenger was instructed to ask women who accept Islam to pledge that they will refrain from the major evils that were prevalent among the womenfolk of pre-Islamic Arab society and to promise that they would follow the ways of goodness that the Messenger may enjoin.

Table 2.2: Pledge of emigrating Believing Women

No	Surah:Verses	Meanings
1	60:012	O Prophet! When believing women come to you to take the oath of fealty to you that they will not associate in worship any other thing whatever with Allah, that they will not steal, that they will not commit adultery (or fornication), that they will not kill their children, that they will not utter slander, intentionally forging falsehood, and that they will not disobey you in any just matter, then receive their fealty, and pray to Allah for the forgiveness (of their sins), for Allah is oft-forgiving, most merciful.

2.2 Assimilation of Emigrating Women at Madinah

There were many Muslim women in Makkah whose husbands were unbelievers. Such women were emigrating and reaching Madinah. Likewise, there were many Muslim men in Madinah whose wives did not convert and had been left behind in Makkah. The question of the validity of the marriage between them was settled when God declared that neither is an unbelieving husband lawful for a believing woman nor is an unbelieving wife lawful for a believing husband. This decision

609

led to some legal and financial consequences for which guidance was provided.

Table 2.1: Believing Women are not Lawful for Unbelievers

No	Surah:Verses	Meanings
		Marriage between **Believers and Unbelievers is Unlawful**
2	60:010	O you who believe! When there come to you believing women refugees, examine (and test) them. Allah knows best as to their faith. If you ascertain that they are believers, then send them not back to the unbelievers. 1. They are not lawful (wives) for the unbelievers, nor are the (unbelievers) lawful (husbands) for them. But pay the unbelievers what they have spent (on their dower), and there will be no blame on you if you marry them on payment of their dower to them. 2. But hold not to the guardianship of unbelieving women. Ask for what you have spent on their dowers, and let the (unbelievers) ask for what they have spent (on the dowers of women who come over to you). Such is the command of Allah. He judges (with justice) between you, and Allah is full of knowledge and wisdom.
		Women should return their dowers **to their Ex-Husbands**
3	60:011	• If any of your wives deserts you to the unbelievers, and you have an accession (by the coming over of a woman from the other side), then pay to those whose wives have deserted the equivalent of what they had spent (on their dower). And fear Allah in Whom you believe.

CHAPTER 48

Striving in the Way of God
FROM SURAH AS-SAFF (61)

Islam is implemented by human pursuance, within the limits of human ability and reasoning. It begins from where an individual is at a certain moment. It goes as far as one's endeavor and capacity can take him, always mindful of one's limitations and capabilities. Islam's main characteristic, however, is that it never neglects human nature and the realities of its physical existence, while allowing a person to reach new heights of progress and achievement. This is unparalleled in any manmade system, and has resulted in new heights of progress having been achieved by Islamic communities in the past. This can always happen again if a serious attempt is made to revive Islam. Human efforts carried out for the implementation of the moral and sociopolitical principles of Islam is Jihad.

Jihad can be a simple action, such as standing firm in the defense of Islamic principles. This may require speaking out in public or in writing articles or books. It may also take the form of reminding people of their Islamic duties and of motivating them to conduct their lives according to Islam. When all else fails, Jihad can also take the form of fighting the enemies of Islam in battle in order to foil their attempts to smother the call of Islam. It was narrated by Ibn Mas'ud that a man asked the Prophet what are the best deeds. In response, the Prophet listed performing the prayers at their fixed times, being good and dutiful to one's own parents, and participating in Jihad in Allah's cause (Sahih Bukhari: 9.93.625). This *hadith* points to three major areas of human activity: (1) developing good relation with the Creator, (2) developing good relation among people, and (3) defending human rights and human values. Believers are encouraged to strive sincerely to learn and to fulfill their duties as God's trustee, implementing God's commands to develop just communities on earth.

611

1 WHY JIHAD IS AN ESSENTIAL PART OF ISLAM

1.1 Islamic Principles are Natural and Eternal

There are a number of basic principles on which the foundation of the Islamic faith and its practical aspects are developed. They have nothing to do with changing circumstances and must not be overlooked or underestimated by believers in any situation. One of these principles is Jihad, or striving hard for God's cause and under His banner. It is the one that earns martyrdom for the one who dies fighting. Islam does not defer establishing a principle until the community is ready to implement it. The community needs to practice so that it can learn and be prepared. To deny people their experience of fundamental principles, such as consultative government, is more detrimental to the development of an Islamic community than any outcome that might emerge from that experience. Mistakes, no matter how great or serious, are no justification for invalidating, withdrawing or suspending a particular tenet or principle. This only stunts the development of the community, emasculates its experience, and threatens its whole existence.

1.2 Believers follow their Values and Principles

It is very important for a believing community to keep the values and principles of its way of life pure and intact. It should continually identify and isolate those individuals who misconstrue or misinterpret them, no matter who they are. Their mistakes or misconceptions should never be justified or lent any legitimacy by changing or modifying the values and standards of the system itself. The system is greater and more lasting than any individual. The true history of Islam is not everything that Muslims have done or achieved in their lives, but it is everything they have done and accomplished in total agreement with Islam and its firmly established values and principles. Deviation and mistakes should not be attributed to Islam, but should be credited to the individuals or societies that were responsible for them.

1.3 Muslims are only those who adapt to Islam

The history of Islam and the history of Muslims are not one and the same thing. The history of Islam is represented by those periods when Islam was truly and rightly put into practice, i.e., when its concepts and beliefs, its code of morality, and its way of life for society as a whole were truly implemented. Islam is the firm center around which the nation's life revolves within a well-defined structure. Once people stray away from that framework or abandon the central tents of Islam, they cease to have anything to do with Islam. In this way, Islam should not be held accountable for their behavior, nor should it be interpreted in the light of their actions. Indeed, what justification is there to continue to associate such individuals or groups with Islam if they break away from its central beliefs and principles and refuse to comply with them in their daily lives? Muslims are only Muslims if they adopt Islam as their way of life, and not because they bear Muslim names or because they claim to be Muslims.

1.4 Jihad is the Foundation of Islamic Society

The assumption must never be made that Jihad was only incidental to a particular situation in a particular place and that situation no longer exists. It is not that Islam loves to draw its sword and chop off people's heads with it. The hard facts of life compel Islam to have its sword drawn and to be always ready and careful. God knows that those who hold the reigns of power are hostile to Islam and that they will always try to resist it. This is because Islam points to a way and a method different from theirs. This doesn't just apply to a particular period of past history. It applies to the situation today and tomorrow, in all places, and throughout all generations. Evil is arrogant and can never be fair; it cannot allow the seeds of goodness to grow. It does not matter which peaceful tactics the advocates of goodness adopt, the very fact that goodness begins to grow represents a threat to evil. The very existence of the truth endangers falsehood. Evil will always be aggressive and defend its existence by attempting to smother the truth, never hesitating to use brute force. This is part of human nature, not something incidental to a particular situation or period in history.

Jihad, in every form, is essential. It starts in people's hearts and emerges in the real world. This is the only way to the inevitable confrontation between armed evil and armed goodness. The forces of falsehood, in their great numbers and heavy armament, must be countered with properly equipped forces of goodness.

613

Proper preparation for serious confrontation requires sacrificing possessions and lives, as God required the believers to do, purchasing all these from the believers in return for admitting them into heaven. He either gives them victory or martyrdom. It is all within His prerogative, and He makes His decision on the basis of His wisdom. All people die when the time comes, but only those who die in God's cause can be martyrs.

2 BELIEVERS STRUGGLE HARD IN GOD'S WAY

2.1 Struggle Hard with Your Properties and Lives

The believers are encouraged to be sincere in faith, to strive in the cause of God, and to fulfill all duties as His trustee, implementing His commands to develop just communities on earth. Believers are told that the way to success, both in this world and in the Hereafter, is only through sincerely believing in God and His Messenger and in exerting their utmost in God's way with their selves and their wealth. As a reward, they will get God's help, relief from difficulties, and victory in the world. They will also earn immunity from God's punishment, forgiveness for their weaknesses, and eternal paradise in the Hereafter. God tells the believers: "O you who believe! Shall I lead you to a bargain that will save you from a grievous penalty? (It is) that you believe in Allah and His Messenger and that you strive in the cause of Allah with your property and your persons. That will be best for you if you but knew! He will forgive you your sins and admit you to gardens beneath which rivers flow and to beautiful mansions in gardens of eternity. That is indeed the supreme achievement. And another (favor will He bestow,) which you do love—help from Allah and a speedy victory. So give the glad tidings to the believers (Qur'an 61:10-13)."

2.2 Fight in Ranks like a Firm and Compact Wall

God tells the believers that He hates those people who say one thing and do another and that He loves those who fight in the cause of the truth, standing like a solid structure against the enemies of God. God warns people that their attitude towards their Messenger and their faith should not be like the attitude of the Israelites towards Moses and Jesus. Although they acknowledged Moses as a messenger of God, they continued to malign him as long as he lived. Although they witnessed clear signs from Jesus, most of the Israelites denied him without any hesitation. Consequently, the Israelites became perverse, incapable of benefiting from divine guidance. The attitude of the Muslims should be like that of the true disciples of Jesus who helped him in his mission.

The believers have also been given the good news that no matter how hard the Jews, Christians, and hypocrites may try to extinguish this light of God, it will shine and spread in the world in all its fullness and that Islam shall prevail over every other religion, however hateful it may be to the idolaters and polytheists. "Their intention is to extinguish Allah's light (by blowing) with their mouths, but Allah will complete (the revelation of) His light, even though the unbelievers may detest (it). It is He Who has sent His Messenger with guidance and the religion of truth, (in order) that he may proclaim it over all religion, even though the pagans may detest (it) (Qur'an 61:8)."

Table 2.2: Why Don't You Fight for What You Believe?

No	Surah:Verses	Meanings
		Fight in God's way in ranks like a compact wall
1	61:002-004	• O you who believe! Why you say that which you do not do? It is most hateful to Allah that you should say that which you do not do. • Truly Allah loves those who fight in His cause in battle array, as if they were a solid, cemented structure.
		- Not Like the People of Moses and Jesus
2	61:005-007	• And remember, Moses said to his people: "O my people! Why do you vex and insult me, though you know that I am the messenger of Allah (sent) to you?" Then when they went wrong, Allah let their hearts go wrong. For Allah guides not those who are rebellious transgressors. • And remember, Jesus, the son of Mary, said: "O Children of Israel! I am the messenger of Allah (sent) to you, confirming the Torah (which came) before me and giving glad

		tidings of a messenger to come after me, whose name shall be Ahmad." But when he came to them with clear signs, they said, "This is evident sorcery." Who does greater wrong than one who invents falsehood against Allah, even as he is being invited to Islam? Allah guides not those who do wrong.
		- But like the Disciples of Jesus who Said **- We are the Helpers**
3	61:014	O you who believe! Be helpers of Allah—as said Jesus, the son of Mary, to the disciples, "Who will be my helpers to (the work of) Allah?" 1. Said the disciples: "We are Allah's helpers!" 2. Then a portion of the Children of Israel believed, and a portion disbelieved. 3. But We gave power to those who believed, against their enemies, and they became the ones that prevailed.

CHAPTER 49

Practice What You Believe
FROM SURAH AL-JUMU'AH (62)

Sarah Al-Jumu'ah consists of two sections, each of which was revealed at a different period. That is why their themes, as well as their audiences, are different. However, there is a kind of harmony between them, on account of which they were put together. The first section, in which Jews were addressed for the last time, was probably revealed either on the occasion of the conquest of Khaiber in Jamadi al-Awwal, A.H. 7, or soon after it. Thus, God might have revealed these verses, addressing the Jews, when their last stronghold had fallen to the Muslims, or these verses might have been revealed when, seeing the fate of Khaiber, all Jewish settlements of the northern Hijaz surrendered to the Islamic state.

The second section is about Friday congregation and was revealed shortly after the emigration. The incident referred to in the last verse of this section must have occurred at a time when the people had not yet received full training in the etiquette of religious congregations. God bestowed Friday on the Muslims in place of the Sabbath of the Jews. Hence, God warned the Muslims not to treat their Friday as the Jews had treated their Sabbath.

1 A LESSON FOR THOSE WHO REFLECT

Immediately after the emigration from Makkah to Madinah, Islam faced Jewish efforts to obstruct the message of Islam. The first section of Surah Al-Jumu'ah was revealed at a time when these efforts by the Jews had failed. Three of their powerful tribes had done whatever they could to eliminate Islam, with the result being that these tribes were removed from Madinah. Then by intrigue and conspiracy, they brought many of the Arab tribes together to advance on Madinah, but in the Battle of the Trench they were all repulsed. After this, Khaiber had become a

617

stronghold and refuge for these Jewish tribes. However, Kaiber was taken by the Muslims without any extraordinary effort. With this, Jewish power in Arabia came to an end.

1.1 Being appointed as a Messenger is God's Grace

The Jews refused to believe in the Messenger because he was born among a people whom they called gentiles. They were under the false notion that a messenger must belong to their own community. Believing that the prophetic office had been reserved for their race, they were convinced that anyone from outside their community who claimed to be a prophet must be an imposter. This belief ran contrary to the Qur'an's assertion: "It is He Who has sent among the unlettered a Messenger from among themselves to rehearse to them His signs, to sanctify them, and to instruct them in scripture and wisdom, although they had been before in manifest error—as well as (to confer all these benefits upon) others of them who have not already joined them. And He is exalted in might, wise. Such is the bounty of Allah, which He bestows on whom He wills, and Allah is the Lord of the highest bounty (Qur'an 62:2-4)."

1.2 Believers are those who Practice their Belief

People endowed with knowledge who do not practice their learning as it should be are like donkeys laden with books. These donkeys can belong to any religion or profession, so people should be aware of this and try to avoid being one. God tells the Jews that they were made bearers of the Torah, but they didn't take their responsibility seriously and didn't act on it as they should have. Those with knowledge who do not practice their learning are like donkey loaded down with books who do not know the burden it is bearing. Such a person is worse off than a donkey, for the donkey is devoid of sense, but a person is intelligent. Such a person has the misconception that he is among God's favorites and that apostleship has been reserved for him. However, if such a person is really among God's favorites, and he is so sure of a place of honor reserved for him with God, then why does he fear death so much?

Table 1.1: People with Knowledge who do not Practice

No	Surah:Verses	Meanings
		Like donkeys are those Scholars who Practice not
1	62:005	The similitude of those who were charged with the (obligations of the) Mosaic Law, but Who subsequently failed in those (obligations), is that of a donkey that carries huge tomes (but understands them not). Evil is the similitude of people who falsify the signs of Allah; Allah guides not people who do wrong.
		People are Alike and Equal in the Sight of God
2	62:006-008	• Say: "O you that stand on Judaism! If you think that you are friends to Allah, to the exclusion of (other) men, then express your desire for death if you are truthful." But never will they express their desire (for death) because of the (deeds) their hands have sent on before them! Allah knows well those that do wrong. • Say: "The death from which you flee will truly overtake you. Then will you be sent back to the knower of things secret and open, and He will tell you (the truth of) the things that you did."

2 THE FRIDAY CONGREGATION

2.1 People should pray at the Prayer Times

Verses 62:9-11 were revealed shortly after the Messenger's emigration to Madinah. The incident in which "they see some bargain or some amusement, they disperse headlong to it and leave you standing" must have occurred at a time when the people had not yet received full training in the etiquette of religious congregations. Since God bestowed Friday on Muslims as the Sabbath of the Jews, God commanded Muslims that they should not treat their Friday as the Jews had treated their Sabbath.

619

Table 2.1: Leave off Trade during Friday Prayer Time

No	Surah:Verses	Meanings
		Trade is not Permitted during the Prayer Times
1	62:009-010	• O you who believe! When the call is proclaimed to prayer on Friday (the Day of Assembly), 1. Then hasten earnestly to the remembrance of Allah, 2. And leave off business (and traffic). • That is best for you if you but knew. When the prayer is finished, 1. Then you may disperse through the land, 2. And seek of the bounty of Allah. • And celebrate the praises of Allah often (and without stint), (in order) that you may prosper.
		Seek God's Bounty after the Prayer is Over
2	62:011	• But when they see some bargain or some amusement, they disperse headlong to it and leave you standing. Say: "The (blessing) from the presence of Allah is better than any amusement or bargain!" And Allah is the best to provide (for all needs).

CHAPTER 50

The Behavior of the Hypocrites
FROM SURAH AL-MUNAFIQUN (63)

Surah Al-Munafiqun was revealed either during the Messenger's return journey from his campaign against the Bani al-Mustaliq or immediately after his arrival in Madinah. The campaign against the Bani al-Mustaliq took place in Sha'ban, A. H. 6. The attitude and conduct of the hypocrites is reviewed in this Surah. Believers are commanded to make sure that their own behavior is not hypocritical. They should not seek credit for what they have not done. One may wonder what compels people to adopt an attitude of hypocrisy. Is it a way to safeguard their wealth and children? People resort to all sorts of measures to increase their riches for their families and then forget their Provider. That is why believers are warned against hypocrisy and failing to remember God in Surah Al-Munafiqun.

1 BEWARE OF HYPOCRITES AND HYPOCRISY

1.1 Hypocrites' Personality and Speech
Hypocrites are a type of people who are found in every community that exists today, just as they were present at the time of the Messenger. They are those who do not have the courage of their convictions and fail to stand in defense of that in which they profess to believe. They are not prepared to fulfill the duties imposed by faith; instead, they stand behind, taking no share in the struggle for faith. If those who fight and struggle for their faith suffer a defeat, these hypocrites raise their heads and boast about their wisdom and realism. If the fighters come back victorious, the hypocrites waste no time pretending to have given them their full support. They take credit and seek praise for something that they have not done. This is a type of people who thrives on cowardice and false pretenses.

1.2 Hypocrisy and Hypocritical Behavior

Since hypocrisy is all about pretense, it is very difficult to define who is a hypocrite. However, the Messenger outlined some characteristics that are common in all hypocrites. It was narrated by Abu Huraira that the Prophet said, "The signs of a hypocrite are three. (1) Whenever he speaks, he tells a lie. (2) Whenever he promises, he always breaks it (his promise). (3) If you trust him, he proves to be dishonest. (Sahih Bukhari: 1.2.33)" Another version of this *hadith*, also related by Bukhari, quotes the Messenger as saying if the following four characteristics are part of a person's character, he is a pure hypocrite. If one of them applies to him, he has a characteristic of hypocrisy until he abandons it.

(1) He lies when he speaks	(2) He violates his pledges	(3) He breaks his promises and	(4) When he quarrels with someone, he is shameless.

1.3 Believers Should Beware of Hypocrisy

Hypocritical qualities are an indication of hypocrisy. When such qualities are typical of one's behavior to the extent that they are a part of his nature, he is almost certainly a hypocrite. However, they do not necessarily mean that he is a non-believer who pretends to be a Muslim. A Muslim may have no doubts about the Oneness of God and the fact that Muhammad is His Messenger, and yet he still commits one or more of these actions. They are the type of actions that a hypocrite does all the time. God tells the Messenger: "When the hypocrites come to you, they say, "We bear witness that you are indeed the Messenger of Allah." Yea, Allah knows that you are indeed His Messenger, and Allah bears witness that the hypocrites are indeed liars (Qur'an 63:1)."

Table 1.1: The Character and Behavior of Hypocrites

No	Surah:Verses	Meanings
		Hypocrites are Pleasing in Personality & Speech
1	63:004	When you look at them, their exteriors please you; and when they speak, you listen to their words. They are as (worthless as hollow) pieces of timber propped up, (unable to stand on their own). They think that every cry is against them. They are the enemies; so beware of them. The curse of Allah be on them! How are they deluded (away from the truth)?
		Hypocrites are Liars, Proud, Stingy, & Arrogant
2	63:002-003	1. They have made their oaths a screen (for their misdeeds). Thus, they obstruct (men) from the path of Allah; truly evil are their deeds. That is because they believed; then they rejected faith. So a seal was set on their hearts. Therefore, they understand not.
	63:005-006	2. When it is said to them, "Come; the Messenger of Allah will pray for your forgiveness," they turn aside their heads, and you would see them turning away their faces in arrogance. It is equal to them whether you pray for their forgiveness or not. Allah will not forgive them. Truly, Allah guides not rebellious transgressors.
	63:007	3. They are the ones who say, "Spend nothing on those who are with Allah's Messenger, to the end that they may disperse (and quit Madinah)." But to Allah belong the treasures of the heavens and the earth, but the hypocrites understand not.
	63:008	4. They say: "If we return to Madinah, surely the more honorable (element) will expel therefrom the meaner." But honor belongs to Allah and His Messenger, and to the Believers; but the Hypocrites know not.

1.3 Negligence in Remembering God

Riches and human resources of all kind are sources of enjoyment for people. However, prosperity and children should not turn away any good person from his devotion to God and his remembrance of Him. The remembrance of God includes every act of service and goodness, and every kind thought and deed, for this is the service and sacrifice that God requires from people. If we fail in this, the loss is our own, for it stunts our own growth as God's trustee on earth. God warns in Surah Al-Munafiqun that wealth and children should not make us neglect remembering Him. "O you who believe! Let not your riches or your children divert you from the remembrance of Allah. If any act thus, the loss is their own. Spend something (in charity) out of the substance that We have bestowed on you before death should come to any of you and he should say, 'O my Lord! Why did You not give me respite for a little while? I should then have given (largely) in charity, and I should have been one of the doers of good.' But to no soul will Allah grant respite when the time appointed has come, and Allah is well acquainted with (all) that you do (Qur'an 63:9-11)."

CHAPTER 51

The Behavior of Humankind
FROM SURAH AT-TAGHABUN (64)

God created people in an excellent form and shape. He gave them free will to choose between belief and unbelief, between good and bad, and He is watching how people choose. People are responsible and answerable for their behavior and deeds. We have been told why some nations have ultimately been destroyed in the past. God says that, in reality, people refused to believe in the messengers whom He sent for their guidance. Without divine guidance, they invented their own philosophies of life and went on groping their way from one error to another. To avoid this fate of former communities, people have been invited to obey God, His Messenger, and the guidance that He has revealed.

Believers should sincerely obey God and His Messenger and place their trust in Him alone. Worldly goods and children are a great trial and temptation. One should watch that love of them doesn't tempt a person to ignore God's commands. Although every person is responsible to the extent of his ability, and although God does not demand that people exert themselves beyond their power and ability, believers should try not to transgress, through their own negligence and forgetfulness, the bounds set by God in their speech, behavior, and dealings with other people.

1 OUR BEHAVIOR AND DEEDS IMPACT OUR FATE

1.1 People are Responsible for their Behavior and Deeds
God created the universe, and everything in it confirms His perfection. There is a purpose and wisdom behind its creation. God gave people responsibility, and they are answerable to Him for their behavior and deeds. Ultimately, they have to return to their Creator to give an account of what they did to serve Him as His trustees. In Surah At-Taghabun, God tells people: "It is He Who has created you, and of you are some that are unbelievers

and some that are believers, and Allah sees well all that you do. He has created the heavens and the earth in just proportions and has given you shape and made your shapes beautiful, and to Him is the final goal. He knows what is in the heavens and on earth, and He knows what you conceal and what you reveal. Yea, Allah knows well the (secrets) of hearts (Qur'an 64:2-4)."

1.2 Corruption has Destroyed many Past Communities

Nation after nation has arisen and ultimately gone to its doom. This has persisted throughout history. People have tried to explain this phenomenon in numerous ways, but God says that the real reason is that people refused to believe in the messengers whom He sent for their guidance. As a result, God left them to themselves. Without divine guidance, people invented their own philosophies and went on struggling their way from one error to another. Their assumption was that this life ends with death and that there is no resurrection, at which time their behavior and deeds are judged and rewarded. This corrupted their attitude towards life, degraded their morals and character, and filled the world with corruption, cruelty, and injustice. Eventually, as a consequence of their behavior, the scourge of God descended and eliminated them from the scene.

To avoid the fate of these former communities, unbelievers are invited to believe in the existence of God, His Messenger, and the guidance that He has revealed in the Qur'an. Further, they are reassured of their resurrection. After resurrection, all former and latter generations will be gathered at one place, and the corruption committed by each will be exposed. The fate of each person will be decided on the basis of who adopted the path of faith and righteousness and who followed the way of disbelief and denial of the truth. The first group will be rewarded with Paradise, and the second will be doomed to everlasting Hell.

Table 1.2: The Behavior Determines the Condition of People

No	Surah:Verses	Meanings
		People will face the Evil Result of their Conduct during this life and in the Hereafter
1	64:005-006	Has not the story reached you of those who rejected faith aforetime? 1. So they tasted the evil result of their conduct, and 2. A painful punishment awaits them (in the Hereafter). That was because there came to them messengers with clear signs, but they said: "Shall (mere) human beings direct us?" So they rejected (the message) and turned away. But Allah can do without (them), and Allah is free of all needs, worthy of all praise.
		People should Believe in God, His Messengers, and His Message
2	64:007-008	• The unbelievers think that they will not be raised up (for judgment). Say: "Yea, by my Lord, you shall surely be raised up. Then shall you be told (the truth) of all that you did, and that is easy for Allah. Believe, therefore, in Allah and His Messenger and in the light that we have sent down. Allah is well acquainted with all that you do.
		Resurrection will be a Day of Gain for Some and Loss for others
3	64:009-010	The Day (of Judgment) that He assembles you (all) for a day of assembly—that will be a day of mutual loss and gain (among you). 1. Those who believe in Allah and work righteousness—He will remove from them their ills, and He will admit them to gardens beneath which rivers flow, to dwell therein forever. That will be the supreme achievement. 2. But those who reject faith and treat Our signs as falsehoods—they will be companions of the fire, to dwell therein forever, and evil is that goal.

2 THE GREEDY WILL NEVER BE PROSPEROUS

2.1 Basics and Behavior that Lead to Success

God tells the believers that: whatever affliction befalls a person, it befalls by God's leave; and whoever remains steadfast, God blesses his heart with guidance. After the affirmation of the faith, a believer should trust God alone and should sincerely obey God and His Messenger. If he turns away from obedience, he is responsible for his loss.

Table 2.1: Reform your Behavior and Deeds for Success

No	Surah:Verses	Meanings
		Basics that Facilitate Success
1	64:011-015	No kind of calamity can occur except by the leave of Allah. And if any one believes in Allah, (He) guides his heart (aright), for Allah knows all things. 1. So obey Allah, and obey His Messenger, but if you turn back, the duty of Our Messenger is but to proclaim clearly and openly. Allah! There is no god but He, and on Allah, therefore, let the believers put their trust. 2. O you who believe! Truly, among your wives and your children are (some that are) enemies to yourselves, so beware of them! But if you forgive and overlook and cover up (their faults), verily, Allah is oft-forgiving, most merciful. Your riches and your children may be but a trial, but in the presence of Allah is the highest reward.
		Listen to and Obey the Guidance
2	64:016-017	So fear Allah as much as you can; listen and obey, and spend in charity for the benefit of your own self. • Those saved from the covetousness of their own souls—they are the ones that achieve prosperity. • If you loan to Allah a beautiful loan, He will double it to your (credit), and He will grant you forgiveness: ...

CHAPTER 52

Commandments about Divorce
FROM SURAH AL-BAQARAH (02),
SURAH AL-AHZAB (33), AND SURAH AT-TALAQ (65)

Commands concerning divorce were given in Surah Al-Baqarah for the first time. Although it is difficult to determine precisely the exact date of revelation of Surah At-Talaq, the traditions indicate that when the people, lacking a proper understanding of the commands of Surah Al-Baqarah, began to commit mistakes regarding divorce, God revealed these instructions for their correction.

1 SURAH AL-BAQARAH (02), AND SURAH AL-AHZAB (33)

1.1 The Process of Divorce in Islam

A man can divorce his wife at most three times. In the case of first and second divorces, he is entitled to change his mind. As such, if both desire to remarry, they can remarry: In Surah Al-Baqarah, people are told: "A divorce is only permissible twice. After that, the parties should either hold together on equitable terms or separate with kindness (Qur'an 2:229)." After the husband has pronounced the third divorce, he forfeits his right to keep her as his wife within the waiting period following the third divorce. They cannot remarry unless the woman marries another person, and they subsequently divorce. However, there is no waiting period for a woman who has been divorced before her marriage has been consummated. She can remarry, if she likes, immediately after the divorce. The waiting period of the woman whose husband dies is four months and ten days.

Table 1.1: Waiting Period for Women in Case of Divorce

No	Surah:Verses	Meanings
		The Waiting period after the Divorce
1	02:228, 230	Divorced women shall wait concerning themselves for three monthly periods. ... then 1. (Either) their husbands have the better right to take them back in that period if they wish for reconciliation. (Or) if a husband divorces his wife (irrevocably, third time), He cannot after that remarry her until after she has married another husband and He has divorced her. In that case there is no blame on either of them if they reunite, provided they feel that they can keep the limits ordained by Allah. Such are the limits ordained by Allah, which He makes plain to those who understand.
		Non-consummation of Marriage
2	33:049	O you who believe! When you marry believing women and then divorce them before you have touched them, no period of *'Iddat* (waiting) have you to count with respect to them. So give them a present, and set them free in a handsome manner.
		The Waiting period for a Widow
3	02:234	If any of you die and leave widows behind, they shall wait concerning themselves four months and ten days.

2 SURAH AT-TALAQ (65)

2.1 Reconciliation or Separation with Dignity

Surah At-Talaq was not revealed to annul any of the rules already revealed or to amend them. It was revealed so that men use their right to divorce in judicious ways that do not lead to needless separation. However, if separation does take place, it should only be after all possibilities of mutual reconciliation have been exhausted. The provision for divorce is only an unavoidable necessity; otherwise, God does not approve that the marital relationship should ever be broken. It was narrated by Abdullah ibn 'Umar that the Prophet said: "Of all the lawful acts, the most detestable to Allah is the divorce (Abu Dawud 12.2173)."

Table 2.1 Reconciliation, Waiting Period, and Child Suckling

No	Surah:Verses	Meanings
		Efforts and Time Required for Reconciliation
1	65:001	• O Prophet! When you do divorce women, divorce them at their prescribed periods, and count (accurately) their prescribed periods. Fear Allah, your Lord, and turn them not out of their houses, nor shall they (themselves) leave, except in case they are guilty of some open lewdness. Those are limits set by Allah, and any who transgresses the limits of Allah does, verily, wrong his (own) self...
		Either Retain Honorably or Part Honorably
2	65:002	• Thus, when they fulfill their term appointed, either take them back on equitable terms or part with them on equitable terms. And take for witness two persons from among you, endued with justice, and establish the evidence before Allah, Such is the admonition given to him who believes in Allah and the Last Day.
		Waiting period for the Non-menstruating or Pregnant
3	65:004	• Such of your women as have passed the age of monthly courses, for them the prescribed period, if you have any doubts, is three months, and for those who have no courses (it is the same). For those who carry (life within their wombs), their period is until they deliver their burdens...
		Compensation for Child Suckling
4	65:006-007	Let the women live (in the waiting period) in the same style as you live, according to your means. Annoy them not, so as to restrict them. And if they carry (life in their wombs), then spend (your substance) on them until they deliver their burden. 1. If they suckle your (offspring), give them their recompense, and take mutual counsel together, according to what is just and

		reasonable.
		2. If you find yourselves in difficulties, let another woman suckle (the child) on the (father's) behalf.
		• Let the man of means spend according to his means, and the man whose resources are restricted, let him spend according to what Allah has given him.
		Allah puts no burden on any person beyond what He has given him. After a difficulty, Allah will soon grant relief.

2.2 Implementation of God's Commands Benefits People

God stresses the importance of implementing His commands by reminding people that their welfare in this world, as well as in the Hereafter, depends on the implementation of His commands and on nothing else. History confirms that many towns that rebelled against divine guidance and His messengers were severely punished in this world. They are also destined to receive God's punishment in the Hereafter.

Table 2.2: Fate depends on One's Behavior and Conduct

No	Surah:Verses	Meanings
		Good Conduct and Deeds Benefit People in Both Worlds
5	65:008-010	How many populations that insolently opposed the command of their Lord and of His messengers did We not then call to account—to severe account? We imposed on them an exemplary punishment. Then did they taste the evil result of their conduct, and the end of their conduct was perdition. • Allah has prepared for them a severe punishment (in the Hereafter). Therefore, fear Allah, O you men of understanding who have believed, Allah has indeed sent down to you a message.
		The Messenger leads the Believers from Darkness into Light
6	65:011	A Messenger who recites to you the revelations of Allah, containing clear explanations, that he may lead forth those who believe and do righteous deeds from the depths of darkness into light.

632

		• Those who believe in Allah and work righteousness, He will admit to gardens beneath which rivers flow, to dwell therein forever. Allah has, indeed, granted for them a most excellent provision.
		People should know that **God has Power over all Things**
7	65:012	Allah is He Who created seven skys and of the earth a similar number. Through the midst of them (all) descends His command that you may know that Allah has power over all things and that Allah comprehends all things in (His) knowledge.

CHAPTER 53

Family Relationships and Responsibilities
FROM SURAH AT-TAHRIM (66)

Citing some incidents concerning the wives of the Messenger, guidance is provided on how to make family life successful. In Surah At-Tahrim, which was revealed seven or eight years after the migration to Madinah, people are told that (1) only God has the right to declare something lawful or unlawful; (2) oaths should be guarded and fulfilled, with expiation permitted in the case of unlawful oaths; (3) efforts in the right direction lead to success; and (4) the support and cooperation of each member of the family is essential for the success of the family, and believers should guide their family members away from the fire—the fire of corruption in this world and the fire of Hell in the Hereafter.

1 THE LAWFUL AND UNLAWFUL

1.1 The Lawful Cannot Be Made Unlawful
The power to prescribe the bounds of the lawful and the unlawful, the permissible and the forbidden, is entirely and absolutely in the hand of God, and nothing of this power has been delegated, not even to the Messenger. A messenger can declare something lawful or unlawful only if he receives an inspiration from God to do so, whether that inspiration is a part of the Qur'an or narrated by the Messenger himself. God says: "O Prophet! Why hold you to be forbidden that which Allah has made lawful to you? You seek to please your consorts. But Allah is oft-forgiving, most merciful. Allah has already ordained for you the dissolution of your oaths (in some cases), and Allah is your protector, and He is full of knowledge and wisdom (Qur'an 66:1-2)."

1.2 Oaths Should Be Fulfilled or Expiated
Oaths should be guarded and fulfilled. However, expiation is permitted in the case of an unlawful oath. How one can expiate for an unlawful oath? The answer is found in Surah Al-Maidah:

634

"Allah will not call you to account for what is futile in your oaths, but He will call you to account for your deliberate oaths. For expiation, feed ten indigent persons on a scale of the average for the food of your families, or clothe them, or give a slave his freedom. If that is beyond your means, fast for three days. That is the expiation for the oaths you have sworn. But keep to your oaths. Thus, does Allah make clear to you His revelations that you may be grateful (Qur'an 5:89)."

2 FAMILY RELATIONSHIPS AND RESPONSIBILITIES

2.1 Wives should Guard their Family Secrets
Things told in secret should remain secret. An incident in the Messenger's life is cited to emphasize this. During this incident, a secret told to one of his wives was communicated to the other wives. The Messenger's wives were also told that if they formed a group against their husband, they would only hurt themselves because the Messenger enjoyed God's support, as well as the support of angels and the believers. "When the Prophet disclosed a matter in confidence to one of his consorts and she then divulged it (to another), and Allah made it known to him, he confirmed part thereof and repudiated a part. Then when he told her thereof, she said: 'Who told you this?' He said, 'He told me Who knows and is well-acquainted' (Qur'an 66:3)." Among other lessons to be drawn from this passage, one should see that support and cooperation from each member of the family is essential for the success of the whole family. Additionally, wives should guard family secrets.

Table 2.1: Characteristics of Good Wives

No	Surah:Verses	Meanings
		Good Wives unite not against their Husbands
1	66:004	If you two turn in repentance to Him—your hearts are indeed so inclined, but if you back up each other against him, truly, Allah is his protector, and Gabriel, and (every) righteous one among those who believe—and furthermore, the angels will back (him) up.
		Good Wives are Faithful, Obedient, and Worship God

635

No	Surah:Verses	Meanings
2	66:005	It may be, if he divorced you (all), that Allah will give him in exchange consorts better than you, 1. who submit (their wills), 2. who believe, 3. who are devout, 4. who turn to Allah in repentance, 5. who worship (in humility), 6. who travel (for faith) and fast, (Both) previously married or virgins.

2.2 Parents Should Try to Save their Children from the Fire

Our efforts impact our results, and efforts in the right direction lead to the success. Therefore, believers should repent and reform. All people, both believers and unbelievers, will be told on the Day of Judgment that they will be rewarded only according to their past striving and deeds.

Table 2.2: Believers Guide their Families Away from Fire

No	Surah:Verses	Meanings
		Believers Guide their Families Away from Fire
3	66:006-007	O you who believe! Save yourselves and your families from a fire whose fuel is men and stones, over which are (appointed) angels stern (and) severe, who flinch not (from executing) the commands they receive from Allah, but do what they are commanded. • (They will say), "O you unbelievers! Make no excuses this day! You are being but requited for all that you did."
		Believers Turn to God and Repent Sincerely
4	66:008	O you who believe! Turn to Allah with sincere repentance: • In the hope that your Lord will remove from you your ills and admit you to gardens beneath which rivers flow— The Day that Allah will not permit to be humiliated the Prophet and those who believe with him. Their light will run forward before them and by their right hands, while they say, "Our Lord! Perfect our light for us, and grant us forgiveness, for You have power over all things.

2.3 God Awards People according to their Efforts

It is stressed in Surah At-Tahrim that God is absolutely fair and just. A person becomes worthy only on the basis of faith and efforts. Addressing the Messenger, God commands people: "O Prophet! Strive hard against the unbelievers and the hypocrites, and be firm against them. Their abode is Hell, an evil refuge (Qur'an 66:9)." No relationship or connection, even with the most righteous person, can help one on the Day of Judgment, and no relationship or connection with the most evil and wicked person can damn one. The Qur'an illustrates this by citing the examples of three kinds of women. The wives of Noah and Lot disbelieved, and their being the wives of messengers did not help them. On the other hand, the wife of Pharaoh believed and chose a path of action that was different from that of Pharaoh and his people. Her being the wife of a disbeliever did not cause her any harm, and God made her worthy of Paradise. The third example is that of Mary, the mother of Jesus. She achieved her success because she submitted to the severe test to which God put her.

Table 2.3: Unbelieving and Believing Wives

No	Surah:Verses	Meanings
		Unbelieving Wives
5	66:010	Allah sets forth, for an example to the unbelievers, • The wife of Noah and the wife of Lot. They were (respectively) under two of our righteous servants, but they were false to their (husbands), and they profited nothing before Allah on their account, but were told: "You enter the fire, along with (others) that enter!"
		Believing Wives
6	66:011-012	1. And Allah sets forth, as an example to those who believe the wife of Pharaoh. Behold! She said: "O my Lord! Build for me, in nearness to You, a mansion in the garden, and save me from Pharaoh and his doings, and save me from those that do wrong. 2. And Mary the daughter of Imran, who guarded her chastity, and We breathed into (her body) of Our spirit, and she testified to the truth of the words of her Lord and of His revelations and was one of the devout.

CHAPTER 54

People have Strengths and Weaknesses
FROM SURAH AT-TAHRIM (66), SURAH AL-IMRAN (03),
SURAH AN-NUR (24), SURAH AL-AHZAB (33),
SURAH AL-MUMTAHINAH (60), SURAH JUMU'AH (62),
AND SURAH 'ABASA (80)

God corrected the undesirable behavior or errors of the messengers at several places in the Qur'an. The only reason for mentioning these incidents in the Qur'an is that God wants to acquaint people with the correct way of respecting their great personalities. A messenger is a messenger, not God. He is human and can make a mistake, although not in delivering the revelation given to him. Respect for the messengers has not been enjoined because they are infallible, but because they are the representatives of the divine will, and God has not permitted any of their errors to pass by unnoticed. This gives people the satisfaction that the noble pattern of life left by the messengers fully represents the will of God. Likewise, the companions and the wives of the Messenger were all human, not angels or super people. They could make mistakes. Whatever ranks they achieved became possible only because of the guidance given by God and the training imparted by the Messenger, which molded them into the finest models of human character and behavior. Whatever respect they deserve is on this very basis and not on the presumption that they were infallible. Whenever the Messenger, his wives, or the companions happened to commit an error due to human weakness, they were corrected.

1 THE BELIEVERS STAND CORRECTED

Some errors of judgement are mentioned in the Qur'an, and God corrected them so that the believers wouldn't exaggerate the respect and honor due to their elders and great men, raising them from humanity to the position of gods and goddesses. These instances are told in the Qur'an, in the same Qur'an in which God pays tribute to the Messenger, his companions, and the

638

Messenger's wives for their great merits. Thus, He granted them the certificate of His good pleasure.

1.1 When Disobeyed their Leader, Believers were Punished

In Surah Al-Imran, concerning the battle of Uhud, the companions were told: "Allah did indeed fulfill His promise to you when you, with His permission, were about to annihilate your enemy, until you flinched and fell to disputing about the order, and disobeyed it after He brought you in sight (of the booty) that you covet. Among you are some that hanker after this world and some that desire the Hereafter. Then did He divert you from your foes in order to test you, but He forgave you, for Allah is full of grace to those who believe (Qur'an 3:152)."

1.2 Believers should have a Good Opinion of Themselves

In Surah An-Nur, in connection with the slander against A'ishah, the companions were told: "Why did not the believers, men and women—when you heard of the affair—put the best construction on it in their own minds and say, 'This is an obvious lie'? Why did they not bring four witnesses to prove it? When they have not brought the witnesses, such men, in the sight of Allah, (stand forth) themselves as liars! Were it not for the grace and mercy of Allah on you, in this world and the Hereafter, a grievous penalty would have seized you in that you rushed glibly into this affair. Behold, you received it on your tongues and said out of your mouths things of which you had no knowledge, and you thought it to be a light matter, while it was most serious in the sight of Allah. And why did you not, when you heard it, say, 'It is not right of us to speak of this. Glory to Allah! This is a most serious slander!' Allah does admonish you, that you may never repeat such (conduct) if you are believers (Qur'an 24:12-17)."

1.3 Great Reward is there for those who do Good Deeds

In Surah Al-Ahzab, the wives of the Messenger were addressed: "O Prophet! Say to your consorts: 'If it be that you desire the life of this world and its glitter, then come! I will provide for your enjoyment and set you free in a handsome manner. But if you seek Allah and His Messenger and the Home of the Hereafter, verily, Allah has prepared for the well-doers among you a great reward (Qur'an 33:28-29)."

1.4 When left Prayer for Trade, Believers were Admonished

In Surah Jumu'ah, we are told: "But when they see some bargain or some amusement, they disperse headlong to it and leave you (O Messenger) standing. Say: 'The (blessing) from the presence of Allah is better than any amusement or bargain, and Allah is the best to provide (for all your needs)' (Qur'an 62:11)."

2 PEOPLE HAVE STRENGTHS AND WEAKNESSES

2.1 Only God can make things Lawful or Unlawful

The power to prescribe the bounds of the lawful and the unlawful, the permissible and the forbidden, is entirely and absolutely in the hands of God, and this power hasn't been delegated even to the Messenger, not to speak of any other person. In Surah At-Tahrim, God says that even a Messenger cannot make things lawful or unlawful: "O Prophet! Why hold you to be forbidden that which Allah has made lawful to you? You seek to please your consorts. But Allah is oft-forgiving, most merciful. Allah has already ordained for you the dissolution of your oaths (in some cases), and Allah is your protector, and He is full of knowledge and wisdom (Qur'an 66:1-2)."

2.2 None is Perfect, Not even God's Messengers

The commentators are unanimous about the incident after which Surah 'Abasa was revealed. Once some chiefs of Makkah were sitting in the Messenger's assembly, and he was trying to persuade them to accept Islam. During this meeting, a blind man named Ibn Umm Maktum approached him to seek explanation of some point concerning Islam. The Messenger disliked his interruption and ignored him. Thereupon, God revealed this Surah to guide the Messenger. "(The Prophet) frowned and turned away because there came to him the blind man (interrupting). But what could you tell but that perchance he might grow (in spiritual understanding) or that he might receive admonition and the teaching might profit him? As to one who regards Himself as self-sufficient, to him do you attend, though it is no blame to you if he grows not (in spiritual understanding). But as to him who came to you striving earnestly and with fear (in his heart), of him were you unmindful. By no means (should it be so), for it is indeed a message of instruction. Therefore, let whoso will, keep it in remembrance (Qur'an 80:1-12)."

2.3 God Forbids the Worship of Created Deities

Moderate and balanced teaching about the honor and esteem of great men saved Muslims from falling into the sin of worshiping people, a trap into which the Jews and Christians had fallen. As a result, when people compiled the books on the *hadith*, prepared commentaries on the Qur'an and recorded history, not only did they narrate the great merits of the companions and wives of the Messenger, but they did not show any hesitation in mentioning the incidents relating to their weaknesses. Those scholars were more appreciative of the merits of the great people of Islam and understood the bounds and limits of reverence better than those who claim to be the upholders of reverence today.

CHAPTER 55

The Humanity Under Trial
FROM SURA AL-MULK (67)

The Prophet said: "A Surah of the Qur'an containing thirty verses will intercede for its reader till he will be forgiven. That is: 'Blessed is He in Whose hand is dominion (Qur'an 67:1)' (Abu Dawud: 6. 1395)." The subject matter and style of this Surah indicate that Surah Al-Mulk is one of the earliest Surahs revealed at Makkah. In it, Islam is briefly presented to make people think and to arouse their dormant conscience. People are told that the human mission is to establish justice in this world and that success can only be achieved through righteous behavior and deeds. Bad behavior and fulfillment of selfish desires lead to corrupt societies. Further, the dreadful consequences of unbelief and corruption will also appear in the Hereafter. By sending messengers, God warned people about the consequences of not believing, and in the Hereafter, unbelievers will admit that they deserve the punishment they are being given.

1 THE HUMAN MISSION, SELFISHNESS OR JUSTICE

1.1 Success is through Righteous Deeds and Conduct.
The universe we live in is a well-organized and fortified kingdom that is without any fault, weakness, or flaw. This universe has been created by God Himself, and the powers of controlling, administering, and ruling it belong to Him alone, and His powers are infinite. Humanity was created with a purpose and sent here for a test. In this test, people can succeed only by righteous deeds and conduct. God tells people: "Blessed be He in Whose hands is dominion, and He has power over all things— He Who created death and life that He may try which of you is best in deed. And He is the exalted in might, oft-forgiving—He Who created the seven heavens one above another. No want of proportion will you see in the creation of (Allah) Most Gracious. So turn your vision again; do you see any flaw? Again turn your vision a second time; (your) vision will come back to you dull and discomfited, in a state worn out (Qur'an 67:1-4)."

1.2 Bad Conduct leads Humanity to Failure

Humans have been invited to reflect on the earth on which they move around and from which they obtain their sustenance. It has been subdued for them by God. Otherwise, this earth might at any time start shaking suddenly and cause destruction, or a typhoon might occur, which could annihilate humankind completely. God tells people to look at their own means and resources. If God wants to inflict punishment, none can save them from it. Likewise, if God wants to close the doors of sustenance, none can open them for them. These things are here to make people aware of the truth, but like animals they are unable to draw conclusions from their observations. People do not seem to use the sight, hearing, and wisdom that God has given to them. That is why they do not see things correctly.

Table 1.2: Reward and Punishment in Life and in Hereafter

No	Surah:Verses	Meanings
		Ultimate Accountability will Come
1	67:015-018	It is He Who has made the earth manageable for you, so traverse you through its tracts and enjoy of the sustenance that He furnishes, but unto Him is the resurrection. • Do you feel secure that He Who is in Heaven will not cause you to be swallowed up by the earth when it shakes (as in an earthquake), or do you feel secure that He Who is in Heaven will not send against you a violent tornado (with showers of stones), so that you shall know how (terrible) was My warning? But, indeed, men before them rejected; then how (terrible) was My rejection!
		Unbelievers persist in Rebellion and Aversion
2	67:019-023	Do they not observe the birds above them, spreading their wings and folding them in? None can uphold them except (Allah) Most Gracious. Truly, it is He that watches over all things. Nay, who is there that can help you, (even as) an army, besides (Allah) Most Merciful? In nothing but delusion are the unbelievers. • Or who is there that can provide you with sustenance if He were to withhold His

		provision? Nay, they obstinately persist in insolent impiety and flight (from the truth). Is then one who walks headlong, with his face groveling, better guided, • Or one who walks evenly on a straight way? Say: "It is He Who has created you (and made you grow) and made for you the faculties of hearing, seeing, feeling, and understanding; little thanks it is you give."

2 RESURRECTION, GOD'S JUDGMENT, AND AWARDS

2.1 Humankind has ultimately to appear before God

It was not for the Messenger to tell the exact time and date of the resurrection. His only duty was to warn people of its inevitable occurrence. However, the unbelievers did not listen to him and demanded that he cause the event to appear prematurely before them. When it does occur, they will see it with their own eyes. God tells the unbelievers that they should look after themselves and consider who will save them if they are overtaken by God's punishment. Even though the unbelievers regard those who believe in God and put their trust in Him as being misguided, a time will come when it will become evident to them as to who was actually misguided.

Table 2.1: Muslims believe in God and on Him do They Rely

No	Surah:Verses	Meanings
		Unbelievers ask: When their Punishment will Be?
1	67:024-027	Say: "It is He Who has multiplied you through the earth, and to Him shall you be gathered together." • They ask: "When will this promise be (fulfilled), if you are telling the truth?" • Say: "As to the knowledge of the time, it is with Allah alone. I am (sent) only to warn plainly in public." At length, when they see it close at hand, grieved will be the faces of the unbelievers, and it will be said (to them): "This is (the promise fulfilled), for which you were calling."

		None will be able to protect the Unbelievers
2	67:028-030	• Say: "You See! If Allah were to destroy me and those with me or if He bestows His mercy on us—yet who can deliver the unbelievers from a grievous penalty?" • Say: "He is (Allah) Most Gracious. We have believed in Him, and on Him have we put our trust. So soon will you know which (of us) it is that is in manifest error." Say: "You See! If your stream be some morning lost (in the underground earth), who then can supply you with clear-flowing water?"

2.2 Belief and Good Deeds Earn Forgiveness and Reward

God reminds people that He is aware of their public behavior and hidden secrets and that people should avoid evil, fearing accountability before the unseen God. Only those who adopt righteous conduct in the world will receive forgiveness and a rich reward in the Hereafter. God reassures the believers that, "for those who fear their Lord unseen, for them is forgiveness and a great reward (Qur'an 67:12)."

Table 2.2: Unbelief will lead People to Punishment

No	Surah:Verses	Meanings
3	67:006-011	For those who reject their Lord is the penalty of Hell, and evil is (such) destination. When they are cast therein, they will hear the (terrible) drawing in of its breath even as it blazes forth almost bursting with fury. Every time a group is cast therein, its keepers will ask, "Did no warner come to you?" 1. They will say: "Yes, indeed; a warner did come to us, but we rejected him and said, 'Allah never sent down any (message); you are only in a great error.'" 2. They will further say: "Had we but listened or used our intelligence, we should not (now) be among the companions of the blazing fire. 3. They will then confess their sins, but far will be (forgiveness) from the companions of the blazing fire.

CHAPTER 56

The Doctrine of Efforts & Reward
FROM SURAH AL-HAQQAH (69)

Surah Al-Haqqah is one of the earliest Surahs to be revealed at Makkah. It was during a time when opposition to the Prophet had started but had not yet become tyrannical. In this Surah, people are told that in the Hereafter they will be rewarded for their efforts, the Qur'an is a revelation from God, and the Prophet is His true Messenger. Addressing the unbelievers of Makkah, God repudiates their claims that the Messenger is merely a poet or soothsayer and tells them that the Qur'an is a revelation sent down by Him to the Messenger.

The idea of effort and reward is central to Islamic thinking. Every action can earn a reward from God if it is intended for the right purpose. People's behavior and effort in this life determine their destiny in the Hereafter. Islam, being a system devised by God for human life, regulates all aspects of life in the light of its basic principles of believing in God, His Messenger and His message. Since it is only through effort and good actions that a person attains salvation in the Hereafter, it is natural for Islam to place particular emphasis on hard work. Islam links actions, which are purely for the maintaince of human life and its needs in this world, to what is purely religious and dedicated to the achievement of happiness in the life to come. This is how Islam leads people to an attitude that encourages hard work throughout the community and thus results in the community's development and prosperity. A believer conscious of this requirement of his faith has the best motivation to work hard throughout this life.

In the past, God has completely destroyed nations by natural disasters or some other form of punishment because they arrogantly refused to follow the prophets and messengers sent to them. The fact that God mentions these punishments to people serves as a reminder that He is able to inflict similar punishments at any time in history if people do not admit their mistakes and reform. Continual improvement in human character and behavior is what God demands. Any effort in this direction is bound to be rewarded in the form of better behavior and deeds, postively transforming the quality of life and existence on earth.

1 IMPACT OF PEOPLE'S BEHAVIOR ON SOCIETY

Volcanic eruptions, cyclones, floods, and other natural disasters take place as a result of natural laws that God has set in operation. They can be caused when the balance set by God in the universe is upset. When a cyclone hits certain areas, one cannot say that the people of that area have earned such punishment by God. How can one tell? After all, cyclones regularly hit certain parts of the world when the people there may be better than those who live in another part of the world. However, God is the most just of judges. If He punishes some people, His punishment is just. Yet, it does not follow that those were the only people who deserved punishment. God may choose to delay the punishment of others until the Day of Judgment. No one who disobeys God can escape punishment unless God chooses to forgive himr. Therefore, one should always be concerned about incurring God's anger, lest His punishment takes us unaware. In short, one should always maintain a balance between realizing that God controls all natural laws and that He can easily inflict any type of punishment He chooses.

1.1 Is the Resurrection to benefit People or God?
Some people may ask about the purpose of punishing people here in this world or after the resurrection. They may say that the creation of Hell is meant to pressure humanity to do what they don't want to do or what is not in their interest. They might also ask why God doesn't motivate them by His love. What such people forget is that God created them in various types; some are motivated by love and others by fear. His system of total life caters to the needs of all generations and of all individuals of the same generation. On the other hand, God did not feel it necessary to resurrect animals because He did not give them free will, nor were they endowed with intellect and wisdom. Armed with free will and reason, humanity has a tremendous power to

act in the best interest of humanity or to be selfish and corrupt. Hell is meant for the corrupt because: "If Allah were to punish men for their wrongdoing, He would not leave on the (earth) a single living creature, but He gives them respite for a stated term. When their term expires, they would not be able to delay (the punishment) for a single hour, just as they would not be able to anticipate it (Qur'an 16:61)."

1.2 God commits no Injustice, they were unjust to themselves
God says: "What can Allah gain by your punishment if you are grateful and you believe (Qur'an 4:147)?" After mentioning the fate of unbelieving communities, God tells people: "It was not We that wronged them. They wronged their own selves. The deities, other than Allah, whom they invoked, profited them nothing when there issued the decree of your Lord. Nor did they add anything (to their lot) but perdition! Such is the chastisement of your Lord when He chastises communities while they were doing wrong (Qur'an 11:101-102)." The coming of the resurrection and the occurrence of the Hereafter are truths that will inevitably happen, and people who deny their accountability for their behavior and deeds and continue their sinful lives ultimately earn God's punishment, in this world or the next.

Table 1: People's Corruption destroyed their Communities

No	Surah:Verses	Meanings
		None among Thamud and the 'Ad People Survived
1	69:004-008	The Thamud and the 'Ad People (branded) as false the stunning calamity! 1. But the Thamud—they were destroyed by a terrible storm of thunder and lightning. 2. The 'Ad—they were destroyed by a furious wind, exceedingly violent. He made it rage against them seven nights and eight days in succession, so that you could see the people lying prostrate in its (path), as if they had been roots of hollow palm trees tumbled down! Then do you see any of them left surviving?
		Pharaoh and those who Disobeyed their Messengers were Destroyed
2	69:009-012	Pharaoh and those before him, and the cities

	overthrown, committed habitual sin. (They) disobeyed the messenger of their Lord, so He punished them with an abundant penalty. • We, when the water (of Noah's flood) overflowed beyond its limits, carried you (mankind) in the floating (ark) that We might make it a message unto you and that ears (that should hear the tale and) retain its memory should bear its (lessons) in remembrance.

2 EFFORTS, FORGIVENESS, AND GOD'S MERCY

It is often said that the prosperity of nations cannot come without an attitude that encourages hard work throughout the community. No doctrine that has managed to raise people to the state of nationhood has ever failed to emphasize the need for hard work on the part of individuals and the community as a whole. Striving leads people to a proficiency by which human weaknesses are overcome and forgiven. Success then descends as God's mercy on hardworking people. That is why Islam stresses the importance of hard work, for it is only through good actions that a person attains salvation in the Hereafter. Even when people go about earning their livelihood, they hope their efforts will be rewarded in this life and the next. Believers must steer away the forbidden and link their immediate purpose to the wider one of earning God's pleasure.

2.1 Individual Efforts and their Rewards

The idea of effort and reward is central to Islamic thinking. Every action earns reward from God if it is intended for the right purpose. The Messenger was always keen to point out what action or attitude could earn reward, in order to encourage his companions to do it. He often emphasized the importance of certain types of work by pointing out that they were bound to earn a reward. This can very well be illustrated by a *hadith* in which Anas ibn Malik quoted the Messenger as saying: "There is none among the Muslims who plants a tree or sows a seed, and then a bird or a person or an animal eats from it, but it is regarded as a charitable gift from him (Sahih Bukhari: 3.39.513)" In Islam, work is equated with worship.

2.2 Every Deed has its Inevitable Consequence

Deeds must bear their inevitable fruit. Wrongdoers don't suffer because of divine injusticeor cruelty, nor do they suffer as a deterrent to others. Their suffering is due to their own evil deeds, and they must bear their inevitable recompense. Describing Paradise, God tells people in Surah Az-Zukhruf: "Such will be the garden of which you are made heirs for your (good) deeds (in life). You shall have therein abundance of fruit from which you shall have satisfaction. The sinners will be in the punishment of Hell, to dwell therein (forever). It (the punishment) will not be lightened for them, and in despair will they be there overwhelmed. We are not being unjust to them, but it is they who have been unjust themselves (Qur'an 43:72-76)." God's grace was and is ever ready to offer opportunities for repentance and forgiveness, but the unbelievers reject them. They were and are unjust to themselves.

God reaffirms that unbelievers who turn people away from God's way, He shall render their works ineffective, "Those who reject Allah and hinder (men) from the path of Allah—their deeds will Allah render vain. But those who believe and work deeds of righteousness, and believe in the (revelation) sent down to Muhammad—for it is the truth from their Lord—He will remove from them their ills and improve their condition. This is because those who reject Allah follow vanities, while those who believe follow the truth from their Lord. Thus, does Allah set forth for men their lessons by similitude (Qur'an 47:1-3)."

2.3 God will Reward Good Behavior and Deeds

The real object for which God has destined a second life for humankind after the present worldly life is to reward people for their good behavior and deeds. People are told that upon resurrection, every person will appear in the court of their Lord, where none of their secrets will remain hidden and each person's record will be given to him. Those who spent lives in the world realizing that one day they would have to give an account of their deeds before their Lord, and who worked righteously in the

650

world, will rejoice when they see that they have been acquitted and blessed with the eternal bliss of Paradise. However, those who neither recognized the rights of God nor discharged the rights of other people will have no one to save them from God's punishment, and they will be thrown into Hell.

Table 2.3: The Day of Resurrection and God's Judgment

No	Surah:Verses	Meanings
		What will happen on the Day of Resurrection?
1	69:013-018	1. Then, when one blast is sounded on the trumpet. 2. And the earth is moved, and its mountains and they are crushed to powder at one stroke. On that day shall the (great) event come to pass. 3. And the sky will be rent asunder, for it will that day be flimsy, 4. And the angels will be on its sides, and eight will that day bear the throne of your Lord above them. That day shall you be brought to judgment; not an act of yours that you hide will be hidden.
		Fruits of the Good Deeds: Enjoy with Satisfaction
2	69:019-024	Then he that will be given his record in his right hand will say: "Ah here! You read my record! I did really understand that my account would (one day) reach me." 1. He will be in a life of bliss, in a garden on high, the fruits whereof (will hang in bunches) low and near. 2. "Eat and drink with full satisfaction because of the (good) that you sent before you in the days that are gone."
		The Failed will have their Books in Left Hand
3	69:025-034	And he that will be given his record in his left hand will say: • "Ah! Would that my record had not been given to me and that I had never realized how my account (stood)! • "Ah! Would that (death) had made an end of me. Of no profit to me has been my wealth. My power has perished from me!" (The stern command will say): "Seize him, and

		bind him, and burn him in the blazing fire. Further, make him march in a chain, whereof the length is seventy cubits! 1. This was he that would not believe in Allah most high 2. And would not encourage the feeding of the indigent!"

2.4 The Qur'an, Guidance from the Lord of the Universe

The unbelievers thought that the Qur'an was the word of a poet or soothsayer, whereas it is God's revelation, as presented to His Messenger. The Messenger by himself had no power to add or remove a word in it. If he would have ever forged something of his own composition into it, God would have instantly killed him. This is the truth, and those who reject it will ultimately regret their rejection of it.

Table 2.4: The Qur'an is the Revelation from God

No	Surah:Verses	Meanings
		The Qur'an is a Revelation from your Lord
4	69:038-048	So I do call to witness what you see and what you see not 1. That this is verily the word of an honored messenger. 2. It is not the word of a poet—little it is you believe. 3. Nor is it the word of a soothsayer—little admonition it is you receive. (This is) a message sent down from the Lord of the worlds. • And if the Messenger were to invent any sayings in Our name, We should certainly seize him by his right hand. We should certainly then cut off the artery of his heart, nor could any of you withhold him (from Our wrath). But verily this is a message for the God-fearing.

CHAPTER 57

Endure with a Gracious Patience
FROM SURAH AL-MA'ARIJ (70)

The unbelievers' denial of the resurrection and of their accountability for their behavior and deeds, as well as their challenge to the Messenger to bring on the Day of Judgment if he is being truthful about it, were all answered in Surah Al-Ma'arij. The unbelievers were told that God has His own ways and timescale for doing things. Since His timescale is quite different from human perception, the Messenger was asked to be patient. If God were to punish people immediately after their wrongdoing, no one would exist on the earth; to avoid this situation, God gives people respite for a stated term (Qur'an 16:61). However, for the ultimate accountability for of human behavior and deeds, resurrection is required.

1 RESURRECTION AND ACCOUNTABILITY

1.1 Unbelievers' Yearning for the Resurrection
The Surah opens with the Messenger having been asked about the penalty to come upon the unbelievers. "A questioner asked about a penalty to befall the unbelievers, the which there is none to ward off—(a penalty) from Allah, Lord of the ways of ascent. The angels and the Spirit ascend unto him in a day the measure whereof is fifty thousand years. Therefore, do you hold patience—a patience of beautiful contentment (Qur'an 70:1-5)."

1.2 Resurrection is to Punish the Corrupt
The resurrection allows for the ultimate accountability for one's behavior and deeds. Irrespective of whether people like it or not, it is going to happen. Since humanity is born with the responsibility for being God's trustee, how effectively one fulfills this responsibility must be evaluated and rewarded accordingly. The unbelievers think that the Day of Judgment will never come, and some believers like to reassure themselves that the Day of Judgment is far off in some distant future. However,

653

the Day of Judgment may come suddenly at any time. When it comes, it will cause great distress to the guilty. At that time, the unbelievers and wrongdoers would give away their wives, children, and nearest relatives in ransom to escape the punishment, but they will not be able to escape it.

Table 1.3 Secularists and Capitalists on the Day of Judgment

No	Surah:Verses	Meanings
		Day of Resurrection and Judgment
1	70:006-009	They see the (Day of Judgment), indeed, as a far-off (event), but We see it (quite) near. 1. That day the sky will be like molten brass, 2. And the mountains will be like wool.
		On the Day of Resurrection and Judgment
2	70:010-014	1. No friend will ask after a friend, though they will be put in sight of each other. 2. The sinner's desire will be: would that he could redeem himself from the penalty of that day by (sacrificing) his children, his wife and his brother, his kindred who sheltered him, and all, all that is on earth, so it could deliver him.
		Those Who Disbelieve and Hoard Wealth
3	70:015-018	By no means! For it would be the fire of Hell, plucking out (his being) right to the skull, (and) inviting (all) such as: 1. Turn their back and turn away their faces (from the right), 2. And collect (wealth) and hide it (from use).

2 BELIEF AND CONDUCT-BASED ACCOUNTABILITY

People who fear God's punishment, believe in the Hereafter, keep up the prayer, discharge the rights of the needy, avoid immoral and wicked deeds, practice honesty while dealing with others, fulfill their pledges and trust, and bear true witness will have a place of honor in Paradise during their life after death.

2.1 Only Good Behavior Makes People Human

People are created as embodiments of both weaknesses and strengths. Generally speaking, people are impatient, complain when in difficulty, and become very possessive and selfish in prosperity. Divine guidance helps them to overcome these weaknesses and guide them to true human character and behavior, which makes them successful in this life and in the Hereafter.

Table 2.1: Human Failures and their Best Behavior

No	Surah:Verses	Meanings
		People Complain in Adversity Or are Miserly in Prosperity
1	70:019-021	Truly man was created very impatient, fretful when evil touches him and miserly when good reaches him.
		Divine Guidance Transforms People into real Humans
2	70.022-035	1. Not so those devoted to prayer—those who remain steadfast to their prayer; 2. And those in whose wealth is a recognized right for the (needy) who asks and him who is prevented (for some reason from asking); 3. And those who hold to the truth of the Day of Judgment; 4. And those who fear the displeasure of their Lord—for their Lord's displeasure is the opposite of peace and tranquility; 5. And those who guard their chastity, except with their wives and the (captives) whom their right hands possess—for (then) they are not to be blamed, but those who trespass beyond this are transgressors; 6. And those who respect their trusts and covenants; 7. And those who stand firm in their testimonies; 8. And those who guard (the sacredness) of their worship. Such will be the honored ones in the gardens.

2.2 Their Evil Deeds Destroyed People in the Past

The unbelievers of Makkah, who were always making fun of the Messenger, were warned that if they did not believe, God would replace them with other and better people. "Now I do call to witness the Lord of all points in the East and the West that We can certainly substitute for them better (men) than they, and We are not to be defeated (Qur'an 70:40-41)." In other words, God is telling people that corruption, if not checked, can even destroy contemporary communities. No community, regardless of its time in history, should think that it is superior to all that went before it. We may be heirs to all of the progress in history, but this is no reason for arrogance. On the contrary, it adds to our responsibilities. When people reflect on past civilizations, how they flourished in number and prosperity, what opportunities they were given, and how they perished when they disobeyed God's law, they should feel a sense of humility and see that it was rebellious and selfish behavior that brought down prior civilizations. God was more than just; He was also merciful. However, past civilizations brought about their own ruin by ignoring God's moral and sociopolitical laws. God reminds people: "In the long run, evil in the extreme will be the end of those who do evil, for that they rejected the revelations of Allah and held them up to ridicule (Qur'an 30:10)." The Messenger and the believers consoled in this Surah, were commanded not to worry about the unbelievers' mockery and jesting, and were told to leave the unbelievers to their idle talk and evil conduct, for the unbelievers were bent upon inviting the disgrace and humiliation of the resurrection. "So leave them to plunge in vain talk and play about, until they encounter that day of theirs that they have been promised—the day whereon they will come out of the graves in sudden haste as if they were racing to a goal, their eyes lowered in dejection, ignominy covering them (all over)! Such is the day that they are promised (Qur'an 70:42-44)."

CHAPTER 58

Noah and His People
FROM SARAH NUH (71)

Noah was the most patient of men. He preached to his people for about 950 years, but his people rejected Noah, called him a liar, and asked him to pray to God for their punishment. Noah prayed, and the promised destruction came. The time had come for Noah's people to reap the consequences of their rejection of God's way and guidance.

1 SEEKING GOD'S FORGIVENESS AND HIS MERCY

1.1 Serve God and follow His Commands
Surah Nuh was revealed at Makkah in the period when opposition to the message of Islam had grown very strong and active. The story of Noah was told to warn the unbelievers that they were adopting the same attitude towards Muhammad as Noah's people had adopted towards Noah. If the unbelievers of Makkah did not change this attitude, they would also meet with destruction. While this was not explicitly stated, the background of the conditions under which this story was narrated to the people of Makah made the message obvious. Noah's appointment as God's messenger and his message to his people was described as follows. "We sent Noah to his people (with the command): 'Warn your people before there comes to them a grievous penalty.' He said: 'O my people! I am to you a warner, clear and open, that you should worship Allah, fear Him, and obey me, so He may forgive you your sins and give you respite for a stated term. For when the term given by Allah is accomplished, it cannot be put forward, if you only knew (Qur'an 71:1-4)!'"

1.2 Repent and Reform to Gain Success
For a long time, Noah had suffered hardships and troubles because of his preaching to his people. Noah had told his people to repent and reform, so that they would be candidates for God's

657

forgiveness and mercy, thereby receiving wealth and children in this world and Paradise in the Hereafter. Noah told God how he had been trying to bring his people to the right path and how his people had stubbornly opposed him. "He said: 'O my Lord! I have called to my people night and day, but my call only increases (their) flight (from the right). And every time I have called to them, that You might forgive them, they have (only) thrust their fingers into their ears, covered themselves up with their garments, grown obstinate, and given themselves up to arrogance' (Qur'an 71:5-7)."

Table 1.2: The Guidance for Prosperity and Paradise

No	Surah:Verses	Meanings
		Following Divine Laws Translates into Prosperity
1	71:008-012	(Noah said:) "So I (Noah) have called to them (my people) aloud. Further, I have spoken to them in public and secretly in private, saying, 'Ask forgiveness from your Lord, for He is oft-forgiving. 1. "'He will send rain to you in abundance, 2. "'Give you increase in wealth and sons, 3. "'And bestow on you gardens and bestow on you rivers (of flowing water).'"
		Created by God, the Universe Confirms God's Greatness
2	71:013-020	(Noah said:) "What is the matter with you that you place not your hope for kindness and long-suffering in Allah, seeing that it is He that has created you in diverse stages? 1. "Don't you see how Allah has created the seven heavens, one above another, and made the moon a light in their midst, and made the sun as a (glorious) lamp? 2. "And Allah has produced you from the earth, growing (gradually), and in the end He will return you into the (earth) and raise you forth (again at the resurrection). 3. "And Allah has made the earth for you as a carpet (spread out) that you may go about therein in spacious roads."

1.3 Their Evil Ways Destroyed Noah's People

Eventually, Noah prayed to his Lord, saying that his people had rejected his invitation to believe in God and to follow God's guidance, that they were blindly following their chiefs, that they had devised deceitful and cunning plots, and that there was no longer any hope for their repentance. This was not, however, an expression of impatience by Noah. After all, he had been preaching his message to them for centuries. God confirmed that there was no longer any chance for Noah's people, and God's punishment descended on those people because of their corruption and misdeeds.

Table 1.3: The Fate of Noah's Unbelieving People

No	Surah:Verses	Meanings
		Because of their Corruption, Noah's People were Drowned
3	71:021-025	Noah said: "O my Lord! They have disobeyed me, but they follow (men) whose wealth and children give them no increase but only loss. And they have devised a tremendous plot. And they have said (to each other), 'Abandon not your gods; abandon neither Wadd nor Suwa', neither Yaguth nor Ya'uq, nor Nasr.' They have already misled many, and grant You no increase to the wrongdoers but in straying (from their mark)." • Because of their sins they were drowned (in the flood) and were made to enter the fire (of punishment), and they found—in lieu of Allah—none to help them.
		Forgiveness for the Believers and Destruction for the Unbelievers
4	71:026-028	Noah said: "O my Lord! Leave not of the unbelievers a single one on earth! For if You do leave (any of) them, they will but mislead Your devotees, and they will breed none but wicked ungrateful ones. O my Lord! Forgive me, my parents, all who enter my house in faith, and (all) believing men and believing women. And to the wrongdoers, grant no increase but in perdition.

2 DETAILS OF THE LIFE STORY OF NOAH

While studying Surah Nuh, one should keep in mind the details of Noah's story that have been given in other Surahs of the Qur'an. These are found Surah Al-A'raf (7), Yunus (10), Hud (11), Al-Mu'minun (23), Ash-Shu'ara (26), Al-Ankabut (29), As-Saffat (37), and Al-Qamar (54). A summery that highlights different aspects of Noah and his people is given below.

2.1 Noah's People Denied and called him a Liar

God tells people in Surah Al-A'raf: "We sent Noah to his people. He said: 'O my people! Worship Allah! You have no other god but Him. I fear for you the punishment of a dreadful day!' The leaders of his people said: 'Ah! We see you evidently wandering (in mind)' He said, 'O my people! No wandering is there in my (mind). On the contrary, I am a messenger from the Lord and cherisher of the worlds! I but fulfill towards you the duties of my Lord's mission. Sincere is my advice to you, and I know from Allah something that you know not. Do you wonder that there has come to you a message from your Lord, through a man of your own people, to warn you, so that you may fear Allah and haply receive His mercy?' But they rejected him, and We delivered him and those with him in the ark, but We overwhelmed in the flood those who rejected Our signs. They were indeed a blind people (Qur'an 7:59-64)."

2.2 Noah always relied on God for His Help

In Surah Yunus, God says: "Behold! He (Noah) said to his people: 'O my people, if it be hard on your (mind) that I should stay (with you) and commemorate the signs of Allah, yet I put my trust in Allah. Get you then an agreement about your plan and among your partners, so your plan be not to you dark and dubious. Then pass your sentence on me and give me no respite. But if you turn back, (consider): no reward have I asked of you. My reward is only due from Allah, and I have been commanded to be of those who submit to Allah's will.' They rejected Him, but We delivered him and those with him in the ark, and We made them inherit (the earth), while We overwhelmed in the flood those who rejected Our signs. Then see what was the end of those who were warned (Qur'an 10:71-73)."

660

2.3 God Granted Noah's People their Wish

Narrating the life story of Noah, God says in Surah Hud: "We sent Noah to his people (with a mission): 'I have come to you with a clear warning: that you serve none but Allah. Verily, I do fear for you the penalty of a grievous day.' But the chiefs of the unbelievers among his people said: 'We see (in) you nothing but a man like ourselves, nor do we see that any follow you but the meanest among us, in judgment immature, nor do we see in you any merit above us. In fact, we think you are liars' (Qur'an 11:25-27)."

Noah asked his people to reform: "He said: 'O my people! See if (it be that) I have a clear sign from my Lord and that He has sent mercy unto me from His own presence, but that the mercy has been obscured from your sight? Shall we compel you to accept it when you are averse to it? O my people! I ask you for no wealth in return. My reward is from none but Allah. But I will not drive away (in contempt) those who believe, for verily they are to meet their Lord, and I see you are the ignorant ones! O my people! Who would help me against Allah if I drove them away? Will you not then take heed? I tell you not that with me are the treasures of Allah, nor do I know what is hidden, nor claim I to be an angel. Nor yet do I say of those whom your eyes do despise that Allah will not grant them (all) that is good. Allah knows best what is in their souls. I should, if I did, indeed be a wrongdoer' (Qur'an 11:28-31)."

Rejecting his invitation, Noah's people replied: "They said: 'O Noah! You have disputed with us, and (much) have you prolonged the dispute with us. Now bring upon us what you threaten us with if you speak the truth' (Qur'an 11:32)." In preparation to fulfill Noah's people their wish, "It was revealed to Noah: 'None of your people will believe except those who have believed already! So grieve no longer over their (evil) deeds. But construct an ark under Our eyes and Our inspiration, and address Me no (further) on behalf of those who are in sin, for they are about to be overwhelmed (in the flood)' (Qur'an 11:36-37)." After the flood, God said: "The word came: 'O Noah! Come down (from the ark) with peace from Us, and blessing on you and on some of the peoples (who will spring) from those with you. But (there will be other) peoples to whom We shall grant their pleasures (for a time), but in the end will a grievous penalty reach them from Us' (Qur'an 11:48)." One should learn from this story that only belief saves people. Individual relationships are of no avail when God's judgment comes. This is illustrated by the unbelief and drowning of Noah's son.

Table 2.3: Only belief saves People not their Relationships

No	Surah:Verses	Meanings
		Noah could not save his unbelieving son
1	11:042-043	So the ark floated with them on the waves (towering) like mountains, and Noah called out to his son who had separated himself (from the rest): 1. "O my son! Embark with us, and be not with the unbelievers." 2. The son replied: "I will betake myself to some mountain; it will save me from the water." 3. Noah said: "This day nothing can save from the command of Allah any but those on whom He has mercy!" And the waves came between them, and the son was among those overwhelmed in the flood.
		The unbelieving Son lost his Family
2	11:045-047	And Noah called upon his Lord and said: "O my Lord! Surely my son is of my family! And Your promise is true, and You are the most just of judges." 1. He said: "O Noah! He is not of your family, for his conduct is unrighteous. So ask not of Me that of which you have no knowledge! I give you counsel, lest you act like the ignorant." 2. Noah said: "O my Lord! I do seek refuge with You, lest I ask You for that of which I have no knowledge. And unless You forgive me and have mercy on me, I should indeed be lost."

2.4 God Keeps People Trying and Testing

The leaders among Noah's people told their followers: "'He is no more than a man like yourselves; his wish is to assert his superiority over you. If Allah had wished (to send messengers), He could have sent down angels. Never did we hear such a thing (as he says) among our ancestors of old.' (Someone said): 'He is only a man possessed; wait (and have patience) with him for a time' ... 'Verily in this there are Signs (for men to understand); (thus) do We try (men). Then We raised after them another generation' (Qur'an 23:24-25, 30-31)."

2.5 People should Learn from the Story of Noah

Surely there is a lesson in the story of Noah for the benefit of people. "They said: 'If you desist not, O Noah! You shall be stoned (to death).' He said: 'O my Lord! Truly my people have rejected me. Judge then between me and them openly, and deliver me and those of the believers who are with me.' So We delivered him and those with him in the ark filled (with creatures). Thereafter, We drowned those who remained behind. Verily, in this is a sign, but most of them do not believe (Qur'an 26:116-121)."

2.6 Most Arrogant People in Human History

Noah tried to reform the character and behavior of many generations of his people for about 950 years, but they failed to learn. "We (once) sent Noah to his people, and he tarried among them a thousand years less fifty, but the flood overwhelmed them while they (persisted in) sin. But We saved him and the companions of the ark, and We made the (ark) a sign for all peoples (Qur'an 29:14-15)."

2.7 God Rewards People even for Trying

Citing the story of Noah, God tells us how He rewards those who do good deeds: "We delivered him and his people from the great calamity and made his progeny to endure (on earth). And We left (this blessing) for him among generations to come in later times: 'Peace and salutation to Noah among the nations!' Thus, indeed, do we reward those who do right (Qur'an 37:76-80)."

2.8 People obtain God's Help by trying their Best

After trying for 950 years to reform his people, Noah, still meeting rejection from his people, called out to God for help. "Then he called on his Lord: 'I am one overcome; do You then help (me)!' So We opened the gates of Heaven with water pouring forth, and We caused the earth to gush forth with springs, so the waters met (and rose) to the extent decreed. But We bore him on an (ark) made of broad planks and caulked with palm fiber. She floats under our eyes, a recompense to one who had been rejected! And We have left this as a sign (for all time). Then is there any that will receive admonition? But how (terrible) was My penalty and My warning (Qur'an 54:10-16)!"

CHAPTER 59

The Jinn
FROM SURAH AL-JINN (72)

The Qur'an twice mentions that jinns listened to the Qur'an. The jinns heard the Qur'an when the Messenger stopped at Nakhlah on his return journey from Taif to Makkah, which was in the 10th year after the first revelation. This event is mentioned in Surah Al-Ahqaf. A similar event is mentioned in Surah Al-Jinn. According to Ibn 'Abbas, this occurred during the Messenger's journey to the Fair of Ukaz. On his way back, he led the dawn prayer at Nakhlah. At that time, a company of jinns happened to pass that way. When they heard the Qur'an being recited, they stopped and listened to it attentively (Sahih Bukhari: 1.12.740).

1 THE BELIEVERS AND UNBELIEVERS AMONG JINN

1.1 Jinns believed after listening to the Qur'an
During the Messenger's journey back from the Fair of Ukaz, he led the dawn prayer at Nakhlah. At that time, a company of jinn passed by that way. When they heard the Qur'an being recited, they listened to it and believed. "Say: 'It has been revealed to me that a company of jinns listened (to the Qur'an). They said: 'We have really heard a wonderful recital! It gives guidance to the right, and we have believed therein. We shall not join any (gods) with our Lord, and exalted is the majesty of our Lord. He has taken neither a wife nor a son'' (Qur'an 72:1-3)."

1.2 Teachings of the Qur'an Reformed the Listening Jinns
After listening to the Qur'an, the jinns reflected on its teachings and evaluated their condition and behavior. This enabled them to distinguish between truth and falsehood. Consequently, through learning and through evaluating their condition and behavior, they believed the truth. Their behavior at the time is summarized: "There were some foolish ones among us who used to utter extravagant lies against Allah, but we do think that no man or spirit should say anything that is untrue against Allah

665

(Qur'an 72:4-5)." Other practices prevalent at that time, as highlighted in Surah Al-Jinn, are given in the table below.

Table 1.2: Humankind and Believing and Unbelieving Jinns

No	Surah:Verses	Meanings
		Some Unbelieving People depended on Jinns
1	72:006-007	True, there were persons among mankind 1. Who took shelter with persons among the jinns, 2. But they (the jinns) increased them (the humans) in folly. They (came to) think, as you thought, that Allah would not raise up any one (to judgment).
		Jinns were unable to steel the heavenly Secrets
2	72:008-010	We pried into the secrets of heaven, 1. But we found it filled with stern guards and flaming fires. 2. We used, indeed, to sit there in (hidden) stations, to (steal) a hearing, 3. But any who listen now will find a flaming fire watching him in ambush. We understand not whether ill is intended to those on earth, or whether their Lord (really) intends to guide them to right conduct.
		The Believing and Unbelieving among Jinns
3	72:011-015	There are among us some that are righteous and some the contrary; we follow divergent paths. 1. But we think that we can by no means frustrate Allah throughout the earth, nor can we frustrate Him by flight. 2. As for us, since we have listened to the guidance, we have accepted it, and any who believes in his Lord has no fear, either of a short (account) or of any injustice. Among us are some that submit their wills (to Allah) and some that swerve from justice. • Now those who submit their wills—they have sought out (the path) of right conduct. But those who swerve—they are (but) fuel for Hellfire.

2 PROSPERITY DEPENDS ON PEOPLE'S CONDUCT

2.1 Prosperity or Affliction depends on People's Conduct

The people are told in Surah Al-Jinn that if they refrain from polytheism and firmly follow the way of righteousness, they will be blessed. If, however, they turn away from divine guidance, they will have to meet the consequences in this world, as well as in the Hereafter. "(And Allah's message is): 'If they (the pagans) had (only) remained on the (right) way, We should certainly have bestowed on them rain in abundance, that We might try them by that (means). But if any turns away from the remembrance of his Lord, He will cause him to undergo a severe penalty' (Qur'an 72:16-17)."

2.2 The Messenger's Mission is only to Convey the Guidance

Whenever the Messenger called the unbelievers towards God, they surrounded and mobbed him from every side. However, the only duty of the Messenger was to convey His message. The Messenger did not claim to have any power to bring any gain or to cause any harm. People have free will and wisdom, with which to reflect on the divine laws and to see for themselves the benefits in implementing them. Divine guidance is for the welfare of the people. God observes in Surah Al-Jinn: "And the places of worship are for Allah (alone), so invoke not any one along with Allah. Yet, when the devotee of Allah stands forth to invoke Him, they just make round him a dense crowd (Qur'an 72:18-19)." Therefore, God guides the Messenger: "Say: 'I do no more than invoke my Lord, and I join not with Him any (false god).' Say: 'It is not in my power to cause you harm or to bring you to right conduct.' Say: 'No one can deliver me from Allah (if I were to disobey Him), nor should I find refuge except in Him. Mine is only to convey what I receive from Allah and His messages. For any that disobey Allah and His Messenger—for them is Hell; they shall dwell therein forever' (Qur'an 72:20-23)."

2.3 Their Strength and Number make Unbelievers Arrogant

Generally speaking, corrupt people are arrogant due to their wealth and children. However, God says: "At length, when they see (with their own eyes) that which they are promised, then will they know who it is that is weakest in (his) helper and least important in point of numbers. Say: 'I know not whether the (punishment) that you are promised is near, or whether my Lord will appoint for it a distant term' (Qur'an 72:24-25)." The Messenger only receives that knowledge that God is pleased to give him, and knowledge about his mission is securely revealed to him in a manner that makes it impossible to falsify. "He (God alone) knows the unseen, nor does He make anyone acquainted with His mysteries, except a messenger whom He has chosen. And (even) then, He makes a band of watchers march before him and behind him, (so) that he may know that they have (truly) brought and delivered the messages of their Lord. And He surrounds (all the mysteries) that are with them and takes account of every single thing (Qur'an 72:26-28)."

CHAPTER 60

The Messenger and His Mission
FROM SURAH AL-MUZZAMMIL (73),
AND SURAH AL-MUDDATHTHIR (74)

In Surah Al-Muzzammil, the Messenger was asked to pray and recite the Qur'an at night, in order to be better prepared to carry out his special assignment as a Messenger of God. Such acts of worship helped develop and nurture the Messenger's special relationship with God. Being a member of a family and a society, and being entrusted by God with the divine revelation, the Messenger had manifold duties to perform. With regard to discharging his duties as God's Messenger, he was instructed to work in the presence of God and to retain a sense of God's nearness around about him in all matters and at all times. He was not to expect any worldly gains, and he needed to be patient in periods of great spiritual stress. After being given these instructions, the Messenger was told in Surah Al-Muddaththir to go ahead boldly to deliver the divine message and to proclaim God publically.

1 DIVINE GUIDANCE IS A BLESSING FOR HUMANITY
FROM SURAH AL-MUZZAMMIL (73)

Parts of Surah Al-Muzzammil were revealed at two separate occasions. In the first 19 verses, the Messenger was instructed to arise during the night and worship God so that he might develop the capability to shoulder the burden of his assignment. This command was given during the early period of his assignment. The command to recite the Qur'an for about half of the night indicates a time when enough of the Qur'an had been revealed to the Messenger that its recitation would take at least half of the night. The Messenger was also instructed to have patience in the face of the excesses of his opponents. The verses that warn unbelievers of divine punishment indicate that the time of their revelation was when the Messenger has started preaching Islam

669

openly and when the opposition had grown active and strong. Verse 20 mentions fighting in God's way and also contains a command to pay *Zakah* (the obligatory charity). Fighting in God's way never occurred at Makkah, and the command to pay *Zakah* was enjoined at Madinah. Therefore, this verse was revealed in Madinah.

1.1 Messenger was commanded to recite the Qur'an
The Messenger was commanded to rise at night and recite the Qur'an during the prayer for about half of the night. This was to prepare him to shoulder the responsibilities of his mission. He was also commanded to devote himself exclusively to God Who is the creator and the owner of the universe, to entrust all his affairs to Him with full satisfaction, and to bear with patience whatever his opponents might utter against him. He was also commanded to avoid unbelievers and to leave their affair to God, Who would deal with them.

Table 1.1: Rise to Pray at Night and be Patient

No	Surah:Verses	Meanings
		To Prepare for Your Mission, Rise at Night to Pray
1	73:001-009	O, you folded in garments! Stand (to prayer) by night, but not all nigh—half of it, or a little less, or a little more, • And recite the Qur'an in slow, measured, rhythmic tones. 1. Soon shall We send down to you a weighty message. 2. Truly, the rising by night is most potent for governing (the soul) and most suitable for (framing) the word (of prayer and praise). True, there is for you by day prolonged occupation with ordinary duties, but keep in remembrance the name of your Lord, and devote yourself to Him wholeheartedly. (He is) Lord of the East and the West; there is no god but He. Take Him, therefore, for (your) disposer of affairs.
		Bear Patiently What the Unbelievers Say

670

2	73:010-014	And have patience with what they say, and leave them with noble (dignity). • And leave Me (alone to deal with) those in possession of the good things of life, who (yet) deny the truth, and bear with them for a little while. • With Us are fetters (to bind them) and a fire (to burn them), a food that chokes and a penalty grievous. One day the earth and the mountains will be in violent commotion, and the mountains will be as a heap of sand poured out and flowing down.

1.2 Unbelievers are invited to the Guidance

Citing the fate of Pharaoh and his people, God invites the unbelievers to safeguard their fate by accepting the universal truth of Islam. God tells people: "We have sent to you a messenger to be a witness concerning you, even as We sent a messenger to Pharaoh. But Pharaoh disobeyed the messenger, so We seized him with a heavy punishment. Then how shall you, if you deny (Allah), guard yourselves against a day that will make children grow grey hair? Whereon, the sky will be cleft asunder. His promise must be accomplished. Verily, this is an admonition. Therefore, whoso will, let him take a (straight) path to his Lord (Qur'an 73:15-19)."

1.3 The *Tahajjud* Prayer is made Optional

Verse 20 of Surah Al-Muzzammil was revealed about ten years later. Reciting (reading, understanding, and reflecting on) the Qur'an is the first obligation among the five major obligations of the believers. In this verse, the initial command concerning the *Tahajjud* prayer is curtailed. However, believers are reminded to attend to the obligatory prayers, pay *Zakah* (obligatory charity), and spend out of their wealth for the sake of God. The believers are told that for whatever good they send up from the world, they will be rewarded by God.

Table 1.3: Major Obligations of the Believers

No	Surah:Verses	Meanings
		Believers Be Moderate in God's Worship

3	73:020	Your Lord does know that you stand forth (to prayer) nigh two-thirds of the night, or half the night, or a third of the night, and so does a party of those with you. But Allah does appoint night and day in due measure.
		• He knows that you are unable to keep count thereof, so He has turned to you (in mercy). Read you, therefore, of the Qur'an as much as may be easy for you.
		• He knows that there may be (some) among you in ill health, others traveling through the land, seeking of Allah's bounty, yet others fighting in Allah's cause.
		  1. Read, therefore, as much of the Qur'an as may be easy (for you),
		  2. And establish regular prayer,
		  3. And give regular charity,
		  4. And loan to Allah a beautiful loan.
		And whatever good you send forth for your souls, you shall find it in Allah's presence—yea, better and greater in reward, and seek the grace of Allah, for Allah is oft-forgiving, most merciful.

2 EVERY PERSON IS HOSTAGE TO HIS DEEDS
FROM SURAH AL-MUDDATHTHIR (74)

The first seven verses of Surah Al-Muddaththir belong to the earliest period at Makkah. The first revelation consisted of the first five verses of Surah Al-'Alaq. This was followed by a period with no revelation. Then, when the revelation was resumed, it started with the first seven verses of Surah Al-Muddaththir, in which the Messenger was commanded to do four things: (1) arise and warn, (2) magnify the glory of the Lord, (3) purify his robes, and (4) shun uncleanness. The rest of the Surah, from verses 8 to 56, was revealed when the first Hajj season came after public preaching of Islam had begun in Makkah.

2.1 The Messenger was instructed to Preach Islam

God told the Messenger: "Arise, and deliver your warning! And your Lord glorify, and your garments keep free from stain! And all abomination shun (Qur'an 74:2-5). Further, the Messenger was instructed by God that he was to be a selfless and atruistic leader: "Nor expect in giving any increase (for yourself), but for your Lord's (cause), be patient and constant (Qur'an 74:6-7)." A true leader should not expect or solicit worldly gain and should always be patient with his people.

2.2 Unbelievers have no Guts to face the Truth

The unbelievers were informed that upon resurrection they would have to face the bad result of what they were doing in this life. Without naming him, the people were told how God had blessed Walid bin al-Mughirah and how he had rejected the true faith. Even though he was fully convinced of the truth, he did not want to risk his leadership and position among his people. As such, he went against his conscience and did not accept the truth. To discourage people from believing, he proposed that the Qur'an should be branded as magic. This person, even after his evil inclinations and misdeeds, desired that God should bless him more. However, he had become worthy of Hell and not of additional blessings.

Table 2.2: Attitude and Behavior of the Unbelieving Leaders

No	Surah:Verses	Meanings
		Unbelieving Leaders like Walid bin al-Mughirah
1	74:008-017	Finally, when the trumpet is sounded, that will be that day, a day of distress, far from easy for those without faith. 1. Leave Me alone (to deal) with the (creature) whom I created (bare and) alone, 2. To whom I granted resources in abundance 3. And sons to be by his side, 4. To whom I made (life) smooth and comfortable. 5. Yet, is he greedy that I should add (yet more)! By no means, for to Our signs he has been refractory! Soon will I visit him with a mount of calamities.
		Scheming and the Ruin of Unbelieving Leaders

673

2	74:018-029	For he thought and he plotted—and woe to him! How he plotted! Yea, woe to him; how he plotted! Then he looked round; then he frowned and he scowled; then he turned back and was haughty. Then said he: 1. "This is nothing but magic, derived from of old. 2. "This is nothing but the word of a mortal!" Soon will I cast him into Hellfire! And what will explain to you what Hellfire is? Nothing does it permit to endure, and nothing does it leave alone—darkening and changing the color of man.

2.3 Hell is a Sign that Motivates and Warns People

God has made people accountable for their behavior and deeds. After swearing by the moon, night, and day, God tells unbelievers: "This (Hell) is but one of the mighty (portents), a warning to mankind—to any of you that chooses to press forward, or to follow behind (Qur'an 74:35-37)." One of the characteristics of unbelievers is that they are always skeptical and question things without any regard for the source of the news. That is why God made the number of Hell's keepers a trial for the unbelievers.

Table 2.3: Hell has Nineteen Keepers

No	Surah:Verses	Meanings
		Thus, God Increases Faith of the Believers
3	74:030-031	Over it (Hell) are nineteen (keepers). And We have set none but angels as guardians of the fire, and We have fixed their number only as a trial for unbelievers, in order that • The People of the Book may arrive at certainty, And the believers may increase in faith, And that no doubts may be left for the People of the Book and the believers.
		Thus, God leaves to Stray whom He pleases
4	74:031	And that those in whose hearts is a disease and the unbelievers may say, "What symbol does Allah intend by this?" Thus, Allah leaves to stray whom He pleases and guides whom He pleases, and none can know the forces of your Lord except He. And this is no other than a warning to mankind.

674

2.4 Each Person is a Hostage to his Efforts and Deeds

People's welfare in this life, as well as in the Hereafter, depends on their efforts and good deeds. God tells us: "Every soul will be (held) in pledge for its deeds (74:38)." Unfortunately, some people do not believe in their accountability for their deeds. Thus, they engage in activities that satisfy only their selfish desires and end up deserving Hell. They do not pray and do not feed the poor. They indulge in vain talk and insist that God must directly address them. The root cause of their aversion is that they: (1) are fearless of the Hereafter, (2) take this worldly life as an end in itself, and (3) run away from the Qur'an as though they were wild asses fleeing away from a lion.

As can be seen, the unbelievers propose unreasonable conditions for believing. Further, even if their each and every condition were fulfilled, they would not advance even an inch on the way of faith, secondary to their denial of the Hereafter. It has been explicitly stated that God doesn't need anybody's faith. The Qur'an is an admonition for whoever desires to accept it. It is God's right that people should fear disobeying Him, and He alone has the power to forgive those who adopt piety and an attitude of God-consciousness, even though they may have committed many acts of disobedience.

Table 2.4: Peoples Wellness Depends on their Efforts

No	Surah:Verses	Meanings
		Each Person is a Hostage to one's Deeds
5	74:038-048	Every soul will be (held) in pledge for its deeds, except the companions of the right hand. (They will be) in gardens (of delight) and ask of the sinners: "What led you into Hellfire?" • They (the sinners) will say: 1. "We were not of those who prayed, 2. "Nor were we of those who fed the indigent. 3. "But we used to talk vanities with vain talkers, 4. "And we used to deny the Day of Judgment, until there came to us (the hour) that is certain."

		Then will no intercession of (any) intercessors profit them.
		Why some People refuse to be Guided
6	74:049-056	• Then what is the matter with them that they turn away from admonition, as if they were frightened asses, fleeing from a lion? Forsooth, each one of them wants to be given scrolls (of revelation) spread out. By no means! But they fear not the Hereafter. Nay, this surely is an admonition. Let any who will keep it in remembrance, but none will keep it in remembrance except as Allah wills. He is the Lord of righteousness and Lord of forgiveness.

CHAPTER 61

Resurrection, Accountability, and Awards

FROM SURAH QAF (50), SURAH ADH-DHARIYAT (51),
SURAH AT-TUR (52), SURAH AN-NAJM (53),
SURAH AL-QAMAR (54), AND SURAH AL-WAQI'AH (56).

When the Messenger started preaching in Makkah, what most surprised people was the message that they would be resurrected after death to give an account of their deeds. In Surah Qaf, Surah Adh-Dhariyat, and Surah At-Tur, the resurrection and the accountability for one's deeds are discussed in detail. There is no authentic tradition to indicate exactly when these Surahs were revealed. However, the discussion topic indicates that these Surahs were revealed in Makkah, when the hostility of the unbelievers had become quite intense but had not yet assumed tyrannical proportions.

1 THE CONSEQUENCE OF THE GOOD OR EVIL DEEDS
FROM SURAH QAF (50)

God assures the Messenger and the believers in Surah Qaf that: (1) He knows very well what the unbelievers say, (2) that one is not to force the unbelievers to believe, and (3) that one should use the Qur'an to admonish whoever fears God. This is also affirmed in Surah Al-Baqarah: "Let there be no compulsion in religion. Truth stands out clear from error. Whoever rejects evil and believes in Allah has grasped the most trustworthy handhold that never breaks, and Allah hears and knows all things (Qur'an 2:256)."

1.1 Resurrection will be like Shoots Sprouting after Rain
The unbelievers of Makkah could not comprehend the possibility of resurrection. How could it be possible, when the body had disintegrated into dust, to reassemble the scattered particles into the same living body after hundreds of thousands of years?

677

Although the thought of resurrection after being dead for hundreds, if not thousands, of years may seem difficult to understand and envisage, it is by no means beyond our power of comprehension. After all, Allah is all-powerful, the absolute creator. Therefore, there is nothing that is beyond His power. In Surah Qaf, people are told that when the time comes, they will come out of their graves at one call, just as young shoots sprout up from the earth after the first shower of rain. God then says: "Were We then weary with the first creation that they should be in confused doubt about a new creation (Qur'an 50:15)?" The Creator Who gives life the first time is certainly capable of bringing us back to life on the Day of Judgement. After all, the resurrection is much simpler than our first creation.

Table 1.1: Unbelievers Deny Messengers and Resurrection

No	Surah:Verses	Meanings
		Unbelievers believe in neither Messengers nor Resurrection
1	50:002-005	But they wonder that there has come to them a warner from among themselves. So the unbelievers say: "This is a wonderful thing! What! When we die and become dust, (shall we live again?) That is a (sort of) return far (from our understanding)." 1. We already know how much of them the earth takes away; with Us is a record guarding (the full account). 2. But they deny the truth when it comes to them; so they are in a confused state.
		Resurrection will be there like Vegetation after a Rain
2	50:006-011	1. Do they not look at the sky above them—how We have made it and adorned it? And there are no flaws in it. 2. And the earth—We have spread it out and set thereon mountains standing firm, and (We) produced therein every kind of beautiful growth (in pairs), to be observed and commemorated by every devotee turning (to Allah). 3. And We send down from the sky rain charged with blessing, and We produce

		therewith gardens and grain for harvests; And tall (and stately) palm trees, with shoots of fruit stalks, piled one over another, as sustenance for (Allah's) servants. We give (new) life therewith to land that is dead; thus will be the resurrection.
		Unbelievers suffered for rejecting the Messengers
3	50:012-014	Before them was denied (the Hereafter) by 1. The people of Noah, the Companions of the Rass, the Thamud, 2. The 'Ad, Pharaoh, the brethren of Lot, 3. The Companions of the Wood, and the People of Tubba'. Each one (of them) rejected the messengers, and My warning was duly fulfilled (in them).

1.2 None can escape the Consequences of their Deeds

The unbelievers' assertion that people have been left free to do whatever they wish and that they are answerable to no one is absolutely wrong. God is aware of each act and word of every individual; He even knows the ideas that pass through their minds. Further, His angels are assigned to each person, writing down whatever one does and utters. Although many past generations were destroyed as a consequence of their evil deeds, personal records of individuals will be evaluated and properly compensated in the Hereafter.

Table 1.2: Two Scribes are Recording everything One Does

No	Surah:Verses	Meanings
		God is nearer to an Individual than One's Jugular Vein
4	50:016-018	It was We Who created man, and We know what dark suggestions his soul makes to him, for We are nearer to him than (his) jugular vein. • Behold, two (guardian angels), appointed to learn (his doings), learn (and note them), one sitting on the right and one on the left. Not a word does he utter but there is a sentinel by him, ready (to note it).
		People escape not the sonsequences of their Deeds
5	50:036-037	• But how many generations before them did We destroy (for their sins)—stronger in power

679

		than they? Then did they wander through the land. Was there any place of escape? Verily, in this is a message for any that has a heart and understanding or who gives ear and earnestly witnesses (the truth).

1.3 Death, Resurrection, Accountability, and Awards

God states in Surah Al-An'am: "It is He Who has made you (His) agents, inheritors of the earth. He has raised you in ranks, some above others, that He may try you in the gifts He has given you (Qur'an 6:165)." Therefore, the unbelievers' assertion that people have been left free to do whatever they wish in the world and that they will answer to no one is no more than wishful thinking. Upon resurrection, people will realize that they were created to be responsible in the world and accountable for their deeds. The rewards (Heaven) and punishments (Hell) that the unbelievers regard as impossible and imaginary things will become visible realities.

Due to their enmity and opposition to the truth, the unbelievers will be cast into the same Hell that they denied in their earthly life. However, those who fear God and follow the path of righteousness will be admitted to the Paradise about which the unbelievers scoffed and expressed wonder and surprise. God says in Surah Qaf: "The stupor of death will bring truth (before his eyes). This was the thing that you were trying to escape! And the trumpet shall be blown—that will be the day whereof warning (had been given). There will come forth every soul; with each will be an (angel) to drive and an (angel) to bear witness. (It will be said:) 'You were heedless of this; now have We removed your veil, and sharp is your sight this day!' His companion will say: 'Here is (his record) ready with me' (Qur'an 50:19-23)."

Table 1.3: Afterlife Awards of Hell and Paradise

No	Surah:Verses	Meanings
		Ungrateful People and their punishment of Hell
6	50:024-029	(The sentence will be:) "Throw; throw into Hell every contumacious rejecter (of Allah) who 1. "Forbade what was good, 2. "Transgressed all bounds, 3. "Cast doubts and suspicions, 4. "Who set up another god beside Allah." Throw him into a severe penalty. • His companion will say: "Our Lord! I did not make him transgress, but he was (himself) far astray." He (Allah) will say: "Dispute not with each other in My presence. I had already in advance sent you warning. The word changes not before Me, and I do not the least injustice to My servants.
		God-fearing people Who will be in Paradise
7	50:031-035	The garden will be brought near to the righteous—no more a thing distant. (A voice will say:) "This is what was promised for you— 1. "For every one who turned (to Allah) in sincere repentance, 2. "Who kept (His law), 3. "Who feared (Allah) Most Gracious unseen and brought a heart turned in devotion. Enter therein in peace and security. This is a day of eternal life." There will be for them therein all that they wish—and more besides in Our presence.

1.4 Be Patient, Pray, and Remind People with the Qur'an

God advises the believers to be patient with the unbelievers and to worship Him in this worldly life. "Bear, then, with patience all that they say, and celebrate the praises of your Lord before the rising of the sun (*Fajr* prayer) and before (its) setting (*Zuhr* & *'Asr* prayers). And during part of the night (*Maghrib* & *Isha* prayers), celebrate His praises, and (so likewise, supplementary prayers and remembering God) after the postures of adoration…Verily it is We Who give life and death, and to Us is the final goal (Qur'an 50:39-40, 43)." People are informed that regardless of where a dead person may be, the call of God's caller will reach him. His call will summon him to rise, proceed to his Lord, and render an account to Him. In conclusion, God addressing the Messenger (and the believers) says: "We know best what they say, and you are not one to overawe them by force. So admonish with the Qur'an such as fear My warning (Qur'an 50:45)."

2 THE ULTIMATE INDIVIDUAL ACCOUNTABILITY
FROM SURAH ADH-DHARIYAT (51)

People's different and conflicting beliefs about the end of human life prove that none of these beliefs and creeds is based on knowledge. The unbelievers form an ideology on the basis of guesswork and make it their creed, whether secular or religious. Some think that there will be no life after death; some believe in the transmigration of souls; some believe in the Hereafter with rewards and punishments but invent different ways and means to escape retribution. A wrong interpretation of such a vital subject of fundamental importance could waste people's lifelong work and ruin their future forever.

2.1 Believing in Accountability Makes People Human
Being devoid of knowledge and understanding, the unbelievers are unknowingly heading towards a disastrous end. For if one's ideas about the Hereafter are flawed, any path that one takes is bound to lead to one's failure. God tells the unbelievers: "Truly, you are in a doctrine discordant, through which are deluded (away from the truth) such as would be deluded. Woe to the falsehood mongers—those who (flounder) heedlessly in a flood of confusion. They (sarcastically) ask, 'When will be the Day of Judgment and Justice (Qur'an 51:8-12)?" In contrast, the believers prepare for the Hereafter. Their behavior has a two-fold characteristic: they recognize the claims of their Lord against them; and they fully realize that whatever has been bestowed on them by God, whether little or much, doesn't simply belong to them and their families. Instead, they feel that the needy have a rightful claim on their wealth.

Table 2.1: Their Accountability Makes People Human

No	Surah:Verses	Meanings
		The Hereafter and Day of Judgment are True
1	51:005-006	Verily, that which you are promised is true, and, verily, judgment and justice must, indeed, come to pass.
		Believers Prepare themselves for the Hereafter
2	51:015-019	As to the righteous, they will be in the midst of gardens and springs, taking joy in the things that their Lord gives them because, before then, they lived a good life. 1. They were in the habit of sleeping but little by night. 2. And in the hour of early dawn, they (were found) praying for forgiveness. 3. And in their wealth and possessions (was remembered) the right of the (needy,) him who asked and him who (for some reason) was prevented (from asking).

2.2 The Hereafter, a Subject of Tremendous Importance

It would be a disastrous mistake to build an ideology on the basis of speculation and guesswork. To guard against such a situation, people should contemplate the information given in the Qur'an on the Hereafter. They should reflect on the working of the universe and their own existence. God will lead such people to His numerous signs. "On the earth are signs for those of assured faith, as also in your own selves. Will you not then see? And in heaven is your sustenance, as (also) that which you are promised. Then, by the Lord of Heaven and earth, this is the very truth, as much as the fact that you can speak intelligently to each other (Qur'an 51:20-23)."

Table 2.2: Signs are there in Human history to Reflect

No	Surah:Verses	Meanings
		Nothing is beyond God's Creativity
3	51:024-030	Has the story reached you, of the honored guests of Abraham? • Behold, they entered his presence, and said: "Peace!" He said, "Peace, (and thought, these seem) unusual people. Then he turned quickly to his household, brought out a fatted calf, and

683

		placed it before them. He said: "Will you not eat?"
		• (When they did not eat), He conceived a fear of them. They said, "Fear not," and they gave him glad tidings of a son endowed with knowledge. But his wife came forward (laughing) aloud; she smote her forehead and said: "A barren old woman!" They said: "Even so has your Lord spoken, and He is full of wisdom and knowledge."
		History is Full of Signs for those who Fear God's Punishment
4	51:031-046	1. (Abraham) said: "And what, O you messengers, is your errand (now)?" They said, "We have been sent to a people (Lot's people) in sin - To bring on, on them, (a shower of) stones of clay (brimstone), Marked as from your Lord for those who trespass beyond bounds." Then We evacuated those of the believers who were there, but We found not there any just (Muslim) persons except in one house, and We left there a sign for such as fear the grievous penalty. 2. And in Moses (was another sign): Behold, We sent him to Pharaoh with authority manifest. But (Pharaoh) turned back with his chiefs and said, "A sorcerer or one possessed!" So We took him and his forces and threw them into the sea, and his was the blame. 3. And in the 'Ad (people) (was another sign). Behold, We sent against them the devastating wind. It left nothing whatever that it came up against, but reduced it to ruin and rottenness. 4. And in the Thamud (was another sign): Behold, they were told, "Enjoy for a little while!" But they insolently defied the command of their Lord. So the stunning noise (of an earthquake) seized them, even while they were looking on. Then they could not even stand (on their feet), nor could they help themselves. 5. So were the people of Noah before them, for they wickedly transgressed.

2.3 The Matching Partner of the World is the Hereafter

Everything has been created on the principle of pairs. The whole universe follows this principle. Everything matches another with which it is paired. This brings into existence a wide variety of forms and combinations. There is nothing that is totally unrelated to others or is devoid of a match. Uniting one with its matching partner makes one productive. If one reflects, it is clear that the matching partner of the world is the Hereafter. Without the Hereafter, the world would be utterly meaningless.

God reminds people that He has not created them to serve others, but to serve Him. He is unlike false deities that receive sustenance from others and whose false divinity cannot function without help. He is God Who is the sustainer of all, Who does not stand in need of sustenance from anyone, and Whose universe is functioning by His own power and might.

Table 2.3: Without the Hereafter the World is Meaningless

No	Surah:Verses	Meanings
		Everything God created—He created in pairs
5	51:047-051	With power and skill did We construct the sky, for it is We Who create the vastness of space. And We have spread out the earth—how excellently We do spread out. And of everything, We have created pairs that you may receive instruction. 1. Hasten then (at once) to Allah; I am from Him a warner to you, clear and open. 2. And make not another object of worship with Allah; I am from Him a warner to you, clear and open.
		Unlike deities, God does not need any provision from People
6	51:056-058	I have only created jinns and men that they may serve Me. No sustenance do I require of them, nor do I require that they should feed Me. For Allah is He Who gives (all) sustenance—Lord of power, steadfast (forever).
		Continue to remind, for the Reminder profits the Believers
7	51:052-055	Similarly, no messenger came to the peoples before them, but they said (of him) in like manner,

	"A sorcerer or one possessed." 1. Is this the legacy they have transmitted, one to another? 2. Nay, they are themselves a people transgressing beyond bounds. Then turn away from them; not yours is the blame. But teach (your message), for teaching benefits the believers.

3 BELIEVING FAMALIES WILL BE REUNITED
FROM SURAH AT-TUR (52)

Since arguments for the possibility, necessity, and occurrence of the Hereafter had already been given in Surah Adh-Dhariyat, these were not been repeated in Surah At-Tur. In Surah At-Tur, people are told that their fate in the Hereafter will strictly be decided according to what they did in the world. Believers are assured that their families who follow them in faith will be reunited with them in Paradise.

3.1 The Day of Judgment will come at its Appointed Time

Swearing an oath by some realities and signs that testify to the Hereafter, it was stated most forcefully that the Day of Judgment will take place and that no one has the power to prevent it from happening. The fate of those who deny it was described, along with the reward bestowed on those who believe in it and adopt a behavior of piety and righteousness.

Table 3.1: Every Person is pledged to One's Deeds

No	Surah:Verses	Meanings
		The Day of Judgment will certainly Come
1	52:001-008	By the mount (of revelation), by a decree inscribed in a scroll unfolded, by the much-frequented fane, by the canopy raised high, and by the ocean filled with swell—verily, the doom of your Lord will indeed come to pass. There is none can avert it.
		Hell is Recompense for Evil Deeds
2	52:009-016	• On the day when the firmament will be in a dreadful commotion and the mountains will fly hither and thither,

686

		1. Then woe that day to those that treat (truth) as falsehood— 2. That play (and paddle) in shallow trifles. That day shall they be thrust down to the fire of Hell, irresistibly. "This," it will be said, "is the fire that you were wont to deny! Is this then a fake, or is it you that do not see? Burn you therein. The same is it to you whether you bear it with patience or not. You but receive the recompense of your (own) deeds.
		Paradise is the Reward of the Righteous
3	52:017-021	• As to the righteous, they will be in gardens and in happiness, enjoying the (bliss) that their Lord has bestowed on them, and their Lord shall deliver them from the penalty of the fire. 1. (To them will be said,) "Eat and drink you with profit and health because of your (good) deeds." 2. They will recline (with ease) on thrones (of dignity) arranged in ranks, and We shall join them to companions with beautiful, big, and lustrous eyes. • And those who believe and whose families follow them in faith—to them shall We join their families, nor shall We deprive them (of the fruit) of anything of their works. (Yet) is each individual in pledge for his deeds.

3.2 Reasoning that Refutes the Unbelievers' Assertions

In order to mislead the common people against him and so that they wouldn't pay attention to the message he preached, the unbelievers called the Messenger a sorcerer, a madman, and a poet. They looked upon him as a calamity and wished a disaster to befall him. They accused him of fabricating the Qur'an and presenting it in the name of God. They often taunted him, saying that God could not have appointed an ordinary individual like him. They expressed disgust at his mission and avoided him as if he were asking for compensation. They consulted each other to devise schemes to end his mission, without realizing how selflessly and sincerely the Messenger was trying to guide them out of their error. God then criticized their attitude and refuted their assertions with reason.

Table 3.2
The Unbelievers Argument against the Messenger

No	Surah:Verses	Meanings
		Unbelievers Assertions without support or reason
4	52:030-043	1. Or do they say: " A poet! We await for him some calamity (hatched) by time!" Say you: "Await you! I too will wait along with you!" Is it that their faculties of understanding urge them to this, or are they but a people transgressing beyond bounds? 2. Or do they say, "He fabricated the (message)?" Nay, they have no faith. Nay, they have no faith. Let them then produce a recital like unto it if they speak the truth. Were they created of nothing, or were they themselves the creators, or did they create the heavens and the earth? Nay, they have no firm belief. 3. Or are the treasures of your Lord with them, or are they the managers (of affairs)? 4. Or have they a ladder, by which they can (climb up to heaven and) listen (to its secrets)? Then let (such a) listener of theirs produce a manifest proof. 5. Or has He only daughters and you have sons? 6. Or is it that you (O Messenger) do ask for a reward, So that they are burdened with a load of debt, or that the unseen in it their hands and they write it down? 7. Or do they intend a plot (against you)? But those who defy Allah are themselves involved in a plot. 8. Or have they a god other than Allah? Exalted is Allah far above the things they associate with Him.
		Unbelievers Cannot be Convinced By Reasoning
5	52:044-047	Were they to see a piece of the sky falling (on them), they would say: "Clouds gathered in heaps!"

| | | • So leave them alone until they encounter that day of theirs, wherein they shall overwhelmed—the day when their plotting will avail them nothing and no help shall be given them. Verily, for those who do wrong, there is another punishment besides this, but most of them understand not. |

3.3 Continue Preaching and Inviting People to Islam

Since arrogant people misinterpret what they are shown, in order to avoid affirming faith, it is of no avail to show them a miracle to convince them. However, the Messenger was commanded to continue giving his invitation and preaching his message. He was not to be discouraged by the accusations and objections of his opponents and enemies. "Therefore, continue to remind, for by the grace of your Lord, you are not a soothsayer or a madman (Qur'an 52:29)." The Messenger was reassured that God had not left him alone to face his enemies and that God was constantly watching over him. Likewise, we are encouraged to endure every hardship patiently till the Day of Judgment comes and to prayerfully seek the power that is required for successfully struggling under such conditions. "Now await in patience the command of your Lord, for verily you are in Our eyes, and celebrate the praises of your Lord the while you stand forth, and for part of the night also praise Him—and at the retreat of the stars (Qur'an 52:48-49)."

4 PEOPLE SHALL HAVE THAT FOR WHICH THEY STRIVE
FROM SURAH AN-NAJM (53)

God has reaffirmed the basic principle of a true religion: "Namely, that no bearer of burdens can bear the burden of another; that man can have nothing but what he strives for (Qur'an 53:38-39)." This is the principle that was presented thousands of years before the revelation of the Qur'an in the books of Abraham and Moses, which fact emphasizes that Islam is not a new and novel religion. These fundamental truths of Islam have existed and been the same throughout history.

4.1 Integrity of the Messenger and the Message

God Himself testified to the integrity of the Messenger by saying: "By the star when it goes down, your companion is neither astray nor being misled. Nor does he say (anything) of (his own) desire. It is no less than inspiration sent down to him (Qur'an 53:1- 4)." Whatever the Messenger was presenting was nothing less than a revelation that was revealed to him. He saw the angel through whom this knowledge was conveyed to him. He was also shown the great signs of his Lord. Whatever he says is true.

Table 4.1: How God Revealed the Qur'an

No	Surah:Verses	Meanings
		God revealed the Qur'an through Gabriel
1	53:010-012	So did (Allah) convey the inspiration to His servant—(conveyed) what He (meant) to convey. The (Prophet's mind and) heart in no way falsified that which he saw. Will you then dispute with him concerning what he saw?
		How Gabriel approached the Messenger
2	53:005-009	He was taught by one mighty in power, endued with wisdom, for he appeared (in stately form) while he was in the highest part of the horizon. Then he approached and came closer and was at a distance of but two bow-lengths or (even) nearer.
		The Messenger saw Gabriel during the Night Journey
3	53:013-018	For indeed he saw him at a second descent, near the lote tree beyond which none may pass. Near it is the garden of abode. Behold, the lote tree was shrouded (in mystery unspeakable!) (His) sight never swerved, nor did it go wrong. For truly, he did see the greatest of the signs of his Lord.

4.2 Only Good Deeds will save People upon Resurrection

False deities and their intercession will not help the unbelievers who failed in their duties as God's trustees on earth. The unbelievers' gods are nothing but names that they have devised. Such deities never existed or have no authority to intercede, and they will not be able to help their worshipers on the Day of Judgment. Salvation can only be assured by believing in God, living according as God's commands, and doing good deeds for the welfare of people and others among God's creation.

Table 4.2: False Deities will not be able to Intercede

No	Surah:Verses	Meanings
		The Unbelievers Worship their Conjecture and Low Desires
4	53:019-024	• Have you seen Lat and 'Uzza and another, the third (goddess) Manat? What! For you the male sex, and for Him the female? Behold, such would be indeed a division most unfair! These are nothing but names that you have devised—you and your fathers, for which Allah has sent down no authority (whatever). They follow nothing but conjecture and what their own souls desire, even though there has already come to them guidance from their Lord. Nay, shall man have (just) anything he hankers after?
		Intercession is only granted by God to whom He Pleases
5	53:026-028	• How many so ever be the angels in the heavens, their intercession will avail nothing except after Allah has given leave for whom He pleases and only if he is acceptable to Him. Those who believe not in the Hereafter name the angels with female names, but they have no knowledge therein. They follow nothing but conjecture, and conjecture avails nothing against truth.

4.3 Criteria for the Judgment Remain Unchanged

God is the creator and sovereign of the entire universe. He knows what every person is doing and will requite evil with evil and good with good. The final judgment will not depend on what

691

people consider themselves to be or on tall claims they make of their purity and chastity. The final judgment depends on whether one is pious or impious and righteous or unrighteous in the sight of God. If people refrain from major sins, God in His mercy will overlook their minor errors. With regard to the final judgment, two basic principles should be noted: (1) no bearer of burdens shall bear the burden of another, and (2) people shall have nothing but that for which they strive of the true religion.

Table 4.3: Accountability on the Day of Judgment

No	Surah:Verses	Meanings
		People will be rewarded according to what they have Done
6	53:031-032	Yea, to Allah belongs all that is in the heavens and on earth, so that 1. He rewards those who do evil according to their deeds, and 2. He rewards those who do good with what is best. • Those who avoid great sins and shameful deeds, only (falling into) small faults—verily, your Lord is ample in forgiveness. He knows you well when He brings you out of the earth and when you are hidden in your mothers' wombs. Therefore, justify not yourselves. He knows best who it is that guards against evil.
		Criteria for the Judgment and Awards on Resurrection
7	53:033-041	You see one who turns back, gives a little, then hardens (his heart). • What! Has he knowledge of the unseen so that he can see? Nay, is he not acquainted with what is in the books of Moses and of Abraham who fulfilled his engagements— 1. Namely, that no bearer of burdens can bear the burden of another, 2. That man can have nothing but what he strives for, (and) 3. That (the fruit of) his striving will soon come in sight. Then will he be rewarded with a reward complete.

4.4 The Consequence of Unbelief and Corruption

The books of Abraham and Moses were quoted to confirm the historical facts that the destruction of the 'Ad, the Thamud, and the people of Noah and Lot was not the result of natural calamities. Rather, God destroyed them as a consequence of the same corruption that disbelieving societies have always been committing. People should realize that the resurrection is getting closer and that none but God can avert it or postpone it, and the unbelievers of Mekkah were advised to abandon their corrupt and arrogant attitudes and behavior and to: "Fall down in prostration to Allah, and adore (Him) (Qur'an 53:62)." This statement so overwhelmed even the most hardened deniers of the truth that, when after reciting these verses the Messenger fell down in prostration, the unbelieving listeners could not help falling down in prostration along with him.

Table 4.4: The Resurrection Draws Near

No	Surah:Verses	Meanings
		A Second Creation has been Promised by the Creator
8	53:042-048	1. (It is written in the books of Moses and Abraham) that to your Lord is the final goal, 2. That it is He Who grants laughter and tears, 3. That it is He Who grants death and life, 4. That He did create in pairs, male and female, from a seed when lodged (in its place), 5. That He has promised a second creation (raising of the dead), 6. That it is He Who gives wealth and satisfaction,
		Most Corrupt People have been Destroyed in the Past
9	53:049-054	7. That He is the Lord of Sirius (the mighty star), and that it is He Who destroyed the (powerful) ancient 'Ad (people), and the Thamud, nor gave them a lease of perpetual life. 8. And before them, (He destroyed) the people of Noah, for that they were (all) most unjust and most insolent transgressors. 9. And He destroyed the overthrown cities (of Sodom and Gomorrah), so that (ruins unknown) have covered them up.

693

		Resurrection Draws Near; Prostrate before God
10	53:057-062	The (judgment) ever approaching draws near. None but Allah can lay it bare. • Do you then wonder at this recital (the Qur'an), • And will you laugh and not weep, • Wasting your time in vanities? But fall down in prostration to Allah, and adore (Him)!

5 THE TIME OF RESURRECTION DRAWS NEAR
From Surah Al-Qamar (54)

Traditions and commentators agree that incident of the *Shaqq-al-Qamar* (splitting of the moon) mentioned in Surah Al-Qamar took place at about five years before the Messenger's immigration to Madinah. After citing the incident of the splitting of the moon, God warns the unbelievers about their arrogance and resistance to Islam. The splitting of the moon was a manifest sign, indicating that anything is possible, including the resurrection. Huge stars and planets could be split asunder, disintegrate, or collide with each other before the resurrection. This all could happen at any time that is in accord with the divine plan.

5.1 The Disintegration of the Universe had Begun
The unbelievers were warned about their resistance to Islam. The splitting of the moon was a clear sign that the resurrection can happen and that it was approaching closer. This also confirmed that the universe is neither eternal nor immortal and that it can be disrupted at any time. Everything that has been depicted in the Qur'an to happen in connection with the resurrection could happen at any time. The Messenger invited the people's attention to this event and asked them to note it and to be a witness to it. However, the unbelievers described it as a magical illusion and persisted in their denial.

Table 5.1: Everything is Destined to End

No	Surah:Verses	Meanings
		As a Sign, the Moon did Split Asunder
1	54:001-003	The Hour (of Judgment) is near, and the moon is cleft asunder. • But if they see a sign, they turn away and say, "This is (but) transient magic." They reject (the warning) and follow their (own) lusts, but every matter has its appointed time.
		A Woeful Day Or a New Beginning
2	54:004-008	There have already come to them recitals wherein there is (enough) to check (them), mature wisdom—but (the preaching of) warners profits them not. • Therefore, (O Prophet,) turn away from them. The day that the caller will call (them) to a terrible affair, they will come forth, their eyes humbled, from (their) graves, (torpid) like locusts scattered abroad, hastening with eyes transfixed towards the caller! "Hard is this day!" the unbelievers will say.

5.2 The Qur'an is easy to Understand and Remember

Unbelieving people neither learn from admonition, nor from history, nor affirm faith after witnessing manifest signs with their own eyes. Perhaps, they will believe only when the resurrection has taken place and they will be rushing out of their graves towards the person who will be calling. The historical incidents about the destruction of the peoples of Noah, 'Ad, Thamud, Lot, and the Pharaoh have been described to stress that these nations suffered when they disregarded the warnings given to them by their messengers. After each story, people are told that the Qur'an is an easy means of admonition. If a nation takes it to heart and follows its guidance, then the fate of the former nations can be avoided. However, it would be foolishness to persist in heedless disbelief until the torment itself arrives.

People are asked to reflect that if they adopt the same attitude and conduct for which other nations have been punished, then why shouldn't they be punished? They are not an exception to be treated differently. They have not been granted amnesty from the punishment for the crime for which others have been punished. Their great numbers will be put to rout, and on the Day of Resurrection they will be dealt with severely. God says: "Are your unbelievers, (O Quraysh), better than they? Or have you immunity in the sacred books? Or do they say: 'We acting together can defend ourselves?' Soon will their multitude be put to flight, and they will show their backs. Nay, the Hour (of Judgment) is the time promised them (for their full recompense), and that Hour will be most grievous and most bitter. Truly, those in sin are the ones straying in mind and mad. The day they will be dragged through the fire on their faces, (they will hear:) 'Taste you the touch of Hell (Qur'an 54:43-48)."

Table 5.2
How Awesome was God's Punishment and His Warning

No	Surah:Verses	Meanings
		The People of Noah rejected their Messenger
3	54:009-017	Before them the people of Noah rejected (their messenger). They rejected Our servant and said, "Here is one possessed," and he was driven out. 1. Then he called on his Lord: "I am one overcome; do You then help (me)!" So We opened the gates of Heaven with water pouring forth. We caused the earth to gush forth with springs, so the waters met (and rose) to the extent decreed, but We bore him on an (ark) made of broad planks and caulked with palm fiber. She floats under our eyes (and care)—recompense to one who had been rejected (with scorn)! We have left this as a sign (for all time); then is there any that will receive admonition? But how (terrible) was My penalty and My warning? • We have indeed made the Qur'an easy to understand and remember; then is there any that will receive admonition?
		The 'Ad People treated the Truth as Falsehood
4	54:018-022	The 'Ad (people too) rejected (truth); then how terrible was My penalty and My warning! 2. For We sent against them a furious wind on a day of violent disaster, plucking out men as if

		they were roots of palm trees torn up (from the ground). Yea, how (terrible) was My penalty and My warning! • But We have indeed made the Qur'an easy to understand and remember; then is there any that will receive admonition?
		The Thamud People Rejected the Warning
5	54:023-032	The Thamud (also) rejected (their) warners, for they said: "What! A man, a solitary one from among ourselves—shall we follow such a one? Truly should we then be straying in mind and mad. Is it that the message is sent to him of all people among us? Nay, he is a liar, an insolent one!" 3. Ah! They will know on the morrow which is the liar, the insolent one, for We will send the she-camel by way of trial for them. So watch them, (O Salih), and possess yourself in patience! And tell them that the water is to be divided between them—each one's right to drink being brought forward (by turns). But they called to their companion, and he took a sword in hand, and hamstrung (her). Ah! How (terrible) was My penalty and My warning! For We sent against them a single mighty blast, and they became like the dry stubble used by one who pens cattle. • And We have indeed made the Qur'an easy to understand and remember; then is there any that will receive admonition?
		Lot's people treated the Warning as a Lie
6	54:033-040	The people of Lot rejected (his) warning. 4. We sent against them a violent tornado with showers of stones, (which destroyed them), except Lot's household; them We delivered by early dawn as a grace from Us. Thus do We reward those who give thanks. And (Lot) did warn them of Our punishment, but they disputed about the warning, and they even sought to snatch away his guests from him, but We blinded their eyes. (They heard) "Now taste you My wrath and My warning." Early on the morrow, an abiding

7	54:041-042	punishment seized them. "So taste you My wrath and My warning." • And We have indeed made the Qur'an easy to understand and remember; then is there any that will receive admonition?
		The People of Pharaoh rejected Signs from God
		To the people of Pharaoh, too, aforetime came warners. 5. The (people) rejected all Our signs, but We seized them with such penalty (as comes) from One exalted in power, able to carry out His will.

5.3 The Resurrection will take place at Its Own Time

God does not require lengthy preparations to bring on the resurrection whenever He wills. No sooner does He give a command than it takes place immediately. Like everything else, the universe and humanity have a destiny. Due to this destiny, everything happens at its own appointed time. That is why the resurrection will not occur just because somebody challenges a messenger or believer to convince him of it.

Table 5.3: God Created Everything According to a Measure

No	Surah:Verses	Meanings
		God created things in Proportion and Measure
8	54:049-051	Verily, all things have We created in proportion and measure, and Our command is but a single (act), like the twinkling of an eye. And (often) in the past, We have destroyed gangs like unto you; then is there any that will receive admonition.
		Every matter, small and great, is Recorded
9	54:052-053	All that they do is noted in (their) books (of deeds). Every matter, small and great, is on record.

6 DEATH AND THE AFTERLIFE
FROM SURAH AL-WAQI'AH (56)

The moral and sociopolitical principles given in the Qur'an are as firm as the principles that govern the stars and planets. Since people will be judged according to what God has revealed, they are encouraged to benefit from His sociopolitical laws. God tells people that when the inevitable event of resurrection takes place, there won't be any to refute its happening and that no one has the power to avert it. On that day, people will be separated into three groups and rewarded or punished according to their behavior and deeds in the world.

6.1 Resurrection and Accountability cannot be Denied

The unbelievers think that the resurrection will never take place. They cannot perceive a moment when the entire universe will be altered and dead people will be resurrected and called to account. After the final judgment, the righteous will be admitted to Paradise, and the corrupt will be cast into Hell. Unfortunately, the unbelievers regard this as mere imaginary that could never happen in actual fact. To answer this argument, God says: "When the event inevitable comes to pass, then will no (person) entertain falsehood concerning its coming. (Many) will it bring low; (many) will it exalt—when the earth shall be shaken to its depths and the mountains shall be crumbled to atoms, becoming dust scattered abroad (Qur'an 56:1-6)."

6.2 The Accountability will Result in Three Groups

On the Day of Judgment, people will be divided into three groups: (1) the foremost in rank and position; (2) the common righteous people; and (3) those that denied the Hereafter and persisted in disbelief, polytheism, and major sins till their last day on earth. "And you shall be sorted out into three classes. Then (there will be) the companions of the right hand—what will be the companions of the right hand? And the companions of the left hand—what will be the companions of the left hand? And those foremost (in faith) will be foremost (in the Hereafter) (Qur'an 56:7-10)."

Table 6.2: Three Groups of People and their Achievements

No	Surah:Verses	Meanings
		The Foremost People will be near stationed to God
1	56:011-026	1. These will be those nearest to Allah in gardens of bliss—a number of people from those of old, and a few from those of later times. (They

		will be) on thrones encrusted (with gold and precious stones), reclining on them, facing each other. Round about them will (serve) youths of perpetual (freshness) with goblets, (shining) beakers, and cups (filled) out of clear-flowing fountains. No hangover will they receive there from, nor will they suffer intoxication—and with fruits, any that they may select, and the flesh of fowls, any that they may desire. And (there will be) companions with beautiful, big, and lustrous eyes, like unto pearls well-guarded. (This is) a reward for the deeds of their past (life). No frivolity will they hear therein, nor any taint of ill—only the saying, "Peace! Peace."
		How fortunate will be the People on the Right
2	56:027-040	2. The companions of the right hand—what will be the companions of the right hand! (They will be) among lote trees without thorns, among talh trees with flowers (or fruits) piled one above another—in shade long extended, by water flowing constantly, and fruit in abundance, whose season is not limited, nor (supply) forbidden, and on thrones (of dignity), raised high. We have created (their companions) of special creation and made them virgin, pure (and undefiled), beloved (by nature), equal in age—for the companions of the right hand—a (goodly) number from those of old, and a (goodly) number from those of later times.
		How wretched will be the People on the Left
3	56:041-056	3. The companions of the left hand—what will be the companions of the left hand! (They will be) in the midst of a fierce blast of fire and in boiling water, and in the shades of black smoke. Nothing (will there be) to refresh, nor to please, for that they were wont to be indulged before that in wealth (and luxury) and persisted obstinately in wickedness supreme! And they used to say, "What! When we die and become dust and bones, shall we then indeed be raised up again—(we) and our

		fathers of old? Say: "Yea, those of old and those of later times, all will certainly be gathered together for the meeting appointed for a day well known. Then will you truly—O you that go wrong and treat (truth) as falsehood, you will surely taste of the tree of zaqqum. Then will you fill your insides therewith and drink boiling water on top of it. Indeed, you shall drink like diseased camels raging with thirst. Such will be their entertainment on the Day of Requital.

6.3 The Creator Can Resurrect People after their Death

The very existence of the universe and humankind confirms the truth of the Oneness of God and of the Hereafter, the two fundamental beliefs of Islam that the unbelievers do not accept. Apart from everything else that exists in the universe, people are invited to reflect on their own body, the food they eat, the water they drink, and the fire on which they cook their food. Then they are asked what right they have to behave independently of, or to serve any other than, the God Whose creative power has brought them into existence, and Whose provisions sustain them. How can one entertain the idea that after the first creation, God will be unable to recreate again even if He wills to?

Table 6.3
Who has Created Humankind, Food, Water, and Fire?

No	Surah:Verses	Meanings
		God created You; Why don't You Admit it?
4	56:057-062	• It is We Who have created you; why will you not witness the truth? Do you then see? The (human seed) that you throw out—is it you who creates it, or did We? We have decreed death to be your common lot, and We are not to be frustrated from changing your forms and creating you (again) in (forms) that you know not. And you certainly know already the first form of creation; why then do you not celebrate His praises?
		Have People considered What They Sow?
5	56:063-067	• You see the seed that you sow in the ground? Is it you that causes it to grow, or are We the

701

		cause? Were it Our will, We could crumble it to dry powder, and you would be left in wonderment, (saying), "We are indeed left with debts (for nothing). Indeed, we are shut out (of the fruits of our labor)."
		Have People considered the water they drink?
6	56:068-070	• You see the water that you drink? Do you bring it down (in rain) from the cloud, or do We? Were it Our will, We could make it salt (and unpalatable). Then why do you not give thanks?
		Have People considered the Fire They Kindle?
7	56:071-074	• You see the fire that you kindle? Is it you who grow the tree that feeds the fire, or do We grow it? We have made it a memorial (of Our handiwork) and an article of comfort and convenience for the residents of deserts. Then celebrate with praises the name of your Lord, the supreme.

6.4 People will be Judged by what is in the Qur'an

The Author of the Qur'an is the One Who has created the universe. Nonetheless, instead of deriving any benefit from the guidance given in the Qur'an, the unbelievers of Makkah were treating the Qur'an lightly. God told them: "Furthermore, I call to witness the setting of the stars—and that is indeed a mighty adjuration if you but knew—that this is indeed a Qur'an most honorable, in a Book well-guarded, which none shall touch but those who are clean. (It is) a revelation from the Lord of the worlds. Is it such a message that you would hold in light esteem, and have you made it your livelihood that you should declare it false (Qur'an 56:75-82)?" People will be judged according to what God has revealed. Therefore, they are encouraged to follow the moral and sociopolitical principles described in the Qur'an, in order to safeguard against the adverse consequence of violating them.

6.5 What People can Hope for after their Deaths

People may overlook universal truths due to the combination of arrogance and free will, but death is enough to open their eyes. When it comes to death, they are helpless; they can save no one.

People die in front of their eyes while they look on helplessly. It is beyond their power to stop God from calling people to account and giving rewards or punishments to them according to what they did during their life on earth. They may or may not believe in it, but every dying person will surely see his own end after death.

Table 6.5: Three Types of People after the Resurrection

No	Surah:Verses	Meanings
		People can't bring back the Dying
8	56:083-087	• Then why do you not (intervene) when (the soul of the dying man) reaches the throat, and you at the moment (sit) looking on? But We are nearer to him than you, and yet you don't see it. • Then why do you not, if you are exempt from (future) account, call back the soul, if you are true (in the claim of independence)?
		Near-stationed, On the Right and Unbelievers
9	56:088-094	1. Thus, then, if he be of those nearest to Allah, (there is for him) rest and satisfaction and a garden of delights. 2. And if he be of the companions of the right hand, (for him is the salutation), "Peace be unto you," from the companions of the right hand. 3. And if he be of those who treat (truth) as falsehood, who go wrong, for him is entertainment with boiling water and burning in Hellfire.

CHAPTER 62

Why Resurrection and the Hereafter?

FROM SURAH AL-QIYAMA (75), SURAH AL-INSAN (76),
SURAH AL-MURSALAT (77), SURAH AN-NABA' (78),
SURAH AN-NAZI'AT (79), SURAH AT-TAKWIR (81),
SURAH AL-INFITAR (82), SURAH AL-INSHIQAQ (84),
SURAH AL-GHASHIYA (88), SURAH AL-ZALZALAH (99),
AND SURAH AL-QARI'AH (101)

Due to their content and style, most of the Surahs about life after death seem to have been revealed in the period after the first seven verses of Surah Al-Muddaththir. In these successively revealed Surahs, the fundamental concepts of resurrection and accountability for individual behavior and deeds are presented briefly, and the importance of individual moral character, behavior, and deeds is stressed. Although God does not expect humanity to be perfectly free from errors and deviations, He does expect people to follow His guidance, admit their shortcomings, and keep on improving their character and behavior, in order to succeed in their lives as humans who are acting as God's trustees on earth.

1 THEIR CHARACTER MAKES PEOPLE HUMAN
FROM SURAH AL-QIYAMA (75)

Addressing those who deny the Hereafter, God replies in Surah Al-Qiyama, to the unbelievers' doubts and objections. An argument is also been given to prove the viability, occurrence, and necessity of the resurrection and the Hereafter.

1.1 The Mechanism for the Continual Self-Improvement
The existence of a mechanism for self-improvement is fundamental to the fulfillment of the human mission of being God's trustee on earth. It is also a foundation for the development of a just and peaceful society on earth. Since a just society cannot be built on corruption, discrimination, exploitation, and oppression, it is absolutely essential that a

704

mechanism exist for continual improvement of human character and behavior. The very existence of a conscience bears testimony to the fact that people are answerable for their deeds. It is human conscience that encourages people to admit mistakes and repent. Repentance in itself has a mechanism that triggers a desire to do better, thus motivating people to continue improving their character and behavior.

1.2 Why People Deny the Day of Judgment

One reason for people's denial of the Hereafter is that their selfish motives do not allow them to affirm it. However, the very event that they deny will inevitably take place, and all of their deeds will be brought forth and placed before them. However, even before people see their record, they will know full well what they had done in the world. Each person is on some level aware of his misdeeds, no matter what excuses and pretenses he may offer to deceive the world and his own self.

Table 1.2
The Existence of Conscience Confirms Accountability

No	Surah:Verses	Meanings
		Conscience, the Self-accusing Soul
1	75:001-006	I do call to witness the resurrection day, and I do call to witness the self-reproaching spirit. Does man think that We cannot assemble his bones? Nay, We are able to put together in perfect order the very tips of his fingers. But man wishes to do wrong (even) in the time in front of him. He questions: "When is the day of resurrection?"
		People will be apprised of their deeds on Resurrection Day
2	75:007-015	• At length, when the sight is dazed, and the moon is buried in darkness, and the sun and moon are joined together—that day will man say: "Where is the refuge?" • By no means! No place of safety! Before your Lord (alone), that day will be the place of rest. That day will man be told (all) that he put forward and all that he put back. Nay, man will be evidence against himself, even though he was to put up his excuses.

705

1.4 The Objective of the Resurrection and Accountability?

Resurrection is there to make people responsible for their behavior and actions. So that humankind should use its free will and reasoning discreetly during the fulfillment of one's duties as God's trustee on earth and not in the pursuit of one's selfish desires. Since people have been given free will and reasoning, they may ignore the call of their conscience and use reasoning to justify their selfish motives and misdeeds. Resurrection and the Hereafter have been created just to counter this problem and provide additional motivation for the improvement in human character and behavior. Happiness in the life to come greatly depends on the 'efforts of the humankind to improve the life in this world'. This is very important, as individuals, irrespective of the situation or status in life, each one of us should improve our behavior and try to help others in their struggle in life. What makes us suffer forever or makes us happy is our work. Our actions determine our present and our future. It is the choice one makes, knowing that all actions either good or bad have appropriate consequences.

Table 1.4
Accountability Assures the Proper Working of Conscience

No	Surah:Verses	Meanings
		The Hereafter Starts with an Individual's Death
3	75:026-030	1. Yea, when (the soul) reaches to the collarbone (in its exit), and there will be a cry, "Who is a magician (to restore him)?" 2. And he will conclude that it was (the time) of parting, and one leg will be joined with another. That day the drive will be (all) to your Lord.
		If not Accountable, Then What is a Human Worth
4	75:031-035	1. So he gave nothing in charity, nor did he pray, 2. But on the contrary, he rejected truth and turned away, 3. Then did he stalk to his family in full conceit. Woe to you, (O men!), yea, woe! Again, woe to you, (O men!), yea, woe.
		The Creator has the Power to Resurrect

706

5	75:036-040	Does man think that he will be left uncontrolled, (without purpose)? Was he not a drop of sperm emitted (in lowly form)? Then did he become a clinging clot; then did (Allah) make and fashion (him) in due proportion, and of it He made two sexes, male and female. Has not He (the same) the power to give life to the dead?

2 THE CHARACTER AND BEHAVIOR OF THE GRATEFUL
FROM SURAH AL-INSAN (76)

Most of the commentators and the majority of scholars regard Al-Insan as a Makkan Surah. A special characteristic of the earliest Surahs revealed at Makkah is that, besides briefly introducing the fundamental beliefs and concepts of Islam, some moral qualities and virtuous acts that are praiseworthy, as well as those evils of deed and morality that Islam strives to cleanse from human life, are also mentioned. Although good and evil deeds do entail good and bad results in the transitory life of the world, the enduring results that they will produce for an individual in the eternal and everlasting life of the Hereafter are repeatedly stressed in the Qur'an.

2.1 The Birth and the Trials of Humankind on Earth
People are reminded that there was a time when they did not exist; then a humble beginning was made with a mixed drop of sperm and ovum. Beginning a human's creation in this way, God has developed and shaped people into what they are today in order to test and try them in the world. Unlike other creatures, humans are intelligent and sensible and have been shown both the way of gratitude and the way of ingratitude. Their life on earth shows whether they have emerged as grateful or unbelieving, ungrateful individuals. In Surah Al-Insan God says: "Has there not been over man a long period of time when he was nothing—(not even) mentioned? Verily, We created man from a drop of mingled sperm, in order to try him. So We gave him (the gifts) of hearing and sight. We showed him the way; whether he be grateful or ungrateful (rests on his will) (Qur'an 76:1-3)."

2.2 Grateful People, Their Behavior, and Their Reward

For people to behave in a manner reflective of gratitude to God, they must have a belief in their accountability on the Day of Judgment. Their behavior is such that "They perform (their) vows, and they fear a day whose evil flies far and wide. And they feed, for the love of Allah, the indigent, the orphan, and the captive, (saying), 'We feed you for the sake of Allah alone. No reward do we desire from you, nor thanks. We only fear a day of distressful wrath from the side of our Lord' (Qur'an 76:7-10)." The blessings that will be provided to such people in Paradise are mentioned in detail: "As to the righteous, they shall drink of a cup (of wine) mixed with camphor—a fountain where the devotees of Allah do drink, making it flow in unstinted abundance...But Allah will deliver them from the evil of that day and will shed over them a light of beauty and (blissful) joy. Because they were patient and constant, He will reward them with a garden and (garments of) silk (Qur'an 76:5-6, 11-12)."

2.3 The Qur'an is Guidance and a Reminder from God

The Qur'an is a revelation from God, not a fabrication. It is according to God's wisdom that the Qur'an was revealed piece by piece and not as a whole. "It is We Who have sent down the Qur'an to you by stages. Therefore, be patient with constancy to the command of your Lord, and hearken not to the sinner or the ingrate among them. And celebrate the name of your Lord morning and evening, and part of the night; prostrate yourself to Him, and glorify Him a long night through (Qur'an 76:23-26)." The Qur'an guides people to the way to their Lord. It is an admonition; so whoever desires may accept it. In Surah Al-Insan, God tells people: "This is an admonition. Whoever will, let him take a (straight) path to his Lord. But you will not, except as Allah wills, for Allah is full of knowledge and wisdom. He will admit to His mercy whom He wills. But the wrongdoers—for them has He prepared a grievous penalty (Qur'an 76:29-31)." People's own will and desires are not everything in the world. One's will and desires cannot be fulfilled unless God also so wills. God's willing is not haphazard; whatever He wills, He wills it on the basis of His knowledge and wisdom. He is merciful to whom He regards as worthy of His mercy, and He

708

has prepared a painful torment for those whom He finds unjust and wicked.

2.4 The Unbelievers Attitude towards Life and the Hereafter

The unbelievers love this world and neglect the Hereafter. They pursue this life without taking responsibility for their actions, which is why they like to forget about the Hereafter. God describes this attitude of the unbelievers: "As to these, they love the fleeting life and put away behind them a day (that will be) hard. It is We Who created them, and We have made their joints strong; but when We will, We can substitute the like of them by a complete change (Qur'an 76:27-28)."

3 HUMAN DIGNITY DEMANDS ACCOUNTABILITY
FROM SURAH AL- MURSALAT (77)

The contents of Surah Al-Mursalat indicate that it was revealed in the earliest period at Makkah. If this Surah is read together with the two Surahs preceding it, namely Al-Qiyamah and Al-Insan, and the two Surahs following it, namely An-Naba' and An-Nazi'at, it becomes obvious that all these Surahs are revelations from the same period. They deal with one and the same aspect of human existence, i.e., accountability for one's behavior and deeds. In addition, the resurrection and Hereafter are affirmed, and people are warned about the consequences of their behavior and actions, which ultimately result from either denial or affirmation of divine guidance. In that regard, rejection of divine guidance leads people to animalistic fulfillment of their selfish desires by any means possible, whether legal or illegal. However, a human is not an animal! People are expected to behave as humans and not like animals.

3.1 God's Trustee is Responsible for His Performance

The system of winds is cited as evidence that the resurrection must take place. The power of All-Mighty God Who established this system cannot be helpless in bringing the resurrection. Since no action of an All-Wise Creator can be vain and purposeless, the Hereafter must appear in order that His trustees on earth are held accountable. Without the Hereafter, human life loses

709

purpose. The Day of Judgment is to settle the accounts of all individual people. God has fixed a specific time for it, and when it takes place, it will confound those who frivolously demand its appearance before they will believe in it.

Table 3.1: Surely the Resurrection Will Happen

No	Surah:Verses	Meanings
		What is Promised will be Fulfilled
1	77:001-007	1. By the (winds) sent forth one after another (to man's profit), 2. Which then blow violently in tempestuous gusts and scatter (things) far and wide, 3. Then separate them, one from another. 4. Then spread abroad a message, whether of justification or of warning— Assuredly, what you are promised must come to pass.
		Resurrection will be on the Day
2	77:008-015	1. When the stars become dim, 2. When the heaven is cleft asunder, 3. When the mountains are scattered (to the winds) as dust, 4. And when the messengers are (all) appointed a time (to collect)— • For what day are these (portents) deferred? For the Day of Sorting. And what will explain to you what the Day of Sorting is? Ah, woe that day to the rejecters of truth.

3.2 Human Dignity Demands Accountability for Deeds

Why the Hereafter? If there were no Hereafter, then where would God's trustees be compensated for their job well done? Why should one improve one's character or behavior and do good deeds? Most importantly, why should a person who has been given free will and the authority of being God's trustee not be responsible for his actions and deeds? History tells us that some nations that denied the Hereafter ultimately became corrupt and met with destruction. The Hereafter is a truth. If a nation denies the Hereafter and acts immorally without regard for the accountability for its actions, it will meet the same destiny as did corrupt nations of old.

710

Since, in the present life, retribution does not always take place in its complete and perfect form, the moral law of the universe necessarily demands that there should come a time when things should take their full course and when all those good works and evil deeds, which could not be rewarded or punished in this world, should be fully rewarded or punished. This makes it inevitable that there should be a second life after death. Considering the supreme powers of God, one cannot deny His ability to do this. Considering God's wisdom, one cannot deny that it is the very demand of His wisdom to call people to account for the right and wrong use of the powers that God granted them on the earth. Rather, it would be against wisdom to let people off without rendering an account.

Table 3.2: God Creates and Destroys and thus will Resurrect

No	Surah:Verses	Meanings
		How did God deal with the Guilty
3	77:016-019	Did We not destroy the men of old (for their evil)? So shall We make later (generations) follow them. Thus do We deal with men of sin. • Ah, woe that day to the rejecters of truth.
		How God Created Humankind
4	77:020-024	Have We not created you from a fluid (held) despicable, which We placed in a place of rest firmly fixed, for a period (of gestation) determined (according to need)? For We do determine (according to need), for We are the best to determine (things). • Ah, woe that day to the rejecters of truth.
		How God Created Earth and Water
5	77:025-028	Have We not made the earth (as a place) to draw together the living and the dead, and made therein mountains standing firm, lofty (in stature), and provided for you water sweet (and wholesome)? • Ah, woe that day to the rejecters of truth.

3.3 Woe to the Rejecters of the Truth and the Hereafter

The unbelievers will be ordered to proceed to their abode in Hell without any argument or excuses. This is the fate of those who deny the Hereafter. God challenges the unbelievers that if they have any scheme against Him, they should try it now. On the Day of Judgment, they will not be able to do anything. They are told, "That will be a Day of Sorting! We shall gather you together and those before (you)! Now, if you have a trick (or plot), use it against Me! Ah, woe that day to the rejecters of truth (Qur'an 77:38-40)."

Table 3.3: Unbelievers on the Day of Judgment

No	Surah:Verses	Meanings
		Journey to Hell in Smoke with many Branches
6	77:029-034	(It will be said:) "You depart to that which you used to reject as false! You depart to a shadow (of smoke ascending) in three columns, (which yields) no shade of coolness and is of no use against the fierce blaze. Indeed, it throws about sparks (huge) as forts, as if there were (a string of) yellow camels (marching swiftly). • Ah, woe that day to the rejecters of truth.
		No Argument will be on Day of God's Judgment
7	77:035-037	That will be a day when they shall not be able to speak, nor will it be open to them to put forth pleas. • Ah, woe that day to the rejecters of truth.

3.4 God will Reward those Believers who Do Good Deeds

The people who have faith in the resurrection and the Hereafter during their worldly lives, and who try hard to improve their character and behavior by abstaining from the evils of disbelief in thought and deed, will certainly find reward in the Hereafter, even if such faith and actions were not fully rewarded in this world. God tells people: "As to the righteous, they shall be amidst (cool) shades and springs (of water), and (they shall have) fruits—all they desire. You eat and you drink to your heart's content, for that you worked (righteousness). Thus do We certainly reward the doers of good. Ah, woe that day to the rejecters of truth (Qur'an 77:41-45)."

712

3.5 People should Live their Worldly Lives like the Humans

People will be judged in the Hereafter, whether they lived like humans as God's trustees on earth or whether they only lived like animals, satisfying their own physical needs. Those who deny the Hereafter, who refuse to take their responsibility seriously and turn away from God's servitude, have been told: "(O you unjust!) You eat and enjoy yourselves (but) a little while, for that you are sinners. Ah, woe that day to the rejecters of truth! And when it is said to them, 'Prostrate yourselves,' they do not so. Ah, woe that day to the rejecters of truth! Then what message after that will they believe in (Qur'an 77:46-50)?" A person who fails to obtain guidance from the Qur'an will not find it in any other source.

4 GOD'S TRUSTEES ARE ACCOUNTABLE
FROM SURAH AN-NABA' (78)

Early on in Makkah, preaching consisted of three Islamic principles. These were that (1) no one be held as an associate with God, that (2) God had appointed Muhammad as His Messenger, and that (3) this world will come to an end one day, and another world will be established. At that time, the former and latter generations will be resurrected and judged for their individual beliefs, behavior, and deeds. Those who emerge as believing and righteous will go to Paradise, and those who are proven to be unbelieving and corrupt will be made to live in Hell forever.

4.1 Unbelievers Views on God, the Messenger, and Hereafter

Although *Tauheed,* the belief in One God, was highly unpleasant to the people of Makkah, they were not disbelievers in the existence of God. They believed in His being the Supreme Sustainer, Creator, and Providence, and they also admitted that their deities were themselves created by God. Thus, the only thing they disputed was the Islamic message that their deities had no share in the attributes and powers of God.

713

The people of Makkah were also not prepared to accept Muhammad as the Messenger of God. However, what they could not deny was that during the 40 years of his life before his claim to be a Prophet, they had never found him to be deceitful or to use unlawful methods for selfish ends. They admitted that the Messenger was a man of wisdom, righteousness, and moral superiority. Their dilemma was maintaining that he was both: (1) an honest and upright person in every affair in life, and (2) lying when he claimed to be a prophet.

However, believing in One God and in Muhammad as His Messenger was not as perplexing for the people of Makkah as believing in the resurrection and Hereafter. When these concepts were presented before them, they mocked them and expressed unusual wonder. They regarded such concepts as being remote from reason and as being impossible.

Without believing in the Hereafter and accountability, it is not possible for people to adopt a serious attitude about truth and falsehood, to change their standard of values with respect to good and evil, or to give up the worship of the material world. That is why the earliest Surahs revealed at Makkah stressed the doctrine of the Hereafter more than anything else. However, the argument for the resurrection is such that the doctrine of the Unity of Godhead is also impressed on human minds. Brief arguments, here and there, to confirm the truth of the Messenger and the Qur'an are also given in these Surahs.

4.2 The Performance of God's Trustees will be Judged

Will God Who has created people be unable resurrect them and establish another world? Will God who has created the universe with wisdom and purpose leave life as purposeless? Nothing could be more meaningless than, after appointing people to the office of His trusteeship and granting them powers, not evaluating their work when they have fulfilled their role on earth. How could people neither be rewarded and granted pension for satisfactory work performance nor be punishment for unsatisfactory performance of their duties? God tells people: "Concerning what are they disputing? (It is) about the great news about which they cannot agree. Verily, they shall soon (come to)

714

know! Verily, verily, they shall soon (come to) know (Qur'an 78:1-5)."

Table 4.2: God has the Ability and Power to Resurrect

No	Surah:Verses	Meanings
		Your Lord is Who has Created the Universe
1	78:006-016	1. Have We not made the earth as a wide expanse and the mountains as pegs? 2. (Have We not) created you in pairs and made your sleep for rest— 3. Made the night as a covering and made the day as a means of subsistence? 4. (Have We not) built over you the seven firmaments and placed (therein) a light of splendor? 5. Do We not send down from the clouds water in abundance that We may produce therewith corn and vegetables and gardens of luxurious growth?

4.3 Hell is an Ambush for those who are Irresponsible

The Day of Judgment will arrive at its appointed time. When the trumpet is sounded, whatever is foretold will appear before one's eyes, whether one believes in it today or not. At that time, a person will come out from wherever he was lying dead and buried to render his account. People's denial cannot avert this inevitable event. "Verily, the Day of Sorting is a thing appointed—the day that the trumpet shall be sounded, and you shall come forth in crowds, and the heavens shall be opened as if there were doors, and the mountains shall vanish as if they were a mirage (Qur'an 78:17-20)." The deniers of the resurrection were warned that their every misdeed has been recorded and that Hell is an ambush to punish them for their misdeeds. In contrast, those who lived as responsible persons and did good deeds will be rewarded.

Table 4.3: The Resurrection will occur at its Appointed Time

No	Surah:Verses	Meanings
		Those who are Rebellious and Careless!
2	78:021-030	Truly, Hell is as a place of ambush, for the transgressors a place of destination. 1. They will dwell therein for ages. Nothing cool shall they taste therein, nor any drink 2. Save a boiling fluid and a fluid, dark, murky, intensely cold, a fitting recompense (for them)— 3. For that they used not to fear any account (for their deeds), but they (impudently) treated Our signs as false. And all things have We preserved on record. So you taste (the fruits of your deeds), for no increase shall We grant you, except in punishment.
		Those who fulfilled their Responsibilities!
3	78:031-036	Verily, for the righteous there will be a fulfillment of (the heart's) desires— 1. Gardens enclosed, 2. And grapevines, 3. And companions of equal age, 4. And a cup full (to the brim). No vanity shall they hear therein, nor untruth— recompense from your Lord, a gift (amply) sufficient.

4.4 Judgment will depend on One's Behavior and Deeds

People will be rewarded for their deeds with justice in the divine court of the Hereafter. No one will be able to force the forgiveness of his followers, nor will one be allowed to speak without leave, which will be granted on the condition that intercession is made only by those to whom permission has been granted by God, and the intercessor will say only what is right and just.

Table 4.4: Nobody will be allowed to Transgress Justice

No	Surah:Verses	Meanings
		None is Allowed to transgress Justice
4	78:038-039	The day that the Spirit and the angels will stand forth in ranks, 1. None shall speak except any who is permitted

		by (Allah) Most Gracious, 2. And He will say what is right. That day will be the sure reality. Therefore, whoso will, let him take a (straight) return to his Lord.
		People will see the Fruits of their Deeds
5	78:040	Verily, We have warned you of a penalty near, the day when man will see (the deeds) that his hands have sent forth, and the Unbeliever will say, "Woe unto me! Would that I were (mere) dust!"

5 RESPONSIBILITY DEMANDS ACCOUNTABILITY
FROM SURAH AN-NAZI'AT (79)

According to Abdullah ibn 'Abbas, Surah An-Nazi'at was revealed after Surah An-Naba'. Its subject matter testifies that it belongs to the earliest period at Makkah. Its theme is the affirmation of resurrection and the life in the Hereafter. In addition, citing the incident of Moses and Pharaoh, people are warned of the evil consequences of belying God's messengers.

5.1 A Single Cry Will Initiate People's Resurrection
Swearing by the angels who perform various duties and those who conduct the affairs of the universe according to His will, God assures that the resurrection will take place. People are reminded that the angels who take out the souls today can also be employed to restore the souls tomorrow. The angels who execute God's commands and conduct the affairs of the universe today can also alter the universe tomorrow to accomplish God's will. The resurrection that people think is impossible will not be difficult for God and will not require lengthy preparations. Just a single jolt will upset this system, and a second jolt will be enough to cause people to appear in a new world. People who denied the Hereafter will be trembling with fear and seeing with awestruck eyes all that they thought was impossible (Qur'an 79:1-14).

5.2 With Responsibility Comes Accountability
Citing the story of Moses and Pharaoh, people are reminded that the fate the Pharaoh was a consequence of denying the

717

messenger (Moses), rejecting divine guidance, and endeavoring to defeat Moses' mission. Similarly, those who do not change their disbelieving ways and attitudes will meet a similar fate, either in this world or the next. People who deny the Hereafter are asked if their resurrection is more difficult than the creation of the universe. The question has been left for the human intellect to contemplate which more in keeping with the demands of wisdom is: (1) calling people to account in the Hereafter, or (2) allowing people to remain dead after committing all sorts of misdeeds in the world and thus never being held accountable.

Table 5.2: God has the Ability and Power to Resurrect

No	Surah:Verses	Meanings
		The Creator of the Universe can also Resurrect People
1	79:027-033	1. Are you (people), harder to create or the heaven? He made it; He raised high its height and then put it into a right good state. He made dark its night and brought out its light. 2. And the earth, He expanded it after that. He brought forth from it its water and its pasture. And the mountains, He made them firm, a provision for you and for your cattle.
		Divine Guidance Helps Humankind to Succeed
2	79:015-026	Has the story of Moses reached you? Behold, your Lord did call to him in the sacred valley of Tuwa: "Go to Pharaoh, for he has indeed transgressed all bounds, and say to him, 'Would you that you should be purified (from sin) and that I guide you to your Lord, so you should fear Him?'" Then did (Moses) show him the great sign. • But (Pharaoh) rejected it and disobeyed (guidance). Further, he turned his back, striving hard (against Allah). Then he collected (his men) and made a proclamation, saying, "I am your Lord, most high." But Allah did punish him (and made an) example of him, in the Hereafter, as in this life. Verily, in this is an instructive warning for whosoever fears (Allah).

5.3 Behavior and Deeds Bring Heaven or Hell

When the Hereafter is established, people's future will be determined by the criteria as to (1) who rebelled against God, transgressing the bounds of service to Him and making material benefits and pleasures his objective of life, or (2) who feared his Lord and refrained from fulfilling his unlawful desires. The rational, logical, and moral demands of giving authority and of entrusting responsibilities to the people in the world is that they should ultimately be judged and rewarded or punished accordingly.

Only God knows when the resurrection will take place. A messenger is there only to warn people that it will certainly come. So whoever wishes may mend his ways, fearing its coming, and whoever wishes may behave and conduct himself as he likes, fearless of its coming. When the time comes, people who loved this life and its pleasures as the only objective of life will feel that they have stayed in the world for a very short time and have ruined their future forever for the sake of short-lived pleasures.

Table 5.3: Approaching Calamity of Heaven or Hell

No	Surah:Verses	Meanings
		When will the Calamity of Heaven or Hell Come?
3	79:042-046	They ask you about the Hour (of Judgment)—"When will be its appointed time?" 1. Wherein are you (concerned) with the declaration thereof? With your Lord in the limit fixed therefore. You are but a warner for such as fear it. 2. The day they see it, (it will be) as if they had tarried but a single evening or (at most till) the following morn.
		What will Happen when the Calamity Comes?
4	79:034-041	Therefore, when there comes the great, overwhelming (event), 1. The day when man shall remember (all) that he strove for, and Hellfire shall be placed in full view for (all) to see, 2. Then, for such as had transgressed all bounds

| | | and had preferred the life of this world, the abode will be Hellfire. |
| | 3. | For such as had entertained the fear of standing before their Lord's (tribunal) and had restrained (their) soul from lower desires, their abode will be the garden. |

6 THE HEREAFTER IS TO PUNISH THE CORRUPT
FROM SURAH AT-TAKWIR (81)

The subject and the style of this Surah clearly show that Surah At-Takwir was revealed at Makkah, in order to stress the need for and importance of the Hereafter. It is there to punish unjust and cruel people, while those who were kind and just will be rewarded for their humanity. To safeguard against the punishment of Hell, people have to take the demands of the Messenger and the Qur'an seriously.

6.1 Why the Resurrection and the Hereafter are Needed
If there were no resurrection and accountability, then when would the cruel be punished for their crimes? It stands to reason that people will have to account for their crimes. The resurrection will be like opening up graves for an autopsy in solving murder cases, and this is of utmost importance. When will all this happen? We are told that it will happen, "When the sun (with its spacious light) is folded up; when the stars fall, losing their luster; when the mountains vanish (like a mirage); when the she-camels, ten months with young, are left untended; when the wild beasts are herded together (in human habitations); when the oceans boil over with a swell; when the souls are sorted out, (being joined, like with like) (Qur'an 81:1-7)." What will happen on that day? People are told in Surah At-Takwir that: "When the scrolls are laid open, when the world on high is unveiled, when the blazing fire is kindled to fierce heat, and when the garden is brought near, (then) shall each soul know what it has put forward (Qur'an 81:10-14)."

720

6.2 Why People need Divine Guidance and Messengers

People are reassured that whatever the Messenger is presenting is neither the bragging of a madman nor an evil suggestion inspired by Satan. Instead, it is the word of a noble, exalted, and trustworthy messenger (Angel Gabriel) sent by God, whom the Messenger saw with his own eyes in the bright horizon of the clear sky in broad day light. People are told about the Messenger: "Your companion is not one possessed, and without doubt he saw him in the clear horizon. Neither does he withhold grudgingly knowledge of the unseen, nor is it the word of an evil spirit accursed. Then whither do you go (Qur'an 81:22-26)?

Table 6.2: Messengers and the Divine Message

No	Surah:Verses	Meanings
		The Qur'an is brought to the Messenger by a Trusted Angel
1	81:015-021	So verily I call to witness the planets that recede, go straight, or hide, and the night as it dissipates, and the dawn as it breathes away the darkness. • Verily, this is the word of a most honorable messenger (Angel Gabriel), endued with power, with rank before the Lord of the throne, with authority there, (and) faithful to his trust.
		The Qur'an is Good Council for Everyone
2	81:027-028	Verily this is no less than a message to (all) the worlds, (with profit) to whoever among you wills to go straight.

7 HEREAFTER IS TO MOTIVATE PEOPLE TO BE JUST
FROM SURAH AL-INFITAR (82)

Surah Al-Infitar and the Surah At-Takwir closely resemble each other in their subject matter. This shows that both were revealed in about the same period. Ibn Omar reported that the Messenger said: "The one who wants that he should see the resurrection day, as one would see it with one's eyes, should read Surah At-Takwir, Surah Al-Infitar, and Surah Al-Inshiqaq (Al-Hadith: vol. IV, no. 16, page 104)."

7.1 God has forbidden Himself Injustice

Islam attaches great importance to justice and requires that all believers and their rulers should maintain justice within their communities. Islam threatens every perpetrator of injustice with grievous suffering on the Day of Judgment. It also promises great rewards for just people. The Messenger quoted God as saying: "My servants, I have forbidden Myself injustice and have made it forbidden among you. So do not be unjust to one another (Sahih Muslim: 32.6446)."

7.2 God will establish Justice among People

It is inconceivable that God, Who insists so much on being just to people, should not have any provision for the establishment of absolute justice in the universe. One may ask what it is that makes people think that God, Who brought them into being and by Whose favor and bounty they possess the finest body, limbs, and features among all creatures, is only bountiful and not also just. His being bountiful and generous does not mean that one should become fearless of His justice. People have been warned not to remain involved in any misunderstanding. Each person's complete record is being prepared. There are trustworthy writers who are writing down whatever a person does. God says: "O man! What has seduced you from your Lord, most beneficent— the One Who created you, fashioned you in due proportion, and gave you a just bias? In whatever form He wills does He put you together. Nay! But you do reject right and judgment! But verily over you (are appointed angels) to protect you, kind and honorable, writing down (your deeds). They know (and understand) all that you do (Qur'an 82:6-12)." That is how God reassures that everyone will know on Judgment Day what he did on earth. "When the sky is cleft asunder, when the stars are scattered, when the oceans are suffered to burst forth, and when the graves are turned upside down, (then) shall each soul know what it has sent forward and (what it has) kept back (Qur'an 82.1-5)."

7. 3 The Award will be According to One's Deeds

When the resurrection takes place, the righteous will enjoy every kind of bliss in Paradise, and the wicked and corrupt will be punished in Hell.

Table 7.3
Day of Judgment and Awards

No	Surah:Verses	Meanings
		What the Day of Judgment Is?
1	82:017-019	And what will explain to you what the Day of Judgment is? Again, what will explain to you what the Day of Judgment is? 1. (It will be) the day when no person shall have power (to do) anything for another, for the command that day will be (wholly) with Allah.
		What the Day of Rewards Is?
2	82:013-016	2. As for the righteous, they will be in bliss, and the wicked—they will be in the fire, which they will enter on the Day of Judgment, and they will not be able to keep away there from.

8 HEREAFTER IS TO
MOTIVATE PEOPLE TO REFORM
FROM SURAH AL-INSHIQAQ (84)

Surah Al-Inshiqaq reminds people that they should not deny the resurrection. Rather, they should reform their character, behavior, and deeds in such a way that, when the resurrection takes place and they appear before their Lord to render an account of their deeds, God will judge them to have been righteous trustees.

8.1 People's Journey to their Final Destiny

People are told: "When the sky is rent asunder and hearkens to (the command of) its Lord—and it must needs (do so)—and when the earth is flattened out and casts forth what is within it and becomes empty, and hearkens to (the command of) its Lord—and it must needs (do so)—(then will come home the full reality) (Qur'an 84:1-5)." Whether people are conscious of this fact or not, they will have to present themselves before their Lord at that time, and they will be divided into two groups. Those whose records will be given to them in their right hands will be forgiven without any severe reckoning. Those whose records will be given to them behind their backs will wish that they would die somehow, but they will not die. Instead, they will be cast into Hell. They will meet this fate because they lived their lives as though they would never have to account for them.

Table 8.1
People returning to their Lord – With their Baggage

No	Surah:Verses	Meanings
		People are Certainly born to Work Hard
1	84:006	O you people! Verily you are ever toiling on towards your Lord—painfully toiling, but you shall meet Him (and find the results of the deeds that you did).
		People's Destiny Depends on their Deeds
2	84:007-015	• Then he who is given his record in his right hand—soon will his account be taken by an easy reckoning, and he will turn to his people, rejoicing. But he who is given his record behind his back—soon will he cry for perdition, and he will enter a blazing fire. 1. Truly, did he go about among his people rejoicing? 2. Truly, did he think that he would not have to return (to Us)! Nay, nay! For his Lord was (ever) watchful of him.

8.2 People's Journey from Here to the Hereafter

Peoples' gradual journey from the life of this world to the rewards and punishments of the Hereafter is as sure as the appearance of twilight after sunset, the coming of the night after the day, the returning of men and animals to their respective abodes at night, and the growing of the crescent into a full moon. The unbelievers, who repudiate the Qur'an instead of bowing down to God when they hear it, have been forewarned of a grievous punishment. The good news of limitless rewards has been given to the believers and the righteous.

Table 8.2: People's Journey from Here to the Hereafter

No	Surah:Verses	Meanings
		People are Ever Travelling in Time
3	84:016-019	So I do call to witness the ruddy glow of sunset, the night and its homing, and the moon in her fullness—You shall surely travel from stage to stage.
		Easier it is to Travel with Guidance
4	84:020-025	What then is the matter with them that they believe not? And when the Qur'an is read to them, they fall not prostrate, 1. But on the contrary the unbelievers reject (it). 2. But Allah has full knowledge of what they secrete (in their breasts). 3. So announce to them a penalty grievous. Except to those who believe and work righteous deeds. For them is a reward that will never fail.

9 RESURRECTION IS A SHATTERING CALAMITY
From Surah Al-Ghashiya (88)

Surah Al-Ghashiya was revealed after the Messenger started publically preaching belief in One God and the Hereafter. In this Surah, people who are skeptical about the existence of One God and of the Hereafter are asked to observe and reflect on the things they experience daily.

9.1 Resurrection will be an Overwhelming Calamity

People are asked: "Has the story reached you of the overwhelming (event) (Qur'an 88:1)? The details of what will happen when the impending calamity materializes are given. People will be divided into two separate groups and will meet their separate destinies. One group of the people will go to Hell where they will suffer punishment, while the second group will go to Paradise and will be provided with numerous blessings.

Table 9.1: Two Types of People and their Destinies

No	Surah:Verses	Meanings
		Evildoers after the Overwhelming Event
1	88:002-007	1. Some faces that day will be humiliated, laboring (hard), weary—the while they enter the blazing fire—the while they are given to drink of a boiling hot spring. 2. No food will there be for them but a bitter thorn that will neither nourish nor satisfy hunger.
		The Righteous after the Overwhelming Event
2	88:008-016	1. (Other) faces that day will be joyful, pleased with their striving, in a garden on high where they shall hear no (word) of vanity. 2. Therein will be a bubbling spring: 3. Therein will be thrones, raised on high, goblets placed (ready), and cushions set in rows, and rich carpets (all) spread out.

9. 2 People should reflect on God's Creativity

The unbelievers are asked to reflect on why God created the things they experience daily. They should consider how camels, on whom their whole life activity in the Arabian Desert depends, came into existence, endowed precisely with the characteristics suitable for life in the desert. They should ponder over the sky, the mountains, and the earth, and they should consider how the sky was stretched above them, how the mountains were erected, and how the earth was spread beneath them. Has all this been created without the skill and craftsmanship of an All-Powerful, All Wise Designer? (1) If they acknowledge that a Creator created all this without the help of any associate in their creation, then why do they refuse to accept Him alone as their Lord and Sustainer? (2) If they acknowledge that God has the power to create all this, then what reasons do they have for not acknowledging His power to bring about their resurrection, to recreate humankind, and to make Hell and Heaven?

9. 2 The Messenger's Duty is to keep Reminding People

God told the Messenger that his duty was just to keep guiding the people. If the people did not acknowledge the truth, they had their free will. The Messenger was not to coerce them into believing. His only task was to exhort. Nonetheless, all people will eventually return to Him, and then He will call them to full account and reward or punish according to their individual behavior and deeds.

Table 9.2: Just Keep Reminding People, O Messenger

No	Surah:Verses	Meanings
		O Messenger, Just Keep Reminding People
3	88:017-022	1. Do they not look at the camels—how they are made, 2. And at the sky—how it is raised high, 3. And at the mountains—how they are fixed firm? 4. And at the earth—how it is spread out? Therefore, give admonition, for you are one to admonish. You are not one to manage (people's) affairs.
		Taking the People to Account is unto God
4	88:023-026	• But if any turn away and reject Allah, Allah will punish him with a mighty punishment. For to Us will be their return; then it will be for Us to call them to account.

10 RESURRECTION IS A DAY OF PARTING
FROM SURAH AL-ZALZALAH (99)

Content and style confirm that this Surah was revealed in the earliest stage at Makkah. This was at a time when the fundamental principles and beliefs of Islam were being presented before the people in a concise but highly effective way.

!0.1 Importance of Accountability and Judgment in Islam
The importance of the accountability for individual behavior and deeds is such that it was reported by Ibn 'Abbas and Anas ibn Malek that the Messenger said: "'When it will be shaken' (Surah Al-Zalzalah) is equivalent to half of the Qur'an, and 'Say, 'He is Allah, the One'' (Surah Al-Ikhlas) is equivalent to one-third of the Qur'an, and 'Say, 'O you unbelievers'' (Surah Al-Kafirun) is equivalent to one-fourth of the Qur'an (Al-Hadith: vol.III, no. 44, page 680)." Based on their individual deeds, all people will

be divided into two separate groups, one of good people and one of evil people.

10.2 Resurrection is the Separation of Good and Evil People
How the second life after death will take place will be massively confusing for people. This is demonstrated in Surah Al-Zalzalah, where it says that the resurrection will take place: "When the earth is shaken to her (utmost) convulsion, and the earth throws up her burdens (from within), and man cries (distressed): 'What is the matter with her' (Qur'an 99:1-3)?" People are told that the earth on which they lived and did all kinds of thoughtless deeds, and from which they would never have imagined that speech was possible, will bear witness to their deeds and speak by God's command. It will be a witness over people as to what they did at certain times and places. "On that day will it declare its tidings, for that your Lord will have given it inspiration. On that day will men proceed in companies sorted out, to be shown the deeds that they (had done). Then shall anyone who has done an atom's weight of good see it, and anyone who has done an atom's weight of evil shall see it (Qur'an 99:4-8)."

11 THE RESURECCTION IS A GREAT DISASTER
SURAH AL-QARI'AH (101)

In Surah Al-Qari'ah, God rhetorically asks: "What is the great disaster? And what do you know what the great disaster is (Qur'an 101:2-3)?" Thus, after preparing the listeners for news of the dreadful calamity, the resurrection is depicted. People are then warned that an individual's good or evil end in the Hereafter will depend on whether or not his good deeds outweigh his bad deeds.

11.1 Ultimate Destinies of Righteous and the Evil People
On the day of resurrection, people will be running around in confusion and bewilderment, just like so many scattered moths around a light. The uprooted mountains will be flying around like carded wool. Then, God's court will be established, and people will be judged for their deeds. The people whose good deeds are heavier than their evil deeds will be blessed with bliss

and happiness. The people whose good deeds are lighter than their evil deeds will be cast into the deep pit of burning fire.

Table 11.1: Ultimate Fates of Righteous and Evil People

No	Surah:Verses	Meanings
		The Calamity is **the Beginning of a New Universe**
1	101:001-005	The (day) of noise and clamor (the terrible calamity!)—what is the (day) of noise and clamor? (What is the terrible calamity?) And what will explain to you what the (day) of noise and clamor is? • (It is) a day whereon men will be like moths scattered about, • And the mountains will be like carded wool.
		The Recompense for Righteous and Evil Deeds
2	101:006-011	1. Then, he whose balance (of good deeds) will be (found) heavy will be in a life of good pleasure and satisfaction, 2. But he whose balance (of good deeds) will be light will have his home in a (bottomless) pit. And what will explain to you what this is? (It is) a fire blazing fiercely.

729

CHAPTER 63

Who are the Real People?

FROM SURAH 'ABASA (80) AND SURAH AL-'ASR (103)

It's the human desire to excel that makes people righteous, truthful, and patient, and these are the three most fundamental human qualities required to build humanity. It is an established truth that each individual, each group, each community, and even the entirety of humanity loses if its members are devoid of belief, righteous deeds, and the practice of exhorting others to truth and patience. In Surah 'Abasa, the human desire to excel is depicted by the behavior and the efforts of a blind man (Abdullah ibn Shurayh, aka Ibn Umm Maktoum). Neither his blindness nor his age stood in the way of his finding the truth from the Messenger. Surah Al-'Asr highlights in a very concise form the salient characteristics of people that qualify them to be God's trustee on earth. These are faith, truthfulness, patience, and constancy. God's trustees seek the truth, believe in it, follow the divine guidance, and do good deeds. They join together in the propagation of truth, patience, and constancy among people.

1 ALL PEOPLE ARE EQUAL IN THE EYES OF GOD
FROM SURAH 'ABASA (80)

Historians are unanimous in their opinions about when Surah 'Abasa was revealed. According to them, some chiefs of Makkah were sitting in the Messenger's assembly, and the Messenger was trying to persuade them to accept Islam. At that time, a blind man named Ibn Umm Maktoum, who was one of the earliest converts to Islam, approached the Messenger to seek the explanation for some point concerning Islam. The Messenger disliked the interruption and ignored him. Thereupon, God revealed this Surah to reaffirm the principle that all people have equal access to divine guidance. According to some *Ahadith* that relate this incident, Ibn Umm Maktoum had already accepted Islam. According to other *Ahadith*, he was inclined to accept Islam and had approached the Messenger in search of the truth.

730

1.1 The Desire to Excel increases One's Respect

In the beginning of his mission, the Messenger naturally wanted the influential people in society to accept his message so that his task would become easier. After all, if Islam were only accepted by the poor and weak people, it was thought that it would not have much effect on society at large. However, this was not the correct approach in inviting others to Islam. Islam does not discriminate among people according to their material fortunes. Every person who seeks the truth is important, even if he is weak or poor. Likewise, every person who is not interested in the truth is unimportant, even if he occupies the highest position in society. A messenger should openly proclaim and convey the divine guidance to all. The people who are really worthy of his attention are those who are inclined to accept the guidance.

Table 1.1: Setting Correct Priorities

No	Surah:Verses	Meanings
		The Messenger did not like the Interruption
1	80:001-007	(The Prophet) frowned and turned away because there came to him the blind man (interrupting). 1. But what could tell you that perchance he might grow (in spiritual understanding) or that he might receive admonition, and the teaching might profit him? 2. As to one who regards himself as self-sufficient, to him do you attend, though it is no blame to you if he grows not (in spiritual understanding).
		Striving Earnestly in God's Way earns Respect
2	80:008-016	But as to him who came to you striving earnestly, and with fear (in his heart), of him were you unmindful. • By no means (should it be so), for it is indeed a message of instruction. • Therefore, let whoso will, keep it in remembrance. (It is) in books held (greatly) in honor, exalted (in dignity), kept pure and holy, (written) by the hands of scribes, honorable and pious and just.

1.2 People will surely be resurrected for Judgment

The unbelievers who were repudiating the Messenger's invitation were reminded about their ungrateful attitude against their Creator. They were told not to forget that they will be resurrected and will have to account for their attitude, behavior, and deeds.

Table 1.2: Who Failed to Perform Their Duty Will Suffer

No	Surah:Verses	Meanings
		Ungrateful follow not as God Commanded
3	80:017-023	Woe to man! What has made him reject Allah? 1. From what stuff has He created him? From a sperm-drop, He has created him and then molded him in due proportions. Then does He make His path smooth for him; then He causes him to die and puts him in his grave. Then, when it is His will, He will raise him up (again). By no means has he fulfilled what Allah has commanded him.
		Ungrateful Acknowledge not God's Bounties
4	80:024-032	Then let man look at his food (and how We provide it). For that, We pour forth water in abundance, 2. And We split the earth in fragments and produce therein grains, grapes, nutritious plants, olives, and dates. (We also bring forth) enclosed gardens, dense with lofty trees, and fruits and fodder for the use and convenience of you and your cattle.

1.3 Performance Evaluation for God's Trustees

The unbelievers were warned of the dreadful fate they will meet as a consequence of their conduct on earth, while the believers who have done their duty as commanded will be congratulated. When will this happen? It will happen: "When there comes the deafening noise—that day shall a man flee from his own brother, and from his mother and his father, and from his wife and his children. Each one of them that day will have enough concern (of his own) to make him indifferent to the others (Qur'an 80:33-37)." The fate of the corrupt people on that day will be such that: "Other faces that day will be dust-stained; blackness will cover them. Such will be the rejecters of Allah, the doers of iniquity (Qur'an 80:40-42)." However, the believers have been told: "Some faces that day will be beaming, laughing, and rejoicing (Qur'an 80:38-39)." These will be the faces of those who have done well!

2 RIGHTEOUS, TRUTHFUL AND PATIENT PEOPLE
FROM SURAH AL-'ASR (103)

The contents of Surah Al-'Asr testify that it was revealed in the earliest stage at Makkah, at a time when the message of Islam was being presented in brief but highly impressive verses. Listeners who heard these verses once could not forget them even if they wanted to, for they were automatically committed to memory. If life is considered as a business transaction, people will lose by merely attending to their material gains. When they add up their day's account in the afternoon, they will show a loss. Since faith is an armor that wards off the wounds of the material world, profit will only incur if they have faith, lead a good life, and contribute to the social welfare by following the path of truth, patience, and constancy.

2.1 What is Islam? To Believe and Do Good Deeds
Surah Al-'Asr is a matchless specimen of comprehensiveness and brevity. A whole world of meaning has been compressed into its few brief words, which are too vast in content to be fully expressed even in a book. In a clear and plain way, this Surah describes the way to real success and the way to ruin and destruction. If people follow this Surah well, it alone will suffice them for their guidance.

To swear by time amounts to saying that both past and present human history bear witness that the statement that follows is absolutely true: "By (the token of) time (through the ages), verily man is in loss, except such as have faith, do righteous deeds, and (join together) in teaching each other to be truthful, patient, and constant (Qur'an 103:1-3)."

CHAPTER 64

Corrupt People and Tyrants
FROM SURAH AL-MUTAFFIFIN (83), AND
SURAH AL-BURUJ (85)

The style and contents of Surah Al-Mutaffifin clearly show that it was revealed in an early stage at Makkah when Surah after Surah was being revealed to impress the doctrine of the Hereafter on the people's minds. The ruinous effect of dishonesty in commercial dealings is well known. Unless people realize that they will have to appear before God to give an account for each act they performed in this world, they won't adopt piety and righteousness in their daily affairs. People can develop true and enduring honesty only when they fear God and sincerely believe in the Hereafter.

1 DEFRAUDING AND CORRUPT PEOPLE
FROM SURAH AL-MUTAFFIFIN (83)

1.1 God's Trustees on Earth are Honest
Honesty is a duty and an obligation that people should always practice, regardless of whether it is useful or not in this world. It was narrated by Abu Huraira that God's Messenger said: "Pay the deposit to him who deposited it with you, and do not betray him who betrayed you (Abu Dawud 23.3528)." The importance of honesty is also illustrated by a *hadith* narrated by Um Salama, in which the Prophet said: "I am only human, and you people have disputes. Maybe some one among you can present his case in a more eloquent and convincing manner than the other, and I give my judgment in his favor according to what I hear. Beware! If ever I give (by error) somebody something of his brother's right, then he should not take it, as I have only given him a piece of fire (Sahih Bukhari: 8.86.97)."

Widespread dishonesty among people indicates the approaching end of time. It was narrated by Abu Huraira that: "The Messenger said: 'When honesty is lost, then wait for the Hour

734

(of Judgment).' It was asked, 'How will honesty be lost, O God's Messenger?' He said, 'When authority is given to those who do not deserve it, then wait for the Hour' (Sahih Bukhari: 8.76.503)."

1.2 Woe to those who defraud People

Dishonesty has a very negative impact in commercial dealings in this world. More importantly, a person's dishonesty in this world will negatively impact him in the Hereafter. Thus, people are discouraged from engaging in prevalent evil practices in their commercial dealings. When the unbelievers of Makkah demanded their due from others, they demanded that it be given in full. However, when they had to measure or weigh for others, they would give less than what was due. Using this practice as an example from the countless evils prevalent in society, we are told that such sinful behavior is the inevitable result of being heedless of the Hereafter. "Woe to those that deal in fraud—those who, when they have to receive by measure from men, exact full measure, but when they have to give by measure or weight to men, give less than due. Do they not think that they will be called to account on a mighty day, a day when mankind will stand before the Lord of the worlds (Qur'an 83:1-6)?"

1.3 Woe to those who reject the Hereafter

The deeds of all people, both the wicked and the righteous, are being recorded. Their fate in the Hereafter will depend on the nature of their individual behavior and deeds in this world. Belief in one's eventual accountability impacts positively on one's attitude towards life and motivates a person to do good deeds. However, those who reject the Hereafter deny themselves this opportunity.

Table 1.3: Believers and the Deniers of the Day of Judgment

No	Surah:Verses	Meanings
		Behavior of those who deny Accountability
1	83:007-017	Nay! Surely the record of the wicked is (preserved) in the crevice. And what will explain to you what the crevice is? (There is) a register (fully) inscribed. 1. Woe, that day to those that deny, those that

		deny the Day of Judgment, and none can deny it but the transgressor beyond bounds, the sinner. 2. When Our revelations are rehearsed to him, he says, "Tales of the ancients." • By no means! But on their hearts is the stain of the (ill) that they do. • Verily, from (the light of) their Lord, that day will they be veiled. Further, they will enter the fire of Hell. Further, it will be said to them: "This is the (reality) that you rejected as false."
		Behavior of those who are drawn near to God
2	83:018-020 83:024-028	Nay, verily the record of the righteous is (preserved) in the summit. And what will explain to you what the summit is? (There is) a register (fully) inscribed. 1. You will recognize in their faces the beaming brightness of bliss. Their thirst will be slaked with pure wine sealed. The seal thereof will be musk, and for this let those aspire who have aspirations. 2. With it will be (given) a mixture of pure *Tasnim*, a spring from (the waters) whereof drink those nearest to Allah.

1.4 Woe to Those who Laugh at the Believers

People who are mocking and humiliating the believers and their honest behavior and good deeds will meet with a most dire end on the Day of Judgment as a consequence of their conduct. The believers, on the other hand, will feel comforted when they see their fate.

Table 1.4
Unbelievers will face the Results of their Deeds

No	Surah:Verses	Meanings
		The Unbelievers' Attitude and Behavior
3	83:029-033	• Those in sin used to laugh at those who believed and, whenever they passed by them, used to wink at each other (in mockery). • And when they returned to their own people, they would return jesting. And whenever they

		saw them, they would say, "Behold! These are the people truly astray!" But they had not been sent as keepers over them.
		Unbelievers' will be paid back of what they did
4	83:034-036	1. But on this day, the believers will laugh at the unbelievers. On thrones (of dignity) they will command (a sight) (of all things). 2. Will not the unbelievers have been paid back for what they did?

2 PERSECUTION AND TYRANNY
FROM SURAH AL-BURUJ (85)

Surah Al-Buruj was revealed at Makkah when the persecution of the believers was at its climax and when the unbelievers were trying their utmost by tyranny and coercion to cause the new converts to Islam to renounce their faith. God, showing His displeasure with the unbelievers, tells the believers that He is watching everyone and everything, that the unbelievers will be punished in this life for their disbelief, and that the unbelievers will suffer in the Hereafter for their cruelties. In contrast, those who believe and do good deeds will go to Paradise, which is the supreme success.

2.1 Tyrants have existed throughout History
In the fight between evil and good, tyrants have existed throughout history. Whether they are tyrants from the past (e.g., the armies of Pharaoh, the people of Thamud, and the armies of colonialists) or from the present (e.g., the armies of various dictators), their common denominator has always been that they persecute believers. These tyrants have no grudge against their victims other than that their victims believed in the commands of God and wanted God's commands implemented in society. The believers of the past were willing to sacrifice their lives rather than give up their faith. This model from the past should motivate the believers of today and of the future to endure every persecution instead of giving up their faith.

Table 2.1: Cursed are the Tyrants, the Residents of Hell

No	Surah:Verses	Meanings
		Unbelievers mistreat the Believers Because of their Faith
1	85:001-009	By the sky (displaying) the constellations, by the promised Day (of Judgment), by one that witnesses, and (by) the subject of the witness— 1. Woe to the makers of the pit (of fire), fire supplied (abundantly) with fuel. 2. Behold! They sat over against the (fire), and they witnessed (all) that they were doing against the believers. 3. They ill-treated them for no other reason than that they believed in Allah, exalted in power, worthy of all praise, Him to Whom belongs the dominion of the heavens and the earth! And Allah is witness to all things.
		Only Repentance can Save the Unbelievers from the Fire
2	85.010-011	• Those who persecute (or draw into temptation) the believers, men and women, and do not turn in repentance will have the penalty of Hell. They will have the penalty of the burning fire. For those who believe and do righteous deeds will be gardens beneath which rivers flow. That is the great salvation, (the fulfillment of all desires).

2.2 All Tyrants can have a Similar Fate in this World

The unbelievers are warned that God's grip is very severe. If they are proud of the strength of their armies, they should know that the armies of Pharaoh and Thamud were even stronger and more numerous. Therefore, they should learn a lesson from their fate. The unbelievres cannot escape the encirclement of God's power, and the Qur'an that they are rejecting is unchangeable.

738

Table 2.2
Tyrants' Fates could be like that of Pharaoh or the Thamud

No	Surah:Verses	Meanings
		Truly Strong is the Grip and Power of your Lord
3	85:012-016	• Truly, strong is the grip (and power) of your Lord. It is He Who creates from the very beginning, and He can restore (life). And He is the oft-forgiving, full of loving kindness, Lord of the throne of glory, doer of all that He intends.
		Your Lord can treat unbelievers like He treated Pharaoh
4	85:017-020	• Has the story reached you of the forces of Pharaoh and the Thamud? And yet the unbelievers (persist) in rejecting (the truth)! But Allah does encompass them from behind.

CHAPTER 65

Protection from Tyranny and Injustice
FROM SURAH AT-TARIQ (86), SURAH AL-A'LA (87), SURAH AL-FAJR (89), AND SURAH AL-BALAD (90)

Unbelief is an attitude that promotes injustice and tyranny, while Islam promotes justice and mutual help. The tyrants of today, like those of seventh-century Makkah, are employing all sorts of devices and plans to defeat and frustrate the message of Islam. However, God has provided divine guidance, the future resurrection, and the final judgment in Divine Court, to protect people from the tyranny of those who are unjust and cruel in the World.

1 GOD'S TRUSTEES ON EARTH ARE TRUSTWORTHY
FROM SURAH AT-TARIQ (86)

Surah At-Tariq belongs to the early Makkan period. Its subject matter is the protection afforded to every person even in the darkest period of history. Human nature may have many weaknesses, but the soul provided by God must win a glorious future at the end.

1.1 The Resurrection is to motivate People to be Human
The stars in the sky provide evidence that there is nothing in the universe that may continue to exist and survive without some power that is regulating its existence. One may also reflect on how people have been brought into existence from a mere sperm drop and shaped into a living person. God, Who originally created people, has certainly the power to create them once again. The resurrection will be to scrutinize those secrets of people that remained hidden in the world. After the resurrection, no one will be able to escape the consequences of his deeds by his own efforts, nor will anyone else rescue him.

740

Table 1.1: Resurrection is to Protects People from Tyranny

No	Surah:Verses	Meanings
		The Physical and Moral laws are for our Protection
1	86:001-004	By the sky and the night-visitant (therein)—and what will explain to you what the night-visitant is? (It is) the star of piercing brightness. • There is no soul but has a protector over it.
		The very existence of Humanity Confirms the Resurrection
2	86:005-010	Now let man but think from what he is created! He is created from a drop emitted—proceeding from between the backbone and the ribs. • Surely, (Allah) is able to bring him back (to life)! The day that (all) things secret will be tested, (man) will have no power and no helper.

1.2 The Qur'an contains Moral and Sociopolitical Laws

Physical laws cause the rain to fall and grow plants and crops from the earth. Similarly, the truths expressed in the Qur'an are firm and unchangeable realities. While the unbelievers are falsely confident that their plans and devices will defeat the invitation of the Qur'an, they do not know that God is also planning and that His plans will neutralize all their scheming and planning. God affirms: "By the sky that returns (after completing its cycle), and by the earth that opens out (for the gushing of springs or the sprouting of vegetation), behold, this (Qur'an) is the word that distinguishes (good from evil). It is not a thing for amusement. As for them, they are but plotting a scheme, and I am planning a scheme. Therefore, grant a delay to the unbelievers; give respite to them gently (Qur'an 86:11-17)."

2 GOD'S TRUSTEES ON EARTH ONLY SERVE HIM
FROM SURAH AL-A'LA (87)

The contents of the Surah Al-A'la show that this is one of the earliest Surahs revealed at Makkah. The words: "By degrees shall We teach you to declare (the message), so you shall not forget" of Qur'an 87:6 also indicate that it was revealed in the

741

period when the Messenger was not yet fully accustomed to receiving revelation and that at the time of this revelation he still feared lest he should forget its words.

2.1 The Messenger's Assignment is to convey the Message

The Messenger was told not to worry about remembering the Qur'an, for God would preserve it in his memory. "By degrees shall We teach you to declare (the message), so you shall not forget, except as Allah wills, for He knows what is manifest and what is hidden (Qur'an 87:6-7)." Further, God told the Messenger that he wasn't responsible for bringing everyone to the right path; his duty was only to convey the truth. "We will make it easy for you (to follow) the simple (path). Therefore, give admonition in case the admonition profits (the hearer). The admonition will be received by those who fear (Allah) (Qur'an 87:8-10)." Those who fear the evil consequences of deviation and falsehood will listen to the truth and accept it, while those who avoid listening and reject it will see their evil end.

2.2 Divine Guidance leads People to Success in Both Worlds

Success is for those who adopt purity of belief, live morally, and do good deeds. They remember their Lord and perform the prayer. This will benefit them during their lives on earth as well as in the Hereafter. Unfortunately, some people are completely lost in seeking the ease and pleasures of this world. They should, instead, work for their welfare in the Hereafter. They should know that the world is transitory and the Hereafter is everlasting and that the blessings of the Hereafter are far better than the blessings of this world. These are truths expressed in the Qur'an, as well as in the books of Abraham and Moses.

Table 2: God, His Laws and Guidance

No	Surah:Verses	Meanings
		Only God Ordains Laws and Grant Guidance
1	87:001-005	Glorify the name of your Guardian-Lord most high, 1. Who has created, and further given order and proportion, 2. Who has ordained laws and granted guidance, 3. Who brings out the (green and luscious

		pasture and then makes it (but) swarthy stubble.
		Guidance is for those who fear the Evils of Falsehood
2	87:010-015	The admonition will be received by those who fear (Allah), 1. But it will be avoided by those most unfortunate ones who will enter the great fire in which they will then neither die nor live. 2. But those will prosper who purify themselves, and glorify the name of their Guardian-Lord, and (lift their hearts) in prayer.
		Success in the Hereafter is Better and Lasting
3	87:016-019	Nay (behold), you prefer the life of this world, but the Hereafter is better and more enduring. And this is in the books of the earliest (revelation), the books of Abraham and Moses.

3 GOD'S TRUSTEES ON EARTH ARE NOT CORRUPT
FROM SURAH AL-FAJR (89)

Surah Al-Fajr was revealed when persecution of the new converts to Islam had already begun in Makkah. The people of Makkah were warned not to forget the evil end of 'Ad, Thamud, and Pharaoh. The rewards and punishments in the Hereafter, which the people of Makkah did not acknowledge, were also discussed. Swearing by the dawn, the ten nights, the even and the odd, and the departing night, God asked if these things were not enough to testify to the truth. These four things are symbols of the regularity system that exists in the phenomena of night and day, and swearing by these symbols stresses that, after observing this system established by God, there should be no need for additional evidence to show that it is not beyond the power of the God to establish the Hereafter.

3.1 Trying and Testing People during Life on Earth
The prior destruction of the 'Ad, Thamud, and Pharaoh are cited to show that when people transgress their limits and spread corruption, God destroys them. This confirms that the universe is governed by certain laws. If these these laws are followed, they

743

have built-in consequences of reward. If these laws are ignored, punishment will eventually follow. History confirms that God has blessed those who follow His rules and laws with reason and moral sense. This is how God tries and tests humankind.

Table 3.1: Testing of People in Life on Earth

No	Surah:Verses	Meanings
		An evidence for those with understanding
1	89:001-005	By the break of day, by the nights twice five, by the even and odd (contrasted), and by the night when it passes away, is there (not) in these an evidence for those who understand.
		Communities Punished due to Corruption
2	89:006-014	1. Don't you see how your Lord dealt with the 'Ad (people)—of the (city of) Iram, with lofty pillars, the like of which were not produced in (all) the land? 2. (Don't you see how your Lord dealt) with the Thamud (people), who cut out (huge) rocks in the valley, 3. And with Pharaoh, lord of stakes? (All) these transgressed beyond bounds in the lands and heaped therein mischief (on mischief). Therefore, did your Lord pour on them a scourge of diverse chastisements, for your Lord is (as a guardian) on a watchtower.

3.2 Materialism and Injustice Cause Much Corruption

Materialism and injustice are two of the worst causes known to have destroyed communities throughout history. At the time of the Qur'anic revelation, the general moral state of Arab society was steeped in a materialism leading to injustice. Unfortunately, this is also the case today in most existing societies. Since a materialistic attitude only values the achievement of worldly wealth, rank, and position as the criteria for honor, materialistic people overlook the importance of moral good and forget that riches are not a reward and that poverty is not a punishment. God is trying people to see what attitude they adopt when blessed with wealth and how they behave when afflicted by poverty.

Materialistic inclinations without moral responsibility lead to injustice. Such an attitude encourages people to ignore the weak and to let the orphan child be left destitute on the death of the father. Nobody cares for the poor; whoever can usurps the whole heritage left by the deceased parent and fraudulently drives away the weak heirs. These people are afflicted with an insatiable greed for wealth. Why should such people, one may well ask, not be destroyed for their misdeeds and greed?

Table 3.2: Major Causes of God's Punishment

No	Surah:Verses	Meanings
		Good Conduct and Deeds Earn People Honor
3	89:015-016	• Now, as for man, when his Lord tried him, giving him honor and gifts, then says he, (puffed up), "My Lord has honored me." • But when He tried him, restricting his subsistence for him, then he says (in despair), "My Lord has humiliated me."
		Various Ways People Humiliate Themselves
4	89:017-020	1. Nay, nay! But you honor not the orphans. 2. Nor do you encourage one another to feed the poor. 3. And you devour inheritance—all with greed. 4. And you love wealth with inordinate love.

3.3 The Believers and Unbelievers on the Day of Judgment

People are reminded that the accountability will certainly be held and that it will be held on the day when the divine court will be established. Further, once the resurrection has occurred, it will be too late to amend one's ways. In the Hereafter, the deniers of the judgment will understand exactly what they previously ignored, and their regrets then will not save them from God's punishment. However, as to those people who previously accepted the truth, God will be pleased with them, and they will be overjoyed with the rewards bestowed by Him on the Day of Judgment.

Table 3.3: Believers and Unbelievers on the Day of Judgment

No	Surah:Verses	Meanings
		When the Day of Judgment Arrives
5	89:021-023	Nay! When the earth is pounded to powder and your Lord comes, and His angels, rank upon rank,

		and Hell that day is brought (face to face), on that day will man remember, but how will that remembrance profit him?
		Unbelievers on the Day of Judgment
6	89:024-026	1. He will say: "Ah! Would that I had sent forth (good deeds) for (this) my (future) life!" 2. For that day, His chastisement will be such as none (else) can inflict, and His bonds will be such as none (other) can bind.
		Believers on the Day of Judgment
7	89:027-030	(To the righteous soul will be said:) "O (you) soul, in (complete) rest and satisfaction, come back to your Lord—well pleased (yourself) and well-leasing to Him! Enter then among my devotees! Yea, enter My Heaven.

4 GOD'S TRUSTEES LIVE ON HONEST EARNINGS
FROM SURAH AL-BALAD (90)

The contents and style of Surah Al-Balad resemble those of the earliest Surahs revealed at Makkah in the period when the disbelievers had resolved to oppose the Messenger by means of tyranny and excesses against him. In this Surah, God tells people that the life of His trustees on earth is like a steep road, which helps them to ascend to new heights of good moral character and behavior. Those who tread the steep road believe in God, follow His laws, and join others in the establishment of a just society that strives to fulfill the demands of virtue and righteousness. Their virtue is reflected by their honest earnings and by spending their wealth to help the orphans and needy.

4.1 Life is Hard Work and Accountability
The city of Makkah, the hardships being faced by the Messenger, and the condition of people in general have been cited as a witness to the truth that this world is not a place of rest and ease for people, where they are born to enjoy life; rather, they are created to toil and struggle (Qur'an 90:1-4). People are told: "That man can have nothing but what he strives for (Qur'an 53:39)." This makes it clear that a person's ultimate future depends on his efforts and struggles. In addition, this Surah

refutes some people's mistaken belief that they are in charge of this world without any accountability for their behavior and deeds. The Messenger quotes God in a sacred *hadith* as saying: "My servants, it is but your deeds that I reckon up for you and then recompense you for, so let him who finds good praise Allah and let him who finds other than that blame no one but himself (Sahih Muslim: 32.6246)."

4.2 The road to the Success is in living on Honest Earnings

This Surah points out what a wrong criterion of merit and greatness many people have adopted for themselves. Such people squander heaps of wealth for ostentation and display, take pride in their extravagances, and enthusiastically admire themselves for it. Whereas God, Who is watching over their deeds, sees by what methods they obtained their wealth and in what ways and with what motives and intention they spend it. The road to success is in living on honest earnings and in avoiding extravagance and wasting of resources and wealth.

4.3 People need both Conscience and the Divine Guidance

People are endowed with knowledge and the faculties of thinking and understanding. God has allowed man the free will to chose between the ways of virtue and of vice. The easy way leads to moral depravity, while the other way leads to moral heights, although it is steep like an uphill road. People have to exercise self-restraint in scaling this uphill road. Unfortunately, human weakness is such that it prefers slipping down into the abyss rather than scaling up the cliff.

Table 4: Human Nature and Human Conscience

No	Surah:Verses	Meanings
		God has Created People into Toil and Struggle
1	90:001-005	I do call to witness this city (Makkah); - And you are a freeman of this city; - And (the mystic ties of) parent and child—verily, We have created man into toil and struggle.
		But People Think they are Accountable to None
2	90:005-010	He thinks that none has power over him? He may say, "Wealth have I squandered in abundance!" Does he think that none beholds him?

	1. Have We not made for him a pair of eyes, a tongue, and a pair of lips 2. And shown him the two highways (of good and evil)?

5 GOD'S TRUSTEES EXCEL IN THEIR CHARACTER
FROM SURAH AL-BALAD (90)

5.1 Only Good Character and Behavior Earn God's Mercy

God says that the steep road helps people to ascend to the heights of humanity by adopting moral character and behavior. Only those who strive to ascend on the steep road believe in human values and are motivated to spend their wealth to help the orphans and needy. People who follow this way become worthy of God's mercy. In contrast, the fate of those who go down the wrong way is the fire of Hell, from which there is no escape.

Table 5: Righteous and the Unbelieving People

No	Surah:Verses	Meanings
		People of the Right Hand
1	90:011-018	But he (man) has made no haste on the path that is steep. And what will explain to you the path that is steep? 1. (It is) freeing the bondman or 2. (It is) the giving of food in a day of privation to the orphan with claims of relationship or to the indigent (down) in the dust. 3. Then will he be of those who believe, 4. (who) enjoin patience (constancy and self-restraint), 5. And (who) enjoin deeds of kindness and compassion. Such are the companions of the right hand.
		People of the Left Hand
2	90:019-020	But those who reject Our revelations, they are the (unhappy) companions of the left hand. On them will be fire vaulted over (all round).

748

CHAPTER 66

Human Conscience and Behavior
FROM SURAH ASH-SHAMS (91) AND SURAH AL-LAIL (92)

Content and the style show that both Surahs Ash-Shams and Al-Lail were revealed in the same period at Makkah, at a time when opposition to the Messenger had grown very strong and intense. The contents of both Surahs closely resemble each other, and each Surah seems to be an explanation of the other. The same topic is explained in Surah Ash-Shams in one way and in Surah Al-Lail in another way.

1 LISTENING TO THE HUMAN CONSCIENCE
FROM SURAH ASH-SHAMS (91)

People's fate depends on how they use their sense of discrimination, free will, and judgment to develop their good and suppress their evil tendencies. Progress in developing one's good and in getting rid of one's evil inclinations will attain the ultimate success. However, if one suppresses the good and promotes the evil tendencies of the human self, that will lead to disappointment and failure.

1.1 Good and Evil are not alike in Effects and Results
Like the sun and the moon, the day and the night, and the earth and the sky, which are different from each other and contradictory in their effects and results, so are good and evil deeds different from each other and contradictory in their effects and results. Neither are they alike in their outward appearance, nor can they be alike in their results.

1.2 Conscience helps to Distinguish between Good and Evil
After giving people their bodies, intellect, and wisdom, God has not left them uninformed in the world. He installed into the human unconscious a natural inspiration that distinquishes between good and evil, right and wrong. As such, there is some

749

basic understanding that what is good is beneficial and what is evil is harmful to human survival and success.

Table 1.2: Successful are those who follow their Conscience

No	Surah:Verses	Meanings
		God Swears by His Creation and Human Conscience
1	91:001-008	By the sun and his (glorious) splendor, by the moon as she follows (the sun), by the day as it shows up (the sun's) glory, by the night as it conceals it, by the sky and its (wonderful) structure, by the earth and its (width), by the soul and the proportion and order given to it and its enlightenment as to its wrong and its right—
		That Human Conscience is to be kept pure and not corrupted
2	91:009-010	1. Truly, he succeeds that purifies it, 2. And he fails that corrupts it!

1.3 The Messengers helped interpret Human Conscience

The inspirational knowledge of good and evil that God has placed in human nature is by itself not enough for the guidance of humanity. People sometimes assume wrong criteria and theories of good and evil, and they are thus misled. That is why God sent down clear and definite revelation to the messengers, in order to augment the people's natural inspiration or conscience, so that the messengers might explain to the people what is good and what is evil. The history of the people of Thamud is cited to illustrate the importance of prophethood. Prophet Salih was sent to the people of Thamud, but the people being overwhelmed by their own evil became rebellious and rejected him. When he presented the miracle of she-camel, as demanded by them, one of them killed her, in accordance with the will and desire of the people. Consequently, the people of Thamud were destroyed.

1.4 People's Fates in this World will match their Behaviors

One may ask why the story of Thamud was narrated to the people of Makkah. The situation in Makkah at that time was similar to the situation that had been created by the corrupt among the people of Thamud against Salih. Because of the similarity of situations, the narration of this story was by itself

750

enough to suggest to the people of Makkah: (1) how precisely this historical incident applied to them; and (2) that if they continued acting like the people of Salih, their fate might not be any different from theirs. This incident is highlighted in Surah Ash-Shams: "The Thamud (people) rejected (their prophet) through their inordinate wrongdoing. Behold, the most wicked man among them was deputed (for impiety). But the Messenger of Allah said to them: "It is a she-camel of Allah! And (bar her not from) having her drink!" Then they rejected him (as a false prophet), and they hamstrung her. So their Lord, on account of their crime, obliterated their traces and made them equal (in destruction)... (Qur'an 91:11-14)."

2 BEHAVIOR AND EFFORTS IMPACT THE RESULTS
FROM SURAH AL-LAIL (92)

Moral and immoral lifestyles and the contrast between their ultimate results are explained in Surah Al-Lail. These two lifestyles, both at the individual and collective levels, are as divergent and opposite of each other as are the day and the night.

2.1 God has provided All People with His Guidance
God has taken on Himself the responsibility to guide people with regard to how they spend their lives on earth. That is why He equipped each individual with a conscience. It is also why He sent His books of revelation to explain human conscience and His messengers to live their lives as human role models. "Verily, We take upon Ourselves to guide, and verily unto Us (belong) the end and the beginning (Qur'an 92:12-13)." If one seeks the world, it is He Who will give it, and if one seeks the Hereafter, again it is He Who will give it. Now, it is up to each person to decide what he should seek. Is it not prudent to seek one's welfare in both this world and the Hereafter?

2.2 The Behavior of Believers and Unbelievers
Believers are those who spend their wealth, adopt God-consciousness and piety, and acknowledge the good as good. In contrast, the unbelievers are those who are miserly, care little for

God's pleasure or His displeasure, and repudiate what is good and the right. The behavior of the two being clearly divergent cannot be equal and alike in their results. Just as they are divergent in their nature, so they are divergent in their results. God makes the correct way of life easy for the believers. This makes good easy and evil difficult for them to do. In contrast, God makes it easy for unbelievers to follow the difficult and hard way of life, so that doing evil becomes easy for them and doing good becomes difficult. The worldly wealth for the sake of which people are prepared to risk their lives will not go down with them into the grave; therefore, what will it avail them after death?

Table 2.2
People's Behavior and Efforts Determine their Fate

No	Surah:Verses	Meanings	
		The Results of Your Efforts are Surely Divergent	
1	92:001-004	By the night as it conceals (the light), by the day as it appears in glory, by (the mystery of) the creation of male and female, verily, (the ends) you strive for are diverse.	
		Believers Behavior and Efforts	**Unbelievers Behavior and Efforts**
2	92:005-006, 92:008-009	1. So he who gives (in charity) 2. And fears (Allah) 3. And testifies to the best—	1. But he who is a greedy miser 2. And thinks himself self-sufficient, 3. And gives the lie to the best—
		Results of Believers Efforts	**Results of Unbelievers Efforts**
3	92:007, 92: 010-011	➤ We will indeed make smooth for him the path to bliss.	➤ We will indeed make smooth for him the path to misery; nor will his wealth profit him when he falls headlong (into the pit).

2.3 The Reward will be According to Peoples' Efforts

The corrupt people who reject the truth and righteousness will have a blazing fire ready for them in the Hereafter. God warns them: "Therefore, do I warn you of a fire blazing fiercely; none shall reach it but those most unfortunate ones who give the lie to truth and turn their backs (Qur'an 92:14-16). In marked contrast, God-fearing people, who spend their wealth in good causes, without any selfish motive, for the sake of their Lord's pleasure, their Lord will be pleased with them and will bless them so that they will be well pleased with Him. The behavior and deeds of God-fearing people is described in Surah Al-Lail: "But those most devoted to Allah shall be removed far from it—those who spend their wealth for increase in self-purification and have in their minds no favor from anyone for which a reward is expected in return, but only the desire to seek for the countenance of their Lord most high; and soon will they attain (complete) satisfaction (due to His mercy) (Qur'an 92:17-21)."

CHAPTER 67

With Hardship Comes Relief
FROM SURAH AD-DUHA (93) AND SURAH ASH-SHARH (94)

The contents of Surah Ad-Duha and Surah Ash-Sharh resemble each other, and these Surahs seem to have been revealed in the same period under similar conditions. Both Surahs were revealed to console and encourage the Messenger in the early part of his mission.

1 KINDNESS TO OTHERS EARNS GOD'S BOUNTY
FROM SURAH AD-DUHA (93)

Traditions show that the revelation was suspended for some time. This made the Messenger deeply distressed and grieved. In Surah Ad-Duha, he was consoled and told that the revelation was not stopped because God had forsaken him or because God was displeased with him (Qur'an 93:3). Rather, a pause in the revelation was given in order to give the Messenger time to be accustomed to receiving revelation. Later, when the Messenger developed the stamina to bear the burden of the revelation, there was no longer any need for long gaps between revelations.

1.1 Your Future will be better than the Present
The Messenger was given the good news that the hardships that he was experiencing in the initial stage of his mission would not last long and that his later period of life would be better than the former period. Before long, God would so abundantly bless the Messenger that he would be well pleased. This is one of the prophecies of the Qur'an that was proven true. When this prophecy was made, it seemed that there was no chance that an individual who had come out to wage war against the ignorance of the entire world would ever achieve such a wonderful success.

1.2 To Succeed, neither Oppress nor Repulse Others
God reminded the Messenger that He had been looking after him with kindness since his birth. Although the Messenger was

754

orphaned at a young age, God looked after him, showed him the right way, and elevated him from poverty to wealth. All this showed that the Messenger had been favored by God from the very beginning. Concluding this Surah, God tells people how they should show their gratitude for His blessings by not oppressing others, especially the orphan and the poor. People are told that by giving kindness to others, they will become candidates for still more bounty from their Lord. People should help both the poor people who ask for help and the poor people who endure it silently. If one is bountifully endowed by God, whether in wealth or in knowledge, then it is one's duty to spread it far and wide. One should proclaim it and share it with those who are less fortunate.

Table 1: Proclaim the Bounty of your Lord

No	Surah:Verses	Meanings
		Your Lord has not forsaken you nor is He displeased
1	93:001-003	1. By the glorious morning light 2. And by the night when it is still, Your Guardian-Lord has not forsaken you, nor is He displeased.
		Therefore, neither Oppress nor Repulse others
2	93:004-011	Verily, what comes after is better for you than that which has gone before, and soon will your Guardian-Lord give you (that wherewith) you shall be well pleased. • Did He not find you an orphan and give you shelter (and care)? • And He found you wandering, and He gave you guidance. • And He found you in need and made you independent. 1. Therefore, treat not the orphan with harshness, 2. Nor repulse the petitioner (unheard), 3. And the bounties of the Lord rehearse and proclaim!

2 GOD STRENGTHEN THOSE WHO SEEK HIS HELP
FROM SURAH ASH-SHARH (94)

Surah Ash-Sharh was revealed to console and encourage the Messenger. Before his call, he had never encountered the conditions that he suddenly had to face after embarking on his mission of inviting people to Islam. This was a great change in his life, the magnitude of which was very hard to comprehend. Immediately after he started preaching, the same society that had esteemed him turned hostile to him. The same relatives and friends, the same clansmen and neighbors, who used to treat him with respect, began to shower him with abuse. Very few in Makkah were prepared to listen to him. He was being ridiculed and mocked in the streets, and at every step he had to face new difficulties. Although he gradually became accustomed to the hardships, even much more severe ones than those mentioned above, the initial stage was very discouraging for him. That is why Surah Ad-Duha and Surah Ash-Sharh were revealed.

2.1 With Every Hardship there Comes the Relief

The Messenger's past life is a testimony of God's help. God reminds the Messenger in Surah Ash-Sharh that He had favored the Messenger with three great blessings. God had expanded the Messenger's breast, removed the heavy burden that was weighing down his back, and exalted him. Therefore, the Messenger had no cause to be disheartened. Further, God reassured the Messenger that the period of hardships that he was passing through was not going to be very long. Following close behind the hardships, there would also be a period of ease. This same message has been stressed in Surah Ad-Duha: "Verily, what comes after is better for you than that which has gone before, and soon will your Guardian-Lord give you (that wherewith) you shall be well pleased (Qur'an 93:4-5)."

2.3 Seek God's Help through Patience and Prayer

Although addressed to the Messenger, Surahs Ad-Duha and Ash-Sharh reminds people that they can develop the strength to bear and resist any hardship in life by remembering and worshiping God. When people are free from their occupations, they should devote themselves to His worship and turn all their attention

756

exclusively to Him. God is the source of strength for those who seek His help. God commands, "Nay, seek (Allah's) help with patient perseverance and prayer. It is indeed hard, except for the humble ones (Qur'an 2:45)."

Table 2: Along with every Hardship is the Relief

No	Surah:Verses	Meanings
		Your life testifies to God's Bounties and His Help
1	94:001-006	Have We not expanded you your breast and removed from you your burden, which did gall your back, and raised high the esteem (in which) you (are held)? 1. So, verily, with every difficulty, there is relief. 2. Verily, with every difficulty, there is relief.
		Seek God's Help with the Prayer and Patience
2	94:007-008	Therefore, when you are free (from your immediate task), still labor hard, and to your Lord turn (all) your attention.

CHAPTER 68

With Effort Comes Reward

FROM SURAH AT-TIN (95)

Surah At-Tin belongs to the earliest period of Makkah. It reflects the style of the earliest revelations of the Makkan period. In this Surah, people are told about the judgment of the Hereafter and that rewards and punishments are a necessary and absolutely rational way of motivating people to be God's trustees on earth.

1 GOD CREATED PEOPLE TO BE HIS TRUSTEES

1.1 People are created in the most Excellent of Molds

In Surah At-Tin, swearing by the fig, the olive, and the mountain at which Moses received the Ten Commandments, God states that He has created people in the most excellent of molds. This truth is expressed in different ways at various places in the Qur'an. For example, the Qur'an reports that God appointed humankind to be His vicegerent on the earth and commanded the angels to bow down to him. "Behold, your Lord said to the angels: 'I am about to create man from clay. When I have fashioned him (in due proportion) and breathed into him of My spirit, fall down in obeisance unto him.' So the angels prostrated themselves, all of them together (Qur'an 38:71-73)." Further, humanity has become the bearer of the divine trust, which the earth and the heavens and the mountains did not have the courage to bear. "We did indeed offer the trust to the heavens and the earth and the mountains, but they refused to undertake it, being afraid thereof, but man undertook it. He was indeed unjust and foolish (Qur'an 33:72)." God also says: "We have honored the sons of Adam, provided them with transport on land and sea, given them for sustenance things good and pure, and conferred on them special favors above a great part of our creation (Qur'an 17:70)."

758

1.2 People's Capabilities are enough for Humanity

The oath made in Surah At-Tin that humankind has been created in the finest of molds, signifies that humankind has been blessed with such an excellent mold and nature that it could give birth to people who are capable of achieving excellent character and behavior, like those of God's messengers. God asks in Surah Al-Infitar: "What has seduced you from your Lord most beneficent—Him Who created you, fashioned you in due proportion, and gave you a just bias. In whatever form He wills, He does put you together (Qur'an 82:6-8). Many human body systems are in common with animals. However, people are privileged to posses their own unique mental and spiritual qualities, which are a special favor from God.

1.3 Important Faculties that Distinguish People

How did God perfect human creation and rightly proportion the human mold? One of the most important faculties that distinguish humans from other animals is their powers of comprehension, the nature of which is yet unknown. The mind is the medium of comprehension, but the working of the human mind and how it functions remain incomprehensible. Furthermore, how does one sort out individual words, meanings, events, and pictures to mold them together into a coherent education? How are information and experience transformed into knowledge? The other uniquely human faculty is that wonderful ray of God's spirit that establishes a link between humankind, the beauty of the universe, and its Creator. Through this link, people experience a sense of communion with the Infinite, the Absolute, which prepares them for a blissful eternal life in God's Paradise. Yet, we have no power to comprehend the nature of the spirit, which is God's greatest favor and makes people human. Maybe the proper use of these human faculties was a prerequisite to be God's trustee on earth!

Table 1.2: God Preferred Humankind as His Trustee

No	Surah:Verses	Meanings
		Humankind, God's Trustee on Earth
1	2:030	Behold, your Lord said to the angels: "I will create a vicegerent on earth." They (the angels) said: "Will You place therein one who will make mischief therein and shed blood, while we do celebrate Your praises and glorify Your holy (name)?" He (Allah) said: "I know what you know not."
	2:034	1. Behold, We said to the angels: "Bow down to Adam," and they bowed down. 2. Not so *Iblis*. He refused and was haughty. He was of those who reject faith.
		The Nature and Expectations of People
2	6:165	It is He Who has made you (His) agents, inheritors of the earth. He has raised you in ranks, some above others, that He may try you in the gifts He has given you.
	7:011	1. It is We Who created you and gave you shape; then We bade the angels bow down to Adam, and they prostrated. Not so *Iblis*; he refused to be of those who bow down.
	15:028-029	2. Behold! Your Lord said to the angels:" I am about to create man from sounding clay from mud molded into shape. When I have fashioned him (in due proportion) and breathed into him of My spirit, fall down in obeisance unto him.
	27:062	3. Who listens to the (soul) distressed when it calls on Him, and Who relieves its suffering, and makes you (mankind) inheritors of the earth? (Can there be another) god besides Allah? Little it is that you heed!

2 HUMAN ABALITIES ARE TO BE USED FOR SUCCESS

Although humanity has been created in the finest of molds, there are still two types of people: those who become inclined to evil and whose moral degeneration causes them to be reduced to the lowest of God's creation; and those who, by adopting the way of faith and righteousness, remain secure from degeneration.

2.1 The Direction of Efforts impacts the Reward

It is consistent with the noble position of being God's trustee that humanity should be created in the best of molds. However, both the noble, as well as the mean, nature of humanity has been observed and experienced in society everywhere and at all times. In such situations, the judgment of and retribution for people's behavior and deeds cannot be denied. If the morally degraded people are not punished and the morally pure and exalted are not rewarded, then both end up alike. It would mean that there is no justice in the universe, whereas human nature and common sense demand the existence of justice. How then can one conceive that God, Who is the most just of all judges, would not do justice?

2.2 Reward comes with Belief and Righteous Deeds,

God is the best of the judges. That is why He stresses in Surah At-Tin that the reward comes with belief and righteous deeds. "By the fig and the olive, and the Mount of Sinai, and this city of security, We have indeed created man in the best of molds. Then do We abase him (to be) the lowest of the low, except such as believe and do righteous deeds, for they shall have a reward unfailing. Then what can after this contradict you as to the judgment (to come)? Is not Allah the wisest of judges (Qur'an 95:1-8)?"

CHAPTER 69

Divine Guidance for Humankind
FROM SURAH AL-'ALAQ (96), SURAH AL-QADR (97),
AND SURAH AL-BAYYINAH (98)

Surah Al-'Alaq contains the very first revelation in which the
Messenger was commanded to "Read (the Qur'an) in the name
of your Lord," while Surah Al-Qadr tells when this first
revelation was given, and while Surah Al-Bayyinah explains
why it was necessary to send the Messenger and the Qur'an.

1 GOD'S TRUSTEES SHOULD KNOW THEIR DUTIES
FROM SURAH AL-'ALAQ (96)

Surah Al-'Alaq was revealed in two parts. The first part, i.e., the
first five verses, was the very first revelation received by the
Messenger. The second part, i.e., verses six through 19, was
revealed when the Messenger began to perform the prescribed
prayer in the Ka'bah and Abu Jahl tried to prevent him from this
with threats. The Messenger had begun praying in the vicinity of
the Ka'bah even before he started preaching Islam openly. From
his prayers, the Quraysh concluded for the first time that the
Messenger had adopted a new religion. While many people were
watching with curiosity as the Messenger prayed, it was Abu
Jahl in his arrogance and pride who threatened the Messenger
and forbade him to worship in the Ka'bah.

A number of the *Ahadith* have been related from Abdullah ibn
'Abbas and Abu Huraira, which mention this behavior of Abu
Jahl. "Abu Huraira reported that Abu Jahl asked (people)
whether Muhammad placed his face (on the ground) in their
presence. It was said to him: 'Yes.' He said: 'By Lat and 'Uzza
(two idols), if I were to see him do that (act of worship), I would
trample his neck, or I would besmear his face with dust.' He
came to God's Messenger as he was engaged in prayer and
thought of trampling his neck, (and the people say) that he came
near him but turned upon his heels and tried to repulse

762

something with his hands. It was said to him: 'What is the matter with you?' He said: 'There is between me and him a ditch of fire and terror and wings.' Thereupon, God's Messenger said: 'If he were to have come near me, the angels would have torn him to pieces' (Sahih Muslim: 39.6718)."

1.1 Read In the Name of Your Lord, Who Created

Learning how to manage our affairs on earth is the first obligation of humanity after being appointed as God's trustee on earth. This was the command given in very first verses that were revealed. "Proclaim (or read)! In the name of your Lord and Cherisher, Who created—created man out of a (mere) clot of congealed blood: Proclaim! And your Lord is most bountiful— He Who taught (the use of) the pen—taught man that which he knew not (Qur'an 96:1-5)."

1.2 Do not follow the Corrupt but Submit to God

The second part of Surah Al-'Alaq, was revealed when Abu Jahl tried to prevent the Messenger from performing the prescribed prayer in the Ka'bah. Using Abu Jahl as representative of corrupt people throughout human history, God commanded the Messenger and the believers not to follow corrupt people. Rather, He commanded them to serve their Lord Who created them and then appointed them as His trustees on earth.

Table 1.2: The Corrupt Reject the Truth and Forbid Good

No	Surah:Verses	Meanings
		Denial of the Truth and forbidding Good
1	96:006-014	Nay, but man does transgress all bounds in that he looks upon himself as self-sufficient. Verily, to your Lord is the return (of all). 1. Do you see one who forbids a votary when he (turns) to pray? See if he is on (the road of) guidance or enjoins righteousness? 2. See if he denies and turns away? Does not he know that Allah does see?
		Follow not the Corrupt but Submit to your Lord
2	96:015-019	Let him beware! If he desists not, We will drag him by the forelock, a lying, sinful forelock. 1. Then, let him call (for help) to his council (of

| | | comrades); We will call on the angels of punishment (to deal with him). |
| | | 2. Nay, heed him not. But bow down in adoration, and bring yourself closer (to Allah). |

2 THE QUR'AN DESCRIBES THE DUTIES OF HUMANKIND ON EARTH
FROM SURAH AL-QADR (97)

It is disputed whether Al-Qadr is a Makkan Surah or not. However, reflecting on its contents indicates that it probably was revealed at Makkah. The purpose of the Surah is to acquaint people with the value, worth, and importance of the Qur'an. Being placed just after Surah Al-'Alaq in the arrangement of the Qur'an, Surah Al-Qadr explains that the Qur'an, the revelation that began with the first five verses of Surah Al-'Alaq, was revealed in a destiny-making night. It's a glorious Book, and its revelation is full of blessings for people.

2.1 The Qur'an is not a writing of the Messenger

God says that He has revealed the Qur'an. It is not a composition of Muhammad. God revealed it in the Night of Power. The Night of Power can mean two things, and both are implied here. Firstly, it is the night during which destinies are decided. It is not an ordinary night, but a night in which destinies are made or marred. The revelation of this Book in this night was not merely the revelation of a book; it was an event that changed the destiny of all humanity—not just the destiny of the Quraysh and Arabia.

2.2 The Destiny-Making Event for Humankind

The unbelievers of all ages have been told that on account of their ignorance, they regard this Book as a calamity and complain that a disaster has fallen on them. In reality, the night in which the revelation to the Messenger began was a blessed night, one that provided welfare for all people, and one that was better than a thousand months. In Surah Al-Qadr, God describes this night by saying: "We have indeed revealed this (message) in the Night of Power. And what will explain to you what the Night of Power is? The Night of Power is better than a thousand months. Therein come down the angels and the Spirit by Allah's permission, on every errand. Peace—this (lasts) until the rise of morn (Qur'an 97:1-5)."

3 THE MESSENGER EXPLAINS GOD'S COMMANDS
FROM SURAH AL-BAYYINAH (98)

Where Surah Al-Bayyinah was revealed is disputed. There is nothing to indicate in its contents whether it was revealed at Makkah or at Madinah. However, the positioning of this Surah after Surahs Al-'Alaq and Al-Qadr in the Qur'an is very revealing: Surah Al-'Alaq contains the very first revelation; Surah Al-Qadr shows when the Qur'an was revealed, and Surah Al-Bayyinah explains why it was necessary to send the Messenger and the Qur'an.

3.1 Why another Divine Book and Messenger?
The people of the world, be they from among the followers of the earlier scriptures or from among the idolaters, could not possibly be freed from their state of wrong belief until a messenger was sent whose appearance would be a clear proof of his apostleship. He should present the Book of God, containing sound advice, before the people in its original form, free from every mixture of falsehood that corrupted the earlier divine books.

3.2 The Corruption of Previous Divine Books
The real cause of straying into different creeds by the followers of the earlier books was not that God hadn't provided guidance to them, but that they had strayed after a clear statement of the true faith had come to them. They were responsible for their own errors and deviations by making changes in their books that supported their selfish agendas. Now, if after the coming of the Messenger, they continue to stray, they will be responsible for their own loss.

3.3 The New Divine Book needed a New Messenger
The messengers from God and the books revealed by Him did not enjoin anything except that the way of sincere and true

servitude to God be adopted. In other words, one is to worship, serve, and obey only God, and one is to establish prayer and charity. This had been the true religion ever since Adam. However, the followers of the earlier scriptures strayed from this true religion by incorporating extraneous and false things into it. This required that a new messenger come to invite people back to the original faith and present himself as a role model to show them how the faith should be practiced.

3.4 Those Who Follow or Reject the Divine Law
The followers of the earlier books and the idolaters who refuse to acknowledge the Messenger of Islam and who refuse to reform are described as the worst of creatures, "Those who reject (truth) among the People of the Book and among the polytheists were not going to depart (from their ways) until there should come to them clear evidence—a messenger from Allah, rehearsing scriptures kept pure and holy wherein are laws right and straight. Nor did the People of the Book make schisms until after there came to them clear evidence, and they have been commanded no more than this: to worship Allah, offering Him sincere devotion, being true (in faith); to establish regular prayer; and to practice regular charity. And that is the religion right and straight. Those who reject (truth) among the People of the Book and among the polytheists will be in Hellfire, to dwell therein (forever). They are the worst of creatures (98:1-6)."

In contrast, people who believe, act righteously, and spend the life of this world serving God are the best of creatures. Their reward is Paradise where they will live eternally, "Those who have faith and do righteous deeds—they are the best of creatures. Their reward is with Allah. Gardens of eternity beneath which rivers flow—they will dwell therein forever, Allah well pleased with them, and they with Him. All this (is) for such as fear their Lord and Cherisher (98:7-8)."

CHAPTER 70

The Passionate Love for Wealth
FROM SURAH AL-'ADIYAT (100),
AND SURAH AL-TAKATHUR (102)

The content and style of Surah Al-'Adiyat suggest that this Surah was revealed in the earliest period at Makkah. Surah Al-Takathur, according to a great majority of the commentators is Makkan in origin. Its contents and style confirm this. In both Surahs, the miserable effects of the passionate love of wealth on both people and society are described.

1 THE DESTINY OF THE UNGRATEFUL PEOPLE
FROM SURAH AL-'ADIYAT (100)

In Surah Al-'Adiyat, people are told that they fail to realize how evil a person becomes when one denies the Hereafter or doesn't care about it. Attention is also drawn to the plundering, looting, bloodshed, and vandalism prevailing in Arabia before Islam. Such atrocities represent the abuse of the powers given to them by God and are nothing less than an expression of sheer ingratitude to Him. People are warned that in the Hereafter both their open and apparent deeds and their intentions and motives will be examined. They will surely be punished for their injustice and corruption.

1.1 Tyranny and Injustice Make Life Miserable
Before Islam, general chaos and confusion prevailed across Arabia. Bloodshed, looting, and plundering raged on every side. Tribes were subjecting other tribes to raids, and no one could have a peaceful night's sleep, secondary to the fear that some enemy tribe might raid one's community early in the morning. Every Arab was fully conscious of this situation and realized that it was wrong. Although the plundered bemoaned their miserable, helpless state and the plunderer rejoiced, when the plunderer himself was plundered, he too realized how miserable the conditions of their communities were.

767

1.2 Ungrateful People and their Eventual Fate

Unaware of the second life after death and their accountability before God, the people of pre-Islamic Arabia became ungrateful to their Lord. They used their God-given powers and abilities for perpetrating tyranny and injustice. Blinded by their love of worldly wealth, they tried to obtain it by every means possible, however impure and filthy. No one would have behaved this way had they believed that the dead will be raised from the graves and their intentions and motives behind their attitudes and deeds will be exposed and judged. God is quite aware of what one did and what punishment or reward one deserves.

Table 1: Those with Evil Deeds and Love for Riches

No	Surah:Verses	Meanings
		The Ungratefulness of Evil and Greedy People
1	100:001-008	By the (steeds) that run with panting (breath) and strike sparks of fire, and push home the charge in the morning, and raise the dust in clouds the while, and penetrate forthwith into the midst (of the foe) en masse— Truly man is, to his Lord, ungrateful. 1. And to that (fact) he bears witness (by his deeds), 2. And violent is he in his love of wealth.
		The Corrupt should Know that they are Accountable
2	100:009-011	Does he not know, 1. When that which is in the graves is raised 2. And that which is (locked up) in (human) breasts is made manifest), That their Lord had been well-acquainted with them, (even to) that day.

2 THE MATERIALISM AND RUTHLESS COMPITATION
FROM SURAH AL-TAKATHUR (102)

In Surah At-Takathur, people are criticized for their materialistic mentality due to which they remained occupied in seeking an increase in worldly benefits, pleasures, comforts, position, etc. and in vying with one another for abundance of everything up

768

until death. Then, warning them of the evil consequences of their heedlessness, people are told that the world is not an open table of food for them to pick and choose as they please, but for every single blessing that they are enjoying, they will have to render an account to their Lord as to how they obtained it and how they used it. The torment of the grave, which some people will face, is also mentioned in this Surah, as well as in some other Makkan Surahs like Surah Al-An'am, Surah An-Nahl, Surah Al-Mu'minun, and Surah Al-Ghafir.

2.1 Torment in Graves before the Day of Judgment
If the accountability is to take place on the Day of Judgment, then why did the Messenger teach his companions to seek refuge with God from the torment of the grave? Although its details are not given, certain people will be subjected to this torment. In Surah Al-Ghafir, the situation of the people of Pharaoh is described. They were the unbelievers who confirmed their unbelief with their deeds in life. The Day of Judgment is not to establish whether a person is a non-believer, a hardened sinner, or an obedient servant of God. He knows the outcome of everyone's test in life. The Day of Judgment is for people's benefit in that they will see the deeds they did in life and come to realize their situation. Then if they are punished, it is due to their own deeds, and if they are forgiven and admitted to Heaven, it is God's mercy.

2.2 The Consequences of an excessive Materialism
People have been warned of the evil consequences of worshiping the world instead of merely to using it. Many people spend most of their lives in acquiring more and more of this world's wealth, material benefits, and pleasures associated with position and power. Such people spend much effort and time in vying with one another and in bragging and boasting about their acquisitions. This pursuit has so occupied them that they are left with no time or opportunity for pursuing the higher things in life.

769

Table 2.2: Torment of the Grave

No	Surah:Verses	Meanings
		The Agony of the Unjust, Dying People
1	6:093 16:027-028	• Who can be more wicked than one who invents a lie against Allah or says, "I have received inspiration," when he has received none, or (again) who says, "I can reveal the like of what Allah has revealed"? If you could but see how the wicked (do fare) in the flood of confusion at death! The angels stretch forth their hands, (saying), "Yield up your souls; this day shall you receive your reward, a penalty of shame for that you used to tell lies against Allah and scornfully rejected His signs... Then on the Day of Judgment, He will cover them with shame and say: "Where are My 'partners' concerning whom you used to dispute (with the godly)?" Those endued with knowledge will say: "This day, indeed, are the unbelievers covered with shame and misery—(namely) those whose lives the angels take in a state of wrongdoing to their own souls. Then would they offer submission (with the pretence), "We did no evil (knowingly)." (The angels will reply), "Nay, but verily Allah knows all that you did."
		The Unbeliever's Conversation in the Grave
2	23:099-100	• (In falsehood will they be) until when death comes to one of them, he says: "O my Lord! Send me back (to life), in order that I may work righteousness in the things I neglected." "By no means! It is but a word he says." Before them is a partition till the day they are raised up.
		Pharaoh's People's condition in the Grave
3	40:045-046	Allah saved him (Moses) from (every) ill that they plotted (against him), but the brunt of the penalty encompassed on all sides the people of Pharaoh. 1. In front of the fire will they be brought, morning and evening (in their graves), 2. And (the sentence will be) on the Day that Judgment will be established: "Cast the people of Pharaoh into the severest penalty."

2.3 The Maximization of the Return on the Capital

Cut-throat competition and materialism can lead people to suffering in this world and to Hell in the Hereafter. Commenting on Alan Corey's book, A Million Bucks by 30, John Bolyard of Pensacola, Florida, USA wrote in US News and World Report (May 26 – June 02, 2008) that when he asked his university students what their goal in life was, they increasingly (and depressingly) responded that it was to make a lot of money. What Corey claimed in his book, i.e., that he was just being creative, perpetuated the idea that ethics does not matter when it comes to getting ahead financially, and it helped Professor Bolyard understand why his students rarely claim their life goals are to serve humanity.

Table 2.3: Materialism Keeps People Away from Good Deeds

No	Surah:Verses	Meanings
		Craving for Greater Worldly Gains
4	102:001-002	The mutual rivalry for piling up (the good things of this world) diverts you (from the more serious things), until you visit the graves.
		Unbelievers' Torment of the Grave
5	102:003-007	But nay, you soon shall know (the reality). Again, you soon shall know. Nay, were you to know with certainty of mind (you would beware)! You shall certainly see Hellfire! Again, you shall see it with certainty of sight.
		Peoples' Accountability in the Hereafter
6	102:008	Then, you shall be questioned that day about the joy (you indulged in)!

771

CHAPTER 71

The Morally Sick People
FROM SURAH AL-HUMAZAH (104)
AND SURAH AL-MA'UN (107)

The contents of these Surahs testify that their revelation was in the earliest stage at Makkah, when the message of Islam was being presented in a brief but highly impressive way so that the listeners could not forget it even if they wanted to, for they were automatically committed to their memory. (However, people differ about the place where Surah Al-Ma'un was revealed. There is evidence in this Surah that points to it being a Madinah revelation. For example, it warns of destruction to those who are unmindful of their prayers and who pray only to be seen. This kind of hypocrite only lived in Madinah.) In these Surahs, people have been informed about those human weaknesses that, if not improved, could lead them to their eventual failure.

1 MATERIALISTIC HOARDERS OF WEALTH
FROM SURAH AL-HUMAZAH (104)

If Surah Al-Humazah is studied in the sequence of the Surahs beginning with Surah Az-Zilzal, one can fully understand how the fundamental beliefs of Islam and its teachings were impressed on people's minds in the earliest stage in Makkah.

1.1 Materialism in the pre-Islamic Society
Some of the evils present among the materialistic hoarders of wealth in the pre-Islamic era are condemned in Surah Al-Humazah. The Arabs knew that these evils existed in their society. They considered them wrong, and no one thought they were good. After describing the character of backbiters and wealth hoarders, the destiny of such people in the Hereafter is stated. Both their character and their fate are narrated in a way that makes the listener automatically reach the conclusion that such people rightly deserve the terrible fate that awaits them. Since such people do not generally suffer any punishment in this

772

world, but seem to be thriving, the Hereafter becomes absolutely essential and thus inevitable.

1.2 Materialism in the Contemporary Society

Although humanity has very much advanced in science and technology, enabling people to harness God's bounties with greater success, humanity's sick mentality has not improved much. In the pre-Islamic days, people considered the hoarding of wealth to be an evil of characteristic; now, people consider it to be normal. Are we better or worse off now? It is a materialist or capitalist society all over the world! These forces people into ruthless competition via the followers of Darwinism's and secularism's slogan of "the survival of the fittest." Furthermore, people today do not like to contribute for the welfare of the sick and the needy. Given such facts, it appears that modern society has actually deteriorated when compared to the pre-Islamic society of Arabia.

1.3 Wealth should neither be Hoarded nor Wasted

In Surah Al-Humazah, backbiting and amassing wealth as one's life objective is criticized. Such people criticized as being those "...who pile up wealth and lay it by... (Qur'an 104:2)." They are those who "...collect (wealth) and hide it (from use) (Qur'an 70:18)" and who "...love wealth with inordinate love (Qur'an 89:20)!" Such people say, "Wealth have I squandered in abundance (Qur'an 90:6)." God describes such a person as being, "...violent is he in his love of wealth (Qur'an 100:8)." Needless to say, this is the description of an extremely corrupt society where materialism keeps people away from doing good deeds.

1.4 A Believer is neither a Backbiter nor a Miser

Backbiting and miserliness neither make people human nor a believer. That is why God warns in Surah Al-Ma'un that, "Woe to every (kind of) scandalmonger and backbiter. Who piles up wealth and lays it by; thinking that his wealth would make him last forever (Qur'an 104:1-3)." Instead, such behavior will lead people to be thrown into that 'which breaks to pieces', "And what will explain to you that which breaks to pieces? (It is) the fire of (the wrath of) Allah kindled (to a blaze), which does mount (right) to the hearts. It shall be made into a vault over them, in columns outstretched (Qur'an 104:5-9)."

2 WITHOUT ACCOUNTABILITY HUMANITY DEGRADES
FROM SURAH AL-MA'UN (107)

People who refuse to believe in the Hereafter develop a character and behavior that is very much below human dignity. They have nothing to motivate them to be kind and helpful. Hypocrisy is another moral disease that thrives on the lack of a belief in the resurrection and in the final accountability for one's behavior and deeds. Unless people believe that they will have to appear before God to give an account of their deeds, they will not adopt piety and righteousness in their daily affairs.

2.1 Denial of the Accountability makes people Cruel
The unbelievers who reject the Hereafter tend to be cruel to orphans and the poor people, "Do you see one who denies the judgment (to come)? Then such is the (man) who repulses the orphan (with harshness) and encourages not the feeding of the indigent (107:1-3)."

2.2 Denial of the Hereafter makes people Hypocrites
Hypocracy is a serious moral sickness among the believers. Besides, the hypocrites either have no idea or reject the concepts of the Hereafter, the Day of Judgment, and rewards and punishment according to one's behavior and deeds. Such people are not serious about their prayers, do good only to show off, and even deny small favors to people, "So woe to the worshipers, who are neglectful of their prayers, those who (want but) to be seen (by men), but refuse (to supply even) neighborly needs (107:4-7)." Quite simply, people cannot develop a strong, stable, and pure character unless they believe in the Hereafter.

CHAPTER 72

God's Will and His Own Divine Ways
FROM SURAH AL-FIL (105) AND SURAH AL-QURAYSH (106)

Historical background of Surah Al-Fil confirms that this Surah must have been revealed quite early at Makkah. The Arabs describe the year in which the event mentioned in this Surah took place as Am al-Fil (the year of the elephants). During the same year, the Messenger was born. Most historians confirm that this event to which this Surah refers occurred in Muharram and that the Prophet was born in Rabi al-Awwal. According to the majority of them, the Messenger was born 50 days after this event.

A great majority of the commentators say that Surah Al-Quraysh is Makkan in origin. The words "Lord of this House," which are stated in this Surah, provide the evidence. Had it been revealed at Madinah, the words "this House" for the Ka'bah would not be relevant. Besides, its contents so closely relate to Surah Al-Fil that it was probably revealed immediately after it.

1 THE DIVINE PROTECTION OF GOD'S HOUSE
FROM SURAH AL-FIL (105)

God has His own divine ways to accomplish His will. Surah Al-Fil describes an incident in which swarms of birds brought God's punishment to an invading army of soldiers and elephants, in order to save the Ka'bah at Makkah. God asks people, "Don't you see how your Lord dealt with the people of the elephant? Did He not make their treacherous plan go astray? And He sent against them flights of birds, striking them with stones of baked clay. Then did He make them like an empty field of stalks and straw, (of which the grain) has been eaten up (105:1-5)." God's punishment to the people of the elephant has been described very briefly because, at the time of this revelation, it was a very recent event, and everyone in Makkah and Arabia knew about it.

Therefore, there was no need to mention the details of the incident in Surah al-Fil.

2 DIVINE PROTECTION FROM HUNGER AND FEAR
FROM SURAH AL-QURAYSH (106)

After reminding people of His favors to them, God invites people to His guidance and servitude in Surah Al-Quraysh. That is why, in the four brief sentences of this Surah, God says to the Quraysh that when they: (1) acknowledge this house, the Ka'bah, to be God's house—not the house of idols; 2) honestly know that it is God alone Who has granted them peace by virtue of His House; (3) accept that it is God Who has made their trade and commerce flourish; and (4) understand that it is God Who is saving them from destitution and favoring them with prosperity; (5) they should then worship and serve God alone.

Table 2: God Provides Protection from Hunger and Fear

No	Surah:Verses	Meanings
2	106:001-004	For the covenants (of security and safeguard enjoyed) by the Quraysh—their covenants (covering) journeys by winter and summer— So let them serve the Lord of this House. 1. Who feeds them against hunger and 2. Gives them security against fear.

CHAPTER 73

Gratitude for God's Bounties
FROM SURAH AL-KAWTHAR (108)

The contents indicate that Surah Al-Kawthar was revealed at
Makkah during a period when the Messenger was passing
through extremely discouraging conditions.

1 DIVINE HELP AND ENCOURAGEMENT

Before Surah Al-Kawthar, when the Messenger was passing
through the most striving conditions and the whole community
had turned hostile, there was resistance and opposition from
every side. The Messenger and a handful of his companions did
not see any chance of success. During this time, God sent several
revelations to encourage the Messenger and console his
companions.

1.1 During Times of Need, God's Help is always There
During difficult times in the life of the Messenger and the
believers, God revealed several verses in Surah Ad-Duha and
Surah Ash-Sharh to console and encourage them. In Surah Ad-
Duha, it was said: "Verily, what comes after is better for you
than that which has gone before, and soon will your Guardian-
Lord give you (that wherewith) you shall be well pleased
(Qur'an 93:4-5)." In Surah Ash-Sharh, God told the Messenger
that even though enemies were trying to defame him, God
arranged to exalt the Messenger's name and fame and that along
with every hardship there is also relief (Qur'an 94:4-5).

1.2 God Consoles and Encourages His People
Hence, the Messenger was told not to be disheartened by the
severity of conditions at this time. This period of hardships
would soon pass, and the period of success and victory would
follow. Although, these verses were revealed for the consolation
of the Messenger and the believers at a certain time and under
specific conditions, they are equally applicable to all believers in

777

all times and in all difficult situations. The fact is that along with every hardship there is relief, which follows the hardship. Therefore, believers should not lose heart, but they should swim through hardship with patience and prayer.

2 THE LEGACY OF CORRUPT PEOPLE

2.1 Corrupt People will never have their Roots

Besides consoling the Messenger in Surah Al-Kawthar, God also foretold the destruction of his opponents. The Quraysh used to say that the Messenger was cut off from his community and reduced to a powerless and helpless individual. There are many *Ahadith* concerning this and similar comments. The Quraysh were angry with him because he worshiped and served only One God, and because he publicly repudiated their idolatry. For this, he was deprived of the rank, esteem, and honors that he had formerly enjoyed among his people, and he was then cut off from his community. His few companions were helpless, poor people who were being persecuted and tyrannized. In addition, the Messenger was bereaved by the death of his two sons, one after the other. Meanwhile, his near relatives and the people of his clan, brotherhood, and neighborhood were rejoicing and uttering disheartening and disturbing words to the Messenger, a person who had treated even his enemies most kindly. At this moment of crisis, God reassured the Messenger that it would be his opponents who would be cut off from their root; it would not be the Messenger.

2.2 Thank God for His Help and His Bounties

Surah Al-Kawthar also teaches us how one could show gratitude to God for all His bounties and help. God commands us to pray and sacrifice: "To you We have granted the fount (of abundance). Therefore, to your Lord turn in prayer and sacrifice. For he who hates you—he will be cut off (from future hope) (Qur'an 108:1-3)." It was those who taunted the Messenger after he lost his infant sons that were cut off from all future hope, in this world and the next, and not the Messenger. (These verses could also mean that corrupt people do not leave anything good behind.)

CHAPTER 74

Nothing in Islam can be Compromised
FROM SURAH AL-KAFIRUN (109)

The majority of commentators say that Al-Kafirun is a Makkan Surah. Its contents confirm this. This Surah was not revealed to preach religious tolerance, as some contemporary people seem to think. Rather, it was revealed to distance the Muslims away from the unbelievers' religion, their rites of worship, and their false gods. It was to express the Muslims' total disgust and unconcern with their beliefs and to tell them that Islam and unbelief had nothing in common. There was absolutely no possibility of them being combined and mixed into one entity. The esteem and importance of this Surah can be judged from many *Ahadith* in which the Messenger recommended its recital before one goes to bed, for this is immunity from polytheism. "Farwah bin Naufal reported from his father who asked, 'O Apostle of Allah, teach me something that I shall read when I shall take shelter to my bed.' He said: 'Read: 'O you that reject faith (Surah Al-Kafirun),' because it is immunity from polytheism' (Al-Hadith: vol. III, no. 49, page 682)."

1 GOD ASSURES FREEDOM OF BELIEF

God commands in the Qur'an, "Let there be no compulsion in religion. Truth stands out clear from error. Whoever rejects evil and believes in Allah has grasped the most trustworthy handhold that never breaks … (Qur'an 2:256)." Islam came to declare and establish the universal principle that there should be no compulsion in religion. This illustrates the great honor that God has given to humanity. The high regard in which one's free will, thought, and emotions are held is due to the fact that this freedom has been given by God Himself to humankind. Hence, the freedom to choose one's beliefs is granted. Here lies the essence of human emancipation that 20th-century authoritarian and oppressive ideologies and regimes have denied mankind. People have been deprived of the right to choose and live other

779

than according to what is dictated by the state. People are given no choice and must adhere only to the secular state system, a system that does not allow for a belief in God as the Creator and Master of the world.

Freedom of belief is a basic right that identifies people as human beings. To deny anyone this right is to deny one his humanity. Freedom of belief also implies the freedom to express and propagate one's belief without fear of threat or persecution; otherwise, that freedom is hollow and meaningless. Islam, undoubtedly the most enlightened view of life and the world, establishes a most sensible human and social system and takes the lead in declaring freedom of belief and religion to be a fundamental principle. It teaches its adherents that they are forbidden to compel or force others to embrace Islam. Islam absolutely forbids the use of force to convert people. Force was not used by the Messenger, not even to reform the hypocrites. People convert to Islam because the implementation of its commands assures the wellbeing of humankind, both in this world and in the Hereafter.

1.1 Islam and Unbelief have nothing in Common
Islam declares that you shall have your religion, and I shall have mine. There is neither any compulsion nor any compromise in Islam. Although it was addressed in the beginning to the unbelieving Quraysh in response to their proposals of compromise, this principle was not confined to that particular situation. As a part of the Qur'an, God gives the believers the eternal teaching that they should exonerate themselves by word and by deeds from unbelief, wherever and in whatever form it may be. The believers should declare without any reservation that they cannot make any compromise with the unbelievers in the matter of faith. Since previous religions were corrupted by incorporating compromises for selfish or political reasons and worldly gains, Islam does not allow any distortion or omission of God's commands.

1.2 The Believers' Objective and Pursuit in Life
Objectives and pursuits in life very much determine the success or failure of individual lives, both in this world and in the

Hereafter. Believers are God's trustees, born to serve Him by following His commands to set up just societies on earth. In contrast, the unbelievers' lives are spent in self-promotion and the fulfillment of their selfish desires. Surah Al-Kafirun commands the believers to tell the unbelievers that they can have their religion but that the believers will uphold Islam.

God commands the believers: "Say: 'O you that reject faith! I worship not that which you worship, nor will you worship that which I worship. And I will not worship that which you have been wont to worship, nor will you worship that which I worship. To you be your way and to me mine (Qur'an 109:1-6).'"

2 THERE IS NO FREEDOM IN RELIGION

There was a time in Makkah, although a storm of opposition had arisen in the unbelieving community of Quraysh against the message of Islam, when the Quraysh chiefs had not lost hope that they would be able to reach some sort of a compromise with the Messenger. Therefore, from time to time, they would visit him with different proposals of compromise so that he might accept one of them to end the dispute. Some of their proposals, as given in the Introduction to this Surah by Maududi in his Tafhim-ul-Qur'an, are summarized below.

2.1 Proposals of Compromise to God's Messenger
According to Abdullah ibn 'Abbas, the Quraysh proposed to the Prophet that they would give the Messenger so much wealth that he would be the richest man in Makkah, give him whichever woman he would like in marriage, and be prepared to follow and obey him as their leader if only he would not speak ill of their gods. If this compromise was not acceptable to him, the Quraysh also offered another proposal. When the Prophet asked what it was, they said that if he would worship their gods, Lat and Uzza, for a year, they would worship God for the same period. The Prophet then asked for time to see what God commanded in this regard.

781

Said bin Mina reported that Walid bin Mughirah, As bin Wail, Aswad bin al-Muttalib, and Umayyah bin Khalaf then met with the Messenger and basically said to him: "O Muhammad, let us agree that we will worship your God and you will worship our gods, and we would make you a partner in all our works. If what you have brought is better than what we possess, we will be partners in it with you and have our share in it. However, if what we possess is better than what you have brought, you will be a partner in it with us and have your share of it." At this point, God then revealed Surah Al-Kafirun

2.2 There is no Compromise in Religion

The Quraysh proposed compromises to the Messenger not just once in one sitting, but at different times and on different occasions, and there was a need that they should be given a definite, decisive response, so that their hope that the Messenger would come to terms with them on the principle of give and take was frustrated forever. These traditions also show that no compromise in or freedom to make any changes in the discipline of Islam is permitted by God. Islam is a complete and final, divine religion that demands from its followers its complete implementation in their personal lives, as well as in society. Believers cannot and should not skip any of their obligations by saying that they have freedom of choice. They have already used up their freedom of choice by choosing Islam as their way of life. Only hypocrites waver in its full implementation. Believers are required to take their religion seriously.

CHAPTER 75

The Acknowledgement of Divine Support
FROM SURAH AN-NASR (110)

Surah An-Nasr is the last Surah to be revealed as a whole. It was revealed only a few months before the passing away of the Messenger from this world, either in the precincts of Makkah at his farewell pilgrimage or in Madinah after he returned from the Hajj in 10 A.H.

1 WHEN THE MISSION IS ACCOMPLISHED

1.1 When the Purpose of One's Life is Achieved

When the purpose of one's life is accomplished, it is the time to depart this world. Baihaqi in Kitab al-Hajj has related from the tradition of Sarra bint-Nabhan, the sermon that the Messenger gave on this occasion. She says: "At the farewell pilgrimage, I heard the Prophet say: 'O people, do you know what day it is?' They said: 'God and His messenger have the best knowledge.' He said: 'This is the middle day of the *Tashriq* Days.' Then he said: 'Do you know what place it is?' They said: 'God and His messenger have the best knowledge.' He said: 'This is *Masharil-Haram*.' Then he said: 'I do not know whether I would meet you here again. Beware your bloods and your honors are forbidden until you appear before your Lord and He questions you about your deeds. Listen: let the one who is near convey it to him who is far away. Listen: have I conveyed the message to you?' Then, when we returned to Madinah, the Prophet passed away not many days after that (Maududi: Tafhim-ul-Qur'an)."

1.2 The Messenger's Attitude towards Victory

As described in many traditions, God in Surah An-Nasr has informed His messenger that when Islam attained complete victory in Arabia and the people started embracing God's religion in great numbers, it would mean that the mission for which he had been sent to the world had been fulfilled. Then, he was enjoined to busy himself in praising and glorifying God by

Whose bounty he had been able to accomplish such a great task, and he should implore God to forgive whatever failings and frailties he might have shown in the performance of his duties.

2 BELIEVERS ATTITUDE TOWARDS SUCCESS

2.1 The Messenger is the Believers' Role Model

One can easily see a great difference between a believing leader and an unbelieving leader. If a worldly leader in his own lifetime is able to bring about a revolution that was the aim and objective of his struggle, this would be an occasion for celebration and exultation. However, the Messenger of God, in a brief period of 23 years, was able to revolutionize an entire nation with regard to its beliefs, thoughts, customs, morals, civilization, economy, politics, and fighting ability. By raising his nation from ignorance and barbarism, the Messenger enabled it to conquer the world and become the leader of nations. Yet, when he had accomplished this unique task, he did not celebrate this as being the result of his own accomplishments. Rather, he glorified, praised God, and prayed to God to forgive him.

2.2 Believers' Acknowledgement of God's Help

Ibn 'Abbas stated that after the revelation of this Surah, the Messenger began to labor more intensely and devotedly for the Hereafter than he had ever done before (Maududi: Tafhim-ul-Qur'an). Surah An-Nasr highlights that victory always humbles the true believers. As a result, they remember God much and ask for their forgiveness. "When comes the help of Allah and victory, and you do see the people enter Allah's religion in crowds, celebrate the praises of your Lord, and pray for His forgiveness, for He is oft-returning (in grace and mercy) (Qur'an 110:1-4)."

784

CHAPTER 76

Arrogance Eventually Destroys
FROM SURAH AL-LAHAB (111)

Although the commentators are agreed that Surah Al-Lahab is a Makkan Surah, it is difficult to determine precisely when it was revealed. However, in view of Abu Lahab's role and conduct against the divine message, one assumes that it must have been revealed in the period when he had transgressed all limits in his hostility to the Messenger and his attitude was becoming a serious obstruction in the progress of Islam. It may well have been revealed in the period when the Quraysh were boycotting the Messenger and his tribe and were besieging them in Shi'b Abi Talib. Abu Lahab, who was the Messenger's uncle, was the only close relative of the Messenger to side with the Messenger's enemies. Public condemnation of an uncle by his nephew could not be considered proper until the extreme excesses committed by the uncle had become visible to everyone. If the Surah had been revealed before this, in the very beginning, the people would have regarded it as morally discourteous that the nephew should so condemn this uncle.

1 EQUALITY DO NOT SUITS THE ARROGANT

According to Ibn Zaid, "One day Abu Lahab asked the Prophet, 'If I were to accept your religion, what would I get?' The Prophet replied: 'You would get what the other believers would get.' He said, 'Is there no preference or distinction for me?' The Prophet replied, 'What else do you want?' Thereupon he said, 'May this religion perishes in which I and all other people should be equal and alike' (Maududi: Tafhim-ul-Qur'an).

2 TIES OF BLOOD ARE IRRELEVANT IN RELIGION

The Messenger's own uncle opposed him in front of the Arabs who came for Hajj from outside Makkah. Since it was against

785

the established traditions of Arabia that an uncle should publicly oppose his nephew without a reason, they were, therefore, influenced by what Abu Lahab said, and doubts were created about the Messenger and his message. But when Surah Al-Lahab was revealed, Abu Lahab was filled with rage and started uttering nonsense. This made the people realize that what Abu Lahab said in opposition to the Messenger was not at all reliable. Besides, when the uncle was condemned by name, the people's expectation that the Messenger would treat some of his relatives leniently in the matter of religion was frustrated forever. The people understood that there was no room for preference or partiality in their faith. A non-relative could become a near and dear one if he believed and a near relation a non-relative if he disbelieved. Thus, there is no place in Islam for unfair favoritism based on ties of blood.

3 CORRUPT LEADERS EVENTUALLY PERISH

God says in Surah Al-Lahab that corrupt leaders eventually perish: "Perish the hands of the Father of Flame! Perish he! No profit to him from all his wealth and all his gains! Burnt soon will he be in a fire of blazing flame! His wife shall carry the wood as fuel, a twisted rope of palm leaf fiber round her (own) neck (Qur'an 111:1-5)."

786

CHAPTER 77

The Lord of the Universe
FROM SURAH AL-IKHLAS (112)

Since this Surah deals exclusively with the Oneness of God, *Al-Ikhlas* (pure faith) is not only the name of this Surah, but it is also the title of its contents. The other Surahs generally have been designated after a word occurring in them, but in this Surah the word *Ikhlas* has occurred nowhere. This name has been given in view of its meaning and contents. Whoever believes in its teaching, will get rid of *Shirk* (polytheism) completely and sincerely.

1 REVELATION OF SURAH AL-IKHLAS

There are several traditions that show that different people on different occasions had questioned the Messenger about the essence and nature of God, to Whose service and worship he invited the people. On each occasion, he recited by God's command this very Surah in response. At first, the pagans of Quraysh asked him this question in Makkah, and in reply this Surah was revealed. Then at Madinah, sometimes Christians and sometimes the other people of Arabia asked him similar questions, and every time God inspired him to recite this very Surah in an answer to them.

In each of these traditions, it has been said that this Surah was revealed on this or that occasion. From this, one should not form the impression that all these traditions are mutually contradictory. The fact is that whenever there existed with the Prophet a previously revealed verse or Surah that addressed a particular question or matter, and later the same question was presented before him, God inspired him to recite the same verse or Surah, as it contained the answer to their question. Given the above, it can be concluded that this Surah is Makkan, that it was revealed in the earliest period at Makkah when detailed verses of the Qur'an dealing with the essence and attributes of God

Almighty had not yet been revealed, and that the people, hearing the Messenger's invitation to God, wanted to know what God was like (Maududi: Tafhim-ul-Qur'an).

2 PRE-ISLAMIC CONCEPTS OF GOD

The traditions relevant to the religious concepts prevalent at the time of the revelation of Surah Al-Ikhlas show that idolatrous polytheists were worshiping gods made of wood, stone, gold, silver, and other materials These gods had a form, shape, and body, and the polytheists believed that these gods and goddesses were descended from each other. No goddess was without a husband, and no god was without a wife. These false gods stood in need of food and drink, and their devotees arranged these for them. A large number of the polytheists believed that God had assumed human form, and there were some people who were descended from Him. Although the Christians claimed to believe in One God, they defined God as being three persons (Father, Son, and Holy Spirit) in one substance. While their emphasis on one substance made their belief monotheistic, by incorporating Jesus and the Holy Spirit into their godhead, they were making associates in the godhead. The Jews also claimed to believe in One God, but their God was not without physical, material and other human qualities and characteristics. He went for a stroll, appeared in human form, and wrestled with one of His servants.

Besides these communities, there were Zoroastrian fire worshipers and Sabian star worshipers. Under such conditions when the people were invited to believe in God, the One, Who has no associate, it was inevitable that questions arose as to what kind of god was God, Who was the One and Only Lord for Whom an invitation to believe was being given, at the expense of all other gods and deities. It is a miracle of the Qur'an that in a few brief words it answered all the questions and presented such a clear concept of God. It destroyed all polytheistic concepts, without leaving any room for associating human traits with God.

3 *TAUHEED*, THE ISLAMIC CONCEPT OF GOD

The Messenger held this Surah in great esteem. He made the believers realize its importance in different ways, so that they recited it frequently and disseminated its meaning among the people. The religion of Islam is based on three doctrines: *Tauheed*, Apostleship and the Hereafter. This Surah teaches *Tauheed*, the fundamental doctrine of Islam, in four brief sentences that are immediately impressed on human memory and that can be read and recited easily.

There are a great number of *Ahadith* that show that the Messenger on different occasions and in different ways told people that this Surah was equivalent to one third of the Qur'an. The commentators have given many explanations about this, but it could simply mean that the religion presented by the Qur'an is based on three doctrines and that since this Surah teaches one of the three, the Messenger regarded it as equal to one-third of the Qur'an. It was narrated by Abu Said Al-Khudri: "The Prophet said to his companions, 'Is it difficult for any of you to recite one third of the Qur'an in one night?' This suggestion was difficult for them, so they said, 'Who among us has the power to do so, O Allah's Messenger?' Allah Messenger replied: 'Allah (the) One, the self-sufficient master Whom all creatures need is equal to one third of the Qur'an (Sahih Bukhari: 6.1.534)."

Who is the Creator of universe? Surah Al-Ikhlas tells people: "Say: 'He is Allah, the One and Only; Allah, the eternal, absolute. He begets not, nor is He begotten, and there is none like unto Him (Qur'an 112:1-4)."

CHAPTER 78

Seeking Refuge from Evil Behavior
FROM SURAH AL-FALAQ (113) AND SURAH AN-NAS (114)

Although Surah Al-Falaq and Surah An-Nas are separate Surahs as given in the Qur'an under separate names, they are so deeply related and their content so closely resembles each other's that they have been given a common name of Mu'awwidhatan. The two Surahs in which refuge with God has been sought were also revealed together. This is another reason why the combined name of both is Mu'awwidhatan. It was narrated by A'ishah: "Whenever the Prophet went to bed every night, he used to cup his hands together and blow over them after reciting Surah Al-Ikhlas, Surah Al-Falaq, and Surah An-Nas, and then rub his hands over whatever parts of his body he was able to rub, starting with his head, face, and front of his body. He used to do that three times (Sahih Bukhari: 6.61.536)."

1 THE SITUATION WHEN THESE SURAHS WERE REVEALED

1.1 A Surah could have been revealed on Several Occasions
According to some traditions, these Surahs were revealed at Makkah. According to other traditions, these Surahs were revealed when the Jews had placed a magic spell on the Messenger in Madinah, causing him to fall ill. When a Surah or verse is said to be revealed on this or that occasion, it does not necessarily mean that it was revealed for the first time on that very occasion. If a previously revealed Surah or verse could answer a particular incident or situation, the Messenger's attention was drawn to it by God for the second time, or even again and again. This was likely the case with the Mu'awwidhatan.

1.2 First time these Surahs were revealed in Makkah
The content of these Surahs indicate that they were first revealed in Makkah at a time when opposition to the Messenger had

790

grown very intense. Later at Madinah, when storms of opposition were raised by the hypocrites, Jews, and polytheists, the Messenger was instructed to recite these very Surahs. This has been mentioned in a tradition from Uqbah bin Amir. After this, when magic was worked on him and his illness grew intense, Gabriel came and instructed him by God's command to recite these Surahs. Considering these Surahs as connected exclusively with the incident of magic is difficult to do, for only one verse is related to this incident.

2 THE UNBELIEVERS' RESPONSE AGAINST ISLAM

Immediately after the Messenger began to preach Islam, it seemed as if he had provoked all the classes of people around him. Further, the opposition of the unbelieving Quraysh increased in intensity with the spread of his message. Their hostility did was not yet very intense when the polytheists still had some hope of tempting the Messenger to prevent him from preaching his message or of striking some bargain with him. However, they were disappointed when in Surah Al-Kafirun they were plainly told that: the Messenger would not worship those that they worshiped; they would not worship the One God Whom the Messenger worshiped; and their religion was for them and the Messenger's religion was for him. At that point, the hostility increased manifold (Maududi: Tafhim-ul-Qur'an).

2.1 People sought all Means to Harm the Messenger

Those families who had some of their members accept Islam were especially furious against the Messenger. They were cursing him and holding secret consultations to kill him quietly in the dark of the night, so that his clan, i.e., the Bani Hashim, could not discover the murderer and take revenge. Magic and charms were also being worked on him in a fruitless effort to cause his death, make him fall ill, or become mentally unblanced. Satans from among both mankind and the jinn became active in whispering evil thoughts into the hearts of the people, against both him and the Qur'an, so that they would became suspicious and abandon him.

2.2 Some were Jealous of the Messenger's Position

There were many individuals who were jealous of the Messenger, for they could not tolerate that a man from another family or tribe than their own should flourish and become prominent. The reason why Abu Jahl was hostile to the Messenger was explained by him as being due to the fact that his clan and the Bani 'Abd Manaf, the clan to which the Messenger belonged, were rivals of each other in feeding others, in providing conveyances to, and in giving donations. As such, the two clans were seen as being equal in honor and nobility. However, when the Messenger's clan proclaimed that they had a messenger who was inspired from Heaven, there was no way that Abu Jahl's clan could compete with this claim. As such, Abu Jahl's clan refused to acknowledge the Messenger and to affirm faith in him (Ibn Hisham, Volume I, pp. 337-338).

3 SEEKING REFUGE WITH LORD OF THE UNIVERSE

3.1 Seek Refuge from the Evil of Everything Created

It was in an environment of extreme hostility that the Messenger was commanded to tell the people that he sought refuge with the Lord of the dawn from the evil of everything that God had created, from the evil of the darkness of night, from the evil of those men and women who attempt to practice magic, and from the evil of the envious (Qur'an 113:1-5). Further, he was to tell them that he sought refuge with the Lord, King, and God of mankind from the evil of the whisperer, who returns over and over again, and who whispers evil into the hearts of men, whether he be from among the jinn or men (Qur'an 114:1-6). This is similar to what Moses was told to say when Pharaoh expressed his design before his full court to kill him: "I have indeed called upon my Lord and your Lord (for protection) from every arrogant one who believes not in the Day of Account (Qur'an 40:27)." Moses also said: "I have sought safety with my Lord and your Lord against your injuring me (Qur'an 44:20)."

3.2 The Power of the Lord of the Universe is Supreme

Both Moses and Muhammad were confronted with well-equipped, resourceful, and powerful enemies. They both upheld their message against strong opponents, even though they had no material power with which to fight their oppressors. They both utterly disregarded their enemies' threats, dangerous plans, and hostility, and both took refuge from their enemies with the Lord of the universe. Obviously, such firmness and steadfastness can be shown only by a person who is convinced that the power of his Lord is supreme and supercedes all other powers. No one can harm the one who takes God's refuge, and only such a person can resolutely say that he won't give up preaching the truth, regardless of what others may say or do.

4 GOD ANSWERED THE PRAYERS OF HIS PEOPLE

Surah Al-Fatihah and the Mu'awwidhatan are the beginning and the completion of the Qur'an. Although the Qur'an has not been arranged chronologically, the Messenger arranged the present order of the verses and Surahs that were revealed on different occasions during a period of 23 years, in order to meet different needs and situations. This ordering was not done by the Messenger's own whim, but by the command of God Who revealed the revelations in the first place. According to this order, the Qur'an opens with the Surah Al-Fatihah and ends with the Mu'awwidhatan.

Surah Al-Fatihah is a prayer that God has taught to all those who want to benefit from His guidance. It has been placed in beginning to tell the reader that if he sincerely wants to benefit from the Qur'an, he should offer this prayer. This is to create a strong desire in people's hearts and minds to seek guidance from God, Who alone can grant it. Thus, this Surah leads people to pray for guidance to the straight path, to study the Qur'an with an attitude of a seeker of truth, and to recognize the fact that the Lord of the universe is the source of all knowledge. The early Muslims prayed to God to show them guidance, and their Lord placed the whole Qur'an before them in answer to their prayer, telling them that the Qur'an is the guidance for which you asked. Just follow it, and you will be successful.

793

Books Cited or Recommended

Akbar, Muhammad (trans. Tafhim-ul-Qur'an). *The Meaning of Holy Qur'an by Syed Abul Ala Maududi.* Lahore: Islamic Publications (Pvt) Limited, 2000.

'Ali, 'Abdullah Yusuf. *The Meaning of Holy Qur'an.* Beltsville, Maryland: Amana Publications, 11th ed., 2009.

Al-Ghazali, Muhammad. *Muslim's Character.* Riyadh, Saudi Arabia: Mubarat Sk. Hassan Tahir Al-Islmiah.

Al-Muhtaj, Sheikh Abdullah Bin Muhammad. *Insan, (Urdu).* Riyadh, Saudi Arabia: Darussalam, 1998.

At-Tarjumana, A'isha 'Abdarahman and Johnson, Ya'qub, (trans.). *Malik's Muwatta.* http://www.usc.edu/org/cmje/religious-texts/hadith/

Hafeez, Dr. Muhammad A. *Human Character and Behavior: An Islamic Perspective.* Beltsville, MD, USA. Amana Publications, 2011.

Hasan Prof. Ahmad, (trans.). *Sunan Abu-Dawud.* http://www.usc.edu/org/cmje/religious-texts/hadith/

Irving, Thomas Ballantine, Ahmed, Khurshid and Ahsan, Muhammad Manazir. *The Qur'an Basic Teaching(s).* Leicester, England: The Islamic Foundation, 1994.

Karim, Maulana Fazlul. *Al-Hadith*, trans.Mishkat-ul-Masabih. New Delhi: Islamic Book Service, 2006.

Khan, Dr. Muhammad Muhsin and al-Hilali, Dr. Taqi-ud-Din. *The Noble Qur'an.* Riyadh, Saudi Arabia: Darussalam, 1996.

Khan, Dr. Muhammad Muhsin (trans.). *Sahih Bukhari.* Hadith Software: www.Islamasoft.co.uk

Maududi, Syed Abul Ala, *Tafhim-ul-Qur'an.* Lahore, Pakistan: Idara Tarjuman -ul-Qur'an, 2003

Maududi, Syed Abul Ala, *Surah Introductions to the Qur'an.* http://www.usc.edu/org/cmje/religious-texts/maududi/index.php

Maududi, Syed Abul Ala, (trans. Ansari, Zafar Iqbal). *Towards Understanding the Qur'an,* Leicester, England: The Islamic Foundation, 2006.

Pickthall, Muhammad Marmaduke. *Holy Qur'an.* Karachi, Pakistan: Taj Company Ltd., 1969

Salahi, Adil, (ed.). *Our Dialogue.* www.ourdialogue.com.

Siddique, Abdul Hamid, (trans.). *Sahih Muslim.* Hadith Software: www.Islamasoft.co.uk

Shakir, Muhammad Habib. *The Qur'an.* http://www.usc.edu/org/cmje/religious-texts/quran/

Tantavi, Sheikh Ali. *Introduction to Islam.* Lahore, Pakistan: the Qur'an Ahsan Tareek, 2004.

Yusuf, Hamza. *Purification of the Heart.* www.starlatch.com: Starlatch Press, 2004.

About the Author

The author, Dr. Muhammad Abdul Hafeez, was born in 1942. He holds a master's degree in history, a master's degree in chemical technology from the University of Panjab, Lahore, Pakistan, and a Ph.D. in chemical engineering from the City University, London, England. He has extensively researched and studied the religion of Islam within its theological, historical, and cultural perspectives in the light of the Qur'an and the *Ahadith* of its Prophet. He has been trying to learn what God tells us in the Qur'an and how it was interpreted by His Messenger from translations of the Qur'an and *Sunnah*.

Originally from Pakistan, the author lived and worked in Saudi Arabia for over 20 years (1983 to 2004). His stay in Saudi Arabia tremendously helped him in his study and learning of the religion of Islam from various sources, specifically from study circles of the Qur'an. He has benefited from various religious scholars there who helped him in comprehending Islam as a *"Deen"* compatible with the modern age. He is indebted to all those teachers, commentators, friends, and scholars who have played a role in imparting knowledge of Islamic studies to him. He owes a special gratitude to all those scholars whose works in Urdu, as well as in English, have been of great help and guidance to him.

He migrated to the United States of America in 1973 and lives in Liverpool, New York.

Made in the USA
Middletown, DE
27 September 2022